D0239778

26

COUNCIL

ROTATION
PLAN

THE ROLLING STONES
STONES
Fifty Years

THE ROLLING STONES
Fifty Years

CHRISTOPHER SANDFORD

**SIMON &
SCHUSTER**

London · New York · Sydney · Toronto · New Delhi

A CBS COMPANY

First published in Great Britain by Simon & Schuster UK Ltd, 2012
A CBS COMPANY

Copyright © 2012 by S.E. Sandford

1 3 5 7 9 10 8 6 4 2

Simon & Schuster UK Ltd
1st Floor
222 Gray's Inn Road
London
WC1X 8HB

www.simonandschuster.co.uk

Simon & Schuster Australia, Sydney
Simon & Schuster India, New Delhi

A CIP catalogue for this book is available
from the British Library.

ISBN: 978-0-85720-102-7 (Hardback)
ISBN 978-0-85720-103-4 (Trade Paperback)

Typeset by M Rules
Printed and bound by CPI Group (UK) Ltd, Croydon, CR0 4YY

To the Lorimers

CONTENTS

ACKNOWLEDGEMENTS

After finishing biographies both of Mick Jagger and Keith Richards some years ago, I promised never to write another book about the Rolling Stones. Here it is.

Many people made the book possible. I'm indebted to Colin Midson at Simon & Schuster and to my agent Barbara Levy. My old friend Vince Lorimer helped with some of the more spontaneous research in the 1970s, as did Pete Barnes, Fred Smith and Phil Oppenheim. The late Tom Keylock, who saw the Stones on a daily basis for six years, was an inexhaustible mine of stories about them; I'm grateful to Tom, his widow Joan and their daughters Allison and Betty. I also doff my hat to the late Frank Thorogood, unfairly stigmatised as the man who murdered Brian Jones, and his family. Mick Jagger allowed me to do a long interview of his parents some years ago, which was as unexpected as it was kind of him. I met Jagger, Charlie Watts and Keith Richards (referred to here as 'Richards', not 'Richard') at Keith's English home in February 1977, and have enjoyed one or two Stones 'VIP' passes in the years since. That said, I should make it clear that the surviving members of the band did not actively participate in the book, and several of their friends I approached for interviews told me that, 'after checking', they'd prefer not to talk. A few of them took the opportunity to vent at me. This, then, is an 'unauthorised' biography, so I'm particularly grateful to the 300 or so people who did speak, either by phone or email, or in various restaurants where the Stones were discussed, usually fondly, over a meal – which is how these things should be.

For recollections, input or advice I should thank, institutionally: Abacus, ABC News, the American Clinic (Tarn), ASCAP, *Billboard*, Blue Lena, Bookcase, Bookends, Book Mail, the British Library, British Newspaper Library, Chapters, Cheltenham College, *Chronicles*, CIA, City of Lausanne, City of Toronto, Companies House, the Complete Line, the *Daily Mail*, Dartford Borough Council, *Dartford Chronicle*, Dartford Grammar School, Decca, FBI – Freedom of Information Division, General Register Office, the Gulf Beach Hotel, Helter Skelter, HM Coroner for West Sussex, HM Prison Service, Inca, LipService, *Loaded*, Main Offender, Morey Management, MultiMap, the Music Box, Orbis, Palgrave Macmillan, Performing Right Society, Producers Guild, Playboy Enterprises International, Public Records Office, Renton Public Library, Rock and Roll Hall of Fame, Royal Navy Officers Club, Seattle Public Library, *Seattle Times*, the *Smoking Gun*, the *Spectator*, State of California, the *Sunday Times*, *The Times*, *Toronto Star*, UK Family Records Centre, UK Music, UK National Archives, *Vanity Fair*, Variety.com, Vital Records, *Vogue*.

Professionally: Christina Alder, Dick Allen, Ellie Altschuler, Luciano Amore, Jan Andres, the late Walter Annenberg, Jeffrey Archer, the late Hal Ashby, Bob Beckwith, Ross Benson, Byron Berline, the late Jeffrey Bernard, Chuck Berry, Hal Blaine, Stanley Booth, Angie Bowie, Jonathan Boyd, Pattie Boyd, Randy Brecker, Ben Brierley, Gary Brooker, Jack Bruce, Bebe Buell, the late William Burroughs, Noel Chelberg, Dan Chernow, Allan Clarke, the late Albert Clinton, Austin Cooper, Lol Creme, Janice Crotch, Sam Cutler, Roger Daltrey, Alan Deane, Rene Defourneaux, Andrew Dellow, Mike Dent, Derek Diamond, the late John Diefenbaker, Manja Dolan, Micky Dolenz, the late Lonnie Donegan, Michael Dorr, David Drinkwater, Alan Edwards, Tony Edwards, Josh Epstein, Alan Etherington, Winifred Etherington, the late Adam Faith, Georgie Fame, Chris Farlowe, Vanetta Fields, Anton Fig, Tom Finn, Judy Flanders, Jan Frances, the late Robert Fraser, Lucy Gentry, Eileen Giles, Tony Gill, the late Charlie Gillett, Lynn Goldsmith, Nick Gough, Jane Graffey, Freddy Gray, Ryan Grice, Jeff Griffin, Ted Haley, Charles Hannah, Bob Harris, Trudie Harris, Roger Hayes, the late Reg Hayter, Alan Hazen, the late Dick Heckstall-Smith, Gill Hickman, Peter Holland, Barney Hoskins, the late Colin Ingleby-Mackenzie, Walter Isaacs, David Jacobs, Ronnie Jacobson, Bianca Jagger, the late Joe and Eva Jagger, Tommy James, Lorraine Jerram, Norman Jewison, Paul Jones, Tom Jones, Phil Kaufman, Lenny Kaye, Edith Keep, Alan Kennington, Allison Keylock, Joan Keylock, the late Tom Keylock, Max King, Matthew Kite, the late Alexis Korner, Alan Lane, Donovan Leitch, Juliana Lessa, Barbara Levy, Cecilia Lewis, the late Carlo Little, Nick Lowe, Angie McCartney, Ruth McCartney, Henry McCullough, Mark McEntee, Roger McGough, Ron and Russell Mael, John Major, Harvey Mandel, Dave Mason, Robin Medley, Nancy Meyer, Colin Midson, Nick Miles, Andrew Miller, Judith Miller, Gary Morris, the late Mickie Most, Cecilia Nixon, Mike Oldfield, Andrew Oldham, Hugh O'Neill, Paul Ovenden, Chris Page, May Pang, Graham Parker, Andy Peebles, Peter Perchard, Wayne Perkins, the late Harold Pinter, Ken Pitt, Bill Plummer, P.J. Proby, the late Carl Radle, Terry Reid, Jim Repard, Tim Rice, Cliff Richard, Julia Richards, Mike Richards, Clive Robson, Pytor Sachin, Saran, Ronnie Schneider, Isobel Scott, David Scutts, Neil Sedaka, Norman Seeff, Pete Seeger, Feargal Sharkey, Sandie Shaw, the late Ned Sherrin, Don Short, Ron Simms, Nancy Sinatra, David Sinclair, Grace Slick, James Sliman, G.E. Smith, the late Peter Smith, Tony Smith, Gill Snow, Benny Spangler, Chris Spedding, Bethany Staelens, Winston Stagers, Walter Stern, Eric Stewart, the late Ian Stewart, Robert Stigwood, the Supremes, the Sweet, Lindsay Symons, Dick Taylor, Don Taylor, George Terry, Irma Thomas, the late Frank Thorogood, Glenn Tillbrook, Peter Tork, Rob Townsend, Charles Vann, the Villars, Lisbeth Vogl, Rick Wakeman, Graham Walder, David Waldman, Scott Walker, Suzanne Walker, Carol Ward, Steven Ward, Simon Ware, Adele Warlow, Erica Warren, Ernie Watts, Patricia Watts, Alan Weyer, Mark White, Bobby Whitlock, Walton Wilkinson, Mary Wilson, Johnny Winter, Tom Wolfe, Betty Wolstenholme, the late Krissy Wood, David Wood, Nanette Workman, Tony Yeo.

Personally: Adis, Air Canada, Ann Allsop, Arvid Anderson, Rev. Maynard Atik, Sam and Barbara Banner, the late Angela Barnes, Pete Barnes, Don Bates, Ann Bevan, Clare Bevan, the late Terry Bland,

Bob Bridge, Hilary and Robert Bruce, Don Carson, Cocina, Common Ground, John Cottrell-Dormer, Ken Crabtrey, Richard Cranfield, Roz Cranstoun-Corby, Celia Culpan, Danubius Hotel, Deb K. Das, the Davenport, Mark Demos, Monty Dennison, the Dowdall family, John and Barbara Dungee, the late Godfrey Evans, Mary Evans, Malcolm Galfe, the Gay Hussar, the Gees, Audrey Godwin, Colleen Graffy, the Grafton on Sunset, James Graham, Tom Graveney, Grumbles, Alastair Hignell, Richard Hill, Charles Hillman, the late Amy Hofstetter, Alex Holmes, Hotel Vancouver, Sarah Horn, Jon Jackson, Jo Jacobius, the Jamiesons, the late Johnny Johnson, Lincoln Kamell, the late David Kelly, Imran Khan, Terry Lambert, Belinda Lawson, Barbara Levy, Cindy Link, Todd Linse, the late Richard Lloyd-Roberts, Antoinette Lorimer, Dominica Lorimer, Vince Lorimer, the late Jackie McBride, Les McBride, the Macris, Lee Mattson, Teri Mayo, Jim and Rana Meyersahm, Missoula Doubletree, Sheila Mohn, the Morgans, Colleen Murray, John Murray, National Gallery Sackler Room, Chuck Ogmund, Phil Oppenheim, Valya Page, Robin Parish, Greg Phillips, Chris Pickrell, PNB, Roman Polanski, Princes Square Hotel, the Prins family, the late Prof. John Prins, Don Richardson, Scott P. Richert, Amanda Ripley, the late Malcolm Robinson, Fatima Roque, St Patrick Hospital Missoula, Debbie Saks, Sam, Delia Sandford, my father Sefton Sandford, Sue Sandford, Peter Scaramanga, Seattle Cricket Club, John Shepherd, the late Cat Sinclair, Fred and Cindy Smith, Rev. and Mrs Harry Smith, Spruce Street School, the Stanleys, Airie Stuart, Andrew Stuart, Thaddeus Stuart, Jack Surendranath, Dave Thomas, the Travel Team, Ben and Mary Tyvand, William Underhill, University of Montana, University of Puget Sound, Syra Vahidy, Diana Villar, the late Roger Villar, Tony Vinter, Lisbeth Vogl, John and Mary Wainwright, Chris West, West London Chemists, Richard Wigmore, the late Peg Willis Fleming, Willis Fleming family, Aaron Wolf, Rusty Zainoulline.

And a low bow, as always, to Karen and Nicholas Sandford.

C.S.
2012

'God's in the star, the stone, the flesh, the soul, and the clod'

ROBERT BROWNING

'We piss anywhere, man'

ATTRIBUTED TO THE ROLLING STONES, 1965

'Anything worth doing is worth overdoing'

MICK JAGGER

1

CONNECTION

How did the Rolling Stones achieve this curious headlock on our affections? If anything, it seems to get stronger over time. The 147 concerts they played between August 2005 and August 2007, known collectively, and with good cause, as *A Bigger Bang*, grossed them around $560million, making it comfortably the most lucrative rock music tour in history at the time. By then the Stones had already been in business for some forty-five years, which raises the question of how they would have felt if in 1967, the season of *Their Satanic Majesties* and sundry drug busts, the top international box-office draws of the day had been Rudy Vallée and other Jazz Age crooners who sang through a megaphone. Or to give it another twist: fifty years have elapsed since the group's commercial debut in 1962; someone looking back then that same amount of time in to the past might be reminiscing about the loss of the *Titanic*. There's a school of thought that believes that hitting the road again in their mid-sixties is the single most outrageous thing the Stones have done – far eclipsing all the stories about Mars bars, coke, and Margaret Trudeau. It's not just that the band refuse to grow up. They seem actually to live in a time warp; in an era when most modern rock stars dress like they work at Ryman and offer a relentless diet of screwed-up nihilism and phoney salves, the Stones are still out there in their skimpy, Day-Glo T-shirts and leather pants chasing lingerie-clad babes, or at least they are in their videos (politically incorrect before the term was invented), serving up great, meat-and-potato rock songs garnished with lyrics about sex and cars.

And that's surely the core attraction. Like it or not, there's a vicarious buzz in seeing these old codgers behaving badly. Because they're so brazen, so funny, and so astonishingly up-front about it, they've gradually acquired special status as the officially tolerated moral slobs of the middle class. On some fundamental level, we *need* the Rolling Stones, if only as a living reminder that one of rock music's chief initial functions was to act as an emotional pick-me-up for a weary public. We want to be entertained by stories about them swaggering around crashing their cars and snorting drugs off the enormous bare breasts of their groupies. What a sad lot most of today's stars are by comparison. No sooner have they made it than they start slagging the very people – the public and press – who got them there in the first place. The Stones love the sound of a crowd. They've heard its roar perhaps more often than any other men alive, and in some choice locations too.

Once, in August 1998, in Moscow's Red Square, some 30,000 people squeezed on to special buses, jammed the metro station and pressed through the streets and out on to the cobblestones in front of Lenin's tomb to become part of a giant parade in honour of the visiting Brits. Workers from a local colliery with pictures of pit-boys on their banners, two grandmotherly women with the unsarcastic slogan 'ROLLING STONES FRIENDS OF THE PEOPLE' on theirs, jack-booted militiamen, bearded young journalists, excited schoolkids and an officially delegated government honour-guard, 'massive in physique, black suited, unsmiling, walking solidly and steadily four abreast like a firing squad', to quote *Time* magazine, the curious and the disturbed, all swarmed around the four mildly bemused-looking dignitaries. They had come to welcome what the Tass agency – until six years earlier, the official news outlet of the Soviet politburo – called 'a truly heroic liberating force for all time and all mankind', an effusion which seemed to echo the banners held aloft by the two elderly women, and many others. In their Russia democracy hadn't yet been perfected, but here among them were the very men who had apparently been at the forefront of the great social upheaval in the West thirty years earlier. On one side of the square by the Kremlin wall, near Stalin's bones, a huge, brightly coloured poster of the Stones in the middle of a row of billboards filled with dire government warnings and statistics adorned the scene like a jewel in the head of a toad. The point couldn't have been made any more clearly. First in Britain and then globally, the Stones had led a movement that Tass called 'a beacon of light for all [who] sought to live in personal, political and artistic freedom. The Rolling Stones are the cultural liberators of the world!'

Or, that's one theory. Another explanation of the Stones' appeal is their sheer longevity: you visit them as you might a once magnificent stately house, still historically vital whatever its current state of ruin. The Rolling Stones have been with us so long that even the jokes about how long they have been with us seem slightly old. *Melody Maker* is thought to have begun calling them 'the Strolling Bones' around 1973, while unflattering references to the group's physical appearance have been doing the rounds almost as long. The antiquity and the air of mild dissipation hovering around the band have their own showbusiness forerunner, a great posthumous favourite today and one I can never think about without recalling the happy likeness. Watching the Stones perform, those with long memories will instantly make the connection to four other late-middle-aged men lurching around the stage, haranguing the audience from behind their Jack Daniel's, and ogling their broads. Any resemblance of the band to the *Ocean's Eleven*-era Rat Pack is purely intentional. The notion, in particular, that Frank Sinatra's touch of macho swagger and Dean Martin's endearing slur might have been handed down to, respectively, Mick Jagger and Keith Richards seems only fitting, while Sammy Davis Jr visibly lives on in the hammy, spindly legged Ron Wood. Music, history, marketing – it's enough to turn a band in to an institution, and it has. But only in retrospect do the Stones' phenomenal endurance and commercial pull seem inevitable. It's one of the intriguing facts about the group that for long stretches of the last fifty years their basic story has been one of unbridled professional and personal tension between Jagger and Richards, as well as among their respective women, employees and fixers, with periodic truces brought about only by the financial bonanza of their latest tour. To give just a flavour of the core relationship: when Jagger released his solo album *Goddess in the Doorway* in 2001, many of the press broadly agreed with the eminent BBC critic who described the record as 'a gutsy Big Statement, showcas[ing] Mick's ever-deepening interpretative skills and use of subtle phrasing techniques to broaden the scope of even the simplest lyrics.' Keith, by contrast, called it 'dogshit'.

There aren't many groups whose looks, clothes, moods, rap sheets, even their in-house tiffs and derogatory remarks about each other's private parts regularly occupy the 'people' pages in everything from *Vibe* to the *Wall Street Journal*. Unfold the personal-finance section of the *New York Times*, and as likely as not there's a front-page article about the Stones' canny use of Dutch-based trusts to allow them to pay only a modest 1.6 per cent in tax on earnings of over $100million annually. Turn to the health supplement of the *Sunday Telegraph* and there's an item about Jagger's discreet use of an oxygen tank backstage to help him get through those gruelling live shows, as well as one about Charlie Watts' battles with cancer. Flip to the gossip columns of the *Daily Mail* and there's the seemingly never-ending saga of Ron Wood's trips to rehab, and associated girlfriend woes. And over in the *Guardian* the featured heavyweight interview is with Keith Richards, who confides that he went 'fucking berserk' when in 2002 Jagger accepted a knighthood – an honour bestowed by 'the Establishment that did their very best to throw us in jail and kill us'. Meanwhile, looming above it all – the subject of a six-page spread in *Fortune* magazine – is the 'Plutonian offshore business empire' which has recently proved itself more financially durable than some of the world's longest-established consumer brands. After forty years, that tongue logo in particular is as well-known, and well-nigh as universal, as the Nike tick.

Which just leaves the Stones' music, in the best of which they took the blues and wrung out the grief and sadness until all that was left in most cases was a sense of fun (if, it has to be said, mildly demented or sadistic fun) which so thrillingly caught its time. Here, clearly, most of us have the same relation to the band as they do to their materially grim but essentially serene childhoods. The operative word is nostalgia. To hear 'Satisfaction' again, amid crowds cheering both the song and our own capacity to cheer, is to fleetingly warp back through the decades. As long as we're experiencing the Stones in the flesh, we're not old. The new stuff – anything since, say, the dog days of the Heath Government – may be a bit on the ropey side, but some of those 60s riffs and hooks, all shattering opening bolts and slurped vocals, reflected changing rock and roll styles so brilliantly that they became one. The prospect of seeing a bit of history keeps us coming back, tour after 'last ever' tour, while the Stones themselves appear to have escaped the artistic bankruptcy of repetitive slog and resultant loss of pride and morale that befell Elvis, for one. As Keith Richards has remarked, with unanswerable logic, 'Why should we stop? It's fun.'

Of course it is. Who wouldn't want to travel around the world and get treated like King Farouk while being paid a million dollars or so for every two-hour show you can perform?

No band, to be sure, could endure a more searching test of its survival skills than the recurrent arrest of its three principal members on, it seems, largely spurious drug charges and the subsequent drowning of one of the three in still keenly debated circumstances. And with the pressure on Jagger and Richards to keep performing and turning out hits, the challenge sometimes seemed to get the better of them. The latter, in particular, would come to acquire a full set of rock-star accessories, including a thatched house in the country, a royal-born Bavarian financial adviser and an initially discreet but long-running heroin addiction.

The late Tom Keylock, a friend and employee of Richards' in the 1960s, offered a more nuanced view of Keith as a solidly English figure ambling around his green and slightly prim nook of West Sussex. Keylock added that, quite uncharacteristically, he'd snapped at his own wife while on the phone at Richards' house one day in

1967. 'Keith overheard me and I got a bollocking – it was all about "She's your lady" and "show some respect". I admired him for that.'

By then, even so, Richards had perhaps seen rather more of life than the average 23-year-old English squire. On the Stones' first American tour, in 1964, the group had been sitting around back-stage in Omaha drinking whiskey and Coke out of paper cups when the police walked in and said, 'What's in that cup?' Richards replied, 'Whiskey, sir.' A policeman said, 'You can't drink that here; it's a public place. Throw it down the drain.' Keith said, 'No'. When he looked up again, a loaded revolver was pointed at his head. 'It was,' confirmed Tom Keylock, 'all fucking heavy.'

Who among the small if animated basement crowd shouting for the Rolling Stones at their debut performance in July 1962 could have possibly imagined that some of their grandchildren would be shout-ing for the same band, echoing back at them among the drink cans and soggy programmes of the world's biggest sports stadiums, more than forty years later?

The times certainly militated against any hopes of longevity the early Stones may have had for themselves. In 1962, even the sort of people who went to 'jungle music' concerts, as the press referred to them, seemed to belong to some Jurassic social order, with a taste in both sexes for shapeless, Utility-style clothes, stout shoes and goofy square glasses. It's remarkable quite how many young men of their generation seemed to resemble Buddy Holly. To lend some historical context, Winston Churchill was still an MP and Harold Macmillan currently embodied the hopes of the Conservative Party, though he would be replaced the following year by the Earl of Home, a Scottish laird who made his predecessor look like Elvis; critics noted the gentlemanly self-deprecation, the faint suggestion of bumbling and the general air of one born to the 'incestuous bar-tering-house for vested interests' as John Osborne termed the ruling class, in a hint of the coming end of deference.

The period in Britain from around 1944 to 1960, when most of that first-night audience were growing up, was probably the hard-est of the twentieth century. Even for a relatively pampered boy like

Mike Jagger, it was an era characterised by icy nights in gaslit rooms, initially to the accompaniment of German rocket attacks, of whale fat and tinned beef – the comically vile ingredients of a serious sacrifice he never forgot. Clothing coupons and food queues long remained a way of life; fourteen years of rationing ended only in July 1954, and even then luxury commodities like butter and petrol were hard to come by. It's true that, within eighteen months of the Rolling Stones' debut, Terence Conran's brightly coloured, brilliantly packaged Habitat had become a flagship of hip, officially declaring the traditional three-piece suite 'grotty' and 'far too boring' a concept. Instead customers would be buying a basic cotton–covered Larnaca sofa with a couple of related beanbags. Other, similarly enterprising retailers would compete to introduce the UK to such exotic concepts as fresh fruit and shops that stayed open until after five in the afternoon. John Stephen and Mary Quant were soon showing that you didn't need to go to Savile Row or Bond Street for fashionable tailoring; out went old fogeys in sensible suits, in came 'with it' young professionals in flares and miniskirts. Finally, and by a lucky bit of timing, the rapid availability of the contraceptive pill happened to coincide with the arrival of that other defining symbol of swinging bedroom etiquette, the duvet.

No such air of sexual possibility appeared to imbue that first-night audience in 1962. It was a sober-suited crowd of some eighty men and thirty women, among whom the ambient smell was of boiled cabbage ground deep in to worsted jackets, and the ubiquitous Players Weights cigarettes. No one there conspicuously appeared to be part of any revolution under way against the Britain of *Hancock's Half Hour*, with its grinding conformity and identical redbrick houses furnished just like grandmother's. It seems fair to say that 'jungle music' took its place against a normal existence, for them and millions of others, of cricket, knitting and pottering about the garden. A night out at *The Sound of Music* followed by the Berni Inn Family Platter remained the height of most middle-class Britons' aspirations. The Rolling Stones were not exactly pushing at an open door.

For most young people in early-60s Britain, life was barely distinguishable from the 1940s. While the war may have ended seventeen years previously, there were still reminders of it everywhere in the capital's bombed-out streets, as well as in the pinched appearance of many of its citizens.

The movement of men's fashion was glacial, and while the modern woman might risk an experiment with her hemline, six inches was still the orthodox clearance from the ground. It would also be fair to say that the average observer of the time would have had little difficulty differentiating the sexes. In 1962, short-haired women, like long-haired men, were associated with dangerous radicalism, if not with free love.

British society was also more sharply divided than it is now. For those passing the eleven-plus exam there was grammar school, with its prospect of university, the professions or the civil service. The alternative was the secondary modern, and a likely unqualified arrival on the job market at the age of fifteen. So an eighteen-year-old might, like Jagger himself, be diligently studying for a degree course, or he or she might be screwing caps on to bottles on a provincial assembly line for a take-home wage of two or three pounds a day. In either case, they would almost certainly never have heard of Concorde, colour TV or Bob Dylan, of Neil Armstrong, home computers, ATMs, flower power, Abbey Road, Muhammad Ali, the Kray twins, the Vietnam war, *Dr. Who*, gay rights, valium or Charles Manson.

The Swinging Decade lay before them.

Young people were, however, already creating a certain amount of consternation. Not the romantic violin but the barbaric saxophone now dominated the orchestra, and to its passionate crooning and wailing the dancers moved in what the Archbishop of York reprovingly called a 'syncopated embrace'. Perhaps inspired by Hank Marvin and the Shadows and their string of five British hits in 1962 alone, things were also looking up for the electric guitar. In just one such case study, a somewhat tragic secondary modern student living in suburban Ripley, Surrey, pleaded with his grandparents to take him to the local musical supply shop on his seventeenth birthday that March and buy him what he later called the 'coolest thing I'd ever seen' displayed in the front window. The instrument in question was a Kay 'Red Devil' guitar; the teenager was Eric Clapton.

There were other signs, too, that a revolt against the accepted cultural order was at least tentatively under way. After enduring *The Music Man*'s dire season in 1962, a young person could have enjoyed an unusually rich bill of fare at the cinema – *Lawrence of Arabia*, *Dr. No* and Marlon Brando's *Mutiny on the Bounty* were all out that autumn – or bought the first edition of *A Clockwork Orange*, published in November at 16 shillings (80p). That summer, meanwhile, the Beatles had signed for George Martin and his Parlophone label, hitherto the preserve of easy listening and comic-dialogue LPs, but not yet released their debut single. The company brass at Parlophone's parent EMI had fallen about laughing when Martin told them the name of his new act, assuming that the man behind such fare as Peter Sellers' *Songs for Swinging Sellers* was having another of his 'Goon jokes'. But set against this were the 2,471 licensed places of entertainment in London noted by the 1961 census, of which an estimated 300 catered in one way or another to those groups busy evolving from 'trad' jazz to American-style rhythm and blues in a not always seamless transition. One such venue was the Marquee Club, which opened downstairs at 165 Oxford Street in April 1958 and which was now hosting a variety of impromptu blues and pop performances. It was here that the Rolling Stones first confronted an audience.

They were officially billed for the occasion as 'Mick Jagger and the Rollin' Stones', though the lead vocalist, it was agreed, was by no means their most compelling personality. Jagger, Richards and the self-styled 'Cheltenham Shagger' Brian Jones (who'd recently come up with the group's name) were the front line. Mick wore a striped sweater and corduroys, Keith a funereally dark suit, and Brian is just remembered as 'pogo-ing up and down, leering at the women'. Behind them was the already comically deadpan rhythm section, which for now consisted of Keith's art-school friend Dick Taylor on bass and the future Kinks drummer Mick Avory, who sat in for the night. A 23-year-old shipping clerk named Ian Stewart, or 'Stu', stood to the side, occasionally munching a pork pie with one hand while playing piano in a loping, barrelhouse style with the other.

The fifty-minute show that followed was paced at the speed of booze – the tempo of scotches and brandies they all downed throughout to calm their nerves. Dick Taylor recalled that there had been some initial catcalls from the house, possibly due to the band's apparent unfamiliarity with their chosen repertoire of southern American blues. (The next week's *Melody Maker* seemed to confirm this theory, reproachfully noting the Stones' 'very suspect tuning and internal balance'.) After three or four more 'well-meaning but interminable songs about sharecroppers', things then suddenly picked up with a loud, catalytic burst of 'Down the Road Apiece', played in the style of Chuck Berry. At that, some of the young men in their worsted jackets started to dance. According to the set-list Stu jotted down in his diary, the band went on to pack nine more numbers in to their remaining thirty minutes on stage, finishing big with Elmore James' 'Happy Home'. Even then they took their sense of urgency not from the singer, but from the chap-faced second guitarist, dressed completely in black, who called out each title and encouraged the drummer both by hammering one spindly leg up and down and yelling 'Fuck you! Faster!'

Not coincidentally, the Stones had great rhythm.

After the show everyone went up in to the foyer of the tiny cinema above the club, walked down the street unrecognised and had a drink in the Tottenham pub, leaving Brian Jones' friend Dick Hattrell to hump their gear upstairs and eventually load it on to a passing bus. They split the thirty-guinea performance fee six ways, which somehow meant that Brian got six pounds ten shillings and everyone else got a fiver. The mood was generally upbeat, even so, although no one there would have guessed that the Stones were twenty-first-century bound, least of all the band themselves. They seemed unlikely to survive until Christmas.

Later that night, Brian Jones took the Northern Line back to Hendon, where he currently shared a room with his on-off girl-friend Pat Andrews, the third of the three young women he'd impregnated so far. Their son Julian Mark had been born in

October 1961. When not rehearsing with the Rolling Stones, Brian was officially working at the local Civil Service clothes shop, where he regularly augmented his wages by helping himself from the till. Keith Richards was in the throes of leaving the parental home in Dartford, shortly before his father, Bert, made a similar decision to decamp. After that Keith and Brian would pool their resources to share basement digs in London's Powis Square, until a visiting bailiff put an end to the arrangement. Mick Jagger went home to his mum and dad. He would have to get up the next morning and take the train back to attend his lectures at the London School of Economics. Before they parted for the night, everyone had a last drink with a professional acquaintance who happened to have been in the audience at the Marquee, and who wandered in to the pub afterwards. He thought the Stones 'had an obvious appeal for the kids that wanted to dance. My band was a joke to look at, but this lot crossed the barrier. They actually *looked* like rock stars.' A dapper, 21-year-old layout artist and weekend drummer whose family called him Chas Boy, they knew him as Charlie Watts.

Lewis Brian Hopkin-Jones, born in to a displaced Welsh family in February 1942, was not one of those pupils to have worried unduly about the eleven-plus. After passing effortlessly in to Cheltenham Grammar School, Brian seemed to be an intelligent and musically gifted boy who could casually pick up an instrument and master it by ear. 'Then, all of a sudden,' his father Lewis recalled, 'he became very difficult. He started to rebel against everything – mainly me.'

Adolescence proved a stormy period for the Cheltenham Shagger, later effectively run out of town for theft, multiple impregnations and playing noisy blues guitar. Music, at least, seems to have given Jones a degree of self-confidence, without puncturing his formidable reserve or involving him in any real responsibilities. In time it also provided him with something else he needed, an audience. At fifteen, Brian had been in the vanguard of those trading in their classical instruments for a saxophone. His parents were appalled by the move, fearing that it would become the starting point for a broader moral decline. It did. At first this took the form of a headlong dive in to jazz and the blues, with a matching zeal for their practitioners. Far away the most important was Charlie Parker, the troubled but inimitable genius of the alto-sax, who had died in 1955 at the age of thirty-four; then there were Champion Jack Dupree, Sonny Boy Williamson and Jimmy Reed; Elmore James, whose name Brian took for a while; Julian Adderley, for whom he named his first three sons; and many others. Those who had known Brian as a lively and outgoing boy with freckled, Milky Bar Kid good looks on entering grammar school noticed a marked change a year or two later: he became sullen and uptight, preferring to slope off on his own, or, failing that, with one of the numerous 'birds' he seems to have attracted with a mixture of soft-spoken charm and latent sadism. 'Brian possessed a hidden cruelty,' Mick Jagger would later remark admiringly, 'which in its way was very sensual.'

After a premature departure from Cheltenham Grammar, Brian found himself working a variety of dead-end jobs in London. For a while he gravitated between a room with Pat Andrews and the baby, and crashing at the small Bayswater flat of a woolly haired, blues-playing bohemian named Alexis Korner. Music ultimately won out over domesticity. Performing with Korner in a dank cellar club in west London, Brian met Mick Jagger and Keith Richards, up for the night from Dartford with their friend Dick Taylor. By the following week, they were rehearsing together. Most of the early try-outs took place in dusty rooms above various Soho pubs like the White Bear or (after the Bear's landlord caught Jones pilfering) the Bricklayer's Arms. This was where musicians drifted in, sat around and played a few Muddy Waters songs, and where Brian, in keeping with his long-standing policy, insisted that each pay him a 'session fee' for their trouble. The first to audition was Ian Stewart, a breezy, no-bullshit Scot with a vast Cro-Magnon jaw and a generous beer gut. Stu, a true pub piano player, was in. He joined Jones, Jagger, Richards, Dick Taylor and anyone they could find on drums. Brian was after Charlie Watts, but he was too expensive for them.

This would be the line-up, Jones announced, that would 'change the face of British music'. After the laughter had died down, Brian also insisted that they join the Jazz Federation to boost their (Jones admitted) only fair prospects of work. He brought the papers in to the Bricklayer's on 2 July 1962. At the line marked 'title of artiste', Brian, in Keith's words, 'looked down: there's a Muddy Waters record, and the first song on it was "Rollin' Stone Blues".' Later, Stu thought the name made them sound like 'a bunch of fucking Irish acrobats'.

It was to take Mike Jagger several years longer than it took Brian Jones to acquire a comparable sense of direction. By July 1960, when he turned seventeen, Jagger was still studying diligently at Dartford Grammar School, where they had high hopes for him as a future schoolteacher or civil servant. In December of that year, the headmaster, one 'Lofty' Hudson, wrote a report noting:

> Michael Philip Jagger has been a pupil at this School since 1954. His general record has been satisfactory. In the sixth form he has applied himself well on the whole and has shown a greater intellectual determination than we had expected. He should be successful in most fields though he is unlikely to do brilliantly in any of them.
>
> Jagger is a lad of good general character though he has been rather slow to mature. The pleasing quality which is now emerging is that of persistence when he makes up his mind to tackle something. His interests are wide. He has been a member of several School Societies and is prominent in Games, being Secretary of our Basketball Club, a member of the First Cricket Eleven and he plays Rugby Football for his House. Out of school he is involved in Camping, Climbing, Canoeing, Music and he is also a member of the local Historical Association.

As a result of this encomium, Jagger won a place at the London School of Economics. His tutor there, Walter Stern, found him 'very shy, very polite and obviously nervous at being at university . . . He announced his intention of going in to business but was worried about mathematics . . . Figures were his weak point.' They addressed each other respectively as 'Mr Jagger' and 'Sir'. Although some of his fellow undergraduates displayed a taste for radical politics, Jagger seems not to have been interested: his academic reports continued to describe him as respectful, friendly and hard-working, if a bit pedestrian. A grammar-school master named Walton Wilkinson remembers seeing Jagger in October 1961, 'standing on the platform at Dartford station, in a grey suit, reading the *Daily Telegraph*. He looked like a young fogey.'

But unknown to the academics, Jagger was also leading something of a double life. Like Brian Jones, he too had discovered the thrilling, primitive strains of what he admiringly called 'jungle music'. In March 1958, Jagger and Dick Taylor had taken a bus to the Woolwich Granada, where Des O'Connor, the compere for the night, oozed on to introduce a bespectacled young Texan who went by the name of 'Buddy' Holly. Taylor remembers how his companion seemed to come alive during Holly's brisk rendition of 'Not Fade Away', 'jumping around with his hair puffing over his eyes'. Not long after that Jagger began his own crash course in pop and blues, fixating briefly on the home-grown (or Scots) figure of Lonnie Donegan, the inspiration for the skiffle boom with household utensils pressed in to service as instruments and a role model for British kids who, like Donegan himself, took songs from the American South, dusted them off and shook them inside out until they were as clean and crisp – if not as starchy – as a freshly laundered sheet. The influence wasn't just musical, either: every British teenager had read the story of how Donegan had taken half an hour to record his hit 'Rock Island Line', and his first quarterly royalty cheque had been for TWENTY-SEVEN THOUSAND POUNDS – always in capitals. Jagger wanted some of that. One day in 1960 Dick Taylor asked his friend what he wanted most in the world and, without batting an eye, Mike said: 'A pink Cadillac.'

In the autumn of 1961, Jagger ran in to a childhood friend who was standing at Dartford station waiting for the same train: Keith Richards. The reunion had an immediate and intoxicating effect. Later that morning, Walter Stern remembered a tutorial in which an 'unusually excited' Jagger 'proceeded to extol the "jazz scene" at some length'. According to Stern's diary note of their meeting, 'Mr Jagger sat with his boots resting on the low table in between us. That was new. Apropos music, he remarked that he hoped to be "doing some blowing"' – a gnomic utterance he delivered with a 'Cheshire-cat grin'. A week later, he reappeared to inform his tutor that from now on he wished to be called 'Mick', not a name automatically associated with probity. In the course of that winter, says Stern, Jagger went from a 'scrupulously polite boy from the provinces' to 'a Ted', who 'lounged around and smoked his way through our appointments'. In time Stern came to think of him as two people: 'shy, polite and intelligent one day, a cocky sod the next'.

Some disparity exists between the raised-by-wolves legend of Keith Richards' upbringing and the reality, with its emphasis on duty, rank and sound traditional values. Richards' paternal grandparents were both well-respected councillors in the London borough of Walthamstow, where his grandmother served as the first female mayor. His maternal grandfather, Gus Dupree, was a First World War hero who subsequently fronted a popular dance band. Keith's father Bert, a private in the Bedfordshire & Hertfordshire Regiment, was among the first to storm the Normandy beaches on D-Day and was badly wounded as a result. He was later cited for conspicuous gallantry. Showing a vein of 1950s traditionalism, Keith himself was one of the lucky few chosen from some 3,000 applicants to sing in the children's choir at a concert following the present Queen's coronation. He was also a model Boy Scout, as well as a dab hand at most sports. Years later in Jamaica, Mick Jagger would challenge Richards – then deep in his 'elegantly wasted' phase – to a game of tennis. Sir Mick appeared for the contest dressed for Wimbledon; his opponent sported ragged jeans and kept a butt-end clamped to his lip throughout. Keith won the match 6–1.

Around 1960, it's true, Richards had embarked on a path that was to deviate appreciably from this background of service and asceticism. Having made an early exit from Dartford Tech, he was then studying at Sidcup Art College. 'We were both on a pretty steady diet of speed and other stuff,' Dick Taylor notes. 'Right across the street was this little wood with an aviary that had a cockatoo in it. Keith liked to go over and feed it pep pills. When he was bored he'd bung the bird another leaper and watch it flap around on its perch.'

Another day, Taylor would recall, Keith tossed a well-aimed match in to a bath of flammable silk-screen wash. 'When I think of him at Sidcup, I think of cockatoos and stuff burning.' In time the drugs and pyromania (both something of a Richards forte in later years) completed a caricature role as the school misfit. When Sidcup's graphic design class went on a field trip to Heal's, the London furniture store, Keith sat down on a leather sofa and dropped hot cigarette ash on it. For half an hour.

Keith's musical tastes, too, were already sharper than those even of a Jones or Jagger. It wasn't just that his imagination ran wilder, or that his sense of rhythm was deeper. It was more magical: his flashes of inspiration on the guitar seemed to come from out of the blue. Like Gus Dupree, Keith heard the sounds in his head first and learned how to play them later. 'He wasn't one of us,' a young Dartford musician (and future Anglican vicar) named Ron Simms remembers fondly. Once when visiting Richards, Simms forgot himself and played him the Shadows' 'Apache', then well on its way to selling its first million, and widely considered essential listening for most musically inclined teenagers. 'Fuckin' awful,' Keith said immediately the record finished. 'They're just wanking around.' He then picked up his guitar and, in Simms' words, 'played a beautiful blues run, the simplest kind possible'. Right there in his poky council-house bedroom, Richards began improvising a song, accompanying himself in a reedy but, to Simms, 'spine-tingling' voice. He embodied the blues so hauntingly, 'it suddenly seemed possible to imagine you were thousands of miles away, riding that lonesome freight-train through the night'. As Simms reeled back on to the street he found he was strangely moved.

'The way Keith played, he could literally bring tears to your eyes.'

'He wanted to stand out,' another Dartford friend adds. When reporting for their first day at art college, each new student was called upon to write his or her name on one of the two blackboards that flanked the main drawing studio. The other 'freshers' wrote their names small, and just the once; for six or seven weeks, whenever Keith appeared he'd reach up and scrawl his name in capital letters so huge that they took up not one but both blackboards. His classmates can remember today – fifty years later – that vast self-introductory KEITH on the left blackboard and RICHARDS on the right.

Three years later, in the spring of 1962, Keith left college with an impressive knowledge of the blues, and a role as the anchorman of a locally popular combo named the Sidcup Trio (currently down to just two members), but no other tangible qualifications. With a few rare exceptions, staff and students had long since learned to give him a wide berth rather than stop to chat. Hardened educators declined to enter in to the briar patch of teaching him, and classmates blanched when they saw him coming down the corridor, 'all fag ash and spots', as one of them recalls, lugging his new Hofner guitar. At Bert's insistence, Keith later took his portfolio to the top London designers – including the man soon to do the titles for *Goldfinger*, Robert Brownjohn – but all of them declined his services. (In 1969, Keith would commission Brownjohn, one of the few to be civil to him, to design the cover of *Let it Bleed*.) Apart from one or two friendly hipsters who talked to him about music, most couldn't wait to get the pill-chewing young punk out of their offices, at least until four or five years later, when some of them suddenly began remembering him and ringing him back. As Keith said, 'A kick in the nuts from those guys – that counted as a warm hello by their standards.' With a certain inevitability, he later burned his portfolio.

On 15 March 1962 – the ides – Keith was browsing through the interminable jazz reviews in *New Musical Express*, when out of the haze a small ad brought him awake:

> Alexis Korner Blues Incorporated
> The Most Exciting Event of the Year
> Ealing Broadway Station
> Turn left, cross the zebra and go down steps
> between ABC teashop and jewellers.
> Saturday at 7.30pm.

Jagger, Richards and assorted alumni of the Sidcup Trio would make it to west London – there'd been some trouble raising the fare – on Saturday 7 April. The Ealing club had no pretension to elegance. An iron gate gave on to sixteen foul-smelling steps, the stone worn to the thinness of paper, leading down to a sort of crypt. This Stygian pit shook whenever a train passed by, and rainwater frequently seeped through the brickwork. A canvas tarp was strung up under the skylight to prevent the musicians from electrocuting themselves.

Nine o'clock on Easter Saturday and six or seven middle-aged men were milling about playing instrumental blues, along with a smattering of 'trad' standards. Korner himself was sitting on an office chair, strumming a Spanish guitar. He looked arresting, with his aura of black fuzz, sweat-rag and Rupert the Bear check trousers, a 33-year-old exotic whose enthusiasm exceeded his, frankly, meagre ability. In fact, Korner barely played audibly at all, leaving most of the heavy lifting to a hunched figure at his side named Cyril Davies, a big Welshman who worked in a junkyard and more pertinently blew a lusty, Chicago-style harmonica. There was a bit of amplified grunting and some groaningly banal whistling and finger-snapping to accompany the faster numbers. But otherwise, Korner's fragmentary contributions were limited to a few semi-spoken lines in the manner of Rex Harrison.

After half an hour or so, Keith had just turned to Mick with the verdict 'This is a wank', when his attention was drawn to something occurring on stage. Korner came forward. 'This' – he indicated a blond bouffant in the shadows – 'is Elmo Lewis. He's come from Cheltenham to play for you.' The individual in question bowed and did a jig, a cigarette sticking out of a sardonic smile. For the next ten minutes, Korner's group performed like a Ferrari swiftly being run-in. An Elmore James medley of 'I Believe' and 'Dust My Broom', with stinging bar-slide guitar, ended to wild applause.

A kick in the groin couldn't have affected Keith more powerfully. When Jagger and Richards beheld Elmo Lewis – in reality, Brian Jones, capering around the stage like an oversexed chimp – they knew what it was to, quite literally, feel the earth move. Backed by a tube-train percussion, Brian's guitar slithered and swooped, slicing through any last vestige of Dixieland.

'Fucking hell,' Keith whispered to his companions, 'that guy's a *star.*'

And Mick Jagger, who not only remembered, but more than once had recourse to quote that line in the years ahead, went up to introduce himself.

2

WOULD YOU LET YOUR SISTER GO WITH A ROLLING STONE?

The Dartford Jagger and Richards grew up in had a mixed reputation. The town, around 15 miles southeast of London, enjoyed
a long history of religious, industrial and cultural achievement; the
Romans built roads here, the medieval monks founded hospitals,
and a series of paper mills, pharmaceutical plants and munitions
works flourished from around the mid-nineteenth century until the
Great Depression eighty years later. By 1944, when the two future
Stones were a year old, most people would have regarded Dartford
as a dull, dispiriting place – not to mention a dangerous one, as the
first of Hitler's V1s, the so-called miracle weapons, began to fall.
The local *Chronicle* for that June and July conveys the horror: 'Flying
bombs Night and Day . . . Parents, Daughter and Cook Killed . . .
Old Tavern Blasted . . . Child Killed Running for Shelter . . . Tragedy
of Two Sisters.' Of its kind, Dartford followed a classic history among
southeastern English communities: in the 1930s the Depression set
in like a chill North Sea fog, and lifted just in time for the Luftwaffe.
Much of the ancient market town was already lost by 1945. The
civic planners soon finished the job, throwing up entire prefabri-
cated neighbourhoods on old bomb sites or green fields. 'Clearance'
was the word, the result a gaudily modern facelift whose chief physical characteristics were endless one-way systems, roundabouts and

mortuaries. Visiting the 'Thames Gateway' today one finds a Stalinist monstrosity built out of giant glass eggshells adjoining a pristine Norman church, which in turn sits next to the concrete slab of a multistorey car park. The incredible visual patisserie of Dartford's timbered past and modern tat is symbolic of a town that seemingly lost its soul in the 50s, and then for decades found itself forced to endure the lingering acidic reek of its vanished chemical factories, like an industrial phantom limb after an amputation.

Michael Philip Jagger was not born here on 26 July 1944. The date, enthusiastically cited by the Rolling Stones' publicist Les Perrin, was all but universally accepted throughout the 1960s and early 70s, when the group's lead vocalist apparently already wanted to appear younger than he was. Jagger actually arrived with us a year earlier, in Dartford's Livingstone Hospital, a small, redbrick wing attached to an imposing, castellated structure founded in 1866 as the 'London County Lunatic Asylum'. His father was a soft-spoken, 30-year-old schoolmaster and physical-education buff named Basil Fanshawe Jagger, who went by the name Joe, which he told me he thought sounded 'friendlier'. Joe's own father had been a teacher, and his family, originally from West Yorkshire, had moved around the country following his various postings until they reached the Home Counties. Mick Jagger later conceded that he, too, had an inbred touch of the educator about him. In 1938, Joe took up a position at Dartford's East Central School, and the following year met a pert, 26-year-old brunette named Eva Scutts. As a five-year-old, Eva had emigrated with her parents and four brothers from Australia on board the SS *Rotorua*, a vessel subsequently sunk by German submarines with the loss of the entire crew and most of its passengers. In Dartford, the Scuttses bought a small terraced home on Lowfield Street, a then cobbled lane running off the market square, where at sixteen Eva went to work as a hairdresser. The family was musical; most of them played an instrument, and they all liked to sing along to the big bands on the radio. The latter was their only substantial piece of furniture, a vast mock-teak box that could easily have doubled as a coffin. Joe Jagger told me that he'd been 'a bit overwhelmed' by the breezy, self-confident Eva, but he'd persisted. They were married on 7 December 1940 at Dartford's Holy Trinity Church, whose windows had had to be blacked out thanks to the German bombs which had destroyed the County Hospital, with the loss of forty-two lives, only the night before. The first of the Jaggers' two sons arrived early on a Monday morning nearly three years later. Joe liked the initials 'MP', which he thought augured well for 'some sort of government career for the lad'. Eva chiefly remembered sheltering with the baby under the stairs during air raids, while 'Mike screamed himself hoarse' in terror.

Even so, it's widely agreed Jagger grew up with the all-important sense of inner authority that came from being the apple of his parents' eye: the lovingly indulged elder son. He clearly inherited qualities from both sides of the clan, the chirpy self-confidence and musical bent of the Scuttses, and the dour application of the Jaggers. Etymologically, too, it was Mick's lot to be torn evenly down the line. He later liked to tell people that his paternal surname came from the Old English 'jag', meaning to pierce or cut in tatters, although to balance this it might be added that seven or eight centuries ago, a village youth who was considered unduly shifty or timid was apt to be called a 'scutt' – a term originally used of the tail of a hare, particularly noticeable when the animal was fleeing.

On 9 January 1951, Mike Jagger became pupil 112 at Dartford's Wentworth County Primary School. Several contemporaries there remember him both for his intense, almost manic energy and for the pocket chemistry set with which, he announced gravely, he intended to blow up the world. A friend named Peter Holland recalls him as a slim but large-headed boy with bushy brown hair and a dazzling grin that 'lit up like the smile of a model in a toothpaste ad'. In 1954 the Jaggers moved to suburban Wilmington, where they bought a four-bedroomed detached house called Newlands. It was 'a bit of the posh', recalled Joe, now commuting to London as a lecturer and PE instructor, and describing himself as a 'technical representative', while Eva became a part-time cosmetics demonstrator. Later that year, Mike passed his eleven-plus and entered Dartford Grammar School, cycling up West Hill in his new uniform of gold-edged maroon blazer and cap.

The portrait of Jagger that most often emerges from those closest to him around 1953–56 is of a boy who was long on graft and determination and less so on raw intellect. Even some of his later admirers had their doubts about his mental candlepower, although, as at school, no one who knew him ever questioned his perseverance or attention to detail. He was about the first Dartford boy anyone can remember to have picked up, in the summer of 1955, on the American epidemic called rock and roll. It reached England – specifically, the Rialto, Dartford – in the form of *Blackboard Jungle*, a teen drama dealing with student anarchy, whose local audiences 'cheered and actually *danced in the aisles*', as the *Chronicle* put it reproachfully. Jagger saw the film six times. From there the 12-year-old began listening to the likes of Elvis and Little Richard, flirted with a school skiffle group whose surviving promotional flyer describes him as providing 'Miscellaneous background noises', and eventually began sending away for hard-to-get rhythm and blues albums from Chess Records in Chicago, carefully making a note of the discs' matrix numbers in his diary in order to swap these with friends. 'Even then, Mick was the organised one,' Dick Taylor recalled.

We forget how paranoid they were in the 50s about young people and their music. *The Times* was to harrumph that the portly, cheroot-sucking figure of Bill Haley was 'inciting our boys to riot with his primitive tom-tom thumping'. In 1957, Dartford Council banned local screenings of the film *Rock Around the Clock*, which of course boosted its popularity. Even then, Mike Jagger was by no means immune to the inchoate stirrings of a postwar 'youth culture' he later partly came to embody. Aged fifteen, he airily informed a classmate named Clive Robson that 'the States are where it's at' – memorable for one who had never been west of a family package-holiday in Marbella. Jagger later declared his 'first screw' to have occurred around this time 'with two teenage skirts in a garden shed' (an account Robson felt 'unlikely, to say the least'). Life wasn't all suddenly Durex and Chuck Berry discs, however. Jagger was also something of a sportsman who played competitive basketball, cricket and soccer, could swim a length of a pool with seven or eight windmilling strokes, and once appeared with Joe on a mountaineering episode of the ATV series *Seeing Sport*, where he could be seen clambering up and down the High Rocks near Tunbridge Wells, having made his television debut as a close-up of a disembodied foot – 'Here's Michael,' a voiceover intones, 'wearing a nice clean pair of gym shoes.'

Dick Taylor remembers once going out of the Newlands door with Jagger at the very moment his father called, 'Mike, your weight-training.' The teenager duly went back inside and spent half an hour pumping barbells. Jagger, Taylor and two other Dartford friends soon began playing a few blues songs together, normally exiled to one or other of their back gardens, and attended by an invited 'skirt' or two, but even this proto-Stones exercise had an endearingly childish feel to it. Having elected to climb up an apple tree one day in the group's practice area 'for the acoustics', their guitarist Bob Beckwith found he couldn't get down again. Grown-ups had to be sent for to free him. Jagger, who passed a creditable seven O levels, made his only known protest against the grammar school regime when, in November 1959, he signed a petition asking that they provide the student body with a better lunch.

Mike's fortunes wavered uncertainly for the next two years, during most of which he seemed likely to go in to either education or industry. At least some entrepreneurial flair can be seen from the fact that he worked as a part-time beach pedlar of ice cream in summer and a street vendor of his mother's cosmetics in winter. Away from her business, Eva enjoyed a party and danced a mean gavotte, being observed one Friday night in the Glentworth Club leading her 16-year-old son through such a dance, the latter 'dolled up like Fred Astaire'. Mike was also a gifted mimic who, it's remembered, liked to stride confidently in to the Rose and Crown pub at the school gates and put on a 'fruity Terry-Thomas accent' when ordering. According to Dick Taylor, Jagger's musical party-piece at the time was a 'primal, twenty-minute version of "La Bamba", [in] which he bawled out verse after verse of pidgin Spanish while tossing his head around like a mad bull'. Instinct somehow told one that boy would go far. In 1961, Jagger duly passed A levels in English and History and, armed with a £350 government grant, entered university that September.

On the raw, autumnal morning of 17 October, Kent and much of the southeast was covered in fog. The trains that particular Tuesday were running late. On the drab northbound platform at Dartford station, a lone passenger, draped in an overcoat and a purple, black and gold scarf, was waiting for the delayed 8.28 to London, where he was due to attend an Economic History lecture. Clutching his copy of *One Dozen Berrys* under his arm, Mike Jagger was jumping up and down, half from cold, half with his usual nervous energy. The time was shortly before nine. In a career discussion earlier that week with Walter Stern, Jagger had repeated his plans to become a schoolteacher or, failing that, perhaps 'a journalist or historian' of some sort. His father Joe told me he thought he had it in him to be a top economist. Stern, for his part, already had doubts about Jagger's mathematical ability, but high hopes for him in advertising. 'That boy always had some campaign, you know, some scheme.'

Almost anything, they all agreed, but music.

As Jagger peered down the curve of Platform 2, that particular option seemed singularly improbable. A moment later it became inevitable. Emerging out of the depths of the fog was Keith Richards, lugging his guitar.

This seismic moment for the future of rock music had its modest antecedents ten years earlier, when Jagger and Richards had been fellow grey-shorted pupils at primary school. They had also been nearby neighbours. In 1951 the Richardses were renting a flat above a grocer's shop on Dartford's Chastilian Road, while the Jaggers were just three streets away in Denver Road, where they lived in a smart pebble-dashed house that boasted a row of descending garden gnomes and a doorbell that played 'Greensleeves'. Those three sub-urban streets were worlds exquisitely separated. Keith's childhood home was, he recalled, 'dark, cold and smelly', with rancid vegetables heaped up in the shop below, and only deteriorated after taking a hit from a German flying bomb in June 1944. A bright blue tarpaulin stretched over a gaping hole in the roof would remain there for months afterwards, until it worked all but loose from its moorings, keeping up a kind of demented beat as it flapped wildly above Keith's head.

Born at Livingstone Hospital on 18 December 1943, Richards would prove bright enough at school, although he already showed signs of being both self-willed and resistant to the discipline of regular work.* His father Herbert William – Bert – Richards was an apprentice printer who became an electrician and foreman first at General Electric and then the Osram light bulb factory in Hammersmith, west London. Bert's wife Doris, whom he married in 1938, was the daughter of a gregarious, semi-professional jazz musician and the youngest of seven sisters, all of whom played an instrument. Like her father, Doris wasn't much given to self-doubt. Richards, then, enjoyed some of the same parental chemistry as Jagger, both being the sons of an emotionally restrained man and a more obviously extrovert woman. For the astrologically minded, Mick and Keith are a Leo and a Sagittarian respectively. As such, Richards is said to be freedom-loving, nomadic, idealistic, sincere, broad-minded, truth-seeking, expansive and virile, among several other virtues. While Mike eased compliantly in to adolescence, Keith, a hard-core cowboy fan, was soon learning how to smoke and swivel a six-shooter. As teenagers, one was focused, the other was virtually dead to the world beyond music and the cinema. Jagger was born on a Monday morning, Richards on a Saturday night.

It would be fair to say that the adolescent Keith was mentally tough, rather than physically strong. Ron Simms remembers him as 'bone thin' with dark shadows around his eyes in a 'crabby, Borstal-boy face', his most prominent feature being a pair of toby-jug ears.

---

*It's a little remarked coincidence that Albert Hoffman, a Swiss research scientist, discovered the hallucinogenic properties of the drug LSD when, on the same day Keith Richards was born, he accidentally swallowed some.

As for baths, 'he didn't seem to overdo them'. For some years, Keith would answer to the nickname 'Ricky' at home and 'Monkey' outside it. Things were simpler then, particularly on Chastilian Road. When Keith came home from school, he walked in through the grocery shop and climbed a flight of concrete steps in to a dingy and low-lit parlour. A two-bar fire there gave off as much heat as a 60-watt bulb. If he wanted to watch television, he went downstairs again and peered through the window of a neighbour called Mr Steadman, who was the only local resident to own a set. Unsurprisingly, Keith 'absolutely adored' the mother who 'pampered, praised, protected and fawned on' her only child, bringing him a steady supply of cakes from the bakery where she worked part-time, and encouraging him both to help himself to her collection of big-band records and join her and her sisters for a knees-up around the radio. Keith would later remark that he had grown up in 'a house full of noise', even if this occasionally included the sound of his parents fighting. In short, he enjoyed the classic rock-star upbringing, with a musical and indulgent mother and a dour, hard-working father (affectionately dubbed 'Adolf') who banged angrily on the wall whenever his adolescent son later riffed on the guitar at all hours. Keith survived, rather than excelled, at primary school; early in 1955 he took and failed the eleven-plus and was sent to Dartford Tech for a desultory four years.

Along the way, Keith had begun to come up to London to sing in inter-school competitions at the Albert Hall, and was deemed good enough to be selected as one of three sopranos to perform in an invitation choir in front of the Queen at a concert in St Margaret's Church, Westminster, in May 1955. The latter was his 'greatest ever gig', he would boast, out of a thousand or so to date. Another attraction of Richards' budding music career was that he was excused chemistry class (something he caught up on later) because of his choral excursions. At ten, Keith also joined the local Scouts, 1st Beaver Patrol unit. He's fondly remembered as entertaining the troops on one overnight camping trip with a comic tap-dance routine, performed as if suffering from some painful disease in the lower half of his body. According to an authoritative source, the climax of Keith's act came when he then gave an 'intestinal oratorio in which he actually farted in *tune*. Sensational. One of the kids laughed so hard he had to be taken to hospital.'

Later in 1955, Keith and Mike Jagger drifted apart when Bert Richards put down an eighty-pound deposit on 6 Spielman Road, part of a ghetto of identical redbrick semis on the new Temple Hill estate in east Dartford. The move was both uphill and downmarket from Chastilian Road. Keith soon found himself getting in fights with the more rough-hewn residents, and 'be[ing] a weed physically' grew quite adept at the tactical kick to an opponent's groin, followed by a swift exit. The sheer uniformity and desolation of the place eventually got even to Bert, who coming home to Spielman Road late at night sometimes walked up the wrong driveway to a neighbour's door. 'How are you supposed to tell these dumps apart?' he once asked. After he entered the Tech, Keith at least encountered one sympathetic teacher who advised him to become a teaboy in a graphic design office, 'which may lead to better things', but even this modest encouragement didn't alter the basic pattern: his school reports continued to describe him as 'idle', 'wilful' and 'academically comatose'.

Then overnight, as Richards put it, everything turned, 'Zoom! From black and white to glorious technicolour.'

The role models came to him, as they did to millions, under the covers, shivering and belted on his long bus journey to the Tech, or hunched over the family radio before Bert returned in the evening. Soon the 14-year-old Richards was cutting school to sidle down back streets to the Dartford Woolworth's, where he'd lock himself in a booth and listen to Woolies' own 'house' versions of American songs until closing time. 'I practically lived there,' he noted. Richards 'sat on that little stool playing the same Chuck Berry and Elvis records twenty times over, picking up the arrangements by ear', Ron Simms says. Keith later called Woolworth's 'my music classroom'. Before long, he persuaded Doris to invest seven pounds in a Rosetti's Professional Style Acoustic Guitar. With that and a cheap gramophone, similarly coaxed out of his mum, he began playing along, sitting on the acoustically favoured upstairs landing, tracing the original recordings. A great moment came one day in 1958 when Keith was playing a bluesy adaptation of Ernesto Lecuona's then-popular song 'Malaguena' and Doris called up the stairs, 'Is that you? I thought it was the radio.' Now the much put-upon Bert had something else to worry about. 'Every time the poor sod came in at night,' said Keith, 'he'd find me sitting there with my guitar, playing and banging on the wall for percussion.'

In early 1959 the Tech, irritated by Keith's attendance record, expelled him. He eventually managed to enrol at art school three stops up the line at Sidcup, which adjoins Dartford but lacks any of its neighbour's raw energy, vital nightlife and racy promise. He seems to have spent most of his time there locked in the college lavs, dressed in a pair of drainpipe trousers and fluorescent mauve socks, practising the guitar. In the winter of 1960, he and a fellow student named Michael Ross — the core members of the Sidcup Trio — played their first semi-professional engagement at a dance held in an Eltham scout hall. The facilities were basic. There was a combined chaperon-MC (the local vicar), a table lamp, and two malfunctioning radios (which more than once interpolated a burst of the Light Programme in to the performance) serving as amps. The vicar leaped on stage after the final number to urge everyone to leave quietly, but there was no problem — most of the subdued audience had already shuffled off. After this inauspicious debut, Keith missed the last train home and 'spent the night freezing in a bus shelter with a local slag. That was my introduction to showbusiness.'

It was an uncertain professional future, then, Richards was facing at the time of his fateful reunion with Mike Jagger. Had his career in rock and roll not worked out, a life as 'some sort of permanent juvenile delinquent' struck him as a 'pretty fair alternative bet' and, to be honest, not all that different. Over the following few weeks, Keith and Mick (as he now called himself) bonded over Chuck Berry and Muddy Waters and, after paternal objections, began practising together at Dick Taylor's home in nearby Bexleyheath. When the Richardses took a rare family holiday that winter, to Devon, Jagger accompanied them. The two teens pulled up stools and

crooned some songs together in the local pub, striking a man named
Ted Haley, who made a note of it in his diary, as 'like an English
Everly Brothers', if not quite as tuneful. Following the performance,
Keith remarked that they 'really needed a manager'. Mick noted
merely that there weren't enough 'skirts' for his liking in the audience. On the way home the battery went out in the family's old
Vauxhall, and Mick's mother was standing on the doorstep waiting
for them by the time they got him home to Wilmington, not the
last time a Jagger would comment on a Richards' punctuality.

Three months later, they came across Brian Jones in the basement
room at Ealing, an experience Keith would compare to Crusoe
finding Man Friday's footsteps. After that the three of them regularly began sitting in with Alexis Korner, though this seems to have
been the source of some debate among the goateed swingers who
ran proceedings at Ealing. Korner's sax player Dick Heckstall-Smith
later confided that Richards, for one, had struck him as 'a grease-
ball'. Generally speaking, the jazz crowd much preferred Jagger,
who proved just the ticket to sell old men's music to a young audience – 'tossing his head around like a hair fetishist'. Korner later
spoke about the Rolling Stones having taken shape 'right there in
that subterranean dump like Hitler's bunker'. His memory isn't
entirely supported by other accounts, however, and the statement
seems premature, because Mick, Keith and Brian hadn't yet figured
out what to do musically in the absence of the more established
players. They learned that at the Marquee Club, on 12 July.

The young man playing the bar-slide guitar at the Ealing jazz club
was a different Brian Jones from the provocative figure who would
later capture the world's imagination and provoke years of outraged
headlines. Apart from his musical gift, there was little about him that
seemed out of the ordinary to his peers Mick and Keith (at least
until they heard about his alter ego, the Cheltenham Shagger).
Although older than either of them, Brian was also physically slight,
a short, wispy youth, only 5 foot 5, with squat shoulders and stubby
legs which propelled him with a low, scuttling gait. Perhaps his
most striking features were his searching green eyes and impudent,

full-lipped mouth. The luxuriant bouffant hair that would become so familiar in later life was clipped in a short, wavy fringe. Internally, too, Jones was still rather more the ex-Cheltenham choirboy who spoke in a lilting, effete voice than the cloaca-tongued rocker of later repute. Five years after that first night in Ealing, a court-appointed psychiatrist would tell a judge, deciding whether or not to send Brian to jail, that he was intelligent but 'emotionally unstable, with neurotic tendencies'. The shrink concluded, 'This individual vacillates between a passive, pathetically weak child on the one hand, and a pop idol on the other.'

As Jones climbed down from the stage for his historic first meeting with Mick and Keith, Korner's bass player toppled drunkenly in to the drum kit. It went over with a molten crash.

'There goes yer fuckin' rhythm,' said Brian to Korner. He had Mick's own gift of tongues; when he turned to Jagger and Richards, he was his old fruity self. 'A new band?' he said. 'Let's chat upstairs. The air here gives me the croup.'

Brian, too, had enjoyed the sort of upbringing that seems to presage becoming a rock star. He was the eldest of three children, one of whom, Pamela, died of leukaemia when Brian was four. He would remember thinking for years afterwards that his parents had given her away and worrying that the same might happen to him. Jones' mother Louisa was a piano teacher who encouraged his musical career right up to the point when he part-exchanged his clarinet for what she termed a 'coon' alto-sax at the age of fifteen. Brian's father Lewis, who also played piano and organ at his local church, does not present an immediately sympathetic figure. A dour, puritanical Welshman, who worked as an engineer at Cheltenham's aeronautical plant, you frequently hear the word 'affection' when talking to Mr Jones' former associates; they say he was extremely sparing with it. There's little evidence that he was ever physically violent or in any way 'abusive' in the modern sense, but it's fair to say that, like many fathers of his generation, he took a restrained approach to showing his emotions. As a boy, the centre of Brian's world was his pet cat and a succession of model train sets, the second of which passions lasted the rest of his life. Although adept at most sports, he was prone to asthma and various other respiratory problems and finished many a session with the sax by sucking frantically on a pocket inhaler.

Brian did well enough at Cheltenham's Dean Close junior school, although he already showed a latent aversion to most forms of authority, and to wearing a uniform in particular. A move up to the local grammar, however, proved disastrous. As he recalled, he 'hated' obeying the rules there, and most of the time he didn't. Whenever he felt like it, Brian would excuse himself from class and wander off in search of a fresh supply of brown ale, which he preferred to the regulation milk. As he progressed through the school there was to be a protracted dispute about his taste for blue 'brothel-creeper' shoes, which also deviated from the standard issue. Nor did Brian neglect the presence of some 600 nubile inmates of the nearby Cheltenham Ladies' College, an estimated 2 to 3 per cent of whom would go on to join him in various displays of mutual abandon. Many of those who knew Jones at the time describe him as an unusually fluid personality. When not in the grip of some sudden rage, he seems to have been an enchanting companion with a natural warmth and mischievous wit that came like an explosion of pagan mirth. 'One never knew which Brian you were going to get,' a woman told me.

Jones' impregnation in early 1959 of a 15-year-old girl would win him his first national press coverage, a small item under the headline 'Vicar "Appalled" by today's Teen-agers', in the *Sunday People*. Another underage partner bore his second child, a daughter, in August 1960. Despite impressive exam results, Brian, an affront to Cheltenham's blue-rinse image, subsequently made a hurried exit first from school and then from the family home. For a time he lived with his friend Dick Hattrell in digs by the town's art college, and took a variety of short-term jobs. In the winter of 1960–61, Jones was successively a coalman, a shop assistant and a factory worker, until an accident with the works' van put paid to the last. A brief spell in the architects' department of Gloucestershire County Council also ended in some disarray, chiefly concerning Brian's excessively relaxed approach both to timekeeping and helping himself to the office's petty cash. He continued to play the sax and guitar, and found a berth in a local combo called the Ramrods, until the band's singer choked to death while eating a bag of chips.

Shortly afterwards, Brian went to see Alexis Korner perform at Cheltenham Town Hall, and bought Korner a drink in the pub afterwards, where they traded phone numbers. The exchange took place in the same month Jagger saw Richards looming at him out of the fog on Dartford station, and was just as pivotal for the development of the Rolling Stones. Brian soon moved to London, where he somehow neglected to marry Pat Andrews, the mother of his third child, as he had promised her. Lewis Jones made various efforts to urge his son to think seriously about his future, including paying for him to study at the London College of Applied Optics, but this, too, ended in a premature exit. After that, Brian's parents wouldn't hear from him again until he was all over the papers as one of the five most notorious young men in Britain.

The summer of 1962 was an unsettled time for the Rollin' Stones, as they still billed themselves, not least when it came to establishing who was in charge. Mick Jagger, still very much the LSE student in his corduroy trousers and floppy roll-neck sweater, could at least lay claim to some higher academic pretension than either Keith or Brian. Ian Stewart – Stu – had no known ambitions beyond playing his beloved boogie-woogie piano and sinking an improbable number of pints of beer. He also enjoyed a round of golf. Stu had a respectable daytime job as an order clerk for ICI, and no reason to believe that the beatnik rabble he'd fallen in with would last for more than a few ill-paid gigs. Dick Taylor and the group's rotational drummer – most often Mick Avory or Tony Chapman, who also played in a Penge rock and roll combo doing Jerry Lee Lewis covers – were 'talented also-rans', Taylor noted, adding that he'd been 'a bit overawed' by even the prospect of turning professional.

Brian Jones, obviously, was the Stones' most conventionally good-looking member, which still counted for something in the pop culture of the day, and patently didn't do well under anyone else's direction. In the brief lull between his moving to London and encountering Jagger and Richards, Brian had met a 20-year-old named Paul Jones (no relation) and asked him if he was interested in joining a band he was thinking of forming. Paul, then an undergraduate at Oxford, declined. A few days later, he asked Brian to join his own group, 'and Brian stiffly replied that he had no wish to be part of a band unless he was its leader'. This was to remain Brian's core conviction throughout the next seven years, and brought the Stones a certain amount of internal strife as a result. In time, Brian's messianic self-belief would steadily fade due to the creative talents of Jagger and Richards and other more self-destructive factors, but he never quite abandoned the idea that his alluring package of musicianship, charisma and good looks elevated him from the pack. This was what he meant when, with a straight face, he told an early interviewer from *Jazz News*, 'Our band can be summed up in two words – Brian Jones.'

Brian was, it's true, a stickler for rehearsals, which comfortably outnumbered the band's paying engagements for the rest of 1962. While Jagger took the train in to the LSE every morning and back to Dartford every night, Jones and Richards briefly inhabited a mouldering squat in London's Notting Hill. This arrangement lasted until – as they always did at Brian's, sooner or later – the bailiffs called. The two bandmates then made a hurried retreat to a shared room in Brackley Road, Beckenham, where, as Keith says, they used to 'lay around, read *Billboard* and play all day, Brian on his Gibson guitar and me on my Hofner': the birth-cry of the Rolling Stones. When that, too, ended in eviction Mick, Keith and Brian all moved back to London and a second-floor flat located in, aptly enough, World's End, Chelsea.

Number 102 Edith Grove was a place which Richards would say made even Spielman Road 'look like fucking Balmoral' by contrast. It was a two-room slum with a gas meter, naked light bulbs and a few sticks of utility furniture. The one armchair was reserved for visiting dignitaries like Korner, under whom it repeatedly collapsed, dumping him on to the cement floor. The walls were painted, if at all, with the ramshackle expediency of a squat, and increasingly came to be daubed with graffiti etched in indelible candle smoke. Hygiene was not an Edith Grove priority. 'The first time I walked in,' said Stu, no shrinking violet, 'the stink almost knocked me over. There was mouldy food and old cigarette butts all over the place, dirty clothes flung around and that disgusting smell, like rotting cabbages.' Washing up for the lads simply meant throwing crockery, cutlery and utensils out of the kitchen window in to the communal garden below. Soon, Richards began wondering aloud about buying a revolver to shoot at the rats who shared the premises.

While Jagger – the flat's official lessee – still dutifully took the bus in to college every morning, Keith and Brian holed up at World's End, listening to records whose raw, fast-paced riffs they accompanied on guitar. The idea of Mick taking care of business while his sleepy-eyed colleagues lolled around in bed was to prove an enduring Rolling Stones image in later years. It was the two guitarists' favourite hobby, playing Muddy or Howlin' Wolf and tracing licks put down in Chicago twenty years earlier. Ian Stewart noted the core competitiveness and tension between Mick on the one hand, and Keith and Brian on the other, though sometimes new factions formed. A shake of the kaleidoscope, and 'those buggers suddenly changed sides'. Stu saw this fickleness at work one night when he was driving the three of them home to Edith Grove from a party. Brian had insisted on squashing down in the back seat between Mick and Keith, and was murmuring intrigue in both their ears. Suddenly, Stu said, 'they all started shouting at each other . . . Brian flung a punch at Keith, and Keith hit him back. I pulled up and told them to piss off and fight it out between them . . . Those three always had some triangle going.' Decades later, Jagger told *Rolling Stone*, 'I wasn't totally committed to [music]. It was a good, fun thing to do, but Keith and Brian were beyond that. They wanted to play *all* the time.'

In October 1962 the Stones had four gigs, in November six. On all too many days, Richards would remember, 'we didn't bother getting out of bed. Nothing to do.' One Ealing engagement ended poorly when Korner's friend Cyril Davies booted the Stones off the stage. Nor were prospects improved when, on a return visit there, Harold Pendleton, manager of the Marquee Club, muttered the word 'greasers' as the ill-clad group strolled on. Keith retaliated by trying to brain Pendleton with his guitar. After that it would be eight years before the Stones went back to play at the Marquee. Keith took a swing at Pendleton on that occasion, too.

Brian Jones, it's worth repeating, was clearly out in front of the others, revered as the group's founder, treated (at least by himself) like a superstar, a tireless writer of unpublished press releases and slightly earnest letters to *Jazz News* (informing them, for instance, 'Rhythm and blues can hardly be considered a form of jazz. It is not based on improvisation as is the latter . . . The impact is, and can only be, emotional') and, even then, considered a sex symbol – exuding 'a kind of drowsy arrogance,' one friend remembers. Young women had already been known to cast their underwear towards him in feints of admiration as he mounted the rickety stages of London's Flamingo Club or the Woodstock Hotel, North Cheam. Brian responded to the acclaim by awarding himself a share and a half of the group's income. Admittedly, this generally involved his pocketing something of the order of seven pounds ten while Mick, Keith, Stu and the two rhythm players made do with a fiver each, but it did little for collective harmony. Jagger's university grant was largely paying the rent and Stu, prefiguring his later role in the band, was already driving them around in his battered Transit van.

Late that October, as the Cuban Missile Crisis played itself out across the Atlantic, the Rolling Stones, as they now officially called themselves, entered a recording studio for the first time. Jones paid four pounds and Jagger and Richards six pounds apiece to cut a three-song demo, which Brian sent to a contact named Neville Skrimshire at EMI. Skrimshire took all of a minute to reject it. Thoroughly demoralised, Dick Taylor left the band. His replacement, who auditioned one snowy night at the Wetherby Arms, a pub near Edith Grove, was a 26-year-old, Brylcreemed ex-bookie called Bill Perks, a name he'd recently changed to Wyman. The impression he made on the band could hardly have been worse. Wyman arrived punctually and neatly dressed, as always, and stood fiddling with his pearl cuff links while Keith and Brian studiously ignored him. Stu would always marvel at the cool, phlegmatic strength with which Bill handled the mass rejection. The ice was broken only by Wyman's wheeling in two massive Vox amps and the sensational discovery, shortly thereafter, that he could really play. To seal the arrangement, Bill then bought everyone a round of drinks and offered cigarettes, 'which were jumped on as if I were delivering famine relief'.

Wyman, then, was in, albeit with reservations. To Bill's prim sensibility, the Stones, with their sullen faces, jumping Negroid music and unheated, fetid shithole of a flat, were 'disgusting ... squalid beatniks'. Wyman, born on 24 October 1936 (or 1941, in Les Perrin's press kit), was the son of a fitfully employed south London bricklayer and – yes – a musical, kindly mother. There were no frills around the family home in Miall Road, Lower Sydenham, a terraced house with, Bill recalls, 'a small front garden and hedge, gas lighting, no bathroom or hot water and a toilet in the back yard'. He was to be the oldest of six children, each of whom was briefly plunged in to a zinc bath placed on the kitchen floor every Saturday night. Bill was miserable at school, had rocks thrown at him because he walked around the streets of Penge in a blazer and cap, got evacuated after the Blitz, and was later knocked around by his father when he started playing boogie-woogie piano instead of concentrating on his homework. At eighteen, Bill was called up for National Service in the RAF, where he listened to rock and roll on British Forces Network and appropriated the surname of a fellow airman called Lee Wyman. Demobbed in 1957, he worked variously as a Penge bookmaker's assistant, an East Ham meat importer and a storekeeper with a diesel engineering firm in Streatham. The Rolling Stones have naturally attracted the interest of psychiatrists, and several studies have been published paying particular attention to Jagger and Richards' on-off creative relationship. It's possible the most interesting, and most neglected, case study is still the one tracing Bill Wyman's evolution from an impoverished, physically unprepossessing self-styled 'south London herbert' in to the canny financial accumulator, debauched King Charles lookalike and tireless sex machine of later legend.

On his twenty-third birthday in 1959, Wyman married a girl named Diane Cory, honeymooned in the Birmingham suburb of Smethwick, and then settled down with her in a room above a Sydenham garage. Their son Stephen was born in March 1962. Having abandoned both the piano and the lead guitar owing to his small hands, Bill began playing bass in several semi-professional groups including the Cliftons, home of the Stones' sometime drummer Tony Chapman. Chapman introduced Wyman, which is how he came to be pushing his Vox amps in to the back room of a Chelsea pub that Dickensian night in December 1962. 'For musicians,' he says, 'their appearance surprised me: they had hair down over their ears and looked very scruffy. In the pop world I came from, smartness was automatic.' Middle-aged and married, Bill, with his Tony Curtis hairdo, was clearly a being apart from the other Stones, as all parties came to recognise at regular intervals over the next thirty years.

If you were going to launch an R&B-inclined British pop group on the world, the early weeks of 1963 were probably as good a time as any to do it. War children like the Stones were finally enjoying a glimmering rise in standards of living, even if the band members themselves weren't yet taking full advantage. The 'good times' heralded by PM Harold Macmillan didn't always cut very deep, but sheer pressure of numbers (with the UK's annual birth rate peaking at around 900,000 in 1947) inevitably brought a certain youth-friendly apparatus in to being by the early 60s. Academics debate to this day the chicken-and-egg dilemma of which came first, the boomer audiences' taste for freewheeling innovations in pop music, fashion, art and photography, or a sudden awakening on the part of the entrepreneurs and money-lenders who made it commercially possible. The answer, at least in rock and roll's case, was a bit of both.

In one scenario of particular note to the Stones, 27-year-old

Brian Epstein had recently wandered in out of the rain to the HMV store in London's Oxford Street, clutching two heavy reel-to-reel audition tapes of a band unknown outside Merseyside called the Beatles. On the first floor of the shop was a small studio, where customers could cut their own lightweight discs, which struck Epstein as a fair plan. As the engineer on duty was making the transfer he casually remarked that some of the stuff wasn't too bad, and that there was a music publisher named Ardmore and Beechwood on the top floor. Their manager, Syd Coleman, in turn listened to the newly minted demo and asked Epstein whether he was at all interested in speaking to someone at their affiliated record company. Epstein replied that he was, rather. Three months later the Beatles were at work in EMI's Abbey Road studios, when, at around seven in the evening, an original song called 'Love Me Do' moved the duty producer to fetch his boss, George Martin. On 5 October 1962, as the Rolling Stones hovered between music, college and the imposing squalor of Edith Grove, the Beatles' debut single was released, followed in February 1963 by a national tour. Not only did the band come to appeal to several million adolescents worldwide, they soon persuaded even the middle-aged men who ran the British recording industry that it was high time to slough off the past and join the Age of Aquarius, where the emphasis would henceforth be on giving the public what it wanted rather than on moral niceties.

Back in World's End, Mick, Keith and Brian could have been forgiven for not instantly recognising that they stood on the brink of commercial success. After twenty-nine years together, twenty-four of them married, Doris Richards had recently left her husband for another man (also named Richards) and now often came up to London to do the boys' laundry and attempt to scrape together a meal. She would remember conditions at Edith Grove as, if anything, worse than her wartime ordeal. 'It was a terrible place, mould everywhere and broken crockery ... like a bomb had gone off.' Ian Stewart would add that relations between the flat's three principal tenants were similarly volatile, with the usual arrangement being that any two members of the household would periodically team up to 'shit all over' the third. Stu recalled that late one night the graffiti 'FUCK OFF MICK YOU TWAT' had mysteriously appeared on the slimy wall of the communal 'bog', one floor up. By morning, the last two words had been erased by an unknown tenant who evidently still agreed with the main thesis. 'All very weird,' Stu noted. 'I think Jagger was beginning to feel left out. Mick didn't have much to contribute, but he had a lot of ambition and vanity and he was damn smart, and I could see him looking at Brian in a way that was a little menacing. I could sense back then the beginning of Mick's desire to distance Keith from Brian ... I used to think they were all fucking insane at times.'

To Richards, 21 December 1962 was probably the low point: the Stones arrived at the Piccadilly Jazz Club 'Rave of the Year' to find exactly six people waiting for them. Helped by a bottle of Hirondelle wine, Keith eventually managed to fall off the stage. A protracted row ensued about the band's performance fee. The next morning, Keith signed on as a relief carrier at St Stephen's sorting office but was caught sleeping on the job, thus ending his career as a postman. By Christmas Day Edith Grove's water pipes were frozen solid, everyone was subsisting on stale bread and spuds, and even Mick's habitual cool seemed to wilt. 'I want somebody to share everything with, someone to respect, not just someone to sleep with,' he wrote to a 17-year-old schoolgirl named Cleo Sylvester, whom he met at the Marquee. 'Please make me happy, it's the one thing missing from my life now.' (One of Brian Jones' many partners heard from him in similar vein that Christmas. 'He told me that my hair was a silken thread and that my smile was painted across the sky in stars. Anything to get those knickers down.') Unlike Mick, Brian – who even in the face of this austerity, was somehow still able to shampoo and blow-dry his hair twice a day – would remain unfailingly upbeat about the band's prospects. His unquenchable optimism led him, during a brief interview with *Jazz News*, to single out the one missing ingredient needed to turn the poverty-racked Stones in to a Beatles-like success. 'All we want,' Brian insisted, effortlessly slipping in to that paper's preferred idiom, 'is a cool new cat on drums. Then watch us!'

★

The answer to Jones' prayers came in the second week of January 1963, when Brian approached a suitably 'cool cat' who played in a relaxed, jazzy style, yet whose backbeat could make the stage jump up and down the street. Charlie Watts had been the drummer sitting in with Alexis Korner's band on that fateful April night when Jones had looked down and seen Jagger and Richards looking back at him. Charlie, who liked to keep it simple, had watched with some alarm when Korner had originally appeared at Ealing with a tiny, portable amplifier and hung it on the wall immediately behind the drum kit. 'When I first played [there], I thought, "What the fuck is happening?"' recalled Watts, who had never worked with electrified instruments before. 'It was an amazing band,' he added, 'but a total cacophony of sound. On a good night, it was a cross between R&B and Charlie Mingus, which was what Alexis wanted.' Even before people went down the stairs to that foul-smelling room under the tube, they could already feel Watts at work. 'What struck me was the beat of his drums,' Keith Richards recalled thirty-five years later. 'Before you saw the band, you heard it.'

It was a curious path that was to take the impeccably polite, suave Watts in to a group that were to hear themselves described as 'morons' by a High Court judge, and to read newspaper accounts citing their 'UGLY LOOKS! UGLY SPEECH! UGLY MANNERS!' among other unattractive characteristics. Charlie, born on 2 June 1941, grew up in and around Islington, north London, at a time when the area was still a byword for urban decay rather than the spiritual home of Britain's left-wing intelligentsia. His father, also called Charles, was a lorry driver for a precursor of British Rail and his mother, Lilian, had been a factory cleaner. Immaculately well organised even then, Charlie sailed through school and was admitted to Harrow Art College under the modest handicap of being 'awkward' in written English. For some years afterwards he struggled with his prose, which could be suggestive of a light fog moving over a hazy landscape. Often, he preferred to communicate in a series of wittily drawn cartoons rather than the traditional letter. Watts was later to remark that, 'Part of my problem was that I was never a teenager. I'd be off in the corner talking about Kierkegaard. I always took myself too seriously and thought Buddy Holly was a great joke.' It's true there was something a bit melancholic about the boy with the long, Buster Keaton face who only ever wanted to read about cowboys or play the drums. He acquired his first kit at Christmas 1955, after at least a year of practising nonstop on his mother's pots and pans. At fifteen, Watts had only one ambition, which was to somehow find himself at Birdland in New York, wearing a hipster suit and sitting in behind the likes of John Coltrane, Stan Getz or Miles Davis – difficult to achieve from Tylers Croft Secondary Modern school, although a few years later Charlie was able to publish a book called *Ode to a High-Flying Bird*, which told the Charlie Parker story in a series of engaging stick insect-like doodles.

By late 1962, Watts drummed for a Korner offshoot called Blues by Six by night and worked as a trainee artist at Gray's advertising agency by day. Korner's line-up was a fluid one, and allowed for some interplay with the early Rolling Stones. Among other things, the band members came to admire the way Charlie looked when seated at his kit, remaining almost motionless in even the fastest number, and the little trick he had of pulling back his stick on two of the standard four beats, effectively meaning that he played only half as much as the conventional rock and roll tub-thumper. Watts' lean but serviceable style was the percussive equivalent of Keith Richards' guitar. For a while, Brian Jones walked around with Charlie's phone number scribbled on an empty cigarette packet in his pocket, and the two bumped in to each other one Saturday night that winter at Leicester Square tube, when Brian was on his way to a gig and Charlie was neatly folding up his drum kit prior to storing it in the station's left-luggage office for the weekend. Mick and Keith also sometimes called at Mr and Mrs Watts' prim north London home to enquire about their son's professional availability. Charlie liked the Stones and told them they needed 'a fucking great drummer', but modestly never considered he himself might fit the bill. 'He was always incredibly polite,' said Carlo Little, a fellow drummer, and Stones trialist, who saw Charlie frequently in 1962–63. 'The family had moved in to this prefab council house in Brent, which they were very chuffed about. Immaculately neat little rooms, doilies on all the armchairs. I sometimes went up there for tea, and all three of them would line up in a row and shake your hand as you came in the door. Here I am in my black-leather Elvis gear, and all we'd ever do was sit in the front room and talk about cricket. The parents themselves were very simple people. They didn't put on airs; they were very shy and reserved and obviously very proud. I liked him better for his mum and dad.'

The Stones tolerated Tony Chapman for a few more gigs, until an unsatisfactory Saturday night performance at the Red Lion pub in Sutton. 'Sorry,' Brian told him as Stu drove them back to town, 'but you have to fuck off.' Still working at the ad agency by day, Charlie had begun to suspect that there might be a more interesting and lucrative way to make a living when the Beatles had recently begun performing their new hit 'Please Please Me' on British television. When Lennon and McCartney stepped to the mike for the song's 'Whoa yeah' chorus, which they sang in falsetto, all four musicians, including the seated Ringo, shook their pudding-bowl hair. At that precise moment the dominant noise from the studio audience invariably changed from one of polite applause to frenzied screaming. So when the Stones again came calling, they found Watts in a receptive mood. Even then, he was to warily admit only that he was 'interested', and later telephoned Korner and his wife for their opinion. They told him to try the Stones out, and not long after that Ian Stewart arrived at the Watts' front door in his van. Stu later noted, 'I said to Charlie, "Look, you're in the band. That's it." And Charlie said, "Yeah, all right then, but I don't know what my mum's gonna say."'

Visually, the Stones were now two bands. There was the disturbing spectacle of the front line, three young gargoyles who looked like the Beatles with hangovers, and behind them the comparatively normal-seeming trio of Stewart, Wyman and the comically impassive figure in a neat shirt and tie, incongruously pounding away on the drums. The new line-up gave its first performance at the Flamingo Club in Piccadilly on 14 January 1963. Brian Jones actually stopped and looked around when he first heard Charlie pick up the beat on Chuck Berry's 'Back in the USA'. Soon

Brian was telling everyone that they had the coolest young drummer in London, while privately he told Charlie to take off his tie
and grow his hair. Ian Stewart also knew exactly what was
happening. After the Flamingo, he wrote in his diary, 'Best Stones
show ever'.

The six weeks that followed were the coldest in living memory. By
day fog descended, leaving spectacular rime deposits on streets and
houses. At night the sea froze solid. Most of the time Keith and
Brian didn't bother to get out of bed at Edith Grove, and before
long Mick took to carrying a blow-torch around to thaw the pipes
in the little box-room at the back where he went to brood over
Keynes or practise the harmonica. Sharing the front lounge in to
which was crowded a (never used) crib for Brian's baby, assorted
guitars and drums and Bill Wyman's spare amp, the Stones now
realised their dream of becoming professional musicians in London.
A local teenager named Eileen Giles, whose mother knew the
Jaggers, sometimes came in to take a stab at cleaning the flat. Forty
years later, she could still vividly recall the kitchen, a room in which
Brian Jones appeared to be conducting a disastrous biological experiment, and where the residents communicated by daubing the walls
in a solution of snot and chewing gum. Even then, Giles made a
sharp distinction between Richards and Jones – 'total slobs' – and
Jagger, who 'seemed to be living there because it amused him'.
Brian, in particular, was already a 'strange bunch of guys' who could
'flip at a second's notice', 'wasn't to be trusted', 'never forgot a
slight', and 'never forgave anyone who made a mistake'. Keith, talking wistfully about becoming a millionaire while lolling around the
unheated flat, was 'always charming enough when it suited him'.
When Giles got distracted doing the ironing one afternoon and
burned a hole in Keith's prize purple shirt, he 'thought about it for
a minute and then volunteered the solution that I should take off my
shirt and give it to him in exchange', an offer she eventually
accepted. A little later still, 'Keith sat me down and played me the
most beautiful song. The way [he and Jones] worked together was
incredible.'

What Giles was hearing, amid all the scorched clothes and festering dishes, was the birth of the Rolling Stones. The whole
alchemy, as Keith often says, 'is the way we work two guitars'. The
sound he and Brian were chasing turned out to be equal parts R&B,
with a rich lode of country and western – big in Britain in 1962 –
and trace elements of Elvis and Buddy Holly. The two room-
mates wrote at least one song together in Edith Grove, but this
turned out to be mannered and trite – 'utter shit', in Keith's bleak
assessment. 'It sounded like a 1920s musical . . . Brian was utterly
impossible to work with. He would dominate anything he was in
to – there was no way you could suggest anything.' A key problem with Jones' songwriting was that it tended to be derivative,
mainly derivative, and unfortunately, of the works of
J.R.R. Tolkien. When the Stones' first manager came on the
scene, he was quickly to establish 'just who had the virtuoso
touch, and who had the pop sensibility'. Brian, who all agreed
could make a guitar ring like a bell, was 'away with the pixies cre-
atively'. 'There was no spark there,' Keith confirmed forty-three
years later. '[Jones] was a gifted musician, but he didn't have the
drive to write. He wanted to, because he saw where the money
was. It drove him nuts when he figured that out.'

Jones did hustle the Stones a few ill-paid engagements around the
Home Counties, including a recurring spot at the Ricky Tick club,
Windsor. Perhaps rashly, the first time they played there the band let
Brian do the driving. It was snowing. Heavily. 'We finally pulled up
to this place and started to get out to go inside,' Stu recalled, 'except
Mr Jones forgot to put the brake on, and the van rolled straight in
to a row of motorcycles owned by these tough-looking rocker
types. Brian started jabbering something apologetic to these guys,
and then jumped back behind the wheel and promptly lost control
again on the ice. He went bumping over the curb and scaring the
shit out of everybody. I remember looking at Mick, who by now
was standing by the front door, whiter than a sheet.' Once inside,
the club's owner, John Mansfield, initially took some time to warm
to the band. 'They looked a bit like the Beverly Hillbillies,' he
recalls, 'and afterwards I took them to a restaurant up by the castle

because they were ravenously hungry. They were being a bit unruly and they kept throwing things at each other. There was a guy sitting behind us with his twin teenage daughters, and eventually he stood up with his arm wrapped protectively around the girls and uttered the immortal line: "I wouldn't let *my* child go out with a Rolling Stone."'

In the middle of what was now officially the worst winter in 200 years, Jones met another well-heeled blues fanatic and father figure, this one a Russian émigré named Giorgio Gomelsky, and wheedled him in to booking the Stones in to the back room of the Station Hotel in Richmond, south London, which Gomelsky quaintly named the Crawdaddy Club. 'I had the Stones on the bill at another place,' he says, 'and Brian walked in, looking much as we remember him now, in black, with that weird, bow-legged gait of his, and then proceeded to order everyone around.' Despite thinking their playing that pre-Charlie Watts night 'abysmal', Gomelsky persevered with the Stones, if only because Jones 'kept lisping at me: "Pleathe, *pleathe*, Giorgio, get us some gigs."' To make the booking, Gomelsky had to phone Ian Stewart in the warehouse at ICI, and he in turn drove out to tell Mick, Keith and Brian at Edith Grove. Gomelsky offered the band seven pounds, which Jones found it convenient to split between the six musicians by awarding himself a double share. The others found out about it, and weren't pleased. Gomelsky's intervention in the band's career quite possibly saved the day. Before taking the District Line down to Richmond, the Stones had played another concert in front of some twenty customers in a London pub, which was depressing enough even before the volume on everyone's instruments suddenly went down to half power owing to industrial action by striking electricity workers. After a subsequent provincial engagement that month, there had been a distressing incident when Keith Richards was leaving the premises pursued by a small but animated crowd of young girls. Ian Stewart swiftly assessed the situation and backed his van up to the stage door of the club. Keith reached for the van's door handle, but this came off in his hand, leaving him at the mercy of his admirers. The promoter of the concert in question then saw fit to withhold the Stones' fee, citing the damage done to his venue by the band's entourage. So under the circumstances the sort of relatively well-structured, paying engagement Gomelsky seemed to promise the Stones at Richmond would have struck them as a godsend.

Stu's first impression as he – a man in his mid-twenties – entered the Crawdaddy was that in doing so he'd raised the average age in the place to about nineteen. 'It was like falling in to a swamp,' he said. The jostling-room-only club, where attendances rose from an initial dozen or so of the curious or obsessed to an estimated 400-plus, with the boys carrying their girlfriends in to the room on their shoulders, soon became a weekly Sunday night date for the Stones. They might not be the world's best musicians, some there would sniff, and to make it more interesting there were gigs when they downed tools and began to fight among themselves, loudly accusing one another of 'wanking off' during a song. The band's rougher edges, however, only served to emphasise the tribal stomp of the Chuck Berry and Bo Diddley fare with which they enlivened the proceedings. From the first bars of 'Talkin' 'Bout You', Keith would be off and chugging, working the gruff, low end of the guitar, with Bill and Charlie doing the locomotion behind him, and soon enough 'the kids', as Stu said, 'would look at each other – they'd heard nothing remotely like it – and go mental'. Mass audience sing-alongs inside British suburban pubs were still a novelty in 1963. Word soon got around and crowds began to form outside on Kew Road early every Sunday afternoon.

Big crowds. Those loud, teeming nights in Richmond, where the steam rose, girls rushed the stage and Mick Jagger learned how to dance, soon took on a comic-strip vitality as the cartoon figures on deck landed one musical knockout after another; you could almost see the capitalised 'POW!' and 'WHAMMO!' concussion sounds in their little spiky speech-bubbles. One of the young women 'sent nearly batty' by the occasion was a 17-year-old trainee secretary named Chrissie Shrimpton. She had already made the acquaintance of the Stones at the Ricky Tick club, where, in a pioneering display of crowd surfing, she'd clambered over the heads of the audience and proceeded to crawl towards the stage, where she planted a kiss on the band's 'weirdly compelling' lead singer. Soon, Jagger found himself forgetting about his girlfriend Cleo Sylvester and his platonic ambitions on her, and he and Shrimpton were an item. 'It was all primal stuff,' Cecilia Nixon, one of Mick's back-up partners of the same era, says. 'The Stones were already fantastic on stage by mid-'63. There was the beat, and there was the visual drama of the singer hopping around with his maracas in between the two evil-looking guitarists. Basic, basic stuff. You saw boys fighting. Girls touching themselves in inappropriate places. I remember walking in to that first concert at Richmond as this very prim young lady, and by the time they stopped playing I was pogoing up and down and I couldn't stop myself screaming. *That's* what I mean by primal.' Clever, cocky and not overburdened by technique, the Stones now gave classic black R&B a face-lift without smoothing the wrinkles.

On 7 April 1963, the first anniversary of Mick and Keith meeting 'Elmo Lewis' in Ealing, the band played a concert to an overflow audience of 425, not bad for a room with an official capacity of 110. While Jagger took the bus to college the next morning, Richards, Jones and Gomelsky, now the group's de facto manager, plastered fly-posters – 'R&B with the Inimitable, Incomparable, Exhilarating Rollin' Stones' – over west London, mixing up the paste in the bath at Edith Grove (its only known function). On 13 April the band was noticed, sensationally, in the *Richmond and Twickenham Times*. The next night, the Beatles and their manager came to pay homage at the Crawdaddy.

They stood right at the front, in their matching German leather overcoats and suede 'twat' hats, with just a few feet between them and the Stones. Mick Jagger would remember thinking, 'Fuckin' hell! I want one of those coats!' – a key moment in his decision to subsequently abandon the blues and launch his band on the hit parade. Immediately after coming off stage that night, Mick excitedly rang his mother to tell her who he had just played in front of, and how he was now well on his way to success as a pop star. 'That's nice, Michael,' she told him. At the impromptu party following the show, Mick was seen to take Brian Epstein aside and quiz him at some length on matters specifically pertaining to copyrights and royalties. Around midnight, Brian Jones arrived back at Edith Grove with his new friends Lennon and McCartney, still high on adrenaline. Years later, Brian remembered how he had felt his poise crumble as he opened the door: Mick and Keith were huddled in bed together – for warmth, obviously – writing a song.

The following Thursday, the Beatles returned the favour and invited the Stones backstage to their concert at the Albert Hall. On his way in to the building, Jones was mobbed by several teenage girls who mistook him for one of the Moptops, an error he did not immediately correct. Bill Wyman remained outside, inspecting the various phone numbers daubed in lipstick on the windows of the Beatles' van, which Bill carefully wrote down in a black notebook. Meanwhile, Brian, Mick and Keith made their way to the dressing room, and watched in awe as the Beatles calmly applied their makeup and triggered a riot the instant they walked on stage to a non-stop barrage of bras and undies sailing over the footlights. Paul McCartney said that when he next saw the Rolling Stones, 'Mick was made up like a tart.'

The Stones' life as a band began to come together on 28 April, when they heard from a semi-obscure former record plugger and failed pop singer (trading under the name Sandy Beach) called Andrew Loog Oldham. Oldham came to see them at Richmond that night. No less an authority than Brian Jones found him an 'incredible hustler'. Younger even than the Stones themselves, Oldham was born in January 1944 to an English mother and a Dutch-American father who was killed in the war. Of those baby-boom entrepreneurs whom the 1960s escalator propelled from the bottom to the top of British life, 'the Loog', that ultimate social climber, was a classic type: tactically brilliant, strategically flexible and not overburdened by false modesty. Ian Stewart believed there was also a pronounced 'feminine streak' in Oldham's nature, a quality that later enabled him to 'think about it from the chick's perspective' when it came to making the Stones ever more attractive to a female audience. There was 'something of the Hayley Mills about Andrew', his business partner Eric Easton agreed. Oldham was slight in build, dainty of feature and, like many another privately educated English boy, had more than once fetchingly donned a frock in a school musical. The idea that the Loog was sexually ambiguous occasionally flitted through the gossip surrounding him, but, at that time, he had stout conventional scorn for 'fairies'. (There was to be a memorable 1965 duet, even so, when he and Mick Jagger crooned 'I Got You, Babe' on *Ready Steady Go!* while stroking one another's hair.)

By April 1963, Oldham, already an ex-employee of both Mary Quant and Brian Epstein, among many others, was that rare mixture of a slightly foppish, Edwardian Jekyll and a beatnik, pill-fuelled Hyde, swaying around Soho in hip-hugging black as though on some permanent audition for the Laurence Harvey role in *Expresso Bongo* (he saw the film nine times). He had already achieved two-thirds of his burning ambition to become a 'teenage tycoon shit'. Calling in on a friend one afternoon at the *Record Mirror*, Oldham was to hear about the new group with their weekly residency in the back room of the otherwise stuffy Victorian pub in Richmond. He appeared there the next Sunday, bringing with him his balding and middle-aged managerial partner Eric Easton, a sometime cinema organist who was unhappy about missing his favourite television show, the variety programme *Sunday Night at the London Palladium*. After seeing the Stones perform, Oldham squeezed his way on stage and asked Charlie Watts who the group's leader was. Charlie pointed a drumstick at the blond mop of hair already deep in conversation with several fans and said, 'Brian is.'

Jones, not one for long-term relationships, soon fell out with Oldham, with whom he had possibly too much in common for any other outcome: both were maddening, touching, intermittently sadistic, very nearly very great, self-created and self-destroyed. But early on, Brian readily acknowledged, 'Andy's chutzpah [was] what put the Stones on the map.' Oldham 'had a way of carrying himself as if he were a rock star', Ian Stewart added, only half-affectionately. 'He would make appointments with you, very precise as if his schedule was extremely tight, instead of just dropping around, even when he was a total dosser. The guy's arrogance was off the wall.' A page-boy cap was habitually pushed rakishly back on Oldham's sandy hair, and in general he projected the slightly manic assurance and panache of a hip Colonel Parker. Before him, British showbiz was still dom-inated by middle-aged men in bad wigs who tended to play things by the book. Oldham tore it up. Twenty-four hours after seeing the Stones, he and Easton took Jones up to their rented office in Regent Street and presented him with a three-year management contract for the band, which Brian was agreeable to signing providing he secretly received five pounds more a week than the other musicians.

Oldham was in. The Stones waited for Gomelsky to come back from his father's funeral and then fired him.

Andrew promptly put the band in waist-cinching black jeans, black sweaters and Beatle boots, and ordered everyone to grow their hair. Next, in the subtlest name change in pop, Keith Richards became the 'more *Clockwork Orange'* Keith Richard. A number of other small stylistic touches followed. Eric Easton took the oppor-tunity to express reservations about the technical quality of Mick Jagger's singing, not least because 'the BBC' – here Easton's own voice fell to a reverential murmur – 'won't like him'. Oldham's magisterial reply was that it was precisely this fact that would make them all a fortune. He then dropped a bombshell when he told Brian, Mick and Keith that Ian Stewart – already struggling with his snug, boy-band uniform – would have to go. The others had always admired Stu, not only for his ability but because he was the only member of the group, apart from Charlie, who was normal and uncompetitive. Unfortunately, it was this very quality that was the cause of his downfall. Looking straight, said Andrew, was dead wrong for the band, whom he was already peddling to an impres-sively wide raft of publications, including the likes of *Sixteen*, although he generously allowed that Stewart could be kept on as a roadie. Eighteen years later, the mild-mannered Stu expressed the opinion that, 'I wouldn't piss on Loog Oldham if he were on fire.' A source close to the band recalled that Bill Wyman, seven years older than Jagger and Richards, had very nearly failed to make the cut for similar reasons, until Eric Easton intervened on his behalf.

The Stones formally signed papers with Oldham and Easton on 6 May 1963. Brian did the negotiating for the band (giving away a full 25 per cent of their gross earnings) and relayed the details to Mick and Keith, who waited for him in a Wimpy Bar around the corner. Stu remembered the three of them immediately talking excitedly about their becoming millionaires and 'buying themselves mansions in Hollywood'. Later that week, everyone except Easton and Wyman had to have their parents co-sign the contract, since they were still legally minors (the age of majority in the UK then being twenty-one). The eventual deal gave the Stones a 6 per cent royalty, split five ways, on future record sales. Despite Brian's promises to the contrary, Stu was never cut in on the action.

Oldham's next move was to swiftly sell the band to Decca's Dick Rowe, the A&R man who in 1962 had famously refused a group of mumbling and − it then seemed − deeply uncommercial Liverpudlians crooning 'Your Feet's Too Big' and 'Besame Mucho'. Forever stigmatised as The Man Who Turned Down The Beatles, Rowe responded to the Stones with a rapid nod, an excited and spluttering puff of cigar smoke, and the high-pitched word 'Fabulous'. The band signed with Decca on 16 May.

Mick Jagger now arranged to take what he called a 'leave of absence' from the LSE. He had just sat his BSc Part One exam with remarkably consistent results, scoring a 'C' in all five of his subjects. Should the 'musical thing' not work out, he let it be known that he would be back to complete the full three-year course. Walter Stern remembered thinking that his former student would more likely 'disappear in to some sales or marketing position, better suited to a mind that was bluff and entrepreneurial, rather than brilliant'. It's worth dwelling on Jagger's academic prowess for a moment, if only to show that he wasn't always the mental colossus later widely feted in the entertainment industry. Mick was, however, both ambitious and adaptable. It was a bolder step for him to throw his hat in to the rock and roll ring than it was for Keith or Brian, who had few other career options. Unlike his father and grandfather, Mick would not spend his life as a teacher.

With Decca now calling for product, Oldham and 'the gang', as he referred to them, began pondering the band's first single. The Stones rehearsed several blues standards, sung by Brian and Mick, with Keith adding a queasy descant. Dick Rowe and his colleagues listened politely to Oldham's claim that the group members themselves might be capable of writing their own material. Having heard the demo tape of Jones' latest effort, Rowe could only remark that even a three-minute extract of such bluesy languor, punctuated by a series of grating vocal eruptions, however worthy, might not strike the BBC as a sufficiently commercial debut. In the end, all parties compromised on an obscure Chuck Berry ditty with which to introduce the Stones. Released on 7 June, 'Come On' was shorn of its distinctive rumba beat and instead given a punk tempo; the finished product broke the two-minute barrier. Mick Jagger deemed it best to sing the words 'stupid guy' instead of, as Berry had, 'stupid jerk'. In a further stylistic lapse, Mick trilled the chorus in falsetto. 'Come On' peaked at number 21, a modestly successful start which nonetheless thrilled the Stones. Eileen Giles remembers Jagger and Richards 'run[ning] back to Edith Grove, waving a copy of the record aloft. Mick put it on the turntable and shouted: "It's here!" and "We're pros now!" That meant a lot to him.'*

On 7 July, Oldham got the Stones £143 and matching Carnaby Street gear for their TV debut on *Thank Your Lucky Stars*. Even when they were dolled up in their prissy hound's-tooth jackets, black pants and shiny new Beatle boots, the compere, Pete Murray, treated them like a disease. Around the Stones in '63 there was always the sound of fans braying and squealing, MCs sternly asking for order and police chiefs rumbling 'Disgraceful!' The headlines followed suit: 'THUGS ... CAVEMEN ... APES' was the consensus, thus sadly undermining Andrew's PR campaign with the teen magazines. After offending the morals of several rural communities over the summer, the Stones began their first national tour on 29 September, when they appeared on the under-card to the

---

*Berry himself happened to be in federal prison at the time, after being convicted of having sex with a 14-year-old white girl, but still received his full royalties.

Everly Brothers. Everyone froze in place for a moment when the municipal red curtain went up on opening night at London's 700-seat New Victoria Theatre. Before that, Keith remarked, 'we'd rarely played a place much bigger than an apartment. When we looked out over the lights for the first time we thought we were in the Superdome. Suddenly we had *all this room!*'

Mick recovered first, celebrating his new-found freedom by spinning round to shake his bony posterior at the crowd before camping his way through most of the ensuing thirty-minute concert. He also minced, swayed, frisked and primped, all the while managing to look supremely bored, and indeed there were long stretches in many songs when he did little else. The classic Stones visuals were fast falling in to place. There was that little harlequinade of lip-pursing and bum-wiggling that Jagger strutted out when not busy appraising the floor. The absurdly deadpan rhythm section. Leering down at the front row, the frock-coated Brian Jones seemed less like a pop guitarist than some randy young Regency buck eyeing up the local talent. Keith Richards was compelling precisely because he stood stock still, right up against Charlie's kit in order to hear the beat over all the screams. Occasionally he crouched down with the guitar, combat-style, also for better acoustics. 'It was a struggle,' Keith later confirmed, but the music 'just about held its own' within the banshee stage act.

By early October, with the Stones sliding around trying to hold on to something in the back of Stu's new VW minibus as it ploughed between identical-looking redbrick provincial cinemas, the shows were becoming a case study of both the possibilities and the limitations of a 1963-style package tour. The depredations included a poverty format that involved being paid £35 for each of their sixty-one sold-out shows, of which the Stones saw roughly two pounds apiece; a succession of brilliantined house managers, on hand as a Greek chorus of disapproval, telling everyone to get their bloody hair cut; wolfed-down transport café meals; nondescript hotels; and a provincial landscape so desolate that, as Ian Stewart remarked, a compass of the sort he carried in his bulging jeans pocket was as important a tool as the roadie's ubiquitous gaffer tape.

Of the band's internal dynamic, Stu noted, 'You really see the worst in someone when you're in the back of a van with your face stuck in his armpit all day,' an irrefutable truth.

Musically, at least, the Stones were bullet-proof. After a particularly well-received performance, there were some 'good times', Stu said. 'It was like a rugby tour – we had a lot of fun.' This would typically involve 'drinking our way through all the booze backstage', after which 'we'd look for some more'. As Stu himself loaded the gear, one or more of his colleagues might enjoy a swift 'knee-trembler' with a local fan. 'The basic pattern went on like that for a couple of years,' Stu said. Set against these modest perks, however, was the fact that the band's front line were still periodically 'fucking each other about', he added. Recently, the simmering rivalry between Jagger and Jones had taken on a new layer of complexity when Mick had come home to Edith Grove late one night and, finding Brian's sometime girlfriend Pat Andrews alone there, 'bonked her'. A coolness had subsequently descended between the Stones' two principal members. It did not take Mick and the others long to discover the truth about Jones' financial arrangements. A friend named Dave Thomson would remember going to see the band in Glasgow, and after the concert finding Brian with his ear pressed to the door of a room where Oldham and the other Stones were talking. 'They're all in there,' Jones murmured. 'They're trying to get rid of me.' Nor was this mere paranoia on Brian's part. 'The basic routine after a gig was always, "Let's fuck off and leave him here",' said Stu. 'More than once, Brian took a cab.'

On 3 October, Keith Richards treated himself to a takeaway chicken dinner backstage at the Southend Odeon. When he returned from a few minutes off in a side room, 'with a well-known groupie', he says, the meal was but skin and bones.

'Who ate me chicken?' Keith asked.

'Brian ate it,' said Bill.

'And just at that moment,' Keith noted, 'the stage manager sticks his head in the door and yells, "You're on!" So we're picking up guitars and heading for the stage, and as we're walking downstairs Brian passes me and I say, "You *cunt*, you ate me chicken!" and bopped him in the eye. We went onstage, and as we're playing Brian's face starts to swell up and change colours.'

On the credit side, those hopped-up, half-hour concerts also taught the Stones how to 'put over' not only a song, but themselves. Slouching on stage with no visible pretence of enthusiasm, the group's singer typically glared at the audience for some moments while his colleagues did a largely perfunctory inspection of their instruments. At length, one or other of them might then belch loudly to signal the first number. A fast-moving package of percussive R&B and whirling, anti-virtuosic dance moves followed, all the more compelling after the Stones' initial apparent show of indifference. The band's jiggly front trio and studiously bored back line quickly became a pop archetype, and a role model for new entries in this exciting growth field: an electrician's mate from Bromley named Dave Jones, later relaunched as Bowie, and the twelve-year-old Gordon Sumner (aka Sting) were among those packing their local Gaumonts and Odeons to enjoy Mick's Tiller-girl hoofing, a lusty beat, and Brian Jones progressing backwards and forwards in a series of malignant hops, mouthing lewd endearments to the female members of the audience. The latter's reaction was, understandably, a trifle demonstrative. Meanwhile, the 18-year-old Pete Townshend, backstage at St Mary's Hall, Putney, watched Keith Richards windmilling his right arm over his head just as the curtain went up, ready to twang the first crash-chord of Leiber and Stoller's 'Poison Ivy'. Townshend nicked the gesture as his own. Keith himself later called the tour his 'higher education', learning how to perform amid a mob orgy. He was in the best possible company to do so. By the second week in October, the Stones were fourth on the bill to an expanded line-up featuring the Everlys, Little Richard and Bo Diddley; a sound sculpture of the whole history of pop.

On 11 September 1963, Oldham and Easton formed company 00821988, otherwise known as Nanker Phelge, in homage to a young friend of the band who sometimes enlivened proceedings at Edith Grove by walking around with his underpants on his head. It aimed for breadth: 'to carry on the business of writers, composers, licensers, distributors, publishers and dealers in radio and television shows, cinematographic film, plays, dramas, opera, pantomimes, revues, song, sketches and entertainments and productions of all kinds.' (The debut work, a Stax rip-off in which Jagger barked, 'Stoned ... Stoned ... Stoned outta mah mind' gave due warning that the main product would be something other than all-round family entertainment.) Later that same week, Oldham was walking around Soho one afternoon worrying about the band's next single, when John Lennon and Paul McCartney drew up in a taxi and told him they had the answer to his problem – a hard rock song with a topical lilt of Bo Diddley they called 'I Wanna Be Your Man'. Whether first presented in the back of the cab or – memories are vague, even by the fuzzy standards of the 60s – the basement of Studio 51, it required only thirty or forty minutes to write, and an hour more to run it through for the Stones. Released as a single on 1 November, it made number 12. Andrew, Mick and Keith were suitably impressed by this ready-made hit, rendered vertebrate by Brian's slide guitar, which the trade press agreed to be 'absolutely, completely wonderful' in every way. *Disc* gave it five stars. Lennon and McCartney thought so much of 'I Wanna Be Your Man' that they gave the Beatles' own version of it to Ringo to sing.

Jagger and Richards moved out of Edith Grove that month in to a flat at 33 Mapesbury Road, Kilburn, where they were joined by Oldham. Not surprisingly after the Southend chicken incident, Jones made other arrangements, eventually moving in with his new girlfriend, Linda Lawrence, a 16-year-old hairdressing student who lived with her parents in a small, semidetached home around the corner from the Ricky Tick club in Windsor. Brian had brought Linda back late one evening after dinner, and Mr and Mrs Lawrence made the broad-minded suggestion that he spend the night at their place. Linda soon got pregnant, a development her parents didn't take well. Despite some initial talk about marriage, Jones ultimately resisted the lure of a settled family life. The following July, Linda gave birth to Brian's son, whom he called Julian, the same name as his son by Pat Andrews; it was to be his last significant contribution to the boy's welfare. Meanwhile, Charlie was commuting up and down to his parents' council house in Brent, before taking over a spare room down the hall from Oldham's new office in Ivor Court, Marylebone, and Bill was still living with his wife and young son above the garage in Sydenham.

Lennon and McCartney's easy gift to the Stones had left a 'major mark', Keith Richards noted, not least on Oldham's appreciation of the financial rewards of the self-written hit single. As soon as they got in the door at Mapesbury Road, Andrew famously 'locked [Mick and Keith] in the kitchen for a day and a night and said, "I'm not letting you out until you've got a song."' The first fruits were an uncategorisable mishmash, swiftly followed by tear-jerkers with titles like 'My Only Girl' and 'It Should Be You', foisted on Easton's protégé, the crooner George Bean. The second result was the further demotion of Brian Jones, who proved sadly unsuited to the gerbil existence the daily slog of writing can be. When it came to the contract between a star and his public, it seemed that Mick and Keith had read the fine print and Brian hadn't. 'One whiff of success and he went nuts,' Stu remarked, of the man who had both hired and fired him. Brian did cut some-thing of a dash in suburban Windsor, where he continued to live with the Lawrence family in the winter of 1963–64. The neigh-bours' view of the Rolling Stones periodically driving up in their van was perhaps the town's major talking point, although the sight of Brian calmly strolling up the high street with a white goat on a leash also made a strong impression. While Jones was becoming the 60s prototype of a debauched pop idol, Jagger and Richards limbered up by penning a half-dozen increasingly assured and lucrative ballads. Within a year, they would be blasting the parochial shackles off British pop in a way not even the Beatles could top.*

*It's just possible Oldham was speaking metaphorically about confining Jagger and Richards in the kitchen at Mapesbury Road. Although some sort of intense creative burst undoubtedly took place in the house, the kitchen itself was a compact 6 x 8-foot room, with no lock on the door, and not seemingly that conducive to a protracted songwriting session. It's a small point, but perhaps another example of how certain Stones anecdotes become more amusing, or dramatic, over the years.

But first there was the troubling matter of the contract Easton had just signed to supply advertising music to the Kellogg's company. The two young turks came up with a jingle and a lyric that went:

Wake up in the morning,
There's a pop that really says,
'Rice Krispies for you and you and *you!*'

When Keith Richards then revamped 'Not Fade Away' in to a stylistic pile-up between Buddy Holly and Bo Diddley, he virtually invented the Stones sound for the next forty years. This pivotal moment came about as much from sheer hard slog as it did from creative inspiration: Keith and the band worked their way through eighteen takes of the song before they emerged with something that felt raw and completely spontaneous. Released in February 1964, 'Not Fade Away' hit number 3 on the chart in the same week that the Stones headlined at the Woolwich Granada, where the teenaged Jagger had jumped out of his seat when Holly himself played the song just six years earlier.

By now the group had organised a fan club, and Easton, having relieved Brian Jones of the duty, was handing each of them a weekly pay packet of around forty pounds, or roughly what Bert Richards brought home from the Osram factory in a month. The fact that not everyone was thrilled by the band's apparent overnight success was brought home to them by a series of public altercations: on 7 January, the Stones were enjoying a late-night meal at Heathrow airport when a party of three or four middle-aged Americans started hurling 'Fag!' insults at them, the trigger for a brief but spirited punch-up of the sort the band was getting used to seeing on stage. 'It was like they had the Battle of the Crimea going on,' Keith Richards noted of this latest tour. 'People gasping, tits hanging out ... You took your life in your hands just to walk out there. I was strangled twice ... It was climbing over rooftops, getaways down fire escapes, through laundry chutes, in to bakery vans. It was all mad. We ended up like the Monkees without even realising it.'

Sitting around at Mapesbury Road one night, Keith began

playing a child's keyboard and doodled a riff, which he gave to Mick
Jagger. Several hours later, Mick had managed to come up with a
chorus and the title 'Shang A Doo Lang'. On 17 March, they sold
it to the singer and later *Carry On* actress Adrienne Posta at her six-
teenth birthday party. Also present were Paul McCartney,
McCartney's friend John Dunbar and Dunbar's 'chick', a slim,
tooth-white girl who looked like something out of a Scott
Fitzgerald novel: Marianne Faithfull. Appraising Faithfull's blonde
hair and generous figure, Oldham had a sudden vision of 'an angel
with big tits', and signed her on the spot. A leering Mick soon
ambled up and introduced himself by pouring his glass of wine
down Faithfull's dress. Keith followed in turn, asked Faithfull a perfunctory question about her singing voice, and drove off to
Mapesbury Road to write the melody of 'As Tears Go By', whicht
went top ten that summer. The song particularly impressed Brian
Jones, who would come ruefully to note that 'it actually took Keith
three minutes to write a three-minute tune', and to rapidly curtail
his own compositional ambitions as a result. It was also an early
career high for Marianne Faithfull, who spent much of the rest of
the 60s as a celebrity without portfolio.

17 April 1964: the Stones' first album was released in Britain. An
early hint that this might be the beginning of something unusual
came with the cover, which eschewed the Beatles' corporate smiles
for five skulking profiles, with no identifying names or title. On the
reverse, Oldham's immortal quip: 'The Rolling Stones aren't just a
group, they're a way of life.' The dozen songs within burn with the
zeal of live instrumentation, not least because there was little or no
money for retakes. There's only one original tune, the warbling 'Tell
Me', but the record's raw power – with Watts and Wyman pumping up the rhythm at a time when studio technology typically made
this sound like a weakly snapped rubber band – offers living proof
that white kids from Cheltenham and Dartford can cross over to a
vast, multiracial audience. Everything was infused with a sense of
frenetic, primal energy and passion that went far beyond mere
homage. The result was a sparkling, unselfconscious celebration of

R&B – a last chance to get in to the Stones at entry level before they became an institution.

In all, it remains one of the two or three truly great debut LPs in rock. Of the 60,000 fans who bought it overnight, a fair percentage were encouraged to go on to greater things. Among them would be an enterprising teenager in Freehold, New Jersey, who snapped up a mail order copy of the record, played it 'thirty or forty' times in rapid succession, and then immediately began badgering his father, a prison guard named Doug Springsteen, for a guitar.

Inside a week *The Rolling Stones* would hit number one, dethroning the Beatles.

On vinyl and in the flesh, it was the same story. On 30 March, the Stones set an attendance record (netting them £318/10sh) in the heady atmosphere of the Plaza Ballroom, Guildford. Fans had been queuing up outside the doors from seven in the morning. 'Most kids [would] never go for indifference,' Oldham had repeatedly impressed on the band, but outright contempt would work every time. When the Stones eventually lounged on stage at Guildford an hour and a quarter late, they neither acknowledged the house nor made any overt display of excitement to be there. After glaring around the room for a moment or two, Keith Richards then counted the band in for the klaxon-like intro of 'Talkin' 'Bout You'. The place immediately erupted. A frantic pop party then followed, with stretcher cases and arrests. Mick was in prime motivational form throughout. 'Now we'd like to do "Roll Over Beethoven", that famous hit written by the Beatles,' he announced, in a rare lull between numbers. The crowd said nothing. 'You're thicker than I thought,' Mick remarked. 'Chuck Berry wrote the song.' Brian laughed maniacally, and Charlie did a ba-*boom* roll of the drums. The chafing from the stage only roused the crowd to greater transports of delight. As the curtain came down there was a full-scale riot in progress, suddenly ended, as if by a thrown switch, by everyone freezing in place for the national anthem. The show closed with Brian being pulled to the floor by several young girls, an experience he seemed not to actively dislike.

On 16 April, the Stones went up in Stu's minibus to the newly opened Cubi-Klub in Rochdale, Lancashire. Before long the place looked like a Hieronymus Bosch painting of hell, with waves of girls swarming across the footlights to clutch even at members of the support act. Police refused to let the Stones go on, and instead gave them a high-speed escort down the A58 to Manchester. Two nights later at a northern music hall, an elderly lady pianist, Miss Olivia Dunn, warmed up the audience with a selection of show tunes. When the Stones appeared the crowd stood up as one and rushed down to the front, trampling Miss Dunn and her piano underfoot.

On 30 April, the Majestic Ballroom, Birkenhead, was rocking to a lusty chant of 'Mick! Brian!' that had already soared up to the pain threshold several hours before the Stones eventually arrived. When Keith then opened proceedings with the guitar chop of 'Not Fade Away', 'there were suddenly 500 kids on stage – it was like D-Day', he told me, still fondly remembering the melee thirteen years later. Abandoning their instruments, the band exited hastily. Peeking out from behind the velvet curtain, they watched as Ian Stewart was left to pad lugubriously around the stage, muttering 'Excuse me' as he went, to retrieve their equipment as best he could. After Oldham intervened, the Stones were paid their full fee – now £385/15sh – for their roughly ten-second performance. The *Daily Express* considered the affair 'Shocking!' and the Stones themselves a 'cause of growing concern'. They weren't just a pop group, they were news.

The Stones' first contact with North America, later that spring, came as something of a mutual shock. There were initially encouraging signs in New York, where the group landed on the cloudy evening of 1 June 1964 at the recently christened John F. Kennedy airport. According to the *New York Times*, 'the young men with shoulder-length haircuts were greeted on arrival by more than 500 teenage girls. About 50 Port Authority and New York policemen were on hand to maintain order.' (This would have been even more promising a welcome but for the fact that Oldham and Easton had paid for the girls to be bused in.) Also on the upside, Decca's US subsidiary, London Records, followed the Beatles' lead and produced a notably accessory-heavy tour; if 1963 had been the year a mass market discovered the Stones, 1964 was the year the Stones discovered mass marketing. As well as their management's cheer-leader campaign, there would be press kits, photos, badges, buttons, posters, programmes and 'exclusive merchandise' – everything from socks to pageboy caps. If a teenager could wear it, Mick, Brian and the boys were on it.

On the downside, the label also hired Murray 'the K' Kaufman, a hyperactive Manhattan DJ and the self-proclaimed Fifth Beatle, to squire the Stones around town. Their chaperon did a good job of plugging both the band and himself; as well as hosting the Stones on his show, where Kaufman sold them on recording the Valentinos' 'It's All Over Now' – a take notable for Keith Richards' ferocious if somewhat monotone solo – he bullied them in to wear-ing 'Radio WINS' T-shirts, among several other promotional indignities. Keith would call Murray the K 'Murray the Kunt'.

There were similarly mixed fortunes when it came to the group's first major television appearance two days later, on the old *Hollywood Palace Show*, compered by Dean Martin. Martin and the Stones loathed one another. The generational clash started the moment they arrived, and continued through the band's brisk performance of 'I Just Wanna Make Love to You', during which Brian appeared to repeatedly flip his host off while playing the harmonica. Lurching towards the old-fashioned stand mike, Dino then delivered his monologue about the Stones having 'low foreheads and high eye-brows' before introducing a trampolinist as 'the father of the band – he's been trying to kill himself ever since'. With half the American press now going nuts for the Stones, the other half became tetchy, making it a point of honour to show their independence by carp-ing. One wag at Radio WNEW announced that 'I Wanna Be Your Man' ought to be retitled 'We Wanna Hold Our Noses'. The Nebraska *World Herald* judged that the Stones 'belonged to a sci-ence-fiction movie. They came out in a kind of crouch [and] stared at the crowd with furtive, almost hostile eyes', mild stuff compared to the band's anonymous critics who offered to tar and feather them, if not bash their fucking skulls in. Keith Richards, who had his first run-in with the law when enjoying a backstage drink in Omaha, would later remark how so many people in America (where 'nobody reads books', he noted) had seemed so strangely uptight. For all its size and sweep, there was 'nothing that hip' about a society whose choice of presidency lay between Lyndon Johnson and Barry Goldwater.

On 5 June, the Stones played their first live concert at the Swing Auditorium, San Bernardino. Thanks in large part to name-checking the town in the opening number, 'Route 66', the band went down a storm. Such was the accompanying din that nobody on stage noticed when a teenaged boy flipped out, wrestled a policeman's gun away from him, and shot a bullet in to the plywood floor just feet from where Mick Jagger was dancing around with his maracas. Four generally less well-received performances followed in Texas, where the Stones appeared to a backdrop of straw bales and horse shit at the San Antonio State Fair. The band's local warm-up was a tank of trained seals, and immediately afterwards came a performing monkey, who, unlike them, was called back for an encore. After Keith Richards got in to a shoving match with an irate customer backstage, he and Bill Wyman went downtown and, for $35 apiece, bought themselves Browning automatics. Keith would never again be without a gun when touring America.

2120 South Michigan Avenue, Chicago. For years, the Stones had all revered the place like an American Mecca; now reality struck as the band pulled to a stop at the kerb in front of a drab 1950s bunker marked Chess Studios. 'That boy'll help you,' their driver told them. 'He works here.'

The Stones glanced across the forecourt and saw a rumpled-looking black man of about fifty, dressed in overalls, shuffling through the studio door ahead of them. It was Muddy Waters.

Keith: 'He was painting the goddamn ceiling. He wasn't selling records at the time, and this is the way he got treated. My first meeting with Muddy Waters is over the paintbrush, dripping, covered in crap. I'm *dying*, right? I get to meet The Man – he's my fucking god – and he's out of work.' The Stones were both shocked and also smart enough to absorb the obvious lesson for their own career.★

In Detroit, Mo Schulman of London Records took the band to a music store and told them to help themselves to whatever they wanted. Jones took fifty-five albums, Wyman took eight and Jagger took one. Bill was already also running up an impressive tally of overnight partners, each of whom he treated with elaborate respect for the few hours of her tenure. If one of the other band members happened to say 'Damn' or 'Fuck', Bill would invariably turn around to his girl and say, 'Sorry, love.' While they were in Detroit, Schulman invited Charlie Watts up for a drink in his hotel suite, which was awash in champagne, caviar and an impressive variety of recreational drugs. When Schulman was then urgently called away on business, he affably told his guest to help himself from the display. 'Anything you want,' he stressed. Charlie took a bottle of beer, leaving both a five-dollar bill and a polite thank-you note on the counter.

Back in New York, the Stones closed their tour with two riotous concerts at Carnegie Hall. Forty-seven arrests, 120 fainting cases. At the afternoon show, Murray the K bounded on stage to ask the audience, 'Do you want to see Charlie?' (roars) 'Bill?' (roars) 'Keith?' (roars) 'Mick?' (roars) 'Brian?' (mayhem). From there, the Stones were content to yell back in to the teeth of the storm for thirty minutes. For the evening performance, Kaufman kept it short: 'Lezz 'n' gennlemun, the Rolling Stones. *Let's hit it!'* It wouldn't have mattered had he been reciting the Republican Party manifesto, because the words were lost in a cyclotron of

★Keith Richards has often spoken of his first meeting with Muddy Waters. It's only fair to add that a number of those who knew Waters best aren't sure about the specifics of the story, but, perhaps significantly, do remember a large amount of whiskey being drunk on the historic day in question. What's not in dispute is that the Stones recorded their next single, and most of both a second EP and second LP, in a 24-hour creative burst at Chess, and that when they left both Waters and Chuck Berry, the latter of whom appeared at speed after hearing that 'some skinny English kids were down there cutting my songs', lined up to shake their hands.

hormonal abandon. Amid ear-splitting screams throughout, the Stones blasted out an eleven-song set, threw down their instruments and ran. In fifteen days, they had played twelve shows, made eight meticulously sullen television appearances, and recorded enough new material to last them a year. They weren't entirely pleased with the experience. Mick was particularly disillusioned by the advance arrangements in Detroit, where he'd performed in front of an audience of 371 dotted around the 14,000-seat Olympia Stadium. 'We feel we've been given the business here,' he noted at an eve-of-departure press conference. 'We'll never get involved in this kind of tour again.'

By their early twenties, the Stones had peaked as musicians. Despite some satirical comment to the contrary, they were all proficient enough at their instruments. Unlike such guitar virtuosos as Jimi Hendrix, Eric Clapton and Jeff Beck, Keith Richards had already developed a signature technique – a barbed, percussive phrasing – that would come to sustain an entire body of pop classics. Brian Jones was the most innately musical of the group, but was showing signs of losing focus. Often, Brian elected to forego the guitar while on stage and concentrate instead on inciting the audience by shaking a tambourine in their faces. Charlie and Bill took the deceptively lazy approach, seemingly bored by the job of pumping out some of the greatest rock songs in history. As Keith remarked, all any of them could do for now was to 'rehearse the art of the getaway – there was no time for anything else'.

The band was, however, also becoming a brand that was far more commercially valuable than the mere individuals who sheltered beneath it. One obvious sign of the direction things were going was the front-page splash in spring 1964 in *Melody Maker*. After reading some of the things the press had to say about them in America, Andrew Oldham was able to suggest the classic headline, 'WOULD YOU LET YOUR SISTER GO WITH A ROLLING STONE?' The question echoed the sentiments not only of the band's fellow diner in Windsor a year earlier, but of a growing number of worried parents on both sides of the Atlantic. The Beatles, the general theory went, wanted to hold your hand, while the Stones' aim was elsewhere. It was to be an enduring and, in Mick Jagger's case, timeless image, although Oldham's caricature of the band as priapic shaggers may have been a touch ahead of reality. FBI records of the first American tour characterise all five Stones as 'liberals' [sic], who had apparently 'announced their intention to financially support Dr Martin Luther King', but, so far as could be ascertained, 'had not consorted with any women of loose morals'. Such self-denial was still the rule for the Stones in mid-1964, Bill Wyman excepted. They were blooming late.

But they caught on. Mick Jagger was now seeing more and more of Chrissie Shrimpton, the elfin but precocious teenager who had climbed over the heads of the audience to kiss him, and who was there to meet him at the airport when he returned from the States. Although only just eighteen, she was to reflect that even then she'd known 'Mick liked a party, and he liked young women. He indulged that liking when he travelled – and he had to travel a lot.' Meanwhile, Keith Richards had recently started dating a glamorous, dark-eyed model named Linda Keith. When he and the Stones were flying back from New York, Linda was in a crash driving home from a Midsummer Solstice rave at Stonehenge and went through the windscreen of her car. 'My face was messed up so badly my family had been and couldn't recognise me,' she remembered, 'and Keith came to the hospital, leaned down and kissed me on the face and showed me that I wasn't a monster and I wasn't revolting. And *that* was Keith.'

We're indebted to Bill Wyman for the information that Jagger, Richards and he had 30, 6, and 278 women respectively in the two years after fame struck. Meticulously well organised in such matters, Bill kept a running tally of his conquests. 'People made a dead [wrong] assumption about who was active sexually,' the bassist would note with some pride. As for Jones, the downward spiral continued: he 'got drunk, took drugs when they were new, hung out too much, stayed up too late', Mick Jagger recalled. 'He started to let his talent slide.' Brian's core duality could sometimes be seen when, suddenly tiring of the miniature train set he still kept on his bedroom floor, he would spray the toy carriages with lighter fuel and gleefully set them on fire. Nor would the Cheltenham Shagger seem to have been the model parent. Pat Andrews had recently taken to visiting the Stones' management office in London, where on six occasions between late February and early May 1964 she took the opportunity to suggest that the father of her son might care to contribute something towards his upkeep. Andrew Oldham and Eric Easton denied knowing anything about the matter.

Brian himself now divided his time between Linda Lawrence and a new girlfriend named Dawn Molloy, whom he duly impregnated. Their son was born in March 1965, named – in a departure – John, and later given up for adoption. Meanwhile, Charlie Watts was going steady with a 23-year-old Hornsey art school graduate named Shirley Shepherd. He still went home most evenings to his parents' house on the Brent council estate. Mrs Watts was bemused to read that her son was involved in a group with such an equivocal repu-tation. 'He's always been a good boy,' she noted. 'Never had any police knocking on the door or anything like that. And he's always been terribly kind to old people. He was always a neat dresser. That's why I get nonplussed when he's called ugly and dirty. When he's home you can't get him out of the bathroom.' Mr Watts was equally perplexed, especially because Charlie (who never learned to drive) came up on the tube every Friday night he possibly could 'with a lovely fresh cake for me and his mum'.

The hundred or so days from 22 June 1964, when a jet-lagged Stones honoured a commitment to play the Magdalen Ball at Oxford for a fee of twelve pounds, until they re-toured America, this time triumphantly, were probably the headiest of their career: the start of both superstardom and 'the Sixties'. The single most star-tling image of the year, and the first that Middle Britain had seen of the group, was the 4 July transmission of *Juke Box Jury*, the popular BBC panel show in which celebrities were asked to judge recent records, forecasting which would be a 'hit' or a 'miss', complete with appropriate studio sound effects. Long-standing convention required that there be a generous minimum 'hit' quota to each broadcast, and even the Beatles had played along on their appearance on the show some months earlier by giving five of the proffered nine selections a cheery thumbs-up. When their turn came, the Stones voted every song a resounding miss. The critic Fergus Cashin of the *Daily Sketch* was unimpressed: 'A group of moronic young men called the Rolling Stones sat in judgement ... It was a mockery of a trial as the gum-chewing, ill-mannered jurors indicated their verdict by catarrhal grunts that an ear, trained in the illiterate school of young people, could sometimes distinguish as, "Well, yeah er, I mean, like, well it's, ha-ha, awful then. Naw, definitely not, in'it?"' The *Daily Mail* cut to the chase: 'The Rolling Stones scandalised parents everywhere by their behaviour on our television.' Since first going on air in 1959, *Juke Box Jury* had typically attracted a weekly audience of between 10 and 11 million viewers. On the night the Stones appeared as panelists, the show was watched by 18.7 million Britons, easily the most in its eight-year history, and not far behind the total enjoyed by a major state event like the 1960 wedding of Princess Margaret.

Two weeks later, the Stones appeared live in concert at the Empress Ballroom, Blackpool. It was a Scots holiday weekend and the hall was packed with day-tripping Glaswegians ('many of them,' Ian Stewart noted, 'drunk'). First on the bill was the 24-year-old Tom Jones, belting out his debut single 'Chills and Fever'. Nearly fifty years later, a fan named Matthew Kite could recall that it was so hot in the room that the fireman on duty backstage, with total immersion in the role, had taken to throwing buckets of water over both the performers and the front rows of the audience. (Mick Jagger would sometimes employ the same tactic in later years.) Metaphorically fanning the flames, Jones then writhed and poked his crotch at the crowd throughout his peak-decibel set, thus launching a long-running tradition: amid the screams, the first pairs of lingerie came sailing over the footlights on to the stage.

Next, the Rolling Stones. Excited by the obvious potential for chaos, Brian Jones immediately began taunting the male members of the audience while mouthing lewd endearments to their women. The Stones in turn came under a barrage not of bras and knickers but of insults and shaken fists. Characteristically, Mick Jagger kept his distance while Keith Richards moved over to the centre of the action and gave the ringleader some verbal between songs. Minutes later, the intro to 'Not Fade Away' was cut short by the guitarist taking a gob of spittle to the face.

Those who witnessed Keith's fury would long marvel at the scene, speaking of it like old salts recalling a historic hurricane. 'You Scotch *cunt*,' he shouted. At that Keith took one step forward, looked down, and plunged a steel-toed boot in to his assailant's teeth.

In the ensuing riot some £2,000-worth of musical equipment was immediately demolished, the theatre's red and gold curtains were torn to shreds and a well-aimed bottle of beer brought down an antique chandelier. A few minutes later a group of disgruntled ticket-holders succeeded in pushing a Steinway grand piano over the edge of the stage to the concrete floor below, where it 'exploded like a bomb', in Ian Stewart's phrase. Brian Jones later claimed that he had been hit over the head with a microphone by a mob chanting 'Scotland, Scotland!', and then 'nearly decapitated' by a cymbal through the air. 'Sensing trouble', as he later remarked, Stu noted that he had promptly shouted to the band to 'for fuck's sake, run', although a young fan named Jane Graffey insists that at least one of the musicians had found time to pause to unzip himself and 'wee all over a photograph of the mayor displayed on a wall'. The Stones were then spirited out of the building over a roof and placed in a police van, which eventually deposited them some miles away, leaving a reported £10,000-worth of damage, thirty-five arrests and sixty injuries in their wake. It took Blackpool City Council forty-four years to lift their ban on the Stones performing in their town.

Impressive as this was, in some ways it was eclipsed by what followed two weeks later at the Kurhaus theatre in The Hague. Overexcited fans removed the band's microphone leads during the first number, leaving Mick and Charlie to perform as a duet with drums, tambourine and maracas. Soon even this arrangement came to an abrupt end in the face of a full-scale stage invasion. Keith

Richards remembered turning to look at Ian Stewart at the piano, and seeing only 'a pool of blood and a broken chair – he'd been hit over the head and taken to hospital.' Keith would add that the thought had then occurred to him that this might not be one of those 60s outpourings of peace and love. 'I fucked off at top speed,' he noted. The subsequent damage to the hall itself was extensive, with Bill reporting that 'Chairs were hanging from chandeliers [and] tapestries were torn off the walls.' But this was to prove only a prelude to a night of city-wide looting and vandalism. 'Flames lighted the heavens,' the weekly *Haagsche Courant* wrote of the scene. 'One heard shots coming from the [theatre area], and riot police advanced on the crowd ... The wave of fanatical concertgoers soon spread in to the town, where 6–7,000 chanting teenagers went on the rampage, many of them adorned with banners and flags, although some paraded around naked.'

By and large, the Stones lived frugally. The Hollies' singer Allan Clarke remembers them at their first meeting in mid-1964 as 'five vampire-pale figures tumbling out of the back of a smoke-filled van', whereupon they 'stretched, belched a bit and wandered off for a pre-concert session at the pub'. While the Beatles were busy experimenting with paisley shirts and herbally tinted cigarettes, the Stones generally slouched around in jeans and sweaters, and confined themselves to downing pints of beer and popping amphetamines to get themselves through as many as fifteen shows a week. They were equally careless of what they ate. Their severe lifestyle was partly from necessity; from 11 to 18 July 1964 the Stones performed eight sold-out concerts, played on three national television shows and continued to polarise society in the wake of their *Juke Box Jury* appearance: that Sunday night, Eric Easton presented each of the band members with a cheque for seven pounds ten shillings. At this stage, Brian Jones was still the only one to enjoy drugs, specifically LSD, on a recreational basis. Keith Richards was more interested in listening to or writing songs, Charlie Watts was with his family, and Bill Wyman was generally off somewhere exploring the limits of his wedding vows.

Mick Jagger, it's true, was no longer leading a life of monastic sobriety. On his free nights, Mick had begun to venture out to one of the new ultra-hip London clubs, like the Ad Lib or the UFO, that somehow packed in four or five hundred people, 'throbbing, sweating, dancing the conga and crashing in to the laps of strangers', in Allan Clarke's words. The photographer David Bailey would remember having dinner with Jagger and Richards at the fashionable Casserole restaurant in Chelsea. 'Mick put a ten-bob tip on the plate,' he says, 'but as we were putting our coats on, I noticed his hand slip out and pop the ten shillings back in his pocket.'

Then it was typically on to Mapesbury Road, or to the Stones' new flat at Holly Hill, Hampstead, where a speeding Keith might suggest that they sit down to write a song together at 5 a.m. Mick usually complied. One aphorism he now favoured, Stu would recall, was, 'Things don't just happen, they're made to happen.' Success meant controlling events, facing down or removing whatever stood in his way. Some people thought that there was already a 'daytime Mick' and a 'night-time Mick'. The former was a hard-working, resourceful, somewhat austere and utterly dedicated artist who liked to work to a strict schedule. The latter was an increasingly public figure who could be exquisitely polite or castratingly rude as the mood took him. Stu remembered that you could usually tell which Jagger was in play at any given time according to whether he spoke in his normal voice or 'that Godawful fake cockney accent'.

The folk memory of the early Rolling Stones is of a long-haired rabble of neanderthal sex addicts with dubious personal hygiene. It's an enduring caricature. In fact, as Mick recalled, most of the headlines then doing the rounds were 'utter crap, at best', variations on 'Would You Let Your Sister Go with a Rolling Stone?' or some other tale recording the group's contempt for normal showbusiness protocol. The promoter Robert Stigwood, for instance, was alleged to have short-changed the band by £12,000 during their 72-show British tour that autumn. At the height of the dispute, Keith Richards was rather fancifully said to have met Stigwood in a

London nightclub and, according to the journalist (and later Stones PR man) Keith Altham, 'started to beat the crap out of him. Every time Stigwood tried to get up, Keith would belt him again. "Keith," I said. "Why do you keep hitting him?" "Because he keeps getting up," he said.'

Total bullshit, notes Stigwood.

'It didn't happen. There was no beating, whatever [the] legend. Violence didn't come in to it.' What did was a well-oiled PR machine that was busy turning out 'Brute!' and 'Moron!' headlines as fast as the *Daily Mail* could publish them.

True, the group's internal goodwill sometimes ebbed away. Keith Richards was known to snigger, for example, at the wholly ground-less rumours linking Jagger and Andrew Oldham. For his part, Brian Jones was becoming known, not affectionately, as 'Mr Shampoo', or plain 'Shithead', having already irritated the band by missing several studio sessions due to mysterious 'allergies'. When Jones, whose aptitude for searing guitar was limited by his inabil-ity to pluck the strings, reported to Regent Sound to record the band's fifth British single, 'Little Red Rooster', he found a note from Jagger telling him the track was complete and to 'just do a dub'. Brian in turn enjoyed ribbing the middle-aged Wyman about his being, in so many words, an old perv. Some of the collective Stones humour could be 'a bit sick', Bill observed, targeting not only 'the spastics' who came to their concerts in wheelchairs, but anyone vaguely suspected of harbouring bourgeois ambitions. Even the genial Charlie was briefly transformed in to 'Dimwatts' when, on 14 October, he sheepishly admitted to having married Shirley Shepherd. The ceremony took place in Bradford registry office, with a reception in the local pub. When Andrew Oldham subse-quently commented tartly on the news, Charlie rose from the chair where he was watching television, punched Oldham in the jaw, shot the cuffs of his suit, and sat down again.

Later that week the Stones were in France. Backstage at the Paris Olympia (home of the can-can) they met Robert Fraser, a 27-year-old Old Etonian army officer turned art-dealer-cum-junkie 'who flouted existing drug laws … spent each night with a male acquaintance in his hotel room ... engaging in congress on numerous occasions', the later FBI synopsis of his activities notes. Keith Richards promptly dubbed the prototype 60s swinger 'Groovy Bob'. Fraser in turn introduced the Stones to the film-maker Donald Cammell and the designer Christopher Gibbs; through Gibbs Mick and Keith met the society photographer Cecil Beaton, who brought along 'Prince' Stanislas Klossowski de Rola, aka Stash, a sometime tambourine player and the son of the painter Balthus, beginning a long-running if troubled friendship between him and the band. It became a kind of chain-letter to the more raffish elements of the aristocracy; bewilderingly, these people began actually hanging out with the Stones, not denouncing them in the press. In time, Fraser himself became a generous provider of drugs and other favours, using his extensive connections to ensure that the band members were furnished according to their individual tastes. 'As I recall,' he reminisced, 'Brian was partial to twins, but, lacking a matched pair, often made do with a couple of other accommodating ladies,' whereas at this stage 'a smoke was sufficient' to get the others through the night. 'Mick sometimes wanted to go to posh restaurants, but Keith couldn't give a damn – bangers and mash was his idea of top nosh, and he always drove down to Dartford to visit his mum.' When Fraser, who would spend four months in a London jail after being found in possession of heroin tablets while a guest at Keith's house, ran in to serious health and money problems in the 1980s, he was to remark that of his celebrity friends 'only Paul McCartney' was immediately available to take his call.

The band's return to New York, on 23 October, prompted a pitched battle between pro- and anti-Stones groups at the airport. Four more months of relentless touring and recording – including the definitive cover of Irma Thomas' 'Time Is on My Side' – had worked wonders for their American box office potential. Andrew Oldham's perverse PR campaign didn't hurt, either. 'The Rolling Stones, who haven't bathed in a week, arrived here yesterday,' several papers remarked, having taken the Loog's publicity handout at face value.

In the accompanying photograph, Mick Jagger was seen to be obligingly scratching himself, while Keith Richards examined the inside of his trousers. Even the teen magazines were caught up in the melee, breathlessly cabling back their front-line reports from a society already busy tearing itself apart over Vietnam. 'There were riots and pandemonium when the Rolling Stones got in to Manhattan,' *Disc* announced. 'Hundreds of screaming fans holding banners about the boys or about President Johnson were storming the street and hotel lobby. Inside, it was even worse. Many people were injured in the fracas.' Appraising the orgy of upside-down faces mouthing tributes through his car windscreen as they drove off for their first concert, Keith would calmly turn to Bill Wyman and say, 'Bit different this time, isn't it?'

On the evening of 25 October, 60 million Americans tuned in, as they had every Sunday for the past sixteen years, to the *Ed Sullivan Show*. Although both Elvis and the Beatles had variously graced the bill, for most of that time Sullivan — whose robotic gait and hangdog demeanour had struck more than one guest as reminiscent of an undertaker — had showcased the most familiar, family-oriented fare. This was something different. Amid hysterical screams in the studio audience, the Stones blasted 'Around and Around' and then returned for 'Time Is on My Side', a tightly choreographed package of loud guitar, snarled lyrics and flying Piltdown-man haircuts. The switchboard at CBS (the company that would later buy the rights to four Stones albums at $6million apiece) was immediately jammed with complaints by parents. Next morning, a rattled Sullivan promised the press, 'They'll never be on again. Never. Never. We won't book any more rock and roll groups and we'll ban teenagers from the theatre.' Six months later, he would beg the Stones to headline his show.

Jagger and Richards went up to the roof of the Astor hotel in Times Square that night with Tom Jones and assorted Herman's Hermits, who were also touring the States. 'Hundreds of kids' were down in the street screaming for them. The musicians, who a year or so earlier had all been broke and living with their mums, smiled at each other. By then Mick had already done the one really imperishable thing of the tour, which was to be standing on stage at New York's Academy of Music when the 'new journalism' writer Tom Wolfe had walked in. Wolfe excelled himself in the piece he filed in that week's *Herald Tribune*. 'The girls have Their Experience,' he wrote. 'They stand up on their seats. They ululate, even between songs. The looks on their faces! Rapturous agony! There, right up there, under the sulphur lights, that is *them*. God, they're right there! Mick Jagger takes the microphone with his tabescent hands and puts his huge head against it, opens his giblet lips and begins to sing . . .'

The Stones then topped a bill at the Teen-Age Music International (TAMI) festival in Santa Monica that also boasted Chuck Berry, Marvin Gaye, the Supremes, the Beach Boys, Smokey Robinson and a half-dozen other such household names. But it was the blistering performance of 31-year-old James Brown that everyone remembered. His was a hard act to follow. As his band, the JBs, vamped on 'I'll Go Crazy', Brown would be draped in a king's robes and led from the stage by roadies, only to wrest himself from their grasp, fling the robe from his shoulders, and come running back on stage, repeating the whole over-the-top performance six times. By the end, Brown was crouched on all fours, hollering and whipping the stage with his rhinestone belt in time to the beat. Keith Richards noted that 'going on after him seemed like the biggest mistake of our lives'. Nonetheless, Mick Jagger gave it a go and pulled out all the stops in a thrillingly physical performance that was part athletics, part ballet and part tribal war dance. You could almost see him experimenting with what his body could do. Mary Wilson of the Supremes told me that no one else on the bill had known quite what to make of the Stones up until then, but they soon saw the attraction. 'James Brown was heard saying, "How can they close the show after me?" It was a running joke backstage. James gave the longest show ever to ensure that the Stones had to work hard to beat it. And they did.'

In time, Jagger would come to adopt much of Brown's histrionic floor show, with a full series of pelvic convulsions and burlesque set-pieces like the stage-lashing, part of a growing stage repertoire of lurches, shuffles, struts and – the Stones trademark – scowling immobility. Before this, as even the other TAMI performers proved, pop singers put on a gold lamé jacket before stepping on to the stage, smiled for photographers, and were humble for the press. Not now. 'That's when the Mick Jagger we know began,' says Giorgio Gomelsky. 'After that second trip to America. When Mick got off the plane in London, he was doing the James Brown slide.' Later, Mick and Keith wrote their first big hit using Brown's famous put-on, pleading routine on the fade of 'The Last Time'.

The now familiar riots: Cleveland, Fort Wayne, Dayton . . . after a while the names tended to blur and mingle. Throughout there was a carefully orchestrated image of the Stones as filthy, shaggy-haired bums who wanted to burn your town and steal your women; only half true, as it happened, but it polarised opinion. In Providence, Rhode Island, not hitherto known as a hotbed of youth rebellion, the show came to a premature end when the entire front half of the playing area collapsed under the weight of the revellers. Mick, Keith and Brian managed to run off stage, Charlie was mobbed and Bill stood playing the bass, his face deadpan. The Stones then performed four Midwestern dates as a quartet. While Jagger and Richards went in to the studio and stopped off to drink champagne with James Brown, Jones was admitted to Chicago's Passavant hospital suffering from 'stress' and 'extreme exhaustion'. When Brian's condition deteriorated, he became delirious and had to be fed intravenously. There was some disappointment, both inside and outside the band, at the subsequent enforced change to their classic line-up. After the MC left the stage in Dayton, having announced the Stones were a man short, several hundred teenage girls also made their way out. Respectful applause greeted the four musicians (discreetly backed by Stu), who toned down their act a notch in favour of more melodic arrangements and less adventurous riffing. 'You can't get what you want from the Stones with one guitar,' Keith Richards remarked, mild compared to his more private critique of the Cheltenham Shagger. In the five days and nights he was in hospital, Wyman and Watts were the only two who troubled to visit their bandmate.

On 16 November, a pale Jones flew back to London to find that 'Little Red Rooster', the song largely recorded behind his back, had shot straight to the top of the charts. Stu summed up a group mood when he said, 'Brian's sin was being so fucking stupid about himself. There was no need for him to get in that out-of-it state he used to. He did it because he thought that was the way rock 'n' roll stars should behave.' As if illustrating the point, Brian told the New York reporter Al Aronowitz that 'he'd fucked sixty-four girls' in his nineteen ambulatory days in North America, eclipsing even Bill's record. For his part, Charlie spent his free time sitting anonymously at the back of jazz concerts ('What a gas!' he exclaimed to the one journalist to spot him) and collecting American Civil War memorabilia. Mick and Keith did the interviews and wrote songs.

On 20 November, the band went straight from Heathrow to the *Ready Steady Go!* studios, performed 'Little Red Rooster', then fought their way through a mob orgy at the stage door before being driven across town at wild speed to play the Empire Pool, Wembley. Immediately after the show Keith Richards collapsed, having been up for five straight nights. A doctor was called, who prescribed rest – which was not available. At ten the next morning, Jagger and Richards were back in their Holly Hill flat with an Epiphone guitar and a tape recorder. Sitting knee to knee, Keith would play old Chess or Stax riffs and Mick would mumble along, moving words and music against each other to find new songs forged in the process. It took them 'about two hours' in this posture to hit on the stinging four-note phrase of 'The Last Time', later sufficient to break even *The Times*' pose of critical reserve. 'A caterwauling classic', it noted of the Stones' new single, which hit number one in the spring.

But despite all the attention, the sold-out concerts, the money (London Records would soon post a cheque for $16,000 to each of the group's two songwriters), the fame and the screaming frenzy that accompanied every step he took, Keith Richards would only now realise that he was suddenly one of the biggest pop stars in the world. The revelation occurred when he was out quietly doing his Christmas shopping in his local high street and a shrill, Dame Edna-type woman went berserk, lashing out at him for 'singing trash'.

Within moments, a lively debate had begun. The next thing anyone knew, Keith's critic was swinging at him with her handbag, and a crowd quickly formed to watch this apparent generational clash taking place on the streets of Hampstead. Both parties continued to bellow querulously at one another until the crowd became a mini-riot, and someone plunged through the plate-glass window of a shop in the confusion. At that, the word 'police' was mentioned. A photographer caught Keith as he then took the opportunity to hail a passing cab, eyes bulging in a moment of frozen shock, his convict's striped jersey slipping from his shoulders.

It was 18 December; he was twenty-one.

3

AN INSPECTOR CALLS

In the first months of 1965, the Rolling Stones' appeal to parents, hardly a great success to date, fell to its lowest point yet. The headlines kept coming, and they tended to be on the dark side. While touring Australasia in the new year, the band managed to display a sort of greatest-hits collection of bad behaviour, which included fighting with photographers, trashing successive dressing rooms, dropping whisky glasses from their hotel balcony in to the car park five floors below and, in Brian Jones' case, smuggling in girls hidden inside the room-service trolley. Sydney's *Morning Herald* didn't much care for it, and declared the Stones to be a 'blatantly wild bunch' who ought to be banned. 'They're shockers. Ugly Looks, Ugly Speech, Ugly Manners,' the paper noted.

Mick Jagger then signally failed to improve Anglo-New Zealand relations when the band moved on to Invercargill, which he described as 'the arsehole of the world', adding that the country itself was 'a dump'. To pass the time, Bill Wyman bought a Polaroid camera and, in a not unrelated development, had the road crew deliver groupies to his room in shifts – only the word 'groupie' didn't exist yet, so Bill resourcefully gave his activities a series of innocuous-sounding code words, casually remarking to the band's tour manager, for example: 'Did you arrange my laundry yet?' Keith

Richards confined himself to sparring with a couple of teenage male fans who chased and rammed him when, in an improbable alignment, he put out one afternoon in to a seemingly tranquil Sydney bay in a rowing boat stocked with a picnic hamper and a supply of books. The same qualities that made Keith effective in interviews came in to play here, as he searched for the words with most telling effect. 'Fuck off,' he snarled, at length. Charlie Watts was so distraught to be separated from his new wife that, landing at an airport where she was meant to be waiting for him, he vaulted over the customs barrier without waiting to be cleared, grabbed a record company executive he recognised and panted, 'Where's Shirl?'

Meanwhile, everyone had a good laugh when on the tour's final night in Wellington, Jagger dared the support act Roy Orbison to sing 'the worst record you've ever made'. 'Agreed,' said Orbison, 'if you will', whereupon he performed his 1955 hit 'Ooby Dooby' (chorus: 'Ooby dooby, ooby dooby/Ooby dooby, dooby dooby/Dooby dooby do wah do wah do wah'), only for the Stones to give ... exactly their usual performance. 'Just kidding,' said Mick.

By March 1965, the core Rolling Stones image was such that they'd been described as 'crude' by Ed Sullivan and 'scum' by the *News of the World*. While other pop groups might rate a dig from their local vicar, the Stones were panned by the Archbishop of Canterbury. Nor was the general air of dissipation surrounding their tours lightened by their recorded output. The first thing you noticed about the Stones' second LP, once past the disturbing close-up of Keith Richards' acne-pocked face on the cover, was how the titles sounded angry: 'Grown Up Wrong', 'I Can't Be Satisfied', 'Pain in My Heart'. So did the music. Almost every cut opened with a snarl of Keith guitar, then chugged in to an R&B groove with offhand vocal interjections and Brian's curly little flourishes. A highlight was 'Off the Hook', which set the sound of misogyny to a snappy Motown beat. *The Rolling Stones No. 2* spent thirteen weeks at number one on the British chart, though it's unclear how many customers took advantage of Oldham's liner notes suggesting that they mug the blind for money to buy the disc. In February,

London Records put out *The Rolling Stones, Now!* in America – an ill-titled round-up of unreleased UK singles and old cover songs that also went platinum. With the best-selling British single ('The Last Time') as well as the top LPs on both sides of the Atlantic, the Stones were emerging both as unrepentant moral slobs and diligent custodians of their art. A disbelieving *Daily Express* was forced to report that 'Many of the best critics are inclined to think that Jagger and co. may be here to stay.'

All this led up to the sorry events of 18 March 1965, when the Stones wound up a two-week, 28-date tour of old Art Deco British fleapits with a boisterous performance at the ABC, Romford. It was the town's first real rock concert: the words entered the language, alongside RIOT and ANIMALS, in the next week's *Havering Post*.

Around eleven o'clock that night, Ian Stewart was driving the Stones in Mick Jagger's new black Daimler up the A118 in to central London. Stu turned the car in to the Francis service station where, according to the attendant, 41-year-old Charles Keeley, 'a shaggy-haired monster wearing dark glasses' alighted to enquire, 'Where can we have a leak here?'

Apparently struck by the phrase, Mr Keeley asked the Stones to move on. The forecourt wrangling then became noticeably bitter. Mick Jagger allegedly remarked, 'We piss anywhere, man,' a line that was taken up by Keith and Brian, who repeated it in 'a kind of chant', it was later said in court. Bill Wyman took the opportunity to relieve himself against a nearby wall. A small crowd began to gather, and some of them yelled encouragement to Bill, while Keeley himself yelled the opposite, as Brian jumped up and down pulling his patented 'Nanker' facial contortion. An honourable exception to the growing furore was Charlie, who remained seated in the car, apparently reading the evening newspaper. It's perhaps not impossible to feel sympathy for the middle-aged petrol-pump attendant, whose premises had been so bewilderingly converted in the space of a few minutes from a quiet suburban retail outlet in to the scene of a pagan ritual. After a bit, a dramatically bearded young man referred to as Goatboy wandered over to politely ask a still occupied Wyman for his autograph, and Bill in turn asked him what the fuck he was meant to sign it with. Mick then repeated his mantra. Brian jumped up and down again, pulling the corners of his eyes down while simultaneously sticking his little fingers up his nostrils. This went on until Bill returned to the car, which then accelerated away, one occupant – believed to be Keith Richards – making 'a parting gesture with two fingers'.

Summoned for insulting behaviour, Jagger, Jones and Wyman were each fined five pounds, with costs, when the case reached East Ham magistrates court on 22 July. Keith Richards, in his first ever appearance in the box, was called as a witness. He testified that he saw 'nothing happen' at the service station.

The Stones' third American tour inside a year, opening on 29 April in Albany, New York, presented them with several challenges, not least when their sound system blew up during the first show. Their subsequent flight to Boston was memorable for its unpleasantness. A few nights later, in Philadelphia, Jagger corked off at fresh-faced Peter Noone of Herman's Hermits, who were headlining the show. The two vocalists had a spirited row about who was going to take the bigger dressing room. 'Herman[sic] is a great guy,' Mick diplomatically told the press, though years later he added the bleak rider that 'the most impossible thing in 1965 was going out to have a hamburger, and some guy would go, "Are you guys Herman's Hermits?" It would *kill* us! We'd say, "Fuck you! They're *shit!*"'

Back in Manhattan, the band taped their second Sullivan show, sought out James Brown and, in turn, got death threats from the Ku Klux Klan for consorting with 'niggers'. The Klan nearly got their wish when, a week later, the Stones flew in to Atlanta. The brakes on the band's plane failed and they had to slide down emergency chutes through clouds of smoke and fire.

The Stones live were something else, even after all the local Code of Conduct restrictions dutifully read out to them by some city-hall clerk who came backstage before every show. In Birmingham, Alabama, for instance, 'lewd or suggestive messages', whether appearing in spoken or musical form, were out. This was only one of many constraints that were forced upon Mick Jagger's performance in the town: he was also allowed to 'remove no attire' and to execute the bare minimum of 'abdominal embellishments'. In the event, his most provocative act was to pick up a chicken drumstick thrown on to the stage and hungrily tear off a chunk. Of the two guitarists, Brian did more of the prowling around, smirking and winking and sometimes jabbing a ringed finger in to the crowd to illustrate a lyric, while Keith Richards normally restricted himself to chopping out the rhythm. When pop critics opined weightily on Bill Wyman's own unique playing style (guitar raised almost vertical, shading his face), few could have known that there was a non-musical motivation behind it. 'It was so I could see the birds down below,' the bassist later revealed.

On 6 May, the Stones got through four numbers at the Jack Russell baseball stadium in Clearwater, Florida, before an estimated 2,000 fans rushed the stage, bringing the show to an abrupt close. As the band's Cadillac drove off, the police were busy 'hurling kids about as though they were sacks of potatoes', according to the *Miami Herald*. In the confusion there were sixty-five arrests and a reported thirty injuries, one of them sustained by a young teenaged girl who sobbingly released her hold on the group's car and subsequently slid to the road. 'I love you!' she shouted after them.

Back to the plywood Gulf Motel. A suddenly quiet Thursday night, with Charlie sitting alone by the small pool and Jagger, Jones and Wyman all *in delicto*. Brian beat his girl up and Mike Dorsey, one of the roadies, thumped him, breaking two of Brian's ribs. Bill notes that Dorsey's initiative was well received by the other members of the band. (Back in London, Eric Easton was quietly negotiating a settlement that week with Dawn Molloy, the mother of Brian's latest child. She was given £700, and the boy was put up for adoption.)

While Jones was debating matters with Dorsey. Keith Richards went up to a Room 3 – there were only seventeen in the place – watched the *Tonight Show*, and nodded off. Towards dawn he woke up with a riff – three notes rising a minor third from B to D, or, phonetically, *dunt dunt, da-da-da* – ringing in his head. Keith, who was in the habit of keeping a tape recorder by his bed to capture such moments, grabbed his new Gibson Firebird, taped the lick, then fell asleep again. In the morning, he forgot about the incident, stuffed the cassette in his back pocket, where it narrowly avoided being washed along with his jeans, and was later about to record over it when he stumbled on the riff. Keith listened to it once and then played the famous eight-bar intro to Mick Jagger, whom he told, 'The name of this song is "Satisfaction".'

It took two days to figure out in the studio, where several aborted attempts were made to record it as a brassy, Stax-like raver. Appreciating the core riff, Ian Stewart kept everyone's attention by repeatedly playing it through on a piano and having each of the band suggest an arrangement or tempo for it. Despite this, they soon lost interest and Stu had to assume the role of roadie, driving off to the local musical-supply store to reappear with a Gibson Maestro Distortion Unit, or fuzzbox, for Keith's guitar. That did it. The eventual track cut at RCA, Hollywood, on 12–13 May, boasted some emotionally pent-up lyrics and, courtesy of Charlie Watts, a bullet-train momentum that fairly screamed 'rock anthem'. Some observers, even so, could still make out the song's frustrated Motown roots: the basic hook had echoes of 'Dancing in the Street', while Jagger married Wilson Pickett barking to a sly, pissed-off delivery of lines musing on the perils of stardom – very much the kind of thing a black R&B singer might have done had he ever actually encountered stardom in the first place. Throw in Charlie's punishing 4/4 beat, Bill's rubbery bassline and the most famous intro in rock, and you had musical history.

Released in June 1965, '(I Can't Get No) Satisfaction' doubled pop's specific gravity overnight. It also became one of those standards that works its way under the skin, shedding spin-offs and a slew of re-releases and covers, until it stopped being a hit and became an industry – one of the key factors that turned the 1960s in to 'the Sixties'. In chronological order, it topped both the American and British charts, becoming the summer's great party-rock staple in working-men's bars and college JCRs alike, survived being cut by everyone from Otis Redding to Joe Loss, got itself re-tooled in to a jingle for candy bars and voted the 'greatest song ever' – nosing out 'Stairway to Heaven' and 'Respect' – by a VH1 poll of music-biz insiders, before being rediscovered by the likes of Britney Spears. In later years certain erudite rock critics such as the *New York Times*' Robert Palmer liked to claim 'Satisfaction' as a 'quasi-Marxist blitz on consumerism', while to others the title was more a rumination on the joys of self-abuse. Whatever your take on it, it seems fair to say that Keith Richards' dream was responsible for the most commercial slice of teen angst until Kurt Cobain wrought his unique brand of rock havoc on *Nevermind*, a quarter of a century later.

Ironically, probably the one person under the age of thirty not overjoyed about the song's success was a member of the Rolling Stones. Brian Jones 'hated' 'Satisfaction', although it's a matter of debate whether his objection to it was primarily on artistic grounds or because it effectively killed off his last remaining hopes of doing any serious composing for the band. There had also been a distressing incident when, with some initial enthusiasm, Brian first played the recorded song over the telephone to his parents in Cheltenham. 'That's very nice, son,' Mr Jones had said at length. 'But there's enough of these Americanisms around. Couldn't you sing "(I Can't Get Any) Satisfaction"?' Another theory, offered by Jimi Hendrix's bassist Noel Redding, was that 'It was Brian who actually thought up the riff and played it to [the Stones]. Then the lads said, "Yeah, right, thanks," and took it' – a not unprecedented act of piracy, if true, though it rather jars with every other contemporaneous account of the events in Clearwater. Ian Stewart told me, 'Keith played the basic song through that [Friday] morning, Mick wrote the lyrics out by the pool, everyone grunted, and we got on the plane,' and that that had completed the creative exchange until the fine detail came to be worked out in the studio in California. Whatever its cause, Jones' vocal disenchantment with the song served to further alienate him from the band he had arguably founded. In concert, Brian sometimes expressed his reservations about 'Satisfaction' by playing 'Popeye the Sailor Man' as its countermelody, leading to renewed mutterings about sacking him.

★

The rest of the American tour was an extended riot. There was full-scale civil unrest in Chicago and San Francisco. In Long Beach, fans danced on the Stones' car, nearly crushing their heroes like sardines in a can. The heavily taped-up Jones, dressed in a velvet smoking jacket, was limping around in hot pursuit of 'chicks'. While Jagger and Richards were busy songwriting, Brian's main priority remained getting his nuts off. On 20 May, the Stones performed 'Satisfaction' on ABC Television's *Shindig!* where, at their request, 55-year-old Howlin' Wolf, making his broadcast debut, closed the show. A mark of Mick and Keith's respect for the Wolf was the removal of the butt-ends they otherwise kept clamped to their lips when not actually singing.

With the riots, the busts and now the money, life for the Stones got appreciably crazier in 1965. In the spring of that year, it was decided to hire a gruff cockney minder, Tom Keylock, whose previous jobs had included working as a lorry driver, a fairground barker, an army paratrooper and co-owner of a small minicab firm. Born in 1926, Keylock had been wounded at Arnhem, suffering burns so severe that, as he put it, 'they grafted most of my arse on to my face'. ('So that's why you talk so much crap,' Mick Jagger promptly noted.) Big and bespectacled, with a passing resemblance to a swarthy Michael Caine, Keylock had thick black hair like steel wool and a face that seemed to have been built in a foundry. More importantly, he was as straight as the day was long, and the Stones all loved him. Generally speaking, the feeling was mutual. Mick and Keith, Keylock soon concluded, were essentially 'kosher' and 'admired guys who stood up to them'. Charlie and Bill were 'no trouble', even if the latter 'bonked for Britain' at all times when his wife wasn't present in the same town, and once or twice even then. As for Brian, 'he could drive you mad, the bastard, but there was another side to him, too. I saw the guy dozens of times being nice to animals and kids, and when he wasn't off acting like a poncy rock star he used to stretch out on the floor at my place and play with his toy trains for hours on end. Very polite to my missus, Brian. Well spoken. There were times when you felt genuinely sorry for him.'

In the summer of 1965 the Stones began yet another tour, this one of Britain and northern Europe. In the pre-dawn glow of 24 June, they found themselves walking across a roped-off stretch of tarmac at Oslo airport. Even at that hour, several hundred screaming girls were there to welcome them. Without warning, the band and their admirers were being sprayed by water cannon fired by advancing Norwegian riot police, led by a mounted officer brandishing a sabre. The charge didn't entirely rout the fans but it impressed the Stones, who conferred briefly among themselves and then told the cops they were wankers. Two hundred arrests followed at that night's concert. The next day, the band played an open-air show to 20,000 on a Finnish beach. Flying, Brian performed a lusty 'Popeye' while the rest of the Stones played 'Satisfaction', leading to a frank exchange of views back at the hotel. The basic power struggle within the band would tick away for the next eighteen months, with Jagger, Richards and management generally on one side and Jones on the other. Although Brian was experimenting with more and more drugs, his staple fare during this period remained the hand that fed him.

Meanwhile, the *Out of Our Heads* album was released in America and Britain, on different dates and in different formats. An oddity, there were a few clunkers: 'Gotta Get Away' was folk meets the blues, but not in a good way, and some of the interminable Stax covers cried out for a firm editorial hand, especially when it came to Jagger's over-the-top hooting. *Heads* was, on the face of it, little more than a collection of tacky, would-be soulful ballads. But closer inspection would reveal a pop sensibility as savvy as its principal competition, *Beatles For Sale*, with rather more guitar chug; 'Heart of Stone' mined grittier seams than most British Invasion fare, and contributed to an LP that ranks, after several listens, at the top of the Stones' second division. The same month saw a British EP called *Got Live If You Want It*. Recorded by the expedient of dangling a microphone over a theatre balcony, its own vocal limitations could be traced to the fact that Mick was singing several of the numbers with girls hanging on to his neck.

The Beatles comparison seems fair, not only on artistic grounds, but because they and the Stones were now choreographing the release of their respective discs. The idea was to strategically time the albums and singles so they didn't get in each other's way. Several of the two bands' summits took place in a darkened booth at London's Ad Lib club, although Keylock would recall a party in the summer of 1965 at Lionel (*Oliver!*) Bart's house where 'everyone got plastered while Mick Jagger and Paul McCartney sat off in the corner like two bank managers. Mick then spent the journey home with his head buried in some sort of file or diary ... When he got you alone he'd ask you stuff about what you thought of the economy and the state of the pound and all that, while with Keith it was more like, "Tom, where's the bleeding gig tonight?" But both of them used to talk about not clashing with the Fabs. So did Decca. I remember that.' Even by 1965, the recording industry had begun to undergo its pop-inspired change from a gentleman's club to a profit-oriented corporate business.

As the Stones' creative sub-group, Jagger and Richards had essentially been living on pocket money, just fifty pounds a week apiece up to the release of 'Satisfaction' – and 'quite happy with it', Keylock said. They soon began to conquer their financial shyness with the help of a lawyer, and from there it was a relatively short step to the world of country estates and young women volunteering to service them in the backs of Rolls-Royces. After leaving Hampstead, Mick first moved in to a room at the London Hilton and then a rented flat at Marble Arch, which Chrissie Shrimpton helped him furnish – 'like the Casbah', Keylock noted. Under the surface, a few cracks were now beginning to appear in the nearly three-year affair of what the press called the 'beautiful duo'. Although it was Mick who did the randy shagging while on tour, he wasn't the only one in the relationship to stray; his increasingly self-assured girlfriend, now the London stringer for the American teen magazine *Mod*, had taken advantage of his absence to step out with the exuberantly styled singer P.J. Proby. Forty years later, Proby reminisced, 'There was a party up at Loog Oldham's office. All the Stones and their chicks were there. They were actually painting the place. Some guy I didn't recognise started picking on [Shrimpton]. God knows why. They were really going at it. Then I saw him slap

her. Blood started coming out of her nose. Nobody else did anything, so I walked up, knocked the guy unconscious, and walked off
again. Well, Mick went berserk. "You fucking Texans! Fuck off out
of it!" he was yelling. Chrissie went home with me that night.
Everything went great until about Christmastime, when I happened
to see Jagger again backstage at *Top of the Pops*. On his finger was a
ring I'd given Chrissie. He looked at me, I looked at him. Then
Chrissie walked by, and I saw her and Mick go outside to this Mini
I later found out he'd bought her. They climbed in and drove off.
That was the last I ever saw of either of them.'

For the past two years, Eric Easton had prudently been putting
money in to separate accounts for Jagger and Richards at the
Bradford and Bingley building society to pay off their eventual tax
liability. (In a critical oversight, these funds failed to allow for 'windfall' earnings all the group members would soon start to receive
from their North American record sales and concert receipts.) Again
thanks to Easton, both men had credit arrangements in place at several London stores, where they were able to run up impressive bills
that they waved away airily on presentation. Keith Richards took the
opportunity of his first songwriting royalties from 'Satisfaction' to
buy his mum an Austin 1100 and to take his girlfriend Linda Keith
on holiday to Greece. When the couple got back they took the
lease on a High Court judge's luxury flat in St John's Wood, though
in short order, Keylock recalls, this sank to a state of Edith Grove-
like decor. The two Keiths 'lived [among] crapulous laundry, stale
fag smoke and dirty dishes. The whole place stank like a litter box.'
Further cashing in on his 'Marxist blitz on consumerism', Richards
bought a Bentley S3 Continental, which he first painted turquoise
(dubbing it the 'Blue Lena'), and then set off with a vast
Confederate flag. When that proved an insufficient deterrent to traffic cops, Keith replaced it with first Turkish and then Chinese
government insignia. The intended note of mandarin formality was
rather spoiled by the sound of 'Satisfaction' booming out of the car's
external speakers, which at least got a few good look-at-that-
bugger-jump laughs from behind the tinted glass. In his own way,
Charlie Watts now also cut something of a dash when on the road,

acquiring both a uniformed chauffeur and a second-hand Mini.

Both Charlie and, more plausibly, Brian Jones were hit by paternity suits that summer. The former was quickly dismissed, but Brian was to face a sterner test from Pat Andrews and Linda Lawrence, both of whom now sued him for maintenance, an all-too-real counterpart to his acid-fuelled recurring vision of snakes crawling all over him. Charlie went on to spend £8,850 on a Tudor manor house in Lewes, Sussex, which he bought from Hartley Shawcross, the former Nuremberg war-crimes prosecutor and Labour Attorney General. Although the British Establishment were by and large scathing in their public assessment of the band, few of them appear to have had any qualms about selling them their property. In his spare time, the Rolling Stones' drummer was interested not in scoring drugs but in arranging his collection of nineteenth-century American military uniforms, toy soldiers, and jazz records. When Charlie's mother came to visit the estate, she told the press it was very nice, but that she wished he could have chosen something 'a bit more modern'. Bill Wyman was able to buy a modest house in Keston, Kent, where he lived on and off with his wife and small son. Like Chrissie Shrimpton, the long-suffering Diane Wyman had had a brief affair during the Stones' recent tour. A ticklish moment came when the third party appeared at the door one night, but Bill was magnanimous. 'I told her to get in touch with him and tell him not to come round again, and the incident was forgotten.'

But even as the Stones were being enriched by their management's robust negotiating technique and undoubted PR flair, they were growing increasingly concerned at certain personal eccentricities on Andrew Oldham's part. The Loog appears to have been battling an undiagnosed case of both amphetamine addiction and manic depression, at the lower ends of which he sometimes checked in to a nearby convent to unwind for several days at a time. Emerging from these increasingly frequent periods of voluntary exile, Oldham was chauffeured around London in a lime-green Chevy Impala by a figure known as Reg the Butcher, another exotic, if short-lived, addition to a Stones entourage which already made Elvis' look like the Bloomsbury Group by comparison. Reg was not only present at his boss's various business meetings; he was omnipresent. According to the writer Philip Norman, 'The idea was that Andrew, if thwarted, would say, "Go and thump that guy, Reg," and Reg would thump that guy.' After self-medicating for several years, Oldham would eventually turn for help to a substance-abuse programme named Narconon, part of a group associated with the Church of Scientology. 'The guy was brilliant,' in Tom Keylock's assessment, 'but he was trouble. If you caught him on the upswing, Andy was a cocky bastard and he had a mean streak. Taking the piss out of cripples and such was a big laugh for him – that's where the Stones got it from. It's funny Brian and him hated each other's guts, because actually they were very similar.'

Oldham himself seems to have quickly tired of the day-to-day mechanics of management, because in July 1965 he introduced the band to a pipe-smoking, 33-year-old 'neighbourhood guy' from New Jersey, once and future Hollywood mogul and book-keeper of genius: Allen Klein. Klein was incredible. 'Weird', 'slimy', 'inelegant', 'ineloquent', 'charmless', 'sinister' and 'volcanically rude' in various contemporary accounts, he may have been the most chillingly repulsive rock-business executive of even that golden era. Squat, beady-eyed and built like a bag of spanners – invariably dressed in ill-fitting jeans and a greasy sweater which offered asylum to stray bits of food – he and his wardrobe were so brazen that both defied ridicule. Klein made his name with a titanically aggressive business style which he conducted on his own unvarnished terms, deploying an almost comic machine-gun rattle of street argot, liberally sauced with ripe invective. 'Al's negotiating routine would have raised eyebrows in a Mafia den,' one friend says admiringly. Casting himself as the Robin Hood of Tin Pan Alley, taking on the mighty robber-barons of the music business, Klein convincingly assured clients that he was 'someone who knows how to give these guys some of their own shit back'.

Both the industry and the press would come to treat Klein with suitably awed respect. 'THE TOUGHEST WHEELER-DEALER IN THE POP JUNGLE' was one Fleet Street headline, though many journalists' private assessments were more vivid. In time, he was to be the subject of ten US tax-violation charges, would cross swords with the Securities and Exchange Commission, which suspended trading in his Cameo-Parkway Inc (a previously defunct 1950s record label whose office he bought and turned in to his New York headquarters), and enjoy a virtual season ticket to the Manhattan court system. Not that the various writs and complaints were one-sided. Klein himself was lightning-quick to sue. He would even, as a scorpion when aroused will supposedly sting itself, sue his own lawyer, if he felt a case had been inadequately prosecuted.

Born in December 1931, Klein was the son of Jewish immigrant parents from Budapest. His father was a butcher by trade, and his mother died before his first birthday. Raised largely in an orphanage, he excelled in mental arithmetic at school and eventually put himself through an accountancy course at Upsala College, specialising in the new field of showbusiness audits. His image as a 'fat little kid from Jersey' belied the enormous care with which he served his clients. Klein was justly famous for having nosed out unpaid royalties, sometimes in the hundreds of thousands, on behalf of recording artists like Bobby Darin and Sam Cooke. He once handed the teen crooner Bobby ('Blue Velvet') Vinton a cheque well in to six figures in 'recovered fees'. Having unsuccessfully offered his services to the Beatles on their first American tour in 1964, Klein had turned to the other British supergroup of the day. 'Andrew sold him to us as a gangster figure, someone outside the Establishment,' Mick Jagger recalled. 'We found that rather attractive.' On 26 July, Klein was hired as the band's business manager. For the moment, Oldham would retain control of the records and the 'We piss anywhere'-type publicity. Eric Easton was fired.

Klein's first act became legendary. The Stones were ordered to dress in black, with sunglasses, and accompany him to a showdown at Decca House. There they met Sir Edward Lewis, the florid and supremely dignified company chairman who had abandoned his career as a stockbroker in order to found the label, primarily as an outlet for ecclesiastical music, in 1929.

Klein wasted no time on preliminaries.

'Ed, you've been fucking us over!' Klein shouted. 'Haven't you?'

The next few moments were exciting. The Stones averted their eyes, and Lewis, who abhorred bad language in the boardroom, reddened further, as though keeping his temper in check.

'I can assure—'

Klein smoothly cut in on him with a sudden flip of tone. 'No. Listen to me. You want the Rolling Stones. The feeling is mutual. Let's talk turkey.'

The band members left an hour later a million pounds richer. Mick, Keith, Brian, Charlie and Bill would each receive an annual guarantee, to be paid by London Records, of $7,500 for the next ten years, regardless of whether or not they sold a single unit in the meantime. (In the event, the band's charter members would still be receiving a tidy annuity from this so-called Decca Bounce nearly fifty years later.) Klein also got them a better royalty rate, 9.25 per cent, than even the Beatles enjoyed. Perhaps it was too dark behind the shades for the Stones to read the fine print, which made everything payable to Nanker Phelge Music USA, a company controlled by Allen Klein.

Why did the LSE-trained Jagger and the rest of the band allow so much power to be concentrated in the hands of one man? No one at the time grasped the extent of Klein's ambition or thought of his accumulation of duties in those terms; there were jobs to be done which no one else particularly wanted, and which he was willing to take on. Mick, Brian and Charlie seem to have been happy to go along with what struck them as no more than a bit of in-house administrative tinkering. Keith in turn thought Klein (with whom he shared a birthday) 'fantastic', the Stones' ticket 'out of cheapo-dom', while only Bill worried that 'Fatso' might, on the contrary, end up costing them. As it turned out, both men would be proved right. Meanwhile, the classic 1960s Stones brains trust was nearly complete, and another key part of it would fall in to place just five weeks later.

'I was sorry about how Keith and Brian went at each other,' Tom Keylock told me one day. 'It was pretty bad. Keith thought Brian was all fucked up, and Brian thought Keith had gotten together with Mick to take over his band.' Then Keylock smiled and put his finger on the problem. 'And in a sense,' he said, 'they were both right.'

On 13 September 1965, the Stones played two riotous shows in Hamburg, where armed SWAT teams swiftly dispersed some 800 ticketless fans in the theatre forecourt. Keith Richards responded to this display of Germanic efficiency by taking a half-filled whisky bottle, peeing in it, shaking it up and offering it to the police when several of them came backstage to relax. The Stones, particularly Keith, were all in fits when the cops proceeded to swig away, happily toasting the boys' health. Everyone then went back to the Hotel Lilienhof, where Bill Wyman claims that the candlesticks on the band's dining table suddenly leaned over sideways mid-meal, though whether due to a psychic manifestation or some other agency experienced only by the Stones themselves is unclear. The next night's show in Munich was marred by Brian Jones managing to get in tune just in time to reprise his 'Popeye' riff to 'Satisfaction', leading to further mutterings about his role in the group. The consensus was that Brian had fucked up royally, deserting his various kids – even the Stones drew the line somewhere – and doing nothing for the band except looking both dandified and wasted. Oldham was again planning to fire him.

And then, to everyone's amazement, Jones himself sauntered in with the most ravishing, drop-dead girl on his arm anyone had ever seen. But *gorgeous*. Bone-thin yet built, with a shock of cropped blonde hair and clad in a shiny black nano-skirt; her face corpse-pale but for two droopy, coal-black eyes that gave her an air of boozy languor. Yet, as the Stones were about to learn, she had already starred in films and been on the cover of fashion magazines all over Europe. At twenty-two, she was a veteran both of the dolce vita crowd in Rome and of Andy Warhol's Factory in New York, through which she knew 'everyone' in showbiz. She spoke six languages. And, best of all, she didn't give a toss about the Stones, whom she considered 'little schoolkids' and who went mad for her as a result. She was some piece of work.

Anita Pallenberg.

Friends have recalled that Brian seemed fascinated that evening by the story of Anita's arty upbringing as the daughter of an Italian travel agent, Arnaldo Pallenberg, who was really a 'frustrated composer' and a surrealist painter, and his wife Paula, a low-level Nazi functionary. The Pallenbergs' first child disfigured herself by putting an electric plug in her mouth, and Anita, who arrived two years later, grew up in a 'dark atmosphere ... rather poor with illusions of being rich'. Here were some of the same raw ingredients that went in to Brian's youth. As a teenager, Anita had gone to a German boarding school, been expelled, and briefly studied art conservation before abandoning it to hitchhike around various European capitals and, eventually, hop a boat to New York. A Manhattan model agency signed her and sent her back to Munich on assignment. Hearing the Stones were in town, 'I went straight up to Brian,' Anita recalled. 'He was the one I fancied. I tapped him on the shoulder and had a big smile ready when he turned around. I could hardly believe it, but he was upset, on the verge of tears, and I thought somehow it was my fault ... He was gutted because Mick and Keith had teamed up on him, and I really felt sorry for him. He was in an awful state. He cried in my arms all night. It wasn't a sex thing. He just wanted someone to be with him. We had a little fling together. That was how I met him.'

The next morning the Stones took the train to West Berlin, but two weeks later Anita flew in to join them in London. Before long the gossip columns in *Nova* and *Queen* would keep up a breathless drumbeat. Brian Jones was going to marry his beautiful fraulein! Anita was spotted at a bridal salon! Bob Dylan would be the best man!

None of it happened, but for the first time in two years Brian was smiling again. The Stones brought down the house in Berlin, not least when Mick chose to pass the instrumental break in 'Satisfaction' by goosestepping around the stage giving a stiff-armed Nazi salute. One hundred and forty-nine arrests followed. The East German Communist Party organ *Neues Deutschland* commented on the concert in a front-page editorial. 'This scandalous conduct,' it said, 'shows anew the dangerous extent of crime in West Berlin, and the degeneracy of its art.' After the show, the Stones ran through old Second World War air-raid tunnels to their cars, then left town with a police escort 'and every road junction blocked off by more cops', Wyman recalls. A photographer caught the band as they boarded their charter flight to Vienna. Five of them look like stick-insects while the well-padded Stu brings up the rear, dressed in a pair of lederhosen.

Brian Jones' growing detachment from the rest of the Stones continued on their next British tour. The band's one acknowledged virtuoso had almost abandoned the guitar by now; onstage he only rarely played any sort of audible musical instrument, and when he did it was filler. On his better nights, Brian added an energetic piano to Keith's rhythm assaults. As to his proficiency, not even the most gnarled pop critic could hazard a guess, as the dominant noise was one of frenzied screaming. Brian told everyone that he thought the new batch of Jagger–Richards songs a drag, but that he was prepared to wait the short time necessary before being commissioned to write music for 'Anita's movies'.

Jones didn't, however, disdain the business of entertaining the Stones' fans. He still loved to bait an audience, and effortlessly worked up the crowd on 16 October at the ABC, Northampton, in to a gale of rowdy chants. During the second number someone threw a metal chair leg, which knocked Keith Richards out cold. He collapsed flat at Jagger's feet. While Mick dropped the mike and tended to his fallen comrade, Brian threw his head back in the spot-light and, it seemed to many, chortled. After a few minutes backstage, Keith recovered and continued the show.

Later on, the Stones liked to portray themselves as, if not exactly full-on village idiots, then 'five English herberts', in Keith's phrase, whose phenomenal American success came about as a sort of list-less fluke. Even the market-savvy Jagger told an enquiring journalist merely that, following the fiasco of the band's first US tour, 'We went back and then things started happening for us.' 'Well, why did they start happening?' the journalist asked. 'I really don't know,' Mick shrugged. 'Some ... sort of chemical reaction ... seems to have happened, somehow.' The same reporter later ventured out with a microphone to gauge the reaction of some of the seven or eight hundred screaming girls on hand to greet the band on their arrival at JFK airport. This suggested that the Stones phenomenon was both broader and possibly even more troubling than most parents feared. 'Office receptionist Debbie Guest, twenty-five' and 'her two College-age pals' paused in their tracks long enough to speak for the record.

'I think that the Rolling Stones have a lot more sex appeal than the Beatles ... When the Stones are performing on stage, there's a lot more excitement coming through.'

'Er ... How about you?'

'I think they're the greatest, they dress different and they're the best thing that's ever happened in the United States.'

'Why do *you* like the Rolling Stones?'

'Because ... Keith is beautiful ... and they're so ugly, they're attractive.'

But if the sociological factor loomed large in the Stones' early American tours, it was soon joined by more sharply defined entrepreneurial considerations. As the group crossed the Atlantic again in October 1965 their irresistible, Isley Brothers-on-speed single 'Get Off of My Cloud', went to number one. Meanwhile, Allen Klein arranged for a 100-foot illuminated billboard rather daringly featuring the group's faces in close-up to loom over New York's iconic Times Square. The weekend before the Stones landed *Time* magazine reported that the tour would gross them an estimated $1.5million, 'which Britain's bad-boys announced they might give to the Black Panthers, or any other radical group they fancied'. A New York City councilman, Art Neely, was also quoted: 'Lock up your daughters.'

Opening out of town, in Montreal, the Stones were reviewed by the chief of police as 'the wildest act Canada has ever seen – and we don't want another like it'. One initial cause of concern was the discovery that Keith Richards had again lost his passport; thinking quickly, the mop-haired band members moved through Immigration so fast, jumping in front of one another like a shell game, that nobody in authority noticed. In New York, the assembled reporters immediately began shouting remarks about the band's Cro-Magnon appearance, and Andrew Oldham was forced to demand that one radio interviewer destroy his tape 'because he was asking stupid questions'. 'All the time the manager was remonstrating with the press,' an NBC television reporter was to say, 'Jagger and company never stopped smoking and drinking, largely ignoring the rest of the room, waving away some questions, stubbing out cigarette after cigarette either in ashtrays or, more than once, on the tablecloth, and motioning for fresh supplies from an aide in heavy sunglasses who lurked behind them.'

Banned by the Warwick hotel, the Stones then took up residence in the unsuspecting City Square Motor Lodge. A young English photographer named Gered Mankowitz rode along with them and remembered 'an enormous crowd of little girls blocking the way ... I'd never seen anything like it, but the band took it all in their stride. Even when the weight of the girls on the top of the car was causing the roof to buckle, so that Mick, Keith and I were literally holding it up with our hands, Bill was still trying to chat up the prettiest girls through the window.'

Once on stage in Boston or Newark or Tulsa the Stones would typically do a nine-song, $30,000 set, climaxing in a snarled 'Satisfaction'. On tour, the politically cautious and hitherto rather demure Mick Jagger now came across as a 'composite agitator and sexual athlete', said *Time*, inspiring, Stu added, 'a whole new phenomenon ... the chick wanting to get laid as quickly and often as possible'. Mankowitz similarly remembers 'an endless stream of notes, often pinned to bras and underpants, with telephone numbers, quite lurid love poems and very explicit offers, quite complicated messages like "Mom and Dad are away – ring me before 11.00".' Unlike most other male English singers of the day, Jagger would no longer use the lower half of his body simply to stand on: whipping up what was called 'wet panty hysteria', Mick's rooster-on-acid gyrations meshed perfectly with the faintly macabre-looking guitarists to either side and the laconic, gum-chewing duo skulking at the rear.

There was no holding the Stones now. The 'love 'em or leave 'em' headlines scrolled across a nation already violently polarised by such issues as the Civil Rights Act and Vietnam: HEY! YOU! GET OFFA MY CLOUD! ... MONSTERS ... DEMONS ... ROLLING STONES CONCERT A HOWLING SUCCESS ... KIDS GET SATISFACTION ... CRUDE AND LEWD STONES WHIP 20,000 IN TO FRENZY ... and so on; an image fashioned with Andrew Oldham's customary skill. For the most part, the press conferences remained one-sided social skirmishes, in which the band rarely deigned to speak. Their clothing showed similar disdain for convention – scuffed Cuban boots, tight jeans and loud check or paisley silk shirts splayed open to the waist, although sometimes, when out on the town, Brian Jones would show up at a club or bar clad in a shaggy Afghan vest that led a journalist to coin the phrase 'caveman chic'. With his travelling wardrobe of mauve suits, pink shirts with swastika cuff links, his waves of blond hair, brocade scarves and black boots, the Stones' one incontestable dandy was a Botticelli angel, Beau Brummell and a likely recruit for the SS all rolled in to one. Brian went out with Bob Dylan one night to a Manhattan dive called the Phone Booth, quickly got in to an argument about a girl with another patron, and ended up rolling around with the man on the bathroom floor, discussing the matter. A Stones minder hustled Brian out the side door and back to the hotel, where he spent the next two days 'pilled up and paranoid' about the police coming to arrest him. In contrast to these public altercations, Mick and Keith were busy with more discreet projects, such as composing the next album, finding investment opportunities for their tour money, and slapping Andrew Oldham around when he expressed his concern about certain personal matters by waving a gun in Keith's Chicago hotel room.

On 19 November, Anita Pallenberg flew in from Paris to join the Stones in Miami. Bill notes primly that she and Brian 'spent much of the time alone', while Stu said that on emerging, the nearly identical-looking pair fought 'like kids', trading little pushes and slaps. The photos have Brian floating around the band's hotel wearing one of Anita's flimsy blouses, or apparently rubbing his head in her capacious breasts. Later, it was thought that the violence was far from perfunctory. Brian's friend Dave Thomson stayed with the couple in their new soundproofed flat in Elm Park Lane, Chelsea, where he was made aware of the essentially cyclical nature of the affair. Jones would use his fists on Anita, whom 'I actually saw going in to their room with a bloody great whip. I could hear her whipping him.' Anita herself would comment of the core relationship: 'Brian was taking acid all the time ... When he did, he saw creatures coming out of the ground, the walls, the floors. He was looking in cupboards for all the people: "Where are they?" That's when he said to me, "Make me up like Françoise Hardy." I powdered him and dressed him up like a chick, you know.'

In his euphoria Jones told people he'd broken through to a higher plane, but it proved to be a trampoline, his manic highs followed by suicidal lows.

3 December, Memorial Auditorium, Sacramento. Three lines in to the first verse of 'The Last Time', Keith Richards ran up to sing harmonies on the chorus, nudging the ungrounded mike stand with his electric guitar. There was a bolt of blue flame, followed by an unearthly screech, and Keith fell to the floor. Then a ghastly burning smell. Richards stayed down so long, seven minutes in most estimates, that people began to panic – there were a few screams, then deathly silence from the audience. Police and medical attendants were swarming all around him. Then, suddenly, Keith opened his eyes, absent-mindedly scratched his chin and said, 'Hiya', before enquiring, 'What do I do for an encore?' After a few minutes backstage, where they discovered that three of the strings on Keith's guitar had gone up in flames, the Stones returned to finish the set. Twenty years later, Stu recalled that the sound of Richards' voice as he came round had been the 'defining moment' in the band's career. They all recognised in him the true rock and roller. Compared to Keith, everyone else was just a musician.

Although the tour formally ended that week, there was a suitably dark and wintry sequel to it in the album *December's Children*, which followed later in the month. For the most part this was a grab-bag of rejects, out-takes and what Brian caustically referred to as a 'load of shit left over from the studio'. On the upside there was both 'Get Off of My Cloud' and the definitive treatment of 'Route 66'. *Children* ended with 'Blue Turns to Grey', whose mild dullness could be traced to the fact that it sounded a bit like 'Yesterday' without the string quartet, and 'I'm Movin' On', an old-time favourite of the Sidcup Trio, powered here by Brian's steel guitar.

That album shifted a million too, staying in the American charts for thirty-six weeks.

On paper, then, Klein and his organisation had done the Stones proud. During the six-week tour the band played to 275,000 fans each paying an average of $4: just over a million dollars, exclusive of merchandising. Of this the group netted $542,589, minus 10 per cent withheld by the William Morris agency (though, perhaps significantly in light of future developments, with nothing set aside for UK tax). Each of the Stones, Oldham and Klein thus took home roughly $70,000. Having kicked off at the end of October and finished in the first week of December, Mick, Keith, Brian, Charlie and Bill made $1,855 a day, $13,200 a week or, for purposes of comparison, $687,000 p.a. – some 200 times more than the average British blue-collar worker of the day. Although they were doing significantly better than their own parents ever would, the Stones still faced certain cash-flow problems in the years ahead, particularly when it emerged that Klein would quite legally hold on to the money and dole it out to them in small parcels, leading even Keith to remark that getting their hands on the stuff was 'a wank'.

On 7 December, the Stones went straight from playing their 244th and final show of the year to Hollywood's RCA studio, with its windowless, Vegas-casino atmosphere, where Keith Richards first strummed the chords of '19th Nervous Breakdown' and the band cut half of what became *Aftermath*. On the first day there, Mick Jagger broke off from singing his spirited attacks on traditional English family life and other social mores to send his parents a congratulatory silver-wedding anniversary telegram in Dartford. After this intense creative burst, everyone relaxed in their own fashion.

Mick went off to stay in a Beverly Hills hotel with Chrissie Shrimpton, Keith disappeared for a riding holiday in the McDowell mountains of Arizona, Brian and Bill hosted a party that drew Dylan, the Beach Boys, several scantily clad go-go dancers and, it was said, a white duck waddling around the floor observing the action, while Charlie went up to the home of his friend the session drummer Hal Blaine and spent most of his time there fiddling with his host's garage-door remote control. Blaine remembered that 'Charlie would continually run outside with the gizmo, click the door open and shut again and then come back in, only to repeat the whole exercise a few minutes later. He was like a kid at Christmas.' By the new year, Brian was off in the Virgin Islands with Anita and a tropical virus. Mick told Klein's nephew Ronnie Schneider that he was thinking of marrying Chrissie Shrimpton, and Schneider advised him not to do so in California – 'the alimony'll kill you'. Bill and Charlie went home to their wives, and Keith spent the break with his mum.

'Look at the schedule,' Mick Jagger remarked in 2006, reflecting on the events of forty years earlier. 'It goes tour, tour, tour, tour, studio, studio, tour, tour, tour, studio, studio. The work was absolutely nonstop'; and the band was duly back on the road in early 1966, again scandalising Australia, where Bill Wyman recorded a personal-best total of thirteen groupies in eight nights. By now the Stones were happening like war happens: thirty-minute concerts, take the money and run, twenty-four hours in New York for the *Ed Sullivan Show* – the first ever colour broadcast on US network television – where, in an awkward scene, Keith Richards threw a dustbin at a Sullivan flunkey who failed to recognise him and Ed himself ordered a bleep to cover Mick's reference in 'Satisfaction' to 'tryin' to make some girl'. '19th Nervous Breakdown', with its Bo Diddley hook and mordant lyric about the kind of bird you meet at certain dismal, dull affairs (Chrissie Shrimpton, in most accounts) was going gold, and the band released the first of many hits collections, *High Tide and Green Grass*. Meanwhile, Keith Richards put his name to one of the weirdest classical LPs of all time, *Today's Pop Symphony*, which proved, if nothing else, that Keith and the London Philharmonic were strangers to one another's time scales.

On 6 March, the Stones flew back to Hollywood and RCA. In seventy-two hours there they cut eighteen songs, including the rest of *Aftermath* and three future hit singles. Late on the second night, the engineers called a halt to proceedings when it was found that a buzzing noise emanating from somewhere in the room was interfering with the recording process. This was eventually found to be Brian Jones, who'd fallen asleep in the corner, his slide guitar propped up against a live amplifier. Andrew Oldham thought it a symbolic moment when they subsequently unplugged Jones' guitar, as if Brian himself was being severed from the group.

Then it was back to Europe, where the familiar riots greeted the Stones' arrival in Paris, with Brian demanding, 'Accelerate! I want to see him bounce!' as a fan attached himself to the band's car. Next night they played an eleven-song set at the Olympia – eighty-two arrests – after which Brigitte Bardot appeared backstage. Stu later remarked that Mick Jagger had declined Bardot's offer of a role in her next musical film, but gave the actress a 'consolation shag' in a broom-closet attached to the dressing room. In Marseilles, Mick was badly hurt when a wooden chair hurled from the crowd gashed him over the eye, necessitating six stitches. 'It took thirty minutes to find the emergency ward,' he noted later. 'Then I saw an incredible thing, running down the corridor of the hospital . . . A huge rat!' Next night Mick gave two performances through shut-tight peepers, as Oldham might have put it. On 1 May, everyone regrouped to play the *NME* Poll-Winners' concert at Wembley, which featured fifteen-minute mini-sets by the likes of the Yardbirds, the Small Faces, the Walker Brothers, Cliff Richard and the Shadows, and Roy Orbison – and those were just the warm-up acts. The last three bands on stage were the Who, the Stones and the Beatles.

Out the next week, 'Paint It, Black'. This was one of Brian's shining moments, with his characteristic, seemingly casual endorsement of the novelty item – here, a sitar – giving the song its classic groove. Mick's lyrics were more Joycean psychodrama in shake-your-arse 4/4 time, and put death on *Top of the Pops* thirty years before Marilyn Manson. In the States, London Records then released 'Mother's Little Helper', 'a very strange disc', Mick conceded, 'like a music-hall number, with an electric twelve-string on it which made it very distinctive'. There was certainly nothing else quite like it on American radio. The B-side of 'Helper' was 'Lady Jane', a mock-Tudor ballad which, while unlikely to keep the neighbours awake, still aroused a lively fanzine debate: some took the song's title as a drug reference, while to the more literary-minded the allusion was to *Lady Chatterley's Lover*, where a 'Lady Jane' was code for a vagina.

But the Stones' main occupation that spring was the recording, release and promotion of *Aftermath*. A crafted song-cycle of Jagger–Richards originals, it established the creative duo on only slightly less exalted terms than Lennon–McCartney and, thanks to Mick's barrow-boy grunting, lent weight to the idea of 'classlessness' on which British television, stage and film were now coming to depend. (Even so, *Disc* complained, 'Jagger's vocals here sound like they were recorded down a well' – though with lines like 'The way she powders her nose/Her vanity shows and it shows/She's the worst thing in the world/Well, look at that stupid girl', some tactical blurring was probably wise.) Highlights included (on the album's two different versions) 'Paint It, Black', with Brian providing the trim to Keith's solid-rock foundation; 'I Am Waiting', a dulcimer workout pretty enough to be a Mantovani Christmas single; the Beatlesque 'Out of Time'; and an eccentric drum and marimba groover (and later target of feminist ire), 'Under My Thumb'. All intoxicating stuff, with plenty of highly evocative, fuzzy guitar.

On the downside, the extended piano intro to 'Flight 505' suggested a drunken pub rehearsal included in error; 'High and Dry' flaunted cheesy lyrics and a similarly busted-heart, country-style tune, played for laughs; while a decent three-minute track signalled wildly to be let out of the never-ending 'Goin' Home'. There was also the problem of the Decca punctuation man. The album (initially called *Could You Walk on the Water?*) was spelt *After-Math*, *AfterMath* or *Aftermath* in various pressings, while the rogue comma in 'Paint It, Black' still enjoys a brisk internet review today.

While decay and loss were recurring themes on *Aftermath*, one old friend, missing presumed dead since Chuck Berry's day, turned up safe and well: the commercial blues. It took Keith Richards, famous within the Stones for judging a room's acoustics by merely snapping his fingers, to prove that there was top ten life in the genre, moving the focus back on to exquisitely crafted, rootsy fare that appealed to more than a cult audience. 'Pow! What a stormer!' was *NME*'s verdict. *Aftermath* was an instant hit in both Britain and America.

For all that, the Stones still weren't entirely free of financial worries. If one of the band members needed cash, Bill Wyman remarks, Klein would routinely loan him back his own money at interest. Quite often even this proved impractical, and Mick, Keith or Brian resorted to firing off cables along the lines of 'What the fuck's happening?' and 'The phones and electricity will be cut off tomorrow ... Get off your arse, Al.' While they were touring America, Bill notes, 'Klein had made a big production out of giving us those huge, folder-sized office-type chequebooks in stiff covers for our New York dollar accounts, emphasising that they were our private ones.' These were the funds notionally supplied to the Stones by the 'Decca Bounce'. When the band members took him at his word and began writing cheques for various small purchases around town, 'Allen erupted, saying that we couldn't pay for things that way'.

According to Tom Keylock, some of the initial euphoria of Klein's guerilla raid on Decca had already begun to fade. 'Keith Richards told me that he was pissed off with management. All that "You want it – you got it" bullshit was just for show, he reckoned. The reality is that they all had to beg for money.' Richards' down payment on his new English country home would be extracted from Klein only by deep surgery, and in a subsequent transaction a year later Keylock flew to New York, took a cab to the Cameo-Parkway office on Broadway, jumped over a counter and told the startled receptionist that he wasn't leaving without 'Keith's cash'.

Still, the Stones' credit remained good. They were all doing materially better than before Klein came on the scene. Brian Jones took advantage of his paper wealth to part-exchange his Humber Snipe for a white Rolls-Royce Silver Cloud, which came equipped both with a specially padded driver's seat so that Brian could see over the steering wheel, and the licence plate DD 666 – a satanic homage, some fans felt. Charlie Watts and Bill Wyman were both leading comfortable lives in the English countryside. Mick Jagger remained in town, moving out of his Marble Arch digs in to 52 Harley House, part of a large, battleship-grey mansion block seemingly moored at the southern end of Regent's Park. The flat itself conveyed something of life at sea, with its flaking white paint, long corridors and oval windows, to which Mick added a variety of high-end bric-a-brac, including a surprising number of horizontal mirrors. Tom Keylock thought Jagger's domestic life was fast beginning to resemble 'something out of P.G. Wodehouse crossed with a *Carry On* film'. His lovers in this period, who in later and less reticent times yielded up a fair number of vivid details, agreed that Mick was striking in his energetic directness, his startling virility, his at times robust technique, as well as in his smooth patter. Forty-five years later, one young companion would recall how 'he sat me down in the front room [in] Harley House, with all the potted palms and red velvet furniture, like a Victorian squire, and told me how the words were his experience and the music was his soul. Anything for a leg-over.'

A vivid portrait of Andrew Oldham in action that spring is a pro-file written by Keith Altham, the pioneering rock journalist and future Stones press agent.

The Loog was in the throes of moving. 'I'm late, of course,' he said, heaping together a pile of legal documents appertaining to the action he is taking against Radio Caroline and *Queen* maga-zine for including Mick Jagger in an advertisement about the pirate station. Andrew's next move was to back in to one of the tea chests on the floor and rip his going-away suit. 'They shouldn't leave these packing cases about,' he snarled and made his personal bid for World Cup glory by punting the offending box around the room. His pretty secretary whitened under the accompanying oaths but stood firm, until Andrew's partner Tony Calder and chauffeur arrived to take him away.

Before 1966, the Stones had used drugs mainly to keep themselves going during long days on the road, or in studio sessions where Keith Richards typically liked to kick a song around (thirty-two times, in 'Satisfaction's' case) before recording it. As their income and celebrity status grew, they would indulge on a deeper narcotic level. 'We were taking a few chemicals,' Keith allows. 'The idea behind it was very pure. Everybody at that point was prepared to use himself as a laboratory ... It was very idealistic and very destructive at the same time for a lot of people.' Mike Gruber, one of the Stones' American tour handlers, would refer to this same phenomenon when he said: 'We'd go to a hotel and I'd call the drugstore ... I'd ask for some toothpaste, shaving cream, deodorant and a hundred boxes of amyl nitrate. I'd ask how many amyl nitrates were in stock as they were legal then and only ten dollars a box. We'd get them all.'

A snapshot of the Stones in this period came one warm night that May at Dolly's Club in Mayfair. Keith Richards and Brian Jones met up with Bob Dylan, who was touring Britain and being 'minded', with Keith's blessing, by Tom Keylock. The two Stones had already enjoyed a toke, two hits of Blue Cheer LSD and several cocktails while in their car. 'Everyone overdid it,' notes Keylock. Another trip or two to Dolly's bar and one to the gents and Keith, in particular, was flying. Somehow a discussion began about 'Like a Rolling Stone'. Keith accused Dylan of taking the piss and Bob retorted that, 'I could've written "Satisfaction", but no way you fuckers could've written "Tambourine Man".'

Dylan evidently didn't yet know his fellow rock star well enough to recognise the warning signs. Keith's response was to bring his fist down, hard, on the table between them. Clearly, it wasn't going to be one of those classic Summer of Love encounters.

'Fuck you, man.'

'Fuck *you*, man.'

At that, Keylock intervened. 'I told Keith to piss off, that that night I was working for Dylan and if [Richards] wanted a fight he'd have to come through me. With that I grabbed Bob, pushed him in to the car and took off back to the hotel. Then I look in the rear-view mirror and right behind me are Keith and Brian, in Brian's Rolls-Royce. They're out of their brains, the car's doing about eighty, weaving in and out of traffic. You can just see Brian peering out over the top of the dashboard, laughing his head off. He was a bloody awful driver at the best of times. I get to the hotel and hustle Dylan in, just as I see the Rolls jump the kerb and fucking nearly ram the front door.'

Mick Jagger, for his part, seemed to be fulfilling Walter Stern's LSE review of him as 'shy, polite and intelligent one day, a cocky sod the next', albeit on a higher budget. 'He was a funny bugger,' Tom Keylock recalled of the head Stone, not without a touch of affection. 'I saw how Mick turned in to a public figure around '66. He was at my gaff in Wood Green for dinner and he turned up wearing a sort of ballet outfit and a ton of jewellery. It was a costume for a party, and that image was what he was after, that look. He'd always shown up at my place wearing sweaters, jeans – clothes, not stage gear. My wife took one look at him and said, "Why don't you just wash off some of that lipstick, and then come back for dinner?" He did.'

Mick was also suffering that spring from some kind of physical or nervous condition. On 3 June he was examined by a Harley Street doctor named Samuel Weinstock, who sent him back up the road to Harley House for what was described as 'two weeks of total isolation ... He is completely unfit for work.' By now Mick was at it 'eighteen or twenty hours a day', he recalled, a merry-go-round of 'constant writing, recording, producing and performing'. On many of those days, he would also have to put in various official appearances, sign autographs, and give interviews where he was invariably called on to 'explain' his latest lyric – 'It means paint it black ... "I can't get no satisfaction" means I can't get no satisfaction' – to a waiting public. It's perhaps not surprising he had trouble maintaining such a relentlessly full schedule. Fortunately, Mick rallied in time to join the rest of the Stones for their latest and most lucrative North American tour, which began with a concert in front of

15,000 fans huddled in the pouring rain in Lynn, Massachusetts. Mick ripped off his shirt and did a hula in 'Satisfaction', the cue for several hundred spectators to break through police cordons and attempt to join him on stage. An authentic mob orgy ensued, from which the band escaped as fists flailed down on the roof of their car (a write-off) and tear-gas canisters exploded in the crowd. There would be no more rock concerts in Lynn until 1985.

Allen Klein then rented a motor yacht, the SS *Sea Panther*, and hosted a floating press conference for the Stones as they cruised around New York Harbor one sultry afternoon. A 24-year-old office receptionist and aspiring photographer then named Lin Eastman came on board with her camera. Her candid, frontal images of various band members slumped back in their seats, yawning, legs akimbo, put her on the rock and roll map. At least initially, Eastman seemed particularly drawn to Brian Jones, whose midriff she recorded several times, in extreme close-up. Brian, his appetite for female appreciation whetted but far from satisfied, then wandered off to linger with two bikini-clad guests on the aft deck. According to Bill Wyman, the photographer went on to spend the night with Mick Jagger. Prior to this encounter, Mick had not been in a good mood. 'I want to do a piece about the reality of being a Rolling Stone,' a lady reporter had announced. 'The reality of being me? It's fucking nasty today,' Mick replied. Another guest on the *Sea Panther* was to remark of the event, 'There's a feeling of "Don't touch me, I'm a Rolling Stone." Even that manager of theirs is so hung up on himself, it's unbelievable ... Jagger is a hippy in the true sense of the word. When someone says something honest, he goes blank.' Once back in London, Mick would have a final showdown with Chrissie Shrimpton and effectively tell her he felt 'very bored' and didn't want to see her again. When she took a nearly fatal overdose of sleeping pills and sent Mick the hospital bill, he refused to pay it. Lin Eastman became Linda McCartney.★

★A William Morris agent named Steve Leber was assigned to chaperon the Stones in America, an occasionally exasperating job. 'I did the tours,' he says. 'I had to be with Mick Jagger all the time and kiss his ass. "What's hurting you, Mick? Who are we gonna fuck over this week?"' Leber grew more philosophical with time, remembering that it had all been in a day's work, and that Jagger was also 'a gentleman'.

On 2 July, the Stones played to an audience of 9,400 fans and 375 police at Forest Hills Tennis Stadium in Queens, under the steely gaze of the *New York Times* arts critic:

> During the combo's last number, 'Satisfaction', several girls appeared to be crying uncontrollably. About a dozen youngsters willfully broke through the police lines ... The combo withdrew immediately and within seconds the park lights were up and the Rolling Stones' helicopter took off in to the night.

Keith Richards and Linda Keith then made straight for the Café Wha? in Greenwich Village to see the week's resident act, a hip young guitarist from Seattle going by the name Jimmy James. Both the Keiths gasped as the psychedelic-clad gypsy bounced around the stage playing a Dylan medley at peak volume, adding washes of screeching feedback. Before long, Linda went off with James, who moved to London and became Jimi Hendrix. Richards found solace with one of Bill Wyman's groupies, who described him as a 'shy, lovable guy', but one of the great sack artists of all time as well. 'That tongue!' The whole thing, alas, turned out badly, and both bandmates ended up on a nasty penicillin course.

The tour's thirty-two concerts were some of the most electrifying of the Stones' career. Under the influence of hallucinogens like peyote and LSD, the basic concept began to change in to something a bit more radical, vaguely political, with a great sense of fashion. Brian Jones took to performing in a Henley-like lemon and blue blazer with pink stripes, although the regatta's stewards might not have cared for his accompanying floral blouse and crotch-hugging velvet pants. Plagued by a lack of synchronisation in his movements, Brian frequently made several attempts to successfully plug in his guitar. Sometimes brilliantly musical, at other times he seemed to operate way out in a psychedelic-cabaret zone that was the polar extreme of his image as a blues-jazz purist. On stage, the Stones' division of labour was increasingly out of kilter. Although Brian flitted around between the guitar, keyboards and harp, Mick shouldered the task of working the fans up in to a lather, which he did with unfailing energy and panache. He deserved a Queen's Award for Industry. On 26 July, his twenty-third birthday, Jagger bumped and ground away in front of several hundred screaming San Francisco concert-goers, while a hirsute young man scaled a lighting tower to drop leaflets on to the stage:

> We welcome the ROLLING STONES . . . They themselves are our fellows in the desperate struggle against the mad people who got the power. We fight in guerilla groups against the imperial-ist invader in Asia and South America . . . Fellows, you'll come back to this land when it is free from state tyranny and play your wonderful music in the factories which will be led by workers among one million red flags fluttering above an anarchic com-munity. ROLLING STONES, the young people of California listen to your message – Long live the revolution!

In Harley House, that week, Tom Keylock was taking possession of a Regency bath and a four-poster bed for his master.

Everything wound up two nights later in Hawaii, where Mick Jagger introduced 'Satisfaction' in his mock Southern drawl. 'I can't tell you how wonderful it is to be here, everybody. It's really wonderful, the best audience . . . ever . . . and this is the final show . . . ever.' The Stones ran off. Over the previous month they had netted $720,000, making for a pay-packet of some $80,000 each, though, again, with-out heed of British income tax. By now they all knew it was the end of something, the last of the anarchic 'Battle of the Crimea' tours and, as it turned out, the last American gig for three years. As if in celebration, Anita flew in to join Brian; the couple rowed through-out, and then split for Morocco, where Jones threw a punch, hit a wall instead of Anita, and walked around with his fist in plaster for a month. Mick and Keith went to Acapulco to write songs, and Charlie took his wife pony-trekking in the California hills. Bill Wyman flew home to London, having managed to bed a comely pair of sisters on his last night in Hawaii. 'As none of the group had been able to pick up any girls on this visit,' Bill notes, 'they were well choked with me for having had two.'

Before disappearing on their summer holidays, the Stones had reconvened at RCA to cut a dozen more songs, including the big 'n' brassy 'Have You Seen Your Mother Baby?', still treasured by erudite critics for its intelligent, cool unorthodoxy ('a Rimbauesque declension of the shadow world of illicit sexuality' in one author's assessment), anchored by enough fuzz guitar and low-fi distortion to make you check for dust on your turntable needle. 'Manic' was the word. The Stones' new single was badly recorded, badly mixed and sold (comparatively) badly, hitting only number 9 in Britain – but it did feature the most talked-about sleeve art in pop history.

In hindsight, the portrait of the boys kitted out in full retro-trans-vestite drag, taken by the New York director-photographer Jerry Schatzberg, but choreographed by Andrew Oldham, was probably only a fair idea. It seems to have initially taken root when Brian Jones emerged from a Manhattan boutique one day in possession of a white sequined cocktail dress of the sort popular in the 1920s. Back in their hotel, Anita had been able to supply various period accessories, including pearl necklaces, earrings and even a glittering costume-jewellery tiara. Later that night, Brian had appeared in this ensemble at a reception to honour the Stones in the Waldorf Astoria hotel. The dress fit him like a snake. Schatzberg had immediately told Oldham, 'These guys would look great in drag.' The resulting image was so hideous, or incongruous, that a Decca director's wife vomited over her advance copy, though she was at least spared the accompanying video footage of Brian energetically pleasuring him-self under his skirt that finished up on the cutting-room floor (where it was rescued by Mick Jagger, who later entertained guests at his French château with it). For others, the most disturbing part of the photograph was the sight of the mournful, rattily furred 'Millicent' Watts, looking like a ghastly rock Miss Havisham. After the shoot, the band members calmly strolled in to a bar still gussied

up, had a beer and a smoke, and, this being Lower Manhattan, no
one said a word.

Next night the Stones were back on the Sullivan show. Since
Brian couldn't play because of his fist, everyone mimed to pre-
recorded backing tracks, most of which were lost in a tidal wave of
screams. Immediately after the taping, the band jumped in to taxis
and went downtown to a party at Schatzberg's studio, where they
declined to reprise their drag act. They dressed as Nazis instead.

When *Time* magazine came to officially dub London the Style
Capital of Europe, they concentrated on a few, photogenic locations
and eye-catching developments like miniskirts and the mid-career
makeover of the Beatles. It's debatable how much of a more general revolution was also under way against the Britain of rationing,
deference and petty repressions. Every generation produces its defi-
nition of transgressive behaviour, and the key thing for a successful
counter-culture is surely to be disapproved of by conventional opinion. Conjuring up a spirit of revolt was a relatively easy task given
the overall state of affairs at about the time *Aftermath* was released.
It's sometimes forgotten that the Lord Chamberlain was still cen-
soring plays until 1968, and raids by the Vice Squad on galleries
such as Robert Fraser's, where officers seized a variety of erotic
prints and sculptures, remained a feature of the British arts scene.

So, on one level, the Stones and others would seem to have been
in the forefront of a highly organised and brilliantly successful coup
against a social order essentially unchanged since their grandparents'
day. Most retrospectives duly take the Summer of Love (loosely
agreed as being the period from about the time England won the
World Cup in July 1966 to the Beatles' ill-fated retreat with the
Maharishi Yogi, during the course of which their manager Brian
Epstein died, thirteen months later) on its own terms. 'Society was
shaken to its foundations!' a recent BBC documentary on the subject shouted. 'All the rules came off, all the brakes came off . . . the
floodgates were unlocked . . . a youthquake hit Britain,' and so on.
For most people, what this mainly seems to have meant was some
very silly shirts, better furniture and a slight increase in the use of

9-year-old Mike Jagger (right) at home with Dartford schoolfriends, 1952.

School outing to Wembley Stadium, May 1954. Jagger in centre, holding cat; Keith Richards front row, fourth from left. They were to return to the venue in some style 28 years later.

The classic 1963 Rolling Stones line-up that Brian Jones said would 'change the face of British music'. Back row, left to right: Charlie Watts, Bill Wyman; front row, left to right: Mick Jagger, BJ, Keith Richards.

The Stones on *Ready Steady Go!* in April 1964, moments before triggering their latest riot.

Landfall in North America, June 1964. Although the Stones enjoyed a Beatles-like reception in New York, elsewhere it was a different story.

On the evening of 25 October 1964, 60m American television viewers watched the Stones perform on *The Ed Sullivan Show*. For the next two days, Sullivan's switchboard was jammed with complaints from parents.

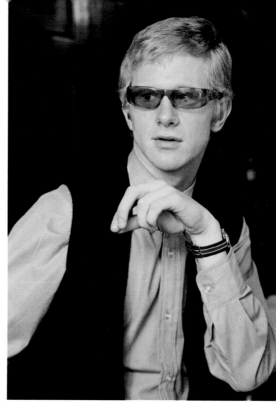

Allen Klein, who took over the Stones' business affairs in July 1965, enjoyed a reputation both as a tough negotiator and a serial litigant. Five years later, his relationship with the band duly ended in court.

The Rolling Stones' legendary image-maker Andrew Loog Oldham, London, 1964.

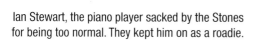

Ian Stewart, the piano player sacked by the Stones for being too normal. They kept him on as a roadie.

Marianne Faithfull (left) and Anita Pallenberg en route to the fateful holiday in Morocco, March 1967.

Mick Jagger and Keith Richards laughing on the way home from their committal on drugs charges in May 1967. At the trial seven weeks later, the judge told the jury to put out of their minds any prejudice they might have about the Stones' looks, clothes, lifestyle or their views on 'petty morals'. They were also to ignore everything they had read and heard about a nude girl who had been lying in front of the fireplace when the police arrived, and not to let her rum behaviour in any way influence their verdict. The jury found Mick and Keith guilty.

Tom Driberg, the former gossip columnist, swashbuckling wartime double agent and occultist, who tried and failed to recruit Mick to the Labour Party.

Brian Jones and Tom Keylock on their way to Brian's second and final drug-possession trial in London, September 1968. The judge gave Brian a fine. 'For goodness' sake, don't get into trouble again,' he told him.

The swimming pool at Cotchford Farm seen on 3 July 1969, hours after Brian Jones drowned in it. Brian's dogs are still looking for him.

Tom Keylock briefs the press later that day, assuring them it was all an accident.

The Stones introduce their new line-up: left to right, Charlie Watts, Mick Taylor, Mick Jagger, Keith Richards, Bill Wyman.

The Hyde Park concert, 5 July 1969. Brian Jones had died two days earlier; Marianne Faithfull, seen here just behind the photographers, tried to kill herself the following week.

Crowd control at Altamont, 6 December 1969.

Performance, which saw Mick Jagger hopelessly miscast as a jaded rock star holed up with a pair of sexually ambiguous girlfriends (Michelle Breton, left, and Anita Pallenberg, right) and a large stash of magic mushrooms. It soon dawned on the Warner Brothers board that the film wasn't quite the 'Stones' version of *A Hard Day's Night*' that an early studio memo had promised. One executive's wife vomited at the premiere.

Les Perrin (left) gets Mick and Bianca Jagger to the church in St Tropez on 12 May 1971. The bride later said that her marriage ended on her wedding day.

Keith Richards' home in Cheyne Walk. When the former owner dropped by to collect his post, he took one look at the décor and had to sit down. In June 1973, police raided the house and charged Keith with 26 drugs and firearms offences.

Mick and Keith at Redlands, shortly before it burnt down.

soft drugs. The contraceptive pill also meant that a few more young women spent the night together with their boyfriends.

Ian Stewart, for one, inclined more to the empirical view of Swinging London and the Peace and Love Generation in general when he referred to it collectively as 'a load of bollocks'. To the practical-minded Stu, 'Nobody in the Rolling Stones was sitting around plotting to overthrow the government or put LSD in the water supply. It was all we could do to cut the records and get to the next fucking gig. If you're talking about having an agenda, we were about as revolutionary as my granny.'

On 23 September, eight weeks after Mick Jagger announced their 'final show ever', the Stones were back on the road for a 24-date British tour. The opening night was at London's Royal Albert Hall. Long before the warm-up Terry Reid performed, the joint was rocking to a communal chant of 'Mick! Keef!!' which soared up to the rafters as showtime approached, and then went on from there to get rowdy. Soon Reid found himself eyeing up the room, hoping to locate an emergency exit he could reach in the event of trouble, while periodically calling for 'calm'. Despite these appeals, 'it was fucking chaos', he remembers. 'The Stones eventually appeared, Keith Richards hits "Paint It, Black", goodnight. There were about a thousand kids on the charge.' Abandoning their posts, Mick, Brian, Charlie and Bill hastily left down the nearest orchestra tunnel. Peeking out from behind a curtain, Reid and the four Stones then watched the bizarre scene of Keith Richards apparently being torn to shreds by the audience. 'He finally staggered, surrounded by a flying wedge of commissionaires, backstage. "You fucking bastards! Thanks for leaving me!" Keith's strategy had been to save his prize guitar from being trashed, at all costs, which I rather admired. I mean, the rest of them just *ran*.'

Also on hand that night was the Stones' new press agent, a balding and conservatively suited 46-year-old former *Daily Mirror* reporter named Les Perrin. At the height of the melee, Perrin could be seen gnawing on a white handkerchief wound around his fist like a pair of worry-beads. 'My first appearance with the Stones was bloody nearly my last,' he remarked. 'Some shows didn't make enough to buy a pork pie. The kids would wreck the hall and the promoter took the damages out of the fee.' After that, Perrin would spend much of his time fire-fighting, denying all the rumours about the band splitting up or retiring, while simultaneously teasing a few, hip titles in to a state of arousal over the release of the latest album. Every week, he sent Mick Jagger a large cuttings file he marked 'Stray Thoughts & Trivia from Fleet Street's Finest'.

And what an evil bunch of tossers they all were, Mick concluded, especially the ones who gleefully splashed Klein's prediction that the Stones would enjoy overseas earnings of $20million in the next year. This was a figure later quoted back to the band by the Inland Revenue.

As the tour progressed, Mick took to spending much of his free time with members of the Ike & Tina Turner Revue – and particularly their miniskirted backing singers – who were also on the bill. Although particularly friendly with an 'Ikette' named Pat Arnold, Mick seems to have been chiefly drawn to the group by his characteristic mix of professional zeal and self-improving ambition. Tina Turner recalled Jagger 'wanting to learn a dance I did with my girls, the pony. I knew he'd been watching us every night from the wings. He tried, and I said, "Look at the rhythm on this guy! God, Mick, come on!" We laughed because Mick was serious – he wanted to get it. He didn't care about us laughing at him. And finally he got it . . . in his own kind of way.' Tom Keylock also remembered that Mick and Tina had had a more personal tutorial immediately before a show at Colston Hall in Bristol. 'I tripped over them with their gear round their ankles backstage.'

Socially, Jagger remained in a transitional state, a big star, but not big enough to mind a certain amount of press scrutiny of his private life. After a London show, he sometimes stepped out with his Ikette friend to restaurants like the Savoy Grill or the Ritz, where there was a reasonable chance of being seen. When in public there would be a bit of mutual fondling that other diners sometimes found unseemly, and the cameras often caught a boyishly happy leer on Mick's face. Though still based at Harley House, he was looking for somewhere bigger. Keith Richards, meanwhile, had recently left his St John's Wood flat after a sulphurous row with the landlord. The distressing inventory check revealed numerous cracked or missing items, messages daubed in smoke on the walls and cigarette burns throughout. With the necessary exception of hotels, Keith would never again resort to living in rented accommodation. From the autumn of 1966 he moved in to Redlands, a timbered cottage some 300 years old, near the sea in West Wittering, Sussex. The property was surrounded by a shallow moat and trees 'that were here when Shakespeare was jiving around'. Keith shipped in a copper garden fountain, exotic Moroccan drapes and rugs, and Ratbag, a dog of dubions pedigree who would be joined by a second such mutt named Syphilis. In time, Redlands also came to feature a small but well-stocked greenhouse.

Over the years, Richards built up an impressive collection of records and books, which he enjoyed while sprawled in front of the home's baronial log fire. There was little furniture in the usual sense, Keith preferring slabs of stone, wolfskin rugs and brightly coloured beanbags to the sordidly conventional world of tables, chairs and beds. Inside the lid of the downstairs lavatory was a collage of photos of Mick and the band. Between Redlands' rustic setting and pop-art interior, the overall vibe was of a 60s crash pad with submerged Olde English charm. Sharp-eyed fans had noticed that Keith had appeared for the Stones' most recent Sullivan show dressed in a khaki Panzerkorps tunic, a style he enjoyed. Over the years he would take the opportunity to step up his collection of Nazi regalia (bought from a shop called Hollywood Military Hobbies), occasionally clanking around West Wittering in a full-length leather coat with accessories. But Keith was also 'a very English kind of rebel', Tom Keylock recalled, and 'nothing like the Midnight Rambler of later legend'. Shortly after coming off the American tour, he had been sufficiently worried about Linda Keith to phone her parents with a 'horrifying report' – mentioning drugs, for starters – bad enough for them to make her a ward of court and fly to New York to rescue her. A certain coolness had subsequently descended between Richards and his ex-girlfriend. Friends also remember Keith's absent-mindedness and extravagant, generous nature, all traits that made his life endlessly complicated, not only for Keith himself but for Keylock, who was forced to run a permanent lost-and-found agency for him, among other duties. 'Keith took his driving test three times and failed it each time. The fourth time I went there, told them I was him, and took it for him. That's how he got his licence.'

Bill Wyman, meanwhile, broke up with his wife of seven years and no longer fooled around with other women while he was away on tour. Now he did so all the time. Wyman was at the wheel of his new Mercedes with two girls beside him one night when he crashed the car in the fog on a northern motorway. Everyone walked away unhurt and Bill went on to find a release for his frustrated songwriting and managerial ambitions with a variety of outside bands. 'The End were particularly successful with one single I produced, rising to number four in Spain,' he reports. Charlie Watts headed back to family life in the Sussex countryside. Although newly moustachioed, 'I was the only rock star never to wear beads,' Charlie reflected. 'I wish I could have done, but it never looked right on me.'

Bill may have done the bulk of the shagging, but he wasn't the only member of the principal cast to swing. Brian Jones and Anita Pallenberg were now cohabiting in their new eyrie at 1 Courtfield Road, South Kensington. For Jones, the relationship still seemed to be having a beneficial effect. Among other things, he was writing the soundtrack music to Volker Schlöndorff's film *A Degree of Murder*, in which Anita herself was hopelessly miscast as a sexually precocious assassin. The commission appeared to have done wonders for Brian's fragile self-confidence. Gone was the fey ex-choirboy, and in his place was a languorously arrogant pop star. Taking a sartorial leaf out of Keith's book, Brian now agreed to pose for a series of photographs showing him dressed in black SS uniform with his boot heel resting on a child's doll. This was too much even for the editors of the magazine *Rolling Stone Monthly*, which folded shortly afterwards after some forty issues. (The group's undoing as a teen attraction had been to go on a sado-Nazi bender 'quite incompatible with the requirements of family entertainment', the *Daily Mail* said.) With its split-level living room, minstrel's gallery and specially installed 'trippy' lighting, Courtfield Road quickly became a band hangout, and Keith Richards was often to be found on the premises while Redlands was being decorated. The proximity of high-quality hash and Dylan's *Blonde on Blonde* (a tribute, some felt, to Courtfield Road's principal tenants) both rounded out this 60s prototype of a rock-star pad.

Before long, Andrew Oldham's other protégé also began to appear at Courtfield Road. Somewhat belying her image as a pop ingénue with pigtails and a heaving bosom hanging out of a schoolgirl uniform, Marianne Faithfull was now a 20-year-old wife and mother with a stalled career. Some time earlier, Robert Fraser had given her a first, 'mountainous' line of cocaine, which she devoured in one snort. She was violently sick, but not discouraged.

Marianne was the scion of an unlikely marriage between Glynn Faithfull, an English philologist and wartime spy, and one Eva Sacher-Masoch, Baroness Erisso, a descendant of the novelist who gave his name to the enjoyment of pain for sexual pleasure. After her parents separated she went to live with her mother, a childhood incest victim, in Reading, prior to being sent to 'finish' at a convent. While there she was required to wear a smock in the bath in order to conceal her own nakedness. Marianne's career as a novice nun was to be short-lived. In 1965 she married a Cambridge undergraduate and aspiring pop artist named John Dunbar, with whom she had a son. This, too, proved a fleeting arrangement, and Faithfull threw in her lot first with Brian Jones ('leaning over me, like an asthmatic god') and then Keith Richards, an experience she describes as 'the best night of my life'. (For years, Keith himself remained tactfully silent on the subject, though there was to be some falling-off from this code of gentlemanly reticence when, in his 2010 autobiography, he wrote of lying with his head 'nestled between [Marianne's] two beautiful jugs'.) Bob Dylan, Andrew Oldham and Allen Klein were only three of the many other industry figures smitten by this voluptuous but somehow virginal-seeming figure. Only a day or two later, Keith would unselfishly confirm what Faithfull already knew.

'Mick's really stuck on you. Go on, luv, give him a bell. He's not so bad.'

Marianne would, after that, phone Jagger, 'this powerful guy promising me the moon', and so go on to be popularly, if harshly, stigmatised as 'rock totty' throughout the late 60s. Her first night together with Mick was at a hotel in Bristol, a few hours after the concert where he had had a private backstage moment with Tina Turner. In a somewhat jaundiced review, Faithfull would later remark that Jagger was 'the last person in the world I would discuss anything with ... We never talked about anything really personal, anything that mattered ... After the beginning Mick was never very interested in having sex. I always felt that whatever sexual drive Mick had, he used it up on stage and there was little left over for his personal life ... Even when we climbed in to our draped, four-poster bed Mick was only interested in reading a book.' She and Richards, at least, lusted vaguely after one another for years. 'The whole time I was with Mick,' Faithfull says, 'I fancied Keith.'

In the weeks that followed, the Stones virtually lived at south London's Olympic studio, a large, cluttered room – built as a sound-stage – sub-divided by baffle boards to give each musician his own semi-private nook, where the band kept its usual vampire hours. Dusk until dawn was the general routine. Any lingering daylight was barred by the heavy wooden shutters and strips of sheeting that sealed off such nightlife as there was on Barnes High Street. Tom Keylock soon grew accustomed to the twilight world of recording with the Stones and their house engineer Glyn Johns. Without the constant cigarette glow and the coloured flickering from the con-trol room, they might as well have been in a tomb.

That Christmas, Marianne Faithfull moved in with Mick, whom the news agencies began reporting was dead. Rising to the occasion, Les Perrin issued a magisterial press statement: 'Mr Jagger wishes to deny that he is deceased, and says that the rumours have been greatly exaggerated. A retraction is required.' One litmus test for classifying journalists of the period is how they treated Jagger: those who called him 'Mick' – or, in the teen magazines' case, 'Magic Mick' – tended to be musical pundits and swingers, or aspired to be; those who rolled their eyes at such cosiness and deference tended to work in Fleet Street. In fact, Perrin's client was suffering from nothing worse than a few cuts and bruises and the ensuing repair bills from a late-night incident when he crashed his new Aston Martin in to the Countess of Carlisle's car.

Early on a biting December morning, the Stones went straight from an all-nighter at Olympic to Primrose Hill in north London to shoot the cover for their new album. The atmosphere was unpleasant, because Jagger and Richards were squabbling about the song mixes and Brian Jones wasn't speaking to the rest of the band. After sixteen hours in the studio, Bill and Charlie looked as though they'd just been exhumed. When the pictures were taken, a red-eyed Brian sank down in to his coat and pulled a variety of 'Nanker' faces. It was his old Edith Grove party trick, although now nobody was laughing – Mick told his colleague to fuck off, and Les Perrin went on to complain about the spectacle more formally. 'I personally regarded the whole thing as quite dreadful.'

Some sort of truce ensued, because Keith, Brian and Anita Pallenberg then went to Paris together for Christmas. Among their thirty-eight pieces of luggage was an acetate of the new album, which in a Ringo-like moment Charlie had named *Between the Buttons*. It was another flawed masterpiece. Only three years after writing that Rice Krispies jingle, Jagger and Richards were now composing twentieth-century pop standards, like the two songs they had brought in to Olympic on successive winter nights. The rest of the Stones had listened to these in rapt silence. 'Title 8', which became 'Ruby Tuesday', was all Keith's, an exquisitely turned ballad about Linda. Deftly stepping through a fusion minefield of skewed folk-blues and cello-inflected madrigal, this was the sort of lush, haunting fare Paul McCartney could only dream about, and thus not, perhaps, a conventional Stones single. As later developments proved, few rock stars could voice broken-hearted resilience, rancour and regret quite like Keith, who also lent a tenderness and melancholy to his portrait of faded love. Mick Jagger, meanwhile, knocked off the lyrics to the jumpy, piano-pop 'Let's Spend the Night Together', his ode to Marianne Faithfull. If 'Ruby Tuesday' sounded like healing music, Mick's cunnilingual rap here – 'I'm goin' red/and my mouth's getting tired' – marked the moment when Jagger-the-priapic-stud was born. This expertly curated image, which Marianne herself, for one, thought a bit of a stretch, remains proverbial some forty-five years later.

On 17 December the Stones' friend Tara Browne, heir to the Guinness fortune and soon-to-be subject of the Beatles' 'A Day in the Life', died when he smashed his Lotus Elan in to the back of a parked van early in the morning in west London. He was twenty-one. Brian Jones had been particularly taken by the 'Tara set', a collective of Swinging London's beautiful people, who invited him in to their homes and offered him the finest LSD and cocaine. Jones didn't need a subpoena. Browne's death 'devastated Brian', Anita Pallenberg said. 'It made it seem like the whole thing was a lie.'

Tripping in their George V hotel suite a week later, Keith turned to his bandmate and remarked casually, '*You'll* never make thirty, man.' 'I know,' said Brian, for once speaking quite seriously. He had no intention of ending up on the rock and roll slag heap, he said, 'playing "Satisfaction" in a Las Vegas ballroom'.

There were two things you could reliably say about Stones albums. They ran about thirty-five minutes, and the band would be glowering furiously on the front cover. Their latest effort, however, was longer and lighter. As varied in quality as in range, *Between the Buttons* at its best was speedy and camp, hopped up on the same chassis of trippy tunes and Edwardian music-hall whimsy as a *Kink Kontroversy*. According to Keith Richards, much of the record's overall vibe can be attributed to various 'psychoactive agents' on hand at Olympic. The narcotics may not have conspicuously helped the Stones recover that hit-making magic, but they seem to have done wonders for their technical prowess. Brian Jones continued to serve as the band's colourist, contributing the Mellotron on 'Please

Go Home' and the brass lines on the larky 'Something Happened to Me Yesterday', while Keith himself kept everything in a steady, soulful groove. Mick Jagger never attempted Motown's regulation whoops, growls and melismatic calisthenics, but his scratchy, resigned drawl seemed right for the material. Charlie was on peak form throughout, while Bill tagged gamely along, ready to give a shove when needed. The worst that could be said of *Buttons* was that some of the songs were too pointedly hookless, and veered either to the mundane ('Please Go Home', 'Cool, Calm and Collected') or the mawkish ('She Smiled Sweetly'). There was even a waltz called 'Back Street Girl', augmented by Brian on an 1870s bal-musette-style accordion. Mick later thought that some of the songs on *Between the Buttons* had been 'lost' in the recording process. For much of the album, the Stones seemed uneasily like shot-putting champions who'd strayed inadvertently on to the badminton court. *Buttons* was a number 2 hit on both sides of the Atlantic.

Included on the American version, 'Ruby Tuesday' came complete with Keith and Bill on cello, Brian on recorder and sweet – yes, sweet – harmonies. 'Let's Spend the Night Together' made the great pop leap forward, incendiary at the time and, even today, well-made music to Stairmaster to. A little-commented-on fact is that the song happily brings out some of the more obvious implications of the lyric by building steadily, after a sudden, brief, tempo drop, to a celebratory vocal climax, while a buzzing organ swells and accel-erates to underscore the general mood. (The tune's bridge is also enlivened by a few seconds of a tapping noise which Oldham insists was produced by two policemen beating their truncheons together under his direction. Having called in at the studio to bust the Stones for drugs, they stayed to contribute percussion instead.) Released as a double-A side, the two songs rounded out a cycle of ten classic singles inside three years.

15 January 1967. Back to New York to plug 'Night', which was being bleeped or banned by DJs from coast to coast. The Stones' car took them to the stage door at the back of the Ed Sullivan Theater, which unfortunately was locked. The front doors were glass, and locked as well. Several dozen highly vociferous fans were

in position there. A melee ensued, and eventually the band smashed a glass panel and forced their way in. Mick Jagger cut his hand. Keith Richards punched Sullivan's doorman to express his dissatisfaction at the arrangements, and then had a misunderstanding with Ed himself about the latter's policy on toking backstage. But the main issue was again the song title. 'Either it goes,' Sullivan boomed, 'or you go.' It was close; in the end Mick compromised, altering 'the night' to 'some time', while rolling his eyes around to register protest.

Three days later, *Melody Maker* prominently reported Allen Klein's boast that the Stones would earn 'as much as $20m, or £7m', in 1967. 'The band will all be millionaires within that time,' he noted. For the musicians themselves, the day-to-day reality remained less exalted. On that same day, Stan Blackbourn, the book-keeper at Rolling Stones Promotions, sent Klein a telex begging for '£763/13sh for running cash, needed [by] 11 am our time tomorrow. Bank has refused further credit.' Over the next two and a half years, there would be a steady flow of transatlantic cables similarly demanding 'urgent' – sometimes 'fucking urgent' – cash transfers to one or more of the band's accounts. According to Keylock, both Jagger and Richards 'continually pounded in to me that we were skint', although Keith, at least, 'still ran up pretty useful bills for cars, food and dope'. In the week *Between the Buttons* was released, Bill Wyman's current account showed a balance of twenty-six pounds. A cleaner employed by Brian and Anita at four pounds a week was suing the Stones office for non-payment. More pertinently, perhaps, the Inland Revenue had opened a file on the band's overseas earnings; each time one of Klein's multimillion-dollar forecasts appeared in print, or a new song hit the chart, this latest financial harvest was being carefully noted by the authorities.

On 22 January, the Stones continued their recent run of television controversy with an appearance on *Sunday Night at the London Palladium*. The show was a much loved British ritual, with its bill of fare consisting of choice, family-oriented acts, from Nureyev and

Fontaine to Sooty and Sweep. Tradition demanded that, at the climax of proceedings, the entire cast mount a revolving stage to blow kisses and bid cheery farewells to the viewing audience. This was too much. No way, the Stones hastily agreed: they wouldn't rotate. The show's producer, Albert Locke, told the band that they were insulting everything the Palladium and 'centuries of show-business' stood for. Mick told Locke to fuck off. Keith, also blunt, added that it was 'just this sort of shit' they'd been fighting for five years. Andrew Oldham, whose own showbiz blood perhaps ran deeper than anyone supposed, sided with the producer and called the Stones' behaviour 'atrocious'. Jagger and Richards in turn yelled at Oldham, who walked out.

The Stones then mimed to four songs and sidled away from the Palladium with a cheque for £1,500. Their refusal to truckle soon netted them far more than that – the press coverage lasted for weeks. Both *The Times* and the *Daily Express* told their readers that the band had become incorrigible, and the Archbishop of Canterbury called them decadent. As if in celebration, 'Let's Spend the Night Together' then went gold. Keith, Brian and Anita took the opportunity to fly to Munich to visit the set of *A Degree of Murder*. Tom Keylock, who waved them off, remembered that the trio was 'crammed with dope' and that it was perhaps fortunate these were the days before full-body scanners at the airport. Continuing her transformation from angelic balladeer to Rolling Stones concubine, Marianne Faithfull then went on the BBC to announce, 'Marijuana's perfectly safe, you know … And something like LSD – it's as important as Christianity. *More* important … I'd like to see the whole structure of society collapse.' Fleet Street again deployed its most scandalised headlines. 'There was a certain amount of flak in the air,' Les Perrin later noted.

To confirm his misgivings, on Sunday 5 February the *News of the World* libellously outed Mick Jagger as a pill-popper. Jagger had allegedly shocked the paper's undercover investigators by sitting in a club and 'tak[ing] about six Benzedrine tablets … Later, he showed a companion and two girls a small piece of hash (marijuana) and invited them to his flat for "a smoke".' Mick claimed the story was a pack of lies and that he intended to 'put down a marker', not just for himself but for others in the public eye. On 7 February, his solicitor started proceedings. Keith and Brian then came back from Germany, flying on acid.

Four nights later, Jagger, Richards and Faithfull drove to Redlands for the weekend. Also present were Christopher Gibbs, the photographer Michael Cooper, 'Groovy Bob' Fraser, Fraser's Moroccan houseboy Ali Mohammed, George and Pattie Harrison and two hangers-on of dubious aspect, David Schneidermann and Nicky Kramer. According to Keylock, Kramer was a 'woolly-haired hippy nutter', spending most of his time 'hanging around the King's Road smoking weed', while Schneidermann was more the entrepreneurial type; the Stones had met him when he appeared at their New York hotel in July 1966 with a briefcase full of pharmaceutical LSD, sufficient for Keith to invite him to drop by when he was in England.

The folk memory of what happened next is that 'the Establishment' somehow colluded to tip off the nascent Chichester drugs squad that an orgy of dope, sex and pop, possibly all three simultaneously, was about to engulf West Wittering, and that the law responded by swarming over Keith Richards' house. It's a caricature, if one with a grain of truth. An unlikely coalition of liverish ITV executives, newspaper editorial writers and overambitious politicians all played their part in the backlash against the Stones' successive snubs of first Sullivan and then the Palladium's 'centuries of showbusiness', not to mention the band's apparent disdain for Britain's existing drug laws. In the first week of February there were several unappreciative press references to Mick and Keith, in particular, as 'well-heeled slobs' (in the words of the *Daily Mirror*) whose recent behaviour went far beyond mere Beatle cheekiness. It seems fair to say there was a predisposition to think that the authorities should act. But the real cue for the raid was a more specific call made to the *News of the World* on 9 February by what the newspaper's archive calls a 'troubled employee' of the group. The paper's editor Stafford Somerfield in turn made the civic-minded decision to notify the police.

Tom Keylock remembered that 'someone closely associated with the Stones' had subsequently asked him to 'duff up that poncy Nicky Kramer', who was considered the most likely traitor in the ranks. Keylock wouldn't do it, so the job fell to an aspiring East London artist and sometime Kray Brothers associate named David Litvinoff. Litvinoff duffed up Kramer sufficiently to break three of his ribs, but not to extract a confession. This wasn't altogether surprising, since Keylock, for one, believed the wrong man was doing the beating. 'I'm bloody certain it was Dave Litvinoff who rang the press,' he told me. 'The guy was a loon. I remember he was living in this little room in the same house as Eric Clapton, and God knows what he did for money. He looked like a fat snake. Beady little eyes, and an ear-to-ear scar where Ronnie Kray had shoved a sword in to his gob. Tasty character.' David Litvinoff later committed suicide while staying at Christopher Gibbs' home by swallowing a bottle of sleeping pills washed down with detergent.

12 February 1967. Everyone at Redlands was tripping on David Schneidermann's high-quality LSD. Sunday was gorgeous, exquisitely balanced between the olde scenery and this giddy sign of the times, people stumbling around on drugs. Most of them later made it outside for a constitutional, successfully navigating the moat before heading through the surrounding fields and on to the shingle beach south of Redlands. It was a characteristic Rolling Stones party – large, loud, happy, with satiric laughs and dazed, sheepskin-clad guests. Keith Richards later remarked that up to that point it had been one of the best days of his life. As he got back inside and settled down to lunch at around seven that evening, someone began ringing the home's 'secure' number, Birdham 513508. Each time Keith picked up the phone, the caller hung up.

An hour later, a convoy of police cars turned up Redlands Lane. Four vans, nineteen officers in all. After extracting a fallen colleague from the moat, the party fanned out to reconnoitre the property. Following this, the official report notes that the visitors regrouped at a side door by the greenhouse and began knocking. Robert Fraser would remember having caught sight of a blurred face ducking down at a window, and, in his cups, deciding that this was a

'dwarf dressed up in blue'. There was no initial sense of alarm. Keith
Richards remarked that the intrusion was 'probably kids', and that
he and Mick would deal with them. Rising from his place in front
of the fire, he opened the door. Before him stood not Rolling
Stones fans but the impressive bulk of Chief Inspector Gordon
Dineley of West Sussex police. 'I have a warrant,' he announced,
'pursuant to the Dangerous Drugs Act.'

A kind of grimace had crossed Keith's face when he saw the law.
Apart from this brief, scarcely perceptible contraction of nose and
lips he expressed no further welcome. However, he stood aside.

Keith then turned to Mick and the others, calmly announced,
'We're being busted,' and flicked on a strobe light for dramatic
effect.

The events that followed can be quickly recalled: the police fanning through the galleried living room, hung with ornate tapestries
and silks, wheezing in the incense and smoke; Marianne Faithfull,
later described under oath as 'in a merry mood and one of vague
unconcern' being led upstairs to be searched, or – since she was
wearing only a fur rug which she promptly dropped to the floor –
ogled; the remaining eight (the Harrisons having left) being frisked;
the instant acceptance of Schneidermann's acid collection as 'unex-
posed film'; the discovery of twenty-four heroin jacks ('for diabetes',
he explained) on Fraser, and of four pep pills in a velvet jacket
belonging to Jagger; the removal of these and sundry tins, pipes,
bowls and even soap and ketchup sachets; the surreal dazzle of the
strobe; the cautioning of Richards that, if dangerous drugs were
identified without specific proof of ownership he, as householder,
would be held responsible. Did he understand?

'Yeah,' Keith deadpanned. 'You pin it all on me.'

This being England, Chief Inspector Dineley then shook everyone's hands and assured them that they weren't necessarily being
charged. At that he withdrew. As the convoy moved off, Keith
Richards serenaded it in to the night with Dylan's 'Rainy Day
Women' and its insistent wail, '*Every*body must get stoned!'

The raid on Redlands turned out to be one of those events
whose actual success – four pills on Jagger, nothing on Richards –

was the least important factor in its public reception. From now on the Stones would be as polarising in their way as the Great Train Robbers: either heinous thugs or plucky scapegoats. In Britain in 1967 you loved Mick 'n' Keith or you hated them. What few people did was to ignore them. Perhaps unsurprisingly, a report of the raid was splashed across the *News of the World* on 19 February, and appeared in most of the following week's broadsheets. A month later the *Daily Mirror* confirmed that Jagger, Richards, Robert Fraser and Schneidermann (who left the country, never to be seen again) were to be charged and tried. Emissaries from the Stones had sought to bribe the police with £7,000, but the money went to the wrong man. In time the Redlands bust hit almost iconographic status, a 60s 'scene' which legend demanded – and the law never denied – had taken place amid an orgy of diabolism, voodoo or worse. The story of Mick having been found in an unusual combination with Marianne Faithfull and a Mars bar only surfaced later. Alas, 'it never happened', said Keylock. 'Keith had a sweet tooth – there was a virtual chocolate factory at Redlands. That's all there was to it, dozens of candy bars and some copper's vivid imagination.' Some forty years later, the owner of the Old Candies Tuck Shop in West Wittering would open for business one wet morning to find Keith Richards waiting on his doorstep, requesting 'about a ton' of bull's-eyes and other confectionery.

The Stones' first response to Inspector Dineley's visit to Redlands was to summon Allen Klein, who flew in for a meeting at the London Hilton on 20 February. Klein's bustling arrival on the scene did wonders for band morale, particularly when he promptly hired his clients the best possible criminal lawyers, including Michael Havers, QC, a future Attorney General. The high-priced defence team listened sympathetically as Keith and Mick (who was dressed for the summit in a white linen suit and yachting cap) complained that the press were out to 'get' them. There was a suspicion that phones had been tapped, and Keith reported being followed. With a month to kill before the next tour started, everyone thought it advisable to leave the country while the 'Stones on Drug

Charges' headlines played themselves out. They settled on Morocco.

In Klein's opinion, Jagger, in particular, was the picture of remorse at the meeting, 'looking like a small boy who'd been caught with his fingers in the cookie jar'. As Klein later described it, in a gesture of almost childlike contrition, Mick stopped before leaving the room and 'put his head on my shoulder'. This caused his cap to fall off and tumble across the floor. The whole interview struck Tom Keylock as 'bizarre'. Only minutes after his arrival, Michael Havers had informed everyone that, in a worst-case scenario, the defendants could go to jail for as much as three years. Before packing for their trip, Mick and Keith both wrote 'Don't worry' letters to their parents, although Bert Richards, estranged from his son for the past four years, declined to reply.

Keith also took the opportunity to improve security arrangements at Redlands. Keylock sub-contracted the job to a north London neighbour and schoolfriend named Frank Thorogood, who initially planned to build a 6-foot-high wall around the home. On Richards' orders, this became a 10-foot wall. After that, 'Redlands looked like the fucking Alamo,' Thorogood remembered.

Tom Keylock ferried the Blue Lena to Paris, where he was joined by Keith, Brian, Anita and a traffic-stopping beauty named Deborah Dixon, the long-time partner of filmmaker Donald Cammell. There was a misunderstanding at the George V hotel about the party's bill. Keylock's French proved just barely adequate to the challenge and, in the end, there were hissed 'Sod you, froggy's as everyone made for the car. Richards tolerated the administrative lapse with composure. He was in festive mood. Keylock remembered that there was already a certain amount of sexual by-play among the party, not least because the two women had recently participated in a *ménage à trois* with Donald Cammell while mutually staying in a north London rehab clinic, Bowden House. 'So there was a bit of slap and tickle.' Keith eyeing Dixon, Brian eyeing Anita and Keylock surveying his four shag-haired passengers 'like fucking

Johnny Morris', the Bentley turned on to the Quai d'Austerlitz, heading south.

It was an unseasonably warm day, and the car was furnished with a cocktail cabinet, fresh flowers, the best food and drugs and a tape deck blasting out an advance copy of the Beatles' 'Strawberry Fields'. No trip with Brian Jones could be entirely tranquil, even so, and by Limoges, after a full day of drinking brandy and toking in the back seat, he was complaining of a 'funny turn'. By Bordeaux, Jones was turning blue. At the American clinic in Tarn, near Toulouse, Brian was told he had an enlarged heart, advanced fatty degeneration and blood in the lungs. No problem, he said: the four of them should carry on to Tangier, and he'd catch up with them there. Jones spent his twenty-fifth birthday alone in the hospital.

Deborah Dixon left the next morning, muttering her premonition of 'bad vibes' ahead to Keylock. 'This is getting weird,' she told him, apparently struck by Anita's behaviour. 'God knows where it'll end.'

For the next twenty-four hours, Keylock spent his time either looking straight ahead at the snow-capped mountains and winding rivers of Catalonia, or glancing in his rear-view mirror at Keith and Anita making love. In a Valencia bar, there was yet another to-do involving a credit card. Soon the management started yelling at Keith, who turned to Keylock and told him to 'sort it'; the dagos would respect a big guy like him, with an English accent. 'Oi doutit,' Tom said, and a merry row then ensued at the police station. When everyone got out a telegram was waiting for them, ordering Pallenberg to return to Toulouse for Brian. Anita tore it up. When they pulled over at a hotel that night, Richards told Keylock to book only two rooms.

Finally crossing on the *Mons Calpe*, they reached Tangier on 5 March; Richards and Keylock made for the tenth floor of the Hotel Minzah where, according to the latter, 'Mick Jagger was already installed like a young lord, lying on a huge bed and asking what the hell there was to do in a dump like this.' Tom himself had the answer, strolling across the market square to score everyone some hash. Also present were 'Groovy Bob' Fraser and Michael Cooper. Anita belatedly returned to Toulouse to collect Brian.

As the week progressed, at least at first, the local hospitality flowed. It was a scene to make the Sixties swing.

Tom Keylock: 'We took over the top floor of the best hotel. Keith's lounging around with his guitar, Mick doing little dances. Lots of toking in the moonlight. The first I knew of Brian's arrival was the sound of his voice coming from a room along the corridor. He was screaming at Anita. The little bugger obviously knew something had gone on . . . Brian started drinking, getting himself in to a state. Next thing anyone knew he'd picked up this pair of dodgy Berber whores, tattooed all over, and made for Anita's room. Brian had the idea that he was going to get her to perform with these two birds. That was typical of the guy.'★

A lot of rock and rollers enjoy combinations, but most manage a better pitch than Jones, a stickler for decorum in other circumstances, but happy to proposition his girlfriend here with 'Get 'em off!' Anita declined the offer and Brian went berserk, smashing up both the room and her.

That was enough for Keith. He and Keylock made up a story about a plane-load of *News of the World* reporters landing in Marrakech, hustling Jones off with his friend Brion Gysin to the local sook. No sooner had he gone, Keith and Anita were packing her eighteen pieces of luggage in to the Bentley. 'What about Brian?' asked Keylock. 'Sod him,' said Keith. 'We're leaving the bastard here and you're driving.' Mick and Marianne Faithfull, the former still grousing about his hotel bill, flew out. The Spanish police gave the Bentley and its three passengers a thorough going-over at the ferry terminal. Tom again saved everyone's skin, hiding the pot under the car's petrol cap.

★Adding to Brian Jones' bad mood was a curious incident that had occurred when he and Anita, joined by Marianne Faithfull, briefly found themselves in Gibraltar while en route to Tangier. As a lark, Jones had started playing one of the local apes a tape of his home-recorded music and it went mad, shrieking at Brian and trying to vault the retaining wall between them. A keeper had to be sent for to restore order.

When Brian got back from the sook, clutching a long-stemmed hash pipe he couldn't resist buying, he found only a few of Pallenberg's things, forgotten in the rush, and a curt note telling him what had happened. He was not pleased at the news. According to Gysin, 'His colour rose to a heated red and his face was unrecognisable ... After a lengthy outburst, Brian sank in to a stupor. A doctor came to give him a shot, and I stuck around long enough to see it take hold on him. I didn't want him jumping down ten storeys in to the pool.' The next day, Jones got on a plane to Paris, where he made for his friend Donald Cammell's flat. Cammell remembered that Brian arrived on his doorstep 'in a terrible state', looking more like a tramp than a moneyed pop star, and so broke that he had to pay off his taxi for him. 'They left me,' Brian kept muttering to his host. 'They just fucked off and left me!'

Jones' first thought back in London was revenge, and there was a furious scene when he caught up with the fugitive pair at their hotel. It took the form of a violent tirade which left everyone who witnessed it, or even heard it from outside the room, shaken and exhausted. He had been double-crossed, he shouted. Even his best mate had shafted him. Brian's essential pitch was that Anita leave Keith, who was 'going to jail' and give him, instead, another chance. It was a spectacularly ambitious proposal to a woman who was still black and blue from Brian's fists. When Anita turned him down, he flipped. Rejection was the signal for one of those sudden reversals in behaviour that constitute the basic pattern of Jones' life. 'Fuck you!' he growled. 'I'm a rock star! I can have any chick I want.'

Brian immediately started dating Linda Keith.

On 25 March, the Stones began a brief but tempestuous European tour. This was not, perhaps, the ideal moment for Keith and Brian to be travelling in close proximity, particularly when Anita joined up with the group in Paris. 'Her switch [of affections] was a major landmark,' Bill Wyman notes, with characteristic understatement. 'Brian was completely isolated ... He leaned increasingly on drink, LSD and marijuana to help him through; he was obviously shattered.' Nobody in the band was speaking to him.

In certain towns, Jones and his colleagues thought it best to stay the night in different hotels. Tom Keylock's photos of the Stones in concert show Brian and Keith routinely standing at opposite ends of the stage, each straining at his guitar lead for maximum separation. The overall mood wasn't helped by their communal reception on the road, which, in the wake of the Redlands bust, tended to be on the brusque side.

'It was wicked,' Keylock remarked. 'I lost track of the number of flights that were over-booked, or hotels that mysteriously lost our reservations. We were treated like lepers.' At airports the Stones were routinely greeted by the sound not of squealing fans but of snarling dogs and the snapping of rubber gloves. In Malmo, Mick Jagger and Bill Wyman were taken aside for what Bill describes as 'intense' body searches. A French customs official later punched Keith Richards on his arrival at Le Bourget, in yet another row about passports. Keith promptly retaliated, and the two of them were still going at it when Keylock intervened. Mick wore a floor-length satin gown to entertain the crowd at the Paris Olympia that night, and at the end of the show threw tulips down to the fans.

While the Stones were performing, someone familiar with their schedule entered their rooms at the George V hotel and relieved them of around £20,000 (some £125,000 today) in cash and jewellery. It was never recovered, and they never stayed in the hotel again as a group. Taking the loss in their stride, Keith and Anita threw a party in a restaurant on the Champs-Élysées, where Mick and Marianne, Charlie, Bill and the long-suffering Ian Stewart did some further damage to their corporate credit card. Keylock remembers Brian, stuffed with acid, then 'playing the next two gigs without even knowing he'd done them ... The guy was bouncing off the furniture like a pinball.' A small but cruel twist of the knife followed when the Stones' office sent a chauffeured car to Heathrow to collect Keith and Anita. Due to a book-keeping error, the bill for the journey was charged to Jones' account.

On 13 April, the Stones played at Warsaw's Palace of Culture, their first visit behind the Iron Curtain, where the best 2,000 seats

had been reserved for Communist Party officials and their families –
a significant presence in a hall holding 2,700. 'I looked down and
all you could see was row after row of men, women and kids all
dressed in grey, sitting there with their fingers in their ears,' Keylock
said. Three songs in, as 'Paint It, Black' struggled for momentum,
there was a sudden intervention from stage left. Pointing furiously
across his guitar, Keith Richards shouted to Charlie Watts to stop
drumming. Mick Jagger tried to continue the song, but Keith kept
pointing and yelling, 'You bastards, get out and let those guys in the
back down front . . .'

'Er – *I see a red door* . . .' Jagger began again.

'Leave those kids alone,' Keith shouted, now holding the guitar
aloft. The back rows kept chanting *Icantgetno! Icantgetno!* for
'Satisfaction', and Keith kept yelling at the police, who were bouncing billy-clubs on the audience's heads. Outside the hall, the army
would disperse a crowd of three to four thousand ticketless fans by
firing rubber bullets and tear gas at them. This would prove to be
Poland's last official dalliance with rock and roll music for twenty-
three years. The next day's press: 'EASTERN BLOC PLANNING
COMPLETE BAN OF "UNACCEPTABLE" STONES.'

After a more tranquil interlude in Switzerland and Holland, the
tour wound up at the national football stadium in Athens. Being on
the eve of a right-wing coup d'état, Greece, too, was in no particular mood to host a riot by the Rolling Stones (or 'Mushroom
Heads', as they were known locally). The emphasis throughout was
on the vast and menacing military presence rather than on the
music. At the end of an abbreviated set, Mick Jagger jogged over to
where Tom Keylock was standing in the wings and thrust a bouquet
of carnations in to his arms. He was to hurl these at 'the cats', Mick
said, for the traditional climactic act of the night. As Tom did so, in
a reciprocal spray of water-cannon fire from the police, he became
uneasily aware that he was alone on stage; the band themselves had
dropped their instruments and run.

It was 17 April 1967, the Stones' last full public concert for two
and a half years, and the last ever by the original band. Mick, Brian
and Charlie got the first plane out to London, Bill stayed on for a

Greek holiday which was interrupted by the Colonels' coup, and Keith flew to Rome, where Anita was auditioning successfully for the role of the vampire-lesbian Black Queen in Roger Vadim's *Barbarella*. Asked by the producers of the film what particular technical expertise she might bring to the part, Anita was succinct: 'Sex'.

Two weeks later, Richards and Pallenberg were in Cannes for the premiere of *A Degree of Murder*. Following a warmly acclaimed showing of the film, Brian Jones arrived in the hotel late at night and arranged a private interview with Anita. They spoke for a while in his room, and then he beat her up again. In due course, the hotel manager appeared and remonstrated with Jones about the late hour and loud noise. Brian offhandedly told the manager to shut up and get the hell out. At that, the manager dropped even the pretence of civility and called Brian a short-arsed English twat. Brian took a swing at the guy, and it connected. The guy swung back. Taking advantage of the melee, Anita fled back to Keith's room down the corridor.

Brian flew home first thing the next morning. 'That was the final nail in the coffin,' Keith says. 'He never forgave me after that. I don't blame him.' Back in London, Mick bluntly announced that the band stood to lose their entire Decca advance if they broke up, and called a meeting at Olympic to impress everyone with the seriousness of the situation. 'The Rolling Stones are enjoying life tremendously, and plan to be together for many, many more years,' Les Perrin said in a written statement.

On 9 May 1967, Mick, Keith and Robert Fraser lunched at a London gentleman's club, spent the afternoon at Lord's cricket ground, and then drove to Chichester to face charges of menacing society.

At the hearing the next morning, the two Stones wore sober dark suits and expressions of mild amusement; they expected a fine. Mick stood in the dock first to hear himself described as a 'popular vocalist', and to be accused of 'possessing four tablets of amphetamine sulphate and methyl amphetamine hydrochloride'.

Keith followed, to be charged with 'permitting [Redlands] to be used for the purpose of smoking controlled substances', the fruits of the various ashtrays and bowls removed by Inspector Dineley and his men. Each in turn nodded affably to his name and legal address (Les Perrin's office in Oxford Street) before pleading not guilty. All three defendants elected trial by jury in a higher court. They were bailed to appear at West Sussex Quarter Sessions on 27 June.

At the very moment of his colleagues' committal, a pilled-up Brian Jones was answering a thunderous knocking at his front door in London's Courtfield Road. It was the drugs squad. The scene that greeted them was like a life-slice exhibit of junkie degeneracy: the fourteen officers took away water pipes, hookahs, bongs, spoons, ashtrays, cigarette ends and a phial bearing traces of white powder. Brian himself, dressed in a Japanese kimono, happened to be in the throes of one of his familiar acid nightmares about snakes. 'I do smoke,' he allegedly told the enquiring officers, 'but I'm not a junkie.' Jones was then escorted downstairs to a car and driven the short distance to Kensington police station. Several dozen journalists were already waiting for him there, not all of them friendly. Brian was charged with possession and spent the next six months on bail. He later claimed that he had been invited to pay £1,000 in order for the law to 'lose' the evidence. After being photographed and fingerprinted at the station, Brian got on the phone to Les Perrin, shouting: 'What the fuck? I pay you, and you can't even come out and fucking bail me out?' The next morning, Jones made a brief appearance at Great Marlborough Street magistrates court, where he elected trial by jury and posted a bond of £250 supplied by Klein's office. While the press ran the familiar 'Stone arrested' headlines, Brian sent a telegram to his family in Cheltenham. It read: 'Please don't worry. Don't jump to nasty conclusions. And don't judge me too harshly.'

The exquisite coincidence of the authorities variously detaining the Stones' entire front row on the same day led some to wonder whether the Establishment really might be a bit down on the band. Formalising their estrangement, Brian's lawyers now told him not to have any contact with Mick and Keith pending their respective trials. Tom Keylock drove the band in to Olympic one night during this period – probably to record their Morocco-drenched single 'We Love You' – and remembered a 'bloody heavy atmosphere' around the studio. For the next several hours, a 'mightily pissed off' Keith was content to stand in the shadows hammering a riff to death while Mick took up position in the control room for a series of press interviews. Brian was nowhere to be seen. Bill and Charlie sat around yawning and eating fish and chips.

'Rather too keen on the infernal WIRELESS' was the verdict on a wartime lieutenant of his ship's commanding officer, Leslie Kenneth Block. Eight years later, as Fleet Navigating Officer, Block entered in the Portsmouth Royal Naval Club's suggestion book a plea for 'pray, SILENCE in the library'. He was a man inordinately given to capitals, with an equally pronounced aversion to modern music and musicians of all sorts; Block 'despised [and] scorned the lot of them as effete, unproductive members of society', he wrote unambiguously in a 1961 edition of *Navy News* (while acknowedging the role played by 'traditional shanties and airs' over the years), and later entertained the annual banquet of the Horsham Ploughing and Agricultural Society by suggesting that the words 'dung' and 'Beatles' 'indeed belong in close proximity to one another'. After the war, Block returned to the bar, serving as a judge on the Mayor's and City of London courts, a commissioner of the Central Criminal Court and later as Chairman of West Sussex Quarter Assizes. It was as the last that he appeared on 27 June 1967, a 61-year-old Tory landowner of naval mien, and perhaps the very last person whom the frilly-shirted figures in the dock would have chosen to confront. 'Mick and Keith,' said Keylock, 'came up against the brick wall of reality.'

While the ensuing trial took many ducks and turns, one image dominated the proceedings from the start. This was the Crown's prompt reference to 'the young lady wearing only a fur rug which, from time to time, she allowed to fall, exposing her *bare body*'. At the last two words there was an audible *frisson* from the public gallery, where Marianne Faithfull herself sat demurely throughout. The 'nude girl' headlines duly proved irresistible and ran for days, along with shrill, though unprintable, rumours about Mars bars and other unusual domestic practices. One juror later told *International Times* that the whole case 'revolved on this axis ... we were really trying people's morals, weren't we?' This was the trial that had it all: drugs, rock and roll, and an intoxicating whiff of sex. According to the opening testimony of Sergeant John Challon, which the court greeted with a shocked hush, 'The lady in question was taken upstairs and, when she got to the bedroom door, she let the rug fall. She had nothing on. The woman giggled and I heard a laugh from two men in the bedroom.'

After a perfunctory defence, which restricted itself to noting that he had once served his country in the Kenyan Mau–Mau emergency, the jury took six minutes to find Robert Fraser guilty. Half an hour later, it returned the same verdict for Mick Jagger.

The other highlight of the proceedings, which eventually stretched in to three days, was the cross-examination of Keith Richards. Richards calmly informed Malcolm Morris, the prose-cuting counsel, that neither he nor any of his friends smoked hash, and that if drugs had been found at Redlands they must have been planted there. With a certain inevitability, the Crown then asked Keith about the woman in the fur rug.

MM: Would you agree that in the ordinary course of events you would expect a young lady to be embarrassed if she had noth-ing on in front of several men?

KR: Not at all. We are not old men and we're not worried about petty morals. [Loud cheering from the gallery]

MM: Did it not come as a great surprise to you that she was pre-pared to go back downstairs still only wearing a rug in front of twenty police officers?

KR: I thought the rug was big enough to cover three women. There was nothing improper in the way she was wearing it.

MM: I wasn't talking about impropriety, but embarrassment.

KR: She doesn't embarrass easily. Nor do I

In his summing-up, Judge Block told the jury to put completely out of their minds any prejudice they might have about Richards' looks, clothes, habits, lifestyle, or his views on 'petty morals'. They were to disregard the testimony describing the interior of his house as a scene of smoke-filled decadence out of some banned Arabian erotica, to ignore everything they had read and heard about the nude girl who had been lying in front of the Redlands fireplace in full view of eight men, and above all not to let her rum behaviour in any way influence their verdict. The jury found Keith guilty. Jagger and Fraser were then brought up from the cells and given three and six months' respectively, the latter saluting with an ironic click of his heels. The judge sentenced Richards to a full year, and ordered him to pay £500 costs. There were high-pitched cries of 'No!' from the gallery, which was packed with young Stones fans. Keith shrugged, raised his eyes to the ceiling, and said nothing.

All three defendants were marched out in handcuffs, Richards and Fraser to be delivered to London's notorious Wormwood Scrubs, and Jagger to the no-more-inviting Brixton Jail. Both the Stones were photographed and deloused, exchanging their velvet frock coats for blue donkey jackets and regulation black shoes. There was no haircut, though that was the one humiliation spared them. They adapted according to type: Mick went to work in the prison library and later sat up in his cell writing the lyrics of a song called '2000 Light Years from Home'; Keith haphazardly sewed a few mailbags, wrote to his mum and quickly befriended many of his fellow inmates, several of whom offered him great drugs, priced to move.

Michael Havers, meanwhile, worked overnight to obtain leave for Jagger and Richards to appeal. On 30 June, three High Court judges granted them bail in their own recognisance of £5,000 each, after Havers had been taken aside by Malcolm Morris, the prosecuting counsel, and told that he had 'direct instructions' not to oppose the application. At five o'clock that afternoon Keylock duly edged the Bentley 'to the gates of the nick, where Mick emerged and collapsed in to the back seat of the car. His first words were, "I need a drink".' An hour later, after collecting Keith from the Scrubs, they were in the Feathers pub in Fleet Street, where Les Perrin hurriedly convened a press conference.

There is nothing to show how far the editorial U-turn subsequently performed by several newspapers was due to Perrin's formidable power of persuasion, and how far to a general feeling that the Stones might just conceivably have been harshly treated. Whatever their motives, a number of papers rapidly revised their view of recent events. 'For many hundreds of thousands of youngsters, it is a troubling matter,' the *Daily Mail* admitted. 'Teenagers ask why there is no stigma in being a heavy drinker, while smoking pot, which they consider less harmful, is banned.'

Something very curious was going on in Fleet Street. A truly populist title like the *News of the World*, with its pictures of footballers and pouting models on the masthead, was calling for the Stones to be jailed. The old bulletin-boards of the Establishment were preaching forgiveness. New lines were being drawn, most famously by *The Times* in its 'Who Breaks a Butterfly' editorial of 1 July:

> It is no offence to be in the same building or the same company as people possessing or even using drugs, nor could it reasonably be made so . . . One has to ask, therefore, how it is that this technical offence, divorced as it must be from other people's offences, was thought to deserve the penalty of imprisonment . . .
>
> If we are going to make any case a symbol of the conflict between the sound traditional values of Britain and the new hedonism, then we must be sure that the sound traditional values include those of tolerance and equity. It should be the particular quality of British justice to ensure that Mr Jagger is treated exactly the same as anyone else, no better and no worse. There must remain a suspicion in this case that Mr Jagger received a more severe sentence than would have been thought proper for any purely anonymous young man.

Eva Jagger told me that she and her husband had been woken in their suburban Dartford home by an early phone call that morning.

'It was Mike,' she said, 'reading out the page from *The Times*. He told us that everything was going to be all right.'

On 31 July, Jagger and Richards came up for an appeal personally presided over by Judge Hubert Lister Parker, the Lord Chief Justice of England. Although a less obviously malign figure than his predecessor Lord Goddard, he was not necessarily a man to cross: just three years earlier, Parker had sent shock waves through Fleet Street by imprisoning several journalists who refused to reveal their sources during the Vassall espionage trial, before going on to send the spy George Blake to jail for forty-two years, then the longest sentence ever imposed by an English court. It was with good cause, therefore, that Michael Havers had advised his two clients not to get their hopes up. A doll-like Mick, wearing a khaki suit, went in to the dock first. The court, he was told, 'thoroughly upheld' his conviction, but would reduce his sentence to one of twelve months' probation, with costs. 'You are, whether you like it or not, the idol of a large number of the young in this country,' the Lord Chief Justice added, somewhat deviating from *The Times'* line. 'Being in that position, you have very grave responsibilities. If you do come to be punished, it is only natural that those responsibilities should carry higher penalties.' Some time later, the *News of the World* carried a small announcement stating that Mick's libel action against them had been settled 'by mutual consent'.

Keith Richards was not physically present in the dock to hear his own appeal, although by cupping his ear to the ceiling he could hear the occasional groans and cheers coming from the courtroom above him. This unusual arrangement was made necessary because Keith had caught a dose of chickenpox following his release from jail, and was thus kept in a cell downstairs for fear of infecting the nation's top judge. Two hours later an official went to tell him that both his conviction and his sentence had been quashed. The Chief Justice ruled that the whole 'nude girl' section of the original trial should never have been allowed. There were whoops of congratulation outside the court, and a celebratory 'be-in' that night in Hyde Park.

Mick Jagger hurriedly changed in to a silk smock, took some

valium and was whisked off by helicopter to debate the trial on television with a panel of politicians and bishops, the first of dozens of such appearances, editorials and ministerial statements that sought to give 'meaning' to the whole saga. Keith, by contrast, seemed to take the somewhat surreal events of the last month as the kind of temporary setback bound to occur in showbiz, and would admit only to feeling 'spotty'. That same afternoon he flew to Rome to join Anita, now heavily in to the lesbian shtick of *Barbarella*. There were no reporters present when Robert Fraser lost his appeal and went back to Wormwood Scrubs to serve his full sentence.

At this point, something akin to panic began to spread among what remained of the British Establishment. As recent events had borne out, Mick and Keith – and by extension Brian, Bill and Charlie – were, unlike the Beatles, rather more than the pop successors to such cheeky-chappy northern music-hall performers as Billy 'Almost a Gentleman' Bennett, George Formby and Ken Dodd. After 31 July 1967, the Stones were 'the most notorious gang alive', says Wyman, not one to be easily impressed, having effectively fought the law to a bloody draw. As well as the criminal proceedings, the lurid headlines and the debauched consorts, there was the matter of the shag haircut – a period rock-star detail in itself – with which Keith returned from Rome, all evidence, apparently, that these five middle-class, Home Counties lads truly wanted to burn your town down. The indictment against the Stones included every crime in the tabloid calendar, from taking drugs to adversely affecting the currency exchange rate by 'giving a bad impression abroad'. They might have won over the softer hearts in Fleet Street, but, Bill recalls, 'Mick and Keith still couldn't find a taxi anywhere in London willing to pick them up.'

In fact, the Stones were even less radical than the Beatles. Interviewing Mick Jagger immediately following his appeal, the editor of *The Times*, William Rees-Mogg, was astonished to discover 'a right-wing libertarian' who insisted, 'I don't really want to format a new code of living, a new code of morals.' ('No one's recruiting *me* to anything,' Mick later confirmed to Tom Keylock.) Over the years,

Brian, Bill and Charlie all proved similarly reticent when it came to moving the guardrails defining the limits of normal behaviour. No one quite knew what Keith Richards' agenda then was, but based on his penchant for eating shepherd's pie and watching old war films like Trevor Howard in *The Cockleshell Heroes* it, too, contained a large vein of English traditionalism. If the Stones were 'political' at all, it was only in the internecine sense of the word.

By the tail-end of the Summer of Love, Brian Jones was on the outs with Keith, and wasn't speaking to Jagger, Stu or Anita. Anita shunned Keylock, who couldn't abide either her or Keith's in-house drug fixer 'Spanish Tony' Sanchez. Sanchez fell out with Mick and Keith over Brian. Bill was uptight about money and more particularly about Allen Klein, who retained his distaste for signing cheques. Everyone was pissed off with Andrew Oldham, who had suffered some sort of psychotic episode following the Redlands bust and checked himself in to a clinic. Charlie just played the drums.

On 18 June 1967, Brian Jones, bombed on hog tranquillisers and dressed in an Afghan fur coat decorated with Berber jewellery and a crystal swastika, floated out on stage to whisperingly announce his friend Jimi Hendrix as 'the most exciting performer I've ever seen' to the 70,000-strong audience at the Monterey International Pop Festival. The printed words perhaps don't quite convey the zonked impression made by Brian at this moment. Although he didn't play a note, people still talk about his show-stopping appearance at Monterey. In a mercurial moment, Jones and his gasped-out speech had given the crowd an inner glimpse of the man who by turns enthralled and exasperated his colleagues.

Less publicly, Brian also spent some of his time while on bail paying twice-weekly visits to a Harley Street psychiatrist named, somewhat improbably, Lenny Henry. Dr Henry eventually arranged for his patient to be admitted to a south London rest clinic, where Brian arrived in his Rolls-Royce, imperiously demanding a suite for his latest girlfriend and himself and 'a room for my man Tom [Keylock]'. Disabusing him of the notion that he had checked in to a luxury hotel, he was promptly shown to a sparsely furnished cubicle and put to sleep for two days. Jones, the clinic's director Anthony Flood noted, was 'anxious, depressed and even suicidal ... without a great deal of confidence in himself ... Still trying to grow up in many ways.' Brian was particularly distressed to hear that some Cheltenham youths had shouted abuse in the street at his mother following his arrest. It was 'another crushing blow', Dr Flood reported.

Back in Olympic, the four-piece Stones were eking out their latest album, a psychedelic folly then called simply *Satanic Majesties*. The proceedings were not distinguished by their sense of artistic focus or urgency. 'People were sitting around playing the bongos,' Tom Keylock recalled. 'Nobody gave a toss ... I remember Mick was pleased as punch because he bought a brand-new synthesizer, one of the first people in England to own one, and when I got it to the studio he couldn't even get a note out of it. It ended up being sold for scrap to a guy I knew in Camden Town.' In the creative vacuum, Bill Wyman eventually came up with a number called 'Acid in the Grass'. Jagger declared this a load of crap and refused to sing on it, while Richards signalled his own verdict on the song by leaving the studio. After some more in this vein, Wyman did the vocal himself, smothering it in a queasy vibrato, and the Stones put out 'In Another Land', as it became, as an American single; it peaked at number 89 on the *Billboard* chart. As a laugh, Jagger and Richards later added a snippet of the sound of Bill snoring to the end of the album version of the track.

Ten years later, Mick confided to his mother that he had been 'overdoing it' throughout the *Satanic Majesties* experience, and that the lyrics of the song 'Jumpin' Jack Flash', which followed a year later, were his coded way of expressing relief at being able to pull himself together and snap out of it. Eva remembered that she had told him she was proud of him.

After the Inspector called and Anita took up with Keith, things would never be quite the same for the Stones. Apart from the professional challenge of keeping a band together in the shades of the prison-house, there were ructions ahead with women that made *Dallas* look like *Playschool*. While touring West Germany, Keith had met a beautiful blonde model and left-wing firebrand named Uschi Obermaier. Uschi had already attained a certain celebrity by the time of her eighteenth birthday by appearing nude in *Stern* magazine while rolling a joint. Despite the twin handicaps of a prior fling with Mick Jagger and a limited command of English, she and Keith had begun a brief but intense affair that would reignite six years later. In order to make the necessary hotel arrangements during the band's stay in Cologne, Richards fired off a memo to Tom Keylock about the need to be discreet given the 'other scene' currently unfolding in his domestic life. Evidently written late at night, the rest of the note defies Keith's customary reserve: 'I love her [Anita] a lot more than the whole beads and bells bullshit', a declaration of intent as well as a sardonic commentary on the Summer of Love. Richards and Pallenberg were back together within a week.

Meanwhile, after tiring of Linda Keith, who went on to take an overdose of sleeping pills in his flat, Brian Jones took up with Tina and Nicky, a pair of near-identical lesbian go-go dancers who moved in to Courtfield Road for several weeks, much to the mirth of the rest of the band. In time, Keith made the good-natured suggestion that the *ménage à trois* might like to take advantage of his visit to Rome and spend a country weekend together at Redlands.

'Brian went down there,' Tom Keylock said, 'promptly got pissed and challenged the girls to a midnight dip. Everyone was loaded, but that didn't stop them from stripping off, diving in and doing a lap of the moat. After about a minute of this, I suddenly realised Brian had disappeared from view. All I could see was a tuft of his hair swirling around on the surface like seaweed. I waded in to get him. But the moat was only about 3 feet deep, and Brian was only pretending to be in trouble. I grabbed him by the hair and pulled him out. Everyone was laughing at the time, but about a year later when I got the call about Brian it didn't seem so funny.'

In June 1967, Tina and Nicky moved out of Courtfield Road and a stunning Anita-lookalike named Suki Potier moved in. She had been Tara Browne's fiancée, surviving the car crash that had killed him outside Jones' flat six months earlier. 'Brian gave me a shoulder to cry on,' she said. 'He picked up the pieces and made me feel like a woman again.' Suki Potier was to die in a car accident in Portugal in June 1981; she was thirty-three.

Early in 1967, 30-year-old Bill Wyman had enjoyed a night out at his friend Chas Chandler's flat, where he met a 17-year-old Swedish schoolgirl and aspiring model named Astrid Lundström. 'There were about twenty people there, many of them openly smoking marijuana cigarettes,' Bill notes primly. 'This was neither my scene nor Astrid's but we drank a lot, and when she wanted to leave we returned to my car. She got in. I suddenly felt very ill and vanished, spending a very long time throwing up nearby.'

Despite this unpromising start, Bill and Astrid would be together for the next seventeen years, although for most of them Bill continued to 'bonk for Britain', as Tom Keylock cheerfully put it. Calling in at Wyman's suburban home in Keston at around nine one morning, Keylock met a young brunette dressed in what appeared to be a leotard 'sitting meekly on a chair in the hall, [like] a job applicant'. Bill himself soon appeared, descending the 'big staircase, sporting a red silk shirt splayed open to display an impressive variety of medallions', with a 'ravishing blonde' in tow. Another party who visited the house confirms that Bill and Astrid's was a non-exclusive arrangement. 'Wyman's practice was to invite every pretty face he met to go to bed with him, and one by one they took him up on the offer.'

If the Stones' domestic relationships generally fell short of the traditional monogamous ideal, Charlie Watts was the honourable exception to the rule. Working long days in the studio, the band's laconic, and consistently brilliant, drummer would get in his chauffeur-driven Mini every night and go home to the Sussex countryside to cook dinner with his wife. The Watts' only child, Serafina, was born in March 1968. In his quiet way, Charlie was also an avid English sportsman, passionately devoted to horse riding, football and cricket. As if to throw off the confinements of his day job, he took in every jazz concert he could and spent nearly every free weekend of his life tapping along to Thelonious Monk or Charlie Parker records in a little soundproofed den in the garage of his home, formerly the country estate of the Archbishop of Canterbury.

Mick Jagger, too, enjoyed some of the trappings of domesticity, particularly after he paid £40,000 for 48 Cheyne Walk, a Queen Anne mansion by the Thames near Albert Bridge. Mick, Marianne Faithfull and her 3-year-old son Nicholas moved in that same summer. The couple's semi-conjugal state soon became a talking point in Swinging London, not least when Marianne announced that she was going to have Mick's baby. Jagger went on the *David Frost Show* to defend their right to bring a child in to the world without 'some bloody silly piece of paper' (or wedding certificate) and had a heated debate on the subject with 59-year-old Mary Whitehouse, of the morally austere National Viewers' and Listeners' Association. Jagger chose not to mention that he had asked Marianne to marry him several times, and that she had so far declined his offer.

Mick's inconstancy, even so, was no secret, even if he lagged far behind Brian and Bill in sheer volume of women. According to the ever-present Robert Fraser, Jagger was a gastronome whose love of a good meal 'rather mirrored his libido'. Just as no dinner was complete with less than three courses, so 'some of Mick's nights were like a menu, with an entrée, a meat dish and a dessert' in the form of a blonde, a brunette and a redhead. What's more surprising, perhaps, is that over the years Mick also found time to casually score with several of his colleagues' lovers, from Pat Andrews (Brian) through Uschi Obermaier (Keith) and Astrid Lundström (Bill), and eventually Suki Potier (Brian again). The verdict on Mick and Anita Pallenberg is still out, although such was the zeal of their scenes together in the film *Performance* that a ten-minute snippet was entered in a Dutch blue-movie festival, where it won the Golden Dong. Fraser thought this particular tendency 'very much a control trip' for Mick, allowing him to 'swagger past all the males [and] have sex with all the females'. Jagger's first wife was also to comment tartly on this same 'alpha-wolf' side of his character.

'People say that Mick was either a great romantic or a one-man shagging machine,' Fraser reflected years later. 'Well, I think he was probably a little of both.'

4

BLOOD AND CIRCUSES

Andrew Oldham left that autumn. As usual with a Stones firing, the end was brutal, swift and a bit oblique. 'At some stage they realised that Andy's ideas on production were only ideas he'd got from them in the first place,' said Stu, whose own feud with Oldham was of Birnam Wood proportions. 'There must have been some sort of bust-up, because all of a sudden they wanted to get rid of him ... We went in and played a lot of blues as badly as we could. The Loog just walked out. At the time I didn't understand what was going on.' On 29 September, Les Perrin announced that the band had 'split from our recording manager, because the Stones are taking over more and more of their own music ... Andrew himself has expressed a wish to get involved in film and theatrical production.' (This came as news to Oldham.) Others thought that Andrew's main error had been to promptly disappear after the Redlands bust, then re-emerge only to help London Records put out a Stones anthology called *Flowers*, the latest in corporate cynicism. Oldham himself believes, 'It was very simple ... It was like, "We know what's what, let's let Allen Klein work it out." It was at the time of *Satanic Majesties* and I don't think they needed a manager like I'd been managing them before. *That's* hindsight. At the time it was just confusing.'

Oldham's departure wasn't the only change happening to the Stones brains trust while the boys themselves were deciding if they wanted to be tabloid acid casualties or a blues band. From late 1967 the group set up shop in a chandeliered top-floor office at 46 Maddox Street, Mayfair (today an antiques store), run by a young Californian named Jo Bergman who took her orders, to Bill Wyman's vocal displeasure, from Mick and Keith. Along with this gesture to corporate efficiency, the Stones would soon go on to commission a fully equipped mobile recording studio that they hauled around the country on the back of a British Leyland lorry; since it was still being hired out for use thirty years later, it proved to be one of their better investments of the era. Counterbalancing the group's new-found role as young entrepreneurs was the increasing presence of 'Spanish Tony' Sanchez, the swarthy Soho hustler who scored drugs for Mick, Keith and Brian, and part of what Tom Keylock called the 'dodgy end' of the entourage that formed in Oldham's absence. 'Tony grovelled to the band but muscled everyone else,' Keylock reflected. 'Or he thought he did. "Just let me know if anybody bothers you and I'll take care of it," he told Mick and Keith. They loved that sort of Al Capone bullshit. I mean, the guy was five feet tall – what the fuck would he do to someone who "bothered" them?' Keylock also fondly remembered having carried Mick Jagger out of Olympic on a couch one night after the latter overdid it on Sanchez's wares (drink, not drugs, it should be said), and Stu later remarking that he wouldn't be surprised if 'the band didn't even make it to '68'. Thanks to Klein and Decca, at least, the hits still came on schedule: 'We Love You', 'Dandelion' and Bill's opus 'In Another Land', all evidence that truckloads of hash were being smoked in the studio.

New York, Wednesday 13 September. Keith Richards flew in to join the rest of the band for a business meeting and to shoot the new album cover. He was welcomed by US Immigration with a full cavity search. Naturally, Richards wasn't carrying any drugs in to America; he got them locally. Keith spent much of the next day at Michael Cooper's studio in suburban Mount Vernon, blasted out of his mind on acid. Everyone eventually wandered in with their own stories to tell of their airport reception. Brian Jones arrived draped in a floral kimono over a pair of leggings and pixie boots, drawing sidelong glances from Mick. In time Brian went off to change in to his 'psychedelic gear'. Bill and Charlie pottered around looking out of sorts in their black capes, face glitter and mascara. 'I dunno about this,' the latter was heard to mumble, perhaps thinking back to the streets of Neasden. When their cue came, however, the Stones were ready. Walking out on to the set with a couple of recent hits under his belt, Keith, in particular, looked the part of a stoned troubadour. Over the next four hours he and the band posed in a variety of attitudes, adding decorative touches of their own with spray cans, while the room filled with the enticing aroma of Afghan flake.

'The whole thing, we were on acid,' Mick Jagger recalled. 'We were on acid during the cover picture. It was like being at school, sticking on the bits of shiny paper and things.' In something of a departure, the eventual photo was then processed in to multi-coloured 3D and given a special 'trippy' backdrop of mountains and revolving planets. The result was a rock equivalent of a William Blake etching of the Beyond, with something of Salvador Dali's hallucinatory high finish. Up until then, Decca's normal policy had been to dummy up a quick publicity shot for its album covers at a cost of forty or fifty quid. Inclusive of all the travel arrangements and hospitality, this one cost them £17,000. The end result was both a representative slice of 60s pop art and, not coincidentally, a clone of Cooper's own *Sergeant Pepper* cover.

Although all the Stones enjoyed a toke or a drink, and often both, Brian Jones' intake had clearly crossed the line separating recreational use from addiction. By late 1967 it was beginning to look as if Anita's defection had ushered in something more than a mere case of mate swapping. Brian was in total freefall. First the police broke down the door at Courtfield Road after someone phoned them to wrongly say that a man inside had overdosed. A few weeks later Brian celebrated his conditional release on drugs charges by swallowing a bottle of pills that landed him in St George's Hospital for 'exhaustion'. After that he moved out of

Courtfield Road and in to a flat in Chesham Street, off Sloane Square. Following yet another visit by the emergency services, Brian's landlord evicted him by the expedient of throwing all his belongings in to the road. Mick Jagger, for one, was not pleased at the possible implications for the Stones' overseas earnings. 'There's a tour coming up, and there's obvious difficulties with Brian, who can't leave the country,' Mick told a press conference, referring to his colleague's work-permit issues. Everyone apparently wanted to play in Japan, 'except Brian, again, who can't get in to Tokyo because he's a druggie'.

'Brian was extremely unhappy,' Les Perrin's wife Janie confirmed. 'Once he called me from the Dorchester Hotel and said he was going to throw himself out of the window. I told him to go down a few floors before he did it, so he wouldn't make too much mess on the pavement.' After that Brian seemed to calm down a bit and even went in to do a few sessions at Olympic, adding a suitably spacey (and brilliantly played) Mellotron to Mick's '2000 Light Years from Home'. But he hated the kind of 'druggy shit' characteristic of the album as a whole, and hardly bothered to go in to the studio again after that. At the band's request, the Keylocks and the Perrins both took him in to their homes to get him out of harm's way for a while. The older generation liked Brian; he was a nice kid, like an adopted son, trying to figure himself out.

'But he was a needy guy,' Tom Keylock said. 'If you were Brian's friend you had to be there for him twenty-four hours a day. You'd get calls at four in the morning: "Tom, there's been a bit of an accident here. I don't know what happened. Can you come over?" You'd drive round there and Suki would be lying on the floor with a black eye.'

By October 1967, Jones seemed to have 'physically shrunk', Keylock noted, living as he now did on a diet of brandy, animal tranquillisers and LSD. 'He was twenty-five, and looked twenty years older.' For Jones intoxication was increasingly the rule, and prolonged consciousness the exception. Friends had to remind him to eat. Brian was a familiar figure on the King's Road, wobbling to the off-licence on platform heels for his cigarettes and booze, hunched down in his Afghan coat, his fingers nicotine-stained, his eyes pouchy and glazed. After his last trip to Olympic he'd all but stopped lobbing his little jolts of joy and fury at the Stones, and instead took more and more overseas holidays – nine in 1967, including the ill-fated tour of Morocco. In time Mick and Keith both phoned the band's mentor Alexis Korner to say they were worried about Jones, and Brian himself put in late-night calls to Korner sobbing that the Stones were about to fire him and hire Eric Clapton in his place.

Once, while out on bail, Jones was driving a rental car around Marbella with Suki Potier when somebody cut them up. At a stop sign, Brian got out, went up to the other car, opened the driver's door, punched the guy, came back, got in, and drove around him. The next morning, there were more problems when Brian tried to send the couple's hotel bill to Allen Klein for payment. According to Wyman, Klein dragged his feet and Jones 'borrowed the money from a Major Dawson at the hotel ... Several days after Brian had returned to London, a cable from the major to the Stones office said the cash had not arrived from New York, and that he (Major Dawson) "required it soonest".' Brian was obliged to fire off three successive telexes to Klein, none of which elicited his funds. A fourth message read, 'Please! Is there any chance of an immediate reply?' At last, an answer. It read: 'No'. While the Stones were going multi-platinum and changing the whole face of rock, the band's founder was sitting in a corner at Maddox Street worrying about his living expenses. One part of him was permanently wound up, spending his time gobbling acid and shagging – very much the legend. The other was a sentimental and endearingly shy man who loved his mum. The two halves would try to control one another; both were Brian. Keylock, despite everything, still cared about him, and he took the long view. The problem was how Jones had been treated from the beginning. 'When he was a kid in Cheltenham, his only entertainment was sitting alone in his room with his record player. Then it was all pregnancies and scandals and being kicked out of home. They threw the man away!'

The final blow to Jones' morale came on 30 October, when he

went on trial for possession. Brian immediately pleaded guilty, and heard himself described in court by his therapist Anthony Flood as 'a very sick boy', 'deeply disturbed' and 'paranoic'.

The judge asked, 'A potential suicide?'

Dr Flood: 'Certainly.'

Brian got nine months. Like Keith before him, he did a day and a night in Wormwood Scrubs, while the lawyers worked on his appeal. On Mick Jagger's orders, Keylock was sent to collect him the next afternoon. 'After waiting an hour, I saw Brian being escorted across the yard . . . He had the two biggest coppers I'd ever seen in my life, manacled to him either side, tugging him along. Brian looked a sad sight. He could drive you mad, the bastard, but I felt desperately sorry for him that day.' At Jones' appeal on 12 December, an independently appointed psychiatrist spoke of his 'extremely precarious state of emotional adjustment' and 'fragile grasp of reality'. The Lord Chief Justice, noting that 'this is a degree of mercy . . . not a let-off', again quashed a prison sentence and sub-stituted probation. Early the next morning, Brian was found unconscious on the floor of his latest flat. After checking himself out of hospital he was meant to go up to Maddox Street for a meeting with the rest of the band. Brian never showed. He did make use of the credit card the office eventually gave him, though. Over Christmas Brian went on holiday to Ceylon (now Sri Lanka), then announced that he was going back to Morocco to record the G'naoua tribesmen and their massed drums. One way or another, the Stones saw their lead guitarist less and less.

As Brian withdrew, Keith Richards took the opportunity to 'listen to thousands of old records I'd collected but never had time for', traced along to some of the riffs, and improved as an all-round instrumentalist. Before long Keith was toying with country tunings, and taught himself to play slide and bottleneck guitar. Many of his work-ups took place in the timbered staff cottage across the field from Redlands, where Frank Thorogood knocked down the walls to create a cavernous music room furnished by a well-stocked bar at one end and a statue of Buddha at the other, with Moroccan rugs scattered around and tie-dyed scarves draped over the lamps for atmosphere. A pair of technically minded friends wired the place up for sound. People began hanging out at Redlands to jam, and once or twice the Stones arrived en masse to rehearse there. One spring evening, Keylock remembers everyone 'lying around on cushions, knocking up a song called "Sister Morphine"', which Marianne Faithfull was talking about recording. The tune took time to grow, and somewhere towards dawn the band's arranger Jack Nitzsche introduced his friend Ry Cooder in to the proceedings. Cooder had just turned twenty and was building a reputation as a hot young guitar-for-hire around Los Angeles. Before long he was flaying away, and Keith leaned over and said, 'That's a gas, what you're playing; how'd you do it? You tune the E strings down to a D, right, and you can get a groove going, yeah, that's very cool', and Cooder showed him the lot. By this time, the room was already resounding to the buzz of open-tune riffing and a chunky chord sequence very much like the intro to 'Honky Tonk Women'. There's of course absolutely no question of piracy on Keith's part but, like many a songwriter before him, he knew when he was on to a good thing. Soon enough, he would be mingling his deft Chuck Berry homages with a sure, sculpted sound that rocked the paint off arena walls.

Cooder went ballistic a year or so later and publicly charged the Stones with stealing his best licks. 'They're *bloodsuckers*, man.'

Meanwhile, *Their Satanic Majesties Request,* an LP that supposedly drove a psychedelic stake through the heart of the band's blues career. No one who had access to a stereo and a bong in the late 60s will ever forget it. *Satanic Majesties* loomed just behind *Sergeant Pepper*, which it shamelessly aped: both albums featured opening numbers later reprised; both included background chat, static and tape loops in the normally sacrosanct silence between grooves; both had a trippy cover by Michael Cooper. Alas, where *Pepper* offered proper songs, *Majesties* opted for 'amorphous and aimless instrumental styles ... We get oscillators and vacuum cleaners, pathetic doodling on the guitar, fuzz-tones without end, and we get the mandatory eight-minute freakout,' in *Rolling Stone's* generally unappreciative review. Jagger's chameleonic vocal style was also all over the map; Wilson Pickett and Nancy Sinatra were just two points of reference among many, while on 'Gomper' Mick sounds as if he'd been recorded from deep down a mine. A whole lot of shaking, banging, whacking and general percussive merriment enlivened all too many of the tracks, though when Charlie took the opportunity simply to rock out, as he did on 'Citadel', 'you suddenly remembered what you dug about the band in the first place', to again quote *Rolling Stone*.

Other redeeming moments included 'The Lantern', where Keith Richards did away with all the performing-seal pyrotechnics and just played the guitar, as only he could. 'She's a Rainbow' was a smoochy, reflective affair where the Stones ventured outside their normal safety blanket of solid-rock riffing with some Mozart piano fills, and a lyric that just might have been influenced by Marianne Faithfull. Brian dusted off the Mellotron to good effect on '2000 Light Years'. But most of the rest was a retro, Beatles-lite confection that sounded closer to a pot party than an album.

Residual loyalty meant the LP 'shipped gold', hitting the *Billboard* chart on the day it was released. London Records sent an overexcited cable to Sir Edward Lewis at Decca: 'It's not a hit, it's an epidemic!' Les Perrin promptly released this to the press, allowing the Inland Revenue, in turn, to add it to its file. *Satanic Majesties* would earn the Stones the biggest royalties and worst reviews of their career so far.

The week the album came out Keith and Anita flew to Paris and then joined 'Groovy Bob' Fraser, just out of jail, for Christmas in Marrakech. As soon as they arrived, Keith went across the street and scored from their old friend Achmed the hash dealer. Achmed would grade his kif 10-, 12- or – for discerning customers – 18-denier, according to purity. Over the next fortnight everyone smoked a lot of 18-denier. As an extra thrill, Richards rolled his joints in HM Prison-issue papers, a souvenir of the Scrubs. Fraser would remember listening to Keith playing his guitar while lying around in the moonlight by the pool and thinking that what he heard was better than the new album. Some of the embryonic songs resurfaced a year later on *Beggar's Banquet*. In the new year everyone drove back to Paris, where on a whim Richards decided to buy a flat in the rue du Faubourg Saint-Honoré. He started to decorate it in classic Keith style – Moroccan tapestries, lots of wolfskin – but in the end spent only a few nights there over the next ten years.

Home, instead, meant Redlands, where Richards passed his days with Pallenberg and a constantly replenished guest-list that occasionally included Jones and Suki Potier: a there'll-always-be-an-England arrangement that lasted some six months, until Brian was busted again. The house 'was like stepping off the planet', said Frank Thorogood, still busy fortifying it against another visit by Inspector Dineley. 'You went in to a no-daylight zone where there were places to crash strewn all over the floor, with hookahs and drug gear and constant music, and these bloody great evil dogs wandering around crapping everywhere.' West Wittering had seen nothing like it. Up until 1966, the place had been a quiet birdwatcher's haven with two churches, a campsite and a pub. After Keith moved in, and more particularly after February 1967, it was like the setting for one of those Roger Corman films where the decent folk are suddenly invaded by Hell's Angels. In time Redlands' decadent squalor was enriched by the 40-year-old American underground filmmaker Kenneth Anger, then scouting locations for his seminal short *Invocation of my Demon Brother*. Anger came down for several long weekends, liked the free-form vibe, and later suggested that Keith and Anita go through a pagan marriage ritual with himself officiating. Anita was reportedly keen. Anger got as far as painting the Redlands front door gold, as tradition requires, though history fails to relate whether he also secured the necessary druidical clothes and sacrificial long-horned ram. Keith eventually put the whole thing off, apparently worried what his mum might have to say, if not for other factors. Friends of the intending couple were still never quite sure when their relationship would spin out of control, once or twice violently so.

It was a point not lost on Ian Stewart, who was in charge of most of the Stones' travel arrangements. As part of his duties (for which he was paid £1,872 p.a., or roughly 2 per cent of the sum being earned by the other founder members of the band) he kept a list of airlines willing or unwilling to fly them. By late 1967, Stu recalled, there were already two or three major carriers where Keith's business wasn't actively sought. He was banned from Alitalia, for one, 'for stayin' in the restroom from Rome to London punchin' that crazy Anita'.

Mick and Marianne Faithfull spent a more traditional Christmas season decorating their new Chelsea home (£6,000 for the dining-room chandelier) and buying a 35-acre country pile near Newbury, Berkshire, implausibly named Stargroves, before enjoying an extended holiday in Rio, Barbados and Tangier. Their Moroccan hotel featured a one-legged bellhop who was also the bouncer in the nearby brothel. Soon Mick and Marianne were enjoying a spirited threesome with one of the veiled local girls. Back in London, the *Sunday Telegraph* journalist Gina Richardson went to interview the couple, whose wispy appearance gave them 'the air of children left in charge while grown-ups are away'. Marianne, we learn, was introducing her partner to ballet and opera and supplying 'literally hundreds' of books, like William Burroughs' *Naked Lunch*, for the bibliophilic Mick to read. The elder Mr and Mrs Jagger later remembered that their outlaw son still drove down to Dartford whenever he could, and always greeted the kids inevitably waiting for him at the door with 'exuberant wit and affection', in Eva Jagger's precise phrase.

According to Peter Swales, a young publicist who worked with the Stones, 'Brian Jones was just a wreck' by 1968. 'He was on the border-line of obesity, in his body and his face, although his hair hid that bit. He perspired all the time and smelled of brandy.' The general feeling in the band was that while Brian could flip from one persona to another, being charming and witty when he wanted to be, he wasn't a fun drunk. Christopher Gibbs remembers that when Jones went back to Morocco with Suki Potier there was an unpleasant scene in the hotel where they were all staying. 'She jolly nearly died there,' Gibbs says. 'She had smashed her wrists on a mirror and was bleeding badly. And Brian, instead of calling a doctor or the concierge, rang *me*. "Can you come and sort this out for me? Can you ring the doctor? Can you talk to the management? Can you clean up the blood? Do you know how a tourniquet works?".' For a man so consistently ahead of his time, Jones was not good at keeping to a schedule. The G'naoua tribesmen and their drums were all left waiting for him up in the hills, and in the end Brian postponed the sessions indefinitely when he experienced technical difficulties with his tape recorder.

Meanwhile, Bill Wyman went off to Sweden to meet his new girlfriend's family, ricking his back when he shovelled the snow off their driveway, and Charlie Watts stayed home to design the Stones' Christmas card to their fans, which assured everyone that they were 'alive and well'.

On 17 March 1968, Mick Jagger took part in a demonstration organised by the British Vietnam Solidarity Campaign, marching down London's Park Lane with some 10,000 other protesters to assemble in front of the 'imperialist fortress', as they called the American Embassy. The timing of the rally was ironic, because the US and its allies happened to be fighting a desperate rearguard action just then against a series of spectacular Vietcong offensives which had been launched on the Tet holiday in January. Despite their ultimate defeat on the battlefields during Tet, the Communists won the sitting-room war for civilian hearts and minds, particularly those with a new and lingering appetite for disorder. Even Mick flirted briefly with a revolutionary attitude, declaring himself against both 'fatcats' and private property (before going on to join the Country Gentlemen's Association) and punching his fist in the air when Vanessa Redgrave told the London marchers, 'A Vietcong victory is the only way to peace.' Jagger did not, however, participate in the widespread looting that followed: he'd only shown up to feel the 'love' flowing from the crowd, he later said – and, besides, he was on probation.

Not long after these events, Mick went down to Redlands to hear Keith play him a new song called 'Primo Grande'. After kicking it around overnight, Jagger added the title 'Everybody Pays Their Dues', which in turn became 'Street Fighting Man'. Back at Olympic, the Stones worked the riff up in to a driving acoustic strum, powered by Charlie's toy drum kit (small enough to fold in to a suitcase) and Keith himself overdubbing bass. Most of the critics completely missed the irony of Mick's central lament in the song about the impotence of direct action: all he could do, he rued, was to sing in a rock 'n' roll band. The track was one of Keith's greatest forays outside his normal comfort zone of roaring electric guitar. Released as a single in the US, it was promptly banned amid the riots, murders and political carnage of the long hot summer of 1968.

Keith himself 'didn't give a stuff' about reaching anyone's mind, only their gut. The energy he put in to 'Street Fighting Man' could have powered a small town, let alone a song.

The Stones' main political point of reference that year wasn't Vietnam, however; it was a wiry, 62-year-old maverick Labour MP, former gossip columnist, swashbuckling wartime double agent and sometime occultist named Tom Driberg. Driberg, a homosexual, had first met Mick at Harley House, where he took a leisurely look at his host, lingering particularly over his mid-section, and remarked 'Oh my God, what a *big* box you have,' an icebreaker that led to merry laughter all round. After more companionable advances were declined, Driberg settled on a role as Mick's political mentor, tabling a Commons motion in support of the Stones and later signing a letter in *The Times* calling for the legalisation of soft drugs in the wake of Mick and Keith's trial. For the next year, Jagger and Driberg met regularly, and aptly, in the Gay Hussar, a narrow, panelled Soho restaurant – somehow giving the impression of the dining car in a royal train – where they discussed what the MP called the 'proletarianisation' of the Stones' music. Although evocatively titled songs like 'Street Fighting Man', 'Salt of the Earth' and 'Factory Girl' all date from this era, it's debatable whether Driberg's mélange of utopian-socialist slogans had any lasting effect on the band's chief lyricist, whose dazzling charm offensive sometimes masked his lack of any deeper commitment. When Driberg once suggested that Jagger stand for his local council, or even parliament, the latter 'literally pissed himself laughing about it', according to Keylock. 'You weren't going to see *him* hobnobbing with the

Establishment – not yet, anyway.' When Driberg appeared for a
meal at Cheyne Walk a few days later, it was to be told by Faithfull
that Mick was 'unexpectedly detained'. Albert Clinton, who managed the Gay Hussar at the time, remembers 'the elder gentleman
always doing the talking, and the younger one the eating'.

While Mick was flirting with Driberg, Keith continued his musical education by attaching himself to the Byrds on their first British
tour that summer – 'a straight gas', he said. While other bands were
busy experimenting with Moogs and wah-wah pedals, the Byrds
retreated through the swing doors of a western saloon-bar with their
twangy steel guitars, bluegrass fiddles and upright pianos. They
brought the house down: sundry Stones and Beatles pummelled the
railings of the upper boxes and jaded critics broke in to wide grins
after their triumphant London debut at the Albert Hall. Country
rock was born. Keith soon befriended the Byrds' presiding genius
Gram Parsons, a 22-year-old musician of brain-teasing agility who
also happened to be a trust-fund millionaire and connoisseur of the
finest drugs. When the Byrds flew on to South Africa, Parsons
struck a blow against apartheid by quitting the band and staying
behind to play cowboy songs and smoke hash at Redlands. Keith's
own rural pursuits at the time included tinkering with guns and
knives, lying prone in a hammock, drawing on a bubble pipe and
noting the strange preponderance of 'weird lights' hovering over the
South Downs. No wonder, perhaps, Les Perrin stopped arranging
visits from the likes of *Teen* and *Valentine*. Later that year, Perrin and
Tom Keylock would help get Richards in to the Lena, up the A3,
through Immigration at Heathrow, on to a jet, and, seven hours
later, safely down the ramp in New York. Keith remained asleep
throughout. But it's only fair to say that he also put his down-time
to good professional use, blueprinting a whole new line of guitar
attack: open tunings, often with a distinct Nashville flavour, plenty
of acoustic, and the self-confidence to play *less*. As Keith liked to
summarise his art, 'Five strings, three notes, two fingers, one arsehole and you've got it.'

Apparently Mick Jagger wasn't so enamoured of Gram Parsons.
Just over a year later the Stones and their inner circle moved in to

a house owned by Peter Tork, of the Monkees, in the Hollywood Hills. Soon the home experienced a distinct transformation. Tork's kitchen had to be temporarily closed off following some disastrous episode with his drink blender, and the previously neat living room, all white and beige except for the gold records on the wall, had become a brocaded lair strewn with drugs, groupies, long scarves, festering bowls of food and a honky-tonk piano where Keith and his new best mate liked to bang out Hank Williams and Jimmie Rodgers songs at all hours. Surveying this scene one night, Mick turned to Parsons and said tetchily, 'We've got to keep this place *tidy*, man.'

Domestic arrangements were only one area of concern, according to a well-placed source who travelled with the Stones. 'Mick insisted on ordering every aspect of the band's lives – the way they dressed down to what they smoked or drank: or their women's weight, hairdo and make-up. "Eating enough, are we?" he'd say to a chick.' If such hints didn't produce the desired result, Mick could be more direct – sometimes excluding Parsons from the room, to Keith's annoyance, while the Stones talked business; or 'pretty well constantly' insisting that Gram and his fiancée Gretchen clean up both their act and the house itself, which 'Mick always wanted to look less like a drug den and more like a modern-art museum'.

Luckily, the mutual tension between the Stones' creative team was also a source of inspiration. The fruits of this collaboration would be heard to good effect on the band's next four albums, although their post-*Satanic Majesties* comeback really began when Bill Wyman carelessly picked out the riff of a lifetime one night on a dusty south London rehearsal-room piano. Jagger and Richards listened to Bill's casual gift, grunted an acknowledgement and quickly drove back to Redlands.

Keith: 'It was about six in the morning and we'd been up all night. The sky was beginning to go grey and it was pissing down rain. I started to fool around, singing, and Mick [comes] in. And suddenly we had this wonderful phrase. So we woke up and knocked it together.'

Working from Bill's lick, Richards hit first on a ll-V-l chord run and then a taut, three-note hook, E, F-sharp and A, that paid savvy and perhaps opportunistic homage to the past. Buried within was the timeless 'Satisfaction' riff, played backwards, and in Nashville key. Mick swiftly added lyrics 'about having a hard time and getting out … a metaphor for all the acid things'. The title was an in-joke twitting Keith's big-footed (size 14) gardener, Jack Dyer, whom they could just make out through the rain, padding mournfully around the Redlands moat.

Jumpin' Jack Flash.

That great syncopated intro, later to kick the likes of 'Honky Tonk Women' and 'Start Me Up' in to gear, soon became a Stones trademark. Within seconds, the band had reclaimed their music from dozens of 'roots-rock' groups that had taken advantage of their recent psychedelic detour. Sane critics later compared 'Jumpin' Jack Flash' to Beethoven's Fifth, although Keith more modestly called it only 'my fucking favourite of all our shit'. It promptly went to number one on both sides of the Atlantic and quite probably saved the band's career. The song not only sounded great on radio, but also packed a fair number of rude shocks in to the accompanying video: warpaint, tight pants and low-slung guitars, not to mention Jagger's mike – used as suggestively as in a Cadbury's Flake commercial – for starters. Keith Richards, with jungle-green shades and matching complexion, a shark's tooth dangling, turned in to the Human Riff at that instant. Who says television doesn't innovate?

Perhaps the only person not thrilled by the worldwide crossover success of 'Jumpin' Jack Flash' was Bill Wyman, who thought up the core riff in the first place. Forty-five years on, Bill is yet to bank any songwriting royalties for his contribution.

Not long after his all-night session at Redlands, Mick turned up at Charlie's house in the Sussex countryside one spring afternoon, sat down on the lawn, took up a guitar, and began strumming a 'very "Blowin' in the Windish" kind of folk song'. The lyrics owed something to Mikhail Bulgakov's newly translated novel *The Master and Margarita*, a copy of which Marianne Faithfull had left lying around Cheyne Walk. As well as being mordantly funny in its own right, the book remains the definitive satire on the old-style Soviet system, with Stalin's regime juxtaposed to that of Pontius Pilate, and a dramatis personae that includes a naked witch on a broomstick and a cheroot-smoking black cat. Out of this all came 'Sympathy for the Devil'. Tom Keylock watched as, over two nights at Olympic, Keith 'tossed the discount-Dylan strum for a samba beat and Charlie kicked in with the voodoo percussion', while Tom himself, a bit implausibly, helped out on the falsetto chorus. 'It was fucking brilliant how they reshuffled the whole thing,' he said, still smiling about it twenty-five years later. 'And what's more, no one ever seemed to tell anyone else what to do. You maybe heard Mick or Keith grunt something from time to time – "that's a wank" or "that's a gas" – but basically they just blasted away until they had something completely different from what they started with.' There had always been a whiff of sulphur about the Stones, but with 'Sympathy' they were right out there on the cutting edge – '*totally evil*', in *Billboard*'s admiring phrase.

All in all, then, a golden era at Olympic, where the Stones' summer sessions soon took on the brisk, down-to-business tone that attends a major comeback. The band threw every radio-friendly beat they had in to these new anthems, and got some great performances – notably from Jimmy Miller, a moustachioed 26-year-old New York session drummer and, more to the point, record mixer of genius. 'Jimmy was great,' even Allen Klein allowed. 'He'd book the studio and run the sessions, get the artists, arrange all the cars and hotels – everything.' In time, Miller's CV included producing the Spencer Davis Group and their breakthrough hit 'Gimme Some Lovin'', the ill-fated supergroup Blind Faith and yet another Steve Winwood act, Traffic. Keith Richards called Miller the 'great knob twiddler', although occasionally coming to drop the 'twiddler' as the band's relationship with him deteriorated in the 1970s. Mick Jagger is said to have written 'You Can't Always Get What You Want', which name-checks 'Mr Jimmy', at least partly as a reply to his producer's request for a pay rise.

Miller left his fingerprints all over the Stones' best mid-career work, and played the drums for them whenever Charlie was unavailable. An early hint of his cut-to-the-chase professional credo came when Mick and Keith sat down in front of him with their acoustic guitars to play the rather fey original version of 'Sympathy for the Devil' and Miller asked them, 'Where's the groove?' Nobody except Stu had talked to them like that before then. But problems began when 'I became more and more involved, and as that happened I got more and more in to the lifestyle,' Miller said. Five years later, he was burned out. 'Jimmy went in a lion and came out a lamb,' Keith Richards recalled. 'We wore him out completely. Jimmy was great, but the more successful he became, the more he became like Brian. He ended up spending three months carving swastikas in to the wooden console at Island studios.' The Stones parted company with their producer shortly afterwards. Twenty years later, the band gave Miller $50,000 after he and his wife were diagnosed with liver disease and cancer respectively; he died in October 1994, aged fifty-two.

The Stones also made use of some great ancillary musicians, including the pianist Nicky Hopkins (Jeff Beck Group, the Who) and the multi-instrumentalist Ric Grech, of Family, both of whom, quite coincidentally, were also to die prematurely of liver problems. Dave Mason of Traffic walked in to the upstairs studio at Olympic one day. 'The Stones were sitting there surrounded by a pile of African instruments which Brian Jones had brought back with him on his travels. I remember there were some full-scale Moroccan drums lying around, a bass covered with goat skin, sitars, maybe some pipes and bells. Brian himself wasn't there, and nobody seemed quite sure what to make of all this gear. Anyway, they asked me in. Propped up in the corner was a shehnai [or tribal oboe], so I played that over the last part of what became "Street Fighting Man". Everyone was very nice. No, I didn't get paid.'

On 12 May, the Stones agreed to appear on the bill of the *NME* Poll-Winners' concert at Wembley. The band made a ten-minute cameo amid almost nostalgic chaos: commissionaires fought with fans as Keith ground out the power chords to 'Jumpin' Jack Flash'. Mick tossed his silver ballet shoes in to the crowd. It was Brian Jones' last public performance.

Nine days later the narcs came for Brian in a dawn raid on his

new flat in Royal Avenue House, King's Road. While one detachment of officers banged loudly on the front door another slid in via
the interior rubbish chute. After questioning, they took Brian away
along with a ball of twine with a chunk of hash hidden inside. He
told them it wasn't his, that he 'never took the stuff [because] it
makes me so paranoid'. Jo Bergman bailed him out pending his
trial.

Over the next eight weeks, the Stones forged ahead with their
masterpiece. Some of the Redlands jams made it on to the new
album, and others were left to marinate for years: 'Two Trains
Running' turned in to 'Midnight Rambler', and 'Meet Me at the
Station' in to 'No Expectations', while the anodyne-sounding
'Blues 1' became 'Gimme Shelter'. Keith Richards wrote the lushly
textured 'You Got the Silver' for Anita, with Brian adding a few
mournful grace notes to the fade. In June, Keylock drove everyone
to a ruined castle, where they pretended to play cricket for the
press. The French auteur Jean-Luc Godard arrived at Olympic to
film the sessions, and caught Keith providing the shuffling, hyp-
notic groove to 'Sympathy for the Devil'. Mick was soon on the
phone to Aretha Franklin to enquire whether she might like to
record the song as her next single, but the gospel diva felt obliged
to pass. ('I wouldn't sing that in my crapper,' Franklin allegedly
remarked, which if true was in no way reflective of the broader
mutual respect between her and the Stones.) Later that night,
Godard's klieg lights set the studio ceiling on fire. While Mick,
Keith, Brian and Charlie ran for their lives, Bill and Jimmy Miller
calmly headed back in to rescue the tapes. Brian's bail was renewed.
Following the hearing, he wrote to his parents again to tell them
not to worry. He had bigger plans, now, he added, to record whole
tribal communities and black American choirs, something that
would amaze and inspire everyone who heard it. For Brian, *bigger*
was the stuff of dreams.

In early July, Jagger and Richards flew to Hollywood to mix the
new album. Gram Parsons was having trouble with his trust fund,
so Keith comped him to tag along, everyone scored some great pot
from Phil Kaufman – a local fixer known affectionately as 'King

Con'* – and came back with a photo of a scuzzy toilet wall to put on the record cover. The Stones had never been shy about shivering the timbers at Decca House, but this was too much. Over the next four months the band and their label, the latter deeming the portrait 'prurient' and 'likely to cause offence' to its shareholders, engaged in a heated public debate about censorship. The LP's release date was moved back from late July to early December. Mick told everyone that the Stones would be leaving Decca the second their contract allowed. Keith maintained that the band had never been more than a tax write-off for the suits in the first place, and that their real business priority remained selling weapons systems to the War Office. Eric Easton was suing Andrew Oldham, Decca and Nanker Phelge Music, claiming that they collectively owed him £84,140/15sh for their two-and-a-half year professional association. Nobody had heard from Allen Klein in a while.

Meanwhile, Brian Jones returned to Tangier with Suki Potier to record the master musicians of Jajouka in some local caves, behaving immaculately until he got back to the Hotel Minzah. 'He beat up Suki right off,' says George Chkiantz, an engineer who accompanied the couple. 'A few hours later Brian was wacked, standing on the balcony and insulting Arabs on the street below. I went over to calm him down, and he just blacked out, keeled over and smashed his head on the iron railing. He looked dead to me, and I

---

*Phil Kaufman still remembers his introduction to the Stones. 'At nine that morning I got out of Los Angeles Jail, where I'd done time for drugs. A friend picked me up and said, "Mick Jagger and Marianne Faithfull are coming to town. They need someone to look after them." I had no money. For that matter, I had no shoes. Eventually I got the bus up to Hollywood and knocked on a door. Jimmy Miller was there, very businesslike. He gave me a typed schedule. Marianne was lying nude on a couch, getting a massage. Mick was friendly. There was a brand new Cadillac convertible in the driveway. Before long we're cruising down to Sunset Sound, where I hop out and ring the buzzer. "I got the Rolling Stones here," I say. "Open up." They open up. I took care of business in the studio. Around 4 a.m. Mick called a wrap and went off in a limo somewhere. He passed me in the hallway. I still hadn't eaten anything since I got out of jail, though by now I at least had some shoes. Mick looked me up and down. "Thanks, man," he said, and gave me all the money in his pocket – about $1,500 – and the keys to the Caddy. "See you tomorrow." I woke up in prison and I went to sleep in a mansion rented by the Rolling Stones. That was my first day in showbusiness.'

began to panic. "What do we do now?" "Nothing," said Suki. "It happens all the time."'

In London, Mick signed on to play a jaded pop star in the film *Performance*, and Keith gave an interview in which he talked about seeing UFOs floating above Redlands and complained of being 'totally skint'. Bill had £47 in his bank account, and had to have the office send the familiar pleading telex to New York. Charlie, having parted company with his chauffeur, was worried about the cost of taking a taxi to the studio. With one thing and another, there were a few thumped fists when all parties met for a late-July summit at Maddox Street, a motion that never disturbed Brian, sleeping face down on the boardroom table.

Donald Cammell and Nic Roeg's *Performance* began shooting around London that summer. Mick Jagger was set to play a retired rock and roll singer holed up with a couple of sexually ambiguous girlfriends and a large stash of magic mushrooms, as they so often are. A fleeing hoodlum (James Fox), introduced in a scene in which he ritualistically shaves the head of a trussed-up gangland chauffeur, joins the ménage to mutually disquieting results. After having an abortion, Anita Pallenberg went up for the part of Mick's principal lover, a character required to initiate the other cast members in to communal bathing, voyeurism and other rituals, auditioning against Mia Farrow, hot off being impregnated by the devil in *Rosemary's Baby*. Anita got the job. 'It was soon after *Performance* finished shooting that drug use among our inner circle took a quantum leap,' Marianne Faithfull says. 'Anita went off her rocker for years. In to an abyss.' Marianne herself lost the baby that she had carried almost to term. She was later to say that her doctor had reached across her bed, taken her left arm at the wrist, and turned it silently and slowly until the inside of her elbow was face up. 'The message was that I [miscarried] because I was a junkie.' Marianne never forgot this devastating reproach. The child, had it lived, would have been a girl named Carina.

On 26 September Brian Jones was back in London to face trial for unlawful possession. Mick, Keith and Tom Keylock sat in the public gallery to hear the judge remind the jury that the burden of proof rested not on Jones (who very plausibly insisted he'd been 'fitted up' on this occasion) but the police, 'whose case is circumstantial. No evidence of his using cannabis was found ... If you think the prosecution has proved without a doubt that the defendant knew the drug was in his flat, you may find him guilty. Otherwise, he is innocent.'

'Groovy,' said Mick.

Outside in the hall he and Keith signed autographs. A beaming Keylock timed the jury: forty-seven minutes. 'For once in Brian's life, the poor bastard was telling the truth,' he said. 'The cops planted him; it's almost moronic, it's so obvious.' As the foreman announced his verdict of 'guilty' Brian slumped back to his seat, head in hands. Suki Potier started yelling, and Keith thumped the railing in front of him. The judge said: 'I think this was a lapse and I don't want to interfere with the probation order that already applies to this man. I am going to fine you according to your means. [Fifty pounds with a hundred guineas costs.] You must keep clear of this stuff. For goodness' sake, don't get in to trouble again.'

Outside, Jagger and Jones danced for the cameras.

Six weeks later, the Stones recorded 'You Can't Always Get What You Want' while Brian Jones lay sprawled in a corner, toking and reading a magazine. As the evening progressed, various technical personnel made creative suggestions to Brian over the in-house tannoy, while Tom Keylock preferred the old-fashioned method of 'marching over there and shouting in the bugger's ear. Didn't do any good. He was gone.' It was a strange session, even by Stones standards: Mick appeared in a shaggy fur coat, and Keith sat cross-legged on the floor wearing a tweed hat with a feather stuck in the band. For once, Charlie couldn't find the groove, so Jimmy Miller did the honours on drums. Keylock remembered the scene later turning in to a marathon drinking session. The next evening on Radio One, Mick Jagger revealed that the band 'definitely want to tour America [but] there are major hassles with visas'.

Mick eventually gave up the fight about the new album cover, opting for a plain white one just like the Beatles had. He continued to express misgivings about Decca's overall treatment of the group, particularly after the company managed to blunder when it came to actually pressing the disc, meaning that the songs were both fractionally slower, and in a different key, than originally recorded. Those responsible were 'old men' and 'total wankers', Jagger fumed. Keylock later explained that the real reason Mick had gone after the label so aggressively was that 'it pissed him off that they always seemed to patronise him. Mick saw the band as serious figures, and Decca saw them as these spoilt little brats.' 'Since the commencement of our relationship,' Jagger wrote Sir Edward Lewis in November, 'we have specifically requested the exclusion of all Rolling Stones' records from your "Bulk Advertisements". We are therefore most sorry to see that you have included *Beggar's Banquet* along with a number of other Decca LPs [*We're the Banana Splits, Thoroughly Modern Millie,* etc.] in *Record Retailer . . . Please make sure this will never happen again – never ever.'*

That same month Brian Jones took possession of Cotchford Farm, the mid-Sussex estate where A.A. Milne wrote *Winnie the Pooh.* Jones particularly liked to sit on the back terrace that overlooked Milne's swimming pool and, beyond it, a grand lawn decorated with bear-shaped topiary. Keylock arranged for Frank Thorogood to drive over from Redlands and help Brian refurbish the place.

On 5 December, the Stones finally launched *Beggar's Banquet* at the Elizabethan Room of the Gore hotel, where guests enjoyed a seven-course feast of boar's head and dumplings and an extensive wine list. Later in the proceedings serving wenches handed round cream pies. Les Perrin finally snapped and smashed two on either side of Brian's head, which hung there like fluffy earmuffs. According to Keylock, there had been certain difficulties arranging the event – originally planned for the Tower of London – in the first place. At issue had been not only the Stones' deserved reputation for public debauchery and mayhem, but also the more specific matter of Brian's chosen outfit for the night, over which he insisted he, not Mick, had final approval. 'He ended up in a very weird costume of [his and Suki's] creation,' Keylock said. 'Brian put on beet-red lipstick and wore a white rhinestone suit that looked like the sort of thing Elvis later ponced around in in Vegas. Halfway through, he nipped off and changed in to a top hat and a pair of tights. I had to talk him out of adding a codpiece the size of a rugby ball.' Bill and Charlie sat either side of their almost luminous colleague, their faces deadpan. Keith somehow got lost and spent most of the evening driving around London in the Lena, but later told a reporter he was 'chuffed' at the album, which he had no doubt would annoy Decca and get itself banned by the BBC. The future looked rosy.

In fact *Banquet* was a brilliant weave of bluesy simplicity and right-on lyrics, and a big hit both on radio and most university campuses. Punchy, mid-tempo guitar, sing-along choruses and crafty background effects were the main ingredients, Jimmy Miller's skill at the mixing desk sometimes masking the paucity of the actual tunes. After some seven years, the Stones showed that they were still at their best when they were mining American blues, soul and R&B, and giving those styles a new twist. 'Parachute woman, will you blow me out? Parachute woman, will you blow me out? Well my heavy throbber's itchin', Just to lay a solid rhythm down,' Jagger noted on 'Parachute Woman', and certainly Bill and Charlie, if not Mick's throbber, were on peak form throughout.

The kickoff, 'Sympathy for the Devil', was a perfect showcase for Jagger's game retelling of *The Master and Margarita*, spinning together an eerie collection of tales about Anastasia, the blitzkrieg and dead Kennedys. 'Prodigal Son' was a throwback to the days when Keith and Brian had jammed in Edith Grove, had a bratty swagger, and didn't need electricity to be heard – 'the charge came from within', as Stu said. Elsewhere, *Banquet*'s songs flowed naturally on classic blues licks instead of 'clever' inside musical jokes like *Satanic Majesties*. The requisitely trippy lyrics and nods to country rock were in the tradition of Dylan and Gram Parsons, respectively. 'Stray Cat Blues', which sounded like something Mick had hashed out with Lou Reed, managed to be both dark and catchy at the same time. Standing above it all, 'Street Fighting Man' balanced lo-fi technology and acoustic guitars against a riff that was so massive it deserved its own STD code.

Beggar's Banquet was released a year to the day after *Satanic Majesties*. In rock a 'roots' album has often served as a prop rather than a springboard for artistic growth. By risking everything, the Stones had performed the ultimate rescue act on their career.

From 10–12 December, the Stones rented the old *Ready Steady Go!* studios in north London to host a Christmas revue they called *The Rock and Roll Circus,* for an invited audience. The whole show was arranged on a handshake basis (something the various guest artists' lawyers would discuss at regular intervals until 1996), Bill noting that it was 'conceived by Mick, financed by us'. Allen Klein hadn't bothered answering the band's telegrams begging for seed money. As well as performances by the Who, Jethro Tull, Taj Mahal and other musicians, there were various fey, late-60s touches like a fire-eater, circus costumes for the rock stars and silly hats for the fans, and the arresting spectacle of a female trapeze artist hanging over-head as the terminally ill philosopher-pianist Julius Katchen played Brahms. A cowboy on horseback eventually announced the Stones, whose dawn set climaxed with six separate takes of 'Sympathy', in the final stages of which the audience was barely conscious. As a side-show attraction the band then paraded around the big top: Jagger appeared dressed as a ringmaster, Richards looked like one of the *Sergeant Pepper* dandies after a hard night, and Brian retreated in to his wispy, stoned, soft-featured self. Later, Keith elbowed Bill Wyman aside to play bass in a hastily assembled 'supergroup' with John Lennon, Eric Clapton and Mitch Mitchell. After performing Lennon's 'Yer Blues' they were abruptly joined by Yoko Ono, with Keith dutifully providing back-up for her glass-shattering shrieks. The surreal aspects of the *Circus* were reinforced by the presence of Elsa Smith, one of Jagger's teachers at Maypole Infant school, who was found hectoring the crowd about 'young Mike' and his alleged personal habits twenty years before. Tom Keylock was delegated to quietly remove her. The Stones seem to have been in two minds about their performance, and Keylock remembered driving Mick and Keith home, 'both of them pissed off because they'd gone on so late and tired, and the Who had upstaged them'. The film and album of *The Rock and Roll Circus* were shelved for the next twenty-eight years, becoming the Dead Sea Scrolls of lost 1960s documentaries.

Performance also languished on its completion that winter, after a decidedly mixed reception at a private screening for the Warner Brothers board who were financing the project. Even as the opening credits appeared, over disturbing scenes of homoerotic sadism (giving way to the gender fluidity and rock decadence of the film's later sequences) it had occurred to them that this wasn't quite the 'Stones version of *A Hard Day's Night*', as an early studio memo had put it. It's said that one elderly executive was physically ill at the preview, while other audience members 'fled in revulsion'. Having been cast as an androgynous, sex-mad rock god, Mick was strangely impressive in the role. Such was the zest of his and Anita's love-making scenes that Keith Richards refused to have anything to do with the *Performance* soundtrack, which Mick and Jack Nitzsche had to record using American session men. (Keith would, however, later remark that he had solaced the void during Anita's absence by again 'knocking Marianne', and that he'd been forced to exit rapidly through an upstairs window at Cheyne Walk one night when Mick came home unexpectedly early from filming.) According to Donald Cammell, Jagger burst in to tears when he remonstrated with him about the music. '"I'm sorry," he said. "I blew it." From then on, after all that indecisiveness, the decisions were made like *lightning*.' Tom Keylock recalled that while Keith was waiting for the money to buy a London property he often stayed at Robert Fraser's place in Mount Street. 'As you can imagine, he wasn't exactly chuffed that his girlfriend and best mate were off shagging on a film stage a few miles away. It was the same sort of triangle as Morocco, and Keith didn't like it a bit. I'd take him up to the set sometimes and he wouldn't get out of the car. We'd go back to Bob's place and I'd listen to him mutter about Mick, Anita and Donald Cammell, who he thought was a wanker.' Sitting there one rainy night among

Fraser's voodoo fetishes and Tibetan skull collection, Keith polished off the words and music of 'Gimme Shelter'.

Even after extensive editing, *Performance* horrified Warner Brothers no less than it did Keith, and the movie 'died in the can'; it was shelved for more than two years and finally opened at New York's Public Theater, an orphanage for lost films, in January 1971. It has never had a general release. *Performance*'s collage of fast cuts, swirling camerawork, drugs, S&M and disturbing close-ups of the normally suave James Fox in drag made it a cult classic. Midnight screenings of it were raided once or twice. The whole controversy dragged on for years, Mick once firing off a cable to Warners insisting they release it 'or sell it fast and no more bullshit', with some occasionally tragic results. One or two of the cast members' later lives, much like the film, proved unhappy, macabre, obscure and downright bleak. Fox's career suffered a sharp decline in the early 70s, following which he took a ten-year break from acting to join a religious sect called the Navigators. *Performance*'s co-director Donald Cammell and its technical adviser, the sometime Stones minder David Litvinoff, both committed suicide. Anita's lesbian interest in the film, Michelle Breton, a petite young Frenchwoman with cropped, boyish hair and incongruously full breasts, became a heroin pusher and disappeared in to the Marseilles underworld. Long presumed dead, the writer Mick Brown eventually located her living in Berlin. 'I've done nothing with my life,' she told him. 'Where did it start going wrong? I can't remember. It's something like destiny.' Breton's co-star John Bindon was tried for murder; acquitted, he later died in poverty. Mick Jagger has never acted as well since. Like Fox, Jagger spent much of *Performance* wearing female cosmetics and preparing for his scenes by smoking DMT, a drug so violently hallucinogenic it causes tiny haemorrhages around the brain. Despite or because of this unusual technique, Mick's performance remains the definitive portrait of 60s rock royalty, captured here in amber, living at the pinnacle of fame. For Keith Richards, meanwhile, the film's most enduring legacy may lie in the fact that, as he told Keylock as they drove up to collect Anita Pallenberg on the final day of shooting, 'I love the bitch, and I ain't letting her go.'

Inside a month, Anita was pregnant again.

On 18 December, Keith's twenty-fifth birthday, he, Mick, Anita and Marianne Faithfull flew to Lisbon and from there set sail for Peru.* Both couples were squabbling. In between visiting the ship's surgeon for shots of laudanum, Anita teased Keith about the paternity of the baby she was carrying. Although going on to suffer a violent haemorrhage, alluded to in 'Sister Morphine', she kept her child. Mick mingled with his fellow passengers in the first-class lounge clad in a transparent blouse, distressed red leather gaucho pants and a Bolivian army cap. After further offending the dress code at Lima's venerable Crillon Hotel, everyone moved on to a beach house in Rio de Janeiro, where they were joined by Marianne's 3-year-old son Nicholas and several dozen paparazzi. In time the Stones' creative unit found themselves on a besieged Christmas holiday with their respective partners, both of whom they'd each previously slept with, one of whom was pregnant with one or other of their children, and the other of whom was recovering from an allegedly drug-induced miscarriage, while her small son from her estranged husband played underfoot. Rock stars are different from you and me.

The press in Rio, with their uniquely relaxed libel laws, were soon reporting that the debauched *turistas* in their midst were dabbling in drugs, free sex and Satanism. 'We're hoping to see this magician,' noted Keith, a bit cryptically.

They were upcountry, staying at a cattle ranch for the weekend, when Richards casually took out a guitar and played Jagger the chord changes and melody of 'Let It Bleed'. The Stones' family break was beginning to assume a sanguinary theme. A few days later, Keith was fooling around with the open-G tuning and hit on the 'Honky Tonk Women' riff again. Mick wandered over and started tapping his foot, turning the plaintiff cowboy ballad in to a

---

*This festive cruise included the famous night when an elderly American passenger they dubbed 'Spiderwoman' squinted at Mick and Keith and said, 'You're *someone*, aren't you? Give me a glimmer.' The word stuck, and they billed themselves as the Glimmer Twins on and off for the next forty years.

ballsy, good-time rocker about laying a divorcee in New York City, and other romantic exploits. Back in London, they played the track to Gram Parsons, who told them he still heard a great country song there and that they should call his friend the fiddle player Byron Berline the moment he got out of his enforced stretch in the US Army. Six months later, Jimmy Miller recorded Berline playing in the parking lot of Hollywood's Elektra studio, as Miller cued in an associate to toot a car horn for added back-porch ambience. Berline remembers doing seven perfect takes 'before the bow slipped and I made a mistake, and that's the take they used'. 'Country Honk', as the number became, was both grainy and catchy, so languid in parts it was barely conscious, and absolutely nothing like any other song ever arranged by the Stones. It was credited to Jagger–Richards.

The Stones' friend Christopher Gibbs had gone along with Mick and Marianne when they drove out to see Stargroves for the first time, 'stopping at various hostelries along the way for a little sharpening up – a joint here, a line there – and arrived at the house to meet the then owner, a rather buttoned-up chap called Sir Henry Garden.' Like other Tory grandees who had expressed their misgivings about the Stones, Sir Henry had no qualms about selling them his property. Although Mick loved the pile's Gothic façade and sweeping grounds, he seems to have been less enamoured by its general air of dilapidation. Soon Frank Thorogood was spending long hours at Stargroves, making repairs designed to 'tart it up for resale, while knocking the central hallway around so you could record there'. Over the years, the manor's sixteenth-century rafters would be regularly shaken by the likes of the Who, Led Zeppelin and the Stones themselves – while up the gravel drive crunched a convoy of horse-drawn caravans led by Sir Mark Palmer, a baronet and former pageboy to the Queen, and now the head of a rather well-heeled band of New Age travellers. Mick tolerated the use of his back lawn as a campsite, and villagers grew used to the sight of Palmer's druidically robed acolytes appearing in the local shop to buy cigarette papers or a magazine of astrological data. At night bonfires could be seen flickering in the distance. 'In reality it was a grim place,' Palmer recalls, 'and Mick never really intended to fix it up and move in ... It did have big stables and all that sort of thing, so when winter came and we couldn't graze the horses any more, we all moved inside. We did that for a couple of winters ... Great masses of people were coming down from London to join us ... We had communal eating, and at night we listened to music together and smoked dope ... Everyone looking up at the stars, touching ... arms around ... sex ... Life as it should be lived. I'm not sure Jagger was as comfortable with all this as he pretended to be; Marianne was.'

Faithfull's miscarriage and the several professional disappointments that followed saw the beginning of a serious drug addiction that mocked the constrictions of her virginal, early-60s image. Soon, while Jagger was at the studio working on the new Stones album (also to be called *Let it Bleed*), Marianne was having sex with 'Spanish Tony' Sanchez in return for a steady supply of cocaine and, ultimately, heroin. From that point on, things began to deteriorate rapidly. 'My mother had me locked up in an insane asylum the first time I told her I was doing smack,' Marianne said. 'A really heavy place. Mick came and got me out.'

Meanwhile, Keith Richards and Anita Pallenberg were still based at Robert Fraser's flat, which the producers of *Performance* rented for them long after the film itself had wrapped. In March 1969, Keith finally prised enough cash out of Allen Klein to put down a deposit on 3 Cheyne Walk, a Queen Anne mansion immediately next to the one where the novelist George Eliot lived and died and, more to the point, down the road from Mick's house. The vendor was a former Conservative under-secretary of state named Sir Anthony Nutting, another case of the Establishment selling out to the Stones. Like Redlands before it, the property soon underwent a significant makeover. While Keith was working on *Let it Bleed,* Anita refurbished the home in a way designed to make even a Tory minister feel queasy. When Anthony Nutting casually dropped by to collect his post about a month later, he took one look at the front hallway and had to sit down. The house where Nutting had once entertained Winston Churchill to dinner was now furnished to rock-star perfection, from the glittering mirror-ball hanging from the ceiling to the black candlesticks and occult hieroglyphics daubed in the grand upstairs reception room. Anita had converted the oak-panelled library in to a scale-model of the casbah, with plump Moroccan cushions and joss-sticks throughout. The study where government officials had debated the Suez Crisis in 1956 was now occupied by a large hookah. A hunchbacked caretaker named Luigi habitually padded up and down the psychedelic-painted stairs with an antique mirror heaped with coke, in the aspect of a butler with a tea tray. When Keith and Anita were in residence, they shared the Regency bed on which she had done her sex scenes in *Performance*.

The underlying idea behind buying the house was to facilitate Keith's creative relationship with Mick Jagger, only 400 hundred yards away to the west. That quarter-mile or so neatly separated their two worlds. Mick's home had its exotic touches, including a Buddhist altar in an upstairs study overlooking the Thames, but it also had yellowed lace curtains at the windows, a floral sofa, and neatly fanned magazines on the coffee table. To Tom Keylock, 'What was most shocking about it was how normal it was. Keith's place was a Hammer-film set by comparison.'

Bill Wyman chose somewhat more conventional surroundings for himself, taking out a £40,000 mortgage on Gedding Hall, a moated and formally landscaped manor house near Bury St Edmunds in Suffolk. Although originally built in the thirteenth century, Wyman's country seat had a lively modern history. Bill bought the estate from an associate of the Kray twins, who had fled there on the night following their killing of Jack 'the Hat' McVitie in October 1967. The place was also said to be haunted by the ghost of a Victorian actress who had retired to the hall when her career failed and ended up hanging herself in the master bedroom. On taking possession, Bill officially became Lord of the Manor of Gedding and Thornwood. Five years earlier, he'd still been living in the room above the Sydenham garage. Brian Jones, meanwhile, was at Cotchford Farm, although he, too, sometimes stayed at Cheyne Walk, where Christopher Gibbs had a flat. 'It was a nightmare,' Gibbs, who was fond of Jones, recalled. 'Brian would appear, creating absolute chaos and burning holes in the sheets. I couldn't wait to be rid of him.' Charlie Watts was still in the Sussex countryside with his wife and infant daughter. Later that spring the film mogul Carlo Ponti, hot off his mordant Swinging Sixties study in *Blowup*, arrived in London with a 'trippy' science-fiction script called *Maxigasm*, in which he planned to cast Mick, Keith and Brian opposite a colony of hermaphrodite 'sky people', with whom they would make music and then engage in vigorous interplanetary sex. 'Charlie and I were obviously regarded as too straight for the project,' Bill notes. 'Fortunately for us, this was not a band investment.'

In fact, nothing united the Stones quite like their collective frustrations about money. The gist of the band's complaint was that Allen Klein was sweating them, making them beg for their own hard-earned cash. By late 1968 the initial 'You want it – you got it' euphoria had waned, and relations with 'Fatso' in New York had cooled to open enmity. Mick Jagger was said to be 'incandescent' when his younger brother Chris was once stranded in Kathmandu by Klein's failure to wire funds, and Mick himself went on to parody his business manager in a scene deleted from *The Rock and Roll Circus*. Before long, the Stones were being regularly threatened with eviction from their office and rehearsal studio, and there were problems even cashing their cheques. While albums like *Beggar's Banquet* and *Let It Bleed* were revolutionising modern rock, the songs' authors were trudging up the stairs at Maddox Street worrying about gas, phones and electricity. Jagger and Richards put their names to one telex ending, 'The power will be cut off tomorrow. Also the rent is due. We're having to run the office despite your wishes. If you would like to remedy this, please do so.' Even this plea failed to stir the remote presence in New York, and the Stones took out a bridging loan from their High Street bank. Jo Bergman, in a memo to the band, added: 'The Klein thing is more than a drag. We're puppets. How can you work, or the office, if we have to spend so much time pleading for bread? It's never going to be different till that's straightened out.'

Compounding the problem, Klein, Oldham and Eric Easton

were fighting a sulphurous three-way court battle over publishing rights, and the judge had frozen some £400,000 of the Stones' assets pending a settlement. As a result, ready cash was even tighter than usual. Mick was forced to keep up the pressure for funds to refurbish Stargroves: Klein ignored at least eight such cables between late August and early November, and eventually the Stones' book-keeper, Fred Trowbridge, had to write, 'Allen, what the fuck is happening? Where are Mick's cheques? Also, Berger Oliver [solicitors] are screaming for the balance of Bill's money . . . What about Brian's £6,000?' It then transpired that the £1 million Klein had extracted from Decca in July 1965 had been paid not in to a group account, as everyone had assumed, but in to an offshore company with himself as president and sole shareholder. In due course, Andrew Oldham was to claim in court that this had been used as 'a vehicle for the diversion of assets and income' from both him and the Stones. The judge seemed broadly to agree, dismissing Klein's testimony in the case as 'the prattling of a second-class salesman'. Meanwhile, the band's accountants had sent a recorded letter to New York, dated 28 October 1968: 'There is a continuing problem with the outstanding information that we need to complete the Stones' personal Income Tax Returns and Partnership Accounts to date. Allen, our clients' best interests are being prejudiced . . . Unless you act, this matter can prove ruinous to all concerned.'

In March 1969, as students occupied Mick's old college buildings to express their disapproval of the Vietnam War, the Stones were back in Olympic studios to record *Let it Bleed*. Brian was an only fitful presence. Tom Keylock saw one such session where the man he calls the band's 'moron-genius' laid down some African drums on 'Midnight Rambler'. 'It took him a fuck of a long time,' said Keylock, who went on to make a diary note of the precise order of events. 'Everything first ground to a halt because Brian went to hit the drums, missed them completely and fell over backwards in to an amp, which knocked over its neighbour like a row of dominoes. No one blinked. "Bad luck," Charlie muttered after a bit. "Is it the snakes again, man?" On the next take, Brian dropped his fag end down the front of his shirt, tripped on a guitar lead and collided head first with a pillar, which again brought things to a screeching stop.' There were, in all, fourteen takes before Keith said 'Fuck it' and marched off to his Bentley. Peter Swales would remember Jagger later complaining, 'We can't deal with this any more. If Brian doesn't fucking perform tonight, he's out of the band,' an ultimatum Swales himself delivered 'at least six times'.

Jones eventually checked in for another rehab stint, this time at the Priory clinic, accompanied not by Suki Potier but a 19-year-old Swedish student and aspiring professional disco dancer named Anna Wohlin. Friends smiled that Brian's partners had become, like Russian dolls, diminishing or at least younger versions of the same basic type – 'and they all look exactly like Anita', Tom Keylock wrote in his diary. Keylock thought the free-spirited but vehemently anti-drug Wohlin was good news for Brian, and that 'Mick and Keith also indulged him a lot. They were pissed off with the guy, but I think they were genuinely worried, too.' There was some talk about flying Phil Kaufman in from California to look after Jones full-time, but this collapsed in the face of various visa and cash problems. Keith seems to have been particularly saddened by recent events, and told Keylock to arrange a delivery of roses from Chivers the Florist 'whenever Brian seems down'. Over the next few months, Keylock would run up a heavy bill with Chivers.

Mick Jagger, meanwhile, was beginning to wonder whether being a major rock star was all that life had to offer. Later that spring, he invested £10,000 in a British edition of *Rolling Stone* magazine, which its editor Jann Wenner had named after his favourite band. On 21 March, Mick registered the name Trans-Oceanic Comic Company for the project, and took offices for it in Hanover Square. Although the venture collapsed after Allen Klein withheld his support, Mick was clearly keen to expand in to new fields. Later that month, he signed up for the title role in Tony Richardson's bush-outlaw film *Ned Kelly*, and there was talk of him following Marianne Faithfull on to the 'straight' stage, possibly even in a production of *Hamlet*. Mick was also the guiding force behind the Rolling Stones' Mobile, often consulting an accounts book where, according to Keylock, 'he kept a detailed record of every mile the lorry drove and every hour its equipment was in use'.

The realisation that life as a rock singer might not sate his ambitions represented a major turning point in Jagger's career. By mid-1969 he exercised almost total control of the Stones' corporate expenses (begging letters from radical political groups, in particular, were 'promptly binned', says Keylock) and soon linked up with 'Prince' Rupert Loewenstein, a Mozart-loving Bavarian aristocrat and chairman of the London merchant bankers Leopold Joseph, who went on to become the band's financial adviser for the next forty years. Loewenstein had never heard a Rolling Stones song at the time he took over their affairs, although he had read – and 'rather disapproved of' – *The Times* editorial supporting Mick and Keith at the time of their drugs trial. Jagger also kept a tight rein on his own expenditure. The general feeling seemed to be that the money could go just as fast as it had come. 'Mick,' Ian Stewart said, 'could always sit down to dinner and remember three hours later who had the scampi and who had the prawn curry,' while Marianne Faithfull enjoyed an allowance of just £25 a week throughout the late 1960s.

It's debatable how much of Jagger's increasingly stringent management of the Stones reflected his own nature and LSE training, and how much was a reaction to events unfolding around him. As well as the corporate frustrations with both Klein and Decca, and the band's delicate visa status thanks to their various court appearances, Keith Richards was now busily expanding his drug intake to something approaching its classic 1970s levels. 'Maybe the frenetic pace of life had something to do with it,' Keith later reflected of his morning routine at the time. 'I would take a barbiturate to wake up, a recreational high compared to heroin, though just as dangerous in its own way. That was breakfast. A Tuinal, pin it, put a needle in it so it would come on quicker. And then take a hot cup of tea, and then consider getting up or not. And later maybe a Mandrax or Quaalude, [followed by] downers to keep going ... I would use drugs like gears – [they] smoothed my path in to the day.' Full-scale smack addiction wasn't long in coming. Keith solved his core supply problem by installing a married couple who happened to be registered users – and thus eligible, under the law of the day, for a regular state-sponsored fix – in the spare room of his staff cottage. Once or twice a week, the couple would take the bus in to Boots in Chichester and come back again with a bag of heroin pills which, in a mutually convenient arrangement, they would share with their landlord in lieu of rent. Keith had been so wrecked at *The Rock and Roll Circus* that even Brian Jones had been alarmed at his condition. Brian later told his friend Helen Spittal he'd 'never seen Keith as high on drugs as he had been that day. And he was worried about it. He was really genuinely concerned about it. From experience, I guess, seeing the way Keith could go if he wasn't careful.'

They saw a lot of Keith at Redlands that spring of 1969. After some three years the place was at last fully furnished, the heavy Moroccan drapes shutting out the scenes of wanton drug use and sexual debauchery – inappropriate here in West Wittering. Keith spent long hours in front of the fire or out on the back terrace, shirt splayed open as if for heart surgery, a joint and a guitar typically close at hand. Keylock remembered a sunny day there when 'Brian turned up ... He, Mick and Keith were inside drinking and talking about trying to get the show back on the road. Pretty soon it turned in to a shouting match with Mick and Brian going at each other, and the next thing I know Brian was running full steam across the lawn yelling that he was going to top himself. At that he leaped back in to the moat. "Fuck 'im," said Keith, switching on the telly. Eventually Mick had to wade in and do a search and rescue job. What he didn't know, which Keith and me did, was that Brian was squatting down in about two feet of water. He couldn't have drowned if he'd tried. Mick wasn't pleased. There was a lot of "You fucking bastard" and "Look at these fucking velvet trousers", I remember. Very bitter about it, he was.'

Relations between Redlands' jaded-looking squire and the community were also sometimes rocky. A man named Nick Gough who saw the Blue Lena making off towards London remembers watching with great interest, not least because the car happened to be the exact same make and model as the one used by the Lord Lieutenant of Sussex, who had just paid a visit to the area. Gough was peering as best he could through the tinted glass, when Anita leaned out of the window and bellowed at him, 'Peese off!' before adding what Charles Keeley would have called 'a parting gesture with two fingers'. It suddenly occurred to Gough that perhaps the Bentley wasn't on official business, after all, but he bears Keith and Anita no ill will. Twenty-five years later, one of Gough's closest friends was to write a letter on behalf of West Sussex Council, appealing for funds to save the village memorial hall. The committee wondered whether local residents might each be willing to donate £30. No problem, said Keith, and wrote out a cheque for £30,000.

Ry Cooder came back to play on the Stones sessions in May 1969. He later complained that the band 'weren't doing well and were just messing around the studio. There were a lot of very weird people hanging around the place, but the music wasn't going anywhere. When there'd be a lull in the rehearsals, I'd start to play my guitar. Keith Richards would leave the room immediately and never return, [but] the tapes kept rolling' – later producing the cult album *Jamming with Edward*. For a while, at least, Cooder was in the frame to replace Brian Jones, and Tom Keylock later heard 'Mick, in his usual roundabout way, ask Eric Clapton if he had any plans'. Clapton happened to be forming Blind Faith at the time, and so declined the offer. (Mick then put in a call to a young, good-time guitarist named Ron Wood, of the Faces, only for the band's bassist Ronnie Lane to pick up the phone and politely pass on Woody's behalf.) Keith returned the minute Cooder left, sending waves of energy through the remaining *Let it Bleed* sessions. The Stones cut the raw tracks of 'Monkey Man' and 'Jiving Sister Fanny' (later inexplicably left off the album) in one take. A shimmeringly fluid version of Robert Johnson's 'Love in Vain', oddly credited to 'Trad', soon followed. Keith's guitar gave up the fight and fell in half on the climactic meltdown note of 'Gimme Shelter'. The rest of the music went well, though production hassles and personnel changes kept the band at Olympic until mid-June. On the last night, in a Cinderella moment in the empty studio after the basic album was finished and the gear was being stowed, Keith turned to Ian Stewart as the latter balanced an amp on his broad shoulders. 'That was a gas, man,' he laughed. Stu's response was a masterpiece of courtesy and tact. 'Yeah, I'm glad I made the gig.'

Meanwhile, Mick was dividing his time between sorting out the Stones' finances and establishing himself at the top of the 'A' list for parties and premieres. Jack Nitzsche would remember 'Jagger turn[ing] up at the Royal Opera House in the back of an open-top yellow sports car driven by a minder, cigarette in one hand and unspilled drink in the other ... Later everyone sat down in a restaurant, and Mick immediately split. I think he did it just to make an entrance.' But Jagger also went to the wall for Marianne Faithfull when Decca first released and then, two days later, abruptly withdrew her single of 'Sister Morphine', apparently horrified to discover that it was about drugs. Still fuming from the long and fruitless saga of the *Beggar's Banquet* artwork, Mick saw red at this latest display of corporate censorship, promising that it spelled the end of the Stones' own association with the label. He was to remain outspokenly loyal to Faithfull and her musical ambitions right through their four-year relationship. Mick may have strayed from the monogamous ideal, but 'no one fucked with Marianne's career while he was around', Keylock observed.

Over time, various extracurricular Stones projects would meet with similar frustrations. Bill Wyman was forced to cable Klein, 'The End are fed up waiting for their record to be shipped and with promises you have given them,' while even the genial Charlie complained about the delay in releasing a jazz album he'd produced for the People Band. Charlie himself never stooped to threats, but Peter Swales telexed Klein on his behalf: 'He has asked me to do what I can to get [the album] released ... Charlie has heard nothing ... At this stage he would be very pleased to get just the cost of it back. He doesn't honestly envisage any incredible sales. In fact people might go so far as to say it's crap. But remember there is a large market for these sort of things in Germany.' Jo Bergman, mean-

while, was firing off daily enquiries about Brian Jones' recording of
the master musicians of Jajouka. 'Elektra wants Brian's album.
What's happening? Brian hysterical.'

In time, his assorted physical ailments convinced Brian that he
could actually die before the record was out. When one of his
heroes, the American jazz saxophonist Coleman Hawkins, went
prematurely that May, Brian told friends like the Korners and the
Perrins that the end was near and began preparing himself and his
family for it. 'I'm getting everything together for you,' he calmly
informed his parents when they came down to Cotchford Farm for
the weekend of 24–25 May, as he spread out his huge collection of
photographs, newspaper cuttings, tour souvenirs, contracts and fan
mail from as far back as 1961 on to the oak breakfast table. A muted
effort had been afoot over the late winter and spring to persuade
Lewis and Louisa Jones to move in to a staff flat on the premises, an
offer they politely refused. Frank Thorogood would remember how
Brian's parents had pored over his display at the kitchen table with
a mixture of pride and mounting apprehension, and how Brian had
later referred to them as 'clueless'. Jones also began planning his
funeral in some detail, repeatedly telling both Thorogood and Tom
Keylock that he wanted to be 'buried, not burned', and specifying
a quiet corner of the garden at Cotchford, near one of the statues
of Winnie the Pooh, for the interment. Keylock recalled that he'd
even spoken about the design of the coffin ('the lining had to be in
either satin or silk of a precise shade of blue') he wanted for the
occasion, as he'd seen and 'fallen in love with' that particular style
when strolling past an undertaker's shop window in New York a
few years earlier. At twenty-seven, Jones didn't find this at all
morbid.

Two days after seeing his parents off for the last time, Brian made
his final recorded contribution to the Stones. Sitting in a corner by
himself, he laid down a few haunting notes on 'You Got the Silver',
Keith's great love song to Anita. 'It's fair to say Brian was badly
depressed,' Thorogood reflected. 'For such a cocky man he har-
boured enormous insecurities and fears. At the same time as he was
a big rock star he was also a nice Cheltenham boy, and despite

everything you read later on I got to like him a lot. When you were alone with Brian over a bottle of wine he was just this shy kid with a bit of a lisp. Always asking you about your family. "Oh, Frank, you must bring your daughter down," that sort of thing. Remembered everybody's birthday. We had these hard-core builders coming down from south London prepared to hate him, and they all went away again thinking he was the nicest guy in the world': not the words of someone likely, just a few weeks later, to attack Brian in a sustained homicidal rage.

On 28 May, Mick Jagger and Marianne Faithfull were visited at Cheyne Walk by Detective Sergeant Robin Constable and half a dozen colleagues. Constable happened to be the very officer who had last busted Brian a year earlier. Reports vary as to what happened next. 'I didn't get a chance to say anything,' Jagger complained. 'One of the coppers put his hand over my mouth, another stuck his foot in the door, and the rest came barging in' – while in later court testimony Mick was said to have 'seen police in the street and dashed home through a window shouting, "Marianne, Marianne, don't open the door! They're after the weed!".' But the narcs got in anyway, pushed Mick in to the dining room and returned a few minutes later holding a small Cartier box which had previously held a collection of sea-shells from Margate beach, but now contained white powder. Mick and Marianne were taken to Chelsea police station, charged with possession, and bailed at fifty pounds each. Mick later claimed in an interview that he'd been invited to pay 'around a grand' in order for the law to lose the evidence. Sergeant Constable then sued for libel, though subsequently dropped his case before it came to court.

Thirty-five years later, the British National Archives released the details of the internal Metropolitan Police investigation in to the matter. Although they don't settle the question of who was telling the truth, they do offer some insight in to the culture clash of the late 1960s. According to the file, 'both Mr Constable and Jagger examined the powder on its discovery. The latter dipped his finger in and licked it. "I would not know what heroin is like," he said, "but this tastes like talcum powder to me."' Robert Huntley, the commander of the Metropolitan Police complaints unit, summed up the case like this: 'The private persons interviewed during the course of this enquiry represent extreme ends of a scale. At one end are respected law-enforcement officers and public figures whilst at the other are the dregs of society. It is interesting to note that those who purport to give first-hand evidence in support of [Jagger's] allegation are at the lower end of the scale, being drug users or pop stars.' (On one of the copies of the report, an unknown hand amended this to ask: 'What's the difference?') Notwithstanding the 'very persuasive evidence that Mr Constable acted properly in the affair', it was deemed best to transfer him to the Surrey Police and out of the Rolling Stones' lives forever.

Two nights later, a young, vegetarian, teetotal guitar player named Mick Taylor got a call from Keith Richards. It was a surprising approach on a number of levels. Hertfordshire born and raised, Taylor was the son of a fitter in an aircraft factory, and thus more 'working class' than any of the Stones, with the possible exception of Charlie Watts. He had never been abroad. He had hardly been to London. He had, however, been playing the guitar since he was eight years old. In 1965, when he was sixteen, Taylor had gone to see a concert by John Mayall's Bluesbreakers near his home in Welwyn Garden City. When Mayall's featured sideman, Eric Clapton, failed to appear (he was later found on a beach in Greece), Taylor shyly offered his services for the night. Eighteen months later, he was a full-time member of Mayall's band and attracting widespread attention for his melodic, blues-based playing, which could keep it short and sharp or soar off in to extended jazzy instrumentals. In time, Mayall selflessly recommended him to the Stones. Taylor had been a 13-year-old schoolboy when the band made their debut at the Marquee, and just fourteen when they had their first hits. He'd never bought one of the Stones' records, or seen them perform live; he preferred the Beatles. Even now, at twenty, Taylor looked almost impossibly young, peering up at people from bulging blue eyes out of an aura of blond fuzz.

Tom Keylock was there to witness the guitarist's first late-night arrival at Olympic. 'They'd actually had about six session men in to audition already. The trouble was, all those other guys were trying to play like they thought the Rolling Stones did, not the way they played themselves. So after all the Keith-clones had been and gone, Taylor plugged in and immediately started ripping off these wild Latin solos that sounded like absolutely nothing any of the Stones, including Brian, had ever done before. I looked over at Jagger and his mouth was open. I mean, he was *gone*.' Taylor's first job was to provide the slow and stately fills to Keith's guitar stabs on 'Live with Me', which he accomplished with a few flicks of his exquisitely delicate, bony fingers. No one had ever sculpted such sounds, with such apparent ease, on to a Rolling Stones record. It was irresistible.★ 'I thought they were all a bit vain and full of themselves,' Taylor recalls of his first Stones session. 'I said to Mick and Keith, "If you guys are just going to sit and mess around, I'm going home. I've got things to do." I told them to give me a call if they wanted me to do anything else.'

The next night, the Stones sent a chauffeured car for Taylor. 'I wasn't impressed by all that and I think they kind of liked my attitude.' When he got to Olympic, Taylor found a representative group scene awaiting him: while Ian Stewart humped in the gear, Bill and Charlie sat at their instruments idly swapping cricket scores, and Mick could be seen off to the side doing an interview for *International Times*. As the band lounged around, whole careers were actually beginning and ending. Keith finally lurched in hours late, looking heavy-lidded, grabbed his Fender, exhaled a cloud of smoke and, take one – after Stu had refreshed his memory of it on the piano – nailed the 'Honky Tonk Women' riff. Charlie started a drum pattern (a fraction off-time, and all the better for it) and Jimmy Miller picked up the beat on a cowbell. Jagger's slurped vocals, then brass and more crackling guitar. Like all true originals, 'Honky Tonk Women' had a past to which it simultaneously paid tribute and waved goodbye. Its roots lay in a fusion of Richards' new, countrified open-tunings and a reworking of 'I Heard It through the Grapevine', wrapped

★Six months later, Bobby Keys, the Texan sax player, and a Stones satellite ever since, went in to Elektra studios in Los Angeles to rasp out a solo on the same song, which thus assumed a significance above and beyond its considerable charms as a barrelhouse rocker.

around a soulful, James Brown groove. Keith and Charlie brought the deft syncopation and equally smart ear for a killer hook, goosing the song to a shouted, orgasmic finish. Mick Taylor was there and thought he was listening to the greatest single ever recorded. 'Honky Tonk Women' was radio heaven, a collage of classic pop ideas wedged in to exactly three minutes.

Next day, Mick and Keith offered Taylor a job.

7 June 1969: Keith Richards wrecked his new customised Mercedes convertible (a remodelled Nazi tank), taking a narrow corner outside Redlands at 70mph. The car spun in the air twice, ejecting Keith as it did so. He was unhurt. A heavily pregnant Anita broke her collarbone and suffered cuts and bruises, but otherwise she, and her baby, were fine. 'Spanish Tony' Sanchez helped Keith empty the glove compartment of 'bags of heroin, cocaine, grass and opium', which they hid in the branches of a nearby oak tree, and got everyone to hospital in Chichester. The drugs squad was waiting for them on their release. By now several of the Stones and their women were on terms of some intimacy with their local law enforcement. The first policeman in to the interview room at Chichester, after squinting at Richards and Pallenberg, both of them still covered in blood, said, 'I know you – I raided your gaff.' A subsequent 'cavity search' turned up three disposable syringes and a half-dozen phials tucked in to Anita's underwear, but she successfully persuaded the rozzers they all contained 'vitamins'. Keith and Tony Sanchez later discreetly recovered the drugs from the oak tree.

Next day, Keith mixed 'Honky Tonk Women' from 2 p.m. to 7 p.m., then he, Mick and Charlie drove to Cotchford Farm. Brian had been drinking steadily all evening and was waiting for them. Alexis Korner had been down to visit earlier in the week, and was shocked when he saw what the famous dandy now looked like: Brian had grown plump, and Korner would remember him settling down after a meal with his acoustic guitar, spreading beyond the narrow confines of his dining room chair 'like a ripe cheese'. Brian talked about the Stones rarely, and about Anita constantly.

Keith Richards: 'We had to go down and virtually tell him, "Hey, old cock, you're fired." Because there was no serious way we could go on the road with Brian. The fact that he was expecting it made it easier. He wasn't surprised. I don't think he even took it all in. He was already up in the stratosphere. He was like, "Yeah, man, OK."' Jones was still sharp enough to remind his guests that it was he who'd come up with the name 'the Rolling Stones' in the first place, but after making his point he affably agreed to a statement citing 'musical differences', a then-popular euphemism for the atmosphere of mutual loathing that characterised many a pop group's demise. 'Whatever you guys do is fine by me,' Brian added. He declined, however, to share a no-hard-feelings joint with his old mates, insisting he wanted to 'stay clean'. As the interview ended, Frank Thorogood came down from the flat at the top of the house, and long remembered Jones standing by the front door, bidding the Stones a cheery farewell, smiling and waving until their car disappeared round a bend, before walking slowly back to the terrace overlooking the swimming pool. At first, Brian had seemed 'almost amused' by the whole visit. 'Mick kept talking about how another trial could screw up our chances of ever getting in to the States again ... *I'm* not the one who's just been fucking busted,' he remarked, with some justification. But Thorogood had learned to adjust to his employer's moods. After a few more brandies, Jones seemed to fall in to a sort of funk. For a long time, he sat silently watching the water fade in the night. Then Brian's lips moved, though just barely, and he spoke in a voice so soft Thorogood had to strain to hear it from 3 feet away.

'Bastards,' he said.

On Friday 13 June, the first of 200 journalists pulled up behind a small, roped-off enclosure in the southeast corner of Hyde Park. There they met a hearty Jagger and a stoned Richards, who announced both the name of their new recruit, and the date – Saturday 5 July – of their biggest ever concert. The Stones were back: official.

The two Micks, Keith, Bill and Charlie limbered up for the event with a week of all-night rehearsals in the Beatles' basement studio at their office in Savile Row. 'I couldn't believe it,' says Taylor, for whom professional disillusionment came on fast, 'because there was such a huge difference between the way the Stones sounded on record and the way we sounded down there. Everything was out of tune, sloppy ... Most of the magic was down to the people who were producing. We had Jimmy Miller and great musicians like Nicky Hopkins and Billy Preston. Otherwise they could have sounded like any old Camden Town blues band.' Mick Jagger and, latterly, Marianne Faithfull were also preparing for their roles in *Ned Kelly*, which would be shot on location in Australia. Bill was concerned about repairs to his country home, and Charlie, distressed both about Brian's departure and the latest 'Stone Busted' headlines his mum and dad had rung him up about, was talking about packing it all in to join a jazz band. As usual, everyone was uptight about money. Brian had been offered a settlement of £20,000 a year for as long as the Stones lasted. Mick Taylor was on £120 a week, which was better than the dole but still only about what a provincial head teacher earned, and Keith was busy sending a telex to Allen Klein's office in New York: 'I was promised £55,000 and I must have it by Tuesday at the outside. Get it together. No, repeat *no* excuses, will be accepted for any delay whatsoever.' 'Will I also be getting my $72,000 for my country-house repairs, too?' Mick added in a plaintive postscript.

Wednesday 2 July. Back at Cotchford, Brian Jones spent that afternoon and evening wheezing with asthma, medicating himself with his inhaler and several bottles of Blue Nun wine. Frank Thorogood and his girlfriend Janet Lawson, a nurse, were spending the night in the flat at the top of the house. Around nine o'clock, Brian knocked on the door and asked if they'd care to join Anna Wohlin and him for a drink out by the pool. Contrary to reports, there were no other builders, disgruntled ex-employees or mysterious hired assassins of any sort on the premises. If Jones and Thorogood argued, as has been said, neither Lawson nor Wohlin thought to mention it in their quite extensive statements at the time. It's true Brian was often a mixture of charm and chaos, but no one who saw him that warm summer evening said he was anything but agreeably tipsy. Twenty-one years later, Thorogood told me that reports that Jones had just given him the sack, and/or owed him money, thus contributing to the strained relations that in turn led him to drown Brian, were 'Cobblers ... First of all, I was getting paid direct by the Stones' office, not out of Brian's back pocket, so I never had any problems there. And second, I was working [for Brian] at most two days a week, along with doing up David Bailey's place in Regent's Park and about half a dozen other jobs. In those days, I had more work than I needed. Much as I liked Brian, he was just another part-time client.'

Thorogood did, however, mention that on the morning of 2 July, he'd set the thermostat in Jones' pool to 'somewhere between the high eighties and low nineties' – the police later found it at 92°F – 'after Brian had complained it was "fucking freezing" the night before'. The water temperature was thus close to that of an average warm to hot bath. It's true that, under normal circumstances, Jones was a strong swimmer and had once impressed his bandmates by venturing out in to the breakers off Fiji while the other Stones watched nervously from the beach. But set against this was the fact that Brian had been steadily downing wine followed by double brandies, giving him a blood-alcohol level equivalent to 2.2 mg per ml, or some three times the current UK drink-driving limit, as well as taking a variety of Mandrax and Tuinals throughout the late afternoon and evening of 2 July. It seems fair to say, too, that his overall physical condition had deteriorated significantly in the seven years since he had picked up the phone to *Jazz News* and, on the spot, casually come up with the name of his new band. As the coroner's report found, Jones was now suffering from 'liver dysfunction due to extensive fatty degeneration', as well as a dangerously enlarged heart, incipient pleurisy and asthma, not the best state of affairs in which to dive in to hot water late at night. For all the rumours about Brian's death, still regularly exercising the press and conspiracy-mongers today, the most plausible verdict remains the official one, misadventure, as both the coroner's inquest and the Stones' own quite thorough in-house inquiry found at the time.

Whatever the truth about Frank Thorogood's involvement, if any, it's hard to see how he could be said to have gained from the events of that summer night; the Stones' office dispensed with his services just a week later, and as other jobs evaporated in the wake of the continuing rumours about his role in Brian's death, Thorogood steadily fell in to debt and ill health. He died in October 1993, aged sixty-seven.

After finishing his sixth or seventh brandy of the evening, Jones – 'seeming anxious to be occupied', Janet Lawson recalled – suggested a swim. It's thought to have been around 11 p.m., based on the sounds of a wrestling match on television they could hear echoing out through the French doors. All parties agree Brian staggered noticeably on the diving board and hit the water like a depth charge. His two Afghan hounds, the home's principal security system, immediately began barking in alarm. Frank Thorogood paused in the process of discreetly changing in to his trunks, and 'half-ran, half-hopped' to the edge of the pool. But when Brian came up for air he was laughing, and in Janet Lawson's words, as quoted in the police report, 'started swimming quite merrily'. Thorogood joined him in the water and the two women walked back to the house, taking the dogs with them. A minute later, the television went off. Lawson also noted that in her medical opinion, 'Frank and Brian were in no condition to swim ... I wanted to disassociate myself [from] them.' Thorogood himself would recall Brian murmuring softly 'I love this place' – his last words – and then settling back to float silently around the deep end. By now the garden was quite still, head-high in mist, the clouds seeping in the pool like fluid, the surface of the water acting as a filter. All around, the Pooh effigies were fading fast. The two men drifted about, without speaking further, for some twenty minutes. Thorogood remembered that the scene gradually took on a sinister hue as everything around them disappeared, leaving only a patch of brilliantly tiled, floodlit water. When he announced he was going in, Brian merely grunted. It was midnight.

By the time Thorogood walked the twenty yards to the house, dried, and lit a cigarette, five minutes may have passed. At that point a phone rang, a not uncommon late-night occurrence at Cotchford, and Janet Lawson came downstairs to ask where Brian was. Without waiting for the reply, she pushed past an apparently 'sweating' – or possibly just still damp – Thorogood and ran back out to the garden. Those inside the house heard her give a loud scream. Thorogood and Wohlin in turn quickly made their way back to the terrace, over-looking the deep end of the pool. Brian was lying face down there, his arms and legs spread out in a cross formation, his hair swirling like seaweed. At the third try, Thorogood managed to get him out of the water and on to his back in the warm grass. Years later, Wohlin would recall how Brian seemed to squeeze her hand when she felt for a pulse, yet he never actually regained consciousness. Half an hour later, the police pronounced him dead at the scene.

The Stones were back at Olympic, tinkering with a Stevie Wonder song called 'I Don't Know Why', when the call came.

Keith Richards: 'We were at a session and someone rang us up at midnight and said, "Brian's dead." Well, what the fuck's going on? I don't know, man, I just don't know what happened that night. If anybody was going to kill Brian, it was going to be me.' Richards later remarked that he was more shocked than surprised at the news. In 2002, when *Rolling Stone* asked Keith who he missed most among the friends and colleagues he had known who had died over the years, he failed to mention Brian.

Mick Jagger immediately summoned Frank Thorogood to ask him in detail what had happened that night and initially, at least, seemed inclined to the theory that Brian was depressed and had somehow killed himself, as he'd often threatened to do in the past. Charlie Watts dismissed the conspiracy theories even before they began. 'I think he took an overdose. He took a load of downers, which is what he used to like, and drank, and I think he went for a swim in a very hot bath.' Years later, Mick seemed to come round to this same point of view when he said, 'Brian drowned in his pool. The other stuff is people trying to make money.'

Twelve hours after hearing the devastating news of Jones' death, the Rolling Stones were strutting out 'Honky Tonk Women' on

Top of the Pops. Backstage, a BBC reporter with a film crew in tow introduced himself with the provocative remark: 'Excuse me, Mr Richards. How do you carry on, under the circumstances?' Keith allegedly grabbed the man by the tie, lifted him up and threw him against a wall. The new single was out the next day: Keith's serrated riff and Charlie's classic drum groove made it the Stones' biggest hit yet. Mick Taylor had been in the band just over a month, and had already experienced more real-life dramas than in his previous three years as a musician. Watching Bill and Charlie pace up and down the Maddox Street office, alternately cursing and crying, Taylor would remember 'a sense of inevitability, as if everyone had been half-expecting it to happen'.

Two days later, Taylor gave his first public performance with the Stones, a free concert for 300,000 people in Hyde Park. The stage was dominated by a huge blow-up poster of Brian Jones, a drunken leer on his pasty face. Mick Jagger appeared in a white frock, blew kisses from his fingertips, and addressed the overflow audience: 'Aawrite ... OK, now listen ... Will you just *cool it* for a minute ... 'Cause I really would like to say something for Brian ... And I'd really dig it if you'd be with us for what I'm going to say. I really don't know how to do this' – a conclusion much of the crowd had reached already – 'but I'm going to try ... I hope you can just cool it before we start ... I'd really appreciate it if I could just say a few words about what I feel about Brian ... and I'm sure you do ... what we feel about him just *going'* – here Jagger's hand floated upwards – 'when we didn't expect him to ... OK?'

Mick then picked up a book and read some lines from Shelley's *Adonais*. In a rock-comeback performance almost visibly straining at the leash, he began to pump his foot up and down in the final verses. As the recital ended, Tom Keylock and his crew produced cardboard boxes at the side of the stage and released 2,000 white butterflies in to the sky, while several hundred more fell to the ground, having already perished in their confinement. At that, Mick let out a yell, spun round and, signifying one of those rapid mood swings that form the basic theme of his career, energetically shook his can at the audience, before cuing in the power chords of Johnny

Winter's 'I'm Yours, She's Mine'. Keith got off some snaky, Nashville-style guitar fills, but the anticlimax came on fast: halfway through the opening number, everybody was out of tune. Jagger chose to perform a subsequent song while bent double over a hand-mike squeezed between his thighs, an unorthodox way to honour a fallen colleague. A group of what Les Perrin's press release described as 'specially imported South African tribal dancers and warriors' then joined the Stones for an extended version of 'Sympathy for the Devil', until Mick drew his finger across his throat in the time-honoured way, and the Zulus went off to wait patiently for Tom Keylock to drive them home to Brixton.

In the course of the concert, 425 fans fainted in the heat. There were no significant public-order disturbances. After an hour, the Stones themselves sidled off to a combined party and business meeting with Allen Klein at the nearby Londonderry House hotel. Unbeknown to Klein, Jagger was already negotiating with the suave, 36-year-old banker Rupert Loewenstein to take control of the Stones' finances. The band's original seven-year contract with Decca was due to expire in May 1970, and Mick, having grown weary of 'Fatso's' dilatory accounting procedures, wanted to capitalise on the event. Earlier in the day, Tom Keylock had found himself alone in the hotel lift with Klein, and took the opportunity to tell him, 'You've screwed this band rotten.' 'It's a rotten business,' Klein replied, apparently unfazed by the indictment. Keylock later described the Stones' incoming and outgoing business managers as respectively 'a Crufts champion and a pit-bull'.

Five days later, Brian Jones was buried in Cheltenham. Keylock made all the arrangements, losing the argument about Brian's resting-place to his parents, but successfully flying in the blue silk-lined coffin from New York. More than 600 mourners gathered outside the parish church where Jones had sung as a choirboy. Among those who attended were Charlie, Bill, Stu, Frank Thorogood and several former lovers clutching Brian's children. Among those who didn't were Keith Richards, Anita Pallenberg and Andrew Oldham.

Mick Jagger and Marianne Faithfull were already in Sydney, preparing for their roles in *Ned Kelly*. Over the past six months,

Mick had spent an increasing amount of time both recording with the Stones and seeing a 22-year-old black American singer-actress, Marsha Hunt, whom he affectionately dubbed 'Fuzzy-Wuzzy', while, back at Cheyne Walk, his 'old lady' gradually succumbed to heroin addiction. Jagger and Hunt had a child together in November 1970. After mulling things over on the flight to Australia, Marianne lay down next to a sleeping Mick in their hotel suite that night and took 150 Tuinal sleeping pills, roughly four times the normally fatal dose. He saved her life. Six days later, she woke up in hospital and told Mick, 'I was in this big, grey, still place where there was no climate at all. And Brian Jones was there.'

Back in Cheltenham, Canon Hugh Hopkins offered a prayer for Marianne's recovery, before telling the congregation, 'Brian had little patience with authority, convention and tradition. In this he was typical of many of his generation who have come to see in the Stones an expression of their whole attitude to life. Much that this ancient church has stood for in 900 years seems irrelevant to them.' The canon then quoted from Luke 15, the parable of the Prodigal Son, and from the telegram Brian had sent his parents at the time of his first drugs arrest – 'Please don't judge me too harshly.'

As Brian's coffin was lowered in to the grave (12 feet deep, to deter souvenir hunters), an unidentified woman threw down a single yellow rose on top of it. Several photographers craned in for their final shots. Of all the haunting memories Tom Keylock had of that day, none stayed with him longer than the sight of a 'large blue policeman who, just as the gravediggers started shovelling the dirt on top of Brian, looked down and suddenly snapped to attention. Then he saluted.'

5

TROPICAL DISEASE

Five days after Brian Jones' funeral, Mick Jagger gave orders for the first Rolling Stones tour of North America in over three years. Allen Klein was busy dealing with the breakup of his other marquee British act, the Beatles, as well as trying to buy a controlling interest in MGM, leaving much of the day-to-day tour negotiations to his 25-year-old accountant nephew Ronnie Schneider. Schneider had helped drive the band and haul their luggage around the country when they last performed in America. Sam Cutler, the Hyde Park MC and subsequently a full-time Stones employee, remembers going with Keith Richards to Klein's headquarters for some pre-tour logistical talk. This apparently went poorly, because Klein ended the meeting by shouting at his two guests to leave his office, reminding them as they did so that he carried a weapon – but then so did Keith, burying a switchblade in Klein's desk on his way out. Schneider was to present American promoters with a 52-page contract that gave the Stones a generous 60–40 cut of their concerts' gross receipts, as well as itemising precisely what sort of food, drink and other amenities the band would tolerate backstage. With ticket prices set at a then-swingeing $6.50 to $8.50, the five musicians and their entourage would gross some $2million – roughly $11million today – from their 23-show, 15-city tour. The money would be paid not in to Klein's account but the group's own off-the-shelf, and offshore, company. For the first time, the Stones also travelled with their own stage manager and full-scale road crew, and selected their own support acts – Ike and Tina Turner, Chuck Berry, Terry Reid and B.B. King, a fair line-up in itself. Some five months later, Schneider would turn to Mick Jagger in a helicopter careening in a tropical storm over a riotous Florida concert site and announce, 'I figure you'll each take home a hundred Gs.' 'Ninety-five,' Mick said immediately.

Jagger himself had necessarily taken a back seat during the extensive pre-tour haggling, preoccupied as he was by *Ned Kelly*. From the beginning, things had not gone well for him in the Australian outback. The production had got off to a bad start when Mick was forced to walk a gauntlet of protesters on arrival at Sydney airport, indignant that their nation's outlaw hero would be portrayed by, as the signs put it, a 'pommy faggot'. Following that, there was Marianne Faithfull's overdose, which again saw the words 'Stones' and 'drugs' deployed in close proximity to one another in the world's tabloid headlines. Tony Richardson dropped Marianne from the cast of *Ned Kelly*, which would go on to grace all the 'Worst Movies in History' lists, following its albeit limited release in June 1970. Adding injury to insult, Mick was badly hurt when, out on location, a prop pistol exploded in his hand. The unit nurse stitched him up and told him to keep his right arm immobile. Preferring to doctor himself, Jagger instead picked up a guitar one afternoon and strummed a two-bar phrase around the C, G and F chords, then threw in some bondage fantasy lyrics. This happy collision between boredom and physical therapy would be the best thing to come out of *Ned Kelly*. Once back in London, Mick and Keith swiftly worked up the riff in to 'Brown Sugar'.

Meanwhile, Anita and Keith's first child was born in London on 10 August 1969. Robert Fraser, now heavily in to smack and LSD addiction, produced a beautifully hand-painted psychedelic crib for the occasion. It happened to be the day after Sharon Tate and four of her friends were butchered in Los Angeles by the Manson clan, and the week before half a million fans assembled at Max Yasgur's farm in Bethel, New York, for the start of a three-day festival known to history as Woodstock. 'Heady times,' Fraser noted. Keith and Anita, now sporting matching bone earrings (and rotting front teeth) called their son Marlon Leon Sundeep, evidence, perhaps, that Groovy Bob wasn't alone in enjoying a toot. In other Stones family news, Bill Wyman finally divorced his wife, allowing the press to gleefully publish his real age, thirty-three, while Charlie Watts seemed content between his performances with the world's most notorious rock group to potter around his Sussex manor with his wife, daughter, six dogs, three cats and pet donkey. Charlie also had an extensive library of American Civil War history books, each of which he wrapped in protective brown paper.

In September, shortly before leaving on tour, the Stones put out their latest hits package, *Through the Past, Darkly*, which they dedicated with the words: 'Brian Jones (1943–1969). When this you see, remember me/and bear me in your mind/Let all the world say what they may/speak of me as you find.' The excerpt from Gertrude Stein and the date given for Brian's birth were both wrong.

The Stones now toured with an entourage of twenty, including Stu, Jo Bergman, Gram Parsons and sundry writers, filmmakers and photographers. Holing up at Stephen Stills' Hollywood mansion for two weeks of rehearsals and illicit recording, they were again joined by Phil Kaufman, the tie-dyed, moustachioed roadie who had carried their bags when they were in town eighteen months earlier to mix *Beggar's Banquet*. Stills himself rented the home from Peter Tork, and Kaufman remembers the glee with which the Stones helped themselves to the 'shitload of Monkees memorabilia up in the attic – Keith Richards walked around with a plastic Davy Jones doll and a matching lunchbox for the next week'. Keith also found some solace for having to part from Anita and their newborn son in the arms of an exotic black singer named Emeretta Marks, like Marsha Hunt, an Afro-wigged veteran of the rock musical *Hair*. Mick Jagger travelled through several short-lived tour partners boasting such names as Miss Mercy, Susie Suck, the Plaster Casters, Suzie

Creamcheese and Kathy Kleevage – half of 'Kathy and Mary, the Dynamic Duo' – having left Marianne Faithfull at home in London.

Mick Taylor, for his part, soon grew in to his new role. 'There was plenty of sex,' he confirmed. Nor did life on the road with the Rolling Stones actively discourage drug use. 'Mick had already begun to dally with the hard stuff,' Bill Wyman noted. Within a relatively short time, Bill adds, it was feared 'even his life might be at risk'. Having joined the Stones as a fresh-faced fitness buff, Taylor would eventually leave them as a professionally embittered smack user. 'One of the reasons I don't bother to make records on my own is because I don't get paid for some of the biggest-selling records of all time,' he later remarked. 'Frankly, I was ripped off.'

One night, the Stones went down to Elektra studios to record overdubs for *Let it Bleed*. The fiddle player Byron Berline was there to add his contribution to 'Country Honk'. 'As I was doing my part out on the sidewalk, I remember this tough-looking Mexican guy working right next to us in a bulldozer, doing some sort of construction job on the road. We obviously couldn't tape with him blasting away, so after a while Mick Jagger came out in his pink suit and make-up, went up to the guy and asked him to stop. You'd expect the guy to say fuck off, but in fact he just cut the engine and politely waited for us. That was the charm of Mick. The guy knew how to talk to the Kennedys, and he knew how to talk to some Mexican hard-hat. When I think of the *Let it Bleed* session, I think of parking lots and bulldozers.'

When Wyman's birthday came around again in late October, Phil Kaufman sought to lighten the heavy mood around the house by baking him a three-tiered hash cake. Unfortunately, Kaufman's well-meaning gesture had the opposite of the desired effect. 'Bill got so fucked-up he had some sort of panic attack and fell backwards in to the buffet table,' Kaufman says. 'The Stones cancelled their session for the night.' Considering the level of drug use as a whole, it was a wonder everyone made it downtown for the few desultory rehearsals they did. Keith typically arrived for these several hours late, Charlie bided his time by reading a book while seated at his drums, and it seemed to rankle with big Mick that after seven years on stage together, he and his bass player still remained unacquainted with each other's time signatures. 'He keeps turning around and looking at me like I'm playing bad notes or I'm out of tune,' Bill complained. 'And I'm not.'

Phil Kaufman more or less kept the Tork household on track until, at nine one morning, there was a thunderous knocking at the front door. It was Allen Klein. After some protracted shouting, he was admitted to the home. The ensuing visit rather jarred with the air of stoned lethargy that tended to prevail at that hour of the day. Kaufman watched as Klein promptly flung off his trousers, demanding they be repaired, then issued several other brisk directives around the room, before picking up the phone to the local radio station to ask why they weren't playing any of the hits off *Through the Past, Darkly*. 'Allen was already pissed off because he was being edged out by the Stones,' Kaufman says. 'When he was on the phone, his voice sounded like an air horn on a truck. "Fuck you! Just *play* 'em!" People were literally cowering behind the furniture. He was so incensed, he started storming around the room in his underwear.'

On 3 November, for the first time, Richard Nixon appealed publicly to the 'great silent majority of Americans' to support escalation of the war in Vietnam. Riots promptly broke out in Washington DC and elsewhere. Four days later, the Stones opened their tour at the State University in Fort Collins, Colorado. That same week, news broke of the massacre of South Vietnamese civilians at My Lai, Nixon maintaining that protesters had 'remained noticeably uncritical of worse Vietcong atrocities'. Meanwhile, much of southern California, if not the nation as a whole, remained in the grip of what was to be retrospectively called 'Manson fever'. Someone still out there, it was widely feared, was responsible not just for five but as many as thirty or forty particularly vicious unsolved homicides and, presumably, could be expected to strike again. All in all, things were 'fucking heavy', Mick Jagger confirmed, not just in the Stones camp but the wider community. In 1966, many of Mick's fans had been delirious 11- and 12-year-olds, for whom pop music was a kind of hormonal gym. They worshipped the Stones, and wrote impassioned letters to the managers of hotels where the band had stayed. The height of their ambitions was to be allowed to gaze reverently on their heroes' bed linen, a demand more than one hotel satisfied by cutting up the boys' sheets and selling squares of them as souvenirs. By 1969, at least half of those venturing their $8.50 ticket money wanted to burn down the White House.

The first sight that most US audiences had of the new-look Rolling Stones was of Keith Richards tooling up the power chords of 'Jumpin' Jack Flash', while bent over his guitar dressed with his usual panache: scuffed snakeskin boots, distressed gaucho pants studded with silver beads, and spangly red shirt flung open to the waist. Following this shattering onslaught, half music, half siren, Mick Jagger emerged in a tall hat and a long scarf, scatting and shouting, prancing furiously, pursing those lips, instantly shrinking the largest arena down to a nightclub and effortlessly dominating a stage that also included the impeccably businesslike Charlie and Mick Taylor, and Bill Wyman's mortician persona on bass. The Stones got rave reviews in Los Angeles, particularly for the violent head show of 'Midnight Rambler', although there were backstage issues with the promoter Bill Graham at the next night's stop in Oakland. Essentially, the Stones thought Graham overattentive to contractual detail, and Graham thought the Stones 'total cunts' for their contempt of their audience. As the band took the stage for the second of their two sets at 3.15 in the morning, five hours after the scheduled start, he may have had a point.

Terry Reid, a fine blues singer who famously turned down the chance to join Led Zeppelin, travelled in the Stones juggernaut and thus had the chance to observe the two sides of the band's most compelling personality, Keith Richards. At one midwestern hotel stop, Richards could be seen 'crashed out on the bathroom floor with one arm held stiffly aloft, while twelve or fifteen people he didn't know milled around calling for more food and booze to be added to his room-service tab'. The suite itself bore little resemblance to the standard Holiday Inn issue, instead seeming to honour its occupant's Dartford roots crossed with a Moorish hash den: a world of ashtrays, HP Sauce bottles and dartboards, all shut in by velvet shawls and batik scarves flung over lamps, and generally accompanied by a throbbing Otis Redding soundtrack. Reid also thought Keith 'absolutely the nicest guy on the tour ... He was the one who used to worry about whether your laundry was getting done or if your meals were OK.'

Late one night after leaving the stage in Los Angeles, Richards fell over in his hotel. In itself, this was nothing new. As Keith's lawyer would reveal at a later drugs trial, 'My client began snorting heroin in 1969 because he was exhausted, and was soon doing two-and-a-half grams a day just to keep normal.' While on tour, Keith also liked to chug Jack Daniel's and beer, quite often in the same glass, and frequently lost consciousness at inappropriate moments, such as in mid-conversation with one of the band's accountants. But when Richards went over backwards this time and crashed to the ground, he managed to gash his riff hand, instantly turning his thumbnail blue. There were horrified gasps from the entourage as they calculated the likely implications of postponing or cancelling the tour's remaining shows. But a moment later, Keith bounced up again and dusted himself off. 'I thought I'd do that,' he said calmly. Stu remembered his friend then going upstairs 'to ring home for the next two hours ... Anita would put Marlon by the phone and Keith would just *beam*.' A prince of darkness, perhaps, but a prince nonetheless.

According to the FBI field memo of 19 November 1969, 'This group [the Stones] are an outrageous affront to accepted morals, with a great emphasis on titillation, [and] are considered by our Los Angeles office to be in the vanguard of the student upheavals there': clearly a provocative situation for all concerned. Nor was the Bureau alone in thinking these 'five herberts with guitars', as Keith Richards had termed them, could actually subvert the American way of life. As the Stones crossed California by limo, the small towns' signs and clapped-out neon wheeled and fell away to reveal the country's main visual drama of late 1969, their own name, alongside a daubed 'NUKE HANOI' or 'PEACE'. That the band themselves were essentially traditional, if not endearingly conservative, landowning Englishmen rather than rabid agitators seems not to have occurred to many on the pristine ideological left. Although several prominent anti-war activists, such as Abbie Hoffman, continued to try and claim the Stones as a rallying point for the social revolution, the actual musicians had no such interest. When Hoffman managed to get backstage in Chicago to ask for money for his upcoming trial on conspiracy charges, Jagger declined to contribute. 'I got my own trials, man,' Mick told him.

Apart from their political apathy, there were two things you could safely say about the Stones by mid-tour. They'd be hours late on stage and, once there, they'd belt out red-hot versions of their last two albums. On 18 November, they taped their sixth and final appearance on the *Ed Sullivan Show*. Reversing his previous position on the band, Sullivan moved his entire production to LA for the week just to accommodate them. The Stones arrived wearing black leather and make-up, with, in Mick's case, a smudge of puce-red lipstick. Even rock music could have produced few odder sights than that of the broadcast's 68-year-old, grey-suited host clanking up to the camera to introduce 'Gimme Shelter'. Meanwhile, Sam Cutler had gotten in the habit of announcing the live shows by booming out over the PA: 'Now . . . The greatest rock 'n' roll band in the world . . . the ROLLING STONES!' It was pure hokum, but all heart. With certain rare exceptions, the Stones delivered on the boast over the course of that month with some of the consistently hottest shows of their career.

Before the Stones left Chicago, a reporter with a London connection took Mick Jagger aside and told him that Marianne Faithfull had left him and flown to Rome with one of Anita's exes, the painter Mario Schifano. He was possibly more mortified than shocked at the news. When the tabloids ran with the story on 20 November, this put pop music's most celebrated lothario in the unwonted role of a cuckold. Although Mick's distress was plain to see, he was soon to console himself with Claudia Linnear, another of the exuberantly styled, whirling Ikettes, at the same time as Keith was accepting an invitation from the pistol-packing Ike himself to teach him his 'new shit' with the open-guitar tunings. How constant Mick was to Marianne in general remains a point of contention. According to Ronnie Schneider, 'Teenage girls followed us all over America. A large group of them grabbed Jagger once when we were running for a plane, a scene he'd obviously faced before, and I remember him spinning round, like Bruce Lee, to assume a karate pose' – but this, like Mick's occasional attempts to disguise himself on tour, wasn't entirely a success. An effort to evade the groupies outside his New York hotel by dressing as an 'ordinary businessman' in a wide-lapelled suit with pink Garbo-esque sunglasses proved counterproductive. Sometimes Mick didn't even bother, and simply let nature take its course. Ian Stewart once sat in on a dressing-room conversation in which Jagger quizzed Charlie Watts on how the latter could find contentment with 'just one woman'. 'You could see a thick fog in Mick's eyes,' said Stu, a science buff, 'as if he'd been asking Charlie to explain Einstein's quantum theory.'

Towards the end of the tour, a reporter asked Mick at a press conference in New York if he and the Stones were any more 'satisfied' now.

'Sexually, d'you mean, or philosophically?'

'Both.'

'Sexually, more satisfied,' Mick replied, to widespread laughter. 'Financially, dissatisfied' – Klein was standing immediately behind him – 'philosophically, tryin'.'

The next night, the Stones held the stage for the first of three sold-out shows at Madison Square Garden. Keith Richards, in particularly high swagger, started proceedings with a spare but shimmering 'Jumpin' Jack Flash' and Chuck Berry's 'Carol', and would go on from there to get raunchy. Swooping Mick Taylor solos over a voodoo beat in 'Sympathy'. The first new songs of the evening come in a tidal wave of noise. Then the communal knees-up of 'I'm Free', with Jagger leaping open-legged in the air in the chorus. Following that, Mick goes jogging downstage in 'Stray Cat Blues', before a brief acoustic interlude and a rocked-up version of

'Under My Thumb', which the Stones bring to a runaway-freight-train finale. The centrepiece of the show is again 'Midnight Rambler', with its multiple fake climaxes and stabs of red light, Mick whipping the deck with his studded belt to illustrate the song's rape suite. Everything ends in a gale of Keith chords – I'll stick my knife right down your *throat!* – and a whooping crash of cymbals. Mick: 'Charlie's good tonight, inne?' Keith Richards would remember that from the stage that night you could watch the arena's concrete walkways and balconies bounce up and down. 'You saw the place actually rocking. That's the real turn-on. When the audience decides to *join*. That's when it really knocks you out.'

On their last night in New York, the Stones went uptown to help Jimi Hendrix celebrate his twenty-seventh and final birthday. Mick Jagger snubbed Hendrix but stole his girlfriend, Devon Wilson. Keith Richards left early and spent most of the night with Charlie Watts, Mick Taylor and their friends at a Greenwich Village jazz club. Around dawn, Keith went back up to his hotel room with the writer Stanley Booth, opened a drawer of his bedside table and took out a capsule filled with white powder. 'This is heroin,' he announced, perhaps unnecessarily. On 30 November, flying in to the last official concert in Florida hopelessly late, Ronnie Schneider allowed that 'maybe we should cancel – except we made the guy who's promoting it pay everything in front; we've already got the bread'. Keith looked at him straight-faced and said, 'Well, let's fly over and drop the money on the crowd.' The blues guitarist Johnny Winter was also on the bill for the show. 'It was a fucking cold, dark day,' he says, 'and my main memory is of Mick Jagger taking umbrage at the weather and starting to hop around and do this weird Indian chant backstage to get the attention of the sun god. Didn't work.' The eventual gig took place amid semi-tropical rain and mud, on a derelict drag-car racing circuit strewn with lovemaking couples, makeshift communes, strolling drug vendors, LSD freakouts, nursing young mothers, campfires, uninhibited bathing, tribal sleeping arrangements, periodic clashes with authority, and other vignettes of 60s hippydom, a scene that foreshadowed what would happen just six nights later in the barren moonscape of a demolition-derby track in Altamont, California.

On 3–4 December, the Rolling Stones moved in to Muscle Shoals studio, a former coffin factory just off Highway 43 in northern Alabama. Though not a place one might immediately associate with the creation of great rock and roll music, for those two days it housed a number of key Stones ancillaries, including Jimmy Miller, Ian Stewart and Keith Richards' friend and future biographer Stanley Booth, loyally sporting the Keith haircut, as well as much of the technical crew behind the likes of Aretha Franklin, Wilson Pickett and other soul legends. Since the band wanted to keep their new recordings for themselves rather than hand them over to Allen Klein, the arrangements for the sessions were more intricate than usual. The Stones checked in to the nearby Holiday Inn under assumed names, went upstairs, and at a prearranged moment around ten o'clock that night turned off all the lights in their rooms as if, somewhat improbably, they were going to bed. Thirty minutes later, in scenes reminiscent of *Mission: Impossible*, a decoy car drove up to the front of the hotel while the band themselves scurried down-stairs, through the kitchen and out the service exit. After a fast ride past the town cemetery and down Jackson Highway, a van with smoked windows deposited them at the back door of the studio, which was then bolted behind them. Since it was thought Klein might try to physically seize the tapes if he knew his clients were there, everyone took to ducking down each time they passed by one of the front windows.

It has to be said there was method to the Stones' apparent mad-ness. Mick and Keith believed there would be a bidding war for their services when their Decca contract expired in 1970, and that this was also the opportunity for a long-awaited change of mana-gerial arrangements. The band had already hinted at their preferred future direction by handing the master-tapes of their Hyde Park concert to Peter Swales and telling him that under no circumstances were these to be given to 'Fatso'. Swales had done his best, but finally succumbed when Klein arrived at the Maddox Street office and secured the tapes by the expedient of kicking in the door of the closet where they were stored. So there was necessarily something of a siege mentality afoot when the Stones went to work at Muscle Shoals late on the night of 3 December, kicking off with a take of Fred ('I Don't Play no Rock'n'roll') McDowell's classic spiritual 'You Gotta Move', which they sang in to a mike positioned in a toilet bowl for that 'shitty sound', as Keith admiringly put it. Next, 'Brown Sugar'. Mick's rehab exercise from the Australian bush came out of the gate like a stock-car race involving Elvis, Bo Diddley and Marc Bolan, with a booming bass drum channelled from Freddy Cannon's 1959 hit 'Tallahassee Lassie', and Bobby Keys' rasping tenor-sax solo to come. The Stones' frothy new raver would soon get its debut amid the blood and muck of a murder scene.

Lastly, 'Wild Horses', which Keith wrote 'because I was doing good at home with my old lady ... and I gave it to Mick, and Marianne just ran off with this guy and he changed it all round. But it's still beautiful.' (Faithfull would leave Mario Schifano and fly back to Jagger as soon as she heard the song.) Stu wanted nothing to do with any 'Chinese shit', as he termed music with minor chords, so the Memphis bluesman Jim Dickinson, who happened to be present, played the piano. The song finally came together at five in the morning, with Mick slumped in a tiny, blue-lit vocal booth, the two guitarists sitting on folding plastic chairs over the porcelain mike stand, and a steady supply of Gram Parsons' finest coke keeping everyone artistically focused. Following that, the Stones left town as fast as they had come. Not a trace of their recordings would be left behind, nor would a forwarding address when Allen Klein came asking after them just twenty-four hours later.

Meanwhile, *Let it Bleed*. The Stones' new album was out a year to the day after *Beggar's Banquet*, which had followed a year after *Satanic Majesties*. But where *Banquet* seemed motivated less by adventure than by a tactical retreat in to the blues, *Bleed* was the great leap forward. Kicking things off with the banshee wail of 'Gimme Shelter', the band went on from there to deliver an eclectic mix of free-flowing, elegantly extemporised folk, soul, country, and rock and roll, consistently balancing ragged guitars against powerhouse melodies and apocalypse-now lyrics. Among the high-lights: the title track, in which Mick Jagger's emotional distress was revealed to moving effect – his girlfriend had offered him a space in her parking lot, but had then knifed him in his dirty, filthy base-ment. (These blows notwithstanding, Mick graciously extended an offer to 'cream all over' him.) 'Midnight Rambler', one of the few tracks generally slower than a fleeing getaway car, married a classic blues groove with a killer tempo change and a headline ripped from the pages of the *Chicago Sun-Times* of 22 October 1968; even though polite compared to the live version, the song's key reference points – rape, knives, mutilated women – were stark enough. It remains one of the few enduring rock anthems to commemorate the Boston Strangler. On the woozily laid-back 'You Got the Silver', Brian Jones' posthumous riff lent ballast to Keith Richards' engagingly nasal voice, extolling the charms of Anita Pallenberg. 'Monkey Man', by contrast, started off smooth and silky and ended in a sound distressingly like that of Captain Beefheart being sick. The whole thing then ratcheted up to a climax on 'You Can't Always Get What You Want', which, if nothing else, proved that the Stones were still able to toss off terse pop hooks in the presence of a French horn and a choir.

Wrapped in a cover displaying a surreal clock, tyre and food sculpture by Robert Brownjohn (with a cake baked by the then struggling cookery writer Delia Smith), *Let it Bleed* sailed to the top of a British chart otherwise dominated by the likes of Simon and Garfunkel, Elvis in cabaret, and Lee Marvin and the rest of the cast of *Paint Your Wagon* warbling their way through 'Wand'rin' Star'. It deposed *Abbey Road* at number one. The album was the best cross-section yet of the elements that made the Stones untouchable on vinyl for ten years. No set of songs has ever been more topical when it came to capturing, if not defining, a sense of end-of-an-era dis-solution and moral decay. As it turned out, *Let it Bleed* was almost too cleverly titled for its own good.

Since some twenty-five books, not to mention forty-three years' worth of scholarly articles, tabloid headlines and a continuing lively internet exchange among Stones fans and detractors are all available on the subject, it's perhaps best to be brief on the band's headlining appearance at the Altamont Speedway Free Festival on Saturday 6 December 1969, sometimes called the worst day in rock music history.

The whole idea began as a well-meaning reply to loud complaints in *Rolling Stone* and elsewhere about the tour's ticket prices, and seemed to be a golden opportunity for another Woodstock-like demonstration of 'togetherness'. 'You expected everyone in San Francisco . . . because they were so mellow and nice and organised, that it was going to be all those things,' Mick Jagger recalled twenty years later. The vibes were positive enough when Mick and Keith drove out the night before to look over the site, and found roughly a quarter of a million fans already camped out awaiting their performance. A closer inspection, even so, might have revealed certain facility-management issues that a further twenty-four hours of cheap red wine, abundant LSD and periodic interaction with the leather-clad Hell's Angels notionally providing security for the event would only exacerbate. For one thing, the 83-acre concert site was almost totally self-contained, or, put another way, isolated. No one ever forgot their first sight of the spot. As Stu said of the morning of the show, 'It looked more like a stoned holiday camp than an organised rock and roll event.' A single grey road wound across a high plateau, then up and down through scrub-covered hills, around a slope of forest to a dip where you could suddenly see the crowds, the queues, and the worryingly small number of bright red 'staff' T-shirts that darted around the still-disassembled sound and lighting equipment like a shoal of tropical fish. The stage itself was a mere 3 feet high.

By midnight on 5 December, the two-lane highway leading out of San Francisco up to the hills where the gig was to be held already looked like Dunkirk, and would soon be clogged for 10 or 12 miles in either direction. All around, Altamont was littered with tents, trailers, fires, bin-liners and the wreckage of drugs. Stoned Hell's Angels wheeled their 'hogs' through nude hippies. The convoy of bikes churned up thick dust clouds as an eerie, crescent-shaped moon rose behind the Diablo mountains. Shadowy-looking parties could be seen foraging for mushrooms. There was a powerful reek of pot in the air. It did not take a wild leap of imagination or a consultation with a tarot-card reader, of whom there were many present, to predict that this was a likely crucible for a certain amount of deviant behaviour. Keith Richards immediately took in the astonishing scene, declared it groovy, and decided to abandon his suite at the well-appointed Huntingdon Hotel downtown and instead spend what was left of the night wandering about Altamont.

Now all that remained was the actual festival, which did not go well.

Around two o'clock on Saturday afternoon, the Stones' helicopter headed off between crags and hills which suddenly dissolved in a startling close-up of a crowd now estimated at some 450,000. The craft swooped over the top, then hovered above the brightly tented backstage area. Gazing down on fans whose own heads strained upwards, Charlie Watts said, 'This is the business.'

They were perhaps the last truly cheerful words of the day, at least as spoken by anyone on the stage. The first overt hint of violence came only moments later, when Mick Jagger disembarked from the helicopter and a teenaged boy rushed forward and punched him in the face, screaming, 'I hate you, I hate you!' By then the Jefferson Airplane had already been and gone, their set truncated when Hell's Angels bludgeoned the singer Marty Balin unconscious. A long interval of Sam Cutler appealing over the PA for calm was followed in turn by Crosby, Stills and Nash, who scrubbed furiously at their guitars as if late for an appointment. The Grateful Dead arrived backstage, took one look at the mounting anarchy, and got back in their helicopter and left again without performing. It's probable the Stones would have gone on there and then, at least giving them the chance to play in daylight, except that Bill Wyman had missed his ride from San Francisco and for once in his life the band were waiting for him, not the other way round. The Angels themselves, some riding the tools of their trade through the crowd, were effectively the next act. For an hour they flailed, fought, belched, spewed and spat. Most used a sharpened pool cue to the ribs as their preferred means of crowd control. Soon scores of the Angels had climbed on to the stage, fists swinging, until, lest anybody out there still be wondering, Cutler explained: 'The reason we can't start is that nobody can fuckin' move . . . I've done all I can.' More muttering, then the nuclear deterrent: 'The Stones won't come out until everybody gets off. *Everybody.*'

Darkness fell. Bill Wyman appeared from his hotel in San Francisco.

When the Stones eventually ran on, in a zap of blood-red light, they were accompanied by twenty-five to thirty Angels and at least one large, unleashed Alsatian sniffing menacingly at the guitarists' legs. 'Fellas,' Mick Jagger kept murmuring. 'Will you gimme some room? Will you move back, *please?*' Both the PA and the stage lights kept cutting in and out, the sky stabbed with green, mauve, red. Somehow they got through two numbers. 'Whoo, whoo! Ah, yeah!' Jagger swigged from a bottle of Jack Daniel's on the amp. The whole place was churning, Mick swinging his stripper's belt, and Keith let rip with 'Sympathy'. As Jagger sang about Jesus and His moment of doubt and pain there was an explosion and a hole opened up in the crowd. 'H-e-e-e-e-ey . . . Keith – Keith – *Keith!*' Mick's voice rose in counterpoint to the music, proving that Keith wasn't easily deterred from a good riff. 'Will you cool it and I'll try and stop it.' Richards unstrapped his guitar. 'Sisters,' said Jagger. 'Brothers and sisters . . . Come *on*, now . . . That means everybody just cool *out*. Just be cool now, come on . . .'

'Somebody's bike blew up, man.'

'I know. I'm hip. Everybody be cool now, come on . . . Can everybody just . . . I don't know what happened, I couldn't see . . . Everyone just cool down . . . Is there anyone who's hurt? . . . Good . . . We can groove . . . Something very funny happens when we start that number.'

Next, a 200-pound naked girl, pinned in the red and green spots, lumbered on to the stage, where half a dozen Hell's Angels made ready to receive her. Soon they swarmed over her like maggots on a carcass. 'Fellas,' Jagger enquired, 'Surely *one* of you can handle it?' A denim-clad individual with a pool cue duly rendered the girl senseless. Keith got the guitar going once more and Mick again sang about being Lucifer, in need of some restraint. Moments later, a long-haired boy clambered up to join the band in a mistaken display of togetherness just before he, too, went down in a cartoon-like whirl of stabbing and punching. Mick Jagger, though probably unused to being interrupted in the instrumental break to 'Sympathy' by an acid-crazed Hell's Angel in a black sombrero whispering in his ear, seemed to take the event in his stride. More scenes of carnage followed as the song finally ground to a halt. Jagger stood there for a moment, wrapped incongruously in an orange and black silk cape, clutching hard at the remnants of his hippy goodwill. 'Who ... who ... I mean, like people, who's fighting and what for? Hey, people ... I mean, who's fighting and what for? Why are we fighting? I mean, like ... every other scene has been cool ... Like we're—'

'Either those cats cool it,' Keith Richards snapped. 'Or we don't play.'

Everybody looked at Keith, fell silent. Seizing his moment, Stu, as ever the voice of reason, took the mike and appealed for help. 'Can you let the doctor go through, please ... We have also ... lost in the front here a little girl who's five years old.' The scenes facing the Stones now were as replete with menace and violence as anything out of their past, only now there were no reassuring British policemen on hand. 'Play cool-out music,' Keith told Charlie and Bill. After a blues interlude, the band kicked back in with 'Under My Thumb' as the audience suddenly started, bug-eyed, immediately in front of the stage. Twenty feet from where Mick was singing, a beanpole-tall black kid in a lime-green suit was pointing a gun in the air. He seemed to freeze there for a second before going down under a collapsing scrum of Angels. Someone let out a wild scream. People began waving blood-stained hands at the Stones, whose song ended in a high-pitched whistle. Jagger cupped an ear, shielded his eyes, pleading: 'Now there's one thing we need ... Sam, an ambulance ... a doctor by that scaffold there. If there's a doctor can he go there. OK, we gonna, we gonna do ... I don't know what the fuck we gonna do. Everybody just sit down.

Keep cool. Let's just relax . . . get in to a groove . . . Come on . . .
We can get it together. Come *on*.'

The man in the green suit, Meredith Hunter, died later of multiple stab wounds. He was eighteen. According to an eye-witness,
Paul Cox, 'An Angel kept looking over at me and I tried to ignore
him, because . . . he kept trying to cause a fight . . . Next thing I
know, he's hassling this Negro boy . . . The boy yanked away, and
when he yanked away, next thing I know he was flying in the air,
right on the ground . . . He scrambled to his feet, backing up and
trying to run from the Angels . . . and his girlfriend was screaming
at him not to fire, because he pulled out a gun . . . And then some
Angel snuck up from right out of the crowd and leapt up and
brought this knife down in his back.'

According to Paul Cox, Hunter's last audible words were, 'I
wasn't going to shoot you.'

The Stones finished 'Under My Thumb', then blithely debuted
their new stomper about drugs 'n' pussy, 'Brown Sugar'. The rest of
the set passed without event: there are those who watched the show
from the relative comfort of the hillside half a mile away from the
stage who still insist they had a good time. By 'Honky Tonk Women',
Jagger was up and jiving again. 'Well, there's been a few hang-ups . . .
yes . . . but generally . . . I mean, you've been beautiful . . . groovy.'
He started 'Street Fighting Man' with his back to the crowd, then
wheeled to face it, yelling, '*Everywhere I hear the sound of marching,
charging feeeet, boy* . . .' Up in the darkness, dwarfed by a row of electricity pylons, the kids were dancing, and Jagger was setting the
pace, pelvis swivelling, hands flapping, clapping them by the side of
his face, strutting back and forth in time with the beat. 'We're gonna
kiss you goodbye,' Mick trilled. 'Bye-bye. Bye-by-y-y-y-e-bye.' The
drums crashed, and the Stones fled for their helicopter as if from
an invasion. Within moments, there were fifteen passengers
crammed in to a cabin built for eight. With a puff of smoke the craft
limped off eastward between crags and hills, then slowly doubled
back towards San Francisco. It tilted over the concert site, immediately above the stage, now bathed in a sulphurous glow and
apparently the scene of a full-scale Hell's Angels keg party. Gazing

down on the whole folly, Keith Richards turned away, livid, and started cursing.

'They're sick, man. Some people just aren't ready.'

'I'd rather have had cops,' Mick Jagger said.

The Stones would soon take severe flak for their role at Altamont. Much of the press was hostile and, in a book-length feature, *Rolling Stone* placed the blame for the fiasco squarely on its namesakes. David Crosby: 'The big mistake was taking what was essentially a party and turning it in to a star game . . . [The Stones] are on a grotesque, negative ego trip, especially the two leaders.' The whole sorry performance was filmed and later released as *Gimme Shelter*. Co-directors David and Al Maysles gave their picture a stylishly dark and moody look, and the effect was more reflective and dreamlike than stark and gory. Some of the best footage was shot by George Lucas, later of *Star Wars* fame.

Stu, ever the thoughtful core of the Stones party, was the nearest thing to an authority figure at Altamont, and one of the few people there over the age of thirty. Mick and Keith had tended to shy away from anyone in uniform since February 1967, and were both party to the disastrous decision to self-police the show – although, contrary to legend, the Stones never 'hired' the Hell's Angels as muscle in exchange for $500-worth of beer. Altamont had no organised security at all; just roadies shouting to 'get off the fucking stage', and the bikers, with the pool cues, up there braining fans. There were over 300 injuries and serious ODs on the day, with four deaths: one lynched, two run over by a car as they dozed in sleeping bags, one drowned in a sewer. (Contrary to another myth, nobody gave birth.)

The lawsuits began almost immediately, and would rumble on for years. When the Stones next toured America in 1972, there were ugly backstage scenes as bailiffs tried to serve writs at the door of the band's dressing room. In April 1975, the Stones were breaking in their new guitarist, Ron Wood, in a rehearsal on a remote coastal estate in Montauk, New York, arranged for them by Andy Warhol. Woody knew he'd hit the big leagues when he saw two of the band's security men fencing off the house's private beach with

barbed wire. The rumour was that local Hell's Angels wanted to kill
Mick and Keith, and might try an amphibious strike. According to
Mark Young, an FBI agent who worked the case, 'The Angels
wanted their revenge. We know they actually launched out in to
Long Island Sound, armed to the teeth, but the boat was hit by a
storm. The bikers were thrown overboard. They never went back
and reinstituted the plan.'

Ten years earlier, Mick, Keith, Brian and Charlie had all rung in the
1960s while living with their mums and dads in their suburban
English homes, or, in Bill's case, the room above a garage. Now they
were the most notorious rock stars on earth, and one of them was
in the cemetery. On 7 December, Mick flew off to deposit the
band's tour money in a Swiss bank account, then came back to
London for a tearful reconciliation with Marianne Faithfull. The
couple's first public act together was to attend a court hearing to
renew their bail following their May drugs bust. Mick was soon to
plead guilty to possession and be given a £200 fine, which was
enough for the US Justice Department to ban him from working in
the country for the next eighteen months. In the meantime, the
British Treasury would send each of the Stones a tax bill requesting 83 per cent of their recent American earnings, and an additional
15 per cent of their invested income. A consistent theme of the
band's tours through the late 1960s and 70s would be how many of
them were determined not by artistic inspiration or popular
demand, but by judges and immigration authorities.

Meanwhile, Keith Richards had family issues of his own: Anita,
Marlon and several journalists were waiting for him when he landed
at Heathrow two days after Altamont. The tabloids were saying that
the Home Office might deport Pallenberg, an Italian citizen, unless
she and Keith got married. Anita played the scene to the hilt, holding the baby up for the photographers and crying, 'Keith! Keith!
They're throwing me out of the country!'

While Jagger and Richards began to weigh the various advantages
of a life outside England, the Stones came together for four hassle-
free concerts at London theatres. Following the last show, Mick told

a *Guardian* reporter, 'Nobody in the band is thinking about going in to tax exile.' That statement had about the same relationship to the truth as *Let it Bleed* had to family entertainment.

None of the Stones or their representatives was present when, on 10 December, Meredith Hunter was laid to rest by his immediate family and four of his high school classmates at a small church in the San Francisco suburb of Vallejo. He was buried in an unmarked grave. Hunter's mother Altha later sued the Stones for $500,000, but found them to be an elusive and determined opponent. In 1972, Altha's lawyer presented the judge in the case with a statement from a process-server who had pursued Mick Jagger around the lobby of the Miyako hotel in San Francisco, tapping him on the arm with the papers as Jagger ran out of the door in to a waiting car. The Stones eventually settled with the Hunter family for a reported $10,000. In January 1971, a jury in Alameda County, California, found a Hell's Angel named Alan Passaro not guilty of Meredith Hunter's murder, on the grounds of self-defence. During the trial, it was said that the deceased had been high on amphetamines at the time of his death, and had been 'disrespectful' when repeatedly asked to move away from the stage by 'duly authorised personnel'. Fourteen years later, Passaro himself turned up floating face down in a nearby lake, with a waterproof bag strapped to his back. It contained $10,000. The Alameda Sheriff's Department still lists the case as unsolved.

Mick Jagger's country mansion, Stargroves, had been a source of both pleasure and grief for him ever since he'd put down a hard-earned £37,000 to buy the crumbling estate in December 1967. On the downside, the place was under nearly continual repair during the twelve years Jagger owned it. If he stayed there at all, it was generally only for a week or two in the guest cottage at the end of the drive. At various times Mick's parents, his brother, and even Maldwyn Thomas, his London hairdresser, acted as caretakers, co-habiting with Frank Thorogood's (or his successors') constantly replenished teams of builders padding around the Elizabethan house with their paint-pots and careworn denim overalls. Stargroves did, however, provide a badly needed opportunity for Mick and his main girlfriend to get away from their more onerous responsibilities in London. Life was slow and quiet there. Only the most hardened Stones fans ever showed up at the door, and both the house and the surrounding countryside also had the distinct advantage of being off the radar of the Metropolitan Police drug squad. It was one of the few spots in the world where Jagger could relax, just as Marianne Faithfull's 4-year-old son Nicholas was one of the few people in the world with whom he felt entirely comfortable. Only at Stargroves could Mick stroll down to the local shops without being hassled. He especially enjoyed walking hand-in-hand with Nicholas around the narrow lanes of East Woodhay, whose elderly postmaster, Alan Deane, remembered the couple often popping in for bags of crisps, McVities biscuits and ice cream.

But in March 1970, Mick Jagger, lead vocalist of the Rolling Stones, discovered that such simple human pleasures were no longer possible. Early that month, the entire band and their entourage moved in for six weeks of recording, roadies threaded dozens of cables in to the front hall, and everyone plugged in against a back-drop of musty chandeliers and baronial coats of arms. Soon the ancient house was ringing to the sounds of 'Bitch', one of several horn-drenched blowouts that went on to grace albums like *Sticky Fingers* and *Exile on Main Street*. Other Stargroves tunes included 'Good Time Woman', 'Sway' and 'Cocksucker Blues'. Sidemen like Bobby Keys on sax and Jim Price on trumpet came in to their own on the new tracks, if only because Keith Richards often wasn't there to supervise them, being increasingly prone to what he later called 'junkie time'. If a session was called for ten o'clock at night, Keith might stroll in around three in the morning. There were frequent arguments and absences elsewhere in the band. Several colleagues noted that even the consummately professional Mick Jagger would down tools, if the phrase weren't so inappropriate, whenever Marsha Hunt or one of his other specially favoured friends appeared at Stargroves. 'Suddenly,' said Stu, 'there were days when Mick dis-appeared upstairs.'

Not that it was all play for the lads. Everyone came together in a rare full-band performance on the gloriously eccentric 'Can't You Hear Me Knocking', a rock-guitar groove that swerved, halfway through, in to a mariachi jam session. But a more typical experience was the night Keith first strummed the moody chords to 'The Japanese Thing', which eventually became 'Moonlight Mile'. Initially, there was something of a skeleton crew present for the song, with just Charlie Watts on drums and Jim Price tinkling a piano. Mick Jagger was in his boudoir, Bill Wyman had also retired, and nobody knew exactly where Mick Taylor was after his co-guitarist had told him, 'Don't bother to play on this. You're so fucking loud.' Six months later, Keith was too stoned to make it to the final session for 'Moonlight Mile', which the two Micks put together at Olympic. Even when everyone was physically together in the same room, a certain amount of debate now ensued between the Stones' principal songwriters about what, exactly, the world's greatest rock and roll band should sound like in the 1970s. Bill Wyman later characterised the creative problem with most Stones records of the time as 'Mick wanted hits, Keith couldn't give a shit.'

Meanwhile, Jagger, Richards and their co-producer Glyn Johns had edited their New York concert tapes, reluctantly – in a final row with Decca – doing without the planned B.B. King and Ike and Tina Turner contributions to the three shows. Such was the promise and letdown of *Get Yer Ya-Ya's Out!* Even as a single album, it was a glorious throwback to the days when the Stones were a two-fisted band, Keith strutting out the solid-rock riffs and Mick Taylor providing the fluid solos. Bill's overamped bass connects with the force of a sustained electric shock, while Charlie's spare but crisp drumming adds the exclamation marks on cue. Caught in its campy prime is Mick's inimitable stage shtick and the band's deft wedding of arena rock and punk attitude.

Whatever 'ya-yas' meant (a voodoo chant, apparently) wasn't explained, but the music steamed like summer asphalt. It went straight to number one.

When Rupert Loewenstein called the Stones together in September 1970 to explain the merits of their spending a minimum of a year in France, while their future recording and tour money was channelled in to a Dutch-based offshore holding company, paying tax at a modest rate of 1.5 per cent, the band members reacted in various ways. After listening to Loewenstein's presentation, Charlie Watts promptly bought a farmhouse in western Provence, and made arrangements for his 2-year-old daughter to begin her formal education on the Riviera. Having travelled abroad for the first time only in October 1969, Mick Taylor also appeared resigned to uprooting himself and his girlfriend Rose, five months pregnant, particularly on learning that after less than a year and a half in the band he already owed the Inland Revenue £22,000.

Bill Wyman was less happy. Loewenstein had been able to extract the Stones' financial records from New York only after protracted discussion, and tempers grew shorter as he and the band awaited the reply. The files Klein provided did not make easy reading. Although the US Treasury Department had generally taken its cut of the Stones' earnings at source, no one had thought to address the needs of the British authority, who now wrote to enquire about the shortfall. 'Telling Bill he owed a hundred grand back tax was like dropping a match in to a petrol tank,' Tom Keylock recalled. 'A major blowup' ensued. After cursing Klein at some length, Wyman seemed to slip from anger to despair, remarking that he found himself forced to work and live with colleagues he had 'nothing in common with' – a verdict at least one of them would have endorsed. Keith Richards later reflected that, other than exchanging strictly musical shop-talk, he and his bass player wouldn't say a word to one another again for the next ten years. Wyman cheered up only when he eventually arrived in the south of France and found that he was in the right place to indulge his hobby of photographing topless women. More than once, Bill sat in a boat anchored off the nude beach at St Tropez, aiming his camera at the obliging sunbathers, although often even this mild ruse wasn't necessary. According to the journalist Robert Greenfield, who visited the Stones in exile, Bill would 'simply ask the most attractive woman at the dinner table to slip in to another room for a moment and remove her blouse so he could snap a quick photo to add to his collection'.

For Keith Richards, meanwhile, the winter of 1970–71 presented a more personal challenge, as both he and Anita embarked on a roller coaster of drink and drug addiction, pausing only to alight at various discreet rehab clinics. Nick Gough remembers an incident around Christmas 1970 when Keith, a serious military buff, somewhat unexpectedly appeared with some friends at a re-dedication ceremony for the West Wittering war memorial, a mile or two from Redlands. When the 'Last Post' played, a surge of patriotism evidently flowed through Keith's group, and there was an awkward attempt to pay respect to the fallen by standing at attention. Not everyone managed to stay upright. The writer Stanley Booth went to stay at Redlands for some weeks, and notes that the basic routine was, 'We'd get up in the morning and get wacked. As Keith was still renting out his cottage to the registered junkie couple whom the National Health obligingly prescribed with heroin, the basic supply wasn't a problem. If anything, we had too *much* dope.' Keith himself later remarked he was 'highly selective' in his intake, enjoying 'pharmaceutical cocaine, the best heroin [and] acid', but drawing the line at 'Mexican shoe scrapings'. He eventually installed a no-nonsense Scottish nurse known as Smitty to help him through a painful but relatively quick withdrawal, apparently with the idea of making a fresh start of things on the Riviera. Keith resented the move on principle, seeing it as another vindictive act by 'the Establishment', but gradually reconciled himself to the idea of a family life characterised by sun, sea and palm trees.

When the time came, however, Keith and Marlon would fly to France without Anita, who was undergoing her own four-week detox course at Bowden House, a private clinic located just across the road from Harrow School in north London. Keith did, to his credit, drive up to visit Anita shortly before boarding the charter jet to Nice. Unfortunately, Gram Parsons had arrived from California earlier that same afternoon, and took the opportunity to introduce his host to the heroin-cocaine speedball. This sorry lapse from Smitty's regime was followed in turn by Keith's nodding off at the wheel of the Bentley, plunging the now Pink Lena through an iron fence and in to the middle of a Neasden traffic island. The front of the car was completely crushed, with steam pouring out of the burst radiator – though, even as Richards legged it over a nearby wall, the sound system continued to blast out 'Brown Sugar' over the car's external speakers. As Keith began frantically digging a hole in the ground in which to bury his drugs, he looked up to see the Stones' urbane piano player Nicky Hopkins staring down at him. Hopkins lived in the next-door house, so he politely invited Keith in for a cup of tea. When Keith then rang Anita to tell her he might be late for their appointment, she screamed back at him, 'Just get me some H or I'm checking out of here. Right now!' This was not a couple who were preoccupied with the long-term implications of international tax laws so much as with the more pressing challenges of their daily lives.

Mick Jagger *was* worried about money. By the summer of 1970, the former LSE student spent more of his time in boardroom meetings with the portly Rupert Loewenstein and his colleagues at Leopold Joseph than he did sprawled across a bed with his latest groupie. The eventual deal hammered out that October with the help of a Paris lawyer, Maître Michard-Pellissier, was that the Stones would collectively spend between £150,000 and £200,000, or roughly $600,000, each year of their exile in France, and that the French Government in return would waive any claim it might have to tax the band's corporate earnings.

Prince Rupert's alternative arrangements for these soon proved quite lucrative: in the accounting period up to April 2007, according to details disclosed by the Handelsregister, the trade registry of the Netherlands, the founding members of the Stones would pay just $7.2million in total taxes on accumulated income of some $500million, rather lower than the average prevailing British or American tax rates of around 40 per cent (or up to 93 per cent, in the 1970s). Part of the band's Amsterdam-based assets would be funnelled through the Netherlands Antilles, a Dutch protectorate and a popular Caribbean tax haven, making them one of about 20,000 such 'mailbox companies', according to a 2009 report by the Centre for Research on Multinational Corporations. It was a highly effective long-term strategy for the Stones, if one that raised certain questions about a band still associated in some quarters with street fighting, anarchy and revolution. As he approached his thirtieth birthday, Mick also had a more specific, genetic concern on his mind. 'His great fear was that he'd lose his hair like his father,' Eva Jagger once told me.

Although spared baldness, Mick had other personal issues to contend with – girlfriend problems, for one, as his initially successful campaign to win back Marianne Faithfull ultimately backfired. Marianne was now as heavily in to smack as Anita was, and when Mick took her out to dinner with well-heeled friends like Rupert Loewenstein or Jonathan Guinness she more than once flaked out in to her soup. After hearing Ahmet Ertegun, the Stones' new record-label boss, describe her as a corporate liability, Marianne bundled up her young son and a few clothes from Cheyne Walk and left for good. 'I didn't take anything else, out of pride,' she says. 'It gives me an edge on Mick, because he really feels that women are terrible, grasping creatures.' Later Marianne would say she suffered some sort of breakdown during this period, though her memory of it was mercifully vague. Prior to intensive psychotherapy, all she could recall was her regular appointment in an alley off London's Great Windmill Street to score drugs, and the time, having read about Mick's wedding in the evening paper, she wandered in to an Indian restaurant, nodded off in to her curry, and spent the night at the local police station. Marianne seemed a lost cause for some years before she resurfaced in 1979 with her extraordinary self-penned song of struggle and redemption, 'Broken English', followed by a series of critically acclaimed albums and occasional film parts. Recovering from a cancer operation in 2006, she picked up a phone in a Paris clinic to hear a familiar voice say, 'Hello, darling. How are you?' It was the first time Mick Jagger had called her in thirty-six years. 'He went to a lot of trouble to get my number in the hospital,' she says today. 'That's a classy guy.'

Other departures from the Stones entourage in the early 1970s included the long-serving Tom Keylock, whose role as the band's indispensable Man Friday passed to his friend Alan Dunn. A few of Tom's more ad hoc duties were assumed by 'Spanish Tony' Sanchez, a man Marianne Faithfull describes as 'dreadful . . . You only had to see him eat to know how loathsome he was. He was a lowlife, a small-time spiv, but a total weakling at the same time.' (And she slept with him.) This particular transition wasn't necessarily conducive to a sense of stability or order. When Keith Richards' emotions flared, he was known to occasionally lob things at Sanchez, who at first picked them up quietly. Over the next few years, however, the balance of power shifted. Sanchez not only shouted back at his employer, he once or twice took the initiative and shouted first. In March 1971, Spanish Tony happened to come down with laryngitis shortly before joining Keith and the other Stones on the Riviera. It was a change: a few days of brooding silence instead of mutual fuck-yous.

On 2 September 1970, the Stones opened a European tour in Helsinki. Booked to perform, with Scandinavian precision, at 8.05p.m., they finally went on at 1.45 in the morning. Keith Richards took his family along for the whole ride, so the Stones tended to run both on 'junkie time' and the 1-year-old Marlon's schedule. Keith also took the opportunity to bond with the good ol' Texan boy Bobby Keys, who fully shared his love of the recreational side of rock and roll. A certain 007 ingenuity, a hollowed-out pen concealing two grams of coke, would be as much a part of the tour as a certain musical high of a time gone by. There was also the fake shaving-cream can, the mysterious extra ivory key on Nicky Hopkins' piano, and the false bottom built in to Keith's amp. When the dope ran low, the Stones had the local promoter go out and hustle some more.

On 22 September, Decca, apparently still anxious for the Stones' business, rashly offered to pay the band's overnight Paris hotel bill, which thanks to generous room-service and other extras amounted to 16,275 francs, or roughly £35,000 today, for the five musicians and their immediate guests. Later, Mick Jagger went off with an olive-skinned beauty with high cheekbones, named Bianca Pérez-Mora Macias, who struck some as a female, and haughtier, version of Mick himself. Bianca was twenty-five, calling herself twenty-one, and not that big on rock and roll. But she was given a warm cocaine welcome to the tour, and Mick soon flew her back with him to London. At Heathrow, Bianca assured reporters that the couple were 'just good friends', adding, 'I 'ave no name. I speek no English' – not strictly so, as in the eight years since leaving her native Nicaragua, she'd been both a regular on the London club circuit and at least informally engaged to the actor Michael Caine. Reaction among the Stones was mixed: Bill and Charlie were polite, little Mick – no longer the newcomer – was friendly, and Keith kept his own counsel. 'At first I thought Bianca was just some bimbo,' he would admit. 'But as I got to know her, I discovered that she's bright [and] strong ... a very forceful character. The only drawback was that she was never one for a joke.' (Years later, Bianca admitted to her friend Ross Benson, 'I hate to smile – it makes me look so dumb.') There was no such shading in Anita Pallenberg's opinion of the new arrival. She loathed 'the stuck-up bitch' on sight. According to Tony Sanchez, Anita was obsessed with the idea that nobody (except Mick Jagger) had ever seen Bianca with her clothes off, and this proved either that she had 'droopy tits', or 'was really a man who'd had a sex-change operation'. Mick himself was sufficiently smitten to now dispense with his other back-up girlfriends, including the heavily pregnant Marsha Hunt. 'We had a baby on purpose,' Hunt told the press after giving birth to the couple's daughter, Karis, in November. 'Now he's no longer involved with us.'

Meanwhile, over Christmas 1970, the Stones formally marked their disaffection from Allen Klein by suing him in New York State's supreme court for $29.2million. The band's complaint noted that their business manager of the past five years had 'used his position ... solely for his own personal profit and advantage'. Decca was sacked with similar dispatch that same week. The Stones were then in the pleasant position of fielding offers for their services, and at one stage nearly joined Elvis at RCA. At the last moment, a sinister, allegedly Mafia-backed, American parking lot- and mortuary-based concern called Kinney Group, parent company of Ahmet Ertegun's Atlantic, came through with a $5.7million worldwide distribution deal. (The albums would actually be released on Rolling Stones Records, a vanity label which would prove curiously inert when it came to signing the 'hot young talent' promised in the initial press announcement.) The new deal got under way when the band hired 29-year-old Marshall Chess, the man who'd sent Mike Jagger his prize Chuck Berry albums from Chicago ten years before, as their label's first president. Mick and Keith came up with the famous trademark, inspired by the Thug goddess Kali and actually drawn by the young Royal College of Art student John Pasche. Pasche was paid his standard design fee, fifty guineas. That tongue logo, slavering in a cunnilingual leer, would soon become recognisable to millions of people around the world who never bought a rock record or attended a concert. In a final departure from the Decca regime, Mick also elected to give all the band's records from now on the serial letters COC, until 1978, at which point he opted for CUN.*

On 4 March 1971, the Stones began a short, pre-exile tour of Britain. It went ahead in a strange, often ugly atmosphere. Many of the critics were hostile, and even the *Daily Telegraph* chided the band for whom 'personal taxation advantage' appeared to be the sole factor. Several papers claimed the Stones' songs had grossed them £83million in seven years, and Jagger and Richards took out a full-page ad claiming they were nearly broke. (As it happened, each of the band's composers had banked a cheque for $805,629 earlier that week.) Junkie time still prevailed, and there were boos and catcalls most nights as the Stones' fans awaited them. On 12 March, Keith Richards managed to miss his train from London to a gig in Liverpool. A private jet, hurriedly chartered for him at Heathrow, broke down on the runway. A second plane was then summoned, and also broke down. Keith, Anita, Marlon and their puppy Boogie

---

*Another up-and-coming English artist, Pete Webb, went to a meeting at Maddox Street at around this time, and outlined his plan for photographing the band for the cover of *Sticky Fingers*. He told them he wanted to dress them up in striped blazers and boaters, and put them in a 'surreal Henley Regatta' montage. No one quite seemed to know what to make of the idea, and in the end Webb had to make do with taking the album's inside pictures. Andy Warhol got the cover.

finally arrived at the theatre five hours after the band had been due on stage. The shows themselves were sloppy at best, though not without a ragged, Faces-like charm, particularly in the extended 'Brown Sugar'/Chuck Berry runout. Everyone's parents came to the final shows at the Roundhouse in London. Mr and Mrs Watts sat primly in the front row wearing their Sunday-best clothes, and Doris Richards handed round biscuits. 'It was weird wigglin' me bum at me mum,' Mick Jagger allowed. 'Like an incestuous thing.'

On 26 March, the Stones played a televised gig at the Marquee Club. It was the same venue as their debut in 1962, with the same manager, Harold Pendleton, muttering '*Still* shit' behind their backs. History repeated itself as Keith Richards swung his guitar at Pendleton's head, before being dragged backwards, still seething, by Mick and Charlie. Heated discussions followed. Keith screamed some more and Mick loudly demanded that the club be cleared before the band performed. 'The Rolling Stones Farewell Special' was never commercially aired. Clearly, pre-exile jitters were show-ing. Mick's own turn came four days later, when the Stones threw their friends and themselves a going-away party at Skindles Hotel in Maidenhead. According to Kenneth Anger, 'everyone was get-ting loose around 2 a.m., when the sound system went dead . . . Mick asked why this had happened, and was told that a village ordi-nance forbade music after then. Mick promptly picked up the table and threw it through an enormous plate-glass window that over-looked the Thames. The piece of glass must have cost £20,000 . . . That was *his* gesture toward having the music turned off.'

The last sight that most Britons thought they would ever have of the Rolling Stones was of the band camping its way through 'Brown Sugar' on *Top of the Pops*. Mick Jagger vamped it up in a pink satin suit, Keith's chugging guitar drove the teenaged audience in to a synchronised boogie, and the rest of the band mimed frantically away as best they could. By the time the clip aired on the evening of 15 April, the Stones themselves were already safely ensconced in their Riviera hideaways. The full enormity of their position had only finally dawned on them when they discovered that neither Allen Klein, nor anyone else working on their behalf, had paid a penny of the steadily accumulating interest and penalties on their outstanding tax bills, leaving Mick and Keith each some £240,000 in arrears. The result of this oversight was to be an extended period spent living in some of the most palatial villas on the Côte d'Azur, although Keith, in particular, long rued the fact that 'the Establishment – a lot of fuckin' judges and politicians – kicked us out of our own country', even if his ire might have been better directed at the Stones' highly paid business managers for getting them to that pass in the first place. Whatever the cause, the result was a certain mutual sense of resentment towards that same Establishment. As the Stones finally prepared to absent themselves, 'the old farts at Decca', as Keith characterised his outgoing employers, informed them that under the terms of their original contract they still owed the label one more single. Always a stickler for such detail, Mick went up to Decca House for the last time and personally delivered the tape of a rollicking number entitled 'Cocksucker Blues'.

Keith's initial displeasure at leaving Britain was somewhat mollified when he saw the house selected for his exile. Boasting a pair of 20-foot-high wrought-iron front doors, a grand living room, a sweeping staircase, eight bedrooms and cool, tiled floors and frescoed ceilings throughout, Villa Nellcôte stood perched on a clifftop overlooking the sparkling Cap Ferrat. For various occult reasons, the house's original owner, a retired British admiral, had thrown himself off the back balcony to his death. It's said by at least one renowned rock biographer that Nellcôte had been used as a Gestapo interrogation centre 'during five long years of wartime Nazi rule', although this claim can perhaps be modified by the fact that the Germans occupied that part of France only from March 1943 to July 1944. (Nor were there any 'dried bloodstains' or 'sinister iron shackles' in the house's cellar.) Ian Stewart, a more reliable source, would remember Nellcôte as 'a Scott Fitzgerald trip, ten people for lunch ... fifteen for dinner'. There were also jungle-like gardens where palm and fig trees, and musky lavender bushes, blew about in the sea breeze. Along with a new E-type Jaguar, Keith soon bought a powerful Riva speedboat and a schooner he named *Mandrax* to buzz around the harbour. Meanwhile, Bill Wyman and Mick Taylor, now the father of a baby girl, Chloe, were both in rented villas in Grasse, 30 miles inland, Charlie had his farmhouse, and Mick Jagger was installed with Bianca in the presidential suite of the Hotel Byblos in St Tropez. In general, this was a rather well-heeled exile.

On 6 April 1971, the Rolling Stones cruised in to Cannes on a chartered yacht, flying their corporate logo, to formally sign their new, four-year record deal with Kinney-Atlantic. At least in terms of longevity, the great Beatles–Stones debate was now settled in the latter's favour. There was a celebration that night at the Carlton hotel. Scantily clad guests were soon jumping up on the dais where a band played, peeling their tops off, bumping and grinding against each other. Bill Wyman had his camera out. One teenager strutted across stage, pumping her arms in a homage to Mick Jagger's famous 'rooster on acid' dance, which he'd first trotted out when she was in primary school. Mick himself was mobbed by photographers, much taken by his flaming pink suit, and the pregnant Bianca's provocatively low-slung blouse.

Keith Richards left early. 'I have to find my dog,' he said. 'He's my only friend at the party, man.'

Sticky Fingers. Even without the bulging crotch on the front cover, and the lubricious advertising, those forty-five minutes would capture the debauched essence of the Stones in all their fucked-up, 70s glory. The album is soaked in sex, drugs and rock and roll. But the band also jump a few borders, slipping in some gentle country and soul grooves, not to mention a nod to Carlos Santana, among the dirtier guitar slashes. Similarly, *Fingers* knows no lyrical bounds: everything is fair game, from social commentary to dope – 'cocaine eyes', 'speed freak jive', 'head full of snow', 'needle and a spoon' – quite apart from the harrowing lilt of 'Sister Morphine', which earned a BBC ban for its brazen use of the word 'score'. From the frothy, open-G rave-up of 'Brown Sugar' to the soporific finale of 'Moonlight Mile', the album's infectious swagger and panoramic breadth make it the finest slab of white blues-rock for years; since, in fact, *Let it Bleed*. Too slick for traditionalists, perhaps, but a stone masterpiece for everyone else.

By midsummer, *Sticky Fingers* was number one in Britain, America and fourteen other markets.

Mick Jagger and Bianca Macias went down the aisle on Wednesday 12 May at the small, whitewashed chapel of St Anne on a hill above St Tropez. The groom wore a three-piece suit, his bride a floppy hat and a white St Laurent jacket cut to her quite prominent nipples. A chaotic civil ceremony had taken place earlier that morning, with Bianca visibly seething after Mick had presented her with a 28-page prenuptial contract, and half the world's entertainment press swarming in to the local town hall from the nearby Cannes film festival, which also started that week. Mick had told everyone he wanted a low-key wedding, for which he chose the Riviera on the opening day of the summer season, as well as flying in a chartered jetload of seventy-five rock-star guests and their families. Among those attending were Paul and Ringo (who were suing each other, and not speaking), Eric Clapton, Keith Moon, Ron Wood and the actress Nathalie Delon, whose previous lover had just been found dumped in a Paris garbage can with two bullets in the back of his head, and who now took up with the Stones' sideman Bobby Keys as an alternative. Among those declining was the author William Burroughs, who told me that he had been asked to pay fifty pounds towards the cost of his airfare and that this had been 'too much, under the circumstances'. Mick's parents came and 'hated it', Eva Jagger recalled. 'The press were like something out of a bad film, and I had a splitting headache for two days. These awful rock-music people kept dragging Mick off in to a corner. We never did manage to give him his present.' At an uneasy eve-of-wedding family do at the Byblos, the elder Mrs Jagger had sat silently appraising her future daughter-in-law's perhaps overgenerous application of mascara, diaphanous silk blouse and miniskirt. 'She was lovely to a fault.' Keith Richards was the only one of the Stones invited to the actual ceremony. He arrived late, arguing furiously with Anita, and couldn't initially get through the scrum of fans, demonstrators and

Paris Match photographers at the chapel door. Pallenberg could tell that a few seconds of sharing a confined space with the mob was already imposing unbearable strain on her partner's fragile PR sense. At the height of the melee, a Fleet Street tabloid reporter tapped him on the shoulder wanting an interview. This was short and sharp and none of it was printable. When Keith finally squeezed in, he threw an ashtray at the verger. The bride was then given away by the Queen's cousin, Lord Lichfield. At Bianca's request, the organist played snatches of Bach's 'Wedding March' and, interminably, the theme from *Love Story*.

Later, back in the Hotel Byblos, Terry Reid and some of Mick's other celebrity guests were changing for the reception.

'By and by we could hear a clanking noise growing ever louder, coming down the corridor towards us. At that time the Byblos had wooden floors, so you could really hear it echoing away, getting nearer and nearer. Clanking and rattling; very weird. All of a sudden it stopped right outside. The door swung open, and everyone did a double take. A man stood on the threshold. He was in full Nazi uniform. He seemed to be standing to attention, all SS tunic, with an Iron Cross dangling round his neck, and black jackboots. It was Keith.'

'Hi, guys,' he said.

The party that night took place in a private theatre at the Café des Arts. Celebrities embraced and grew ecstatic at the sight of one another as Terry Reid sang. Keith, still in his field gear, and after encountering a friendly coke dealer in the Byblos gents, blacked out in a corner. A turbanned Bianca danced once with 60-year-old Joe Jagger, and left alone. But her evening wasn't quite over. Hours later, she awoke to find a stark-naked Keith Moon abseiling through her sixth-floor bedroom window. Although unclothed, Moon was wearing a pair of novelty glasses whose eyeballs bounced around in front of him on springs, and sported a set of women's underpants on his head. Years later, Bianca gave it as her opinion that her marriage had ended on her wedding day.

After that, there was little to do but spend the summer at Nellcôte with Gram Parsons and a constantly shifting cast of friends,

musicians and drug dealers. The house's formal salons were decorated with antique brocade chairs, its floors inlaid with purple and
white tiles, with gilt-edged mirrors on the walls and upstairs
ceilings. White silk curtains flowed from the tall windows, which
offered a commanding view of hills almost obscenely bright with
bougainvillea. Down the twisting back steps lay a private beach.
Keith himself rarely went there, preferring to lie in darkened rooms,
toking and listening to thunderous Chuck Berry records. A cordon
bleu chef named Jacques, or 'Fat Jack', served exquisite meals at all
hours of the day and night. Keith drove him mad by asking for
bangers and mash, with plenty of brown sauce.

The Stones had generally enjoyed working at Stargroves and,
given the lack of quality studios locally – Stu characterised the few
available on the Riviera as 'fucking awful . . . the loos were always
backed up and you could smell the sewage' – the band eventually
decided to record their next album onsite, in the cellar of Keith's
house. Even though some early tracks had been cut at Olympic,
and the final product was mixed in LA, *Exile on Main Street* duly
became the greatest and most profitable rock and roll ever to
emerge from a basement. As widely reported, it proceeded in some
domestic turmoil. Thanks to his Scottish nurse, Keith himself had
actually arrived on the Riviera relatively 'clean', in the sense that
he was taking coke, LSD, pills and pot, but not heroin, which
almost counted as abstemious by prevailing Stones standards.
Unfortunately, Keith then managed to fall off a go-kart he was
racing around a local track, scraping most of the skin off his back
in the process. A 33-year-old occasional Grand Prix driver, socialite
and drug runner named Tommy Weber had befriended the Stones
in their final pre-exile days in London, a relationship that survived
the seduction by Anita Pallenberg of Weber's lovely but fragile wife
Susan, or 'Puss', while in Bowden House. In May 1971, Puss
would check in to a London hotel and kill herself with a cocktail
of champagne and sleeping pills. According to Tommy Weber,
'Keith and Anita were simply marvellous and insisted I stay at
Nellcôte', although, like the registered 'junkie couple' at Redlands,
he was soon to find that Richards' hospitality came at a price. 'A

little after the go-kart incident,' Weber recalled, 'Keith looked at me and he said: "OK, Tommy, I think it's about time you went to the doctor and get him to get us some you-know-what." Which everyone had been staying away from. And that was the beginning of it. The go-kart accident instigated the opiates.'

The inevitable followed. Playing host to twenty-five or thirty stoned musicians and friends, Nellcôte soon became the Riviera's answer to Graceland, with in-house connections like Tommy Weber and Tony Sanchez joined by a regular procession of late-night visitors from Marseilles who invariably arrived wearing shades and carrying identical black briefcases chained to their wrists. 'Everyone was so out of it,' Mick Jagger would confirm. 'And the engineers, the producers – all the people that were supposed to be organised – were worse than anybody.' Before long, even the once-austere Jimmy Miller was walking around with his tattooed right hand clamped to a pint mug of tequila, and more than once called a halt to the proceedings in order to be violently ill at the mixing desk. 'Do you want to die?' Miller shouted for no apparent reason one evening. 'I'll see if you fuckers want to die!' At that he attempted to introduce a match to a wadded-up handkerchief he held over his drink, seemingly in an effort to fashion a Molotov cocktail, but quick intervention from Stu and a nearby golf club saved the day. A Stones accountant later noted in a court deposition that Nellcôte had cost Richards some £4,000 a week: £500 each on food and drink, £1,200 on rent and £1,800 on 'cotton candy', or pure Thai heroin. Keith would have no difficulty meeting the French government's requirement that he invest some £30,000 for each year of his residency in their country.

Apart from the drugs, there were the logistics. Agreeing to work in one of their own homes was no guarantee that the Stones would actually all be there at the same time. Mick Jagger particularly disliked the communal vibe – 'you didn't know whether you [were] recording or having dinner', he complained – and he also had his heavily pregnant, and vocally unhappy, wife to consider. Before long, Bianca decamped to Paris, effectively forcing Mick to commute across France for the remaining sessions. More than once, she threatened to leave him for good. The band sometimes called her 'Bianca the Wanker' behind her back. Mick himself had now exchanged cheek for *chic*, dressing like a Frenchman in a beret and tight suede maxicoat, also the subject of some in-house chafing around Nellcôte in his absence. Jimmy Miller remembered 'many mornings after great nights of recording, coming over to Keith's for lunch, and within a few minutes of seeing him, realising something was wrong. He'd say, "Jagger's pissed off to Paris again." I sensed resentment, because he felt we were starting to get something and when Mick returned the magic might be gone.' Later that summer, when Anita fell pregnant, she spread the obviously base rumour that the baby was Mick's. According to Marshall Chess, 'it was tossed around whose kid it was. [Anita] thought it was Jagger's. There were major problems between Mick and Keith over it.' Meanwhile, both Bill and Mick Taylor found themselves sitting around Nellcôte's mouldy basement at all hours while Keith himself was 'putting Marlon to bed' upstairs, an exercise that often took several hours. Charlie, for his part, was driven in from his farmhouse 125 miles away in the foothills of the Massif Central, arriving punctually every Monday morning at nine, and leaving again every Friday evening exactly at five. He slept in a small upstairs guest room, spending his ample leisure time at Nellcôte sketching pictures of flowers and birds. If inspiration suddenly struck and Keith wanted to record something at the weekend, as happened with 'Happy', either he or Jimmy Miller played the drums.

In hindsight, Villa Nellcôte was perhaps too close to Marseilles for Keith's good. While his bandmates sweltered downstairs, sometimes eking out a little music, he organised a heroin supply chain with the local Corsican mafia – nicknamed *les cowboys* – an arrangement which soon came to the attention of the Toulon *prefecture* narcotics bureau. By midsummer, Fat Jack, the Nellcôte chef, was also spilling to *les flics*, after Anita Pallenberg allegedly gave his teenage daughter heroin. Jack tried to blackmail Keith, who told him to fuck off. The gendarmes arrived the next morning, took statements, and asked why internationally known drug couriers had been seen wandering around the premises. Richards told them they were technical crew on the new album. Stu believed the police had subsequently planted a paid informer on the Nellcôte staff. When Keith picked up the phone, he was convinced he could hear someone breathing on the line. This perhaps wasn't the best time for Eric Clapton, then bouncing between one crash cure and another for his own addiction, to invite himself down for a quiet weekend, most of which he spent passed out in Nellcôte's downstairs bathroom with a needle in his arm. Following that, Eric went back to his Surrey mansion and bolted the door for the next two years. John Lennon, with Yoko in tow, followed for a visit – but exited rapidly after vomiting on the marbled floor. The strain of trying to mobilise the Stones while at the same time entertaining his 2-year-old son sometimes proved too much even for Keith. 'You're getting up my nose,' he would eventually remark to Gram Parsons, if so by no means the only substance to do so. Parsons spent weeks at Nellcôte strung out on coke and irritating Anita. This wouldn't do; Keith threw his best work friend out and made a new one in Bobby Keys.

Exile ground on, through the hottest late summer and early autumn in recorded Provence history. It was the last non-airconditioned album the Stones would ever make, and even at night the temperature in Keith's crypt, where the musicians sat around in their underwear bathed in a ghastly grotto-blue light, reached 100°F. Before long, the sessions were going under the working title of 'Tropical Disease'. Unsurprisingly, the music that resulted was sludgy, chaotic and often tired-sounding. It was also the Stones' greatest and most enduring moment, with songs like 'Rocks Off', 'All Down the Line' and 'Sweet Virginia' all emerging from the field-project approach in which the band typically jammed their way through a continuous twelve-hour flow of blues music from which the crew later extracted palatable three- and four-minute chunks. One night, Mick and Keith removed the joints from their mouths long enough to lay down the vocals for 'Tumbling Dice', which is believed to have taken 117 shots to get right, after the Nellcôte housekeeper, partial to the nearby casinos, helped out with the lyrics. The masterly and aptly titled 'Ventilator Blues' was also cooked up in these musty surroundings. As usual, Bill Wyman was irked at being detained from his other pursuits, and was sometimes heard to remark that it would be nice to know exactly what song it was they were actually recording. To expedite things, the whole band moved in to Nellcôte for the final sessions. One afternoon, Keith sent a secretary up to everyone's rooms to present the Stones with bills of £100 each for bed and board. Wyman got so upset that he broke his self-imposed vow of silence. 'It's a joke, isn't it?' he asked over the dinner table that night.

'No,' said Keith, with some venom. 'It's not. You're getting accommodation dirt cheap at that price, and anyone who doesn't like it can piss off.'

The Stones paid up.

Relations between Nellcôte's primary tenants and the wider community were also sometimes rocky. One afternoon, Keith Richards and 'Spanish Tony' Sanchez got in to a minor traffic accident in the nearby town of Beaulieu. The harbourmaster, one Jacques Raymond, wandered out of his office to investigate and Keith addressed him as a 'fuckin' Frog'. From this point on, things began to deteriorate rapidly. Keith pulled out a toy gun belonging to Marlon, and M. Raymond drew his own very real revolver before calling the law. Spanish Tony deemed it best to fly back to England that night, leaving Keith to face a judicial investigation that eventually petered out after the local mayor came up to Nellcôte for dinner and a few autographed albums. Back in London, Sanchez thoughtfully obtained an ounce of pharmaceutical coke and concealed this in a hand-carved toy piano, which he then shipped back for Marlon's, or, rather, his parents' attention. Richards and Pallenberg smashed open the gift on arrival and devoured the contents.

According to documents obtained from the FBI, 'local law enforcement officials [now] put the house under daily surveillance', alerted not only by the comings and goings of *les cowboys* but by 'an individual identif[ied] as Mick Jagger, seen to enter the grounds on a motorcycle accompanied by a woman passenger not his wife'. Apparently, the police detail weren't yet at their posts early one

Monday morning, when thieves broke in and stole eleven of Keith's guitars.

In fact, many of *Exile*'s best tracks worked in close connection with the chaotic and increasingly paranoid atmosphere at Nellcôte. 'Rip this Joint' was comfortably the fastest thing the Stones had ever recorded, sounding as if they were in a collective race to finish it before the police kicked down the door. By the time it came to 'Casino Boogie', 'Mick and I had run ourselves ragged,' Keith says, so they resorted to William Burroughs' cut-up technique for the lyrics, which perhaps helps explain lines like: 'Sky diver inside her, skip rope, stunt flyer/wounded lover, got no time on hand'. Friends could almost hear the banished Gram Parsons on 'Sweet Virginia', like a musical demon limb after an amputation. Likewise, 'Soul Survivor' seethed with subversive energy and a riff that lingered long after it was over. According to Anita, the final part of *Exile* was recorded with power diverted from the French railway system. Mostly, though, it drew its electrical charge from an interior source, the tension between Mick and Keith.

The Jaggers' daughter was born at a nursing home in Paris on 21 October 1971. After prolonged discussion she was christened Jade, 'because,' said Mick, 'it fits. She's precious and quite, quite perfect; she looks a little like Bianca and a lot like me.' (The child's middle names were 'Sheena' and 'Jezebel'.) Mick phoned Keith later that night to say that he wouldn't be coming back to Nellcôte. The band was to finish up the basic tracks and he would lay down his vocals when *Exile* was mixed in Hollywood. Keith was not pleased. It was ten years since the old friends had met up on the platform at Dartford station, and with the notable exception of their music they no longer had much in common.

With the law now taking up residence in an unmarked van parked under some low-hanging palm trees outside Nellcôte's front gate, Richards and Pallenberg deemed it wise to move in to a small guest bedroom at the rear of the house. Stu in turn parked the Mobile immediately underneath the window, so that in the event of a bust Keith and Anita could jump down on to the top of the truck and make their escape. It was never explained how a four-ton recording studio was then expected to outrun the police on the twisting cliff road that led away from the house, but Keith wasn't one for details. By early November, as *Exile* wound down, Nellcôte was beset on every front. The narcs were making their surveillance more obvious by the day. Burglars walked off with Keith's replacement guitars. A stoned Anita then managed to set the couple's bed on fire. Dave, the chauffeur, broke down the door to find them lying there, comatose, with the mattress in flames all around them. This incident was to prove a critical wake-up call, because twenty-four hours later, on 30 November, Keith, Anita, Marlon, Charlie Watts and most of the crew took a midnight flight from Nice to Paris, and on to Los Angeles, where they were joined by the rest of the band. In their haste to decamp, they abandoned most of Keith's record collection, his two boats and his E-type Jaguar. Some doubt exists about the exact nature of the mass breakout. In one version, the French authorities had let Keith leave the country only on condition that he continue to rent the house while abroad, as proof that he meant to return. In another popular account, the local force was unaware that its wrecked-looking prey had moved on. In either case, neither Keith nor anyone else in the Stones would ever see Nellcôte again.

Exactly two weeks later, on 14 December, a squad of twelve policemen rammed open the gate and poured in to Nellcôte through the doors and windows. According to published reports, they turned up enough heroin, coke and hash to throw the book at Keith and Anita. A maid told them that everybody had suddenly left one night, taking their mysterious canisters of tape with them.

As at Muscle Shoals, not a trace of the Stones' recordings would be left behind, let alone a forwarding address.

Mick, Keith and the engineers spent most of the winter of 1971–72 at Sunset Sound studios in Hollywood, turning Tropical Disease in to *Exile*. Horns and washes of pop-gospel hollering would flesh out 'Tumbling Dice', 'Shine a Light' got the full Billy Preston organ treatment, while 'Let It Loose' was subjected to a week-long revision by the Stones' friend Mac Rebennack (Dr John) and a soul-sister chorus. Wyman apparently wanted nothing to do with any overdubbing, and would be credited on only eight of *Exile's* eighteen finished tracks. In his absence, the Indo-jazz pioneer Bill Plummer came in to play upright bass. 'The Stones weren't exactly the Mormon Tabernacle Choir,' Plummer reveals. 'There was a lot of lubricating going on, and of course it's always a thrill to be asked to play on a song called "Turd on the Run". But they also knew exactly what they wanted. I did four tracks in about two hours, shook everyone's hand, went home. There was a big crowd at the back door, I remember, and people were worried it was the Hell's Angels. Mick and Keith were being hassled by them.' Plummer's rollicking bass helped make *Exile* a major hit in both Britain and America. He was paid his standard fee, 'a couple of hundred bucks', for the session. Venetta Fields, a former Ikette, also spent several days with the Stones in the studio, and could be heard on their new single 'Tumbling Dice', among other numbers. 'Every day when I went in to sing I walked past a store window where they had this big, second-hand fur coat on display. I couldn't possibly afford it. It was freezing that winter. I thought I'd die it was so cold. [*Exile*] may have been about sex, fame and drugs for some people, but for me it was a job. Hard work. I did finally get to buy that coat.'

While in Los Angeles, Mick rented William Randolph Hearst's former mansion in Beverly Hills, Keith and Anita were installed in Nellcôte-like opulence in Bel Air, and the rest of the band were eventually scattered around the purple smudge of Hollywood. Charlie, ever the Stones' style guru, brought in the Swiss-born filmmaker Robert Frank to shoot the album's cover and to produce a documentary of the band's next American tour, a decision they would regret. The former South African professional soccer player and doctor-turned-photographer, Norman Seeff, did *Exile's* inside art. 'Mick,' he says, 'had the idea of parodying the pictures of the Ballet Russe coming down the steps of the plane as they landed in France in the process of defecting from Russia to Monaco. Obviously, he identified with that. The session started at midnight, which is when the Stones' day began. There were a lot of women and gallons of cheap red wine involved, but in the end it was all finished successfully.' Less agreeable was the night Mick and Keith managed to get themselves thrown offstage at a local Chuck Berry concert. One of Berry's managers had waved them up and Keith tore in to a loud 'Sweet Little Sixteen', accompanied by Mick's mad, martial dancing. The audience went nuts. Keith says, 'It developed in to a little ego thing ... people were paying more attention to Chuck's band than they were to him.' Berry's version is even stranger: 'I didn't know who the fuck they were.'

Mick and Keith's love-hate relationship with Brian Jones also found its most public voice that winter, with the release of Jones' posthumous *Jajouka* LP on Rolling Stones Records. Taped in August 1968, the album saw Brian setting aside his fucked-up rocker persona for the role of godfather to the World Music movement: *Jajouka* covered territory from meditative spaciness to full-bore freakout, often in the same song. Stu remembered all the Stones sitting down one night in Hollywood to listen to it and said, 'Everyone was stunned the little fucker had it in him. They were genuinely impressed.'

May 1972. Twenty years before grunge, there was *Exile on Main Street*. The album's legacy will loom large over both the Stones legend and the whole history of rock and roll, ushering in several decades' worth of lo-fi tributes and parodies. 'Rocks Off' announced *Exile*'s intentions – Keith's riff raced by Charlie's neck-snapping beat – and then made the point with honks of sax, juggernaut rhythm and dimly moaned vocal interjections. (With lines like 'Ten liddle nigga/Sittin' on de wall' elsewhere on *Exile*, Mick was probably wise to heed Fats Domino's dictum, 'Never let 'em hear the words.') Jagger and Richards flexed their tag-team skills again on 'Rip this Joint', sung in a raspy burr and apparently accompanied by a vacuum cleaner. 'Just Wanna See His Face' was the most lyrically refined, and eccentric, thing on the album, with Mick favouring a mumbled approach and periodically wandering off-key, or off-mike altogether, as weird female hoots took up the slack. Keith's shrill intro to 'All Down the Line' was similarly out of wack, a noise that managed to sound both tossed off and perfect for the song – a 'really *sour*' guitar, as he put it approvingly. 'Shine a Light' started off like some churchy piano track, then built slowly through Mick T's scorching solo to climax in a massed-voice chorus which, in yet another sonic departure, seemed to have been recorded underwater. Although time has been kind to *Exile*, one of those official classic-rock double albums, like *Blonde on Blonde*, whose reputation ought to be sealed up in an eternal amber of chart and sales statistics, it initially flummoxed many of the same reviewers who had flocked to the more accessible *Sticky Fingers*, and who were now left scratching their heads, not nodding them.

Writing in *Rolling Stone*, the journalist and future Patti Smith guitarist Lenny Kaye said, 'There are songs that are better, there are songs that are worse, there are songs that will become your favorites and others you'll probably lift the needle for when their time is due ... You can leave the album and still feel vaguely unsatisfied, not quite brought to the peaks that this band of bands has always held out as a special prize in the past.' Other critical assessments were that *Exile* was 'an hour of bluesy clatter', sounding as if 'recorded down a pit' (not far off the mark), with an 'overall vibe [like] a gang-fight inside a rusty trash can', while Mick's old antagonist Mary Whitehouse had more specific reservations about the title or content of tunes like 'Turd on the Run'. The album itself was a summer number one and spent six months on the chart before returning on its re-release thirty-eight years later. *Let it Bleed* may have been more organic, but this was a flawed, sprawling masterpiece, the last great extreme work the Stones did.

After three months in Los Angeles, Keith Richards was on the move again, settling in to the same Montreux hotel as Vladimir Nabokov, author of *Lolita*, meaning that two of the twentieth century's more exotic creative talents were under the same Swiss hotel roof. Or they soon would be: Keith actually spent the first week of his new exile in Dr Denber's discreet De Nantes Clinic in nearby Vevey, in order to go through detox. Since he collapsed on arrival at the airport, turned green, and had to be driven off at top speed in an ambulance, this latest intervention seems to have come none too soon. Anita was heavily pregnant, and still fixing three times a day, so she, too, was taken in to Dr Denber's care. The rest of the Stones soon arrived among the lush vineyards, sharply angled roofs and dove-blue sea haze of Montreux, which became an unlikely commune as the band and crew gathered to rehearse their next tour. Mick Jagger never forgot how he was treated in Switzerland, where he could stroll around the local lake with his wife and baby daughter and no one ever hassled them. The tax break didn't hurt, either.

Dandelion Richards was born, with a cleft palate but otherwise perfectly healthy, on 17 April 1972. Keith's mother Doris, who took over most day-to-day responsibility for her granddaughter, quickly renamed her Angela. 'I was a bit unpredictable in those days,' Richards would later concede, when reflecting on his family arrangements. 'It's very difficult living with your old lady who's also a junkie, in fact a bigger one than you are. The only thing Anita ever said to me then was, "Has it arrived?"' Six months later, Keith would come up with the words and music of 'Angie' in his daughter's honour.

Meanwhile, Anita and the baby settled in to a suite in a new hotel, on the outskirts of Geneva.

Spanish Tony: 'Keith and I would take the children out for walks, [while] Anita languished in solitary splendour, smoking her joints, jabbing needles in her bottom ... After three weeks ... there were empty bottles everywhere, fag burns on most of the mock Louis XIV furniture and the sheets were an uninviting shade of grey. The maids stuck with the onerous task of cleaning out the suite insisted on fumigation.'

On 22 May, all five Stones were issued with work permits at the US Embassy in London, and all five proceeded to miss their plane to Los Angeles. Rehearsals eventually resumed on a sound stage at Warner Brothers, 'very larky' (Stu) in a postmodern, it's-only-rock-'n'-roll way. Mick was dressed in a scanty rhinestone catsuit with a pink sash, and silver bells on his shoes.

The Stones settled with Allen Klein that month for $2million, instead of the roughly $30million the band had claimed he owed them. Bill Wyman, for one, was fuming; after legal costs, he and Charlie would each receive around $170,000 for their services as recording artists over the past six years, seven or eight times more than the equivalent skilled blue-collar wage, but still somewhat shy of the $3–4million figure Bill had had in mind. Even this relatively modest sum would be diluted following Rupert Loewenstein's latest negotiations with the Inland Revenue. Klein, meanwhile, wound up with the rights to the entire Stones publishing catalogue through 1970, and later successfully sued for ownership of two other songs, 'Wild Horses' and 'Angie', from 1971 and '73 respectively. Even by prevailing 1970s rock and roll standards, it was a crushing triumph of the managerial 'bread-head' over the creative artist. Although not exactly 'flat broke', as Mick Jagger insisted, the Stones would clearly need to keep turning out the albums and tours, or else forego the sort of Babylonian lifestyle they had come to enjoy over the years. 'The band has resolved all outstanding difficulties with their former business manager,' Les Perrin announced in a typically dignified statement later in May. 'The parties look forward to co-operating together, in their mutual best interests, in the future.' Mick's private verdict on the 'Fatso affair' was considerably more scathing. 'The deal,' he said, 'is that Klein never has anything else to do with us.'

To a certain generation, the Stones' 1972 American tour remains the ultimate in glam rock and roll junketing: the one with all the sex and dope and a documentary about it called *Cocksucker Blues*. A critic has written that 'for years afterwards, every kid – male and female – in every high school lunch room wanted to look like Keith Richards'. Quite apart from the music, there was the Stones' private DC-7 – the Lapping Tongue – a flying *Satyricon* of well-endowed groupies and unusually accommodating stewardesses serving nonstop tequila sunrises; a permanent, travelling entourage that included the band's own doctor and pharmacist, as well as society drop-ins like the writer Truman Capote and his companion Princess Lee Radziwill (Jackie Kennedy's sister); totemic Stones scenes, like Keith Richards defenestrating his tenth-floor hotel-room television, physically evicting a female process server from the band's jet, and later being busted for assaulting a photographer; frequent stage invasions, street riots and other outbreaks of public disorder; four significant bomb scares; one actual explosion; and a climactic rooftop party in New York where the band found themselves being serenaded by Muddy Waters while posing for pictures with the likes of Zsa Zsa Gabor.

Stevie Wonder enjoyed major crossover success as the Stones' warm-up act, but felt shunned by Jagger and Richards 'because I wouldn't get high with them'. When Wonder begged off one show because his drummer had suffered a nervous breakdown and checked himself in to a psychiatric hospital, Keith reacted by punching a steel dressing-room locker. From there things began to deteriorate badly, with Richards yelling, 'That bloody cunt! Fuck that Stevie cunt. He's a cunt!' and various aides frantically trying to protect Keith's hand. Later, Wonder would privately remark that he was 'never quite sure where the Stones were coming from'.

Opening night, Vancouver: thirty-eight Canadian policemen stretchered off after clashes with rioting fans. That was the quiet, out-of-town preview. The Stones' set was a hi-tech marvel that resembled something out of a nocturnal military rally lit by Albert Speer. Bathed in stark-white spots, with a 40 × 16-foot mirror hanging above to reflect the band from all angles ('just like Mick's place', Stu observed), the band jogged on for a nightly ninety-minute mix of big beats, tight britches and classic, chant-along choruses. The stage itself was washed in a solution of warm water and 7-Up to render it danceable, and from the first song – 'Brown Sugar' – Mick was off to the races, bumping and grinding in his skimpy jumpsuit. After an extended medley from *Exile*, and the Marat-Sade head show of 'Midnight Rambler', Keith turned up the juice for the run-out section of 'Honky Tonk Women', 'Bye Bye Johnny' and 'Jumpin' Jack Flash', with smoking solos all round. The hell-for-leather gallop of 'Street Fighting Man' closed the show in a gale of power chords, Mick Taylor's lusty guitar belying his queasy appearance and Bill and Charlie going in to a synchronised frenzy, their own faces totally deadpan. Doing without a signature song like 'Satisfaction' was not the sort of choice any other band lucky enough to have it in its arsenal was likely to make, but no one here seemed to miss it. As Mick Jagger threw rose petals, the 20,000 faithful were generally busy kicking the hall in to matchsticks. Backstage in a mobile recording studio one night, Ian Stewart opened the door and stuck his head outside to see what all the fuss was about. Mick was singing the lines about 'marching, charging feet' and, in eerie synchronicity, the truck was actually shaking around on its wheels. 'So many people were kicking the floor, we were bouncing around like an earthquake.'

Stu thought Mick 'an interesting case on tour ... He'd be up there screaming with froth flying, and then come in to the dressing room and sit down and it would be Mick the vicar again. I admired that about him.' Jagger's old grammar school friend Clive Robson, in town for a law seminar, found himself in the midst of a Stones party in Los Angeles, 'where I saw Mike, or Mick, for the first time in ten years. There he was, surrounded by groupies, sitting in a red velvet chair and wearing a satin suit and make-up. Quite a change from our last encounter. I remember him slipping through three or four different accents before getting the right one, and from then on he was very sweet. When you got him away from the court jesters he was just a normal Dartford guy who you could have a beer and a laugh with, but you were also aware there was a whole organisation out there awaiting his pleasure.' One of Mick's habits was to call up the tour manager Peter Rudge or one of the other sixty-five crew members late at night and ply them with technical questions, a possibility which kept many of them at their posts until the small hours.

In Chicago, the Stones moved in to Hugh Hefner's lakeside Playboy mansion, mingling with the Bunnies in Hef's underwater bar. At some stage in the nonstop carousing, there was a specific party to welcome the band, a double row of Range Rovers and Mercedes wagons out front testifying to the arrival of Roman Polanski, billionaire oil heir John Paul Getty Jr and Andy Warhol. It was that kind of crowd. Keith and his partner in crime Bobby Keys caused some merriment by snapping an amyl nitrate popper under the nose of a passing waiter, then watching as he spun round and round, desperately trying, and failing, to keep control of a fully laden tray of champagne and other goodies. Later, they managed to set one of Hefner's bathrooms on fire.

As Hef acknowledged, the Stones' three-day residency as a whole transcended mere decadence. Dressed in his ubiquitous pyjamas and smoking jacket, the band's 46-year-old host spent his evenings waltzing around the crowded living room with a succession of Playmates, for the most part nude but for their stiletto heels and elaborate jewellery, and one pneumatically built young guest introduced herself to Mick Jagger with the words: 'Shall I put my diaphragm in now?' The customary arrangement during their stay was that, after a little socialising, each Stone would pick the two or three girls who struck his fancy and retire to his own soundproofed room. It may have been Bill Wyman's apogee as a career musician. An honourable exception to the rule was Charlie, who preferred playing snooker.

But if part of the day was recreation, the remainder was business as usual – the Rolling Stones brand of business. 'It wasn't fun,' Jo Bergman would later remark of the tour. 'And it wasn't supposed to be. Be punctual, make money, and don't hurt anyone; that was the given system.' The new-found air of relative propriety occasionally jarred with Keith Richards, not a man who liked to be tucked up early with a mug of cocoa – and one 'marked for death', according to Truman Capote. The author of *In Cold Blood* turned up at a party one night in Keith's hotel suite, which he remembered as looking like a Bedouin encampment. Scarves and flags were draped over lamps, Arabic music thumped out of the sound system, and there was a cauldron of something stewing on the floor. After deciding not to write about the tour, Capote would call the band 'complete idiots . . . That unisex thing is a no-sex thing. Believe me, Mick Jagger's about as sexy as a pissing toad.'

On 12 July, in Indianapolis, Brian's old friend Stash de Rola was beaten up by the Stones' security goons in a misunderstanding about drugs. Keith, who also liked Stash, was extremely upset by this development. The bodyguards were subjected to a brief trial, of the sort popular in Cuba or Burma, before being frogmarched upstairs at gunpoint in order to apologise to their victim, who was suffering from several cracked ribs and a broken nose. 'Keith was on such a rant, he even yelled how mad [Jones] would have been,' Stu

remarked. It happened to be exactly ten years since Brian had first
led the Stones out on stage at the Marquee Club.

A week later, the Lapping Tongue was diverted by fog on its way
in to Boston and forced to land 50 miles away in Warwick, Rhode
Island. The band was already late, tired and irritable when an agency
photographer named Andy Dyckerman pulled up and started taking
'unauthorised' shots, as opposed to the kind usually seen in glossy
magazines. There was a tense standoff as Dyckerman and Peter
Rudge exchanged views on the media's First Amendment rights,
a debate settled only when Keith Richards slugged the paparazzo
as he ran past him on the tarmac. The Port Authority cops arrested
Keith, Jagger trotting alongside shouting, 'Look, man, what are you
doing? We got a show tonight.' After the third or fourth 'fuck you',
Mick then joined Keith in the paddy-wagon. Once in custody, the
latter was relieved of a .38 pistol found concealed in his boot.
Perhaps fortunately, an aide not involved in the fracas was carrying
Keith's drugs for the night, which he remembered as comprising
'three or four pills, some amyls, a half-pound sack of coke and a
hash pipe'. A three-way combination of the Governor of Rhode
Island, the celebrity lawyer F. Lee Bailey and the mayor of Boston,
Kevin White, finally sprang the Stones at midnight, after a judge
agreed it would be in the interests of public safety to get the show
started as quickly as possible, particularly as the streets around the
Boston Garden had just erupted in a race riot. In one of those
sudden reversals of fortune characteristic of the band's career, Jagger
and Richards were then given a high-speed police escort to their
appointment. As their car approached Boston, they could see the
glow of burning rubble out of their window. 'We do that?' Mick
enquired impassively. At 1 a.m., the Stones pulled up at the back
of the hall, ran straight onstage and played one of the killer shows
of the tour. Kevin White later suggested that the band might like
to give a free concert for his family and political supporters in order
to thank him for his help in getting them out of jail. It didn't
happen.

Last stop but one, Pennsylvania. Robert Frank wanted an orgy
scene for his film and two young fans obliged on the plane. It was

all done like a stag movie, wobbling cameras, woeful dialogue and groupies with giant tits. Everyone came out of their private state-rooms to watch, shaking maracas and wailing away in time with the action. Bill Wyman's 10-year-old son happened to be on the flight and Bill, missing out for once, took him up to the front of the jet to look out of the window at Pittsburgh.

New York. Mick Jagger's twenty-ninth birthday and the final concerts came together in a rush that stretched from Madison Square Garden to a glittering reception on the roof of the St Regis hotel. The Stones' three climactic concerts 'touch[ed] the isolated sense of togetherness that many young people came to feel about themselves in the Sixties', the *New York Times* said. 'Their appeal [was] beyond music, beyond theater and in to symbolic expression of generational independence.' They were good gigs. Keith cuffed the riffs, the sound and lights were both exemplary, and nobody needed binoculars. The crew threw cream pies around at the end of the last show, leaving Mick and the boys to entertain the crowd for several minutes without the benefit of musical accompaniment. An hour or so later, the band was partying in the elegant environs of the St Regis with the likes of Tennessee Williams, Woody Allen and Bob Dylan, while Andy Warhol took Polaroids. Mick received his birthday dues when Bianca toasted his health and a stripper leaped out of a cake. Bill brought his camera. Following that, every-one went out on the terrace to watch the total eclipse of the moon.

During the eight-week tour the Stones played to 462,000 fans each paying $6.50: three million bucks. Of this the group (via their hold-ing company, Promo Tours) grossed two million, minus 30 per cent prudently withheld for tax. Having kicked off at the beginning of June and finished in the last week of July, each of the band took home the equivalent of $5,180 a day, or $36,260 a week, roughly 200 times more than Joe Jagger earned as a physical-education lecturer and 300 times more than Bert Richards did at the Osram light bulb factory, where he still worked. But the rock and roll life wouldn't be all material grat-ification. Charlie Watts told friends he hated everything about the tour except the hour and a half a day he was actually on stage, and announced he was quitting shortly afterwards – to relent only when

Rupert Loewenstein advised him of the difficulty of maintaining large homes in the English and French countryside as the drummer in an occasional jazz group. Bill remained frustrated about money, and after three years Mick Taylor had had almost enough, remarking that he was 'bored' and 'disliked being surrounded by hangers-on permanently telling us how wonderful we were'.

Meanwhile, there were problems elsewhere in the ranks. The Stones slapped a writ on Robert Frank preventing him from showing his tour documentary, after Frank had told the *Montreal Star* it included some scenes the public might find 'revolting'. Marshall Chess, the band's de facto manager and head of Rolling Stones Records, lapsed in to long-term heroin addiction; the already frail Nicky Hopkins lost twenty-five pounds on the tour and arguably never quite recovered, despite undergoing the Church of Scientology's Purification Rundown, while Bobby Keys cheerfully described himself as 'one hundred per cent fucked up' by the experience. Kicked off the next Stones tour, he returned sixteen years later, when Keith Richards smuggled him on stage to play 'Brown Sugar', leaving Mick Jagger to 'fucking nearly gag' with surprise.

Keith Richards' tenancy at Nellcôte formally expired in October 1972. The house would remain empty for many years afterwards, shut up behind high walls topped by a strand of barbed wire and a sign saying '*Chiens bizarres*'. In a not unprecedented development, it's said the local rental agency was shocked by the overall condition of the property. Its inventory check showed the familiar cigarette burns and breakages, as well as numerous souvenirs of Keith's pet – though not tame – dogs, rabbits and parrot. Nor had Marlon neglected to leave his mark on the premises.

From mid-September, Keith and his family were installed first in Gryon and then in a chalet called Le Pec Varp in Villars, high in the foothills between Montreux and Lausanne. The 83-year-old Charlie Chaplin was a near neighbour. During his Swiss Family Richards period, Keith not only got addicted to heroin again but, more surprisingly, learned to ski. After watching the end of the cricket season in England, Mick Jagger came to visit to talk about a new album.

Mick later told Ian Stewart that this had been a frustrating experience, causing him to 'sit on his arse looking at the mountains' while
Keith either slept or fielded endless phone calls. There were also
various briefcase-carrying friends constantly coming and going.
Mick and the other Stones became quite tetchy. They didn't have
a lot of free time, and they were under pressure from Atlantic's boss,
the suave but insistent Ahmet Ertegun, who wanted more product,
fast. A certain tension consequently developed between Mick and
Keith, just as it had at Nellcôte.

On 2 December, the French police issued a warrant for Richards
and Pallenberg on charges of the 'use, supply and traffic' in drugs.
Front-page stories in Nice correctly reported that all five Stones were
wanted for interview, and wrongly added that they would be arrested
as soon as they set foot on French soil. Two days later, both Micks,
Bill and Charlie flew to the Riviera to 'deny categorically we have
been charged with the buying and use of heroin' and promising to
sue should anyone say otherwise. After protesting their innocence,
some of the band members and their families took the opportunity
to spend a day sailing around the harbour on Keith's abandoned
yacht, the Mandrax. 'Everything went far better than any of us had
hoped,' Bill Wyman would later say of the preliminary court hearing, at which he and Charlie both told the judge that they had never,
under any circumstances, used drugs. 'The police witnesses denied
everything and insisted that they were made to sign false statements.
While this put us in the clear, it still left Keith with a major problem.' Bill was also left to rue the fact that, although only one of the
Stones was charged, the $58,000 bill that came in from the band's
Paris lawyers was split evenly six ways. Anita's was the final share.

On 15 October 1973, a court in Nice found Richards and
Pallenberg guilty in absentia of the use and supply of narcotics. Both
received a suspended sentence and a 5,000-franc fine. The judge
added another provision. It was meant as a punishment, but might
well have come as a relief to the couple whose dream life on the
Riviera had quickly turned in to a nightmare. Keith and Anita were
both banned from France for two years.

6

THE DRACULA GIG

For the Stones, 1973 was the year of living dangerously. After a decade together, the band members were no longer the cohesive fighting unit of old; everyone had wives – or 'old ladies' – and kids, and Jagger and Richards were living not just in different countries but 'a different world', Keith said later. 'It got up my nose, his jet-set shit, and the flaunting of it. But he's a lonely guy, too. He's got his own problems.' With Keith himself at the height of his 'elegantly wasted' phase, barely more than a skeleton topped off by a crow's nest of black hair and a bone earring, Mick assumed total control. When the group slouched in to one of their periodic meetings, it was 'more like a lecture, or a performance', Stu recalled. Standing up to read off a list of points from a typed agenda, Mick would jab the air for emphasis, like 'a conductor', leading the greatest rock and roll band in the world – the band that, for so long, had refused to be led.

A gloomy outlook greeted the Stones as the new year dawned. On 4 January, both the Australian and Japanese governments banned the group, quickly followed by Canada's Ministry of Public Safety and the US Immigration Bureau. This precluded a significant portion of any possible future tour itinerary. There was still a French arrest warrant out for Keith and Anita and, for tax purposes, everyone remained exiled from Britain. Meanwhile, a judge in Warwick, Rhode Island, ruled that Mick and Keith would have to stand trial there as a result of their altercation with a local photographer, although the charges were later dismissed. With Atlantic demanding a new album and England, France and North America all unavailable, the Stones took a lead from Paul Simon and moved in to Dynamic Studios in Kingston, Jamaica. It was a particularly significant choice for Keith, who quickly discovered not only the local skank but what he termed 'marrow music', reggae, while on the island. He soon laid down $152,000 in cash to buy Tommy Steele's villa Point of View, craning out over the fishing village of Ocho Rios on Jamaica's north shore. Apart from the local cricket scene, Mick Jagger seems not to have taken to the place quite as warmly, and went around with a Rasta bodyguard named Winston Stagers after someone sent him, Mick, a package of chicken entrails and a series of death threats at the Terra Nova hotel. Stagers would witness an odd and touching instance of the Glimmer Twins' sibling rivalry when, one day in Kingston, Jagger challenged Richards to a game of tennis. Although Mick's outfit for the contest was of Wimbledon lineage, Keith won the day 6–1. Mick got on perfectly well with his real-life brother Chris (then alternating between landscape gardening and a fledgling career as an R&B singer, easily recognisable for the thick curtain of hair that fell down to his lips), but he and Keith sometimes seemed more like an elderly married couple than anything else. 'I have the feeling that Mick thought I belonged to him,' Keith would write in 2010. 'And I didn't feel like that at all. It's taken me years to even think about that idea. Because I love the man dearly; I'm still his mate. But he makes it very difficult to be his friend.'

On 23 December 1972 an earthquake devastated western Nicaragua, killing 9,000 people and severing communications with the outside world. Mick and Bianca Jagger flew in to Managua three days later, carrying some $7,000-worth of anti-typhoid serum they delivered to the local Red Cross operation. It's hard to think of any other major rock star of the era who would have reacted as quickly and efficiently as Jagger did, albeit at his wife's urging. The Stones themselves headlined a Hollywood benefit concert on 18 January, raising $310,000 for earthquake relief. This was another rock-music first, at least in terms of delivering the money where it was most needed, rather than in to the pockets of the various crooks, charlatans and top-of-the-range Mercedes owners ruling the country. Mick was subsequently thanked in a formal motion of appreciation passed by the US Senate. Coincidentally, both American and Australian immigration services soon lifted their ban on the Stones, and the Rhode Island assault charges were dropped.

A short Far East tour followed in February. Keith Richards travelled with sixteen guitars, a crate of Rebel Yell whiskey and a 51-year-old companion named Fred Sessler, a Polish Holocaust survivor who owned a hair-weave business in New York and, more pertinently, a chain of retail American drugstores. As a result, Keith would never again be short of pharmaceutical cocaine. There was some temporary unpleasantness en route with US Customs in Hawaii when a syringe fell out of one of Bobby Keys' saxophones, but Sessler and the Stones' lawyers kept the show on the road. When opening night in Brisbane came, Richards, Wyman, Watts and Taylor kicked out the jams. Mick Jagger, who appeared to have been watching David Bowie, danced around in ballet tights while holding a rhinestone mask up to his face. You had to be there.

6 April 1973. The Stones put a partial end to their tax exile, returning home at least for the ninety days a year allowed by the Inland Revenue. According to 'Spanish Tony' Sanchez, while Anita Pallenberg stayed back in Jamaica, Keith Richards seemed to go in to Rod Stewart mode that spring, sitting around London clubs like Tramp wearing tight pants and a suggestive leer. Keith evidently thought he'd scored one night with a scantily clad blonde model who introduced herself as Krissy, wife of the Faces' guitarist Ronnie Wood. There was some encouraging talk about a nightcap. Keith seems to have assumed that Wood himself was out of town. Doing the gentlemanly thing, he offered to drive Krissy home in his spiffy new yellow Ferrari. Once at her south London mansion, though,

Keith found that they weren't alone. Down in the basement studio was Ron Wood, working on a hot new song with Mick Jagger.

An awkward moment followed as Keith recognised Mick, but it passed off when Ronnie poured everyone a large brandy. It turned out that Bianca (recent winner of the coveted Hat of the Year award) had been complaining that the Stones' music was nothing more than second-generation pop, with little in the way of a 'serious message'. Mick's response was to pen the song he and Woody were slaving over that night, 'It's Only Rock 'n Roll (But I Like It)'. No one cared to wake up Charlie Watts at home in Sussex at that hour, so when the time came Wood called in his Faces mate Kenney Jones to play drums on the track.

Anita Pallenberg came back to London later that spring, after Jamaican police had dragged her out of Point of View at gunpoint in front of her two young children and charged her with a series of offences ranging from practising voodoo to ganja possession. Imprisoned in medieval conditions (though not, as some writers claim, gang-raped), Anita was eventually deported back to England. She insisted on standing up throughout the nine-hour flight, since every time she sat down she fell asleep and 'saw things crawling around' in her head. After that the Richards family divided their summer between Redlands and London.

Early on the morning of 26 June, Luigi the caretaker opened the door of 3 Cheyne Walk to a party of ten policemen. Moments after leaving the Chelsea Embankment, the officers found themselves in a kind of casbah. There was an impression of purple-painted rooms, gold lamps studded with jewels, overturned bottles and ashtrays, and rotting food underfoot, while a thick haze of incense and cigarette smoke lay over the general Beggar's Banquet squalor of the place. Luigi, as if suffering from some painful disease in the lower half of his body, slowly led the way upstairs to the tripping room. Richards, Pallenberg and their house guest Stash de Rola can have had no illusions about what the dawn visit meant, and they were only partly successful in their attempts to hide the incriminating evidence by swallowing it. Between them, the narcs carried off armfuls of grass, heroin, methadone, Mandrax tablets, water pipes and brass scales, as well as Keith's .38 Special, a miniature antique French blunderbuss, two shotguns, eight boxes of bullets, a collection of Jamaican ratchet knives, several bottles of wine bearing a skull-and-crossbones label, and a plaster bust of Jimi Hendrix that 'looked suspicious'. There were twenty-six charges in all. Four months later, when the case came up at Marlborough Street magistrates court, Keith's lawyer claimed that all the drugs had been left there by a previous tenant – by implication, Sir Anthony Nutting, former Conservative Minister of State for Foreign Affairs. The bench gave Pallenberg a one-year conditional discharge, and Richards a fine. Stash was acquitted. Keith celebrated in the Londonderry House hotel that night, burning his room down.

On 26 July, Richards put on a wide-lapelled brown pinstripe suit, bought specially for court appearances, to do the honours at Mick Jagger's thirtieth birthday. Five days of partying later, Keith, Anita and their children were at Redlands. Some time in the early hours of 1 August, 3-year-old Marlon came running in to his parents' bedroom, threw a nearby glass of wine in to Keith's face and screamed, 'Fire!'

It was a desperate scene. Between them, Richards and Pallenberg managed to get the children and at least some of the antique furniture and vintage guitars to safety. Redlands, though, was all but gutted. The fire gained ground steadily. It smouldered here, flared there, soon ignited the thatched roof, snatched at beams and got its teeth in to trees in the garden, and they in turn set light to the cars. Explosions were heard. Everyone stood helplessly on the back lawn, where Anita shared her displeasure while the emergency services clanked up the lane. 'Fucking hell, Keith. Fucking hell! The only reason for coming down here was so we could get some rest, and now look at it! Go on. Look at it.'

'Not too good,' Keith was forced to admit, as the roof fell in, sending up a shower of sparks, just as Spanish Tony managed to lug the huge refectory table out on to the lawn. Everyone spent the rest of that night giving statements – Keith speculated that a mouse must have chewed through the house's electrical wiring – and then dozing fitfully in the guest cottage. A month later, the Stones' new album, *Goats Head Soup*, was released. Keith was seen on the back cover as if spontaneously combusting, a 'charred' look, as he put it, which some critics thought was the most interesting thing about the whole record.

On 6 September, the Stones hired Blenheim Palace for the album's launch party. Amid all the beautiful people filling the crowded, marbled ballroom, Richards ambled in hours late, looking pale-faced, with a stubbly beard, ashing a cigarette. Anita apparently preferred to wait outside but soon joined him, screaming at Keith to get back in to the fucking limo so they could leave. According to Tony Sanchez, 'all hell broke loose' once in the car. 'Keith punched her hard in the face. Anita grabbed him by his hair and jerked him down to the floor ... Every ten minutes or so, throughout the two-hour drive, they attacked each other again.' A Stones European tour followed. Three weeks later, in a break between concerts, Richards subjected himself to a course of haemodialysis – the filtering out of waste and toxins by a kidney machine – administered by a specialist named Strait, who was flown in from Miami to a villa in Berne rented for the procedure. This was the source of the enduring myth of the 'Dracula gig', as Keith put it, which insists that he had his blood changed wholesale at a Swiss clinic. Spanish Tony had to dissuade the chauffeur driving the party back to the next concert in Munich from taking a short cut through France, since the authorities there had warrants out for Keith and Anita. There was another fire that night in Richards' hotel suite.

When the smoke cleared, Keith found himself not only banned by several hotel chains but effectively without an English home. Redlands would take three years to rebuild and Cheyne Walk was off limits due to security concerns and general paranoia. Instead, he moved in to the cottage at Ron Wood's house, the Wick. The main property sits on top of Richmond Hill, less than a mile from the old Crawdaddy Club. Keith took a long look at the elegant black and white marble bar, comfortably furnished library and home studio, and pronounced it a 'cool scene'. On and off, he lived there for the next three years. Before long, someone at the Wick told someone else's hairdresser who told a journalist that Wood was going to join the Stones if Keith's dope problems got any worse. This particular rumour was the biggest thing in British rock in late 1973. Being intimately familiar with Section 5(A) of the Dangerous Drugs Act, which holds a homeowner responsible for anything illegal found on the premises, Keith considerately buried his massive diamorphine supply deep under a stable block on Wood's grounds. A few days later he all but tore the building apart looking for the stash, but in all probability it remains there to this day.

While Keith was careening between these various crises, Mick Jagger took care of business. As well as doing the interviews for *Goats Head Soup*, Mick was to reassure Ahmet Ertegun about the band's choice of the lushly orchestrated 'Angie' as its new single in preference to another *Exile*-like belter. Nor did Mick's photo on the album, portraying him wearing lipstick and sporting a Victorian motoring bonnet, discourage Ertegun's view that this might be a hard sell to the rocker-dude crowd in Middle America.

When not busy in the Atlantic boardroom, Mick went in to Broadcasting House in London to help the BBC compile the definitive six-part radio series on the band. Jeff Griffin, the programme's producer, remembers asking Jagger about his marriage, 'and he went on for ten minutes about how committed to it he was and how a child needed two parents, et cetera – it was like an advertisement for Victorian family values.' While Mick spoke, a famous female socialite lay on a studio couch, in a state of extreme repose, next to him. It was not Bianca. Later in June, Marsha Hunt filed an application order in Marylebone magistrates court seeking financial support from the alleged father of her 2-year-old daughter Karis. The suit was eventually settled in January 1979, after Hunt had managed to freeze the receipts of a Stones concert in Los Angeles, and a California judge subsequently awarded her $78,000 p.a. maintenance. Another British woman who went on to become a well-known actress fell in to a 'really stupid' affair with Jagger that summer. Mick had a low tolerance for alcohol – 'a couple of pints and he was gaga', she says. After dining with Gore Vidal and some of his circle at a waterfront bistro in Positano, Vidal urged Jagger to stay with him at his nearby villa rather than risk the long drive home

to his hotel in Naples, adding that he would enjoy the pool there –
'No need to wear a swimsuit when among friends, Mick.' The
young actress yielded when Vidal insisted she stay, too.

Meanwhile, Bill Wyman was pursuing his photography studies
back in the Suffolk countryside and Charlie Watts, sporting a three-
piece tweed suit and a crew-cut, was playing in a series of ad hoc
jazz bands around London. The once-abstemious Mick Taylor was
busy overdoing it with the booze and coke. Before long he blew his
septum, started missing sessions, then announced he was 'bored shit-
less' waiting around to do more than supply the occasional bluesy
tang to Keith's anthemic riffs. Taylor quietly let it be known that
Goats Head Soup might be his last album.

Everyone came together for a 42-date European tour, distinguished as much by what the Stones were taking as what they were
playing. The drugs were in charge. Pop critics forgave them, straining for 'Human Riff' metaphors to describe Keith Richards, a
'twitchy figure in black', 'corpse-pale', 'hissing his back-up vocals'
through carious teeth. (He'd had a bad experience with a dentist as
a child.) After coming off stage in Innsbruck, Bobby Keys took
Keith aside and told him that their friend Gram Parsons had died of
a tequila and morphine overdose in a run-down California motel;
he was twenty-six. Ten days later, Keys himself collapsed and
abruptly left the tour. Jimmy Miller and Marshall Chess were both
strung out, couldn't work, and found themselves unceremoniously
fired and left for dead on the floor of a London hotel room, respectively. Spanish Tony checked in to rehab and went on to write his
own version of *Elvis – What Happened?*, entitled *Up and Down with
the Rolling Stones*. One or two of the book's more complex phrases
perhaps owed something to a ghostwriter. Michael Cooper, the
photographer who once roomed with Keith Richards and Anita
Pallenberg, killed himself with an overdose. 'People were dropping
like flies then,' Keith reflected. 'It was nothing to wake up once a
week and hear so-and-so's gone – "What, the usual?" "Yeah, the
usual." Nobody seemed to snuff it of anything but ODs in those
days.'

While the Stones' friends were dying all around them, the band themselves managed to get through seven weeks of sold-out concerts in eight countries. The basic show was a compelling two hours of rock and roll in a street accident sort of way. Other than the deviant dancing, Mick's core act consisted of a series of kicks, jabs and karate-inspired chops, eerily suggestive of the fading Elvis. Keith trucked out such hits as 'Honky Tonk Women', but the narcotic fog never really lifted. Billy Preston joined the band on keyboards, painting many of the best songs thunderously black. Following a concert in Glasgow, Keith Richards convinced Preston to turn down the volume on his piano by the expedient of waving a knife in his face. On 2 October, everyone got stuck in Frankfurt by a German air traffic controllers' strike and took out their collective frustration by trashing their hotel suite's expensive artwork. Keith, Bill, Charlie and Mick Taylor eventually set off for the next gig, in Hamburg, by train, while Mick Jagger flew ahead in the Atlantic company jet. On the tour's final night the Stones enjoyed some Hugh Hefner-style cabaret in a private room at Berlin's Kempinski hotel, where the local promoter arranged a lesbian revue for the band. 'Girls demonstrated stunts with Beaujolais bottles – and one another,' Sanchez reports. Charlie Watts and his wife forwent the show in order to have dinner with his elderly parents, Charlie Snr and Lil, who had come over on the ferry especially for the concert.

August: *Goats Head Soup*, the first stop on a funky continuum that climaxed in *Some Girls*. The album sported butt-wagging horns and clavinets (Bobby Keys and Billy Preston, respectively) and more wah-wah pedals than the theme from *Shaft*. Keith Richards' ode to his daughter, 'Angie', heavily layered with strings, became a number one single in eighteen countries, thus allaying Ahmet Ertegun's fears; it remains the Stones song of choice for many of their Latin American fans. Close behind it in the romantic stakes was an exquisitely dreamy Van Morrison-like number called 'Winter'. Striking a rather different chord was 'Star Star' (aka 'Starfucker'), a balls-out rocker that had Ertegun and his colleagues reaching for the smelling salts. Not only was the one-word chorus slavered some fifty times, but the lyric sheet also made reference to pussy ('Bad', an

Atlantic memo noted) and Steve McQueen (worse). Eventually one was bleeped, the other signed a waiver. It was a classic libidinous Stones track, as 1970s as the three-day week, as well as a cheerful bit of self-parody.

Goats Head Soup went straight to the top of a chart dominated by the likes of Gilbert O'Sullivan, the Carpenters and Donny Osmond. In a natural if also debatable reaction, Mick Taylor privately questioned the paternity of certain songs (all credited Jagger–Richards), and told friends he felt diddled. The Stones didn't know, at this point, that Taylor was now planning to bail on them.

When the Stones went back underground to record in Giorgio Moroder's Musicland studio in the cellar of Munich's Arabella hotel – fondly known as the Bunker – they essentially operated as five separate groups. Mick Jagger and his entourage would stroll around the nearby Englischer Garten and take in a show before dropping him at the studio door at midnight. When Mick left again three or four hours later, Keith would troop in with his local girl-friend Uschi Obermaier and his crew of spliff-wielding Rastas. Bill Wyman recalled: 'They'd do it to each other. Jagger would be on time one night and annoyed because Keith wasn't there; then Keith would feel guilty and make it early the next night [but] Mick would be so pissed off with him he wouldn't show up.' The Glimmer Twins were also fighting about when to tour again. Keith fretted about the Stones getting rusty, Mick wanted to make films and watch cricket. Nor did the grey, Stalinist decor of the hotel imme-diately above them lighten the mood around the workplace. The Arabella roof was a popular spot for suicides, and Billy Preston would remember that the Stones had more than once stepped over 'fresh bloodstains and chalk-marks' immediately outside the studio door.

When an 'ill' Mick Taylor eventually showed up, days late, Keith began squabbling with him too. The Munich sessions finally killed any lingering hopes Taylor may have had about writing Stones songs, particularly after he took a nondescript ballad called 'Time Waits for No One' and gave it a soaring Brazilian coda, instantly turning the track in to a staple of American FM radio, for which he got a grunted 'thanks' but no royalties. Some nights, Richards would wipe his junior colleague's guitar from the tapes and dub in his own. 'It wasn't always fun making the records,' Taylor said later. 'In fact, it was so painful I used to hate listening to them.'

Meanwhile, Bill Wyman began recording his first solo album, *Monkey Grip*, which Keith fondly dubbed 'Monkey Shit', and even Charlie Watts, the consummate professional, 'wasn't just looking bored – he *was* bored', Ian Stewart said. Stu recalled an occasion when Charlie showed up at the studio at two in the morning, did one take, and left, saying, 'That's all you're gonna get from me.' As usual, Mick Jagger was on top of all the logistics, flying the Dutch avant-garde artist Guy Peellaert to Munich to paint the new album cover, which showed the band being adored by 114 wispily clad handmaidens, like something staged by MGM. Mick was reportedly not happy when David Bowie then commissioned Peellaert to design the sleeve of his own new album, *Diamond Dogs*, which scooped the Stones' by four months.* Richards told Jagger to 'just put the fucking thing out in a brown bag' and not to worry about being hip. That concluded their creative exchange on the matter. Sometimes Keith would go AWOL for days on end and when found would be slumped in some Munich bar. Uschi dispatched friends in search of him when his coke-fuelled outings became too prolonged. He told her and others that he could kick dope any time he wanted to, but he seldom wanted to. It began to be said that Keith was actually dying, and the Woody-for-Stones rumours began again.

The band denied it, and Les Perrin still loyally churned out press releases with titles like STONES ENJOY BAVARIA HUGELY and

---

*David Bowie's then wife Angela says: 'Yes, it was a competition. David considered that the Stones were on the way out. It was his turn. In those days we lived around the corner from the Jaggers in Chelsea. Guy Peellaert was introduced to David by Mick. Mick showed David the Stones' new album artwork. David was so excited that he commissioned Peellaert to do the *Diamond Dogs* cover, and how wonderful that he did. It was David's deft way at metaphorically pushing his influences out of the way as he stepped up to take their place. He wasn't only the diamond dog. He was the top dog.'

STONES COMPLETE WORK ON 'BEST EVER ALBUM'.
The cosy atmosphere was tainted only slightly by the fact that Mick
and Keith weren't speaking to each other.

Quite apart from their other issues, Jagger still refused to tour that
summer. When Richards finished work in Munich, he went back
to Richmond to help Ron Wood record his first solo LP, *I've Got
My Own Album to Do*. (The title was a dig at Rod Stewart, who was
busy just then cutting *Smiler* instead of touring with the Faces.) A
mutual friend named Bebe Buell walked in to the Wick one morning to find Keith, Ron, Rod and Eric Clapton passed out at the
foot of a bed, where Angie Bowie lay in splendid isolation.
Richards was 'the sweetest of them all' and a 'very wise man', Buell
insists, 'well versed in philosophy – brilliant, in fact. He was open
to all types of spiritual [beliefs]. He could talk for hours about the
Mayans and the pyramids and we discussed the mystery of
Stonehenge and the universe. He had a theory that whales have
souls.' That Keith could be a tad on the brusque side was all part of
his charm. Richards' long-time neighbour in Cheyne Walk remembers him as a 'good sport', who nonetheless sometimes elected to
make an unorthodox late-night entry to his property through the
next-door garden; when the neighbour questioned him about this,
Keith's response failed to include the word 'sorry' and instead contained the words 'shut' and 'gob'.

'Yes, star crossed in pleasure/The stream flows on by/Yes, as we
are sated in leisure/We watch it fly', Mick Jagger crooned on the
Stones' new album *It's Only Rock 'n Roll*. Just how sated was a question much discussed in the tabloid media. By 1974, Mick had
joined the junk food-chain of celebrity, vying with the likes of
Elizabeth Taylor, Jackie Onassis, cancer cures and Soviet psychic
phenomena. 'STRIP ROW AT STONES PARTY' and 'NAMES
JAGGER OVER LOVE CHILD' ran two representative headlines
in the *National Enquirer*. Dubious as most of the tales were, it seems
fair to say that after three years Mick was straying from his marital
vows with impudent regularity. Bebe Buell, for one, remembers a
'very classy, elegant guy [who] still didn't waste any time. Mick

pulled out all the stops for a girl ... I got middle-of-the-night whispering phone calls, gift baskets, and detailed advice on which shampoos and sprays and body lotions to use. Very precise like that, Mick was. On my twenty-first birthday he took me to this gorgeous Japanese restaurant in New York, poured some champagne, and asked me, other than him, which historical figures I'd most like to have dinner with. Oscar Wilde, Albert Einstein and John Lennon, I told him. Mick made a phone call. After the meal we got in to a cab, drove across town, pulled up at a dark apartment building, went up a narrow flight of stairs and there at the top, with a Polaroid camera, was Lennon. "Happy birthday," Mick told me.'

In July, on the fifth anniversary of Brian Jones' death, *New Musical Express* published an open letter from a fan of his, chiding the Stones for 'completely forgetting' him. 'I think I should elucidate concerning the attitude of other members of the group in connection to Brian,' Les Perrin replied. 'He is forever in their hearts, and considerable thought was given to sending a floral tribute. After much heart-searching it was decided that, rather than the ephemeral salutation of flowers, a donation to charity should be made. Knowing as the boys do of Brian's personal contributions to children [q.v.] it was decided to donate money to the United Nations Children's Fund.' More pertinently, the Stones ensured that the Jones family continued to receive their son's share of the 'Decca Bounce', worth around £3,000 annually, part of a generally robust supervision of the group's finances as a whole. When a meeting in London with Allen Klein to discuss royalty arrangements failed to go as hoped, this ended with Klein fleeing down a corridor of the Savoy Hotel pursued by various band members. Shortly afterwards, Les Perrin put out another press release, announcing, 'The recent talks between the Stones and their former business manager were thoroughly professional, amicable and productive.'

While Perrin waffled, Prince Rupert introduced Mick Jagger to a high-powered young attorney from Little Rock, Arkansas, by the name of Bill Carter. Carter not only counted a hip local law professor and wheeler-dealer called Bill Clinton among his friends, he was also well connected in Washington. Following Richard Nixon's resignation in August, certain key administration officials, such as the hard-line US Solicitor General Erwin N. Griswold (author of a May 1970 memo denouncing this 'prancing Britisher in our midst, perform[ing] to our children whilst draped in a stovepipe hat and American flag') also took early retirement. Carter promptly dressed Mick in a suit and tie and had him visit the Justice Department, where he cheerfully signed autographs and posed for photos with the staff. Soon afterwards, the Stones got their provisional work visas, contingent on Carter personally vouching for their 'good character'. Everyone met back in Maddox Street that October and agreed to tour the following year.

Keith Richards wasn't speaking to Mick Taylor, but did play at Ron Wood's stoned debacle entitled 'A Weekend of Rhythm & Booze' at the Kilburn Gaumont in north London. With their identical dark eyes and pasty skin, Keith and Ron reminded the *NME* journalist Nick Kent of 'degenerate Everly Brothers', if not quite as melodic. The Stones then spent a day with Michael Lindsay-Hogg filming a chaotic promo for 'It's Only Rock 'n Roll'. Although, for some compelling reason, the director nearly drowned Charlie in soapsuds, the clip survived to become a staple of *Top of the Pops* and something of a rock-video pioneer. Despite the hype and a London graffiti campaign orchestrated by Jagger (a particularly striking example appeared on the wall of Lord's cricket ground, where it can be seen today), the single sold modestly. Taylor would call it 'Mick and Keith trying to write something in the classic Stones style', implying that self-parody had stalked the Bunker.

The *It's Only Rock 'n Roll* album was perhaps too well titled for its own good, and once or twice the Stones imitated their imitators on it. The result was pleasantly funky and slightly innocuous – without Jimmy Miller the band lost some of its mid-period clout, and came close to losing its identity. As it was, tracks like 'If You Can't Rock Me' and 'Fingerprint File' sounded uneasily like the Faces and *Aladdin Sane*-era Bowie, respectively. Just for old time's sake, 'If You Really Want to Be My Friend' lifted the gospel chorus from *Exile*'s 'Let it Loose'. A new-found love of reggae informed 'Luxury', which, like one or two other sun-baked tracks, bobbed and wove engagingly, while the gloriously eccentric 'Ain't Too Proud to Beg', a mid-60s hit for the Temptations, welded soul harmonies to a noise like that of Keith Richards slamming his guitar in to a wall. The Chuck Berryish title track remains the only song to have been appropriated by both Twisted Sister and the Christian-rock combo ApologetiX. *It's Only Rock 'n Roll* was the first in a string of productions credited to the Glimmer Twins, which in this case largely meant Mick Jagger. Coincidentally, it was also the first on which the vocals were fully audible.

It's Only Rock 'n Roll sold decently, though Ron Wood learned that his credit for 'Inspiration' didn't necessarily convert in to royalties. Twenty-three years later he ruefully told a reporter, 'It's a hard nut to crack, the Stones' financial side.' Mick Taylor was on turf well beyond that, 'in a virtual coma', according to one source, after Nick Kent showed him an advance copy of the album crediting Jagger–Richards throughout. Taylor's ambitious partner, Rose, reportedly flipped out and promptly rang Keith, who wasn't available to take her call.

Vocal as these reservations were, there was also more muted dissent elsewhere in the ranks. Even the friends-and-family audience at one New York listening party for the new album couldn't help but wince as the greatest rock and roll band in the world chugged from one *Shaft*-cum-reggae groove to another. In a characteristically blunt review, Stu thought at least some of the fare on offer 'utter bollocks'. Several of the professional critics seemed to agree, finding little to like but Mick's great title, which quickly became a catch-phrase. Bill Wyman was again threatening to leave the band, and might have done so had *Monkey Grip* made a better showing than its lone week at number 56 on the *Billboard* chart. Nor was Charlie Watts about to go out of his way to tout either the Stones or their latest product. Ironically, it was the zonked-seeming Keith Richards who did most to talk up *It's Only Rock 'n Roll* to the press, cheerfully agreeing to a month-long round of European interviews. He spent one evening charming Bob Harris on BBC TV's *The Old Grey Whistle Test*. 'Keith appeared in the studio swinging a bottle of Jack Daniel's by his fingertips,' Harris recalls. 'Despite copious draughts from it throughout the evening, we got through the show, after which everyone made for Mr Chow's restaurant in Knightsbridge. There was about ten of us in the party, and we didn't have reservations. After a bit, we were shown to a table in the middle of a crowded room, at which point Keith whips out a sack of cocaine and slaps it down next to his place setting. I say sack because it was the size of a household bag of flour. There it sat in full view for the next two hours, with Keith alternately snorting it up and graciously offering it round the table. With every course, there was another application. To him, it was just another condiment.'

Everyone made it back to Montreux in November to talk some more about an American tour the following year. Mick Taylor kept mum, but a few days later he rang the office in London to say he had had enough. Up against the venerable songwriting firm of Jagger–Richards, and nearly broke, Taylor wanted, instead, to go out on the road with the former Cream bassist Jack Bruce. At least some of the band thought he was bluffing, and reminded him that they were due back in the studio in a few days' time. But Taylor then cornered Jagger at a party for Eric Clapton at Robert Stigwood's house in north London, and told him he wouldn't be returning to Munich. As luck would have it, Ron Wood happened to be sitting in between the two Micks at that moment, and soon took the opportunity to confirm that he would be available to serve if required. On 12 December, Jagger put out a polite press release, noting that Taylor 'wants the chance to try out new ventures. While we are all most sorry that he is going, we wish him great success and much happiness.'

'I don't really know [why he left],' Mick told *Rolling Stone* years later. 'He never explained. He wanted to have a solo career. I think he found it difficult to get on with Keith Richards.' Keith was certainly not pleased at the defection. 'Two days before a fucking new album,' he fumed when the call came through. Just as the Stones won their war with the Feds, they were faced with mutiny from behind the lines. 'No one leaves this band except in a pine box,' Keith added, in the course of various other unappreciative remarks. 'Mick was like Clapton – a lovely player, a brilliant player. But you won't have them in a band because they're not team players. They don't like being kicked up the arse . . . That's why Mick Taylor is a permanent failure to me.'

Taylor was soon to grasp the harsh reality of his decision to leave the Stones. 'When I told the office I was going, they immediately asked for my gold Amex card back,' he says. 'After that, I didn't see any money for a year . . . Mick Jagger tried to persuade me to stay, but I told him I was fed up and how my drug problems were beginning to worry me. Mick suggested taking six months off, but I've never been good at taking advice. Maybe I should have listened.' In time, Taylor found himself enrolled in a methadone clinic on Hollywood Boulevard, having sold his gold records and other memorabilia largely in order to buy drugs. 'In 1982, the Stones stopped paying me,' he adds. 'They'd signed to a different record company and had new contracts and were advised they didn't need to include me . . . I should have got a lawyer, but instead I called them rude words and asked how they could just [cut] me off. They all know it's not right. In fact it's outrageous. They get all the money and I get the plaudits and praise, even from Mick.' In 1974, Taylor had been convinced that 'the band was falling apart – it was in chaos; Mick and Keith weren't talking or working together, and it was taking longer and longer to make the albums. They didn't seem to have a future together.' Like many people, he wasn't to know that back then the Stones were actually still in their relative infancy.★

In January 1975, Mick and Keith used their new German sessions to audition guitarists, turning the lobby of the Munich Hilton in to

---

★In 2009, Taylor went in to the studio to overdub guitar on 'Plundered My Soul' and other *Exile* outtakes for the reissued version of the album. He hadn't recorded with his former band in thirty-five years. This one-off collaboration gave Stones fans new hope that Taylor might be invited back, at least on an ad hoc basis, although Keith Richards' remarks in his autobiography *Life* seem to rule out a full-scale reunion. 'Mick Taylor left us in the lurch,' Keith notes. 'The proof that he didn't really fit in is that he left. He didn't want to fit in, I don't think. I guess he felt that with his credentials from being with the Stones, he'd be able to write songs, produce. But he didn't do anything.'

a scene from *A Chorus Line* as long-haired musicians sat around awaiting the call to play. Over the course of the winter, Jeff Beck, Mick Ronson, Harvey Mandel, Rory Gallagher and even Geoff Bradford, briefly a friend of Brian's in 1962, all drifted in to jam. Alexis Korner happened to be making an album called *Get Off My Cloud* in the next room to the Stones, with Steve Marriott and Peter Frampton helping him out. Marriott spent much of his time trying to prove to Mick and Keith that he was the man for the job, while Bill and Charlie thought highly of Frampton. Nobody gelled. The versatile English session guitarist Chris Spedding, who over the years would rock up songs by everyone from the Sex Pistols to the Wombles, remembers 'how all the music papers ran stories about who was to replace Taylor. It was a bit like when the Pope dies, or when there was a change in the leadership of the Soviet Union. Jeff Beck was top of the list (for the Stones, not for Pope) but months later I got a call from Mick Jagger asking me if I was available. Oddly enough, I wasn't. I had a lot of work coming up, so I told him no.' Three months later, the Stones played a residency at Madison Square Garden while Spedding donned a furry suit to mime 'The Womble Shuffle' on *Top of the Pops*, a fate he 'doesn't regret in the least'. At some stage during the process, Mick Taylor's English house burned down with most of his worldly possessions inside, and there was speculation that, like Brian, he might actually die after leaving the Stones.

Eventually, Keith Richards' eye lit on a 23-year-old part-Cherokee guitarist from Texas by the name of Wayne Perkins. He came well qualified. Keith's favourite song at the time was Jimmy Cliff's reggae anthem 'The Harder They Come', which affected him more profoundly than anything since he had first heard 'Heartbreak Hotel' nineteen years earlier. In March 1975, the Stones were recording with their mobile unit close to their money in Rotterdam, when Eric Clapton ('too dope-sick' to take the job himself) rang to tell them about this guy, Wayne, he was hanging with by the pool in Jamaica, who'd worked with artists as diverse as Perry Como and Bob Marley. What's more, he'd actually *played* on 'The Harder They Come'.

'Send him over,' said Keith.

Perkins arrived in Holland to be met by Stu, who drove him to the small, dark theatre where the Stones were working.

I walked in . . . It was a weird scene; everyone was sitting around, Keith half pulling his pants down, the top of his ass showing as he examined some sore. Bill and Charlie, I think, grunted. That was my introduction. Next thing, I'm playing alone on stage while they watch. Jagger runs on from the wings without me even noticing, grabs a tambourine and starts doing this jitterbug-boogie routine right behind me. Shaking the fucking tambourine in my ear. Mick's messing with my head while Keith's sprawled down front, still ruefully prodding his ass and occasionally glancing up, checking me out . . . That's my audition. Next I'm invited outside to the mobile. I did some stuff on 'Cherry Oh Baby', 'Memory Motel', 'Fool to Cry', only they weren't called that then. Keith and I put together the song 'Hand of Fate'. I obviously did OK, because by now everyone's cool, there's dope bouncing up and down on top of the amps, and Keith's grinning. No problem, I thought, I'm in . . .

But Perkins was soon to find that there was more to joining the Stones than merely auditioning to Keith Richards' satisfaction. 'The guy had to fit in,' he says. 'It wasn't just keeping up with the continuous dope, drink and lack of sleep, there were these little traps they set you, too.' A day or two later, Perkins was back at the Wick, where Anita carried round an antique tray heaped with coke as decorously as if serving tea and biscuits, and the other guests included various Stones and Faces, as well as David Bowie, Gary Glitter and someone recalled as a 'Jamaican male ballet dancer' who amused Mick. At eight one evening, Keith and Wayne set out for a 'quick' drink, which lasted until 5 a.m. Perkins found himself in the passenger seat of the yellow Ferrari, barrelling down Richmond Hill with his host 'doing his usual ninety mph, wearing shades, leaning on the horn as we sped through a series of red lights'. Somehow, in the dead of a London night, Keith found a musical supplier willing to sell him a £12,000 baby-grand piano. Then it was another wild ride, bouncing off various kerbs along the way, up to Jagger's house on Cheyne Walk, where Anita again did the honours. Around breakfast time, Keith disappeared down the road with Marlon, mentioning something about putting the 5-year-old to bed. Mick then placed a phone call summoning the ballet dancer, and Perkins watched the two of them bumping and grinding away to some 'disco bullshit' on the sound system, while Prince Rupert and Bryan Ferry, the latter in a tuxedo, both materialised at the door. It was all getting a long way from rural Texas. Before long the room filled with well-groomed young men in smartly cut suits. Backed in to a corner, Wayne, in his T-shirt and jeans, shifted uncomfortably as Mick's guests stared a hole through him. Everything was 'very weird', he says. 'I guess it was some kind of test.' Next day, back at the Wick, Keith told him to learn the Stones catalogue. 'We're going on tour.'

Perkins was soon practising 'thirty or forty' of the old standards. For the Stones, rehearsals meant plugging in guitars around the time other people went to bed, then bashing away while Keith called out 'Faster!' or 'Cool it' and swarthy aides replenished the various bottles and tins jumping up and down on the amps. 'Lady Jane' and 'Satisfaction' were first in the bag. As Keith and Wayne traded licks in the cottage, fifty yards away in the Wick's oval living room Ron Wood was pondering his career options if, as now seemed likely, the Faces broke up. Two days later, without having a clear recollection of getting there, Perkins was back in Munich. While everyone else slept, Keith was wired up and wanted to visit nearby Dachau. 'It'll be a gas.' There were some more coke-fuelled rehearsals. The waiter at the hotel bar had Keith's written instructions of how to make up his current cocktail, which basically involved pouring out a hefty tumbler of Stolichnaya vodka and adding a splash of fruit juice – the beginning of Keith's long and sometimes troubled relationship with Stoli. Before long, the Jamaican ballet dancer reappeared. Later that same night, the audition process reached its climax when Mick Jagger summoned Perkins upstairs to his suite.

Mick was lying alone on the huge bed. He sort of patted the covers, and I sat down next to him . . . There was a heavy atmosphere; Mick offered me a toot and lay there, kind of fidgeting around. Somehow he started this rap about adolescence and chicks, and before long he leant over and said, 'What was your high school girlfriend like?' Well, I don't know. Maybe it was the drugs, but I felt sick. That's when I puked all over Mick's bathroom. He had to change suites for the night. Right after that there was a phone call between Jagger–Richards, sort of a dogfight about whether or not I was in the band. Keith was definitely rooting for me, but Mick was the guy running things. He mentioned the fact that they were really looking for an Englishman. I didn't get the job.

On Sunday 30 March, Ron Wood was one of the guests at Eric Clapton's thirtieth birthday party. Next afternoon he woke up, found he had nothing particular to do and made a phone call to Munich. Woody flew in that evening. Later that night in the studio, he asked Keith how the search was going.

'We're looking for a Brit who looks cool, with a fucking good sense of humour, who's slightly shorter than you, plays OK, likes a pint, won't freak out on the road, isn't going to jump ship and can get on with Jagger.'

'Where are you gonna find someone like that by next Friday?'

Woody then played on a song called 'Hey Negrita', and was swiftly hired for the tour. Keith commented: 'After literally one number, we thought: "That's it. It's obvious."' The arrangement was that Wood, like Taylor before him, initially join the Stones on probation rather than as a full member. As it turned out, he would be kept on salary for the next nineteen years. Keen-eyed observers didn't miss the point that Woody had finally joined the band to support Keith, not to replace him. In the Stones' transformation back from jaded superstars to active musicians, Wood's ability to simply plug in and get on with it was crucial – he may not have been a virtuoso, but he was prolific. Within a week the band had most of what became *Black and Blue* in the can, as well as dozens of outtakes: one called 'Slave', one called 'Start Me Up', one (working title only) called 'Cunt'. Some of these were recycled years later, and sold in the millions.

Ron Wood was then twenty-seven, and had been playing the guitar professionally for ten years. As the third son of a heavy-drinking family of 'water gypsies' who had left their barge for a council flat near Heathrow airport, he was genuinely working class. His father Arthur, or 'Archie', played in a 24-piece harmonica band that periodically toured the racetracks of England. His mother, Lizzie, brought home a steady weekly wage from her job as a cleaner at the HMV record-pressing factory. Ron had two elder, musical brothers, Ted and Art. At home, there were weekend sing-alongs around the piano that got so boisterous that a crack appeared in the middle of the sitting room. When the Woods eventually moved out, the new owners found 1,700 empty Guinness bottles buried in the back garden. Well in to his seventies, people used to say of Archie Wood that he 'must have a hollow leg' – and in fact he did, having had one of them cut off following a blood clot.

After stints in the Birds, the Jeff Beck group and the Faces, Ron had emerged as a reliable, journeyman guitarist whose core sound was as pneumatic and solid as Mick Taylor's was fluid. Keith-like in general appearance, with spiky black hair, Wood struck the reviewer of one Faces concert as a 'musical bog-brush' whose main contri-bution to the show was to 'scamper about scrubbing at his guitar while smoking an unfeasible number of cigarettes'. He could also sing in a wheezy, Dylanesque rumble.

As Wood himself acknowledged, there were better musicians around. But what he lacked in technique he more than made up for in other ways, contrary to the critics who called him a barely com-petent, bum-note merchant and, at worst, a total joke. The Keith–Ron dream ticket looked great in photos, and Wood was as willing to muck in as Taylor hadn't been. 'He's the one that kept the horse on track,' said Korner. 'To categorise [Wood] as just a tag-along guy who got lucky? No. Not true. There were instrumentalists who could run rings round him, but none of them had his personality.' Stu fondly described the Stones' new recruit as 'like a little kid rushing round doing things to get attention. He'd sit on a hot plate with his bare arse if he thought it would get a rise.' Fortunately, 'that was just what the band wanted in those days – someone to make 'em laugh.'

Before 1975, Wood had made a dozen visits of various kinds to America, but had never once flown in a private jet. In the Stones, the world of airborne orgies and other rock-star perks suddenly opened up to him. It made the Faces tours 'look like a whelk stall by comparison', he later said.

Mick Jagger was always ready to mingle in any class of society, and more than once his high-powered connections proved useful to the Stones. Early in April, Mick's friend Walter Annenberg, US Ambassador to the Court of St James, advised him that the band and their chaperon Bill Carter were welcome to tour America, but that they would each have to pass a full medical before being granted a work permit. At this point, Sanchez says, the haematologist was again discreetly flown in from Miami. 'As soon as the cure had been effected, Keith went to London and presented himself at the US Embassy for examination. The doctor pronounced his blood as pure as spring water, his passport was stamped and he was back on the road again.'

Meanwhile, Mick was busy ordering his Giorgio di Sant' Angelo tour outfits and inspecting the Stones' customised 707, which came complete with two bedrooms furnished with Mylar mirrors and upholstered in a garish shade of gold, a library, a Jacuzzi, a well-stocked bar with a piano and even, Wood adds, 'naked girls running up and down the aisles'. On 21 April, the band started rehearsing at the remote estate in Montauk where the roadies had to fence off the local beach against an amphibian strike by the Hell's Angels. Bianca stayed home in London, so Mick sent the jet to fetch his friend Bebe Buell. Prince Rupert and several of his colleagues were nearby, staying in an establishment called the Memory Motel, about a mile up the road from the Stones. 'Nice name,' said Mick, and used it for a song. Andy Warhol was much in evidence. Some of his pictures of the Stones biting each other ended up on the cover of the band's next live album. The group then had to drive out to an aircraft hangar on a military base in Newburgh, New York, to practise on their new hydraulic, lotus-shaped stage, since it was too big to fit in even their living room. Billy Preston was on keyboards, and Stevie Wonder's drummer Ollie Brown tinkled a variety of cowbells, chimes and gongs. Keith wanted Bobby Keys back in the fold, but Mick demurred; the Stones managed without horns until 1981.

At noon on 1 May, the seven-piece Stones drove down Fifth Avenue atop a flatbed truck to announce the tour. The most illustrious rock group in the world gave its first American performance in three years standing on a wooden plank, belting out 'Brown Sugar' and bringing Lower Manhattan to a screeching halt. For once, playing for free turned out to be the lucrative choice. Half a million tickets were sold in the following week. The *Washington Star News* canonised them:

> The Rolling Stones gave an amazing, traffic-stopping display . . . For sheer spectacle, it compared favorably with the major news events of the year – the jailing of presidential aides convicted of perjury, deception and obstruction of justice, the energy crisis, or the final, heart-rending fall of Saigon. Those stories may be important in their own right, but none of them are exactly uplifting. The Stones render the most gnarled among us happily, helplessly *teenage*. It's a profound accomplishment.

On this reading, the 'five herberts with guitars' were as big as the end of the Vietnam war.

When opening night came around, on 1 June 1975, the Stones pulled out all the stops. Mick Jagger first appeared to the strains of *Fanfare for the Common Man* – the roadies firing off cherry-bombs for added gusto – before cavorting around in his silk pyjamas, straddling a fat balloon of suggestive mien in 'Star Star', swinging on a wire, and generally doing the funky strut with Billy Preston. As for the rest: stage right, Woody demonstrated his woozy good cheer, if not his acumen, often choosing to forgo the guitar in order to somewhat randomly conduct the audience in a mass sing-along. There were similar hijinks from Ollie Brown, who otherwise did little for the Stones' already vast beat. As usual, Bill Wyman barely moved throughout the concert, although his stone-faced demeanour, now framed by a bushy wave of King Charles spaniel hair, may have been more one of concentration than boredom. According to Wood, 'Bill was actually playing a game called "Spot The Tits". He'd come over to me in the middle of the set and start a conversation with the words: "Nice pair over there".' Keith Richards was on peak form throughout, sporting a soiled white jacket, snug leather pants, and a baggy denim cap in whose flap he kept his nightly supply of coke, running up to the mike to hit the down and dirty riff of 'Happy', and throwing in some weak-at-the-knees Elvis moves to accompany a particularly hot solo. As Keith later made clear, he wasn't keen on all the other stage antics: Mick was turning in to 'fucking Danny La Rue' (whose birthday he shares), while some of the props in general and in particular the bank of 3,000 coloured lights, rippling like the façade of a Vegas casino, 'belonged in a panto'. Keith barely concealed a sneer as Jagger and Brown inflated yet more simulacra during the encore – an extended 'Sympathy' – this time of a fire-breathing dragon and a frosty snowman. The show itself blew similarly hot and cold, but nobody could fault the Stones' gamut-running: in two and a half hours the fans got everything from Aaron Copland to a queasily burlesque minstrel act. It seems fair to say that the $8 and $10 seats represented better value than those for John Denver, Donny & Marie and David Cassidy – America's other pop idols that summer.

The frenzy began a few days later, when the band started play-ing the biggest arenas in Texas. Slash-and-burn gigs, sex and drugs: the STONED headlines soon followed, along with rather full pic-tures of Mick's bouncy rubber phallus. In San Antonio, moved by both deep respect, and £4,000 from the *Daily Mirror*, the Stones agreed to pay homage to Davy Crockett and the American heroes who died at the Alamo. The *Mirror* photographer brought along a box of props for the shoot. Bill Wyman was seen to experiment with a coonskin cap in a variety of locations, and Keith Richards, by now almost concave from drugs, bulked up by the expedient of stuffing several flags down the crotch of his jeans. Back in London, the resulting full-page spread of the five leering Stones in their punkish garb, Mick wrapped defiantly in a Union Jack, was widely considered a new low point in Anglo-American relations.

One of the best indices of the Stones' reputation in 1975 was their continuing ban in a variety of countries and individual towns. Apart from their problems in France, they were forbidden to play in New Orleans or anywhere in the state of Alabama, although against the odds Canada's Public Safety ministry reversed itself and allowed the band in on a 72-hour visa. In Toronto, Keith Richards heard about a young blind fan, Rita Bedard, who was hitching from gig to gig. This brought out Keith's humanitarian streak. He began arranging for the roadies to let the girl ride with them, anonymously paying for her to have a hot meal and a bed at night. Keith's simple act of generosity would be repaid, in nearly incredible fashion, three years later.

On 4 July, the Memphis city elders threatened to haul the Stones off stage if they inflated their 'rude and lewd dirigibles', as the writ called them, or sang the lyrics to 'Starfucker'. Bill Carter intervened on the band's behalf, and the 60,000 crowd were able to celebrate Independence Day in style as Mick duly rode the rubber cock to a state of arousal. Earlier, the Stones themselves had refused to perform unless 82-year-old Furry Lewis, the great slide guitar king who never earned enough to give up his day job as a Memphis street cleaner (this despite having a wooden leg) went on before them. Stu believed he was paid 'around ten grand' for his services, which was roughly twice his annual salary. After his ecstatically received set, one of the handlers asked Lewis if he wanted to stay and watch the Stones. 'No, I don't care nothin' 'bout it,' he said.

Six sold-out shows followed in New York, with everyone from Dylan to Raquel Welch partying backstage. Somewhere in the crowd at Madison Square Garden was a pretty 19-year-old blonde from a good Lutheran family, named Patti Hansen. She, too, would resurface in Keith's life three years later. Mick somehow found time to slip off to the studio to record with Eric Clapton, followed by some light rock-star recreation. Clapton's bass player Carl Radle remembered 'a degree of coke snorted and brandy drunk. Then there were the girls ... a big brunette for Mick and a blonde for Eric, both dressed in these come-on, trashy skirts. Hooker clothes. When Clapton came out he was laughing that the chick had wanted butter smeared all over her. "Well," he said, "it beats a Mars bar".' Bianca flew in to join the tour a few days later. While the Stones stadium-hopped in their own 707, their old mentor Alexis Korner followed them around the country in a small van. Del Taylor, Korner's manager, said: 'The idea was that Alexis' album, *Get Off My Cloud*, would be released to tie in with the Stones' tour. Alexis would go to the States and interview the Stones in different towns and cities and the record would be available. CBS managed to screw up every single town on the tour bar one.'

Mick and Keith invited Howlin' Wolf to their Chicago concert, paying gracious tribute to him from the stage but failing to appear for an elaborately home-cooked dinner at Wolf's house later that night. It was left to Bill Wyman to make amends by attending with his 13-year-old son. Some of the Chicago press took exception to the apparently unscripted moment when Billy Preston dropped to his knees, seized Jagger's buttocks and engaged in possibly the first act of simulated fellatio in the same arena where, thirty-one years earlier, Franklin Roosevelt had accepted his fourth and final nomination as President of the United States. There was some difficulty for the Stones when they came to check in to their hotel that night. Surveying the rabble of musicians and groupies who appeared in his lobby at 3 a.m., a panicky night manager asked that the band lodge a cash deposit before taking their rooms. Peter Rudge strode outside to his car and returned with a black briefcase, which he turned upside down on to the front desk. Thousands of dollars rained down like green confetti.

Both Mick and Keith reacted poorly when Bianca then got herself photographed with the current president's son, 'Disco Jack' Ford, and started dragging both him and his Secret Service agents backstage. A year or two later, the Glimmer Twins wrote a song about 'the rag trade girl/the queen of porn/the easiest lay on the White House lawn'. Live, Mick sometimes concluded this ode by bawling 'Get out of my life! Don't fuck my wife! Don't come back!'

From Memphis, Richards, Wood, Freddie Sessler and a Stones heavy named Jim Callaghan decided to drive to the next gig, in Dallas. Late in the afternoon of 5 July, shortly after the four left a burger joint in rural Fordyce, Arkansas, they were stopped on Highway 79 by a state trooper who later said he smelled dope and that there were 'enormous clouds of smoke' pouring out of the limo, which gave him his due cause.

After asking everyone's name and occupation, the officer took a crowbar to the car boot, which allegedly contained coke, the property of Fred Sessler. Keith was also relieved of his favourite hunting knife, though he managed to expel most of his pills and pot in to the nearby bushes by courteously doffing his cap to the police in what the arrest report calls an 'unusually vigorous' style. The cops took everyone to the courthouse, variously charged with possession, carrying a concealed weapon and reckless driving. When 'Billy Bob' Wynne, the presiding judge, was eventually found around seven that evening, it was noticed that he wore a pair of tartan shorts and carried a half-bottle of bourbon tucked in to his boot. He appeared in a benign mood, and professed several times never to have heard of the Rolling Stones. In a vain attempt to avert publicity, Keith and Ron were initially addressed by the bench by their tour aliases of Ziggenpuss and Stockfish, which heightened the general air of a Marx Brothers film.

Bill Carter, the Arkansas native now working for the Stones, flew in by chartered jet within the hour. News crews soon followed from as far afield as Dallas and Atlanta. The BBC called, enquiring about local satellite-feed facilities for a live interview. Before long, a large pro-Stones crowd had gathered in the square outside the picturesque white courthouse. A second Learjet of the evening soon hit Fordyce, carrying a man holding $50,000 in cash to be used as bail, as Carter and the local police chief continued to debate the ethics of the case. Local FM radio stations cancelled their scheduled programming to go live to the scene. It was the biggest news event in Fordyce since 1926, when a local teenager called Paul Bryant, the future football coach of some note, wrestled a bear in the town square. Outside, the 'Free Keith' crowd grew steadily more vociferous in their demands. Carter made an impassioned plea on the grounds of illegal search and seizure, and at this stage, at nine on a Saturday night and the mob beginning to pelt the courthouse with rocks, the judge decided it would be in the interests of public order to set everyone free.

Richards and Sessler (described in news reports as a 'hitchhiker') posted bail of $162 and $5,000, respectively. The Stones party then ran for their limo, which accelerated away to the airport, one occupant waving a bottle of Rebel Yell out of the car window. All the drug charges were later dropped. In 2006, Arkansas governor Mike Huckabee broke off from his failed presidential campaign long enough to grant a somewhat redundant pardon to Richards and Fred Sessler; Sessler had died five years earlier, aged seventy-seven. Keith's knife still hangs on a plaque in the Fordyce courthouse, along with a framed photo of the judge and police chief posing with their famous prisoner.

Ten days later, Elton John 'ruined' a Stones concert in Fort Collins, Colorado. The collaboration 'never really clicked', Stu said with some understatement, remembering that Keith Richards had had 'words' with the band's guest later on in the dressing room. John, who was recording nearby, had rung Mick Jagger the night before and insisted he wanted to play on just one song, 'Honky Tonk Women'. No problem, said Mick. Elton got on stage, did the number, and wouldn't leave. The resulting all-star jam was not a conspicuous success – according to Wood, 'Keith kept shouting "Get the fuck off"', and before long an unseemly struggle ensued between Elton and Billy Preston for possession of the piano stool. This roused Preston's manager to try and physically cut a switch sending 500,000 watts of power to the stage, while jostling a member of Elton's entourage with his free hand; at one point he actually flicked the lever for a second, causing Jagger's orgasmic howl to end in a drone. 'What the fuck?' Mick enquired, when normal service was resumed.

In Greensboro, Richards and Wood relaxed after hours by playing country blues in Keith's hotel suite, with Faye Dunaway, among others, crooning along. The cops tried to bust the dressing room before the final gig in Buffalo. Peter Rudge, Jim Callaghan and assorted lawyers held them off. Jagger, Richards and Wood all dropped LSD, ran on and goofed through a 24-song set, Mick barking the words in the general direction of the tune. 'It's only rock 'n' roll,' Keith yelled after the second encore, 'but I like it.' And there, with him slumped on his knees, it all ended.

For their 68-day, 27-city tour, each founding Stone earned $409,317 post-tax, or just less than $10,000 per two-hour show. Woody was paid $225,000 for his services. They also sold a million-plus copies of *Made in the Shade*, the latest official hits collection, and, less agreeably, of *Metamorphosis*, a ragbag of outtakes, demos and rehearsal numbers put out by Allen Klein. A more definitive rarities set known as *The Black Box* and twelve keenly anticipated shows in South America were cancelled by Klein and political unrest respectively. Two chartered C-130 Hercules transport planes, of the sort normally used to carry tanks around the world, flew the Stones' hydraulic stage and lighting equipment back to London. The Who's Keith Moon later bought the entire apparatus and installed it in his back garden as a play-yard for his 10-year-old daughter Mandy.

At tour's end, Mick went back to Los Angeles, toyed with the idea of auditioning for the role of the over-the-hill pop singer in *A Star is Born*, and eventually fell in with John Lennon in the midst of his 'lost weekend'. Lennon and his crew ran around nights drinking impressive amounts of brandy and savouring the city's after-hours clubs. David Bowie, Ringo Starr and Harry Nilsson were all variously part of the group. Around five o'clock one morning, Mick drove everyone back to Bowie's house on North Doheny Drive, where they watched the Thin White Duke get out of the car and stagger up the path to his front door. 'We drove off, and it turned out it wasn't Dave's house after all,' Nilsson said. 'He was sitting there all morning with some bank manager and his wife.' After a while, Mick flew back to New York and bought a house on West 72nd Street.

Keith Richards was in Montreux with a pregnant-again Anita and 6-year-old Marlon, a pocket rock and roller who kept vampire hours, sat around on barstools and swore at his nannies. Richards also allowed himself a few luxuries: long Jamaican weekends, Hollywood boogie nights, trendy London clubs with the likes of Peter Cook and Fred Sessler. Prince Rupert would later tell a court that Keith's casual spending had totalled $175,000 in 1975 and $300,000 in 1976.

Later in the autumn, Jagger let it be known that the next album, still 'steaming ahead' after twelve months, would be called *Black and Blue*; and that, the Faces having finally imploded, Wood could be regarded as a fixture. Woody immediately relocated to a big rock star's villa next to Steve McQueen's pad in Malibu. Like Keith, Ron was soon in to the marching powder and both men smoked heroin-laced 'dirty cigs' on stage.

Now nearly forty, Bill Wyman was cutting another solo album, *Stone Alone*, which peaked at number 166 on the *Billboard* chart, and talking about writing his memoirs. Charlie Watts stayed home in the English countryside with his family.

Mick Jagger never specifically signalled that he didn't appreciate his two guitarists' drug consumption; that wasn't his style. But he had his own sly ways of letting people know he was aware of the problem, and went on to remark of a future possession trial, 'Keith gets busted every fucking year.' One of the crew in Munich noticed the Stones 'didn't really talk when they were together. Bill and Charlie would exchange views on the weather for about twenty seconds, then one of them would sit in one corner and the other would sit in the other corner. Mick and Keith never spoke. The only time they acknowledged each other was when one of them grunted, "What key's this in?" or some other technical chat. Woody was the messenger-boy between the four of them.' Wood also had his own issues. In an unusual duelling-guitarists arrangement, Ron had been having a hot affair with George Harrison's (and later Eric Clapton's) wife Pattie Boyd, while his own wife was stepping out with Jimmy Page of Led Zeppelin. While the Stones were in Munich, the drug squad finally hit Wood's house in Richmond. They kicked down the door, couldn't find any stoned musicians lying around the studio, but carried on up the grand staircase carpeted in royal red to the top bedroom. They found Krissy Wood fast asleep there with a girlfriend. By the time the police left, crowds of reporters and photographers had already gathered at the Wick's front door, and the next day's headlines were full of the 'pink knicker raid', and how the two women had been shamelessly 'embracing' and 'cuddling'. After that, the Woods spent more of their time in Los Angeles. That autumn, Krissy gave birth to a baby boy they called Jesse James, but the good times didn't last. Ron soon started seeing a blonde ex-model named Jo Howard, whom he eventually married in 1985. Krissy Wood later remarked that her husband's joining the Stones disastrously encouraged his already prodigious consumption of 'vintage booze and young women'.

Meanwhile, on 26 March 1976, in Geneva, Anita also had a son. He was several weeks premature, but apparently healthy. She and Keith named him Tara JoJo Gunne, after Tara Browne and a character in an old Chuck Berry song. The following year, Bebe Buell gave birth to a daughter, the future actress Liv Tyler, and Mick told friends that the pretty, full-lipped child was his. Nine years later, Liv learned that her father was Aerosmith's singer Steven Tyler.

On 23 April 1976, the Stones released *Black and Blue*. If you wanted the band who made *Exile*, with its curt guitar, you'd have to wait for their next outing, *Some Girls*, which proved one of the defining moments of their career. Meanwhile, for all its funky Ohio Players allure, this one fell a few tracks shy of a *Soul Train* revue. Other than reggae-and-roll jokes like 'Hot Stuff' (it wasn't), there was the jazzy shuffle 'Melody' and a single, 'Fool to Cry', which made 'Angie' sound rootsy by comparison. Jagger and Richards shared lead vocals on 'Memory Motel', an extended love letter to Hannah, a honey of a girl, layered in synthesisers, from which a decent three-minute ballad signalled wildly to be let out; Keith would actually fall asleep while performing this song at a concert in Germany. Elsewhere, Mick stuck doggedly to the James Brown playbook. 'Hot Stuff' assures us 'you're hot/you're hot/you're hot stuff'; 'Hey Negrita' urges us to 'shake your body/hey, do it up now'; and so on.

Keith Richards later described *Black and Blue* as 'rehearsing guitar players', and even Mick thought it 'not very good – certainly nowhere as good as *Let it Bleed*, flung together under similar conditions. The two albums shared another distinction. Not for the first time, the Stones' back-room staff found themselves cut out of the action. There were no songwriting credits for Ron Wood, Wayne Perkins or Harvey Mandel, the former Canned Heat and John Mayall guitarist who graced 'Hot Stuff' and 'Memory Motel'. Billy Preston got an acknowledgement for 'Inspiration' on 'Melody', a track Bill Wyman says Preston wrote; still no royalties. *Black and Blue* did, however, come with lavish full-page ads that showed a bruised, scantily clad blonde, with her hands bound above her head, legs akimbo, pouting. The caption read: 'I'm black and blue from the Rolling Stones and I love it.'

Black and Blue hit number one on the *Billboard* chart and number 2 in Britain, where it was kept off the top by Abba's *Greatest Hits*.

On 28 April, the Stones played the first of thirty-seven European dates. It was another drug tour. Keith Richards had the crew lay out lines of heroin and coke in compartments built in to the backs of the amps, so he and his fellow chemistry student Ron Wood could refresh themselves between songs. At some gigs, the smack dealers had their own reserved backstage lounge. Charlie, meanwhile, declined to speak to the media, while Keith told them he thought Bill Wyman's new album was a load of crap. Even old friends noticed that the Stones could be a moody lot. The British critic Charles Shaar Murray found his prearranged interview with the band in Frankfurt cut short by a sound 'exactly like Mick Jagger saying in his proletarian voice, "Oi fort your review [of *Black and Blue*] was bahluddy stoopid".' 'Throw these cunts out,' Mick then instructed the heavies, referring to the press corps as a whole. There

was so much criticism of the Stones in heavyweight titles like the
Sunday Times that it couldn't be confined to one section. They got
panned not only in an editorial, but, under the headline 'NOISES
OFF', on the Style pages, while the paper's magazine spoke of the
band's '22 fuel-guzzling lorries' and 'tons of lights and amplification'
at a time when ordinary Britons were feeling the pinch of an energy
crisis.

Mick's marriage to Bianca appeared marginally more stable than
his press relations, but it was still showing signs of strain. Apart from
Bebe Buell, he was seeing the singer Linda Ronstadt and the model
Apollonia von Ravenstein, among others, and was soon to enjoy a
one-off lunchtime encounter with the 18-year-old TV starlet
Mackenzie Phillips, who he'd first met around the time of *Beggar's
Banquet*. 'I've been waiting for this since you were ten years old,'
Mick told her, before making his move.

By contrast, Keith and Anita were enjoying one of their cyclical
bouts of happiness following their son Tara's birth. At one point,
they even contemplated a rock and roll wedding ceremony right on
stage. Keith was 'beginning to feel optimistic about it', he told the
London *Evening Standard*, but shortly afterwards Anita moved out
of the tour hotel and flew back to Switzerland. Marlon stayed on
the road with the Stones. The security detail knew Keith slept with
a gun under his pillow and didn't like to disturb him, so Marlon
would be sent up to his father's room an hour before curtain-up to
get him ready for the night's show. Sometimes the Stones' main creative force went direct from his bed to the stage. Perhaps as a result,
some of the concerts seemed to lose a little zing. Many of the punk
rockers thrashing away in their dives, while making a non-
aggression pact with Keith himself, now claimed to despise the
Stones as 'boring old farts', while the word 'parody' dominated the
print reviews. Every so often, *New Musical Express* issued an
impromptu fatwa on the band, satirically asking that some disgruntled fan do them a favour and 'put everyone out of our misery'.
On opening night, Keith fell down during 'Jumpin' Jack Flash',
couldn't get up, and finished the song flat on his back. Often, the
problem seemed to be the opposite extreme. Keith was so wired, he

reminded Stu of a caged tiger prowling from side to side. Critics like Charles Shaar Murray began to talk about the Stones' 'narco-flop music' . . . 'a total shambles' . . . 'phoned-in funk' . . . 'crudely exaggerated' . . . 'stylized up its own ass'. Mick was flying around on a trapeze for much of the show, while Keith performed in front of tens of thousands of fans wearing a silver necklace with a snorting tube and coke spoon on it.

On 19 May, Richards engaged in another one of those random, long-distance drives which, accompanied by a takeaway fish-and-chip dinner, and enlivened by a pounding reggae album in the tape deck, constituted his idea of a quality night out. Some two hours after leaving a Stones concert in Stafford, Keith was at the wheel of the Pink Lena when he nodded off for a moment, lost control, and bounced the car off a guardrail and in to a field just outside Newport Pagnell. It was four in the morning. When the police arrived they found Keith, wearing sunglasses, his pockets allegedly full of acid, wandering up the side of the M1 with 6-year-old Marlon. A search of the Bentley revealed the snorting tube squeezed under the driver's seat. Charged with possession of coke and LSD, Richards later appeared in the same Aylesbury courthouse where the Great Train Robbers had gone on trial thirteen years earlier. He told the jury he never took drugs and had never seen the snorting gear introduced as evidence against him. 'It could belong to anyone. I don't even know what it is.' The prosecutor then produced a front-page press photograph of the accused wearing a chain and tube identical to the one seized by the police. 'I don't know anything about it,' Keith insisted.

Six sold-out gigs followed at London's Earls Court, some of the worst the Stones ever played. Mick managed a little 1960s-style outrage by publicly referring to the venue as 'the shittiest toilet I've seen', but somewhat undermined the effect later that night by inviting Princess Margaret backstage, the band shuffling up to be introduced like a sick Cup Final team at Wembley. From the sounds of the actual concert, you could tell there had been a catastrophic breakdown in the chemically based creative process and that, as a consequence, a metal din was going to be inflicted on the audience for much of the show. 'Certain songs,' *The Times* reviewer wrote, seeming to allude to this point, 'were accepted rather than seized on.' Charlie concurred: 'It was bloody awful.' After the final gig, Mick went out to dinner with Bryan Ferry and his girlfriend Jerry Hall, a 20-year-old blonde Texan model whose mouth was currently to be seen in extreme close-up adorning the sides of buses and taxis all over Britain, advertising a brand of lip-gloss. When Mick started flirting with her, Ferry walked out of the room. How far things went that night isn't known; later that month, however, during the course of an interview, Ferry announced that he intended to punch Jagger on the nose.

When the Stones played in France, Stu remembered, 'Keith could just barely stand up.' The critics saw a pattern whereby 'Richards would reel on and somehow get through two hours', while Jagger swung around like one of the Flying Tabares on the end of his wire. The French press gave the band some of the worst reviews of their career.

Tara Richards was just seventy-two days old on Sunday 6 June, when Anita found him dead in his crib. He had apparently suffocated. Keith, who was informed by phone, played some blistering solos on his black 'skull' guitar when he went onstage in Paris a few hours later; many of the tracks on *Love You Live* were recorded that night. Tara's tiny remains were cremated in Geneva on 14 June. Following that, Richards and Pallenberg locked up the house in Switzerland, and never set foot in it again. Thirty-four years later, Keith wrote: 'I wasn't about to ask questions at the time. Only Anita knows ... I don't think it's her fault; it was just a crib death. But leaving a newborn is something I can't forgive myself for ... Anita and I, to this day, have never talked about it.' Tony Gill, an AP reporter who interviewed the Stones during the week of 7 June, had the impression from the exchange that 'Keith didn't want to show how much it hurt. It was business-as-usual. The sense elsewhere was that he'd lost the person who held his home life together more than anyone else.'

Anita: 'Keith was very calm and protective and normal and loving. He just said, "Forget it." And everybody else told me the same thing.

They all said, "Forget it. Look after your other children." I'm sure that the drugs had something to do with it. And I always felt very, very bad about the whole thing.'

Keith Richards would probably be the one rock star ever to have nodded off on stage in front of 20,000 screaming fans, shortly after playing the solo on 'Memory Motel' in Munich. The Stones then did a few desultory gigs in eastern Europe, before winding up in Vienna. Mick and Ron wrecked their hotel suite there. The management threatened to call the law and have everyone arrested, but became more cordial when Peter Rudge peeled off £5,000 in crisp £50 notes to help defray the damages.

The next time anyone saw the Stones was on 21 August, when they performed to 200,000 at the Knebworth Festival, their first since Altamont. It was also the last public appearance of the band's long-serving press agent, Les Perrin. Over the past decade, the somewhat spinsterish but supremely capable PR – known to refer to his famous charges as 'my naughty boys' – had been much more than a media wrangler, deftly orchestrating the coverage of Jagger and Richards' 1967 drugs trial, and almost single-handedly salvaging Mick's otherwise anarchic wedding-day arrangements four years later. 'You can call me twenty-four hours a day,' Perrin had always promised clients and press alike, many of whom had taken him up on the offer. Having contracted hepatitis while chaperoning the Stones on their last Far East tour, he was to suffer a series of strokes, and died, aged fifty-nine, in August 1978. One of Perrin's last professional acts was to take a full-scale BBC television crew around Knebworth to film the concert as part of a well-received documentary on the band. Some hours later, travelling back to London, the same crew spotted Bianca Jagger standing alone by the side of the road where her car had broken down, attempting to hitchhike home to Chelsea. Although happy to oblige, it struck the BBC men as odd that rock's most glamorous consort should find herself stranded on the outskirts of Barnet while her husband went on ahead of her by limousine and helicopter. The show itself was a shambling parody.

★

John Phillips, formerly of the Mamas and the Papas, was living around the corner from Jagger and Richards in Chelsea with his wife, the actress Genevieve Waite, and his teenage daughter Mackenzie, who Mick had recently become closer to. During the summer, Phillips began an affair with Bianca. Mick in turn enjoyed a warm relationship with Genevieve, who had just appeared alongside David Bowie in Nic Roeg's film *The Man Who Fell to Earth*. David's wife Angela was reportedly seeing something of both Jaggers, possibly concurrently, which, if true, meant that the sexually omnivorous Bowie and his wife were allegedly sleeping with the same man, clearly a tricky situation for all concerned.

Having lost his shirt producing a film about a boy whose ambition is to take wing and fly inside the Houston Astrodome, Phillips, the composer of such sunny 60s classics as 'California Dreamin'' and 'San Francisco (Be Sure to Wear Flowers in Your Hair)' was busy recording his comeback LP with the Stones' help. Ahmet Ertegun liked the idea and signed the album to Atlantic, with a generous production budget. Keith Richards quite often stayed with the Phillipses in their house on Glebe Place when he needed a safe berth in London. One day Keith and John told young Mackenzie they were going out, and that they'd be back later.

By later, they meant three days. 'There was no telephone and no food,' Mackenzie Phillips says. 'There was just cereal in the cupboard, and I remember sitting in front of a mirror with my journal, writing about how I had been abandoned. I was a kid. I guess I was being dramatic, but that was how I felt. Dad and Keith came back, totally wasted on heroin. They were crawling around on the floor, looking for bits of drugs that had fallen on the carpet. I remember looking at them and thinking how ridiculous they were.'

Richards was then thirty-two, and prone to blackouts and memory gaps. He smoked and drank as if he had no wish to see thirty-three. And yet, deathly as he looked, there was something about him oddly and irrepressibly alive. Later that winter, Keith cut a raucous solo version of Chuck Berry's 'Run Rudolph Run', before dressing up as a cheery if notably gaunt Santa Claus for

Marlon and Angela. When not on the road, he spent much of his time with Peter Cook and members of the Monty Python crew.

While Keith laid back, Mick Jagger assumed full control of the Stones, in league with Prince Rupert and an army of tax lawyers whose advice on when and where to record sometimes seemed to prevail over mere artistic considerations. The strategy worked. For all their drug- and family-related issues, the group's financial position was golden. Their current American record deal was coming to an end, and they anticipated another bidding war for their services. *Black and Blue* may have disappointed the critics, but it was a solid hit around the world, and Mick and Keith already had a batch of hot new songs for the album's follow-up, *Some Girls*. With Ahmet Ertegun promising the Stones a reported $20million to stay with Atlantic in America, and the big names lining up to sign them in Europe, it seemed the band was on a roll, both creatively and commercially.

Then things started to go wrong.

7

'WE WANT TO PLAY.
YOU WANT TO PLAY.
WHERE ARE YOU?'

On 3 January 1977, the US Drugs Enforcement Agency sent a classified letter to the British Home Office. They wanted to be kept up to date with Keith Richards' latest trial.

A week later, Keith appeared at Aylesbury crown court to face charges of coke and LSD possession arising from his traffic mishap at Newport Pagnell the previous May. As TV crews gathered in the bustling market square, something like a mob orgy broke out on the courthouse steps. Monday-morning shoppers jostled with busloads of Stones fans driven in from London, many of whom paraded through the streets in support of the accused. One buxom woman screamed, 'I love you!' at Keith and followed him inside when he pulled up, forty minutes late, in a chauffeured black car.

Adding to the drama, Mick Jagger arrived unexpectedly from LA, where he had been enjoying a winter break with Linda Ronstadt. Half a dozen news crews perched up on the library roof opposite turned on their klieg lights to capture the scene, attracting even larger and louder crowds. By mid-morning two or three hundred people had massed tightly at the courthouse door for a glimpse of their idols and, whenever they got tetchy, a Stones aide came out with a handful of glossy photos. Meanwhile, local opinion provided the flip side of the fans' shrill support. From time to time a few callous souls down in the market yelled, 'Lock 'im up,' and there were soon dull thuds and groans heard from that general area. The trial and surrounding melee led that night's bulletins on both the BBC and ITV, immediately before the story of Britain's latest currency crisis and the resignation from the Commons of the ex-Home Secretary, Roy Jenkins.

Keith pleaded not guilty. Called to the box, he made a persuasive witness in his own defence. He was dressed in a dark suit and spoke in a level, pleasant voice; but there was no hiding the bombed-out eyes and gaunt cheeks. He'd been thin before he discovered heroin, and had lost weight since. For the record, Keith said that he knew absolutely nothing about any drugs and that he'd been sharing driving duties that night with Jim Callaghan, which happened to be the then Prime Minister's name. The judge had to gavel down the laughter. 'May we proceed?' he asked gruffly.

Staring ahead, Keith stayed doggedly on message as he spoke about his career and busy work schedule until his QC, Peter Rawlinson, slipped in a 'What does being a lead guitarist mean?' question. 'It means I make the most noise,' Keith said. Everyone, including Mick, cracked up again. It was a well-rehearsed answer.

On 12 January, Richards was convicted of coke possession and acquitted on the LSD charge. The judge decided against a jail term, noting that the defendant had had every chance to dump the evidence had he known it was in his possession. 'There is some support for your tale,' the bench told him. 'But under the circumstances, another conviction will certainly lead to a prison sentence.' The defendant was ordered to pay a £750 fine and another £250 in court costs. Pouring himself a large vodka in the hastily convened press conference in the pub across the road, Keith commented that the trial struck him as 'a good, old-fashioned bit of British theatre', a warm-up act, as it were, for the altogether more malign events that awaited him six weeks later.

Keith was back at Redlands on the night of 12 February 1977. Mick and Charlie were there too, talking to neatly suited and tied record label executives while 'Brown Sugar' blasted from the stereo. It happened to be ten years to the day since the unpleasantness with

Chief Inspector Dineley and his men. Keith winced when I reminded him of this. 'The fuzz are still a pain in the bum. Well, not really a pain, they're more of a habit.'

He reflected further, and added sadly, 'An expensive habit.'

Everyone was sitting around the galleried living room where a pair of razor-pointed duelling sabres hung somewhat intimidatingly over the roaring log fire. 'Brown Sugar' had finished, and Mick, dressed in a velvet jacket, was tinkling a grand piano in the corner. Keith was wearing jeans, suede boots and a Hawaiian shirt, and Charlie was in a three-piece tweed suit. A large, nearly albino dog was sprawled on a Persian rug, periodically emitting gastric noises and dubious smells in counterpoint to the music. A kaftanned Anita Pallenberg lay next to it, smiling beatifically and not making any sign of distress or reproach. Eventually, one of the label heads started a spiel about 'breaking the band to a whole new demographic', prompting the owner of the house to look over, wink, and surreptitiously make a vigorous rubbing gesture in the air immediately above his crotch. It lasted just a second, but it said as much about Keith's essential outlook on life as the acres of news coverage of his recent trial did.

Four days later, the Stones announced a new £7million distribution deal with EMI for all territories outside North America. Everyone but Keith then caught a flight to Toronto, where Mick had arranged for them to record some club dates for inclusion on *Love You Live*. The band gave him a day or two, then started sending sarcastic telegrams: 'WE WANT TO PLAY. YOU WANT TO PLAY. WHERE ARE YOU?' As the week wore on, Mick arranged for Stu and his crew to set up a round-the-clock watch at Toronto airport. Back at Redlands, Keith had taken the phone off the hook.

On Thursday 24 February, the Richards family finally packed their twenty-eight suitcases and boarded a British Airways flight to Canada. Midway across the Atlantic, Keith excused himself and disappeared in to the first-class lavatory. He didn't come out again for three hours.

Mysteriously, there were no Stones representatives on hand to meet the plane when it landed in heavy rain at around six that evening. Canadian Customs, however, were there in force: their inspection quickly turned up a burned spoon and a 'brick-size' chunk of hash in Anita's handbag, but missed the white powders. Unbeknown to the Richardses, the police had already intercepted a package of assorted drugs posted ahead from London and addressed for Keith's attention at his local hotel. Anita was arrested, and immediately released on a promise-to-appear notice. One of the Customs officers later said that the booking process had been terminated by the unnerving sight of 7-year-old Marlon poking his head round the door to enquire whether his mum was 'ready to go now'.

From Toronto airport, Stu drove Richards and his party downtown, where they were registered, under the name Redlands, on the thirty-second floor of the Harbour Castle hotel. It was a towering grey structure of about the same general decor as the Arabella in Munich. On 25 and 26 February the Stones rehearsed on a soundstage at the nearby Cinevision film studio. On Sunday the 27th, Keith retired to Suite 3224 for one of his deep, Rip van Winkle sleeps.

Around four that afternoon, five members of the Royal Canadian Mounted Police knocked on the door and, after some effort, having managed to slap Keith awake, served a search warrant. In his stupor, Richards thought the Mounties – 'all weeds in anoraks with droopy moustaches and bald heads' – might have been reps from EMI and, in truth, they weren't all that different. The RCMP then swiftly relieved Keith of two plastic bags containing white powder, a razor blade, flick knife, brass lighter, silver bowl, teaspoons, scales and a sheet of tinfoil all with similar traces, three purple pills, a hypodermic needle and two pouches 'believed to contain hashish and heroin'. (The transaction wasn't totally one-sided; the officers also took the opportunity to plant a listening device under the bed.) Keith, who remained calm throughout, told the law that the drugs were his and that he'd been a 'heavy user for four years' who 'purchased in bulk to reduce the risk of detection'. The arresting officer, a 25-year-old Toronto native named Bernie Barbe, called his prisoner 'a gentleman [who] was no trouble at all', although Keith did request that Barbe and his colleagues return a gram or two of his stash to help get him through the evening. Instead, he was taken uptown, where he was formally booked with possession for the purpose of trafficking. The charge carried a potential sentence of seven years to life.

When Richards was bailed and got back to the Harbour Castle that night, one or two of the band dropped by to offer condolences. Bill notes: 'I'll never forget going to Keith's room with Woody to find him writhing on the floor, vomiting. We tried to give him pills, but he threw them up. Nobody seemed to be looking after him.' Afraid that their friend might die, Wyman and Wood scored some heroin for him.

The press coverage that followed Richards' arrest was an even worse disaster than anyone had anticipated. As well as the familiar 'STONE ON DRUGS CHARGE' headlines, there were grounds to believe that Keith might actually go to jail this time, and that 'Mick Jagger and the rest', as the *Toronto Star* revealed, were 'close to calling it quits' as a result. During the next several days, reporters besieged the hotel and swooped in helicopters outside Keith's window while fans brawled down in the street. Mick locked everyone in his room and read them the Riot Act about not blowing the new American record deal. Three thousand miles away, Rupert Loewenstein was installed in the Beverly Hills Hotel, where he had assumed he would be facing the pleasant task of conducting an auction for the band's services. One by one, the suitors retired from the bidding. The morning after Richards' arrest, Robert Stigwood's RSO label publicly announced its decision to 'withdraw a $7million offer to the Rolling Stones for their recording rights to the USA after protracted negotiations', while the US Drugs Enforcement Agency sent another of its registered letters formally asking for details of Keith's charges. In time, they would share this information with their colleagues in the State Department and Immigration Service. A day or two later, Loewenstein was compelled to ring Mick Jagger telling him that his bargaining power had been significantly compromised by recent events. At this point,

Mick slammed the door of his suite and got on the phone to Jerry Hall. Later that night, he started writing a song he called 'Miss You'.

Compounding the problem was the presence in Toronto of Margaret Trudeau. The Canadian prime minister's 28-year-old wife – Madcap Maggie, to friends – had recently been hospitalised for stress, and was spending more and more time apart from her 57-year-old husband Pierre and their three young sons. Friday 4 March happened to be the couple's sixth wedding anniversary. Margaret celebrated the occasion by checking in to a suite on the thirty-second floor of the Harbour Castle hotel. This was an unorthodox way to achieve the 'total peace and quiet away from the press' Mrs Trudeau had insisted she wanted following her release from hospital. That same night the Stones played, brilliantly, at a local dive called El Mocambo, where they elected to do some of their old Crawdaddy Club chestnuts for the first time in fourteen years. The place was an inferno, so young women were soon peeling their tops off and the bar sold $1,242-worth of beer, or an average of roughly six bottles per customer; the club split the proceeds 50–50 with the band. Mick Jagger was on top form throughout, prowling the stage in his tiny catsuit and frequently singing straight in to the face of a pop-eyed young fan ostentatiously enjoying a toot in the front row. As Mick boogied up to introduce 'Starfucker', he spelled it out: 'Aawrite, Margaret?'

The next day's *Toronto Sun* headline – 'C'MON MAGGIE' – signalled the start of a political firestorm. Prince Rupert's intimation of disaster came true. Three more record companies withdrew from the bidding for the Stones' services, and the heavyweight press arrived in Toronto in force. In the course of the week of 7 March, government stocks dropped, followed by the Canadian dollar, which led in turn to disinvestment in the oil industry, financial panic and a parliamentary censure motion. Meanwhile, the entertainment titles were busy flashing their own leads about Madcap Madge and her various late-night hotel capers. 'I wouldn't want *my* wife to be seen with the Rolling Stones,' Charlie Watts quipped. Bill Wyman describes Mrs Trudeau and Ron Wood as enjoying a 'quiet liaison'. It was perhaps more open than that. Pursued by the press down a hotel corridor one night, the couple opened a door and narrowly avoided falling down a lift shaft. Mick was secluded in his room with Mia Farrow. The 32-year-old actress was in Toronto preparing for her role in a horror film called *Full Circle*, in which she finds herself trapped in a tall building inhabited by ghouls. There were also reports, filtered through the mists slowly, like a Kremlin health bulletin, that Keith himself was taking more and more smack. He was in bad shape. Would there even be a trial?

A day or two later, a terrified Marlon Richards knocked on Margaret Trudeau's door. Anita was out shopping and Keith was curled up on his bathroom floor, retching. Margaret and her police protection officer raced down the corridor to Suite 3224. Together they picked Keith up, walked him around, and stayed with him until Anita returned. 'He's my friend. He's my friend. I reached out!' Mrs Trudeau would say in a low, halting voice when later asked about Keith. But the painful ordeal wasn't quite over. Before leaving his room that day, Margaret considerately leaned down to give young Marlon a hug. It was an outreach too many. 'Fuck off,' the 7-year-old told the First Lady of Canada.

Earlier on Friday 4 March, Anita Pallenberg appeared in court and pleaded guilty to possession of heroin and pot. She was fined $200 on each count. Three days later, Keith Richards went to Old City Hall for a preliminary hearing of his own case, and found himself locked in a holding cell for ninety minutes while the judge held a private session with the lawyers. On 8 March, Keith went back to court and was bailed for $25,000. The next day, Mick and the other Stones were smuggled out of the hotel and on to separate flights to New York. The First Lady followed them there. Keith later had some hard words to say on this breach of group etiquette about never leaving a man behind. The swarm of reporters at a subsequent Rockefeller Center press conference had few questions about the Stones' new six-record deal with Atlantic – Ahmet Ertegun had loyally kept faith with the band – which was ostensibly the reason for them being there. All they wanted to know was what Madcap Madge was up to. 'No comment,' Mick told them.

Back in Toronto, Keith went in to a studio accompanied only by Stu and recorded a series of doleful cowboy ballads as he waited to hear, the next day, whether or not he was going to jail. These were extraordinarily moving songs – stuff, said Stu, 'you wanted to listen to, not just hear' – played in rural American style. Keith also traded on his bruised voice, exploring a range of snarls, guttural moans and lower-register sighs as he gasped out his songs about heartbreak and suicide.

Richards nodded off in court the next morning. While he slept, the Crown argued that he was a bad bail risk (residences in London, Paris and Jamaica), but the Stones' counsel prevailed. Bill Carter then immediately petitioned the newly elected President Jimmy Carter (no relation) and his English-born drugs czar Peter Bourne for emergency medical visas on behalf of the Richardses, citing the fact that his principal client was a 'highly creative and sensitive artist who deserves rehabilitation, not punishment', and arguing strongly against 'any further incarceration' over and above the ninety minutes Keith had so far spent in jail. It worked.

For the next month, Keith lived on a rented farm in Paoli, Pennsylvania (the very house where, in 1958, Steve McQueen had starred opposite a man-eating jelly in scenes from the cult film *The Blob*), undergoing a 'black box' cure that sent controlled electric shocks to the brain. During this period, Marlon was housed with a family of evangelical Christians just across the state line in Cherry Hill, New Jersey. It was not a success. At that time, Marlon never wore shoes, rarely bothered with clothes, and his language, even by prevailing Stones standards, was ripe. His primary social intercourse up until then had been with rock musicians and room-service waiters. One Sunday morning, Marlon returned to his room to discover a formal dark suit, a stiff white shirt and a gold crucifix laid out for him, attire that this 'son of Satan', as he once cheerfully called himself, would not likely have selected on his own.

The Richardses were eventually reunited in a white-fenced Colonial home in South Salem, New York, called Frog Hollow, where Keith got hooked on heroin again. It didn't go unnoticed in the tabloid press that this was a part of America historically linked

with witchcraft. In time, the *New York Post* would publish a series
of front-page scoops about 'ritualistic' orgies involving Anita and
various teenage friends and neighbours, adding that a policeman
had been attacked by 'a flock of black-hooded, caped people' a mile
from the house. Mick Jagger was soon driving up and down from
New York with tapes both of the Stones and their favourite reggae
bands for Keith to listen to. This wasn't merely a professional courtesy; Stu or a lesser employee could easily have made the trip. 'Mick
looked after me with great sweetness, never complaining. He ran
things ... Mick looked after me like a brother,' Keith later wrote.

Ten years after the Summer of Love, there was New York's
'summer of Sam' – with the psycho killer David Berkowitz on the
loose, the disco scene taking off like a rocket, and a rampant heroin
epidemic in much of Lower Manhattan. As Berkowitz himself said,
everyone was 'seeking pleasure and finding death'. In July 1977, the
World Economic Forum Travel and Tourism competitiveness index
put New York a lowly ninety-third on its list of leading holiday destinations, eighty-five places below London, though marginally
ahead of Hanoi. So it was a somewhat whimsical choice for Jagger
and Richards to now choose to settle in. Mick was on the Upper
West Side, spending most of his nights at Studio 54, the disused theatre converted by the likes of Andy Warhol and Truman Capote in
to the Oz of discos. On 2 May, Bianca celebrated her thirty-second
birthday there by trotting around the dance floor on a white Arab
stallion led by a big, black male model wearing a pair of gold underpants and nothing else. It seems to have been a climactic act in the
Jaggers' marriage, because just two weeks later Mick was openly hitting the town with Jerry Hall, the fun-loving Texan with the
peek-a-boo hair, whose knowledge of the arts of the *Kama Sutra*
was rumoured far more than cursory. Some people thought Mick's
switch from Bianca to Jerry was akin to the Stones' from Taylor to
Wood, a shot of infectious, over-the-top energy. Keith was still up
in South Salem, undergoing yet another cure at the private Stevens
Psychiatric Clinic in New York, and looking for a place of his own
in Manhattan. Preferring to spend his down-time at reggae clubs in
the Bronx, he was perhaps less fond than Mick of Studio 54, which

he memorably characterised as a room 'full of faggots in boxing shorts waving champagne bottles in your face'.

Kicking the physical dependence on heroin proved to be the least of Keith's problems. There was a growing feeling within the Stones camp that he would also have to part from Anita if he was serious about staying clean. 'I got myself together and she didn't,' he said later. Ron Wood soon took up some of the slack by becoming a major freebase addict, then started missing sessions, nearly went broke, and got busted. All of which might sound familiar, because it was the road first Jones and then Richards had taken. As the sorcerer's apprentice, Woody was learning to out-Keith Keith. Meanwhile, Bill Wyman was again promising to quit the band, a step Mick is thought not to have actively opposed. (In a later correction, Bill said he'd been misquoted.) Given the chance, Charlie Watts liked to stay home and raise sheepdogs. Reflecting on his role in the late-1970s Stones, Charlie said, 'I just [sat] at the back and played the fuckin' drums.' Stu thought the band he had helped found was badly off the rails, and *Black and Blue*, in particular, 'a load of old cobblers', which he hated.

September 1977, *Love You Live*. Heavy on synths and crotch-grabbing references to sex, money, dope and disco, the album's three arena sides made do with perfunctory versions of the Stones' back pages, with whiny, dentists'-drill guitars and intros mired in endless takes on 'How you doin', Paris?' Mick sang as if shouting the lyrics from a passing car. At best, all you could say for *Live* was that everyone's heads had been higher than their feet when they made it, and that the El Mocambo side, at least, sounded like it was 1963 all over again. At worst, heavyweight critics like Lester Bangs thought the album 'boxy', 'hollow' and 'little more than a joke'. It was, however, a singularly practical joke, a top-ten smash on both sides of the Atlantic for the rest of the year.

When the Stones signed their £7million deal with EMI, one of the main perks was free use of the label's famed Pathé-Marconi studios in Paris, the birthplace of brassily melodramatic hits by the likes of Edith Piaf and Charles Aznavour and, more pertinently, the Beatles' 'Can't Buy Me Love'. The band was based there between

October 1977 and April 1978, cutting what began life as 'More Fast Numbers' and would be known to the world as *Some Girls*. ('Because we couldn't remember their fucking names,' Keith observed.) Mick and Keith moved in to apartments with Jerry Hall and a local fashion model respectively, and everyone else lodged at a convenient hotel by the town's main Renault factory. Some of the Stones' subsequent creative renaissance can be put down to Chris Kimsey, a young British engineer who 'got beautiful sounds for me and Charlie', a for-once enthusiastic Bill Wyman said. For the first time since *Let it Bleed*, the band also elected to part with all the 'clever bastard' auxiliaries like Billy Preston. Mick filled in some of the gaps on clangorous rhythm guitar, a contribution that led Ian Stewart to boycott most of the sessions – 'They sound like bloody Status Quo,' Stu complained. A week or so in to the proceedings, the Stones hired the 21-year-old harmonica player James Whiting, who went by the name Sugar Blue, after Rupert Loewenstein heard him play at a Paris cocktail party and gave him a piece of paper with what he claimed was Mick Jagger's private number on it. To Blue's surprise, it was; he would appear on various Stones projects for the next five years. In December, Woody recruited the keyboard player Ian McLagan, his mate in the Faces, who spent a week in the studio performing on such songs as 'Miss You', which went on to become the Stones' eighth number one single in the US and a top-ten hit in seventeen other countries. At the end of his stay, McLagan, who was broke, politely asked Mick about remuneration for his work. Mick paid him out of his own pocket: 120 francs, or roughly £15.

The private Mick Jagger emphasising hard graft, thrift and self-discipline juxtaposed uncomfortably with his public persona as, to many, a morally dissolute social rebel and, to others, a singing phallus. However, all those closest to him in the *Some Girls* era are insistent that behind the outer shell of rock-star glitz lay a vein of English traditionalism, or even romanticism. Mick spent the night of 21 October 1977, his daughter Jade's sixth birthday, at his Cheyne Walk home – the last time, according to sworn court testimony, he made love to his wife. The following month, he bought Jerry Hall a Cartier bracelet and earrings (which she lost on the Paris Metro) before flying with her for a long weekend in Morocco. 'I could see we were really in love. I knew I was going to stick with him,' she reported, before publicly extolling Mick's astonishingly 'weird and dirty' sexual prowess. (Some of the couple's more elaborate means of gratification are said to have made extensive use of role-play, and it's known that Jagger, like a large number of British males, occasionally enjoyed the opportunity to dress up.) Mick himself now put his money where his mouth was, having a tiny diamond set in to his right-upper front tooth. Like him, several of the other Stones were undergoing a transitional phase in their domestic arrangements. Keith Richards had left Anita Pallenberg behind in suburban New York while he wintered in Paris, and Ron Wood's marriage ended abruptly when he got his girlfriend Jo Howard pregnant. Although Bill Wyman had long been spoken for, first with his wife Diane and then his long-time partner Astrid Lundström, this hadn't stopped his pioneering contribution to the rock-groupie industry, even if his early activities in the field had been couched in euphemism. Later, in Paris, the terminology was more specific, as befitted the sexually more explicit 70s. Ian Stewart remarked that the 41-year-old Bill remained partial to a good game of 'Spot the Tits' – 'very keen on it, he was'.

On 15 February 1978, Constable Bill Seward, the chief investigating officer in Keith Richards' drug case, was killed in a car crash. Shortly after that, the Canadian Justice Ministry ordered that the charge against Keith of possession for the purpose of trafficking (potential life sentence) be reduced to one of simple possession. In a separate hearing, a judge ruled that the Crown would not be allowed to read the accused's prior arrest history in to the record. Unless they happened to be rock music fans, none of the jurors would know anything about the various proceedings in Chichester, London, Nice, Fordyce or Aylesbury. Keith failed to appear in court for a scheduled session on 6 March, although he writes of a visit to Toronto at about this time when he fixed up in a public-bathroom cubicle while a Mountie relieved himself just outside the door. The judge eventually set a trial date of 23 October 1978.

Keith had another near-miss with the representatives of the law back in the Paris studio. According to his autobiography, after five days' continual drug-fuelled work on his *cri de coeur* 'Before They Make Me Run', 'I fell asleep under the booth, under all the machinery. I woke up eventually ... and there's the Paris police band. A bloody brass band. That's what woke me up. I sort of rolled out and said, "Oh, my God! I'm terribly sorry," and before they knew it, I was out.' 'I'm gonna find my way to heaven, 'cause I did my time in hell/Wasn't looking too good, but I was feelin' real well', Richards sang on the track, as if reviewing the past seven years. The song was sufficiently commercial to be considered as a single, which would have made it only the second such release to feature Keith on lead vocals, but the idea was shelved when Mick expressed his views on the subject.

Now Keith wanted to go on tour. Mick again demurred, telling the press he would never take to the road 'with a geezer pushin' a heroin charge'. 'Anything I do, he's got to negate,' Richards shot back. Keith was soon able to rally Charlie and Ron Wood to the cause (no one consulted Bill, or apparently cared), with Atlantic and EMI also on board. Mick was unhappy because of his twin yearning for a reasonably settled family life and a solo career, goals that he had discovered were incompatible with travelling the world as the lead singer of the Rolling Stones. But he was also shrewd enough to read the figures prepared by Rupert Loewenstein, predicting take-home pay of some $800,000 a man for six weeks' work. The money would have come in useful, because Bianca was about to sue Mick for $12.5million, or half the total amount he allegedly earned during their eight-year marriage. As an interim measure, she demanded $13,400 a month living expenses, which included the salaries of a chauffeur, a nanny and a live-in maid. Jagger's response was instantly to cut off Bianca's credit cards. After that, workmen arrived to colour-coordinate the interior of Cheyne Walk in vivid red. 'Mr Jagger [has] bragged he's never given any woman anything and never will, no matter what the circumstances,' Bianca noted in her petition. On 22 April, Mick and Keith flew to Jamaica to see their protégé Peter Tosh perform at the One Love

Peace concert (broken up by riot police), pausing to announce that they would go out on stage in America the following June.

First, *Some Girls*. Channelling punk, vintage Lou Reed and the southern boogie tradition of Muddy Waters and Chuck Berry, the Stones returned to their *Exile*-era best. Even the cover art provided some cheap thrills – a collage of a 'Frederick's of Hollywood' lingerie ad, inspired by Jerry Hall, over which Raquel Welch and Lucille Ball got their knickers in a litigious twist. A week or two later it would be Jesse Jackson's turn, railing at Jagger's fey lyrics on the wistful title track. In this tune, Mick's amorous plight was detailed to moving effect. French, Italian, American, English and Chinese girls all had their merits, he allowed, whereas black girls were perhaps overkeen in bed. They 'just want to get fucked all night', Mick sang. ('But they *do*,' he later protested.) Although Keith's 'Beast of Burden' wedged a blues riff in to a Motown-type ballad and Mick gave 'Far Away Eyes' a camp, Nashville-school vocal, the honky tonk women gone rhinestone, *Girls* otherwise stuck to a sleazy itinerary down the alleys of New York. A concept album of sorts, it ended with the stutter-step snarl of 'Shattered', a punk Baedeker tour of Lower Manhattan infused with new depths of alienation and scorn, along with a booty-shaking groove. Keith's riff and Mick's 'Looka me!' vocal both caught the late-70s, coked-up Bombay spirit of the place, a travelogue the local Chamber of Commerce might not have endorsed.

Some Girls resuscitated the Stones, just as *Beggar's Banquet* had ten years earlier. It sold 8 million copies, and actually toppled *Saturday Night Fever* from number one. With Dylan no longer bringing it all back home, the Beatles mummified and Led Zep grounded, this was the Stones searching for – and finding – a new voice.

Keith Richards had told the judge in Toronto that he was a creative soul racked with emotional pain, but that he was 'firmly resolved' to kick drugs. This seemed to be optimistic as handlers carried Keith from his car up a flight of stairs to his apartment on Todd Rundgren's estate in Woodstock, New York, where the Stones convened to rehearse for the tour. Ian Stewart remembered that 'management' swiftly appraised the situation and placed a call to enquire if Jimmy Page might if necessary be available to deputise on guitar. Later that night, Keith hooked up to the black box again. According to Jerry Hall:

> He was lying there wearing these things that looked like head-phones ... Mick and I would feed him. And every time the hooks would fall off we'd clip them back on ... We'd cover him up with a blanket at night. It gave Mick a very good feeling to be able to help Keith.

Hall, now living openly with Jagger for the first time, remembered Keith as having been under their care for the best part of a month. 'You know the feeling when you have a child, and you watch him grow? We were like, "Look, he's having a bath!" and "Oh, did you see what he was doing?"' According to Stu, Keith stayed with Mick for a total of two days.

A week later, Anita Pallenberg called for a car and went back to her house in South Salem. Ron Wood's girlfriend Jo soon brought a visiting Swedish colleague named Lil Wergilis with her to Woodstock, where she moved in with Keith. Lil was another hot blonde, sexy, self-assured, of the school of Marilyn Monroe, and a popular lingerie model. 'That's when it blew,' Keith remarks of his eleven-year relationship with Anita. On 29 May, Bianca Jagger filed for divorce on the grounds of irreconcilable differences. Bill Wyman's partner Astrid Lundström was also in and out of town to discuss her issues with Bill, some of which weren't so much aired as shouted out; she later told the press that she was tired of sharing her man with thousands of other women.

Jagger was running 10 miles daily through the New York woods – 'I have to stay sober, in training,' he told *Rolling Stone*. Keith, who wasn't in training, crashed off a porch early one morning and sprained his ankle. Sharp-eyed reporters didn't miss the ever-mounting crates of dead Stolichnaya bottles piled up at the estate's back gate. The promoter Bill Graham was impressed by the way the Stones managed to function, each after his own fashion. 'I watched Keith chain-smoke one cigarette after another and pour down vodka like he had a date with a firing squad ... Wood took in rivers of smoke and booze, wav[ing] his hands and weaving his long, skinny torso this way and that, all the while plucking the "Miss You" riff while Charlie whammed the drums.'

Mick, meanwhile, was throwing the tour together as best he could, adding and dropping cities faster than the press could list them. Sometimes only he knew where and when the Stones would be playing a day later. On 10 June, 12,000 fans in Lakeland, Florida bought tickets to see what was billed as 'The Great Stoned-Out Wrestling Champions'. The cops busted the dressing room before the show, arresting one of the Stones' minders and a coke dealer, and next morning Keith bought a stolen .38 Special in case he might want to conduct his future drug business in person. Elsewhere in the south the band was billed as both the London Green Shoed Cowboys and the Cockroaches, among other aliases. Ian McLagan returned on keyboards, and Mick Jagger conducted the negotiations for his services with his old LSE touch, bargaining with Mac for a favourable price while mentioning the unhappy experience everyone had had on the previous tour when Billy Preston had held up the live album for a reported 12 per cent of the gross. Under some pressure, McLagan signed his contract: he got a flat fee said to have been 'less than $3000' for each concert, and donated his services whenever the band appeared on TV or radio.

Generally, the Stones' ninth North American tour was a modest success. Thanks both to the last-minute nature of the itinerary and a willingness to downsize, the band played a novel mix of arenas, more intimate theatres and even clubs. Mick camped on, wearing tight red-leatherette pants, a white dinner jacket and, more than once, a rakishly tilted golf cap. Keith laughed out loud when he first saw the outfit. The extensive staging and set list of the *Black and Blue* tour were both pared back. Keith and Woody parodied the punks' thrashing guitar style, revved up the beat and brought in some of the classic Stones anthems in under two minutes. 'Spontaneity' was the buzzword that circled around, with at least some band members apparently only half conversant with the core repertoire – 'a bunch of sozzled people conducting a public rehearsal', as *Time* put it. On the other hand, for once the phrase 'Here's one off the new album' was a cause of celebration, not gloom, and a frantic, beat-the-clock version of 'Shattered' routinely got even the most wizened critics dancing along.

At the Rupp Arena, Lexington, a fan was shot and others plunged through a sheet of plate glass in a dispute about tickets. In Chicago, Richards went backstage at the Quiet Knight club to see Muddy Waters; when he appeared, Keith promptly fell down and kissed him on the feet. A week later, in Fort Worth, the Stones' blind fan Rita Bedard was taken backstage to meet both the band and, significantly, Keith's Toronto lawyer Austin Cooper. Back in the Fairmont hotel, Mick Jagger hosted a fortieth birthday party for Ian Stewart. As the festivities got under way, with reggae blasting from the sound system and a *Playboy* model waltzing around wearing only a red ribbon tied round her neck, Mick calmly turned to a journalist and announced, 'Solzhenitsyn's right in a lot of ways. About America. When we were in France, we were cut off from the media and no one wrote about us . . . Solzhenitsyn said everyone in the US is subject to this terrible TV and radio. I agree.' Bill Wyman fell off the back of the stage in St Paul, injuring his arm. In Arizona, a marquee reading 'Welcome Mick Jagger . . . and the Rolling Stones' raised Keith's hackles. Mick had taken to enlivening some of the band's less robust performances by announcing, 'If we seem slightly lacking in energy, it's because we spent all night fucking' – in Tucson, the cue for a hot-panted Linda Ronstadt to run out on stage and sing 'Tumbling Dice' with him.

At Detroit's Masonic Hall, fans saw a band that was loose enough to make mistakes, like starting a song in two different keys and crashing to a halt, and tight enough to get 4,000 people punching the air in time to the falsetto whoops of 'Miss You', before banging out the inimitable riffs of 'Brown Sugar', 'Jumpin' Jack Flash' and a restored 'Satisfaction'. Mick gave the audience exactly what they expected, including the lewd patter, gaudy outfits (six consecutive jackets, notably a pink tuxedo affair with the word 'Sex' stitched on the back) and caricatured lascivious stage moves. John Lennon came to the New York date and promptly dubbed his old

Swinging London crony 'the Charlie Chaplin of rock'. Steve McQueen showed up in Anaheim, demanding dozens of free passes. (Charlie's response: 'Tell 'im to get on 'is bike'.) As in 1972, the tour ended on Mick's birthday. He and the Stones each took home some $785,000 for forty-seven days' work. Bill Graham threw a party after the final show at the Oakland Coliseum, where Keith shot pool and Mick and Charlie watched a video of the England–New Zealand Test match at The Oval. A blond teenager with a familiar leer was also backstage that night: Brian Jones' second son, Julian.

After that the Stones moved on to RCA Studios in Los Angeles (their first visit there since 1966), where they cut some of the songs that wound up on *Emotional Rescue*. Keith Richards was the moving force behind the sessions, acting on his plan to record the band while they were still hot off the road. Considering Keith's best-publicised recreations of the time were drugs and firearms, everything went relatively smoothly. Mick and Charlie then flew back to London to watch some more cricket and Bill went to the south of France to photograph flowers, among other subjects. Ron Wood and his girlfriend Jo bought a house in the Hollywood Hills, where they became friendly with Kathy Smith, a local drug connection and aspiring singer, who later briefly went to prison for the heroin-related death of John Belushi. Keith Richards and his partner Lil Wergilis rented a home for the summer in nearby Laurel Canyon. Trying to light a flaming torch by the pool one night, Keith managed to set fire to his pants instead, and had to jump in to the deep end to extinguish himself. A week later, a neighbour happened to see black smoke pouring out of the house at eight one morning and called the emergency services. With police and firemen swarming on to the grounds, Keith and Lil climbed out of an upstairs window and leaped to safety. The place was still smouldering an hour later. Richards was pacing up and down wearing only a bed-sheet, with his arm around Lil, in a short T-shirt. Everyone flinched as first Keith's guitars and then his ammunition started exploding inside. The crowd on the lawn became a small mob, and some of them yelled for everyone who wasn't there on city business to clear the area; Keith himself seemed anxious to split,

as a policeman tried to take a statement. As he did so, Lil lay down
on the grass and took a nap. Just then, a sports car pulled up. In one
of those coincidences shunned in fiction but prevalent in Rolling
Stones life, it was driven by a cousin of Anita's who happened to be
passing. Keith and Lil leaped in and, leaving officialdom behind, the
three tore off down Sunset Boulevard.

On 7 October the Stones played on *Saturday Night Live*, their first
major US television appearance since the *Ed Sullivan Show* in 1969.
On the day before taping, everyone came down with laryngitis.
Mick mugged his way through 'Respectable' and a sketch with
comedian Dan Akroyd ('Why Jagger? Because it's my name ... my
father's name') before returning to croak 'Beast of Burden'. During
the tune, a viewing audience of 17 million watched Mick stick his
tongue down his lead guitarist's throat. 'I tried to kick him, but he
was too fast. He loves putting people on the spot,' Woody rued.
Back in Hounslow, Archie Wood later entertained his friends by
repeatedly playing them a clip of this episode. The Stones had a
contract with NBC which allowed them to walk away from the
studio if anyone so much as approached them for an autograph or
intruded on them in any way while they were on the premises. No
one did.

A fortnight later, Keith Richards and Lil Wergilis flew in to
Toronto on a Learjet and made for a suite at the Four Seasons, where
they were registered as Mr and Mrs Thomas Crapper. On the
Monday morning of 23 October, Keith's trial got under way at the
York County courthouse. Despite some typically breezy words to the
press, his comments both to Ian Stewart and in a letter to his father
Bert (living in the back room of a Bexley pub) reflect a certain see-
sawing in the defendant's spirits. On the whole, he was much more
down than up. Keith had started doing heroin again towards the end
of the American tour. His latest attempts to detox remained slow and
painful. Since coming off the road, he'd lost 15 pounds and his
appearance was visibly shrunken, with a complexion that reminded
the Canadian *Daily News* of a stubbed-out cigarette. A whacked
Anita, meanwhile, was living in seclusion with Marlon, whose school
attendance was fitful. One way or another, the Thanksgiving-week

atmosphere in Toronto could hardly have been less festive, nor the
climate of opinion more lacking in goodwill. As Stu put it: 'October
1978 was the lowest point in Keith's life.'

Against this backdrop, Pierre Trudeau's Liberal Government was
in serious trouble. Published polls showed that more than half the
Canadian electorate (76 per cent among Liberal voters) was worried
about the economy; press and TV coverage reflected the widespread
concern over taxes, rising energy costs, soaring unemployment. By
mid-1978, Trudeau was locked in a bitter struggle to reconcile
provincial and ethnic rights to the federal government. The War
Measures Act had been invoked. Radical Quebec separatists personally targeted the First Family, and Trudeau and his three sons
lived under tight security. So it may not have been entirely coinci-
dental that the Liberal Attorney General, Ron Basford, having
passed in to law the 'Universal Human Rights Act' and abolished
the death penalty in Canada, would tell the Cabinet on 21 July
1978: 'This is a compassionate country, historically generous even
towards those who abuse our hospitality.' Soon after that, Mr
Basford's ministry came up with a plan to settle the matter of *The
Crown v Keith Richards*. The prosecution would accept a plea of
guilty to possession of a small amount of heroin, then drop both the
coke and importing charges. All outstanding bench warrants for
Keith's arrest for non-appearance at previous hearings would be
waived. According to a previously unpublished Justice Department
memo of 1 August, 'Keith Richards' admission of guilt, *without a
custodial sentence*, [is] a satisfactory solution [and will] constitute a fair
resolution of the case and give appropriate public relief.' The plan
served several purposes. On a petty level, it would avoid a long and
quite likely embarrassing trial, with testimony about the PM's wife.
An international furore about jailing Keith, and thus scuttling the
Stones, could also mean that, if anything, the government would be
less likely, not more, to shore up plunging confidence in the
Canadian dollar. As the defendant himself put it some thirty years
later, 'The Mounties and their allies were thinking, "Oh, great!
Wonderful job!" And the Trudeaus were thinking, "Uh-uh, pal, this
is the last thing we need."'

Keith entered the court dressed in a three-piece tan suit, white socks and scuffed brown boots. He was sporting an earring. There were gasps, gavelled down by Judge Lloyd Graburn, when the Crown's Paul Kennedy announced the reduced charges. Kennedy then made a rambling speech in which he argued that Keith had been caught with quite a lot of drugs, and had written some songs that mentioned the stuff. Nearly two years of preparation had left the prosecutor apparently only half familiar with the Rolling Stones' *oeuvre*, because he couldn't immediately remember which ones. Nonetheless, he was sure he had. Kennedy suggested that a jail term of three months, or some lesser time, might be appropriate.

In Keith's defence, Austin Cooper said that his client had a poor self-image and problems with other people. The 49-year-old Cooper quoted movingly from a biography of Baudelaire, saying that art is created from 'pieces of the shattered self. Witness our modern greats. Van Gogh was a schizophrenic and cut his ear off. Aldous Huxley was a drug addict.' Cooper then compared Richards to Sylvia Plath and Judy Garland. A conga line of witnesses, including *Saturday Night Live* boss Lorne Michaels, testified that the Stones in general, and Keith in particular, were the world's greatest rock and rollers. Cooper read out glowing reports from the Stevens clinic, insisting Richards hadn't so much as touched heroin since May 1977. He added that Keith would personally raise $1 million for an unspecified drug rehab programme; he still might.

Richards arrived, punctually for once, still wearing his tan suit and tugging nervously at his earring as Judge Graburn read out his ten-page ruling early the next morning. He agreed that the defendant was a heavy drug user. But, the judge added, Keith was doing 'marvellously well' in therapy, more of which was clearly needed. 'The Crown seeks a jail term,' he concluded, 'but I will not incarcerate him for addiction and wealth.' At that, a barely perceptible twitch played over Keith's face.

The judge continued, 'Maybe the Rolling Stones have encouraged drug use in their songs. Still, his efforts have been to move firmly away from the drug culture and can only encourage those who emulate him.' Now it was the turn of the press to crack a smile.

The full sentence ran: no fine, no jail; defendant to be of good behaviour for a year; to continue treatment at the Stevens clinic; lastly, to give a benefit concert within six months on behalf of the Canadian Institute for the Blind. Quite by chance – there could have been no collusion – Richards' fan Rita Bedard had personally lobbied the judge on this final point. As soon as the verdict was in, Keith slowly raised a clenched fist above his head and left the courtroom to loud applause. There was a mixed reaction in the world's press the following morning, and questions were asked in the House of Commons in Ottawa about the 'preposterous and more than lenient sentence imposed on a wealthy pop star. There are Canadians sitting in prison today for lesser drug offences.' A month later the Crown duly lodged an appeal, which came to nothing. Cynics on papers like the Toronto *Sun* were left to openly speculate that an 'expensive and major fix' was in. Pierre Trudeau survived in office until May 1979; he and his wife separated the following year.

Although the Stones made a habit of lending moral support at each others' trials in the 1960s, Keith's bandmates, possibly on legal advice, stayed away from Toronto. Mick Jagger was spending much of his time either with his divorce lawyer or Peter Tosh, the latter of whom had a Stones-financed reggae album, *Bush Doctor*, climbing the pop charts. When Tosh played at the Bottom Line in New York, Mick was lifted up by the crowd and passed over their heads from the back row of the hall to the stage in order to duet on the song 'Don't Look Back'. In a subsequent appearance on *Saturday Night Live*, Mick took the opportunity to reprise his amorous routine with Ron Wood by kissing Tosh on the mouth – 'perhaps too much of a show of support', in *Time*'s opinion. Wood himself was in Los Angeles, where his girlfriend gave birth to their daughter Leah, a future singer-model, on 22 September. Ian Stewart was doing pub gigs with his boogie-woogie side project, Rocket 88. On the first day of rehearsals, Stu had told his bandmates he 'might know a drummer who's quite good' for the job, which proved to be Charlie Watts. Back on the Riviera, Bill Wyman continued to combine his photographic studies and his energetic social life without exciting more comment than was inevitable when an eminent middle-aged man shows a taste for the company of free-spirited young girls. Mick Taylor was in New York, where he released an unsuccessful solo album, sold most of his possessions, and, a true Rolling Stones guitarist at last, spent the money on heroin.

After a post-trial holiday in Jamaica, Keith Richards and his family flew back to spend Christmas in London. It happened to be his thirty-fifth birthday. As Keith walked through the terminal at Heathrow, a number of reporters slapped him on the back and wished him well. None of them recognised the thickset, middle-aged woman with broken teeth and matted, greasy hair hobbling along behind him. It was the once ravishing Anita.

A month later, the Stones reconvened at Compass Point studios in Nassau, where Island Records' boss Chris Blackwell had moved operations after someone fire-bombed his recording facilities in Jamaica. Despite the idyllic surroundings, bickering continued between Jagger and Richards as the latter tried to reassert himself as a fully functioning creative partner. The dispute reached the point where, according to Stu, 'they weren't on speaking terms with each other . . . Mick was making sarcastic comments. Little digs. Rolling his eyes.' Vodka replaced smack as the drug of choice. A blotto Richards annoyed Jagger so much that on 7 February Mick refused to come to work, noting that Keith was 'so out of it nothing [had] been done'. Much of the music was being recycled from *Some Girls*, although the Stones also cut some reggae-and-roll numbers like 'Claudine' and a cover of an old Paragons tune called 'The Tide Is High' that Blondie somehow managed to turn in to a worldwide hit in 1980. (The raw tapes of the Nassau sessions also include Mick Jagger shouting angrily over the tannoy at an overpersistent drug dealer.) But in general, as Stu said, the studio appeared to be echoing not so much to great rock and roll as to the sound of barrels being scraped. One of the engineers told Keith that Mick wished out loud that he'd go back to being a junkie. Before long the Glimmer Twins struck a non-alignment pact, rarely working on the same day and not even speaking when they did. Meanwhile, Wood was taking up the baton from Keith and would come perilously close to killing himself with drugs. Bill Wyman talked about quitting again. Charlie reportedly told the press that he was sick and tired of the whole thing and that all he really wanted to do was raise sheepdogs in the Sussex countryside.

Keith: 'In the Seventies, when I was on dope and I'd do nothing but put the songs together and turn up and not deal with any of the business of the Stones, Mick took all of that work on his shoulders ... When I cleaned up – "Hey, I'm back, I'm clean, I'm ready; I'm back to help and take some of the weight" – immediately I got a sense of resentment ... Mick [saw] it as a power grab.'

Clearly, it was solo career time. In April 1979, Ron Wood released his own new album, *Gimme Some Neck*, some of which sounded more like an extended jam than the finished article, but taken as a whole an engagingly rootsy, faux-*Exile* collection of songs that deserved a wider audience. Buoyed by the critical response to the LP, Woody put together a road band, the New Barbarians, to which he and Columbia Records enlisted several familiar names including Keith Richards, Ian McLagan and Bobby Keys, among others. On 24 April, the Barbarians began a month-long tour of the US. The high point of this was a sold-out concert at Madison Square Garden. The low point was a rainy night in Milwaukee, when fans rioted due to the non-appearance of 'special guests' the morning press had named as Mick Jagger and Rod Stewart. The band generally made a big entrance, a spotlight punching up Woody and Keith looking like twin crows. Unburdened by a fixed repertoire, they went on to rasp out Sam Cooke and Elvis classics along with a few originals, all paced by the Meters' great Ziggy Modeliste on drums. Richards himself performed the parts ordinarily taken by horns, double bass and organ, as well as extraordinary parts that existed only in his brain. Those eighteen North American gigs were some of his finest moments. The Barbarians concluded proceedings on 21 May with a live television special from the LA Forum. Unfortunately, the customised Learjet and individual limos, not to mention all the drugs and room service, did for the tour's profits, leaving Ron Wood a reported $200,000 in debt to the record company. 'Things got so bad for me,' Woody later reflected of his Stones gap-year, 'I convinced my insurance agent to let me have a $70,000 home-improvement loan. When I got the cash, I put tarmac down on a new driveway, painted the kitchen green and spent the rest on dope in just six weeks.'

On 22 April 1979, the Barbarians had made their world debut at the 5,000-seat Civic Auditorium in Oshawa, outside Toronto, fulfilling the terms of Keith Richards' sentence just twenty-four hours before the court-imposed deadline. Over the preceding days, the small lakeside town filled up with the Stones' entire tour apparatus: fleets of limos and equipment trucks, phalanxes of cops, both uniformed and plain-clothes, mingling with the band's sumo-sized security detail; various managers, lawyers, roadies and the all-important fluffers and puffers; reporters and photographers flown in from LA and London; coked-out groupies wearing flimsy Keef T-shirts and screaming that Mick was the father of their children; and, on this occasion, some 2,000 visually impaired fans each paying anything from $10, retail, to $500, scalped, to hear justice served. After the Barbarians' set, the Stones themselves took over, racing through their 1978 *Some Girls* set. Mick, still in his tour outfit of red pants and pink FUNKY BUTT T-shirt, was on top form, even if some of his manic gyrations were presumably lost on the core audience. The Stones, paying their own expenses for the night, lost a great deal of money by voluntarily accompanying Keith, who took the opportunity to visit his local probation officer the following morning and assure him that he was gainfully employed. The band raised $52,000 on behalf of the Canadian blind.

On 20 July, while Richards was back in Paris, kicking around the thirtieth take of a then reggae-style song called 'Start Me Up', Anita Pallenberg was lying on the couple's bed 3,000 miles away in South Salem, watching TV with a 17-year-old friend called Scott Cantrell. Marlon and Fred Sessler's son Larry were downstairs. In what may have been a disastrous game of Russian roulette inspired by the film *The Deer Hunter*, Cantrell blew his brains out with Keith's stolen .38 Special while Anita was 'tidying up' a few feet away. 'He was lying on his back and I turned him over,' she said. 'I heard a gurgling sound. He was choking on his blood. I picked up the revolver and put it on the chest of drawers. I don't like guns.'

Detective Douglas Lamanna, who responded to Marlon's emergency call, said that when he arrived Cantrell was breathing but unconscious. He died ninety minutes later at a nearby hospital. Lamanna wrote in his report that Cantrell was lying on top of the soiled bed covers, barefoot, wearing a shirt and jeans, 'in a room filled with smoke and debris'. In matters of home decor, Anita's mingling of the luxurious and squalid was legendary, but the scene that greeted the police here was truly shocking. Mouldy plaster had fallen from the bedroom ceiling and lay piled up on the oriental rug amid numerous cigarette burns and other marks. One corner of the massive oak bed was broken and propped up with a chair. The *New York Post* would report that the first ambulance crew to arrive on the scene was staggered by the sheer filth and air of decay: 'There was a powerful, unpleasant stench, as if there was a dead cat somewhere.' Over the next few days, the headlines made much of the old Stones associations with sex, drugs and ritualistic practices. The *Post* added that cats and dogs had been found 'sacrificed' in the woods nearby, while nuns at a local convent spoke of hearing 'strange chants, gunshots and loud music'.

The police later cleared Anita of involvement with Scott Cantrell's death, which was ruled a suicide, although charging her with possession of a stolen weapon. She was fined $1,000. The deceased's parents brought a case against Keith and Anita for corruption of a minor, but this was eventually dismissed. The house at South Salem was immediately closed up. An understandably distraught Anita then went on an extended binge that at one stage included swigging horse tranquilliser from out of a bottle. In 1983, she was raided for drugs in London's Grosvenor House hotel. At around the same time, she spent eight weeks on an alcoholic ward. One night, a drunken Anita tore her hip out of its socket by falling out of bed. She stopped drinking in 1987, but then started again in 2004 when she had a second hip operation. Despite this momentary lapse, she was able to successfully detox and move to a halfway house in Notting Hill, around the corner from the pop star's lair she'd so bewitched in *Performance*. No longer the wasted Stones concubine, Anita re-emerged in her forties a much-loved penitent – 'I did a lot of service,' she says – bicycling around London and working on a small suburban allotment. She and Keith eventually became friendly again, spending most New Years together and putting Toronto and Salem and 'all that shit' behind them. Neither party has ever been busted since.

After a protracted legal battle, largely about whether he should pay alimony at the Californian or more modest British rate, Mick and Bianca also formally parted company. In November 1980, their divorce was finalised at the High Court in London for a sum reliably said to be 'not more than a million pounds'. Bianca told her friend Ross Benson that even then the money, payable in instalments, was 'always late' and that attempting to deal with her ex was a 'fucking nightmare'. Custody of their 9-year-old daughter Jade was to be shared. During this period, Bianca was something of a staple of the disco scene in both New York and London, of which her roles in such films as *Cocksucker Blues*, *Flesh Color* and *All You Need is Cash* serve as a poignant memorial. Renouncing café society, she was to re-emerge years later as a social and human rights advocate, with a seat on both the Leadership Council of Amnesty International and the board of the Amazon Charitable Trust. There continues to be talk about her nomination for the Nobel peace prize. Bianca still declines to speak about her ex-husband, other than to remark on his business acumen and extreme shrewdness with money (qualities also noted by Mick's younger brother Chris, when he found himself driving a cab for some time in the early 1980s, and told reporters who asked him about it: 'It's not my family's job to support me').

On 20 May 1979, Eric Clapton threw a party at his home in Surrey to celebrate his wedding to Pattie Boyd. 'Mick and Jerry were clearly an item by then,' the bride says, but adds that when Bryan Ferry arrived in his Ferrari and heard their names he 'promptly did a U-turn, taking half of the drive with him'. Several hours later, Boyd went upstairs to the marital bed only to find 'Mick, Jerry and little Jade all fast asleep on it', leaving her and her husband 'to the floor of the bedroom closet'.

★

There's probably a law that defines the rate at which an album gets worse as its production budget increases. Having begun life in Hollywood and the Bahamas, the Stones' *Emotional Rescue* resumed with extended sessions in Paris and London, before being over-dubbed and mixed in New York and finally wrapped in a cover featuring a series of 'cutting-edge thermographic images like those used in the search and rescue of earthquake- and other natural dis-aster victims', to quote the press blurb, ahead of its June 1980 release.

In the meantime, the New Barbarians played to an audience of nearly a quarter of a million at Knebworth. It was noticed that Keith was downing ever greater quantities of 96 per cent proof vodka. Later that year, back in the studio in Paris, he flaked out after seven or eight nights on the grog, bounced off the side of a speaker cab-inet and shattered his nose. A more controlled physical embellishment came on 18 December 1979, his thirty-sixth birth-day, when a jeweller friend presented him with his trademark silver ring in the shape of a skull, one of those small but decisive factors that helped establish the modern-day Keith, and Stones, image.

The band itself remained on hiatus. Wood was making his next solo album and doing vast amounts of drugs; in January 1980, he and his girlfriend were arrested for coke possession on the Caribbean island of St Maarten. Imprisoned in brutal conditions for five days, the couple were released and deported after publicly com-plaining that the police had planted the evidence. Charlie and Stu were touring with Rocket 88 and Bill Wyman was composing music for a Ryan O'Neal caper called *Green Ice*, which included Bill's pidgin-French hit single 'Si, si (Je Suis un Rock Star)'. Following this, the bassist's thoughts turned, as they often did, to another solo album. Unambiguously called *Bill Wyman*, this was released in July 1981; it peaked at number 69 on the *Billboard* chart. Mick was watching more cricket, taking the opportunity to introduce his friend Paul Getty to the game, before going off on hol-iday with Jerry Hall in Morocco. Richards later got a 'Dear Keith' telegram from Marrakech, scuppering plans for a 1980 Stones tour. He was not pleased. 'Mick waits until he's three thousand miles away and then he just sends a note,' Keith told the press. ('The old *cunt*,' he added, among friends.)

Allen Klein, meanwhile, was surrendering to authorities just a few doors away from the Stones' New York office at Manhattan's downtown Correction Center. A jury had found him innocent of tax evasion, but guilty of filing a false return, in charges that dated back to 1969–70. US District Court Judge Vincent Broderick concluded that Klein had 'lied throughout' his trial, and gave him a two-year sentence, all but two months of it suspended.

Emotional Rescue. Even on *Black and Blue*, the Stones had avoided the ploddingly obvious riffs and glam posturing of most of their peers. Their own spandex debacle came only now, in 1980. Much of the album was filled with spare parts and lazy throwaways from the *Some Girls* sessions. Like its forbear, the record would prove a richly eclectic, unpigeonholable mishmash – the old farts meet punk and disco, with blues and jazz and even a stray mariachi trumpet thrown in. Unhappily there were few real songs this time around, just some raunch-by-rote guitar hooks and unfortunate attempts at rapping on the opening track, 'Dance'. 'Where the Boys Go' and 'Down in the Hole' offered up competent tributes to vintage Chuck Berry and Muddy Waters, respectively. The title cut was a smoothly syncopated, Bee Gees-type romp where Mick Jagger gets protective, obsesses about his girlfriend, dons his shining armour, jumps on a fine Arab charger and rides to Jerry Hall's rescue. You could almost hear Brian Jones creasing himself.

After the tossed-off pop of 'She's So Cold', Keith Richards closed the album with the sublime 'All About You', a welcome variation on *Rescue*'s standard fare. This was mood music raised to high art. At the time, everyone assumed that the lyrics' reference to dogs and bitches and getting laid was a parting swipe at Anita, and it could certainly be so read. Keith later clarified, 'It's about Jagger ... I'd just come off junk and went back to work; in the meantime, Mick had got used to being in charge. I was made to feel like an intruder.'

Keith's bittersweet song, both pissed off and conciliatory, ends in a slew of croaks, whispers and deeply personal ruminations. In the final fade, he puts his lips to the mike and growls, 'So how come/I'm still in *love* with you?'

The critics hated *Emotional Rescue*, using terms like dumb, spiritless, parodic, tinny and flat-out awful. It spent seven weeks at number one.

On 17 March 1979, during a rare visit to Studio 54, Keith Richards had run in to a tall, fresh-faced blonde named Patti Hansen, who was there celebrating her twenty-third birthday. She was the youngest of six children of a Staten Island, New York, bus-driver father and a homemaker mother. The Hansens were hard-working, modest, devoutly Lutheran; Julie Andrews in *The Sound of Music* embodied their idea of a big pop star. Patti came from a background of early nights and clean habits, and parents who expected her in church on Sunday, and somehow managed to move in a world where such things weren't spoken of. In 1971, while selling hot dogs on the beach, she had been discovered by a vacationing manager from the Wilhelmina modelling agency. Three months later, Patti was on the cover of *Seventeen* magazine. Along with the apple-pie looks, her bubbly humour and unspoiled sense of decency made her the 'real thing', a star who charmed not only agents and photographers but also movie moguls like Peter Bogdanovich, with whom she had a brief affair. Patti enjoyed a beer and a pizza, and came across as a cheerful, well-adjusted adult – an anomaly in the profession. At the time she met Keith she had just appeared on the cover of *Esquire*, celebrating 'The Year of the Lusty Woman'.

Nine months after their first meeting, Keith saw Patti again at a party at the Roxy roller rink in New York. Due to some confusion with the arrangements, both Anita and Lil Wergilis were also present. Compounding the scene was the arrival of assorted hookers, strippers and a famed rock-music groupie who seemed intent on meeting Keith alone in a back room. At the end of a long night beset by rival camps, Richards rang Hansen and invited her to join him for a quiet drink. She then spent the next five days and nights cruising around New York in a limousine filled with deafening reggae music and accompanied by Keith and an entourage of large, silent bodyguards, Marlon, Fred Sessler and sundry Rastas. On the sixth day, Patti found herself at a Christmas party in Mick Jagger's apartment on Central Park West. Not surprisingly, all eyes turned to the willowy blonde and her dark-eyed companion with a bottle of Stoli in his hand. They made for a striking couple. When an exhausted Patti decided to leave, Keith turned to Mick and said, 'I'm outta here, too. I'm going with this lady.'

Early in 1980, Keith moved in to Patti's Greenwich Village apartment, an arrangement soon terminated by the neighbours' complaints about the new tenant's stage-quality sound system. Not long after that, Lil Wergilis accepted the inevitable and flew home to Sweden. Anita then happened to come across the couple one night that winter at the Ritz Club in New York. Stealing up behind their table, she greeted Keith by jumping on his lap, wrapping her legs round his head and squeezing it hard between her thighs. The press photographs suggest that she effected this embrace without first having taken the precaution of donning any underwear. '*Please* let me go,' Keith gasped. A day or two later, Patti brought her new man across on the ferry to meet her family. An awkward moment occurred when Keith arrived carrying his own bottle of vodka and proceeded to mark his displeasure at some comments by Patti's brother Rodney, a naval chaplain, by smashing his guitar on the dinner table, but it passed off when he cracked everyone up with some great jokes about Dartford. They loved him on Staten Island.

Mick, meanwhile, was all over the place both physically and personally. The complexity of the Jagger character still fascinated his bandmates. They knew he had a dark side in which vanity, deviousness and personal ambition could come to the fore. There were times when they were offended by the brusqueness of his management style, for example when he met a certain suggestion during the *Emotional Rescue* sessions by replying, 'Oh, shut up, Keith. Don't be stupid,' or announced that he wasn't about to 'put it all on the fucking line' in another tour. Mick could also strike outsiders as a bit glib, as for instance when he met the disc jockey Andy Peebles at a London party in December 1980. Peebles had been the last man to interview John Lennon just before his murder earlier that month.

'When Mick left the party,' says Peebles, 'he looked at me and said in that absurd cockney accent, "'Ere, Andy, someone gonna fuckin' shoot *me* now, are they?"' Yet for all his changes, Jagger could be dazzlingly charming with colleagues, fans and even critics. The BBC's Bob Harris remembers 'driving in to London from the country to interview Mick about *Emotional Rescue*. We got stuck in bumper-to-bumper traffic on the M4, and in those days there was no way to phone ahead. I was sweating bullets. We finally got to Mick's house about three hours late and he couldn't have been nicer about it. I expected a bollocking, or worse, and instead we had one of the most famous people in the world pouring tea for everyone and asking about our journey. It was a bit like meeting the Queen.'

In November 1980, Mick and Jerry Hall jointly paid 2 million francs (some £220,000) for Château de la Fourchette, north of Amboise in the Loire Valley. Fourchette came equipped with ten bedrooms, a garden landscaped by Alvilde Lees-Milne and picnic tables on which Jerry served afternoon teas. 'Everything looked so perfect,' Eva Jagger said, remembering that she'd been 'quite emotional' when she first visited. While Eva saw only the understated elegance of Fourchette, others recall a more exotic atmosphere. 'It was a total knocking shop,' says one 1980s guest, a minor and notably unstuffy royal, who notes she excited Mick's interest by going about braless. 'But the great thing was, you could meet anyone there. The local vicar would be sitting next to Lou Reed.' Along with candlelit suppers for the likes of Princess Margaret went Saturday night cross-dressing parties. 'Everybody loves it,' a fashion-industry guest later told *Vanity Fair* magazine. 'You're staying with Mick and Jerry in France, and everybody comes down in drag, and it's just huge fun. Masses of people sort of screaming, running in and out of each other's bedrooms, applying make-up . . . Mick was terribly dashing one night in a tight black shift and a ratty silver-fox fur. He was so chic, he looked like Coco Chanel.'

On 27 December, Jagger temporarily abandoned this life of luxury to fly to Lima, and from there took a two-day car and canoe journey to the Peruvian interior to star in *Fitzcarraldo*, director Werner Herzog's allegory of a man hauling a river steamer over a mountain. Quite apart from the challenges of its main plot device, the production was beset by a bewildering variety of problems, including malaria, cost overruns and hostile natives. In the midst of the mounting chaos, Herzog had nothing but praise for his distinguished cast member. While various other actors wilted in the incessant tropical rain and primitive living conditions, Jagger remained imperturbable, finding humour in everyone and everything, even the monkey that bit him. 'Somehow, he constantly laughed in the face of adversity,' Herzog said. Although the director recalls him performing 'beautifully' in front of the camera, Mick eventually chose to withdraw from the project and return to London. By then, he had spent six weeks living in a mud hut, and he confessed it had felt more like a lifetime. Early in March, Jagger met Richards in Barbados, and before long the promoter Bill Graham flew in to offer his services as a tour manager. Graham mentioned that with a corporate sponsor and proper merchandising, the four original Stones could expect to net some $22million between them for twelve weeks' work. Not long after that, the other band members and their seventy-two employees got word from Mick that he was ready to 'put it all on the line' again.

8

WORLD WAR THREE

'I don't like rock 'n' roll as a way of life. I think it's awful. Most of the people who are living on rock 'n' roll are living in a dream world,' Ian Stewart commented of the industry whose creative and administrative sides he had come to know well over the last twenty years. 'The money's got them in trouble,' Stu said elsewhere of the Stones themselves. 'They can't even live in their own country. They have to go from one hotel to another.' By 1981, Mick Jagger and Keith Richards had each tentatively settled down with a ravishingly beautiful blonde American girl, although Mick, at least, continued to avoid the lure of excessive domesticity. Rather than a wife and kids, he dreamed of 'some extravagantly beautiful concept called love', he told the writer Jeffrey Bernard in the course of a long, bibulous afternoon in London's Colony club. But something always went wrong. Mick saw women as a vital source of energy, but remarked that 'you can have all these chicks and still be a lonely sod'. His affairs, he told Bernard, 'were at once fun and ultimately unsatisfying', not to mention occasionally dangerous. There had been certain episodes in his life, Mick admitted, when a one-night stand or a casual fling had threatened to turn in to a case of *Fatal Attraction*-like erotomania. Precautions had to be taken. Sometimes an American friend would appear at the Stones' tour

hotel and ask for a 'Mr Kent', say, only to be told that he had
checked out, whereas Mick was really upstairs, registered under the
name 'W.G. Grace' or one of half a dozen other cricketing aliases.

Ron Wood, who was in such poor shape that even Keith
Richards worried about his drug consumption, clearly needed to
tour for financial as much as creative reasons. He stood to lose an
immediate $500,000 if, as rumoured, the Stones replaced him with
either of the young blues virtuosos George Thorogood or Stevie
Ray Vaughan. Keith eventually intervened by signing a formal tour
rider guaranteeing his fellow guitarist would 'not be found in possession of narcotics in any area, [or] be instantly suspended from his
duties'. Although there would be several occasions over the next
few months when Woody was palpably out of his box, he kept his
job, thanks in large part to Keith's loyalty. Money was a factor for
Bill Wyman, too; despite enjoying the biggest solo hit to date by a
Rolling Stone, Bill had large homes to keep in England and France,
as well as an ex-wife, a son at university and a long-time girlfriend
who in 1981 checked in to a private California detox facility to deal
with her coke addiction. 'I found her descent impossible to take,'
Bill notes. 'I hated the fact that after avoiding drugs all my life, I had
a partner to live with who was in to it.' So successful was the Stones'
tour that autumn that each two-hour concert netted Bill some
$95–100,000, or an estimated $5million for the full 51-date itinerary – a figure to compare favourably with the roughly $350 he
earned from the band's first visit to North America, seventeen years
previously.

As for Charlie Watts, the early death of his father and certain
other family issues (a year or two later the Watts' teenage daughter
Serafina would be asked to leave her boarding school, allegedly for
smoking pot) seem to have triggered a decade of discreet but almost
heroically full overindulgence. By the early 1980s, Charlie was regularly blasting himself on alcohol, amphetamines and heroin. Stu
wasn't alone in again thinking it was the end of the road for the
band. Keith Richards, who had taken to displaying a large framed
photo of Charlie at his home in New York, would consistently
advise him during this period that the best therapy was to 'get out

on stage ... You can be feeling like dogshit, and within five minutes you're cured.' Keith seems to have been typically persuasive.
'Should I really tour?' Charlie enquired of another old friend in
1981. 'All that hassle. All that hard work. All those terrible arse-
lickers ... The only reason I could go through with it is that it's
better than the fucking alternative.'

Although the Stones recorded in Paris intermittently during the
winter of 1980–81, they never really did do a new album after
Emotional Rescue. Rather, *Some Girls*' engineer Chris Kimsey came
up with a novel idea for everyone to make a fortune without actually going to the hassle of sitting around the studio for months on
end. This involved dusting off outtakes like *Black and Blue*'s 'Slave'
and several relics ('Tops', 'Waiting on a Friend') from *Goats Head
Soup*. Kimsey went on to give the new record – eventually called
Tattoo You – its one irrefutable claim to fame when he unearthed a
forgotten snippet of rock and roll guitar in the middle of the second
of forty-five takes of the otherwise obscure reggae jam 'Start Me
Up' and persuaded Keith Richards to give it the full open-G treatment. Mick Jagger liked the idea, too, and suggested they gas the
song up by going straight in to Keith's dynamite riff. That three-
note bolt, instantly plunging the tune home, and featuring plenty
of strategically positioned dramatic pauses, would help 'Start Me
Up' become a major worldwide smash – number 2 on the *Billboard*
Hot 100 chart, where it was kept off the summit by 'Arthur's
Theme (Best That You Can Do)' by Christopher Cross – and the
Stones' last UK top ten hit to date.

Tattoo You kept building from there. 'Slave', once thought unwor-
thy even of *Black and Blue*, re-emerged as a vacuum-packed tune
with a soaring Sonny Rollins sax break, one of several mid-70s
rejects to be retooled to 1981 specifications. The Stones took their
past to the bank again with 'Black Limousine', borrowing an old
Jimmy Reed blues lick and scuzzing it up in to a classic radio
anthem. Although the eminent critic Robert Palmer praised the
band for 'drop[ping] the studied decadence and writing about adult
issues' on *Tattoo You*, this was perhaps to overlook one song, an ode
called 'Little T&A', in which Keith Richards cheerfully paid

homage to those features. Mick Taylor balked when he heard himself playing on 'Tops', a 1972 discard whose catchy pop chorus survived its camp-falsetto vocal. Never just a riff factory, Keith strummed through 'Waiting on a Friend', a deft guitar-and-sax ballad which showed the melody under the mayhem, and was soon to follow 'Start Me Up' in to the US chart.

At ten o'clock on the hot August night *Tattoo You* was released, the Stones, who were then rehearsing on a Massachusetts farm, sent out a roadie to buy a dozen copies of the *New York Times*, which contained a rave review of the album. By the time he got back some of the band couldn't read – Mick was off on a horse somewhere – but it was a great party. *Tattoo You* sold over a million copies in America that week, and would do better business than *Sticky Fingers*.

The events of late 1981 weren't only the Stones' creative renaissance; they were also the band's financial salvation. It would be a new kind of tour, with the headliners enjoying an unprecedented 90–10 cut with local promoters and a whole range of tongue-logoed T-shirts, jackets, belt-buckles, panties, shoes, socks, lighters, shot glasses, wallets, patches, badges and dolls. If you could wear it or carry it, Mick and the boys were on it. The last-but-one show in Hampton, Virginia, would gross them a tidy $3.2million thanks to a pay-per-view hook-up with the HBO cable TV network. As a sweetener, Prince Rupert did a quick side deal with Jovan Perfumes, who forked out over $4million merely to print their name on the individual concert tickets: rock's first such sponsorship. Opening night was scheduled for 25 September, in Philadelphia.

Much had changed since the band's last outing.

By 1981 pop stars were working half-naked on custom-built stages that exploded during the encore. Jagger's friend David Bowie pushed the sense of theatre with a set straight out of the Albert Speer drama school, lit by 700 white neon tubes. The Who owned more lasers than the British Government. Rock and roll had gone mad for spectacle, and Mick wanted a part of it. He ordered up a tour of the biggest arenas, and indulged his love of props with a mechanical cherry picker that let him sing while hovering over the front of the stalls – just as Bowie had done on his *Diamond Dogs* tour, seven years earlier. Keith Richards remarks that Mick also 'wanted stilt walkers. Luckily, at dress rehearsals it was raining, and all the stilt walkers fell over.' (Mick, even so, was to persevere with the idea thirteen years later.) Certain other logistical decisions involving the Stones' sound and lighting arrangements and the gaudy, 70-foot-high purple-and-gold murals that would serve as the stage backdrop were being taken unilaterally rather than by band vote. Charlie and Bill both remarked to Bill Graham that Mick had commissioned a million-dollar set, 'and *we're* paying for it'. The 32-page tour contract everyone signed was not, however, entirely one-sided: Clause 9b) indicated that Mick should be 'completely absent from the playing area' while Keith performed his three-minute solo turn, generally a gasped 'Little T&A' with infectious Chuck Berry guitar stylings.

Relations between the Glimmer Twins were formal rather than social, then, and they had a tacit agreement never to venture in to one another's quarters on Long View Farm, the Stones' rehearsal facility located in the rolling hills west of Boston. A reporter from *Life* found a 'vague air of unease' when he went up to interview the band in late August. Other than the songs, 'Jagger and Richards had little to say to one another. While Mick padded around with a cal-culator, Keith's preferred props were a joint and constantly replenished tumbler of vodka over ice . . . I noticed that when he was out of the room, the other musicians regularly referred to their lead vocalist as "Her Majesty".'

Merely getting everyone settled on the farm in the first place had proved a major trial. First, Keith Richards went AWOL at his friend Fred Sessler's house in Florida, prompting a pissed-off Bill Wyman to fly home to England. Charlie Watts rang him there a few days later, the worse for booze and muttering that the band was 'finished'. Both he and Bill were raging about all the delays. Keith's timing had always been limited to his guitar. He was chron-ically late just about everywhere else, now tardily flying off to Rome to get a new US work visa. All five Stones finally straggled back to the farm, where Mick and Keith rowed about who to hire to play second piano to Stu. Eventually, Woody again swung the job for his old Faces mate Ian McLagan. He, too, happened to be a free-base addict.

Although the Stones had suffered some wear and tear, they had also survived while their only real peers had either imploded like the Beatles or succumbed to hammy caricature like the Beach Boys and Bob Dylan. At thirty-eight, Mick, in particular, was a figure of nostalgia, a monument appreciated not just for himself but for having lasted as long as he had. The Stones' fans were growing older, too, and as they matured they seem to have valued their starting heroes more highly, or certainly enough to pay a modest sixteen dollars to see them. The band made its move later that month, simultaneously releasing *Tattoo You* and announcing the tour. Bill Graham Presents fielded 2.5 million ticket applications in the following week, and the US Mail was forced to hire 245 part-time employees to deal with the barrage. It was 'bank time', Mick told Keith.

On 14 September the Stones gave their first performance of the Eighties in a 300-seat dive called Sir Morgan's Cove, a few miles from Long View Farm. It was a riot. Outside, the ticketless brawled with mounted police, prompting the mayor of Boston (the Stones' old friend Kevin White) to ban any future such public rehearsals. Despite the encouraging news from the box office, Mick and Keith had both fretted whether the band still had much to offer, apart from an obvious death-watch curiosity. With one or two notable exceptions, they seemed to have been coasting for ten years. But the whole paradox of the Stones was that, as the music got worse, the personal mythologies got bigger and better. Mick was famous enough, but, thanks to events in Toronto, Keith was now a global icon of debauchery, survival and glamour – Lennon and Moon and Bonham had died, and he was the big fish who'd wriggled out of the net. Those 2.5 million ticket requests became 4 million; Bill Graham added a dozen extra shows.

Eleven days later, the Stones began their latest triennial tour of North America. They played on a vast, sloping stage in front of glitzy pop-art cartoons of pink planes and purple race cars. Much of the decor was apt to cause temporary damage to the retina, and the whole project trod a thin line between vivid and trashy. Mick's cherry picker was cranked up for him to sing 'Jumpin' Jack Flash' while blowing kisses and pelting the fans below with long-stemmed red roses. The Stones still seemed to be rehearsing during the first shows, but by a week or so in they'd polished the act in to a two-hour master class in recorded pop history – 'Twenty Flight Rock' to 'Start Me Up'. There were also plenty of visuals, including a $20,000 firework display in the outdoor venues. Carefully balancing their raucous, rockin' yin with their sensitive yang, the band later threw in a soulful mini-set of 'Beast of Burden' and 'Waiting on a Friend', with Woody playing lead, Keith supplying bluesy jabs, and the auditorium a sea of bobbing lighters. The *Wall Street Journal* spoke for all when it called the basic show 'spectacularly musical and overwhelmingly physical', and even Bianca Jagger remarked diplomatically of the Stones' two-night stand in New York: 'It was superb. They seem to get better as the years go on.'

The shows began with the brassy swing of Duke Ellington's 'Take the "A" Train' over the PA, before the curtains parted to reveal Keith Richards lashing out the chords to 'Under My Thumb'. In Philadelphia, audience participation on the opening number was divided between those who hollered along to the lyrics and others who held up signs protesting that these were unfair to women. Should the song ever appear to be flagging, Keith would turn his back on the crowd, plant himself in front of Charlie's bass drum and bear down on the beat. There was no doubt who was up there directing traffic. One of the core pleasures of Stones-watching over the years was the suspense of waiting to see what Mick Jagger would wear on stage. For his first public performances of the 1980s, Mick favoured sporty, gay-quarterback gear mercilessly co-ordinated in bright pinks and yellows. He put on a slick show. There were hydraulics, platforms that went up and down, dramatic lighting effects. Mick periodically tore across the stage on to one of a pair of catwalks extending in to the crowd, like a labrador chasing a tennis ball. He sang the encore while dressed in tights and a cape fashioned out of the American and British flags. Keith and Woody played their guitar parts as one long, joshing by-play, complete with errors, and Charlie effortlessly battered the drums. Stage left, Bill

Wyman remained stationary throughout, except to neatly shoot the cuffs of his pale-blue suit, but even he looked like a manic rock star compared to Ian Stewart. In Philadelphia, Stu walked on in front of 90,000 fans wearing ancient corduroys and a golf shirt straining over his ample midriff while munching a cheese sandwich, which he carefully placed on top of his piano. He then proceeded to play in a classic, jumping-barrelhouse style that sometimes seemed to be from another song, if not another galaxy, to the chosen repertoire. At what proved to be the last moment, he was finally able to perform a full set of concerts with the band he had joined before anyone else still alive. Between numbers, Stu yawned, took down the sandwich, and continued to eat it impassively.

After playing the Left Coast the Stones headed to the notoriously mellow Pacific Northwest. The Seattle trek wasn't without incident, however. At the afternoon show, on 15 October, a 16-year-old girl named Pamela Melville died of head injuries after falling from an upper balcony of the stadium; Mick and Keith sent flowers. A second woman was arrested for informing the crowd she intended to kill 'that evil cocksucker Jagger'. Down to Candlestick Park, San Francisco, where the scenes of drunken, mud-caked spectators, thuggish security and periodic violence erupting around the more entrepreneurial souvenir outlets reminded some of Altamont. Bad blood flowed within the band, too, notably later that night in the Fairmont hotel when somebody told Keith Richards that Ron Wood was back on the freebase, and Keith decided to intervene by walking downstairs, marching through the public lobby and taking the elevator back up to Woody's room in the far wing of the hotel. 'There was too much stuff going on in there,' Keith noted. 'He had some dodgy people around.'

'He came at me with a broken bottle,' says Woody. The two mates bawled each other out, Keith accusing Ron of fucking up the tour, then had a brief but spectacular punch-up. Several roadies had to pull them apart. Keith dropped the bottle, called Wood a cunt, and kicked the dope dealers out of the room.

Thirteen years later, I asked Wood if he thought Keith could have bottled him. 'Yeah,' he nodded.

'We were doing drugs in the dressing room,' Wood remembered of a *Spinal Tap* moment later on the California leg of the tour. 'Suddenly Bill Graham stuck his head round the door and said, "The police are here!" We all panicked and threw our dope in the bog. Then Sting, Andy Summers and Stewart Copeland walked in.'

While Keith and Ron brawled in their San Francisco hotel, Mick went downtown to join Mayor Dianne Feinstein in a televised 'Save the Cable Cars' appeal before having dinner with Jackie Onassis. Charlie wandered off by himself to a jazz club and Bill preferred to sample the local scenery from the privacy of his room. Nobody found time to meet their old manager Eric Easton, who was running a small nearby record store. It was exactly twenty years since the adolescent Jagger and Richards had met on the foggy platform at Dartford station.

In Los Angeles, the 23-year-old Prince went onstage before the Stones, which he elected to do wearing only a pair of snug-fitting black bikini pants. It was too much for a well-oiled, rocker-dude audience still unacquainted with genre-breaking albums like *1999* and *Lovesexy* that would be released to such acclaim later in the 80s. Watching from the wings, Ian Stewart remembered Prince's LA set as being cut short by a hail of boos and catcalls, 'followed by him taking a full roasted chicken to the gob. He came back to the dressing room in tears and, talented as he was, that was the last we saw of him on the tour.' Through the South, then a three-night stand at New Jersey's Meadowlands, with Tina Turner also on the slate. Backstage, Keith Richards sat toking through an interminable version of 'Proud Mary' with Vitas Gerulaitis and John McEnroe. The tennis stars were reportedly stunned at how their host 'could get fucked up and still play'. Hot topics of conversation: the best pain relievers, lesbianism in sport. Two weeks later, in Pontiac, local boy Iggy Pop opened for the Stones and came out clad in a pair of women's sheer stockings and a black leather miniskirt of singularly sparing cut. 'This time it worked,' said Stu. It needs tact, care and subtle handling if the magic of empathy is to emerge for a performer – 'and at least this guy was in on the joke'.

Sunday 22 November, Chicago. Mick and Keith's first order of business was to call at the 200-seat Checkerboard Lounge, where they jammed with Muddy Waters until dawn. As usual when the Stones were involved, there was a small riot outside. It was also Waters' last ever recorded concert; he died in April 1983, aged any-where between sixty-seven and seventy. Strained bonhomie and dubious guest spots dominated the next two nights. The director Hal Ashby (*Shampoo, Being There*) joined the tour to shoot a con-cert film, which he completed despite having to be carried out of the Stones dressing room on a stretcher after overdosing on heroin. A zonked-looking Mick Taylor sat in with his old band in Kansas City. The reunion overexcited him. According to Wood, 'He shocked us with how loud he was blasting it . . . bulldozing through parts of songs that should have been subtle, ignoring breaks and taking uninvited solos': something of a role-reversal. Tempe was a dream come true for Jerry Hall, who at last got to perform with the Stones. 'I danced around and Mick hit me on the bottom. It was thrilling.' Sometime around now, Keith Richards got in to a hotel-room row with his friend Fred Sessler, took out his gun, squeezed the trigger and shot through the floor. 'There were a bunch of pen-sioners down below and Keith's bullet broke up their party,' says Woody.

Most of the critics were enthusiastic about the tour, and a few lost their pose of reserve altogether. According to the daily *Seattle Post-Intelligencer*, 'Mick Jagger was wonderful . . . prancing across the center of the stage and out on to its long wingways, with his elfin, androgynously erotic grace' . . . 'He was as raw, raunchy, and full of juice as ever' . . . 'a walking, writhing grace note' . . . a 'lovely'. Some of the American press hero-worshipped Mick as a sage and treated his patter between songs – 'Everything's cool, yeah, doncha worry about a thing' – as oracular truths. He remained a great entertainer. Even now, in his late thirties, Jagger's provocative public image kept the American moral-outrage industry going. The hun-dred or so demonstrators in Lexington, Kentucky, many belonging to Reverend Jerry Falwell's evangelical-Christian Moral Majority, finally gave up when they realised the protests were effectively advertising the show.

While Mick romped, Keith Richards often laid back, allowing songs to build, pausing to let Charlie and Bill solo for a moment. Once or twice, it wasn't the concert which was under review but Keith himself, caricatured as the Human Riff, dressed in mouldy jeans tucked in to tatty suede boots, a torn T-shirt and the skull ring, a butt-end permanently clamped in his mouth when he wasn't actually singing, and once or twice even then. This was not a poster-boy for the Reagan Revolution. Happily, it sounded as if Keith was less taken by the image than by the music. Few people worked with the base materials of rock and roll quite as thrillingly as he and Jagger still did, whatever their other differences. After he vetoed Bobby Keys for the tour, Mick had hired the 36-year-old jazz saxophonist Ernie Watts, a veteran of Johnny Carson's *Tonight Show* television orchestra. 'Out of the period of time that I worked with Jagger and Richards, they seemed to get along just great,' Watts says. 'We all rode to the gig together in the same van, we all flew together on the same plane, and their relationship seemed to be just fine. The music always came first. There may have been some things behind the scenes, but I wasn't aware of them.' Watts' namesake, too, was the 'coolest guy'. Audiences often watched in amusement as the Stones' crew ritually dismantled the support-act's multitude of drums and forest of cymbals and replaced them with Charlie's minimalist, 1960s kit. 'He's genuinely eccentric,' Keith would remark, admiringly. 'At the end of the show, we'll leave the stage, and the sirens will be going, limousines waiting, and Charlie will walk back to his zone and change the position of his drumsticks by two millimetres. Then he'll look at it. Then if it looks good, he'll leave.'

18 December, Hampton Roads Coliseum, Virginia. Keith Richards' thirty-eighth birthday and a nationally televised show. Everyone's mums and dads had flown in from England. Mick celebrated by getting the 14,000-strong crowd to sing 'Happy Birthday' to Keith, and Keith reciprocated by unstrapping his guitar and using it to brain a stage-crasher who rushed at Mick during 'Satisfaction'. 'Anyone's on my turf, I'm gonna chop the mother down,' he later clarified of his working terms and conditions. It all wound up the next night with a storming, 27-song set, thousands

of balloons and fireworks. Mick Jagger was a wise-cracking host overseeing a madcap party. After the final notes faded away, Mick's amplified voice – '*Yeahhh! Aaawrite!*' – echoed around the arena, indicative not of his desire to return but just the reverse; the sentiments were expressed by way of a radio mike as he sat demurely in a speeding van between his 70-year-old parents.

When all the numbers were added up, the Stones were found to have played to some 2.9 million fans, roughly the same as had come to their first eight American tours in total. The band might have played the anarchic layabouts to comic perfection, but they also negotiated the toughest tour contract in rock music history, making themselves a mint. They were on top of the world.

For the past seven years, a pert, strikingly handsome New York brunette named Jane Rose (known affectionately to the band as 'Jugs') had been the Stones' interface with the world, travelling around with them carrying a bundle of passports, visas and bail money in her handbag. Among other duties, she had been the first employee on the scene when Scott Cantrell shot himself, and shepherded a blood-spattered Anita Pallenberg in and out of the police station later that night. When Jagger fired Rose at the end of 1981, Richards immediately took her on as his personal assistant and, ultimately, manager. Mick was not happy at the perceived snub. The Glimmer Twins would play thirty-five European shows in 1982 without speaking to one another.

Symbolically restoring the 's' to his surname, Keith also took the opportunity that spring to meet his father Bert for the first time in twenty years, for most of which the elder Richards had been living in a pub. At sixty-eight, the one-time 'Adolf' had mellowed in to a merry, bewhiskered old man with a briar pipe. Bert's rounded, guzzler's belly hung over his jeans, a ragged scarf was tied round his neck, his cloth cap covered a mass of unruly hair, and his frizzy white beard was neither full nor neat. Father and son hit it off instantly. The only note of reproach came when Mr Richards first looked his offspring up and down and good-naturedly said, 'You've been a bit of a bugger, haven't you?' In the months and years ahead,

Keith and Bert bonded over vodka and dominoes; Bert was a fixture at that summer's Stones tour.

On 1 June, the band released its concert album *Still Life*. It was a good title for a record as dull as a waxed-fruit display. The overall sound conjured joyless Midwestern domes where riffs echoed among the sports scoreboards and soggy T-shirts. At one point, Mick enlivened proceedings by urging his audience to 'drink a few beers [and] smoke a few joints', but *Still Life* went downhill from there. It hit number 3 on the chart.

As well as listlessly promoting the album, the Stones spent part of that spring rehearsing on a stage at Shepperton studios outside London. Long faces all round. Keith still travelled with a spliff-wielding Rasta entourage, much to Mick's chagrin. Stevie Ray Vaughan and George Thorogood were both in town, again on standby to replace Ron Wood. Bill and Charlie pottered around looking out-of-sorts in their bandanas and tracksuits. The long-suffering Stu thought they were all 'wanking around trying to make something mildly interesting out of endless repetition', an apt description of the Stones' regimen of all-night rehearsals. Gered Mankowitz, who'd travelled with the group in the 60s, was invited back to photograph them for the first time since *Satanic Majesties*. After a series of phone calls from the band's office ('Mick's just got up, and he's in the bath – we'll call you right back' ... 'Mick's still in the bath, but Keith's up now, and says he's looking forward to seeing you' ... 'Mick's out of the bath now, it's definitely on for tonight') he arrived to find a 'really friendly' Jagger and Richards, who suggested a second session two nights later. Mankowitz returned to a noticeably cooler reception.

'They told me to hop it,' he says. 'Apparently everyone was going through a rough time. Bill was ill and wasn't even coming. After some haggling, I finally did a roll of black-and-white, gave the film to them and left.'

Opening night was 26 May, in Aberdeen. These new shows were full of catchy blues-rock riffs and Mick Jagger's raps about the concerns of the average British youth: sex, the Falklands War and getting high. At a gig in France, Keith finally managed to hijack the cherry picker, taking a lengthy airborne solo while Jagger seethed below. 'Get him *down*,' Mick kept yelling at Wood. In Sweden, by contrast, Keith stretched out and performed 'Beast of Burden' while flat on his back. Charlie was travelling with his wife and mother, the latter of whom once remarked in a room full of journalists that her son's band was 'rather loud'. It was not immediately obvious how Mrs Watts' yearning for tranquillity could be satisfied by touring Europe with the Rolling Stones, but she remained immensely proud of her son.

Some of the press, meanwhile, like the music critic on *La Stampa*, were beginning to take more notice of Bill Wyman following his recent solo success. Bill's face 'was a brown olive ripening on the ancient coast of Liguria', the scribe wrote, after watching him perform with the Stones in Turin. The same reviewer was impressed that this 'wizened little man [could] play the bass as impassively and yet as thrillingly' as he did. As usual, Mick was on top of everything, and often disguised himself in a hooded sweatshirt to wander out and watch the band's support act from among the audience. After his inspection tour in Turin, the local security crew failed to recognise him and refused to let him backstage again. Bill Graham had to resolve the 'major scene' that ensued. Apart from the two hours a day when they were on stage, the Stones saw almost nothing of each other. 'Socially, it was every man for himself,' Stu recalled. After a concert in Nice, Mick went on to dinner with the fugitive director Roman Polanski at his villa in Ramatuelle, an almost excessively quaint fishing village perched on a rock overlooking the bay near St Tropez. Polanski's neighbours' view of the fleet of limousines and motorcycle outriders seemingly necessary for this engagement was the town's major talking point, though the sight, early the next morning, of Mick casually strolling in to the local tobacconist's clad in American football tights and a pink jacket made a strong bid for runner-up.

Keith Richards, while clearly a more relaxed and genial figure than in his lost decade, occasionally still managed to be quite frightening. Following a concert in West Berlin, Keith found himself at a club where the house DJ insisted on playing nonstop disco music over the sound system. Richards was not a man who bent easily to the will of others. That was what had been said about him by his parents. That was what had been said about him by his Dartford schoolteachers. That was what had been said about him by his colleagues in the Stones. And in every setting, Keith's demeanour in conflict had been the same. One of the other guests in the Berlin club recalls that the Human Riff had 'politely asked the DJ to put some Motown music on the PA, and after his pleas were continually ignored, Keith finally settled the matter by putting a Bowie knife to the guy's throat and repeating the request. That seemed to work.' At a show at Wembley Stadium, when he forgot the riff of 'She's So Cold', Richards was so angry with Wood for failing to cover him that he charged over and, once again, punched him in the face. This got a Cup Final-sized cheer from the crowd. Woody's father Archie was backstage in his wheelchair, drinking large quantities of Guinness and telling nautical jokes. 'You haven't lived till you've had a one-legged man,' he declared, exacting raucous giggles from the entourage. A few nights later, Keith corked off at Charlie on the tarmac at Naples airport. The two bandmates had a farcical row about who was going to take which seats on a chartered jet back to London. Keith again proved a hard man to argue with. In the end, Charlie muttered 'Fuck it' and walked off in to the night. In Madrid, Keith's head somehow collided with a heavy brass ashtray in his hotel room, causing Patti to place a panic-stricken call to Bill Graham. Graham arrived to find blood spurting everywhere, Patti hysterical, and Keith himself calmly applying ice to the wound. 'Worse things happen at sea,' he said.

The tour ended in Leeds on 25 July. Mick Jagger turned thirty-nine the next day. Again, as they had every closing night since 1966, the press brought out the 'IT'S ALL OVER NOW' and 'COULD BE THE LAST TIME' headlines. For once, they were nearly right.

The Stones' generally businesslike and lucrative tour was in contrast to their somewhat turbulent home lives. Although Keith had clearly found his soul mate in Patti Hansen, his bandmates each seemed to be suffering a midlife crisis. Bill Wyman and his long-term partner

Astrid Lundström bought a house together in Mulberry Walk, Chelsea, but split up almost immediately afterwards. This left Bill free to begin seeing various younger women, including, in time, Mandy Smith, aged thirteen, thus handing the press a satirical gift for the next few years. Charlie Watts had domestic issues of his own, and would later reflect, 'In the mid-eighties, I hit an all-time low ... I was drinking a lot. I nearly lost my wife and family and everything. I took more speed than heroin. I slept one day in four for two years. I liked speed because I'm naturally lethargic.' Meanwhile, Ron Wood briefly moved out of the home he shared with his girlfriend Jo Howard and in to a hotel room with *The Woman in Red* star Kelly LeBrock, although Woody seems to have reconsidered matters only a week or two later. He and Jo married in January 1985.

Mick Jagger was all over the place, whether watching cricket in London, gardening at his French château, or helicopting in to see the Who open their so-called world farewell tour in Philadelphia.* By the autumn of 1982, Jerry Hall was routinely coming home from modelling assignments to 'find things next to the bed like earrings or a ring ... It [became] impossible to pick up the phone without some girl on the line.' Jerry was sufficiently moved to show Keith Richards 'this note from some other chick that was written backwards – "forever mistress your be I'll",' a formula that might not have unduly troubled the wartime code-breakers of Bletchley Park who Mick later eulogised in his film *Enigma*. In October, the Stones began recording again in Paris. Jagger was reading William Burroughs' *Cities of the Red Night*, writing lyrics about rape and cannibalism while squiring the likes of Texan actress Valerie Perrine (the first woman ever to purposefully appear nude on American

---

*In 1961, Jagger's college tutor Walter Stern had found him to be 'shy and polite' one day and a 'cocky sod' the next. Stern wasn't the only one to make the distinction over the years. In August 1982, Mick spent a day in the press box at Lord's, where he struck Peter Smith, the long-serving cricket correspondent of the *Daily Mail*, as 'genuinely funny, modest and charming, right up to the moment at the end of the day when I politely asked him for his autograph, at which point he invited me to "fuck off".' Smith was left to marvel at Mick's 'amazing ability to turn his public image on and off at will'.

TV) and Venezuelan model Victoria Vicuna around town. Not for the last time, the tabloid media hustled out the 'Love Rat' stories, and took to chasing Mick and his friends up and down the Champs-Élysées. 'I'm fine. I'm fine. There is no tomorrow,' Mick apparently told reporters on 16 November, before 'darting in to an apartment block with two dusky ladies'. If so, there was soon a reconciliation. 'I've gotten him back,' Jerry announced six days later, 'and we're going to have babies.'

Stu, meanwhile, was privy to Keith Richards' true feelings about Jagger's proposed reorganisation of the Stones' archaic recording practices and leisurely songwriting system, and about Mick's proposals to add modern production techniques, like sampling and phasing. 'You can overdo this streamlining shit,' Keith told him. His idea of the ideal creative process was to play 'thirty or forty great songs by other guys, and hope one drops off at the end'. Back in Paris, Keith now made a habit of coming to work wearing a full-length black cape and a fedora. At times of particular professional stress, he started waving a swordstick around the studio for emphasis. Mick's tendency to hop everything up with violent lyrics and tribal riffs was a complete rejection of Keith's musical philosophy of never pandering to fashion. One aimed for timeliness, the other for timelessness. In Paris, Jagger kept telling Richards and Wood that he wanted more 'modern guitar' on *Undercover*, as the new album was called, 'something like Andy Summers'. Keith's roadie Jim Barber duly obliged with some African riffing on 'Too Much Blood', Mick's ode to one Issei Sagawa, a Japanese student at the Sorbonne who murdered his girlfriend and ate her.

On 10 February 1983, Keith dressed in a black suit to serve as a pallbearer at Alfred Hansen's funeral in New York. Patti's father had been particularly fond of his intending son-in-law, telling his churchgoing friends that 'the guy [was] nothing like what you'd think from the press'. That same night, Keith, still wearing his formal suit, joined Mick, Charlie and Woody at the premiere of Hal Ashby's concert movie, *Let's Spend the Night Together*: loud and hip, but sadly lacking the snap of the shows.

Later that month, Mick decided to accept a reported £2million advance from the British publishers Weidenfeld and Nicolson to write his memoirs. A 'technical assistant', John Ryle, deputy literary editor of the *Sunday Times* (and authority on Molière) was hired for £50,000. Sadly, Mick's restless nature proved unsuited to the arid existence of the working author. John Ryle later commented disparagingly on the 'exotic substances' smoked in their few substantive meetings, which had routinely been 'a chore' to arrange. To at least one Weidenfeld director, speaking, perhaps wisely, on condition of anonymity, the eventual manuscript proved something of a disappointment. 'It was crap,' he says. 'No sex. No rock 'n' roll. Just boring stuff about his ordinary parents, his ordinary upbringing. I was surprised at the poor quality.' The *Daily Mirror* later reported that, as a last resort, Jagger had approached Bill Wyman – an early aficionado of the Apple Mac, on which he filed away the band's archives – for help in recalling certain events. 'Get stuffed,' Bill told him. He was writing his own book. Mick finally abandoned the project in April 1985, after returning Weidenfeld's advance. 'I scrapped it,' he told the press. 'I just got sick of talking about the past and thought I'd leave all that book-signing caper till later.'

Mick had better luck domestically. After banking his *Tattoo You* tour money, he would invest $1.5million in a five-bedroom brownstone on New York's West 81st Street, and about half as much in a smaller property he described as 'literally a shack on the beach' on the private Caribbean island of Mustique. This was perhaps to stretch the definition of the word shack. Mick's tropical retreat consisted of a six-room villa, surrounded by a series of adjoining Japanese guest pavilions, a bathhouse with hot tub, a children's cottage and outlying games room, and furnished throughout, according to one visitor, 'with Gauguin prints, kabuki artefacts and sushi prawn chaises longues.' All that was missing was a private yacht, and Mick often rented one. Jerry Hall duly got pregnant that summer. Mick's friend Bebe Buell continued to visit him in New York, and remembers a sunny day 'horse-riding with Jerry and him in Central Park. "Oh no, I've got two Cancerian chicks on my case," he announced. Very in to astrology, was Mick. And sex.' Jagger's appetites in this area are worth mentioning once again, if only because they so obviously defined him at all times when he wasn't actually at work with the Stones, and once or twice even then. 'Every so often,' another friend recalls, 'Mick became intolerably bored and stale. Like any intelligent rock star, he found at least part of what he did ridiculous, and he desperately craved for renewal.' One way to find renewal was with a new woman. 'Sooner or later, he embarked on another affair – there was no shortage of tail willing to participate – although he generally came home again at the end of the day.' On 2 July 1983, Jagger furnished Mr Chow's restaurant in New York with bouquets of white roses to celebrate Jerry Hall's twenty-seventh birthday. For the rest of the summer, the couple rented an estate in Vermont, down the road from both their friend Jackie Onassis and the author John Irving. On 26 July, Mick himself turned forty there.

That same month, Keith Richards happened to run in to his childhood idol Chuck Berry walking through the terminal at Los Angeles airport. On the last occasion they'd met, in a New York club, Berry had punched the younger man in the mouth after again failing to recognise him, before going on to apologise profusely to Ron Wood (whom, compounding the error, he kept calling 'Jack'), thinking he, Woody, was Keith. This time around Berry greeted Richards by name, but then somehow dropped a lit cigarette down the front of his shirt. As Keith later ruefully said, 'Every time him and me get in contact, I end up wounded.'

In August, Keith went to Marlon's fourteenth birthday party held at Anita's rented house in Sands Point, Long Island. One of the Stones' companies had taken over the lease on the property from Mick Taylor, who had moved to more modest accommodations. The next day, Keith was back in Paris, where the Stones inked an American distribution deal with CBS Records. The contract gave them $6million apiece for four new albums, the most lucrative in rock music history, while CBS got the rights to the band's back catalogue from *Sticky Fingers* onwards. Mick Taylor was not a party to the arrangements. The label was represented for the occasion by its 50-year-old president Walter Yetnikoff, a cigar-chomping fast talker who put some in mind of a more aggressive Allen Klein, if such a thing can be imagined. Yetnikoff was the man who nine months earlier had introduced Michael Jackson's *Thriller* to posterity. Everyone at CBS, he confided, was convinced that Mick personally could be as big as Jacko. Mick joined the consensus.

A furious debate would rage in years ahead over whether Keith fully understood that Mick had made any such commitment to develop his solo career. If not, he must have missed the bold-type announcement in *Rolling Stone* of 24 November 1983, which reported:

> The heart of the new deal is that CBS will release the next four Stones albums. In addition, it will also release, for the first time ever, a solo album by Mick Jagger himself. Maybe two or three. This is an unexpected breach in Jagger and Richards' long-standing no solos tradition, and Mick seems excited by it.

In September 1983, Bill Wyman and Charlie Watts played alongside Eric Clapton, Jeff Beck and Jimmy Page in an all-star group assembled to raise funds for multiple sclerosis research. After two sold-out London shows the band did nine American dates, where Ron Wood sat in on guitar. Bill (who was to say of the tour, 'Most of the million dollars we made mysteriously disappeared') was also hard at work on his autobiographical video feature, *Digital Dreams*, a mélange of surrealist cartoon sequences and embarrassed cameos by the likes of James Coburn. It was not well received by the critics. Bill stuck it out and began writing his memoirs, aided by the PC on which he'd stored material pertaining to twenty years of rock music and uncomplicated sex. Charlie Watts and his family had moved on to a stud farm in north Devon, which they shared with a stable of twenty-three Arab horses, and several dozen cows, sheep and dogs. 'The squire', as he was known locally, could sometimes be seen walking in gumboots around the nearby village of Dolton, unmolested by the few residents who associated him with the Rolling Stones. Charlie also continued to play in the chosen anonymity of Rocket 88 and several other pick-up jazz bands. In New York, Ron Wood and his partner Jo had a baby boy, Tyrone.

Everyone met again in Paris to interview 29-year-old Julien Temple, *enfant terrible* of the National Film School, who Mick wanted to direct the promos for *Undercover*. Keith greeted Temple by holding the swordstick to his throat and telling him not to fuck up. The two men then shook hands and drove off to scout locations, Keith 'barrelling down the Quai de Bercy in a red Ferrari going 120 mph'. Temple survived the initiation test and went on to shoot videos for three of the album's songs, doing the interiors in the club Bains-Douches in Paris and the exteriors in Mexico City. In one suggestive setup, Mick would be seen being dragged out of his hotel room by three wild-eyed gunmen. The leader of the gang, who then blew Jagger's brains out, was played by Keith. Like the host album, Temple's videos for *Undercover* did not inspire critical consensus. Back in London, the cutting process was interrupted when one of the female editors at work on the 'assassination sequence' became nauseous and wept, though to the anonymous *Sunday Times* critic, the end result 'suggest[ed] for the first time that a rock-music film may have true artistic potential'.

Mick's solo career got off to a head start on *Undercover*, out that November. He retooled the Stones for the Me Decade with a string of danceable romps and violent, fuck-you lyrics. Among the key reference points: Wall Street, money, murder, *The Texas Chainsaw Massacre*, flagellation, knives, razors and battered babies. Keith's clanging guitar stoked such tracks as 'Pretty Beat Up', but generally the album settled for easy club grooves – 'Too Much Blood', which had kids boogieing along to Mick's cannibalism rap – that showcased the production more than the tunes. *Undercover* never got beyond an icy professionalism. It was flawless, facile and completely forgettable.

The title track, a funky brew of rapid-fire drums and guitars that sound like an angry swarm of wasps, is Mick's lament for political *disparus* in Argentina (where the song was banned in perpetuity), and much the sort of 'serious message' Bianca had lobbied for ten years earlier. Keith's signature riff is paced by Stu's loping piano on 'She Was Hot'; the melody sings, the rhythm swings and even the voice is shot through with character. 'Wanna Hold You' is a straight reworking of 'Happy', and a rare moment of abandon on the album. Keith would raid the Stones playbook again on 'Too Tough' and 'It Must Be Hell', which channelled the *Let it Bleed* outtake 'I'm Going Down' and *Exile*'s 'Soul Survivor', respectively. There are a few good rubbery bass lines. Charlie rocks. Generally, though, the consensus was that *Undercover* was poor fare, pretentiously wrapped (in a trashy blue sleeve that showed a naked, sectioned woman). It hit number 11 in Britain, number 5 in the US; a first commercial flop, relatively speaking, in fifteen years.

By the time the reviews were in, the Richards and Hansen families had gathered for Keith and Patti's wedding in Cabo San Lucas, a resort favoured by American swingers like Hugh Hefner on the tip of Mexico's Baja California peninsula. Over the weekend of 16–17 December, they were joined there by friends including Jane Rose, Gregorio Azar, the Azar Nuts tycoon, and Mick Jagger. None of the three other Stones was invited. Mick and Keith entertained the crowd at the bachelor party by sitting on stools and strumming a selection of Elvis and Buddy Holly hits, just as they had in the pub in Devon twenty-two years earlier. For that hour or so, everything again seemed closer to an early-60s sing-along than to the jaded wrangling of recent days. The ceremony itself took place on the afternoon of 18 December, a mile or so away from Keith and Patti's villa at the luxurious Hotel Finisterra. Everyone gathered on the terrace, under a double row of palm trees and overlooking the beach. Doris and Bert Richards met for the first time in twenty years. It would have been their own forty-fifth wedding anniversary. Patti wore lace, Keith his formal black suit, white shirt, and blue suede shoes. It was a shockingly normal affair for the most part. Religion wasn't Keith's bag, and particularly not Christianity with its 'logo of a guy nailed to a piece of wood'. However, in deference to his in-laws he agreed to 'the full Lutheran gig', conducted in Spanish. Keith added an ecumenical touch of his own by performing the Jewish wedding ritual of smashing a wine glass underfoot. That same day, he turned forty.

There had been well-merited celebrations in and around the Paris Ritz when the Stones signed their record-breaking deal with CBS.

Mick Jagger had given an eloquent speech, which was later typed up and distributed to the label's 400-plus employees at Black Rock, its New York corporate headquarters. 'We are clearly living through one of the most difficult business cycles of recent times,' Mick noted. 'Some say the record industry will pull out of the recession; others believe it's permanent. But I believe that CBS and the Stones will go forward to make some great music together. We're ready to roll.' Mick's optimism was heartfelt. But it was not fully warranted, for 1984 proved to be a trying year. It began on a dismal note when the Stones' old friend and mentor Alexis Korner died of cancer in a London hospital on 1 January. He was fifty-five. The band themselves were embarking on a feud that simmered steadily, and occasionally boiled over, for most of the rest of the 1980s. Mick engaged in a constant derogation of Keith that seemed almost automatic. Keith began calling Mick 'Brenda' after coming on a copy of a book by Brenda Jagger, a British spinster author of historical fiction like *The Barforth Women*. It was not a term of endearment. The Stones released only forty minutes of new music between November 1983 and August 1989, leaving performers like Madonna, with her thin talent and hard edge, a reborn Bruce Springsteen, and the band's old warm-up act Prince to fill the void.

In April, Walter Yetnikoff got Mick and Michael Jackson together to cut a song called 'State of Shock' for the Jackson brothers' album *Victory*. Yetnikoff's two main corporate assets 'got on great', he announced, although Jacko was concerned enough about Mick's voice to insist on him singing two hours of scales before recording began. Some of the teenage entourage in the studio apparently expressed surprise that the head Stone, seemingly out of a Jurassic social order, looked so young. Paradoxically, Jagger's presence there harked back to pop's golden age, when hits were made for kids by clever adults.

Shortly afterwards, Mick began to cut his own solo album at Compass Point in the Bahamas, with the help of friends like Herbie Hancock, Chuck Leavell, Jan Hammer and some twenty-two other musicians. The result was a rather denser sound than for the Stones, as 1980s as *Miami Vice,* with a bouncy synthesiser at the core. A New

York session musician (and future member of David Letterman's TV orchestra) named Anton Fig played some of the drums. 'Mick was very, very particular about it,' he says. 'I remember he would walk back and peer over my shoulder to see exactly what I was doing.' Sometimes Jagger varied the routine by swaying in front of the drum riser so that Fig could pick up a beat based on his body language. Mick 'was on top of everything', often managing to sing, conduct and dance simultaneously, apparently revelling in the freedom to make his own music. In all, there would be plenty of big tunes and lyrical allusions to love, sex and marriage, just as CBS might have prescribed for one of the great male romantic icons of pop history.

Mick certainly showed no signs of slowing down in his forties. One of his London aides remembers him picking her up one morning that spring and driving her to work. 'He was weaving in and out of cars, shouting at their drivers, ming[ling] dictation and diatribes,' she says affectionately. In the summer, Mick was back spending his days mixing his album at the Power Station in New York and his nights at the nearby Kamikaze Klub, where the bartender was Bruce Willis. Many people thought he'd changed significantly, or even matured, since his divorce. Despite his schedule, Mick also found time to be present and 'very supportive' when Jerry Hall gave birth to their daughter Elizabeth that March in Manhattan's Lenox Hill hospital. Three months later, they had the child christened at St Mary Abbot's church in London. Eva Jagger told me it was a 'wonderful family day' (13-year-old Karis and 12-year-old Jade were also on hand), 'although I did rather put my foot in it when I said something about "Mick and Jerry's wedding . . . I mean christening" in my speech'. On 26 June, the Stones met at their new office in Munro Terrace, Chelsea, where Mick told the other three attendees – Woody wasn't invited – that he had plans for the rest of the year. There would be no album or tour in 1984. Bill Wyman (currently seeing an American teenager named Kathy, and an English one named Kelly) wasn't pleased. It wasn't merely money 47-year-old Bill sought. It was mutual respect and a stable working relationship. 'I've lost touch with whoever Mick is now,' he told the

Sun. 'I'm sure he has as well. Seven or eight years ago, I could still talk with him about books, films and intelligent things, but now I just talk to him in asides. Mick is a very difficult person to know.'

While Jagger was busy cutting his solo album in Nassau, Keith Richards and Patti Hansen were an hour's flight away across the Caribbean at their home in Jamaica, Point of View, where Patti soon announced she was pregnant. The newlyweds had moved there after the Cabo police allegedly took Keith aside, showed him some surveillance photographs of men in ill-fitting white suits and sunglasses arriving at his villa in the middle of the night, and advised him of the difficulty of pursuing his career from a Mexican jail cell. With that, the Richardses took off to Ocho Rios for the summer. When they landed at Kingston airport, however, they found that Keith's current tenant, Peter Tosh, had ignored all prior notice of their arrival and was refusing to leave the property. As he observed on the phone, 'If you come anywhere near here, I'll shoot you.'

Keith: 'Then you better load the fucking gun, Peter, because I'll be there in an hour.'

Although Tosh himself had wisely moved on by the time Keith and Patti's car reached the house, they were still able to see evidence of their recently departed guest. Point of View had, at first glance, the air of a dilapidated farm rather than a luxury villa. A large pig, tethered by one hind trotter to the front railings, lay squarely across the driveway. Assorted sheep and goats roamed the once elegant garden. There was also a three-legged dog, which snarled rabidly at Keith and Patti as they edged past. Other pets and friends of Tosh's sprawled around the house itself in varying degrees of stupor. Keith's living room, library and studio had all been thoroughly trashed.

Tosh left Rolling Stones Records shortly after that by mutual agreement. Three years later, on 11 September 1987, he was shot dead in the course of a burglary at his house down the hill.

In August 1984, the four charter Rolling Stones met for another business conference in Paris. Not for the last time, Ron Wood was in a detox facility in London, and so couldn't make it. Mick finally came clean to everyone about his full ambitions to tour behind his solo album, now going under the title *She's the Boss*. 'My attitude,' Keith told the press, with that flair for laconic expression people admired, 'was, fine! Since I'm not gonna have anything to do with it, I don't really want my name coming in to it, anyway. Since I'm not going to be involved, maybe I won't like it. I told him, "Don't make a shit album".' Meanwhile, the Stones put out a stopgap hits collection called *Rewind*, and a video of the same name featuring two relentlessly chirpy presenters for the price of one. Jagger and Wyman duly hammered their way through sixty minutes of disjointed patter, sight gags and boffo *Fawlty Towers* humour. About the only watchable moment came when, asked to explain the band's longevity, Mick and Bill answered as one: 'Charlie Watts'.

As the Stones' creative life slowed to a crawl, so their business schedule accelerated. In New York that October, Jagger, Richards and Wyman got together with Rupert Loewenstein and several sober-suited merchant bankers and tax lawyers to discuss the band's investments. Unfortunately, the intended note of calm debate was offset when Richards arrived in the boardroom brandishing a ratchet knife. According to Bill, 'Keith was still annoyed with Mick for working on solo material. It nearly came to blows.'

The band's next meeting, in Amsterdam, did so. Following Prince Rupert's latest presentation, a more conciliatory-seeming Richards took Jagger out on the town and got him drunk. The latter's usual transition from gregariousness to mindless exuberance was abnormally swift. A blotto Jagger phoned Charlie Watts' hotel room at five in the morning and rashly referred to him as 'my drummer'. Charlie got up, showered, shaved, dressed in a Turnbull and Asser shirt, silk tie and three-piece suit, went downstairs, grabbed Mick and punched his lights out. 'It was like a scene in a movie,' Keith Richards later said of a room containing forty or so well-oiled musicians and their friends. Anyone familiar with *The Island of Dr Moreau*, with its apes and dogs surgically turned in to semi-human form, has only to think of these same fauna dressed in 80s pastels to get a bit of the flavour. The band's ever-present security crew froze in place – nobody seemed quite sure what the protocol was for separating one Rolling Stone from another – leaving Keith himself to grab hold of Mick as he 'landed on a plateful of smoked salmon and slid along the table towards the window'. Keith later remarked that he had been moved less by humanitarianism than by the fact that Jagger happened to be wearing his own favourite silk jacket at the time. His intervention possibly saved Mick from being ejected in to the canal below, but its real motivation was to 'stop my gear being ruined'.

'Don't ever call me your drummer again,' Charlie observed on his way out. 'You're *my* fucking singer.'

On 2 January 1985 Ron Wood married his long-time girlfriend Jo Howard at St Mary's church, Denham. Keith was best man. Charlie, Bill and just about every other British classic-rock star was present. Mick was on holiday in Mustique, installing a new sewage pump at his home there, so was unable to attend. Only fragmentary recollections of what was said have survived. The vicar had a go at the Stones, noting among other things that 'these proceedings are the antithesis of wealth and decadence'. The comedian Peter Cook attempted to seduce the bride, then climbed in to a black limo marked 'Musicians' in the car park. A ticklish moment occurred at the reception when Keith Richards caught sight of the journalist John Blake, Spanish Tony's ghost on *Up and Down with the Rolling Stones*, and took the opportunity to make some unappreciative remarks about the book. As Keith got in to the gist of his review, Blake suddenly remembered a pressing engagement and hurriedly left the room.

Back to Paris. The old Pathé-Marconi studio had been bull-dozed, but the Stones set up shop in its successor on rue de Sèvres. Mick brought no new material to speak of, having just finished *She's the Boss*. Keith then arrived with twenty-seven songs, which went under titles like 'Fight', 'Had It with You' and 'Knock Yer Teeth Out'. The album itself was provisionally called *19 Stitches*, after one of the engineers overdid it in the hospitality room and managed to crash through a plate-glass coffee table. Soon Keith was bringing his Rasta friends and a bearded New York Talmudic scholar-cum-licensed pharmacist named Svi to hang out and watch the Stones record. Mick brought the cricketer Ian Botham. For the most part, Stu was to schedule the sessions so the Glimmer Twins wouldn't be there at the same time. When everyone did meet, it was generally only to offer a muttered 'yep' or 'nope' to the latest playback. Mainly nope. Mick now wanted to record with the Stones in much the same way he'd cut *She's the Boss*. Everything had to be written down, lyrically and musically, before a note was played. He allowed for a few embellishments by the band, but generally a steely discipline ruled – not the other Stones' preferred system. One night in Paris, Mick finally lost it with Keith and told him that he was tired of the ramshackle way the sessions were going. He provided other examples of the shortcomings of the Stones' creative practice, several minutes' worth, then said he could see 'no useful purpose to be served in proceeding in this vein'. Slipping in to a different idiom, he added: 'We're just dicking around here.' Before long, Keith was openly referring to Mick as 'Brenda', even when he happened to be physically present in the room. Only Mick didn't know it meant him. Keith would turn to Woody and say something about 'that bitch Brenda' and Mick would just stand there, apparently assuming it was some new female acquaintance of his guitarist's. According to Stu, the usual practice was that 'Mick would arrive in the studio around 8 p.m. and leave at midnight, just as Keith and co. came through the door. Nobody was speaking.' Another party present in rue de Sèvres compared the core atmosphere to 'spending six months in a designer padded cell'.

On 4 March, Jagger put out *She's the Boss*. It was a perfectly good album on its own terms, buffed up by a busy funk production. Over a month it sold a respectable million-plus copies, and spawned two hit singles. 'Unlike a major Stones album, which yields more ideas and ironies as you live with it, *She's the Boss* just gets more danceable,' *Rolling Stone* wrote, in the course of a highly laudatory review. Keith Richards told journalists he didn't care for the disc. 'Wimpy songs, wimpy performance, bad recording,' he summarised. Keith's mood wasn't improved when Mick started leaving the latest Stones sessions to promote *She's the Boss* in interviews held in a café immediately across the street. 'I very nearly stiffed him at the time,'

Richards noted. 'But there's no joy in punching a wimp. Jagger was around so infrequently . . . it was just Charlie, Ronnie, Bill and me trying to make a record. It was very unprofessional, very stupid.' Although Mick later decided to postpone his solo tour, he wasn't about to hit the road with the Stones either, characterising them to reporters as a 'bunch of pensioners' who were out of touch with the current music scene.

A few days later, Keith decided to leave the studio and fly back to New York. On 17 March, Patti Richards turned twenty-nine. Early the next day, she gave birth to the couple's daughter, Theodora Dupree. For the first time, Keith, the man who death forgot, was present to watch a child of his born. A second girl, Alexandra Nicole, followed sixteen months later. In between these events, the Richardses moved out of New York and in to a two-storeyed Colonial house in the well-heeled town of Weston, Connecticut, 60 miles northeast of Manhattan. The distance would allow for more privacy and unimpeded views of shimmering lakes and rivers, but still be close enough for Keith to take nightly trips down I-95 to the city. Before long, he was working with friends like Bobby Womack, Tom Waits and Patti Scialfa (later Mrs Bruce Springsteen) to fill in for the not-happening Stones. Weston, a town of 6,000 souls and a single stop-light, seemed straight out of a Norman Rockwell painting. Rich in ivy-clad houses and apple-cheeked tots, it had no apartment blocks, offices or public transport. There was one small market, and even that trafficked solely in string, toffee apples and copies of *Farmer's Almanac*. Keith would now spend much of his time either here or in West Wittering.

Richards went back to Paris in mid-April, recording *Dirty Work*, as *19 Stitches* had become, while Jagger promoted *She's the Boss*. The Stones were obviously making each other miserable, and it's easy to say that Mick made a sound decision by stepping aside. He later insisted he'd never wanted to break up the band, merely to give everyone a rest. It's easy to see, too, how his good intentions could have been misconstrued. Having cried off touring with the Stones, Mick then agreed to perform at Live Aid on 13 July, with Hall and Oates' big-haired soul band – and Tina Turner – backing him. Later

that spring, while Richards moved operations to RPM Studios in
New York, Jagger flew back to London and did a record and video
of 'Dancing in the Street' with David Bowie. Here Mick's genuine
if too often unappreciated acting ability came in to play. The drummer for the session, Neil Conti, told me, 'Jagger came off as the
nicest guy in the world, asking about everyone's families, et cetera,
doing all that meeting-the-troops stuff. Then when I ran in to him
a couple of weeks later it was as though we'd never met. "Hi,
Mick," I said. Not a flicker. He literally turned on his heel and left.'
Bill Graham offered Jagger the prime 9 p.m. slot for the
Philadelphia end of Live Aid, just before the night's headliner Bob
Dylan – the one figure ranked above him in the rock pantheon.
The worldwide TV audience at that hour would be 1.5 billion. This
was the sort of exposure Walter Yetnikoff could normally only
dream of for a client. Two days before the show Dylan dropped by
Ron Wood's house on the Upper West Side of New York, mum-
bled something about 'playing this gig on Saturday', and added that
he could really use the help of a good band, preferably consisting of
two guitarists, as he was going on right after Mick and Tina . . .
When he looked up, Bob found that, for once, he was talking to
himself. Woody was already speeding downtown to RPM to find
Keith.

Mick Jagger gave a stunning performance in Philadelphia.
Despite being interminably rehearsed, songs like 'Honky Tonk
Women' managed to sound both fresh and raw. Ninety thousand
sun-baked fans – from beer-gutted geezers to those actually concerned with the famine in Ethiopia – moshed along amid a storm
of noise and strobe lights. Jagger wore a bright lemon suit. It was his
first official performance outside the Stones. Mick's brand of campy,
well-choreographed pop was perfect for the occasion. Somehow, he
even managed to rip Tina's dress off.

Dylan and his hastily assembled crew were, it has to be said, a
sorry letdown. The three of them spent that long, humid afternoon
drinking and jamming in a small trailer. They were allotted only a
few minutes on stage. Keith and Woody couldn't hear a thing
through their monitors, Dylan popped a string on his acoustic guitar,

and the necessarily brief rehearsal process had apparently left them only half acquainted with Bob's opening number, 'The Ballad of Hollis Brown'. Grinning sheepishly, the conscience of a generation and his two heavily mascaraed cohorts were reduced to busking it, while Lionel Richie and his ensemble could be heard, and occasionally seen, vigorously practising the show's big finale 'We Are the World' on the other side of the stage curtain immediately behind them. If you closed your eyes, you could have been forgiven for thinking you were listening to a BBC Sound Effects recording of a protracted car crash. It was the sort of unintentionally slapstick rock and roll performance that endeared itself to Spinal Tap. By the time the gig ended, Jagger had clearly scored several points in the solo-career stakes and would soon again begin planning to tour on his own.

Ron Wood was able to offer his conciliation services later that summer when 'Keith and I were talking on the phone one night [and] the other line rang – it was Mick, saying Keith wouldn't take his calls. After our conversation finished, I told Keith: "Mick really wants to talk to you. He's going to ring you right now." Half an hour later Mick was back on the line and said: "We're talking again".' Jagger's mood may have been lifted by the birth of his first son, James Leroy Augustin, that August. Mick was elated to have a male heir – 'I'll teach him to play cricket' – and talked about him endlessly like any proud parent. Jerry Hall assures us he took his turn at getting up at night and changing nappies, and sometimes sang 'Jumpin' Jack Flash' to lull the infant to sleep. But it was a rule of thumb with the Stones that at least one band member would be facing domestic turmoil at any given time. Just as a wary truce broke out between Mick and Keith, Bill Wyman, forty-eight and officially single for the first time since 1966, began seeing a woman so much younger than him that for a time he reportedly faced being slapped by the authorities with a statutory-rape charge. The siren that initially lured Bill on to the rocks was 15-year-old Nicola Smith, a doe-eyed north London schoolgirl with streaked blonde hair and a tartan miniskirt, and the original claimant to be the 1980s 'Wild Child'. In due course, he took up with Nicola's nearly identical sister Mandy. Bill met his new flame in early 1984, and subsequently introduced her to the Stones in Paris. Their affair, which the band followed as avidly as they did *Dallas*, sent Mick in to paroxysms. Presciently, he saw only 'major aggro' ahead. An aspiring actress and model, Mandy Smith seemed both intelligent and precocious, and had no apparent difficulty adjusting to life among the Rolling Stones. She was, however, only thirteen.

Meanwhile, Charlie Watts began seeing a woman named Sylvie, who at twenty was roughly the same age as his daughter. Although they seem to have done no more than go out to dinner together, it was enough for Charlie's wife Shirley to burst in to the studio one night, scream at her husband, and then throw herself off the nearest balcony. At that time, both Wattses were drinking perhaps more than was wise, and the chaotic circumstances of Charlie's professional life had taken their toll. Fortunately, the balcony was on the first floor of the studio and Shirley sustained only minor injuries. Later in the year, Charlie himself managed to fall down a flight of stairs in his wine cellar in Devon and break a leg.

It was, therefore, a band already facing various personal and professional issues who received the devastating news in late 1985 that their friend and guiding conscience Ian Stewart had died. Stewart, who was complaining of respiratory trouble during the final *Dirty Work* session, had been to see a London specialist on the afternoon of 12 December. The doctor was running late, and his nurse, to whom Stu seemed cheerful enough, asked him to take a seat. During the wait, he suffered a cardiac arrest and died within seconds. He was forty-seven.

A year that had begun with a wedding now ended with a funeral. All the Stones came together for Stu's service on 20 December. Several of them were in tears as his favourite record, 'Boogie-Woogie Dream', was played in the crematorium chapel. Keith reached over and embraced Mick, and then turned to Woody: '*Now* who's gonna tell us off when we fuck up?'

Having toiled on it for more than a year in three different cities, Keith was 'extremely stoked' by the band's eighteenth studio album,

Dirty Work. Early in 1986, he began summoning his favourite journalists to discuss the record, prodding 'Mr Jogger', as he called him, through their pages. 'If Mick was to go out without the Stones,' Keith told *Musician*, 'I'd slit his throat ... That's the way it is. This is the first album in a new contract. We'd be *idiots*; it'd be the dumbest thing in the world to not get behind it. We've got a good thing here! He knows that. Why toss it away?'

Jagger was, in fact, curious to read of his proposed tracheotomy, and distinctly cool on the subject of *Dirty Work*, which he later described as 'not special'. He had one of his staff contact Charlie and Bill to ask them to be by their phones at a certain hour. When Mick came on the line, he talked to them about Keith and what he saw as his problems. 'We all do other things on the side – except him,' he complained. Mick didn't want to tour and, as he somewhat immodestly recalled in *Rolling Stone*, 'I was a hundred per cent right. It would have been the worst. Probably would have been the end of the band.'

On 23 February, everyone did, however, gather at London's 100 Club to pay tribute to Ian Stewart. For an hour the Stones hustled out the sort of R&B chestnuts Stu loved and they started their career playing. It was the band's first performance together in nearly four years. Two nights later they picked up a lifetime-achievement Grammy in a televised ceremony at the Kensington Roof Gardens. The seeds of dissolution sown over recent years were beginning to show in some of the group; while Mick smoothly did the honours, Charlie appeared to stumble in to the arms of the award's presenter, Eric Clapton. It's possible the band's presence there in the first place owed less to communal pride at their 24-year accomplishment than to the producers' promise to air their latest video on national TV if they showed up. Immediately the cameras were turned off, Keith and Ron Wood took a limo over to Clapton's nearby home and, in Woody's account, 'took the fucking place apart'. The two Stones left at seven the next morning after one of the most bibulous nights with which even they were ever associated.

Dirty Work followed on 24 March 1986. With the best will in the world, it's hard to fundamentally disagree with Mick's verdict on the album. Instead of great songwriting, the Stones would give the whole thing a kind of glazed dullness, with some untypically stiff, Led Zep-style drums. In the hideous cover photo, out of a taxidermist's nightmare, the other band members peer up lifelessly while a grizzled-looking Charlie, alone, gazes down at his feet. Richards' left knee appears to be poking Jagger in the crotch. Mick's right foot is cocked behind Keith's back.

The record opens with 'One Hit' and 'Fight', thus returning to *Undercover*'s gory turf: we get lyrics about flesh, blood, pulp, bruises, holes and putting the boot in. From the grungy tub-thumping, through the soul and reggae covers and the howled rave-up 'Winning Ugly', *Dirty Work*'s all over the shop, loud and rambunctious and in your face. Mick's 'Back to Zero' is the voice of late-Cold War reason – 'I worry about my great-grandchildren ... livin' ten miles beneath the ground' – with a riff uncomfortably like that of David Bowie's 'Fashion'. 'Harlem Shuffle' updates the Barry White-arranged R&B oldie, and would go on to become the Stones' first non-original studio single since 1964. Jagger sings Richards' 'Had It with You' and its refrain 'You dirty fucker ... Singin' for your supper ... I had it, had it with you' with surprising equanimity. Keith himself takes vocal duties for the album's sign-off, a throaty country-rock confection backed by an endearingly tinny piano. There's not much melody, but 'Sleep Tonight' is hands-down the best Stones ballad since 'Wild Horses'. It's the sort of thing a Johnny Cash or even a Furry Lewis would have sung, and Keith's cig-tinged wheeze rises to the occasion.

Old and new. New and old. That's the coupling that, yet again, is *Dirty Work*'s selling point, a marriage of Mick's dance-hall grooves and Keith's bluesy shuffles. The album hit number 3 in Britain, number 4 in America. It was dedicated to Ian Stewart.

While Richards kept up a brave front, telling interviewers like Chris Spedding (one of the short-listed candidates to replace Mick Taylor eleven years earlier) the Stones had done a 'fucking great' album and would 'definitely tour' behind it, Mick's attention was elsewhere – fighting a plagiarism lawsuit, overseeing work on his house in

Mustique, and watching cricket in Barbados. On 24 April, Jagger sent Richards a telegram telling him he was going to record a second solo album, this one called *Primitive Cool*. There would be no summer Stones shows. For most of the rest of the spring, Mick and Keith would be busy not exchanging great new song ideas but bickering by telex and fax. Not surprisingly, the band were in Defcon 2 mode when, on 1 May, they met back at Elstree studios to cut a video for *Dirty Work*'s 'One Hit (To the Body)'. Nobody was speaking. Jagger and Richards spent much of the shoot taking flying kicks at one another. Wood somehow smacked Mick on the head with his guitar. Keith later called it a 'fairly good portrayal of things at the time'.

After that, Richards took the *QE2* back to New York, where he arrived in time to attend the birth of his third daughter, Alexandra. In a frenzy of dues-paying, Keith then performed at a Chicago R&B festival and played Los Angeles club dates behind the blues diva Etta James, before flying to Detroit to help Aretha Franklin cut a cover of 'Jumpin' Jack Flash'. Mick provided the title song to the Danny DeVito comedy *Ruthless People* and headlined at a Prince's Trust concert in London, duetting with David Bowie, before going on to dinner with the heir to the throne. (Eva Jagger told me that none of her family was at all interested in wealth or nobility, unless they were also accompanied by 'oodles of humour and charm'.) Later in the summer, Mick began work on *Primitive Cool*, signing up musicians like Jeff Beck, the drummer Simon Phillips and bassist Doug Wimbish in a series of theatrically secretive LA hotel meetings. 'It's strange working without the other [Stones],' Mick allowed. 'Like having a wife and a mistress.' Charlie Watts, having literally hit bottom, was quietly cleaning up in a London clinic. 'I got sober after I fell down the steps when I was in the cellar getting a bottle of wine,' Charlie said. 'It really brought it home to me how far down I'd gone. I just stopped everything – drinking, smoking, taking drugs, every-thing, all at once. I just thought, enough is enough.' In November, Charlie took his 22-piece jazz orchestra on a tour of America, cul-minating in two sold-out shows at the Art-Deco New York Ritz, where Andrew Oldham was among the paying audience.

The Stones remained a gang of four financially, with Ron Wood still on salary rather than a percentage of profits. For most of the 80s, the band's junior member would turn to his on-off solo career, his paintings, and his briefly popular Miami nightclub, Woody's on the Beach, to augment his income.

Late in July, Keith Richards went down to visit Chuck Berry at Berry Park, his commercially troubled amusement centre in Wentzville, Missouri. Located some 20 miles west of St Louis, it had once averaged over a thousand customers a week, each paying two dollars to swim in the guitar-shaped pool or go dancing in the nearby lodge, but had since fallen in to disrepair. In 1990, armed SWAT officers would raid the complex and take away sixty-one videotapes allegedly showing anatomical close-ups of female customers filmed in the ladies' bathroom, and described as 'graphic' in content.★

'Mad keen' to get back on the road, Richards was there to talk to his boyhood hero about putting together a band for some filmed concerts in the autumn. For a variety of reasons, the experience was not quite to be the 'relaxed break [from] the bitchy Stones' Keith initially had in mind. The first hint of trouble came when Berry greeted his illustrious guest by repeatedly calling him 'Jack', his generic name for an inferior. After three spells in federal prison, Berry was, in his own words, 'moody and very schizophrenic', less concerned with artistic fulfilment than with the financial side of the rock business. Even as Keith ploughed dutifully through the figures, he must have known that he was actually there not to 'escape shit', as he told *Rolling Stone*, but to take it. By and by, the two guitar legends and their entourages made their way up to the home projection room, where Berry played everyone some stag movies of white girls rubbing food on each other. He soon tired of it, and slipped in a feature-length film about himself. There was more than a slight air of the unreal to Berry Park, with its rusty funfair, its family diner next

---

★Berry eventually reached an out-of-court settlement with fifty-nine female plaintiffs, and a court also handed down a six-month suspended jail sentence for his possession of the 'copious marijuana plants' found on the premises.

to its lesbian floor-show, all overseen by Chuck's 90-year-old father. A somewhat dazed Keith went home to Jamaica, uneasily aware that Berry would 'manoeuvre and manipulate anything ... It was very like working with Mick.'

After further meetings in Kingston, London and New York, and a lengthy and acrimonious rehearsal process filmed by the director Taylor Hackford (*An Officer and a Gentleman*), Richards successfully got Berry on stage at the Fox theatre in St Louis for two concerts loosely timed around Chuck's sixtieth birthday. Keith was able to recruit an all-star band for the occasion, including Berry's original pianist Johnnie Johnson, sixty-two, who came out of long-time retirement for the gig. (Apparently prompted by Keith, Johnson went on to sue unsuccessfully for a co-writing credit on fifty-seven of Berry's songs.) Richards would refer to himself 'not so much as musical director as an S&M director – social director of the S&M band. When you're playing with Chuck, you've got to be prepared for anything.' Immediately he got to the venue, Keith had the road-ies bury a slave amp three floors below the stage and feed Berry's guitar, instead, through a non-functioning dummy. That way Chuck – who had also partially blown his voice by doing paid con-certs during rehearsals – could blast out anything he wanted without it spoiling the film soundtrack. Keith had no intention of letting him ruin his own party.

The back-to-back shows on 16 October went well enough, punched up by Johnson and Chuck Leavell on keyboards and Bobby Keys on sax. An awkward moment occurred when Berry boogied over during the first number and said that, for a lark, he wanted to change the key to B-flat. Keith told him to fuck off. The eventual result was probably the best live performance of Berry's long career. Taylor Hackford's documentary *Hail! Hail! Rock 'n' Roll*, including footage of the many rehearsal skirmishes, was a popular and critical hit on its release in 1987. Berry would later suffer the indignity of seeing eight full-frontal nude pictures of himself and various dates published in *High Society* magazine, followed in turn by the discov-ery of video cameras reportedly placed 'literally inside' his female customers' toilets. He remains a popular and hard-working musician today. An exhausted Keith went back to Connecticut, telling friends that he had repaid a debt that had begun twenty-six years earlier, when he queued up fourteen times to watch Berry perform in the film *Jazz on a Summer's Day* at the Dartford Odeon.

Meanwhile, the *News of the World* had broken the scoop of Bill Wyman's relationship with Mandy Smith, and stories accusing him of being an apparent serial philanderer (or, as the *Sun* put it, a 'dirty old perv') began appearing in the British tabloids. In October 1986, Wyman's ex-wife Diane gave an interview broadly confirming the rumours about him, and reporters were soon routinely doorstepping Gedding Hall and smuggling themselves in to the band's London headquarters disguised as delivery men. Before long, Bill found it best to retire to his gated estate in the south of France for his prolonged fiftieth birthday celebrations, while the press engaged in one of its cyclical fits of indignation with headlines like 'HEART OF STONE' and 'JAIL THIS WORM WYMAN'.

On 1 January 1987, Jagger, who was in Mustique, rang Richards, who was in Jamaica, to wish him season's greetings. Keith later described their conversation as 'very polite – very formal. He said that we must have a drink when we were back in New York.'

Spokesmen for both sides loudly insisted that the Stones were still a unit – 'inspired by the example of a guy like Muddy Waters to keep going in a mature and graceful way', as Richards put it to Chris Spedding. All questions about the band's alleged breakup were parried with angry jabs of a lawyer's hand. Even as Keith threatened to sue anyone who wrote them off, however, he ruefully acknowledged the outbreak, that spring, of 'World War Three'. The feud went public on 2 March, with a blast by Jagger in the *Daily Mirror*. Complaining that Richards wanted to run the band 'single-handedly', Mick said, 'I love Keith, I admire him . . . but I don't feel we can really work together any more.'

Keith responded twenty-four hours later in the *Sun*. He said that Jagger 'should stop trying to be like Peter Pan and grow up . . . I don't see the point of pretending to be twenty-five when you're not.' When asked if he could forsee any end to 'the bitching going on' between Mick and himself, Keith replied, 'You'd better ask the bitch.'

Furious that Jagger would work with 'some little jerk-off band' rather than the Stones, Richards stopped going to group meetings, hung up whenever 'Brenda' called and, the sharpest slap, apparently tried to replace him with Roger Daltrey. He kept telling the press about Mick being a sad case. 'You can't sit down with a bottle of whisky with him and talk it over. He just changes the subject.' It seemed to some the Stones were beginning to unravel as spectacularly as the Beatles had fifteen years earlier. Bill Wyman was then quoted as calling Jagger 'the guilty one. He's decided he wants to do his own thing . . . be famous in his own right.' This led to another kung-fu round of recriminations and threatened lawsuits. Wyman's London solicitor sent Fleet Street editors a letter describing the interview as 'misquotes, off-the-cuff remarks taken out of context and blown out of proportion'. (Bill later took the opportunity of his 1990 memoirs to clarify his position. 'Mick broke the bond,' he wrote. 'He committed the cardinal sin of putting another project ahead of a band effort.') Later that spring, Jagger wrote a song about Richards called 'Shoot Off Your Mouth'. Keith called Mick a back-stabbing wimp.

The popular conviction that, after twenty-five years, the Stones were finished as a productive unit remained solid, indeed increased, as the back-line musicians pursued their own projects. When not exiled behind the walls of his French home, Bill Wyman both recorded and toured with an ad-hoc R&B group. He gave this combo the name of Willie and the Poor Boys. The band's drum stool was alternately occupied by Charlie Watts and Ringo Starr. Bill had also published some photographs of his neighbour, the modernist painter Marc Chagall, and was hard at work committing the various Stones' archives to computer, a labour of love that would soon lead him to write his own book.

According to Nick Cowan, Ron Wood's manager from 1979 to 2002, Woody, while commendably loyal to the Stones, may not have been entirely true to his wedding vows to Jo Howard. Around 1987, the two men began taking extended business trips to Ireland, where Wood went on to buy a house in the Dublin suburb of Sandymount, 'seeking a shelter for my art and music', Ron said, as well as from the British Exchequer. 'Our schedule was always the same,' says Cowan. 'After spending the day in the local pub, we'd drive to Dublin. First stop was the Horseshoe Bar in the Shelbourne hotel. Then it was on to Renards, staffed by some lovely Irish lasses, then the VIP room in Lillie's Bordello club, and finally ending up in an after-hours bar before returning to Ron's place for a nightcap.' The two 'rarely came back on our own', Cowan adds, perhaps superfluously. Wood eventually transformed the stables on his 60-acre estate in to a private pub called 'Yer Father's Yacht', and did a licensing deal with Guinness to supply it with unlimited quantities of beer. There were thirteen more pubs within a square mile of his front door.

Back in Connecticut, Keith Richards finally seemed ready to forgo a life of rampaging around the globe laying waste to wine, women and nonprescription drugs, if not to abandon the rock scene entirely. On 17 July 1987, Keith signed a contract with Virgin Records for two solo albums. While he was auditioning musicians at the Hit Factory in New York, Mick Jagger was across Broadway at Right Track studios, mixing *Primitive Cool* and dress-rehearsing his long-delayed tour. Mick particularly wanted to take Jeff Beck on the road with him, but it wasn't to be. 'I quit because he offered me peanuts,' Beck told the press. 'It was laughable . . . an insult. I'd love to play with the old geezer, but I can't believe how tight he is.'

Primitive Cool followed that September. 'On my first solo album, I basically wrote whatever first came to me, then recorded it,' Mick admitted. 'I put a little more thought in to this. I wanted to make the songs more varied in mood, so they weren't all variations on the same style.' The result was a landmark record designed to smash borders, and still the single most satisfying Stones solo project. Rather than the integrated, raunchy Richards–Wood attack, there's Beck's precise, spiralling lead guitar on tracks like 'Throwaway' and 'Kow Tow', the latter with its more-in-sadness-than-anger lyrics apparently aimed at Keith. 'I'll be leaving soon, I'm off at high noon/I've got a heavy heart . . ./The future looms, so damn the past,' Jagger sings. The title tune strays briefly in to Steely Dan territory, and seems to consist of Mick interjecting his views on the 60s with his children's, as if he were giving them a history lesson. He strips out the heavy backbeat, sings it straight, throws in some angular piano and pulls it off, just about. Then it was back to business with the Motown bass and big drums of 'Let's Work', whose key message – 'Let's work, be proud, stand tall . . . Be free, kill poverty' could have been a battle hymn of Conservative Central Office. 'War Baby', by contrast, was as close as Mick had ever come to outright protest, and managed to combine his thoughts on the Blitz and D-Day with further ruminations on his children's future. Somehow it worked. Elsewhere, a layered, wide-screen rhythm section, Irish fiddles, various Eurythmics (whose Dave Stewart co-produced the album), aerobic-sounding keyboards and Beck's incendiary riffs combined to create the best album featuring Mick Jagger since *Exile on Main Street*.

Primitive Cool hit number 41 in America and number 19 in Britain. Perversely, it sold less than the inferior *She's the Boss*. 'Let's Work' avoided the singles chart. Five weeks after the album's release, on 19 October 1987 – Black Monday – the Dow-Jones industrial average lost 508 points, nearly a quarter of its total value. As shares dropped vertically with no one buying, traders were sold out as they failed to respond to margin calls, mobs gathered on Broad Street outside the New York Stock Exchange, and by the end of the day even some of the best-managed investors – including a number of prominent rock stars – had lost millions.

Three days later, *Primitive Cool* disappeared from the chart. One of the Rolling Stones began calling the others to talk about putting the band back together. It was Mick Jagger.

The 'Suntory Dry Beer Live Mick Jagger Experience In Japan' tour, as it was officially known, opened in Osaka on 15 March 1988. Eleven thousand fans enjoyed a tightly choreographed two-hour set, including scantily clad back-up singers, giant video screens and sulphurous lighting effects. Jagger performed twenty-six numbers a night. Twenty-one of them were Stones songs, and five of them were solo songs. He was watched by impassive but apparently well-satisfied customers. While in Tokyo, Mick was joined on stage by

Tina Turner. As at Live Aid they duetted on 'It's Only Rock 'n Roll'. He again deftly removed her skirt. Ron Wood also happened to be in town, doing club dates with Bo Diddley, and on the night of 20 March the two Stones sat down for a saké. Several hours later, it was agreed that Ron would pass on a friendly message to Keith.

But first there was the troubling matter of the $7million lawsuit filed by the Bronx-based aspiring reggae musician Patrick Alley, accusing Mick of having stolen the song 'Just Another Night' from him. On 18 April, the parties met in court in White Plains, New York, to hear Sly Dunbar, the primary drummer on *She's the Boss*, sit down at his kit and, in the judge's words, 'make these hallowed precincts rock up and down the block'. In a bizarre twist, Alley then claimed that Dunbar had also played on a number of *his* recent records. Later in the proceedings, Mick himself took the witness box and, at the judge's invitation, repeatedly broke in to song. A juror named Benny Spangler told me he had the impression that his fellow pundits were 'totally confused and bored' by the intricacies of clave patterns and cross rhythms, but riveted by the sight of Mick Jagger leaning forward to croon 'Brown Sugar' to them. 'As I sat there, with the world's number-one rock star turning on that million-watt smile, I feared for [Alley] and the outcome of the case.' On 26 April, Mick was cleared of all charges of copyright infringement. 'It's one of the drags of being well known that people take shots at you,' he remarked, before jumping in to a waiting limo, leaving an unrepentant Alley to call a sparsely attended press conference, where he complained about various 'lying and conniving' individuals. News programmes led with the story on all three American networks.

By early 1988, the Rolling Stones had sold several hundred million albums and singles, and not just for themselves. Countless surrogate acts including the Black Crowes, Guns N' Roses and a reanimated Aerosmith had emerged in their absence, and benefited from adopting much the same mix of traditional blues verities and rock swagger. The band members themselves were all in their mid-forties, except for Bill Wyman, who was fifty-one. Both Mick's and

Charlie's adolescent daughters had recently been expelled from boarding school, triggering a second generation of 'Stone in Sex Shocker' headlines. All five musicians had found other creative outlets for themselves, and Bill was also planning to open a burger restaurant. But for the Wall Street crash, it's possible the band would have taken Rupert Loewenstein's reported advice and quietly folded after twenty-six years together.

On Wednesday, 18 May, the Stones met in the same room for the first time in two years. There was the sense of a momentous encounter that bright spring morning in London's Savoy hotel, a rock and roll version of the Allied leaders converging at Yalta. Mick said that he wanted the band to get together in the autumn, but Keith, in a notable volte-face, refused. He had no intention of inter-rupting his solo album, *Talk Is Cheap*, or of breaking his commitment to take his band, the X-Pensive Winos, out on the road. However, after 'row[ing] like crazy for a day' (during which Keith took to openly calling Mick 'Brenda'), all parties agreed to a full-scale comeback in 1989. Jagger was extremely confident, he said in conclusion, that the demographics were right for a tour.

Then came Keith's own summation.

'Listen, darling,' he chortled. 'This thing is bigger than both of us. *Capisce?*'

At that, Richards went back to New York, wrapped his album, and made plans for his thirteen-city tour of America. (Jagger's own pro-jected US concerts had been cancelled when *Primitive Cool* prematurely left the chart.) Bill Graham took several trans-conti-nental flights with Mick over the next year, and remembered him travelling 'with a briefcase on his knee, dipping in to it for papers, using it as a writing desk when it was closed. He often sat for long periods in an apparent coma staring out the window. Then he would suddenly start to talk. I got the impression he didn't blame Keith for [the feud] as much as he blamed some of the people around him.' The Jagger–Richards reconciliation took another ten-tative step forward when they met again, in Manhattan, together with their families. Eighteen months earlier, Jerry Hall had hit the headlines after being arrested at Barbados airport, allegedly carrying 20 pounds of ganja in her luggage. The subsequent trial – with its parade of tropical self-indulgence – caused a tabloid scandal in an England in the depths both of a recession and the worst winter in twenty-five years. Patti Richards had been among Hall's 'most supportive friend[s]' during the ordeal.

Keith himself still wasn't quite ready to record with Mick, but he was increasingly prepared to take the long view of their thirty-year partnership. 'Ninety-nine per cent of the male population would give a *limb* to live like him,' he told *Rolling Stone*. 'To be *Mick Jagger*. And he's not happy … I'm trying to grow the thing up, and I'm saying we don't need the lemon-yellow tights and the cherry picker to make a good Stones show. There's a more mature way of doing it.'

That New York summit now triggered a very Jaggeresque piece of play-acting. While at the Hit Factory, Keith took the opportunity to blast his guests with a tape of *Talk is Cheap*. Returning from the bathroom, he happened to glimpse Mick, with his back to him, dancing away to the opening track. Keith retraced his steps, coughed, and walked in to find Jagger sitting demurely on a sofa, reading the *New York Times*. Somewhere in this story is the perfect example of the core relationship between the two Stones, who struck more and more people as exhibiting the endearing if self-indulgent dottiness that sometimes flowers in elderly married couples.

Talk is Cheap came out on 4 October 1988, twenty-two years after Keith's whimsical solo debut, *Today's Pop Symphony*. It stayed in the charts for six months. Although there were few classic rockers or party tunes, the record was a likable hybrid of reggae and soul grooves and near-bootleg-quality production values. Generally as gritty as a half-completed road, the overall sound – not to mention the nicotine vocals – stood as an obvious reproach to the sleekness of Jagger's recent solo output. Accusing Mick of greed and selfishness, the lyrics of 'You Don't Move Me' touched specifically on the bargain-bin fate of *She's the Boss* and *Primitive Cool*: 'Now you want to throw the dice/You already crapped out twice', Keith growled, and went on from there to get personal. At worst, *Talk is Cheap* sounded like a collection of demos that Jagger just might, conceivably, have sharpened (a view Mick himself shares). On top form, the work's improvisational fervour in no way embarrassed its illustrious predecessors like *Beggar's Banquet* or *Exile on Main Street*.

That autumn, Mick Jagger played another eighteen concerts in Australia and Indonesia. The shows clomped along, doing all the baseline things you expected from them, with thin but urgent tunes performed by bouffant-haired men on synthesisers and a guitarist who liked to roll up the sleeves of his jacket, without ever coming close to Stones levels of abandon. Richards took the opportunity of several press interviews to comment tartly on Jagger's band, which he thought had about as much pizazz as a set of stuffed owls in bell jars. Mick replied that Keith had been slagging him 'just to get publicity for his record. It was the only way he could get any. He takes things more personally. He's had a more problematic life.' Mick himself remained the extreme example of the rock star whose emotions went up and down in response to actions and events he couldn't control. An 'evil tosser' in one tour insider's account, he was also capable of picking up the phone to call his old Dartford schoolfriend Paul Ovenden, who had since emigrated to Australia and now found himself driving a cab around Melbourne while Mick gave a sold-out show at the local arena. 'He was quite unlike the image people have of him,' Ovenden says, 'and he talked a lot about his parents and cricket, and things that we both missed about England.' Churchillian words followed. 'My wife was ill and I was going through a hard time. Mick gave me some advice about coping with it all that I've never forgotten. The essence of it was "integrity and perseverance". The odd thing was, he said that in some ways he actually despised the rock-star life he lived himself.'

On 24 November, Keith Richards and his band embarked on a three-week American tour at the Fox theatre, Atlanta. To open the show, 'We'd sit down in front of the drum kit and smoke a joint,' Richards later revealed. 'All the audience could see was this light passed around. You felt the mood of the place, and you could feel when it was the right time – "OK, let's break" – and you could open with a different song every gig. It was far more interesting than fireworks going off.' On certain nights, Keith, dressed in a black jacket and white frilly shirt, seemed to be doing stand-up more than performing, joshing with the crowd about his 'other brand' – the Stones – while tapping a long cigarette in to the ash-tray welded to his mike stand. There were a lot of mutual toasts drunk. Improvisation was the rule, and a tightly scripted song-cycle the exception for most of the fifteen sold-out concerts. Depending on what mood Keith and the Winos were in, they might perform heart-rending folk rock or ear-grating punk. Everything wound up at a sports stadium in New Jersey on 18 December 1988, which happened to be the headliner's forty-fifth birthday. Patti and the girls were there, along with Marlon, Bert Richards, Anita Pallenberg and some 200 other friends. Mick Jagger was in Mustique, so sent his regrets.

In London, Prince Rupert Loewenstein was finalising a $70million deal to get Keith's 'other brand' back on the road.

The Wick, Ron Wood's south London mansion that became a Stones commune around 1973–6.

Tom Keylock seen at Redlands with his daughter Betty and Jack Dyer, the inspiration for 'Jumpin' Jack Flash'.

Hot off whipping New York's Madison Square Garden into a frenzy at his twenty-ninth birthday concert, Mick unwinds at the England v Australia Test match at the Oval.

Mick and Keith onstage in September 1973, at about the time of the latter's 'Dracula gig'.

Mick Taylor, the Stones' one undisputed virtuoso of their first 50 years. He went into the band as a fresh-faced teetotaler and left it to enter a methadone clinic.

Woody and Mick entertain Princess Margaret and the paying fans at Earls Court, May 1976.

Keith, Ronnie Wood, Mick, Charlie and Bill desperately promote their 1976 European tour.

Margaret Trudeau in her element at Studio 54.

Keith with his wife Patti Hansen, the youngest daughter of a hardworking Lutheran family from New York.

Shirley, Charlie and Serafina Watts in 1982. When away from the Stones, Charlie liked to collect American Civil War memorabilia or dress up in a motoring cap and goggles to sit behind the wheel of his 1937 Lagonda Rapide. Since he hadn't learnt to drive, the car never left the garage.

Mick and Jerry Hall, together again, celebrate his fortieth birthday in 1983.

Mick's duet with Tina Turner at Live Aid, his first official performance outside the Stones. 'I very nearly stiffed him at the time,' Keith remarked.

The Stones and wives at Bill Wyman's wedding to Mandy Smith, June 1989. The groom was 52, the bride 18.

The band bearing down on New York's Battery Park aboard the Kennedys' old presidential yacht *Honey Fitz* to announce their twelfth American tour, May 1994.

Sir Mick poses outside Buckingham Palace with his 92-year-old father, Joe, and daughters Elizabeth (right) and Karis, in December 2003. Keith went 'fucking berserk' when Jagger accepted the 'paltry honour'.

The Stones sell out at the Don Valley Stadium, during the European leg of the *A Bigger Bang* tour in 2006. After two years and 147 shows the tour grossed some $560m.

The Stones and Martin Scorsese at the *Shine a Light* premiere in New York, March 2008.

Ronnie Wood and his girlfriend Ekaterina Ivanova at a private preview of Ronnie's one-man art show in Los Angeles, March 2009.

In 2010, Charlie, Mick and Keith relaxed their ban on re-releases to give *Exile on Main Street* a second outing 38 years after its original launch. It went straight back to number 1.

Johnny Depp and his role model at the premiere of *Pirates of the Caribbean: On Stranger Tides*, May 2011.

9

THE OLD DEVILS

In February 1981, Mick and Keith and their entourages had met up in Barbados to resolve their differences, plan their forthcoming tour, write some songs and do a little socialising. Eight years later, they chose the same location to put an end to 'World War Three'. If the Genesis 1:1 of Rolling Stones lore is the story of the teenage Jagger and Richards stumbling on each other that foggy morning in 1961 at Dartford station, what happened now, when each of them swooped down on Grantley Adams airport in Bridgetown in their private jets, would eclipse even that historic rendezvous for the sheer drama of the occasion. At the airport that day was a French journalist named Charles Vann, who served as a stringer for *Paris Match*. Was that Mick Jagger who just arrived? Yes, an immigration official told him; Mick was here on a 'strictly private' Caribbean holiday. Two hours later, Vann was mulling this over at the airport bar when the unmistakable figure of Keith Richards and several colourfully attired Rastafarian friends swept past him on their way to a waiting limo. Vann breathlessly phoned in what would have been the showbusiness scoop of the year to his desk in Paris, where his editor, assuming that Vann was drunk, listened politely and then spiked it.

Richards was 'thrilled to bits' to be there, he said, but also wary both about working with 'Brenda', and relaunching the Stones in the era of Guns N' Roses and Nirvana. He told his family that he'd be back in 'either two weeks or two days'. In the event, he and Mick wasted no time on recriminations. Both had songs left over from their solo albums, and the juices flowed under the tropical sun. In the space of the weekend of 14–15 January, they had three tracks, including the full-throated chorus of 'Mixed Emotions', blocked out for the band. Prince Rupert then flew in for some business talk. He brought with him a high-powered New York music attorney, John Branca, who soon convinced the two Stones of the merits of centralising their ticket sales, retail spin-offs and other logistics under a single supremo, a system that had worked well for Branca's other marquee client Michael Jackson. Mick: 'We were in a hotel with the sea crashing outside and the sun shining and drinks, rapping about all the money we're gonna get and how great it was gonna be.' By cutting out Bill Graham and going instead with the Toronto-based promoter Michael Cohl, who in turn oversaw a sponsorship deal with Budweiser and assorted TV and merchandising rights, the prince guaranteed the original Stones a staggering $18million apiece for a fifteen-week tour.

When Keith came back to Connecticut, it was merely to pack.

On 18 January, Mick and Keith made their first public appearance together in three years, when Pete Townshend inducted the Stones in to the Rock and Roll Hall of Fame at a glittering ceremony in New York's Waldorf Astoria hotel. They were joined for the occasion by Ron Wood and a stout-looking Mick Taylor. Townshend cracked the room up by alluding to Jagger's love life and Richards' blood change, and called Woody the only member of the band who 'still has his own teeth'. After the laughter had died down, Mick gave a speech in which he thanked everyone from Brian Jones to Jean Cocteau (but not Andrew Oldham) while Keith ostentatiously studied his nails. 'We're not quite ready to hang up the number yet,' Mick concluded. At that, the three Stones and their ex loosened their cummerbunds and jumped on stage, where they were joined by Townshend, Bruce Springsteen and Stevie Wonder to play 'Satisfaction'. Suddenly the dysfunctional, wheezing geezers were transformed back in to the greatest band in the world. Charlie and Bill arrived in New York the next day.

Early in February, everyone went back to Barbados for the first proper Stones sessions in four years. The music was perfectly competent, and sometimes much more than that, but for the next six weeks what they were really doing was churning out an album to promote a tour, rather than the other way round. The band took some of the final songs up to George Martin's Air studios in Montserrat, booting Bill off the island after his gymslip lover proposed to him by phone and he accepted. Mick and Keith had no intention of breaking off their most productive sessions since *Aftermath* to deal with a posse of women's-page journalists flying in from London.

In May, the Stones moved shop back to Olympic, their first use of the old *Beggar's Banquet* studio in twenty years. Jagger called the new album *Steel Wheels*, apparently a pun on the 'antiques roadshow, old giblet lips' press he was getting. As well as finishing the record and preparing the tour, Mick also found time for several meetings with Michael Cohl, the bearded, dishevelled-looking 42-year-old promoter whose resemblance to a 60s-era roadie belied entrepreneurial skills of a high order. Widely credited with perfecting the concept of 'package' touring, Cohl was also soon to face published, but unproven, allegations of price fixing and tax evasion, as well as rumours of certain personal eccentricities. *Fortune* magazine was later to half admiringly call him 'the Howard Hughes of rock and roll'. One of Cohl's first coups on behalf of the Stones was to sign a deal with Event Transportation Systems (ETS), a Canadian firm that, quite legally, resold concert tickets at up to five times face value as part of a 'VIP' experience. ETS guaranteed Cohl and the band $625,000, and Mick and Keith each received a further share of the profits. Bill Graham had a twenty-year history with the Stones, promoted their wildly successful *Tattoo You* tour, and personally managed Mick's solo concerts in Australia. But it wasn't enough. As he said in his autobiography, 'What happened [in 1989] was like watching my favorite lover become a whore.' Graham eventually managed to put together a counter-offer to Cohl's, which would have guaranteed the Stones marginally less upfront, but a greater potential payday from back-end rights to the various concert movies and merchandising. After making his pitch to Jagger on a Concorde flight to New York, Graham concluded by asking, 'After all this time, what's *really* the difference to you guys between sixteen million dollars and eighteen million?' 'Two million bucks, Bill,' said Mick.

Money succeeded where every other strategy over the years had failed. For the first time, all five Stones were regularly punctual at the studio. It was 'much more of a drill' than before, Mick confirmed. He, Bill and Charlie typically reported for work sporting neatly tailored tropical-weight suits, Ron favoured the primary-coloured look, while Keith still flaunted an engaging mishmash of rock and roll styles and accessories. Everything about his appearance, from the eye-liner down to the scuffed pixie boots, indicated a lifestyle predicated on the transgression of norms associated with the hated pre-60s *ancien régime*. He remained one of rock music's true characters. In Montserrat, one of the lawyers brought in to discuss the tour arrangements took the opportunity to tell Keith he 'really dug' what he'd heard of the new album, but rashly added that with a few embellishments it could be 'so much better'. Over the years, Keith had reacted to his critics with implements including loaded guns, fire irons and cricket bats. His response here was to produce a hunting knife and launch it across the room. It landed between the lawyer's feet. Among the suits in general, Richards had long been known as the 'temperamental genius' of the band. By the time the new tour came around even this mild euphemism was superfluous; in discussions between them, he was known simply, but affectionately, as 'the madman'.

By early June, the Stones' organisation – now with 370 employees – was busy putting together a year-long piece of rock theatre to be pumped out on vast, *Blade Runner*-like stages. The set was so extravagant that some American sports domes were too small to house it. On the outdoor gigs, the tower from which Mick sang 'Sympathy' needed flashing red lights on top in order to wave passing jets away.

The Stones' commercial windfall, however, did not extend to

their cutting in Ron Wood to a piece of the action. After a four-teen-year apprenticeship, Woody remained a salaried employee whose money ran out at least twice during the 1980s, largely as a result of his emulating Mick and Keith's lifestyle while enjoying a fraction of their income. In general, Jagger continued to spend the Stones' cash as carefully as if it were his own, as indeed much of it was: he was now worth an estimated £60million. As Bill Graham could attest, just because you happened to have known the band for a long time, it didn't necessarily mean you could take their con-tinued support for granted. In 1986, the Stones' old friend Robert Fraser died, alone and essentially broke, of an Aids-related disease at the age of forty-nine, while their long-serving publicist Paul Wasserman, having been fired in favour of Michael Cohl's candi-date, attempted suicide and, aged sixty-six, spent a year in a Los Angeles prison for fraud. Around the same time, Mick Jagger heard from Ossie Clark, the 47-year-old one-time style guru who had supplied the glittering silk and velvet, Balinese-inspired outfits that defined the look of the Stones' 1972–73 tours. He asked if Mick could spare him fifty pounds: middle-aged fashion designers some-times have mundane difficulties. Towards the end of his life, Clark commented that, 'of the old gang, only George Harrison' had remembered him; in August 1996, he was stabbed to death in his London council flat by his male Italian lover.

As several of the Stones' friends noted over the years, anyone who relied on them for moral or financial support beyond their legal obligation probably made a mistake. But if they weren't the ultimate caring band, the individual musicians could often be gen-erous. Mick contributed £20,000 to the cricketer Imran Khan's cancer hospital, and Ron Wood taught art classes for sick children. Keith Richards belied his midnight-rambler image by anonymously donating to everything from the worldwide Hurricane Andrew fund to an appeal for a new scout hut in West Wittering. People increasingly thought the permanently tipsy, Dean Martin persona Keith now presented was a comic impersonation, not his real self. The author William Burroughs was on hand for the first annual International Rock Awards ceremony in New York on 31 May

1989. Burroughs told me that Richards had been 'sobriety itself' throughout the evening, but had then 'immediately switched on a slurring, knockabout routine' once at the podium to receive his Living Legend gong. 'We're playing at an incredible level,' Keith told the crowd, apparently referring to the gibes about the Stones being too old. 'Why shouldn't we compete with the kids? If anybody can do it, we can.'

Two days later, Bill Wyman married Mandy Smith at a civil ceremony in Bury St Edmunds. The Stones were livid with Bill for all the tabloid aggro, as well as for opening a fast-food restaurant named Sticky Fingers without checking with anyone. They did, however, turn up en masse for the wedding reception at London's Grosvenor House. Mick Jagger gave the groom a Picasso etching valued at £70,000, and made a series of gracious and witty toasts to the newlyweds and their distinguished guests. Late in the proceedings, some of the bride's young family approached Mick for his autograph. He told them to sod off.

In June 1989, the Rolling Stones plugged themselves back in like a neon sign. Mick and Keith finished up *Steel Wheels*, taking a day trip to Morocco to record some last-minute pipes 'n' drums for the track 'Continental Drift'. (The local Jajouka musicians were still waiting to be paid for their work on Brian Jones' album, twenty-one years earlier.) Judging from the advertisements and posters that suddenly appeared on the billboards and walls of New York and London, CBS lived up to its commitment to promote the new record in a style that befitted a major comeback by the world's greatest rock and roll band. By early July, everyone was housed in a disused girls' school in Washington, Connecticut, an hour's drive north of Keith's place, surrounded by sleepy New England hamlets with names like Dartford and Kent. On 11 July, the Stones pulled in to Track 42 of New York's Grand Central station to announce their eleventh and latest North American tour. One of the 400 reporters present asked if they were doing it for the money. Mick assured her that nothing was further from his mind. 'What about love?' he asked. Keith took the mike and cackled, 'It's for the glory, darlin'. The *glory*.'

From the start, business was brisk: four concerts at Shea Stadium sold out overnight, two in Toronto in six hours. One block of 200,000 seats went at the phone-melting rate of 2,000 per minute. Although a holiday mood prevailed in Connecticut, the hangover from 'World War Three' surfaced from time to time in the various tour arrangements. 'We were getting to the dress rehearsals, and I wasn't too happy with the horns, so I rang Bobby [Keys] and said, get on a plane and hide yourself when you get here,' Keith Richards writes in his memoirs. 'So we're going to play "Brown Sugar", and Bobby was in, but Mick didn't know he was there. I just told Bobby, when we play "Brown Sugar", come in on the solo. So it was solo time, and Mick looked round at me and said, "What the fuck . . . ?" I just said, "See what I mean?"' (Keith adds that Mick failed to speak to Bobby Keys for the next year.) Jagger then announced that he wouldn't go out on tour if Jane Rose was involved, and Richards replied that was fine by him. Rose did the tour. Further ructions involved such concert accessories as stilt walkers, cherry pickers and female dance troupes. Towards the end of rehearsals, Jagger introduced his protégé Matt Clifford, a former cathedral chorister-turned-keyboard player ushered in to twiddle the Korg knobs and give everything a modern, electronic wash. Mick was particularly sold on Clifford, who, he told everyone, would 'punch up' the old Stones sound. Here again, some friction existed with Keith's vision. Jagger let it be known that this time around, the Stones couldn't afford to give one bad concert. 'Everything's gotta be perfect.' The insight was followed by Mick announcing that he was 'worried about the drums coming across', and telling Keith that they needed a click-in track to get the tempos right.

Keith: 'I'll handle the tempos, mate.'

Mick was soon jogging 7 miles a day with a professional coach, while Keith trained on vodka and cigarettes. All the Stones took and passed the pre-tour physical. On 12 August, the band gave its first American concert in eight years at the 200-seat Toad's Place, down on the Connecticut shore. The first anyone knew about it was when a twenty-man crew pulled up in a fleet of vans and began wheeling massive Fender Twin amps through the back door. Any doubts the band might have had about their ability to satisfy a crowd in the late 1980s were resolved the moment Keith loped on and hit the opening chords of 'Start Me Up'. It's tempting to *want* the world's greatest rock and roll band to still be good; it's another thing when the Stones actually deliver the goods, as they did here.

Steel Wheels followed a week later. Once again, the fallout from World War Three was all over the record, which broke down along party lines: Mick's songs (fast and hip) and Keith's songs (warm and lazy), with a rejuvenated Charlie the constant factor. The *Exile*-like 'Sad Sad Sad' wasn't quite 'Rocks Off', but still barrelled ahead like a night train out of Memphis. 'Mixed Emotions' and 'Break the Spell' both somehow ticked the box marked 'commercial' and the one marked 'bluesy'. Mick's 'Blinded by Love', as well as flaunting some edgy lyrics about the Duke of Windsor, was a throwback to 'Blue Turns to Grey' from *December's Children*. Keith, in turn, reworked the 'Bitch' and 'Beast of Burden' riffs to good effect on 'Terrifying' and 'Almost Hear You Sigh' respectively. While most of *Steel Wheels* was tailored to appeal to mainstream American classic-rock radio formats, the Stones also threw in one googly – 'Continental Drift'. This opened with the sound of Keith Richards scraping his ratchet knife over a bicycle wheel and moved from there in to a swirling pattern of nasal Moroccan pipes, tribal chanting and voodoo rhythms, an appropriately spacey if belated tribute to Brian Jones' pioneering role in world music.

Both Mick and Keith would talk about *Steel Wheels* having been made at wild speed. There was clearly no time for any proper artwork, which, in the event, had all the allure of a Soviet department store display. In all, this was one of the most perverse – and catchiest – albums of the band's career. It hit number 2 in Britain and was a number one in America, their best showing there since *Tattoo You*.

31 August 1989. Headlines proclaiming the Stones' return as 'The Year's Triumphant Reaffirmation of Individuality and Self-Expression' (*Spin*) acquired a certain irony in view of the Hungarian Government's decision that week to open its western borders and thus precipitate the end of the Cold War. But it was still a timely celebration of the economic veracity of the classic rock song. The

band drove up to Philadelphia's Veterans Stadium in a royal progress, with flashing lights and a sixty-strong police motorcycle escort. It was their first paying gig in just over seven years. As fireworks exploded and turrets shot out flames, Keith Richards ran on, alone for a second, and again lit the fuse to 'Start Me Up'. Apart from a few loopy, unanchored moments during 'Sympathy', the band was on song throughout, with fierce, no-frills readings of 'Midnight Rambler', 'Gimme Shelter' and 'Satisfaction'. The music was rougher and less clipped; the snake-hipped Mick shimmied around in his britches and tails and tirelessly worked the sports-field-wide stage, itself dressed as a decaying industrial park complete with boilers, girders, trusses, chutes, hoses and flame-belching pipes. For those high up in the bleachers, the band looked like a distant Punch and Judy show, with Mick and Keith circling each other and bopping up and down.

For twenty-five years, Stones tours had been famous for their excesses, for egos run amok in one-night stands hazed over by trashed rooms, dope, strange faces in packed halls, sex, and enough hero-worship for anyone. With *Steel Wheels* the drug-and-chug vibe gave way to one of icy professionalism, the groupies were replaced by wives and kids, and the operation ran like a mobile company. Nowadays, Mick had the use of a pre-show chillout area furnished with Buddhist icons and soothing mood music, and Keith and Ron actually troubled to tune their guitars before taking the stage. The only excesses were ones of scale. Although the Stones came back triumphantly in August 1989, they weren't quite the same group that had disappeared in July 1982. For one thing, there were no fewer than fifteen musicians on stage for each concert: the band itself, a five-man horn section, three backing singers and two keyboard players. Some of the old ramshackle charm was lost forever. What emerged was a well-rehearsed showband, occasionally struggling to cope with all the flame-throwers, fog machines and other props. Even the most humanly evocative songs, like '2000 Light Years from Home', sometimes seemed cipher-like, constrained by the spectacle and all the gaudily flashing neon. There was little hint of the original emotion involved. The number had been written in

a Brixton jail cell. Where was the claustrophobic sense of confinement and hopelessness on a set the size of Lord's? Some songs need
acoustic guitars and moody lighting. Here everything was loud and
kitschy and bathed in abrasive orange. It was all 'fucking immense',
Charlie Watts noted. When the Stones went backstage it was in to
a virtual hamlet of individual changing suites, children's nurseries,
buffets, bars, games rooms and a communal lounge equipped with
Persian rugs, couches and a fireplace. 'Not quite the Manor pub,
Haringey,' Charlie said.

From Philadelphia – where a recovering and foxy-again Anita
Pallenberg appeared backstage – it was on to Toronto. Somehow fittingly, Canadian Customs were waiting for Anita's ex at the airport.
After an intensive search, they relieved him of a small knife. Keith
was not pleased to subsequently find that several hungry roadies had
tucked in to his personal pre-concert shepherd's pie. Both the
Stones themselves and 53,000 expectant fans were made to wait
while a replacement was cooked and delivered. According to the
band's long-time assistant Tony King, 'I had to say to Mick, "Your
show is running late because Keith doesn't want to go on stage until
he gets a shepherd's pie." Mick said, "You can't be serious." And I
said, "I think I can on this occasion."' The dish was finally borne
backstage amid scenes reminiscent of a human-organ hospital mercy
dash, with a full-scale police escort and security guards barking in
to walkie-talkies, 'The pie is in the building!' As several well-placed
observers remarked, none of the Stones was entirely free of the kind
of whimsical self-indulgence that comes from being endlessly
humoured for twenty-five years. Keith was on top form at the
actual show that night, prowling around the vast stage, suddenly piv-
oting or launching in to a histrionic twist, as if he'd been prodded
with a defibrillator just out of camera shot. Jagger's own cherry
picker moment came in 'Sympathy', when he introduced himself
from atop a 100-foot-high scaffold. There was a section Mick then
spent off stage, as Keith led the band through a mini-set of 'Before
They Make Me Run' and 'Happy', trotting out his long public history of troubles and triumphs in his gravel-pit of a voice. In an
operation serviced by at least twelve accountants, part of a travelling

brains trust of 300, this was the show's starkly intimate climax. Some nights Keith substituted 'Little T&A', evincing all the self-confidence of a man with a pair of his wife's panties reportedly stuffed in his pocket.

Coincidentally, Paul McCartney was also touring America that winter, lacing his shows with Golden Greats (fifteen Beatles tunes, and an *Abbey Road* encore), energetically thrashing his mane around in the ravers and wielding a left-handed Hofner bass, just as he had in the 60s. 'It was a gas,' he confirmed to me. For all the wet seats and hot flushes, however, his concerts somehow failed to generate the sort of spontaneity or communal frenzy the Stones' did. It was hard to imagine McCartney starting a song in the wrong key, or shouting 'I got it!' as a solo approached. The one act presented a neatly mown lawn, the other a jungle. Keith walked on stage one night with his riff hand visibly smoking where a stray pyrotechnic spark had hit it, and continued to perform as his finger burned through to the bone. From there he went on to pump out half a dozen classic party tunes before stopping dead and breaking in to a husky cowboy ballad, all conducted under a dense cloud of Marlboro smoke. Ron Wood, for his part, sometimes seemed to lose a little zing in the bigger halls. One minute he'd be centre stage, hitting the shrill solo of 'Tumbling Dice', striking at his guitar in tiny, shocked gestures while smoking a fag and evincing his usual good cheer. Next minute he'd be slumped on the amps, his mind wandering, and an entire number, possibly involving Mick changing in to a gold-lamé suit to sing 'Ruby Tuesday', would go by unnoticed. Bill remained a law to himself, his stone face like a tranche of old ham retrieved from the back of the fridge, content to stand in place for two hours effortlessly playing his similarly – and brilliantly – steady bass. As usual, Charlie rarely drew attention to himself, but his playing had a rubbery power, and was based in rhythmic ideas. For long stretches, Keith parked in front of the drum kit and locked in to a groove.

The chaotic American rock and roll tour scene where the Stones had disported themselves for so long had, like the band itself, changed significantly by 1989. But it still had its moments. On a

night-time helicopter flight in to Washington DC, the band's pilot
complained that the smoke from Keith's and Ron's home-rolled
cigarettes was so thick that he couldn't see his instrument panel –
laughed off at the time, if not two years later when Bill Graham died
in similar circumstances. Four sold-out shows followed at the LA
Coliseum, with Guns N' Roses opening for the Stones after
Aerosmith declined the honour. Eric Clapton came backstage at
Shea Stadium in New York with his girlfriend Carla Bruni. A stun-
ningly svelte brunette, at twenty-two exactly half his age, she'd
recently left a Swiss art school in order to become a model. Clapton
said to Jagger: 'Please, Mick, not this one – I think I'm in love.' By
and large, the great blues guitarist and lothario ascribed the Stones'
successes to technique and marketing, not musical conviction, and
he knew full well that Jagger had once stepped out with his previous long-term companion, and later wife, Pattie Boyd. Mick
assured him that nothing like that would happen here. But by the
time Clapton came to sit in with the Stones at the Atlantic City
convention centre six weeks later, he was forced to do so in the
knowledge that his latest flame, and the future First Lady of France,
was watching the show from the comfort of Mick's private backstage nook. The Stones themselves had initially refused to play at the
faded seaside resort, but changed their minds after Donald Trump
offered them $6million to do so. Trump in turn charged fans $250
a seat, which was roughly nine times more than elsewhere on the
tour. Most of the American public was only too happy to welcome
back the band after a biblical-seeming seven years' absence. But that
wasn't entirely the case here. 'To put it mildly, the Stones impressed
me as a bunch of major jerks,' Trump later wrote, among other
unappreciative remarks, miffed, apparently, that the band had threatened to leave the building if he came anywhere near them.

After four months of impeccable musicianship and fairground
scenery, it all ended there. Three and a half million customers saw
the Stones in sixty shows, with tickets and merchandising grossing
$98million and $40million respectively. It was the most lucrative
rock and roll tour yet staged. The sheer scale of the enterprise guaranteed not just money, but a certain degree of backbiting. Keith,

who wasn't keen on the idea of being sponsored, fumed at having to line up every night to shake hands with beer executives, dubbing the wheeling-dealing Mick 'a smart little motherfucker'. Some of their differing views on high finance weren't so much aired as shouted out. The usual factions formed. 'Mick and Keith's obsession with one another went off the chart,' says a Stones manager. 'Whatever Keith said to Wood, Mick had to know. Whatever Mick said to Clifford, Keith had to know.' Another tour insider likened the core atmosphere to being 'either in Mick's gang or Keith's gang at a dysfunctional boarding school'. Meanwhile, Jagger was playing more and more guitar onstage. Richards told friends that Mick was OK on acoustic, but wasn't to be trusted anywhere near electricity. Jagger's private little tuning room was quickly christened 'the house of God'. Towards the end of his life, Bill Graham remarked that the 'singing businessman' had set the tone and evoked the attitudes that made his own departure from the Stones organisation inevitable. 'But there was another side to Mick that made him a considerable figure and accounts for the Stones surviving all the pitfalls. I admired the self-discipline by which he wrested a sense of direction from the druggy Seventies. He saw the band through one crisis after another.' On the last time they met, Graham, in a simple and eloquent tribute, smiled at Mick, nodded, and doffed his hat to him.

On 5 February 1990, the Stones flew in to Tokyo, watched the Mike Tyson–Buster Douglas title fight six days later, and then played ten sold-out *Steel Wheels* shows. The crowds, a mixture of dour salarymen, mothers and kids, applauded warmly before lapsing – as if by prearranged signal – in to total silence. Even Mick, who had done solo gigs in Japan, looked uncomfortable in the reverential hush between songs. For Keith the greatest shock may have been the 6 p.m. showtime, an hour when he'd been known to be starting breakfast. After a Caribbean break followed by a week's rehearsal at a Norman château, the band played forty-five European gigs that summer. Mick talked to the press about staying fit, while Keith got headlines about how ravaged he looked compared to his last home-town concerts. He had lived far more than eight years since 1982.

A sulky Bill Wyman was rightly concerned about his young wife. Mandy Smith was now in a London clinic suffering from 'multiple allergy problems [that] caused stress to our marriage', Bill wrote in his memoirs, a wild understatement. Compounding his misery, after three years in the RAF and thirty on the road, Bill had now developed a fear of flying. The award-winning British architect Mark Fisher came up with a pared-down set for the new shows, which Jagger named the *Urban Jungle* tour. He was still given plenty of toys to work with: a staircase he ran up and down, girders to swing from, and big balloons to prod with a stick. The only thing Mick didn't do was bungee-jump. Yet although he set a benchmark for spectacle, he was also hip enough to ensure that, for the most part, the props supported the music, not vice versa. Opening night, in Rotterdam, was a killer. The Stones miraculously turned the Olympic Stadium in to a dark and sweaty rock club, with a whirling mosh pit and even the occasional flannel-clad stage diver.

In Berlin, Jagger rashly told Richards that the crowd that night was the largest the Stones had ever played to. Keith turned the amps up to bazooka level, and Mick would soon start working with an earplug on his left side. Back in London, the Stones' old Dartford friend Dick Taylor enquired if his band the Pretty Things could support them at Wembley Stadium. As Taylor waited for a reply, Mick was giving a series of interviews that dwelt on what he called the 'constant shit' of reliving the past (he was against it). Shortly after that, a young band named Gun, currently enjoying a top forty disco hit, was announced as the Stones' London warm-up. On the night of 4 July, Mick sang 'Ruby Tuesday' to an incongruous 70,000-strong Wembley roar as news came in of an England goal in that night's World Cup semi-final tie against West Germany in Turin. By the time 'Satisfaction' came around, the fists shaken aloft stretched up to the highest stands, and off-key audience participation nearly drowned out the band. England lost their match on penalties.

The Stones went through some hard times that summer. There was a recession on, as well as a monsoon, which led to a steep decline in business. In Rome, Mick celebrated his forty-seventh birthday in front of an audience of three or four thousand dotted around the Stadio Flamino. There were conflicting reports about the rate of trade in Spain and France. The band did, however, perform to 110,000 rock and roll-starved fans in Prague, at the personal invitation of Václav Havel. A ticket to the 19 August show also acted as a one-day visa for the crowds travelling west from Poland and Hungary. Havel sent his private jet to pick up the Stones, and workmen erected a giant tongue logo in the nearby Břevnov hills, on a spot recently occupied by a statue of Stalin. There was a highly enthused crowd at the stadium that night. Havel introduced the band while sporting leather trousers and an *Urban Jungle* T-shirt, not an ensemble one would associate with his former Czech government strongmen. An effusive Keith Richards later remarked, 'It was us – rock and roll and blue jeans – that tore down the Berlin Wall' (which, while one takes his point, had actually fallen nine months earlier).

The tour finished at the end of that month, with two shows rearranged after Keith mysteriously injured a finger, exactly a year since the opening night in Philadelphia. Julien Temple broke off from shooting *Earth Girls are Easy* to film the final London concerts with 'rolling loop' Imax cameras. Nobody but Bill himself knew that they would be his last ever Stones gigs. Twenty-eight years earlier, he'd humped his gear on to a bus to make his debut at a Methodist youth hall in Putney, which had paid the band three pounds (filched by Brian) for its services. Now Bill went away in a limousine, with the press still on his case about Mandy and all her allergies.

The Stones tossed themselves an end-of-tour do at the Kensington Roof Gardens, where everyone drank champagne and wolfed kilos of caviar. They could afford it: for the year August 1989 to August 1990, Mick, Keith, Bill and Charlie made a conservatively estimated £11million apiece. When they ordered room service on the road, they often did so from another country: in Rome, it was pork sausages flown in from London's Fortnum and Mason; in Basle, crates of Guinness from Ireland. Apart from their casual crew of carpenters and drivers, the band were supporting thirty-two people full-time, whose mortgages they paid and whose retirement pensions they funded. Later that summer, the Stones were said to be set to tour Australia, but the shows were cancelled due to travel hassles and general burnout. In October, everyone finally got together for a forward-planning meeting, only for Bill Wyman to talk at length about the day when he'd be 'too old to be pumping out "Satisfaction"' – a day, he thought was, at fifty-four, fast approaching. According to Ron Wood, Wyman took the opportunity to air certain other long-standing artistic grievances. 'Bill said, "Fuck you lot, you didn't use any of my songs," and Keith was going, "Haven't you sussed that they're useless songs?"'

Long before the press woke up to the fact in the mid-60s, it was obvious that the Stones in general, and Mick Jagger in particular, had formed a withering contempt for the 'incestuous bartering-house for vested interests', as John Osborne had called the British ruling elite. Mick saw them as the arrogant, toffee-nosed scions of privilege, like the unnamed rich girl he pulverised so superbly in 1965's 'Play with Fire'.

   It was therefore not without amusement that the press discovered, as his tastes matured, that when Mick began to find pleasure in aristocratic society, those who were once the target of his satire became numbered among his closest friends. In a long article in the London *Evening Standard*, the huntsman-journalist Rory Knight Bruce now explained, in some detail, how 'Jagger Joined The Gentry'. There was talk of Mick 'hobnobbing' (a word that was to be slightly foreshortened in a sensational 1993 biography) with Princess Margaret, quizzing his youngest daughter's headmistress about the school's religious education, laying pipes of port rather than groupies, and spending most of his free time either counting his money or landscaping his French château. Mick himself demurred. 'I couldn't give a shit about gardening,' he told *Vanity Fair*. 'I think wine is so boring . . . nor do I play the stock market.' It's a truism that none of the other Stones, let alone the press and public, really knew the inner man. Each member of his entourage was acquainted with a slightly different Jagger, subtly adjusted to Mick's judgement of the individual or to his assessment of the person's background. If there was a through-line to his personality it was probably the dry and often underappreciated sense of humour, which often played on his own priapic, rock-stud image. When announcing the British *Urban Jungle* gigs in March 1990, Mick had capered up to the mike to face yet more bonk-related jibes. 'Maybe the babes don't fancy me any more,' he'd said, thus tucking the press neatly in to his pocket. When he came onstage nowadays people roared with glee, and he gave them just enough – a pelvic thrust, a mike stuffed down his pants – to signal that while it was only rock 'n' roll, the randy old goat was lurking just behind the performance. Sex succeeded where every other image, sooner or later, had failed. When Mick came to choose a new private secretary in the summer of 1990, the short-list boiled down to three equally well-qualified female candidates, named Smith, Snow and Crotch. The last got the job.

The Stones were back in the news that autumn: on 21 November, Mick and Jerry Hall (apparently overlooking the Carla Bruni episode, which she went on to parody in a shampoo commercial) went through a Balinese-beach wedding ritual. In the course of a six-hour ceremony, a holy man named Ida Banjar recited chants, burned incense and advised the respondents to embrace their karma. History fails to record whether, as tradition requires, the groom also beat his wife with a banana. After eleven years of bachelorhood, Mick was seemingly married again. Aristocratic languor 'wasn't his bag', however, he told *The Times*, and he was soon back in London working on the tapes of a new live album. Keith, by contrast, spent most of that winter with his family in Jamaica. Tasks included lying prone in his hammock overlooking the Caribbean, reading, toking, listening to Rasta drum music and strumming 'Guts', his Velazquez classical guitar. Charlie Watts began recording another jazz album, dedicated to Charlie Parker, and Bill Wyman published his memoirs, which made it clear that Bill had gotten less money but more sex than anybody else in the band. 'I could never understand his thing about counting women,' Keith remarked. 'What are you gonna do with a chick in ten minutes, for Chrissake? It takes them half that long to get their drawers off.' Bill and Mandy, whose weight was down to 5 stone, split up soon afterwards, with a reported £4million divorce settlement.

On 12 November, Ron Wood was driving back to London on the M4 after attending his father-in-law's funeral in Devon. Somewhere near Junction 15 outside Swindon, his Mercedes skidded in the rain and hit the back of another car. Woody got out to inspect the damage and was standing in the fast lane of the motorway exchanging views with the other driver when a third vehicle hit him, crushing his legs. Two weeks later, he was able to leave hospital in a wheelchair, giving a cheery thumbs-up and waving a bottle of Guinness for the waiting photographers.

In all, there was a mere three days' slog for the Stones in 1991. On 16 January, just as Allied bombers opened the first Gulf War, the band recorded its seventy-third single, entitled 'Highwire'. If nothing else, it managed to work up the editorial writer of the *Sun* in to a lather. Jagger's biting critique on arms dealing (allowing him to rhyme 'tank' with 'bank') was given the open-G treatment by Richards and a still convalescing Wood, and eventually made it to number 29 on the UK chart. Bill refused to appear on the video. Mick and Keith knocked off a James Brown riff for the B-side, which they called 'Sex Drive'.

In April the Stones accepted $5million to let 'Satisfaction' be turned in to an advertising jingle for Snickers chocolate and put out a vapid live album, *Flashpoint*. It was their fourth and final offering under their old contract. Walter Yetnikoff had had an explosive row with Amnesty International, apparently convinced they were anti-Semitic and possibly exacerbated by his self-admitted 'mountainous' daily coke habit, and then abruptly left CBS. The label itself was soon put on the block and sold to Sony. Richard Branson immediately began courting the Stones for Virgin Music, reportedly offering them $45million. While he was pondering that, Mick hired some lingerie models for a quick 'Sex Drive' video which was part Freud, part Benny Hill. The core ripped-panties theme got it banned in America.

Joe and Eva Jagger celebrated their fiftieth wedding anniversary that winter, and their elder son threw them a glittering party at a seafront hotel near their home in Margate. Eva told me that she and her husband had been thrilled by the 'solid gold chalice thingy' Mick presented them with, but that actually getting in to the do had been 'a nightmare'. A point is usually reached in a rock star's career – it came rather early in Jagger's – where he feels that his daily harassment by the media exhausts his tolerance for their company. As a result, a thick security screen was in place that evening, with the Stones' assistant Jim Callaghan presiding over the full tour apparatus of vast, hatchet-faced bodyguards, liveried chauffeurs and what Mrs Jagger labelled other 'Mob-like' personnel lining up at the head of a row of black limousines parked on Margate high street. Despite the precautions, Eva remembered 'several seedy individuals in raincoats' hovering around the edges of the room. A small ruckus ensued when a journalist introduced himself as 'Mick's brother' to Chris Jagger, but it passed when Callaghan intervened.

Mick and Jerry spent the rest of the winter in Atlanta, appearing alongside the likes of Emilio Estevez and Rene Russo in Geoff Murphy's lavishly budgeted feature *Freejack*. For the most part, this was impeccably acted but unconvincingly scripted, with much of the dialogue apparently on loan from Harold Pinter and at least one scene straight out of the *Carry On* series. Anthony Hopkins, who plays a villainous, mind-stealing millionaire, appears to have wandered in from some comic pastiche being shot on another planet entirely. For his first Hollywood starring role in twenty-two years, Mick chose a futuristic thriller in which healthy humans are catapulted through time to undergo mandatory brain transplants. Playing a black-clad mercenary paid to encourage unwilling donors, he was said to be 'the world's most unlikely hard man', 'a mincing travesty' and 'buttock-clenchingly awful' in a film described by the critic Barry Norman as 'urgently needing' a brain transplant of its own. Several papers were left to speculate that Jagger had taken the role only for the money. In May 1991, Mick paid £2.2million for Downe House, a lofty Georgian mansion opposite the Wick, craning out over Richmond Hill like a pop Berghof. It included ten bedrooms, six reception rooms, original Adam ceilings, a gym and a nursery. By midsummer, Jerry was pregnant again. Mick was also at work on his third solo album, which he called *Wandering Spirit*. A member of the production crew at Capitol studios in Los Angeles admiringly recalls that 'Jagger would be in the vocal booth hollering away. At the end of a take he'd pause, glance round and calmly begin discussing his taxes with Prince Rupert before again breaking off to take a phone call from Václav Havel. One day he exchanged telegrams with Boris Yeltsin. You want to know how much of a Renaissance man he was? I remember him dancing around to the music while someone from a gallery came in with these oil paintings for him to inspect, I presumed for [Downe House]. There was Mick bopping up and down, and meanwhile still carefully appraising the art. "Yes, that one . . ."' Jagger also entered in to talks with Tim Renton, the Conservative Government's arts minister, who he met at a trustees' dinner in the Nubian Room of the British Museum. The eventual result was Britain's inaugural National Music Day, which Mick announced at a parliamentary press conference on 12 February 1992. The first question he was asked was, 'Have you joined the Establishment?' It was exactly twenty-five years since the most famous bust of the 1960s had taken place at Redlands, with Jagger and Richards paraded to the public in handcuffs. Four months later, Mick brought the Music Day festivities to a climax in a short but twitchily charismatic concert at Hammersmith Odeon, accompanied by Charlie Watts and Ron Wood.

Meanwhile, Richard Branson duly signed the Stones to a £30million contract, with a guaranteed upfront payment of £4.5million for each of the band's next three albums. Virgin got the distribution rights to the back catalogue since *Sticky Fingers*. This was a significant cash commitment for a company whose most recent annual accounts recorded post-tax earnings of just £500,000, and assets of some £3million. On the night the deal was consummated Branson took Mick, Keith and Woody for a celebration dinner in a private room at Mosimann's in London. It broke up around 6 a.m. A light pre-dawn rain had begun to fall as the elfin, dark-haired rock stars and their statuesque blonde wives left the restaurant and drove away. Down the road through the drizzle you could see an unbroken line of early-morning commuters making their way to work on foot, on bicycles, or by car. Branson himself emerged with a wide grin. 'How do you feel?' he was asked. 'Tired,' he said, 'but happy.' Stories praising this apparent triumph of British entrepreneurship were splashed all over the morning's press. Those who questioned Virgin's finances, or the company's long-term commitment to its artists, were silenced by the threat of a writ.

Just over three months later, Virgin Music was sold to Thorn EMI for $1billion (£620million), the most ever paid for an independent company in England. Richard Branson used his windfall to start an airline. The Stones deal (which Bill Wyman failed to sign) would reap a quick dividend with *Jump Back*, the latest in a golden-greats continuum that began as long ago as *Big Hits (High Tide and Green Grass)* in 1966.

While Mick was working with the young hip-hop producer Rick Rubin (Run-DMC, Beastie Boys), Keith was in Seville as part of the Guitar Legend show that promoted the following year's Expo 92. Perhaps rashly, he and assorted Winos agreed to perform with Bob Dylan again. The short set that followed was greeted by a range of reactions (mainly shock) that had in common one underlying article of faith: that Dylan was a talented nutcase. Famous for playing his hits in unrecognisable format, he chose Seville to rehearse some completely fresh arrangements – during the concert. Later that night, a reporter asked Richards why Dylan would have done such a thing. 'Because he's a cunt,' Keith replied affably.

The Stones' various other satellite projects brought them a mixed press. After wrapping his latest jazz album, Charlie Watts went back to his farm and took the phone off the hook. In his few interviews, Charlie maintained that his family and his animals were what really mattered in life – the rest was just 'rock star bullshit', he told *Today*. Bill Wyman now had his burger restaurant and a new American-model girlfriend, Suzanne Accosta, who at thirty-two struck some sceptical observers as far too old for him. Bill took the opportunity to sell his former marital bed (which Mick Jagger himself had owned in the 60s) at auction for $24,740. 'I liked the look of it,' said the new owner, an advertising executive named Ray Gaffney. 'And it certainly has a colourful history.' Bill continued to insist that he had made his last public appearance with the Stones. Keith Richards theorised in print that, at fifty-six, his long-time colleague had gone round the bend – 'I reckon he's on his third menopause,' Keith noted.

In December 1991, Virgin put out *Keith Richards & The X-Pensive Winos at the Hollywood Palladium*, a 67-minute shot of the *Talk is Cheap* tour. After *Flashpoint*, it restored the live album's good name. Keith was back at the Rock and Roll Hall of Fame in New York's Waldorf Astoria that January, where he happened to run in to Andrew Loog Oldham in the lobby. With the deaths of Brian Jones and Ian Stewart, there was no institutional resentment against Oldham left in the Stones camp, even if Allen Klein was still heard to comment on the 'little shit' who had been among his most tenacious litigants in the late 1960s. When Keith saw his old manager coming through the door that night he strode over, held out a hand and welcomed him to the party. Oldham joined Anita Pallenberg, Marlon Richards and Chuck Berry at the head table for the ceremonies.

In February, Mick Jagger got pulled over at Narita airport in Tokyo, where he'd flown to promote *Freejack*. He was detained there, to much tabloid mirth, as a 'social deviant' and 'convicted drug felon'. The last time Jagger had been in dope trouble, *Let it Bleed* was climbing the chart and England were still world champions at football. Even so, he was subjected to a five-hour grilling. While investigators took Mick step by step over his entire life, justice ministry officials began debating his 22-year-old pot conviction, for which he had been fined £200. (They must have missed him when he slipped through to perform sold-out concerts in both 1988 and 1990.) After two days Japan finally declared Mick no threat to public morals, and allowed him to enter. *Freejack* died at the box office.

Mick's fifth child, named Georgia May, was born that month. Although Georgia made her appearance at the Portland Hospital in London and largely grew up at Downe House, her birth certificate lists her parents' 'usual domicile' as Mustique. Six months later,

Mick became a grandfather when 20-year-old Jade Jagger and her art-student boyfriend Piers Jackson had a daughter they named Assisi. Despite advancing age, Mick was still flying around the world pursuing girls as young as his two older children. In March, he was seen with a 'mystery teenage beauty' at the Amanpuri hotel in Phuket, prompting Jerry Hall to tell the press: 'I confronted him about it . . . A married man is supposed to be with his wife when she's just had a baby.' A degree of doubt surrounds Mick's own policy on the sanctity of his wedding vows, but in general he seems to have taken the relaxed approach. Later that spring, he was back in Paris for a candlelit-bistro dinner with Carla Bruni, amid a scrum of paparazzi and screaming Stones fans that deprived the occasion of its intended romantic intimacy. Jerry told the *Daily Mail* she was 'devastated' by the humiliation. A less restrained British tabloid then printed the contents of a note they claimed the long-suffering Mrs Jagger had written her husband. 'I want you to have your freedom and I won't be mad if you fuck other girls; I respect, admire, trust, need and love you' it said, among other effusions. Mick and Jerry were reportedly reconciled that summer at their French château, where he rigged up a home studio to cut some of the songs for *Wandering Spirit*. ('I'm as hard as a brick/Hope I never go limp' Mick insisted on the album's opening track.) 'I hope the man comes to his senses,' Keith Richards told *Vanity Fair*, when asked to comment on his old friend's love life. 'He should stop that now, the old black-book bit. Kicking fifty, it's a bit much, a bit manic.'

Keith, for his part, was rehearsing his new album, *Main Offender*. To kick off the creative process, he and the Winos sat around in Connecticut with their guitars, some drums and a case of Stoli, and let inspiration strike. One night the phone in the music room rang three or four times, each of them a wrong number. When someone answered it, a male voice muttered the word, 'Eileen?' Keith started chanting the name and soon set it to a lurching, Stonesy tune, proving his point that the best songs are often accidental. He broke from recording long enough to sit for an interview with Hunter S. Thompson (*Fear and Loathing*), a post-junkie version of a Thatcher–Reagan summit, in which the two principals were said to have communicated in a series of clicks, grunts and squeals – 'like the secret language of dolphins', *Rolling Stone* said. On 20 October 1992, Virgin put out *Main Offender* to warm reviews and tepid sales. Keith began a solo world tour a month later.★

While his fellow guitarist kept playing, Ron Wood put on art exhibitions in London, Dublin and Tokyo. One British critic described the work as 'post-A Level, pre-art school'. Another left with a terse, 'Embarrassing'. Wood had even less luck with his new solo album, *Slide on This*. No major record company wanted to take it, so the lead guitarist of the Rolling Stones had to hawk the tapes around from one specialist label to another. Eventually released on New Jersey-based Continuum Records in late 1992, *Slide on This* failed to chart in either the UK or the US, although it did enjoy a fleeting appearance in the lower reaches of the Japanese Hot 50. Woody was to have the last artistic laugh, however, because he went on to sell a portrait of the Stones in a Jacobean interior, *Beggar's Banquet*, to a private collector for a reported $1.2million. Charlie Watts in turn emerged from seclusion on his Devon farm to release his latest big-band album, which he promoted by a short coast-to-coast American tour. Settling behind his kit for a show at New York's Blue Note club in his three-piece zoot suit without removing his jacket or loosening his tie, it was hard to remember this silver-haired old gentleman was the drummer in the world's most notorious rock and roll band. In July 1992, the 'silent Stone', as he was billed, was to have appeared as the musical guest on NBC television's *Late Night with David Letterman*. This highly coveted spot would have exposed Charlie and his album to an audience of some 6 million potential customers, but it came with an important condition. In keeping with NBC policy, the show's in-house band would have to accompany him. The subsequent discussions had not proceeded far before it became apparent that Charlie would not be

---

★Although an agreeably loose band-leader, Keith once had cause to read the Riot Act to the Winos when it seemed to him they came too close to living up to their name during the *Main Offender* sessions. 'I began to realise,' he said, 'they were pushing it.' One of the musicians confirms this diagnosis. 'That got my attention. I thought, Fuck! Can you imagine Keith Richards telling you you're overdoing it?'

open to this arrangement. Minutes before the programme's scheduled air-time, he left the building with a muttered 'Fuck it' and
wandered off alone in to the warm New York night.

Keith Richards' theatre shows over the winter of 1992–93 stood
at the farthest remove from the Superdome-sized, flashy pomp rock
of *Steel Wheels* days. Playing material mostly from his two solo
albums, Keith threw in some Eddie Cochran and Elvis covers and
a run-out section including 'Happy' and snatches of 'Brown Sugar'.
The familiar formulae were made fresh again by the spare arrangements, with an absence of gospel choirs and, for that matter, of
60-foot-high blow-up dolls and flame-throwers. Old chestnuts like
'Gimme Shelter' sounded as strong as ever, all the better in fact for
being given the lean treatment rather than the stadium glitz.
Although Keith and the band continued to perform to ecstatic
response, there was still no escaping his 'other brand'. At least once
a night, a cry of 'Mick!' or 'Satisfaction!' would surge up from the
stalls.

In Seattle, Keith lurched on in a ruby-red jacket, skinny black suit
pants and distressed boots, his grey hair corralled by a thin red head-
band. He roamed around as he played, sometimes crouching down,
spinning, then shooting sideways like a demented crab. Carefully
polished jokes filled out the gaps between songs. 'Where's my ash-
tray?' Keith growled at one point. A roadie scuttled on stage with
the required item. This was enough to make Keith decide that he
also needed a large glass of vodka, which he drank in one slurp, to
inevitable whoops from the crowd. He eventually ended the concert smiling lopsidedly at the audience and hugging his guitar.
Richards and the Winos went on to play London on 18 December,
his forty-ninth birthday. Mick Jagger came but got hassled by the
press, leaving early. Bill Wyman couldn't make it.

Although Jagger and Richards were as busy with extracurricular
projects in 1992–93 as they had been five years earlier, there was
one important difference this time around. Through all the recent
solo activities, neither Mick nor Keith had ever threatened to leave
the Stones. Nor did they now. Keith told the *New York Times* that
after thirty years the 'old buggers' were still a testament to the power

of creative harmony and brotherly squabbling that seems to have begun almost the moment they met at Dartford station. 'I love my kids and my wife most of the time,' Keith noted elsewhere. 'Music I love all the time. It's the only constant joy in my life. You're never alone with a guitar. It's the one thing you can count on.'

On 9 February 1993, Mick Jagger released his album *Wandering Spirit*. Keith told friends that this one, with its three old soul covers and an Irish sea shanty, wasn't too bad. Although *Wandering Spirit* also had its quota of balls-out rockers, much of Jagger's original material was slow-paced, with pensive lyrics that explored themes of betrayal and domestic upheaval. 'It was love in a minute, it was love in a flash/It brings me no pleasure, just a stab in the back', he sings on 'Don't Tear Me Up', wherein Mick suggests he's been cruelly used by his woman. 'Love is fragile', he notes elsewhere on the album, before complaining in a third song, 'I was your ever-present fool/You turned the heat off and left me standing/Freezing by your swimming pool'. Whatever one makes of the notion of Jagger-the-dupe-in-love, these were some of the stronger songs of any Stones solo album. But as the records themselves got better, their sales performance got worse. *Wandering Spirit* enjoyed only a week in the British chart, and its first single, 'Sweet Thing', stalled at number 84 on the *Billboard* Hot 100. Keith was sympathetic. Leading the Winos around the world had given him new insight in to what 'Brenda' went through with the Stones. The Glimmer Twins got together at Mick's West 81st home in New York later that month. It was now nearly four years since *Steel Wheels*.

'We sat around,' Keith recalled. 'I say, "I got stuff." He says, "Yeah, I got stuff." I came out with one word – focus. We're looking down the same scope this time, we've got all the other ingredients, what we need to do is *focus*.'

At that point Bill Wyman publicly left the Stones, by announcing it live on the television show *London Tonight*. Jagger was thought to be relaxed at the news, but Richards wasn't pleased. Keith put out feelers, got Bill on the phone, told him he was making a big mistake. 'You're walking away from millions of quid,' he said. Still no joy: Bill announced he was getting married again, thinking about starting a blues band and maybe writing another tell-all book. Compounding the fallout from his recent divorce, Wyman's son Stephen, then thirty-one, had gone on to announce his engagement to 47-year-old Patsy Smith, who was none other than Mandy Smith's mother. (Had both romantic partnerships flourished, Bill would have become his son's son-in-law, Mandy would have become both Stephen's step-mother and step-daughter, and Patsy would have become Mandy's daughter-in-law as well as her mother; clearly a ticklish situation for all parties.) There were no more phone calls. The Stones had to deal with only their third team change in thirty-one years.

While Wyman pulled the plug, Keith went back on the road with the Winos for another five weeks, then joined Mick in Barbados to kick songs around and audition bass players. Many Stones fans felt Bill's departure gave Mick and Keith the chance to correct a twenty-year-long error by bringing Mick Taylor back in to the band and switching Ron Wood to bass, the instrument he'd originally played in the Jeff Beck group. Having recently completed treatment at a methadone clinic on Hollywood Boulevard and moved back to England in search of work, Taylor, now forty-four, might have seemed the logical choice. But, as Tom Keylock once said, 'The Stones don't give a shit. It's like the Mafia. They never forget who's crossed them and, once you do, there's no way back.' After several fruitless cattle-calls in New York and London, 30-year-old Darryl Jones finally walked through the door. He was Miles Davis' old bass player, who'd gone on to work with Sting in his bebop phase before touring with the likes of Eric Clapton, Peter Gabriel and Madonna. Charlie, thrilled at the jazz connection, soon voted him in. Jones was hep, black and American. He'd never seen the Stones play. Their first single came out before he was born. However, Mick and Keith put him on wages (said to be $200,000 a tour) like Taylor and Wood before him. After nineteen years and over Mick's reported objection, Woody himself was finally cut in on the action, with points instead of a salary. He celebrated his promotion by promptly disposing of two bottles of vodka. Not long after that, Wood's manager Nick Cowan took him to a doctor in Harley Street for his obligatory annual medical exam. 'When the doctor asked Ron how many units of alcohol he consumed on a regular basis, he started totting up, beginning with draught Guinness and finishing up with late-night vodkas. The doctor looked at the numbers and commented, "Not too bad. As far as the insurance company is concerned, it's about within the acceptable range of units per week." "Per week?" Ronnie replied. "That's my *daily* intake."'

On 9 July 1993 the Stones went to work in earnest, recording at Windmill Lane studios down by the Dublin docks and often unwinding at Wood's nearby home pub. There were some rockin', *Exile*-type songs, with the originals replaced by new tunes that tried to conjure the spirit – if not the substance – of classics like 'Rocks Off', with a few forays ('Blinded by Rainbows') in to social comment. And for the romantically inclined there was Mick's crooning on 'Sparks Will Fly'. (Lyric: 'Gonna fuck your sweet ass!') The band worked at top speed throughout. Keith lived, just as he had twenty years ago in Richmond, in Woody's staff cottage. Later in July, everyone broke for a day to celebrate Mick's fiftieth birthday at a French Revolutionary ball, complete with guillotine – 'for the press', Jerry Hall (dressed as Marie Antoinette) explained.

After that it was back to New York, and then on to Charlie Chaplin's old studios in Hollywood to finish *Voodoo Lounge*, as the new album was being called. At Mick's invitation, the forty-year-old, shock-haired American writer-producer Don Was ('Walk the Dinosaur') came to the final sessions. Keith went ballistic, treating Was to an extended speech on why, nothing personal, he wasn't needed. Was walked out thinking, 'At least I've got something to tell my grandchildren.'

Two days later, Keith phoned him back as though nothing had happened. Was co-produced *Voodoo Lounge*.

Working with the Stones, Was agreed, was very cool. It was also quite strange. When Mick and Keith arrived in the studio 'they'd exchange notes about a soccer match for maybe thirty seconds and then go to opposite corners of the room'. It was left to Was himself to give shape to the vague, seemingly never-ending jams that constituted a typical Stones session, and to mediate between the various band members' cryptic instructions to find a mutually acceptable sound. At one stage, Mick announced that he wanted a faultlessly hip new album of 'groove songs, African licks and stuff'. Keith had more of an 'Elvis vibe' in mind. Charlie expressed no particular preference but, for once, wanted his drums turned up louder. Was presumed that the Stones must be getting together when he wasn't around in order to plan the sessions, but later found out this wasn't the case. 'The only time any of them called one of the others was when Keith hit a speed dial wrong at the Sunset Marquis and Mick was staying at a rented house in the hills and he called Mick and asked for more ice. He thought it was room service.'

When the album finally wrapped, Keith and Woody celebrated by gracing the launch party for Pete and Dud's latest video, which they held on the top floor of the Cobden Working Men's Club in west London. Kensal Road had seen nothing like it since the Coronation. The two Stones arrived in a hand-built 1920s coach, surrounded by five enormous bouncers. Once upstairs, Richards sank several pints and then moved on to the Stoli, impressing even his well-oiled hosts. Peter Cook suggested adding a splash of tonic, but Keith refused, apparently scandalised at the suggestion. 'I don't want to rust,' he said.

On 3 May 1994, the Stones chugged in to New York to announce their twelfth American tour. It was one of the slickest press events since the days of Colonel Parker, if not P.T. Barnum. In the past the band had sparked riots at the airport, snarled up downtown traffic, and, in 1989, brought Grand Central station to a halt. Twenty years before that, Sam Cutler gave them the world heavyweight rock and roll title every night as they hit the stage. This time around, the Stones commandeered the Kennedys' old yacht *Honey Fitz* and bore down on Battery Park like some latter-day British Invasion. The subsequent news conference revealed that age had done nothing to impair their legendary self-confidence. Mick remarked truthfully that 'We're still a fucking good band' and went on to comment disparagingly on the late Kurt Cobain. The prince of grunge and mouthpiece for a generation had committed suicide just a month earlier. According to friends, Cobain had been in a dark mood in the days leading up to his death over reports that both the Stones and the Eagles were set to break American box-office records that summer, commenting acidly, 'We might as well not have happened,' although there were certainly other contributory pressures on him at the end. Elder-statesman reaction to the tragedy was near unanimous. Paul McCartney, Eric Clapton and Bono all sympathised, and Neil Young wrote a moving tribute. David Bowie called Kurt's loss 'one of [the] really crushing blows in my life'. Mick wasn't impressed. As far as he was concerned, 'The guy had a death wish.'

'Go screw the press and their slagging about the Geritol tour,' Keith soon added, in equally feisty vein. 'You assholes. Wait till you get our age and see how you run. I got news for you, we're still a bunch of tough bastards. String us up and we still won't die.'

Keith and his band spent that summer in, of all places, Toronto. Rehearsals began there, in a converted school gym just 5 miles from the scene of the crime in 1977, a 'shithole' he had once promised never to revisit. The Stones chose Canada because it was a 'cool vibe', Mick insisted, but also because they had only six-month US work visas and no wish to interact with the American tax authorities any more than was strictly necessary, if even then.

'Don't worry about copying Wyman,' Keith immediately told Darryl Jones. Jones took that as a vote of confidence, and soon jazzed things up with some snappily done bass licks. Richards then put the new-look Stones through their paces for six weeks. The basic routine was that a roadie would chalk up a song title on a blackboard, while a colleague would sort through a stack of CDs and cue up the track in question – 'Rocks Off', say, from *Exile*. As the classic basement riff boomed over the PA, Keith and Woody then began playing along, tracing the original recording. Charlie in turn picked up the beat and Mick, reading from a lyric book, crooned the verse about his orgasmic dancer friend. Within a minute or two, the old Stones were letting it rip like the young ones. They had the full showband sound, too, with Chuck Leavell, Bobby Keys, two singers and a horn section. Matt Clifford wasn't invited back. Watching a group of taciturn, middle-aged million-aires pottering around a Canadian gym may not sound like a riveting experience, but it had its moments. No semi-public appear-ance by Mick Jagger could be without its accompanying mob of press and photographers, and Charlie enlivened the experience of clocking on and off for rehearsals by the expedient of hanging an old-fashioned shop's 'Open' or 'Closed' sign in front of his kit. Drummers, like goalkeepers, are a bit different.

Elsewhere, in a Toronto aircraft hangar, Mark Fisher and his crew were at work on the latest state-of-the-art stage, a towering bazaar complete with two mainframe computers that stored and executed all the lighting instructions. According to Mick, the basic design this time around said something about the twenty-first century, 'with the future as clean and cool and very, very upbeat'. (If so, the fore-cast must have changed since the wholesale decay of the *Urban Jungle* set.) As well as the 90-ton sound system and 300-foot-long banks of video screens, there was a fire-spewing cantilevered steel arch known as 'the Cobra' positioned over the performers. This delightfully wacky concept was part of a travelling company that would operate for thirteen months in twenty-five countries, selling 8 million seats. In 1989, Michael Cohl had packaged an all-in deal that guaranteed the Stones around $70million. He promised them even more this time.

As a gesture to the whole spectacle, Keith Richards agreed to dye his hair black.

Out that July, *Voodoo Lounge*. What's a band to do when one of its songs is used in a Snickers commercial? Get down and dirty, from all indications. The Stones' twentieth studio album finally earns them a coveted Parental Advisory sticker for some choice lyrics about blood, guts and 'alcoholic cunts', as well as a rubbery sex-toy logo and generally hideous artwork. The music is surprisingly accomplished. After thirty years, most of the familiar chord pro-gressions somehow aren't so much derivative as pleasantly expected, even archetypal – most obviously on crunching rockers like 'Sparks Will Fly' or the 'Lady Jane'-like 'New Faces'. *Voodoo Lounge* also aims for breadth: the album opens with 'Love Is Strong', a good rockin' confection of booming drums, harp breaks and strategic guitar bursts, and winds up with Keith's 'Thru And Thru', a slow blues that wobbles about, barely scaling the ladder to songhood, but eventually turns out highly musical, poetic and sad. Between them, Jagger, Richards and Don Was gave the whole thing a dank, sub-terranean feel, as if they had finally cut out the in-between steps and recorded it in a bank vault. (Mick later complained that his co-producers were too retro, and specifically too *Exile*, for his tastes.) *Voodoo Lounge* was a number one in Britain and went to number 3 in America, selling five million copies, figures that would have sent modern pop gods in to ecstasies. Keith was stoked by the record, and especially generous about Mick's harp playing. 'That was one of our original instruments,' he told *Rolling Stone*. 'And his phrasing is so uncanny. If that can roll over on to the vocals ... After all,' Keith rasped, 'it's just pushing air out of your mouth.'

The tour opened on 1 August, with 55,000 spectators spending an average of $60 and $35 apiece on tickets and merchandising respectively, meaning that the $3million stage paid for itself on its first night. An hour before each concert there was a meet and greet with Budweiser reps and a few lucky VIPs – a Bill Clinton, say, or Brad Pitt. It was generally all over in sixty seconds. Then a sacred half-hour when Keith and Woody shut themselves away in the tuning room. Much concurrent activity backstage as bouncers clear the area of all 'non-essential personnel', a task accomplished with no more fuss than usually attends the change of government of a small country. Then they're ready. Three of the Stones come out draped in foppish floor-length hunting coats, tight pants and boots, and stride off confidently towards the stage. Charlie, dressed for church, sits down at his kit. As a rule, the crowd still has no idea that the show is about to start: they're all too busy screaming at the flame-belching Cobra. The lights dim and there's an almighty roar.

'*I'm gonna tell ya,*' Mick crows, '*how it's gonna be.*'

It's the old, potent spell, big magic. That one phrase sets the night

up. Omigod! They're *right there!* Jagger struts out, and does a wiggle
or two. The band punch up the grainy chords of 'Not Fade Away'.
Intercut with this is a bank of flashing lights, screens and various
explosions. Everything is amped up to the pain threshold. The
Rolling Stones are back to work.

After the opening stomp Keith comes on full tilt with 'Shattered'
and 'Rocks Off'. The first half-hour is irresistible. There seem to
be several Mick Jaggers, all on different parts of the stage, yelling
optimistically '*Yeahh!*' and 'It's a *gas!*' Costumed in cherry red, he
shrieks and honks his way through 'Tumbling Dice' and 'Live With
Me', before, perhaps inevitably, things slump in mid-set. Live, there
are various hoops the Stones feel obliged to jump through, presumably in the interests of selling the new album. Jagger screams, he
spins, he does the mashed potato – but 'Sparks Will Fly' remains
stubbornly earthbound. Rows of coloured light bulbs twinkle
behind him like those of a vast Christmas display. The song ends to
polite applause. 'Everything OK?' asks Mick, still clinging to ves-
tiges of his optimism. Usually a great ad-libber between numbers,
now he had professional joke-writers, on loan from his friend Lorne
Michaels, the producer of *Saturday Night Live*. Mick must have
finally prevailed over Keith when it came to the stilt walkers,
because on opening night two of them, male and female, tottered
out during 'Monkey Man'. Both parties seemed to be dressed as
devils, with a variety of horns and tails, and, in the woman's case,
a pair of pointy breasts that caught Mick a sharp blow to the top of
his head when she leaned down to kiss him. The stilt walkers didn't
appear again during the tour. For fast rockers like 'Start Me Up',
everything was bathed in white; for ballads like 'Angie', it was dark
purple. After Mick, Keith and Ron indulge in a bit of Status Quo-
like shtick, riffing in unison during 'I Go Wild', the band kick back
in with a bazooka-rock finale. 'Honky Tonk Women' goes down
a storm. In the last verse, Keith sidles up behind Chuck Leavell and,
gently nudging him to keep playing at the low end of the keyboard,
reaches in to pick out a wickedly funky right-handed solo.
'Sympathy' erupts against a backdrop of giant dolls, among them
Elvis and the Thug goddess Kali. There are fast changes, lashings of

smoke and mirrors, and the great call-and-response rave-up in
'Brown Sugar'. The night ends in a choric 'Jumpin' Jack Flash'.

Striking a balance between the technical and the emotional, it
was a cleverly packaged concert and a wildly successful tour.
According to those who helped handle their finances, the Stones'
other sources of income over and above basic ticket and merchandising sales in the period August 1994 to August 1995 included a
pay-per-view TV special, two lavishly budgeted nights at the MGM
Grand Casino in Las Vegas – their first concerts ever in the city –
and a robust 'market penetration' campaign, as Michael Cohl called
it, which meant you could buy *Voodoo Lounge* tour jackets not just
outside the stadium but at your local mall, priced at $525. And if,
for instance, you were one of the lucky Stones insiders with a 'VIP'
backstage pass, it still didn't mean that you were actually there as the
band's guest. Even if your name was Jerry Hall or Patti Richards,
you still had to pay for your seat. Literally everything was geared to
maximising the tour's profits, whether it be charging family and
friends a handling fee for the privilege of dealing with the Stones'
own travelling ticket-lady rather than the public box-office, or Mick
negotiating for Keith and him to appear on American television's
top-rated teen show, *Beverly Hills 90210*, presumably in an effort to
familiarise the 'Generation X' crowd with a band already famous
before many of them were born. Michael Cohl's memo to the
troops of 5 October 1994 captures some of the basic flavour of the
enterprise. 'The main benign messages we need to disseminate,' he
wrote, 'are: 1) sell the remaining tickets, 2) publicize the pay per
view, 3) generate merchandise awareness . . . All [other] considerations should be tied to these three points.' 'Benign' was an odd word
to apply to a sales and marketing campaign that had the same general sense of momentum as a Sherman tank. Nowadays, the Stones
were less likely to cavort backstage with drug dealers and groupies
than they were with their numerous business managers and handlers. On 19 October, Richard Branson threw a party for the band
at the American Legion Hall in Hollywood, which made the scene
at the Cobden working club look self-effacing by comparison.
According to Bill German, a journalist who travelled with the

Stones, 'Branson was seated on a giant pillow, playing sitar, as Egyptian-looking servants fed him grapes and fanned him with large feathers.'

Some 3 million fans bought tickets for the North American tour, which ended on 18 December in Vancouver, where the crowd sang 'Happy Birthday' to Keith. Each of the Stones took home around $19million for his previous four and a half months' work. While they were on the road that autumn, the band's old piano player Nicky Hopkins (*Beggar's Banquet, Exile*) died of complications following stomach surgery, aged fifty. In recent years Hopkins had publicly complained that he'd only ever received 'peanuts' for his recording services, although there is no evidence he had any particular sessions in mind. A month later, Jimmy Miller, the band's producer of the same period, succumbed to liver failure. He was fifty-two.

On 14 January 1995, riots broke out around the Rodriguez stadium in Mexico City. Some 15,000 ticketless fans wanted to get inside and watch the Stones. It was the same in Brazil, Argentina, Chile and South Africa. All sellouts. The band spent a similarly productive March in Japan, and April in Australia. On May Day, a planned gig in Beijing was called off because of visa hassles.

'I got some shit from the Chinese Government saying why I couldn't come,' said Keith Richards, never one for fine details. 'Number one on the list is "Cultural Pollution" and about number thirty is "Will cause traffic jams". And in between is a whole load of other crap.'

In May, the Stones, billed as the Toe-Tappers & Wheel Shunters Band, recorded and filmed two acoustic gigs in the relatively bijou setting of Amsterdam's Paradiso club. After Las Vegas, the 550-seat, partially converted cannabis café must have felt like somebody's back room. Added to some songs similarly given the *Unplugged* treatment at EMI studios in Tokyo, these would go on to make up the best live Stones album since *Get Yer Ya-Ya's Out!* The full *Voodoo Lounge* express then got under way again in Stockholm. Volkswagen paid a reported $10million to sponsor the summer's thirty-nine sold-out gigs. Hitler's favourite car firm took the opportunity to launch the 'Fabulous VW Golf Rolling Stones-Mobile', a limited edition saloon with the tongue logo stitched in to the seat fabric, and psychedelic purple floor carpeting. It was a rather dire addition to an otherwise stunning tour.

By and large, the Stones stuck to the well-rehearsed set, enthralling most fans, offending others with the MGM staging, but with a few novelties. Back from the archive: 'Connection', 'I'm Free', 'Let It Bleed'. An acoustic medley dotted the wastes of the stadium din. In a self-referential nod, they started doing Bob Dylan's 'Like a Rolling Stone'. (Dylan himself was the band's warm-up at a stadium show in the south of France.) There was a gig in Sheffield – the Stones' first on home turf in five years – then three more at Wembley. Keith Richards threw a small backstage party there an hour before curtain-up. Everyone from John Major to Jimmy Phelge (an Edith Grove flatmate in 1962 and the inspiration for the 'Nanker Phelge' company name) stood in a lavishly furnished tent and waited for Keith to change out of his street clothes in to his nearly identical stage gear. When the host arrived he was in good spirits. Someone innocently mentioned Marianne Faithfull's new autobiography, in which she extolled Keith's lovemaking technique, and someone else noted that Marlon Richards and his wife were expecting their first child. 'I'm joinin' the crowd,' Keith cackled. 'Designing my little grandpa suit. I'll get a bag of candy in the pocket and grow a beard or something.'

After the tour Mick Jagger went off on an extended cricket holiday with his family. Breaking away from her book-signing duties, Marianne Faithfull appeared one afternoon at Wormsley, Paul Getty's private ground, where, perhaps fortified over the tea interval, she assured Mick's 82-year-old mum that her son, too, had been 'great in bed'. Keith went back to Jamaica and started recording some tropical grooves and reggae chants, which he eventually turned in to an album called *Wingless Angels* and released on his own label, Mindless Records. Ron Wood had a cancer scare but went on to throw a Christmas party at his home in Ireland that accounted for 1,600 bottles of Guinness. Charlie

Watts' mother died. Charlie quietly dealt with the loss, said nothing to the press, and then went off with his wife on an African safari. Apparently miffed that Mick had told a Wembley audience, 'I know you're worried about our new bass player, but this one dances and smiles,' Bill Wyman began commenting that his old band were a bunch of farts, who most people saw by aiming binoculars at a giant video screen.

The tour album *Stripped* followed in November. In a tribute to the staying power of classic rock, it went gold in the same week as the latest Elvis release and the Beatles' *Anthology*. In December, the German weekly *Der Spiegel* rashly claimed that the Stones' guitarists had been in the habit of miming certain *Voodoo Lounge* shows to backing tracks. Keith erupted with blowpipe fury, threatened to sue, and the magazine soon admitted it had made a ghastly error. Later that winter, the Canadian Government launched a criminal probe in to allegations that Michael Cohl had charged a three-dollar surplus on each ticket sold at two Stones concerts in Toronto, which, if true, would have meant he pocketed something like $340,000 over the course of a weekend. Nothing was ever proved, but he was obliged to sell some of his corporate stock back to Labatt's. After that, Cohl's production company underwent a name change to become The Next Adventure, Inc, and immediately began preparing a new Stones tour. Meanwhile, Microsoft paid the band $5million to use 'Start Me Up' in its latest advertising campaign. Mick and Keith turned down an offer of 'a million or two' to write music for the new Bond film.

When Allen Klein finally got around to releasing the album and video of *The Rolling Stones Rock and Roll Circus* in October 1996, twenty-eight years after the event, it fulfilled a long-time hope shared by the project's copyright owners and the fans. The Stones themselves were apparently less thrilled by what Mick had called the 'constant shit' of reliving their past. Although Klein hosted a lavish premiere for the film at New York's Public Theater with a variety of lion-tamers, fire-eaters and other less obviously themed entertainers on display in the lobby, none of the band attended.

A week later, Mick Jagger incorporated his own movie production company – Jagged Films – and went on to buy the Robert Harris novel *Enigma*, which Tom Stoppard would adapt for the screen. Mick was soon seeing the actress Uma Thurman in LA and getting HEART OF STONE headlines back home, where Jerry Hall consulted a lawyer. In January 1997, the rock star with the Herculean libido felt sufficiently secure of his masculinity to put on a dress and appear as a faded drag queen in Sean Mathias' gay concentration camp film *Bent*. Many of the professional critics were impressed by Mick's counter-intuitive performance, and there was even talk of an Oscar nomination. Keith Richards, by contrast, thought it a 'fucking joke'.

Meanwhile, the Charlie Watts Quintet finished a tour of Japan. Woody was resting between projects. Keith took the opportunity to call a band meeting in New York.

Right away, tension. Mick wanted to produce films and record a fourth solo album, rather than spend half the rest of his life 'turning in to a fucking oldies jukebox', as he once put it, with the Stones – and besides, it was still too soon after *Voodoo Lounge*. The Virgin reps balked, talking instead about market share and reworking the proven album-tour-video formula. For once, Keith and the suits were as one. With Michael Cohl speaking of a potential $300million payday, netting each Stone around $35million, Mick was soon able to clear his diary and join the other band members in a Greenwich Village rehearsal studio. In March 1997, everybody was back in Barbados, at the start of the old cycle. Keith was making it up as he went along, while Mick was sitting in his villa painstakingly writing more and more songs about his love life. He again wanted a sharp, digital sound to prevail, and hired hipsters like Danny Saber (Busta Rhymes, Black Grape) and the Dust Brothers to co-produce the new album. This gave Keith the opportunity to share some thoughts on what he termed 'techno-geeks' and 'knob-twiddlers' who, ideally, should never have been let near the Stones. 'You say Dust Brothers,' he growled, 'I say ashes to ashes.' Back in Hollywood's Ocean Way studio, Keith bumped in to Kenny 'Babyface' Edmonds on his way in to the control room one night.

Jagger had invited the 37-year-old prodigy behind Paula Abdul and Toni Braxton to lend another ear to the proceedings. 'You cut with Mick,' Keith told him, 'your face is gonna look like *mine*. You may be Babyface now, but you're gonna be *Fuckface* after you're done with that guy.'

While the Stones worked away in Los Angeles, the on-off northern-English rock band the Verve were giving it yet another go with their single 'Bitter Sweet Symphony', which eventually hit the chart in June 1997. The legal struggle that ensued brought the Stones and their former management several weeks of unwanted headlines, as well as a reported $4million windfall. Although the Verve enjoyed a transatlantic smash with their song, they also paid dearly for using a small sample on it of 'The Last Time' from Andrew Oldham's 1966 masterpiece, *Today's Pop Symphony*. Klein went to work, successfully petitioning a court that the Verve had 'wilfully exploited' Oldham's creation in order to 'brazenly maximise revenue and profits' for themselves. This had apparently detracted from the 'original artistic integrity' of the work in question. 'Bitter Sweet Symphony' was legally removed from the Verve and credited to Jagger–Richards. Klein went on to license the song for use in a TV commercial by Nike.

By late June, Mick and Keith had taken to recording their contributions to the new album in a different room – and often a different town – to one another. Each had his own crew of Stones irregulars: Jagger worked in one studio with Danny Saber and Matt Clifford, Richards in another with Blondie Chaplin (ex-Beach Boys) and Waddy Wachtel from the Winos. Keith polished off the last two tracks without Mick's help. One of them, titled 'Thief in the Night', allegedly referred to problems at home with Patti. At the last minute, Richards hired Jeff Sarli (Bluesiana, Marshall Crenshaw) to add the rockabilly-bass stomp as done by Bill Plummer on *Exile*. By then Jagger was back in London with Jerry Hall, who was pregnant. After discussing it on the phone, he and Keith changed the album's title from *Blessed Poison* to *Bridges to Babylon*, with, aptly, a smoking Tower of Babel in the artwork. Don Was called an end to the whole thing late on 30 June. Next morning, Mick was back on the line complaining that Keith had been given three songs to sing on the album, which he deemed 'unheard of' and 'unacceptable'. Was recalled, 'It was a total standoff between these two guys, neither one was backing down, and we were going to miss the release date and the tour was going to start without a new album out there.' At the last moment, an engineer was able to edit the space between Keith's final two songs so that they effectively became a medley, sufficient for Jagger, who was also busy reading the liner notes with that mixture of professionalism and occasional pedantry that had driven the art director of more than one major record label to distraction, to nod his assent. That everything was safely in the shops six weeks later demonstrates the effectiveness of Mick's business model. Keith then made his final contribution to the album by handing a home-made tape to a driver, who in turn took it to a waiting speedboat, which roared off in the moonlight across Long Island Sound to the mastering studio in New York.

A month later, Richards was listening to the finished *Babylon* tapes at Redlands when, in a Verve moment, his daughter Angela told him there was 'something funny' about one of the tracks. Jagger had quite unconsciously used the tune of k.d. lang's 'Constant Craving' for a new song called 'Anybody Seen My Baby?' Keith got on the phone to Mick right away. Various lawyers then joined in the debate, and negotiated a solution which gave lang and her partner a writing credit and royalties. Keith saw to it that the money came out of Mick's share.

18 August 1997. The Stones rolled in to Manhattan on a Monday morning, tying up the rush-hour Brooklyn Bridge by cruising across it in a cherry-red '55 Cadillac. If happiness is really the fulfilment of childhood dreams, as Freud says, this was a significant step in the right direction for the boys from Dartford and Neasden. It was also another inspired bit of street-drama. Mick Jagger was at the wheel, and the other three were his passengers. On South Street, Mick and Keith jumped out of the car and told the waiting press about the album and tour. Any doubts about the terms of trade still being in their favour were allayed on 27 August, when a million fans tried to buy tickets for the opening shows in Chicago.

By then the Stones themselves were already back in their familiar rehearsal quarters in Toronto. Once there, the band's senior partners seemed to go through one of their periodic role-reversals. While Mick now told everyone he was up for the tour, a tetchy-seeming Keith first throttled Woody when the latter wandered off without permission one night to watch a boxing match on television, and then went on to share some views with *Entertainment Weekly* on Elton John's performance at Princess Di's funeral. Elton's great gift, Keith said, was writing 'songs for dead blondes ... I'd find it difficult to ride on the back of something like that myself, but Reg is so showbiz.' (Asked later if he might like to play at a concert in the princess's memory, Keith replied: 'Sorry, didn't know the chick.') Elton then retorted that Richards was 'like a monkey with arthritis, trying to go on stage and look young. He should have been thrown out of the Stones years ago.' Keith Richards had no known interest in looking young, but the monkey tag stuck. Proving he could take a joke, he named his backstage suite on the new tour the Baboon Cage.

Late September, *Babylon*: the Stones juggernaut rolls on, embracing basic rock and roll, hard-edged funk, slow-boiling reggae, maudlin pop and even a torchy spiritual. There are moments, as in the bullet-train beat of 'Flip the Switch', when the cocky young band of thirty years before reappears, and others when the fifty-something musicians cut the testosterone level: a jazzy, mariachi flavour permeates 'You Don't Have to Mean It', and it's apparently Mick himself who needs the emotional rescue in 'Already Over Me', where he notes, 'I'm so hurt, so confused/I've been burned/I've been bruised'. Among several other treasures, the churchy 'Saint of Me' brings Billy Preston in from the cold after twenty years, and 'Always Suffering' similarly doffs a Stetson to Gram Parsons. The album closes with 'How Can I Stop', which sees Keith Richards in sentimental-gangster vein, singing about his various obsessions in that familiar raspy burr, a voice that increasingly sounds as if Keith took it out and let it marinate in a cask of port in between records. Not everything works quite as seamlessly. Some of the album's busier numbers feature not just the core vocals, guitar and drums, but dozens of overlapping keyboard lines, percussion, squeaky sound effects, extra little tunes squeezed in behind all the riffs underlying the main riff – the sort of funked-up production technique beloved of the Dust Brothers, the men responsible for the Beastie Boys and Beck. But most of the songs 'come off feral without sounding forced, contemporary without succumbing excessively to modern-rock trendiness', in *Rolling Stone*'s measured words. 'It's the band we used to love, who made records that were neither too self-consciously up-to-date nor too giddily nostalgic.'

Bridges to Babylon was the best Stones album since *Exile*. It sold some 6 million copies during the two years the band was on tour.

On 23 September, the *Babylon* experience got off to an explosive start in Chicago. Fans screamed as the Stones began 'Satisfaction', hitting its riff simultaneously with a zap of quasar-white light on the JumboTron screen. Keith Richards loped up in shades and a ratty tiger-fur coat, planting himself stage-left. He was the calm eye of the storm. Elsewhere, cartoon characters raced by on urgent missions. Mick waved as he sped past in his tight black britches, spangly blue frock-coat and white opera scarf. Woody scampered about on high heels, nose aquiver, cranking at his guitar. Darryl Jones chicken-strutted across the boards before coming to a skidding halt in front of the trumpet player, who waved his horn around like a fly-swatter. The choral section bopped from foot to foot. It's a curious sensation to watch so much frenetic activity and not to particularly care about it. About the only composed figures were Keith and Charlie, who both sounded better than ever.

The show itself was Variety, with plenty of quick changes. Mick (who donned nine consecutive jackets, notably a red sequinned number with a feather boa sticking out of the top) owed a lot to the set designer and the props department. And they in turn owed everything to an eclectic crew that included Andy Warhol, Liberace, Siegfried and Roy, U2's *Pop Mart*, *Arabian Nights*, Cecil B. DeMille and, chiefly, Albert Speer. The stage was a hi-tech marvel that resembled something out of a biblical epic shot in Las Vegas. Pineapple-shaped clusters of speakers sat atop giant columns. Busty inflatable nudes crouched, in chains, next to the world's biggest video screen. Halfway through the gig, a bridge rose out of the main stage and, swelling like a fireman's ladder, arched on to a small dais in mid-field, which itself rose up to meet it. The Stones trotted down for a quick blast of R&B classics like 'Little Queenie'. Although a bracing, Crawdaddy Club atmosphere prevailed on the B-stage, it was perhaps less readily spontaneous than had once been the case: when Keith Richards wheeled in to an apparently impromptu version of 'I Just Wanna Make Love to You' one night in front of 70,000 delirious fans at the Texas Motor Speedway, a crew of backstage technicians had to frantically reload the lighting schematics as best they could to accompany the song. Then it was typically back for the Big Three, 'Honky Tonk Women', 'Start Me Up' and 'Jumpin' Jack Flash', echoing out between the gold Roman pillars. (You somehow remembered that the band had spent weeks rehearsing in a Masonic temple.) More eruptions, confetti, fireworks. The applause went on so long that the Stones came back and, seemingly as an afterthought, did 'Brown Sugar'.

As winter approached, the Stones migrated south and west. Keith Richards was steeling himself for the outdoor shows with Stoli and cranberry juice. Woody stuck to pints of Guinness, which he sank in impressive numbers both before and during the gig. Sheryl Crow was the warm-up, sometimes joining the band for a sexually charged duet, Mick thoughtfully licking the sweat off the top of her breasts at one humid Texas arena. Telecoms giant Sprint had replaced Budweiser, and was pumping millions in to the tour. Keith strayed off message by informing the press that he rarely used a mobile phone, and anyway 'the fuckers give you cancer'. In October, the Stones doubled back for two shows at Veterans Stadium, Philadelphia, grossing $7million. Mick came down with flu. He and Keith, enjoying yet another late renaissance, landed on the cover of *Rolling Stone*, their twenty-fourth such appearance between them. In late November the band again played Vegas, packing them in for a glittering night at the MGM Grand, where much of the audience bussed over from an Avon convention across town and sat with their fingers stuffed in their ears throughout the concert. Richards told the media that he still went on stage in

whatever he happened to be wearing, which quite often happened
to be a zebra-print shirt, cut open to the waist, festooned with
several medallions. For relaxation he was reading the Beat poets,
Erotica Universalis and a book called *Hashish* – 'excellent; a whole
education in chemistry and folklore'. One of the crew was shocked
to discover that Keith sometimes pumped himself up for the night's
show by listening to Mozart.

The first leg of the *Babylon* tour ended with a filmed concert in
St Louis; the band had made some $89million over the previous
twelve weeks, with $200million more to come. In January 1998 the
Stones upped the price of a good seat to $300. On 15 February they
played the Hard Rock Casino in Vegas, where tickets were $500.
'It's only money,' Mick observed. 'I'm sure the people who go and
pay $500 don't worry about it. Any more than I would.' Prince
Rupert then brokered a multi-layer deal between the Stones and
Pepsi-Cola. In a 35-year performing career that had had its
moments of strangeness, the band's private concert at a Honolulu
beach resort for 3,000 lucky soft-drink bottlers made a strong bid
for second place behind the likes of Altamont. Pepsi also bought the
rights to 'Brown Sugar' (original working title: 'Black Pussy') to sell
their product. They paid $4million for the show and $2million for
the song.

Not long after that, things began to go wrong. The tour suffered
a spate of postponements and breakdowns due to a bewildering
variety of problems. There were blizzards and floods, broken ribs for
Keith when he fell off a ladder in his library, laryngitis for Mick, and
hassles with the Inland Revenue. A yacht with Charlie and Woody
aboard enigmatically caught fire on a day off in Brazil. For once the
nearby paparazzi came good, rescuing the two Stones. Mick settled
in to a momentary lull of domestic contentment with Jerry Hall,
who gave birth to their fourth child, Gabriel Luke Beauregard, until
a Rio thong model named Luciana Morad announced that she, too,
was carrying Mick's baby; he eventually settled with her for
$4million.

Back for another lucrative stand in New York, the Stones were
joshing around one night in their backstage camp when their old

friend Marshall Chess talked his way in to see them. It had been twenty-one years since Chess abruptly resigned as president of the band's record label, largely due to his ongoing heroin addiction, and he was unsure quite what to expect. In the event, there were big hugs from Keith, Charlie and Ron Wood. A few moments later, Mick Jagger appeared. 'When Mick saw me,' Chess recalls, 'he got real uptight. I put my arm around him and he turned in to a rock. He was shocked ... I know Keith must have loved doing that to him.' But Mick was also consistently charming both to the press and the band's latest corporate sponsors, who invariably found him witty and unassuming. Most nights, Michael Cohl organised a meet-and-greet session with executives from Sprint, which sowed the seeds of many boardroom stories about how Mick had conducted himself like an LSE-trained whizz-kid, speaking to the suits about the most esoteric financial matters moments before running on stage to sing 'Shattered'. In March 1998, Bill Clinton modestly told a reporter that there were only two individuals in the world whose mere announced arrival guaranteed pandemonium on the streets: the Pope and Mick Jagger.

In April, the Stones played South America. Five nights in Brazil scored them another $15million, coincidentally the same amount Jagger reportedly settled on Jerry Hall after Luciana Morad, allegedly aged eighteen, but actually twenty-nine, had his son. In January 1999, Ms Morad told the press that their relationship had been 'much more than physical', and that Mick 'really respected' her. She later reportedly sued him for £10,000 a month child maintenance. In August the Stones finally played Moscow, where the audience once again chanted *Icantgetno! Icantgetno!* for 'Satisfaction', and Keith told them, 'Great to be here. Great to be *any*where.' The good vibes, however, didn't extend to their home country. Four sold-out British shows were blown off by money problems. Under new Labour Government provisions, Britons living abroad had lost their tax-exempt status if they did work of any kind while physically located in the UK. As a result, the Stones organisation would have been liable to pay around £3.3million to the Treasury on gross concert receipts of some £8–9million. Mick claimed he was thinking of the road crew, not himself, in postponing the shows. 'I was tempted to bite the bullet, but I'm not the only one affected,' he said, deeming the 40 per cent tariff a 'rip-off'. After thirty years, the band retained its core wariness of the British tax regime. On 19 September 1998, the *Babylon* tour wound up with a concert to 35,000 ecstatic fans in an Istanbul soccer stadium. Mick Jagger stayed on for a family holiday on the Turkish Riviera. Twenty-one years earlier, he'd chosen the same spot to make a final effort to patch things up with his first wife Bianca. According to Luciana Morad, Mick soon slipped off from Jerry and the kids to join her in a quiet Paris hotel.

Meanwhile, Keith Richards walked his daughter Angela, now twenty-six, down the aisle of a London church. An attractive woman who loved horses, she married a carpenter. Keith flew in the full Stones stage and lighting crew to prepare Redlands for the reception later in the year. Anita, Marlon, the Richards' two young daughters and even Keith's biographer were there. Everyone was very polite. The kids had firm handshakes. No one seemed like demon spawn. Later in the proceedings, Woody, Bobby Keys and Chuck Leavell serenaded the bride with 'Angie'. On 17 December, Keith himself got up on stage at the Life Club in New York and banged out an hour of rock and roll classics with his friend Ronnie Spector. Since coming off the road with the Stones, he'd dyed what remained of his hair blue and then dressed it with a seemingly haphazard row of baubles and ribbons. It made for a late-seasonal effect, like a badly moulting Christmas tree. Conversely, Keith had never sounded better, telling reporters he intended to play until he dropped, and putting all the gibes down to envy. 'They can't understand why I can do what I do "at my age",' he said. 'What is it with these guys? Because they can't do it? Just because chicks still throw their panties at me? Well, stuff you.' The day after his New York show, Keith turned fifty-five.

The Stones put out another live album that holiday season. With its cheesy effects and intros mired in localised takes on 'How you doin', America?' *No Security* opted for musical tourism rather than a sense of place. It died commercially.

On 25 January 1999, the Stones were back on the road. Tommy Hilfiger put up the cash to sponsor the so-called *No Security* leg of the never-ending tour. This time around, the good seats were $300, and in Vegas, $450–600. For skinflints, there were a few 'restricted view' bargains at fifty bucks. The band took the whole show indoors, stripped the stage, and shed some of the old evergreens. Out went warhorses like 'Satisfaction' and 'Miss You', replaced by Mick's poignant commentary on his disintegrating marriage. 'Some Girls' became a pissed-off snarl, while sharp-eared critics noted the ad-libbed 'Get outta my life/go fuck my wife/don't look back' in 'Respectable'. For the first time since 1969, Keith did the ageless 'You Got the Silver', his love ode to Anita Pallenberg.

Also back after thirty years, Byron Berline, the fiddler whose great, alfresco solo had graced the Stones' 'Country Honk', went backstage at the Myriad Arena in Oklahoma City to catch up with the band. 'Meeting the Queen would be easier,' he notes. When Berline arrived at the first of several security checkpoints, he was handed a variety of passes and laminates that allowed him to pro-ceed to the next level. To get in to the heavily fortified inner sanctum, where the Stones relaxed before the concert, even a VIP like Bill Clinton – taking time away from directing the NATO bombing of Yugoslavia to enjoy the show – had to have a special chit, good for one visit, and pass the personal inspection of Jim Callaghan, the band's long-time chief of tour staff (of whom more later). After two of Callaghan's guards escorted Berline through the fifth and final security barrier, he found himself in a room furnished like the royal palace of a Middle Eastern state. There were potted palms, Persian rugs, an ornamental water fountain, elaborate floral displays, wives, children, manservants, strolling Arab musicians, and, somewhat incongruously, a burly chef by the name of Reg flown in from London to keep the band supplied with fresh shepherd's pie and gourmet fish and chips. In the midst of this, Keith Richards was seated at a card table playing dominoes with his 84-year-old father Bert, while Keith's wife Patti sat on a nearby sofa reading the Bible. Berline admits he was uncertain how he might be received by his old colleagues from the *Let it Bleed* days. But 'Keith was sweet,' he says. 'I asked him if he remembered me. "Oh yeah," he said. "I've got a picture of you at home playing the fiddle with a pot plant growing between your legs." I had no idea what he was talking about, but what the hell. He's Keith Richards. He also joked about being a career musician, despite having tried out the likes of carpentry and plumbing as an alternative – "I'm a lifer," he chortled. Great guy, very down to earth. The rest of the Stones sort of grunted.'

While Keith bonded with his family, Mick was being sued for divorce by Jerry Hall. 'Jerry waited until her man was in America before she filed,' an unnamed friend told the *Daily Mail*. 'She wanted him thousands of miles away to avoid any ugly scenes in front of the kids. That way he can do his shouting down the phone.' Hall had apparently learned of her husband's double life with Luciana Morad only in a front-page British newspaper story. Morad herself didn't fail to see the media opportunity and exploit it, displaying her 'bump' while clad in a string bikini on a Rio carnival float. Mick told *The Times* his life was 'like being trapped in a soap opera'.

By contrast, Charlie Watts and his wife Shirley had now been together thirty-five years. Although not entirely starved of offers during that time, Charlie had never strayed from the vows he made at Bradford registry office in October 1964. The Wattses had long since mutually beaten the bottle and settled in to a comfortable domestic routine that centred on their roughly 200 horses and 40 sheepdogs, and that also allowed for a rich vein of the eccentricity occasionally known to flourish in English country life. When Charlie was on the farm, he sometimes liked to sit behind the wheel of a burgundy 1937 Lagonda Rapide, dressed in a matching burgundy check suit, motoring cap and goggles. To communicate with his family and animals he fixed an extra large horn to the ledge of the Lagonda's window, and frequently gave it a toot. (Since Charlie hadn't learned to drive, the car never left his courtyard.) Ron Wood also kept a well-stocked stable of thoroughbreds on his estate in Ireland. Woody, who still famously enjoyed a pint, went on to release his 2000 solo album *Live and Eclectic*, which had been recorded eight years earlier. Bill Wyman was married again and playing a few low-key blues concerts around Europe, which he travelled between in a bus. Bill told reporters he couldn't rely on his Stones royalties to pay his bills. 'The big money wasn't there yet,' he said. 'I had a small nest egg and I can live nicely, but the Stones income doesn't support me. I have to work and I'm not in the same league as the boys who stayed on.' In other interviews, Bill made clear his relief at having left the boys when he did. Five years later, someone working on the Stones' behalf saw fit to airbrush the bass player's image from the archive photograph that appeared on the cover of the band's *Rarities* compilation album. 'Very petty,' said Bill.

The other Stones may have had their personal or domestic foibles, but their family lives seemed positively quaint by comparison to Mick Jagger's. When Jerry Hall filed her petition in January 1999, she reportedly demanded a £30million cash settlement. Mick contested the action on the grounds that they were never formally married, thus in the tabloids' view effectively bastardising his two youngest children. The subsequent stampede of reporters selflessly making their way from midwinter London to the Hall of Records in Bali was seemingly able to confirm Mick's view of the 'purely symbolic' nature of the November 1990 ceremony. 'It's very strange,' noted Parisada Hindu Dharma, an official at Indonesia's interior ministry. 'The couple's "Niskala" – the immaterial side of their union – was taken care of. But there is another side of their wedding – the "Skala", the material side – which is causing some concern. This involves the administration, the filing of documents ... It never happened.' So with sages on both sides of the Atlantic debating abstruse Hindu law and *People* blaring 'IT'S ALL OVER NOW' – one of a half-dozen titles endlessly recycled – Jagger came off the road and headed for New York. In a nationality role reversal, Hall stayed in London. Mick eventually settled a sum reported at anywhere between £4million and £12million ('£9.27million', I was told rather precisely) on his partner of twenty-two years, after DNA tests confirmed he was the father of Lucas Maurice Morad Jagger, born on 18 May 1999 in a private New York hospital.

Perhaps it was optimistic to hope that such a gripping union as that between Mick and Jerry Hall could last. He'd often said, 'Domesticity is death', while she had unfulfilled theatrical ambitions and went on to star in a TV reality series revolving around her search for a 33-year-old 'boy-toy'. The cruel truth might be that even a grand passion rarely compensates for a 5-inch difference in height. In any event, Mick – who all parties agreed doted on his seven children – went on the prowl again in 1999, first being seen with the 19-year-old *Cosmopolitan* cover-girl Sophie Dahl, before reportedly dating the Irish singer-actress Andrea Corr, twenty-two, and finally stepping out with the former British TV siren and aspiring photographer Amanda de Cadenet. If jaws dropped at the news it was only because, at twenty-nine, de Cadenet struck observers as being far too mature for him. Jerry Hall told reporters that Mick was 'the world's best father', but a 'lousy husband'.

The *Babylon/No Security* tour officially ended on 20 April 1999, in San Jose. A brief European leg was bolted on from late May to mid-June. As well as concerts in Spain, Italy and Germany, the Stones finally remembered their British fans and rescheduled two shows at Wembley Stadium. Overnight, London was plastered with huge billboards promoting *Bridges to Babylon* as THE CLASSIC NEW ALBUM. And, as a more realistic slogan: 'First UK appearances in four years'. Hairy and bedraggled, thin smiles pasted over their craggy features, Mick, Keith, Charlie and Ron squinted out from every possible cranny. The shows themselves were a celebration of the Stones' extraordinary staying power. Having arrived backstage wearing a variety of designer jeans, T-shirts and Savile Row suits, the band members emerged from their dressing rooms sporting floor-length duster coats, make-up and identical wraparound shades. This disturbing spectacle appeared first on a giant screen, making them look like a chain gang from a Sam Peckinpah film. What followed was a two-hour master class in rock-pop dynamics. The Stones turned the stadium in to a smoky nightclub for the ballads, while Mick deftly restored the mass aerobics-class feel in knees-ups like 'Brown Sugar'. Jerry Hall, Anita Pallenberg and Shirley Watts

were all backstage with Bert Richards, now confined to a wheelchair after suffering a stroke. Ten days later, the tour wound down
in Cologne. Keith's two younger daughters joined Leah Wood,
twenty, and 15-year-old Elizabeth Jagger for the backing vocals.
Patti Richards surprised her husband by coming out to hand him
his guitar.

The late 1990s belonged to the Rolling Stones. In two separate
bursts, spread over five years, the band had played 282 shows to
some 8.5 million worldwide customers and grossed $665million in
the process. They had also produced one of their best albums in
twenty-five years, even if, with the honourable exception of
Stripped, most of the seemingly unstoppable flow of concert souvenirs and spin-offs did little for the artistic integrity of the Stones
franchise. (Or, as Allen Klein noted when presented with the master
tapes of one North American performance, 'Even I can't polish a
turd.') Impressive as this was, at fifty-six Mick Jagger remained convinced that the Stones' creative and commercial peak lay ahead of
them. 'You either keep moving, or you die,' Mick observed.

He was right. Astonishingly, the Stones' high-water mark was yet
to come, as they managed to gloriously channel all the attitude and
sexuality and freedom of their golden era – the 1960s – amid the
turmoil of the times forty years later. Rock bands have often done
much worse.

10

PERFORMANCE

On 20 October 2001, Mick Jagger and Keith Richards got up on stage together at Madison Square Garden as part of the Concert for New York City, following the 9/11 terrorist attacks. There were emotionally charged scenes both in the auditorium and among the roughly 80 million North American television viewers who watched all or part of the event, 10 million more than had tuned in to the Beatles' historic first appearance on the *Ed Sullivan Show* thirty-seven years earlier. The combination of patriotic speeches, specially themed films, stand-up comedy and musically assisted therapy supplied by the likes of David Bowie, Bon Jovi, Billy Joel, the Who, Elton John and Eric Clapton made even the average all-star charity rock gala seem modest by comparison. Amid the warmly effusive, if necessarily bittersweet audience reaction in the hall that night, three speakers were booed: Susan Sarandon for taking the opportunity to plug her candidate to be the next mayor of New York; Richard Gere for expounding on the need for a non-violent response to terrorism; and Hillary Clinton merely for appearing on stage. (In the DVD version of the concert, it was thought fit to remove the booing and replace it with dubbed applause.) But generally the show was all its producers could have hoped for, a vast communitarian event that acknowledged, if not dwelt on, the horrendous scenes of death and destruction televised worldwide just five weeks earlier. When the night's headliner Paul McCartney saw the faces of some of the victims' families looking up at him from the front row, he broke down and wept.

As it happened, Mick and Keith were going through one of their extended periods of non-communication in the months and weeks leading up to the concert. Earlier in the year, Richards had inducted Elvis Presley's guitarist James Burton and Chuck Berry's sideman Johnnie Johnson in to the Rock and Roll Hall of Fame. In the press room afterwards, the three men were asked if, in retrospect, they might do anything differently in their careers. 'We'd shoot the lead singer,' said Keith. Since he then gazed right at the audience with a straight face and his fists clenching and unclenching, there had been only muted laughter. Nobody knew if there would be another Stones tour. Keith was hot to trot, but Mick and his Jagged Films were busy elsewhere. *Enigma* was in post-production and there was more to come: internet cricket, apparently, as well as *The Man from Elysian Fields* and *Map of Love*. Amid talk of a new solo album, Keith's exasperation with Mick was boiling out of control by the summer of 2001. He engaged in a constant deprecation of his old friend that seemed almost automatic. When Mick went back to Dartford Grammar School to open a new wing and music centre he'd helped pay for, Keith made clear his disdain for all that 'ribbon-cutting shit'. Jagger then went on to record his fourth solo album, *Goddess in the Doorway*, which he celebrated with a vanity TV documentary called *Being Mick* and a major worldwide publicity campaign leading up to its Thanksgiving Day release. Keith listened to an advance pressing of the record in September 2001. Many of the reviewers thought *Goddess*, Jagger's first solo release in eight years, his best yet, and the BBC called it 'a gutsy Big Statement, showcas[ing] Mick's ever-deepening interpretative skills and use of subtle phrasing techniques to broaden the scope of even the simplest lyrics.'

Keith called it dogshit.

'I listened to three tracks,' he revealed, 'and gave up on it.' A reporter then asked him what, in general, he didn't like about

Mick's solo albums to date. 'Wimpy songs, wimpy performance, bad recording,' Keith said. 'That's about it.' When the Stones' business managers or other aides went up to Connecticut to see Keith, they sometimes came back thinking he was a man obsessed, unable to staunch his steady stream of snide remarks about how vain, inept and affected Mick was when he was away from the Stones – and by the same token, how he was 'still fucking electrifying' to watch and work with on a small stage with just Keith, Charlie, Woody and a few mates behind him.

So there was a certain subtext to Jagger and Richards agreeing to perform together again after more than two years at the Concert for New York City. It was their first face-to-face meeting since Keith had attended the London funeral of Mick's mother Eva sixteen months earlier. Most of their exchanges since coming off the road from the *No Security* tour had been conducted through the media. They arrived at Madison Square Garden in separate cars, with their own muscular support crews, and changed in rooms at different ends of the facility. Mick spent much of his remaining time back-stage exchanging pleasantries with his friends Bill and Hillary Clinton, while Keith was content to lurch up against Adam Sandler's party and convivially share a bottle of vodka. The two Stones at no stage acknowledged each other's presence. They had found time for one brief run-through of their set earlier that after-noon, and even then had affected not to actually know one another. Further compounding the challenge, Jagger and Richards were scheduled to go on in mid-concert, immediately after the Who. Pete Townshend, Roger Daltrey and John Entwistle (in his last-ever American concert appearance) duly brought the audience to its feet with a vintage performance, culminating in a rousing version of 'Won't Get Fooled Again'. Daltrey's final words to the crowd of first responders and their families were: 'We could never follow what you did.' It was a statement that might also have resonated with Mick and Keith as they walked nervously to the back of the stage curtain, still not seeming to notice each other, to await their intro-duction.

When the Stones came out, there was bedlam in the hall. It

stopped dead for a brief eulogy to the fallen; but as soon as this ended the yelling started again. Keith then sang the opening verse of 'Salt of the Earth' from *Beggar's Banquet* as Mick stood silent, hands in pockets, behind him. Under other circumstances, the song may have seemed like a ballad of folksy goodwill, and cover acts like Judy Collins and Joan Baez had often treated it as such over the years. But when Keith rasped 'Raise your glass to the good, not the evil' he added a derisive snort and a couple of stabs of guitar, as if to personally put Osama bin Laden on notice that he was on his case. Then Mick joined in the chorus, glaring at the audience, as if in turn daring someone to say a word against his adopted home town. 'And when I look in to this faceless crowd/A swirling mass of greys, and black and white . . .' he went on, and the lyric sounded especially poignant in light of the uniformed emergency workers, and all the widows and orphans, staring back at him. At the end of the number, Mick came forward to tell everyone that it was an honour and a privilege for him to be there. Thank you. You're a great crowd. Really great. The audience, some of whom threw articles of clothing on to the stage, gave him a standing ovation. 'It's great to be back in this wonderful town with you special people,' he continued. Another roar of approval erupted. 'If there's one thing to be learned from this whole experience,' Mick concluded, jabbing a finger towards the front rows for emphasis, 'it's that you *don't fuck with New York*.' The roar this time was truly deafening; he had clearly struck the most responsive possible chord. With the subsequent opening duh-duh-duddle-duh bass notes of 'Miss You', Jagger and Richards slowly began to morph in to something larger than the bickering old couple they'd been in rehearsal just a few hours before. Mick stripped off to jeans and a tight pink shirt and prowled up and down the stage, palpably putting everything in to his singing. Nor did he take a rest during the instrumental parts, playing maracas and harmonica with his whole body thrusting. Keith got a groove going in the song's chorus, and the transformation was complete – they were the *greatest rock and roll band in the world!* And the crowd went crazy.

★

Although Mick's relationship with Jerry Hall formally ended in July 1999 and he's yet to marry again, he was far from celibate in the years ahead. After things cooled with Amanda de Cadenet, Mick was seen around town with the 26-year-old Venezuelan heiress Vanessa Neumann, the so-called Cracker from Caracas. 'But their different lifestyles led to friction,' noted the American tabloid the *Globe*. Ms Neumann was from a 'fabulously wealthy', plantation-owning family. What could the problem have been, journalists asked. Was Mick not posh enough for her, or was it the other way around? In June 2002, Jagger's old chauffeur Keith Badgery briefly went in to print in a memoir called *Baby You Can Drive My Car* to suggest that his former employer was not, perhaps, the quiet, slippers-and-pipe type. Mick won an injunction against the book, and characterised the more lurid accounts of his sex life as 'baloney'. Meanwhile, Jerry Hall went on to appear as Mrs Robinson in a well-received Broadway revival of *The Graduate*, which included a nude scene on stage. She has also starred in the play *Picasso's Women*, and in several touring productions of *The Vagina Monologues*. Hall's later interest in Kabbalah, a sect concerned with the mystical aspect of Rabbinic Judaism, saw her introduce both Mick and Ron Wood to Kabbalah's London headquarters – some wags speculated that Woody had surely confused the name of the group for that of a new Danish lager – although it's thought that all three devotees later ended their active involvement with the faith.

As the Keith Richards phenomenon grew, his psychology and complexes seemed even further removed from Mick Jagger's. Keith was the more impetuous, and vulnerable, of the two: He did not suppress entirely, as Mick often did, the warm and trusting side of his nature, although he was also the more prone to sudden and often volcanic tantrums. He could travel with an approximation of ease, if not enjoyment, in the company of a wide range of rock and roll camp followers, like Fred Sessler; Mick was always in enemy territory. Keith was also infinitely sharper and more focused than his permanently sozzled image suggested. People who got to know him often found that his 'What year is it, man?' persona was a bit of an act. For three decades, Keith had rarely appeared in public without

conspicuously toting a glass (and sometimes two or three glasses) of
a brown fluid. It was widely assumed that this was some fiendish
grog distilled in the hills of Kentucky, and doubtless it often was.
But a well-placed source once took the opportunity of an interview
when Keith was called away to the phone to sip from his 'vase-sized'
tumbler. It contained iced tea. In 1989, William Burroughs had
noted how his friend seemed to 'switch his image on and off like a
light' at a press event in New York. Twelve years later, when Keith
went on stage at a London magazine-awards ceremony, 'an extraordinary transformation took place', the journalist Nigel Williamson
says. 'He scratched his head, mumbled "Yeah, man" several times
and got the name of the award wrong. Everyone clapped and
winked approvingly. Good old Keef. It's only lunch-time and he's
already out of it. Then he returned to the table, and was perfectly
straight again.'

But to repeat: Keith at one time really was the rock and roll buc-
caneer, a role he belatedly illustrated both with the skull ring and
all the fish-hooks and amulets dangling bizarrely from his blue hair.
Apart from writing some of pop music's crown jewels, he'd lived on
a diet of LSD, pot, Mandrax, heroin and cocaine – often inhaled
from off the tip of a switchblade – went cold turkey 'ten or twelve
times', enjoyed a good dust-up and once consumed caviar (if not a
Mars bar) from a most unusual receptacle. He was the heart and soul
of the Stones. A woman named Bethany Staelens went to work for
Keith's New York office in 1995, and was immediately won over by
his natural charm and lack of front. 'I went up to deliver something
to him at the Plaza hotel,' she says. 'I knocked, the door opened,
and I gave the package to Jane Rose. She took it and said, "OK, you
can go now." As the door was closing again a figure jumped up,
grabbed my hand warmly and said, "Hi, we should meet. I'm Keith
Richards."' Another long-serving member of the entourage adds
that Keith was 'always the first to ask about your family, lend you
money, pay your kid's hospital bills if he was sick. Every year, when
Christmas came around you got a ten-dollar bath towel or a scented
candle from Mick. Keith either forgot to shop completely, or gave
you a top-of-the-line DVD player.'

If Keith was the swashbuckling but avuncular pirate, not all his crew was quite as benign. One evening in July 2001, the Richards family enjoyed dinner in New York followed by a concert at Carnegie Hall. When they left through the stage door, a fan pushed out of the crowd, gave Keith a beautifully polished Fender and asked him to sign it. Clearly the street noise intruded, because Keith merely grunted, apparently assuming the guitar was a gift, grabbed it and made for his Cadillac. The car walloped the pavement, swerved from some pedestrians, and headed downtown.

The bewildered fan gave it a moment, then took off down Sixth Avenue in hot pursuit. He caught up with Keith's limo at a light and hammered on the front door. 'Piss off,' the driver invited him.

There was a brief pause, and the fan's eye tracked to the smoky rear window and back again. A goodly crowd had gathered to watch.

'I just want my guitar back.'

'Fuck you,' the driver answered. 'Buy another one.'

In May 2000, Charlie Watts released *The Charlie Watts/Jim Keltner Project*, an album that had begun life when the two drummers collaborated on the *Bridges to Babylon* sessions. 'It's a mishmash kind of thing,' Charlie remarked, alluding to the record's unorthodox mixture of swing jazz and electronica. 'I can see how it's nice to be entertained,' Charlie allowed. 'But this is a different kind of music.' The end result evoked equal parts Miles Davis and Dixieland, with a touch of Kraftwerk. Although warmly reviewed, the album languished commercially. Watts' natural modesty surfaced again in his few public comments on the Stones, who he apparently rated more for their antiquity than their musical chops. 'We're a terrible band really, but we're the oldest,' Charlie said. 'That's some sort of distinction, isn't it – especially in this country. That's our claim to fame, you know. Carry on, lads, regardless.' He added elsewhere, 'The only difference between us and Westminster Abbey is we don't do weddings and coronations.'

Meanwhile, Ron Wood was becoming a kind of court portraitist of the rich and famous, after Andrew Lloyd Webber commissioned him to paint the celebrity patrons at a London restaurant. Woody also bred racehorses on his Irish farm, where he continued to enjoy a licensing deal with Guinness to supply his private pub. In June 2000, he checked in to the Priory clinic for alcohol rehabilitation. Emerging ten days later, Ron swore he would reform and even started drinking mineral water. Unfortunately, he was back at the Priory in April 2001, and the following year spent three weeks at the Cottonwood clinic in Arizona, allegedly on Mick Jagger's orders. In May 2004, Wood was admitted once again to the Priory after being found inebriated under a restaurant table. Nine months later, he checked in to an Irish detox facility after getting drunk at his wife's fiftieth birthday party. Between times, Woody was able to record and release his sixth solo album, *Not for Beginners*, which featured his son Jesse and daughter Leah among his backing band. Affectionately reviewed, it avoided any sales.

Bert Richards died in September 2000 (a date Keith gives in his memoirs as 2002). He was eighty-five. Bert's last words were spoken to his son: 'At least things are going in their natural order.' 'Save a seat for me at the bar, mate,' Keith replied. Their latter-day reunion had lasted eighteen years. Later in the autumn Keith drove his two teenage daughters in to New York from Connecticut to see the boy band 'N Sync. A few days later, he managed to slip back in himself and jam with the blues legend Hubert Sumlin; when Sumlin died in 2011, the Stones paid his funeral costs. On 18 December that year, Keith's fifty-seventh birthday, his friend and travelling companion Fred Sessler died aged seventy-seven. He was buried in his Stones bomber jacket, with his head resting on a pillow containing his backstage passes.

When it came to being a polymath celebrity, and defying the expectations of those who like their rock stars to be skull-faced drug addicts, Mick Jagger had long since cornered the market. He struck many observers as being increasingly in the tradition of great English theatrical player-managers, a seriously dedicated professional with a busy personal life. In March 2000, Mick flew to the rescue of 28-year-old Jade Jagger and her two small girls after they were involved in a car crash in Ibiza, and went on to chaperon his 16-year-old daughter Elizabeth, a would-be model, on the New York catwalks.

But perhaps the most striking sign of his celebrity was when, later that month, he took Jerry Hall and their three eldest children back to Dartford for the opening of the arts centre named after him. £1.7million of the facility's £2.1million construction cost was met by a National Lottery grant, and Mick helped make up the rest. Watching him move around Dartford that day was a bit like watching the *Queen Mary*, with a fleet of tug boats servicing the majestic, purple-suited figure in their midst. As Mick got up to speak at his old school following some introductory remarks by the Duke of Kent, it suddenly struck home that the guiding theme of his discourse was how it had all been accidental. There was no moral to his story except how easily it could have been otherwise. 'I wasn't trying to change anything. I never set myself up as a leader in society,' Mick said, echoing his remarks to the editor of *The Times* thirty-three years earlier. Sadly, Eva Jagger would not live to see her son further honoured by the Establishment. She died from heart failure in May 2000, aged eighty-seven. Joe, Chris and Bianca Jagger, along with Jerry Hall, five children and all three charter members of the Stones attended the funeral, at which Mick movingly sang 'Will the Circle Be Unbroken'. Friends insist that Eva, with her combination of self-discipline, charm and dogged social ambition, was *the* woman in Mick's life.

In later years Jagger would keep company with another statuesque American model, 6-foot-4 L'Wren Scott, who he began dating in 2002. Born Luann Bambrough in April 1967 in Roy, Utah, where she grew up as the adopted daughter of a Mormon family, she had got her start working as a stylist for the erotic photographer Helmut Newton. Newton once told *Vogue* that she was the 'most exotic beast' of his acquaintance. With her long, pale face and mane of waist-length jet-black hair, Scott exuded a faintly sinister glamour that put some in mind of Morticia from *The Addams Family*. Among her first acts in the Stones camp was allegedly to urge Keith Richards and Ron Wood to 'smarten up' their image, and then to suggest that they stop smoking. Keith in turn has referred to Scott as a 'tough chick'. Cynics have called her pushy, vain, touchy, untroubled by self-doubt and – as if there could be anything worse — 'the Yoko Ono of the Stones'. Although not everyone was enraptured by Scott, she was obviously good for Mick, which is what counts. In 2005, the couple spent £6million on a new house in central London, having apparently abandoned plans to live in a flat immediately next door to Jagger's former marital home, Downe House, where Jerry Hall still resides. Prior to that, Mick had spent close to four years camping in a top-floor apartment at Claridge's in Mayfair, at the end of which the hotel presented him with a bill for £1.52million. In May 2007, Hall herself had some harsh things to say about Mick, who she claimed 'made me pay for the kids' throughout their 22-year relationship. 'He always wanted me to take care of everything to do with the home and children, which I didn't mind doing, I guess, because I had the money,' she said. 'Mick's generous with presents, but yeah, he's pretty tight with the day-to-day stuff.'

Goddess in the Doorway dashed some of the high hopes that Mick had had for it. On its first day of release, it sold fewer than 1,000 copies in the UK, compared with the 95,000 Robbie Williams' latest managed. Other market realities were also beginning to bear down that autumn. When the New York stock exchange re-opened after the 9/11 attacks, it lost 684 points in a day and 1,370 points, or 15 per cent, in a week, stirring memories among many investors of the crash of October 1987. Not long after that, a Stones spokesman announced that the band would tour again in 2002.

In the new year, Keith Richards provided a brief but deft foreword to Robert Gordon's biography of Muddy Waters. Richards' prose style wasn't just lucid; it was rich, droll and crisply phrased. He was already thinking about writing his autobiography. Some critics now wondered aloud if they might have got him wrong all along. Richards was all over the straight press that spring, and he and Jagger soon enjoyed the accolade of appearing on *The Simpsons*. Keith balked only when *Fortune* magazine called Mick the 'sole business brain' behind the Stones. 'We're a mom and pop operation,' he corrected them. 'He's mom, I'm pop.'

Later in the spring, the talk turned back to solo projects.

'I think that everybody,' Keith said, 'with the possible exception of Mick himself, has learned the lesson that he's really good when he's with the Stones. But when he ain't, I don't think anybody gives a fuckin' toss.'

On 7 May 2002, the Stones announced their fourteenth North American tour by making a low pass over New York City in a bright yellow blimp emblazoned with the band's logo. It was a flamboyant bit of news management, even by their standards. Presently the craft landed at Van Cortlandt Park in the Bronx, where its famous passengers strolled across the lawn and took the usual questions. Yes, they were back. No, you wouldn't have thought it – not forty years ago, anyway, when it all began. As the band stood there in their shades and bandanas, with an airsick Charlie looking queasy, even their crumpled faces seemed endearing: they were like Merrie Melody cartoon heroes – no matter how often shot, vaporised, tossed off cliffs, they always bounce back and get on with the show. They were doing it, as Keith said so succinctly, because 'it's fun'.

Everyone then moved to a studio in Paris to cut four new tracks for the latest greatest-hits package. Don Was produced. Mick complained that his voice was affected by Woody's habit of constantly smoking in his face, and that Keith drove him nuts by blasting the heavy-metal band AC/DC from his boom box – 'he plays them all fucking night'. Keith in turn remarked on something that had apparently escaped everyone else's notice – that a proposed video image of Jagger performing in front of a pile of corn was 'suicidal', and that the press would make the obvious association.

Somehow, they got through the sessions and flew back for six weeks of rehearsals in Toronto. Prince Rupert, Michael Cohl and various lawyers, accountants and publicists came and went. There were cover stories in everything from *The Economist* to *Vogue*. Alongside L'Wren Scott, Mick now had his own travelling fashion guru, one Maryam Malakpour. He was spending up to two hours every night in wardrobe and make-up. Even Keith, we learn, allowed his hair to be dressed with 'Bumble & Bumble Tonic, Grooming Crème and Lotion, available from selected salons'. Personal trainers and voice coaches had finally replaced the one-time cortege of loose women and drug dealers. When Keith

ventured out of his hotel now, it wasn't to score heroin but to buy
religious books for his wife. Mick Jagger's tour contract specified
that a 'medium white Casablanca lily arrangement with weeping
eucalyptus' be placed in his private exercise room, and that, wher-
ever they were in the world, the band should have access to a
wide-screen television capable of showing cricket. 'That is the
channel we need most of all,' the contract stated. Perhaps in reference to his recent Hollywood activities, one of Mick's stock moves
on first walking in to a hotel room or the backstage area of an arena
was to frame the air with his hands, as if sizing the place up as a film
set. The Stones' old association with death and scandal surfaced only
once, and in muted form, when their long-time roadie 'Chuch'
Magee died of a heart attack one summer night in Toronto while
the Stones rehearsed just a few feet away from him. He was fifty-
four, and had worked for the band half his life.

The entire Stones organisation nearly ground to a halt on 14 June
2002, when Mick rang Keith to share some news. The one-time
Prisoner 7856 at Brixton Prison was being knighted. Keith, who
saw it as rank hypocrisy, was foam-flecked. He vowed to pull out
of the tour – a move that would have left some 300 people jobless
and millions gobsmacked – while Mick kept repeating, 'But Tony
Blair *insists* I take it.' A month later, Richards still wasn't happy. 'I
went berserk and bananas,' he told *Mojo*, 'at [Jagger's] blind stupid-
ity.' Keith particularly objected to his always being told such news
on the phone, not 'direct, over a bottle of Scotch', his own preferred mode of communication. He denied it was just knighthood
envy on his part. 'I doubt they thought of offering me one, because
they know what I would've said ... They knew I'd tell 'em where
they could put it.'
    Keith's good humour gradually returned, along with the carefully
sharpened jokes. By August, he was laughing it off as 'a paltry
honour. I told him, "Hold out for the lordship, mate"'. In private,
Keith sometimes referred to Mick by the slightly extended title of
'His Royal Fucking Highness'.
    In September 2002, the Stones took their past back to the bank

with their new anthology, *Forty Licks*. It was the first to include songs
from the band's pomp as well as from the three decades that followed.
The first of the two CDs was sublime. You marvelled again at how
they could swing out or keep it short and sharp as a ransom note.
The second half sagged a bit by comparison, and the four Paris tracks
were no more than a pastiche of former glories. It had been five
years since the release of *Bridges to Babylon*. The *Guardian* asked Keith
Richards if the Stones were now principally a touring act rather than
a creative band. Certain other 60s' survivors might have met the
question with an indignant denial. 'Yeah,' Keith said. 'One could
look at it like that. I think from our point of view, it's obvious we've
got this body of work and so there's no pressure on us to come up
with new stuff. We carry around a lot of damn good baggage.' *Forty
Licks* hit number one in the UK, number 2 in the US, and made the
top ten in twenty-nine other markets.

On 3 September, in Boston, the Stones played the first of 117
Licks concerts that would take them to 23 countries, in 5 legs, and
gross $301,550,000 in the process. They were sponsored by the
online stock-brokerage service E-Trade. Convening behind the
stage curtain on the opening night, the band were four twitchy figures in black. Ignoring local health and safety regulations, Keith
Richards lit an unusual-looking cigarette, and an on-the-wagon
Ron Wood calmed his nerves by doing a lengthy *Fawlty Towers* skit,
which could have gone better. Mick Jagger expressed his concern
to Charlie Watts that their jackets clashed, among a host of other
such details. 'I can see your white hair sticking out your cap,' Mick
observed to one elderly retainer. 'Please tuck it in. It's a distraction.'
Throughout this, on the other side of the scrim, there was a steady,
abattoir-like lowing. Loud tribal drums played on the PA. On a
nod, Keith stepped forward, Mick following, and literally charged
towards the front of the stage, playing the opening riff from 'Street
Fighting Man' as he did so. The audience went nuts.

The next two hours would be a glorious rebellion against the
march of time. There were generous helpings of *Beggar's Banquet* and
Exile, a sexy, transcendent 'Gimme Shelter' and Mick's playful version of 'Love Train'. 'Midnight Rambler' ranked up there with the

original. Working on its smallest stage in thirty years, the group put the premium back on music rather than showbiz glitz. (The sole props: a $5million screen, and the B-stage.) The prospect of a band led by a knight of the realm and composed of four cricket-loving English squires singing 'Sympathy for the Devil' might be a stretch if it were anybody else but the Stones. They brought it off. Keith's guitar was utterly steady, yet unobtrusive; even in the rockers, he never seemed to be in a particular hurry. Charlie and Ron Wood funked up even the newer Paris numbers, such as the aptly titled 'Don't Stop'. Mick Jagger was singing better than he ever had in his life. His weary, lovelorn vocals carried songs like 'Angie', and his phrasing on the faster tunes was a revelation. 'Satisfaction' was given a thoroughly convincing, if schizophrenic mixture of vulnerability and hostility, which Mick illustrated with karate-like jabs of his hands. On certain other numbers, he was content to flick his fingers vigorously from side to side, as if attempting to dry them in a public lavatory without a towel. He also kept up a nonstop regimen of prowling, prancing, kicking and hip-swivelling. At fifty-nine, Jagger had embarked on his Late Period, and it was an utterly mesmerising routine. He may have been the spiritual Albert Steptoe of rock and roll, as some cynics said, a wizened old codger, lecherously tottering after dolly birds half his age, but while up there with the Stones he seemed powered by pure electricity. Mick's anxious cockerel strut came out gloriously on 'Brown Sugar'. He changed clothes eight times during the set. The big finale: Mick in a Joseph-style 'fantasy coat'. This item had begun quite sensibly, with just a tongue logo stitched to the shoulder, but had evolved beyond all common sense: scraps of denim and leather, silk squares printed with design motifs from previous tours, a Jeff Koons swirl, splashes of red and blue, multiple pockets and zips and shiny brass buttons all went in to the mix. It got a special little gasp.

For the next three months the Stones mixed it up in a variety of domes, arenas and clubs, sometimes all in the same town. As a result, they sold fewer tickets, but at a higher price – in some cases $900 for a ringside seat. On 16 November, they again played in Vegas, at what was billed as the world's most expensive sixtieth birthday party. The hippy turned lawyer David Bonderman paid them $7million to entertain him and his 1,500 guests. With that notable lapse, the Stones still set the standard for remorselessly honest rock and roll, with no gratuitous drum solos or long-winded speeches about saving the whales. In an era of pre-packaged, computer pop they were strutting out sublimely ragged tunes like 'Rocks Off'. Keith Richards' rumpled face was in itself an affront to the scrubbed, aerobicised figures bouncing around on MTV. The Stones smashed records from coast to coast, and went on to headline a festival in front of 550,000 ecstatic fans in Toronto. It was as if rock had decided it was through with all this wholesome crap and gloriously gone back to basics.

I saw the Stones several times that winter, and noticed certain reassuringly familiar aspects to the whole ritual. The truly hardcore fans – the so-called Shidoobees – were always down at the front, regardless of cost, competing to be the first to offer a celebratory high-five at the beginning of each song. Many made copious notes as the performance progressed. This being America, and it being 2002, concertgoers were also subjected to lengthy security checks and a variety of exhortations appearing in either written or spoken form. Sit here. Don't stand up. Give us your cameras, recording devices and lasers. Don't smoke. No outside food or beverages. Don't disrespect the staff. Be courteous. Your patience is appreciated. No latecomers admitted. All rise for the national anthem. Have a nice concert. It was an extraordinary transition when Keith Richards burst through the curtain to put hammer to anvil on 'Street Fighting Man', almost as if the audience, too, was suddenly shoved from the dark in to the light. After thirty-five years of being content merely to bawl it out, Mick now nailed the irony and frustration of the song's lyric for all time, making the whole thing an indelible commentary on the 1960s, an uncomfortable truth with an irresistibly snappy beat.

The Stones had also accumulated a fair-sized entourage over the decades, many of whom patrolled the immediate backstage area during the concert. As well as the security and technical crew, each band member had a personal assistant on standby throughout the two-hour show. An etiquette of finely tuned call and response ruled between the elfin musicians and the burly figures crouching behind the amps: the band communicated with its court in nods or grunts, and the slightest touch of the lips meant 'Get us a drink'. 'Starting a song in the wrong key – I do that,' Keith remarked affably of the typical Stones performance of the time. 'We walk around in the [show], have a couple of pints, smoke a little something. We're a club band. Even though we've played on some of the biggest stages of all time, we're acting very much the opposite.' The longest-running crew members had served either Mick (Alan Dunn, Tony King) or Keith (Jim Callaghan, Jane Rose) since the early 1970s. By and large, the entourage was supremely competent, commendably loyal, fiercely partisan, and absolutely loathed one another. The single aide who had the Stones' collective and wholehearted backing, and knew it, was Rupert Loewenstein, who controlled the money.

On 6 February 2003, for the first time since Altamont, the Stones played a free concert in the sense of waiving their fee for it. Done partly as a favour to Mick's friend Steve Bing (the father of Liz Hurley's son), the Los Angeles event benefited the Resources Defense Council, a politically active environmental lobby. Bill Clinton made the stage announcements. Keith Richards and Ron Wood both smoked their way through the gig, and the former was not immediately able to explain the band's decision to forgo the likes of Live Aid but to support a militant pro-renewable energy and anti-global warming advocacy group when asked to do so following the show. The Stones then played Australia, where they met their old stage MC Sam Cutler for the first time in thirty-three years. He says the reunion was 'generally positive'. Mick and Charlie were friendly, while Keith looked his guest up and down and said, 'Fuck me, Sam Cutler! Or should I say, fuck *you*?' Later in March, the Chinese Government announced that the Stones would finally be allowed to play in Beijing, but refused permission for them to perform 'Brown Sugar', 'Honky Tonk Women', 'Beast of Burden' and 'Let's Spend the Night Together', as these particular songs contained 'spiritual pollution'. ('Sympathy for the Devil' was apparently fine.) Keith then reportedly wrote a letter to Tony Blair supporting him in his decision to invade Iraq. 'Stick to your guns, Tone,' the guitarist professed. On 4 April, in the week Baghdad fell, the Stones gave their first-ever concert on the subcontinent, performing on a specially built stage in the backdrop of Bangalore Palace. Unusually for a rock and roll show, the audience was seated in an open courtyard on granite benches covered with fluorescent blue tiles, and a marble staircase decorated by stained-glass windows ran up the side of the auditorium. There were 33,000 people in the hall, and an estimated 20,000 more listening outside the front gate. In another departure from recent practice, tickets were priced at between $6 and $25 apiece. 'We're happy to be here. Sorry we're about forty years late,' Mick Jagger announced, as monsoon rain began to fall. Even in Indian press conferences, the questions were always the same: sex for Mick, drugs for Keith, and age for them both.

Six weeks passed without a word from the Stones. Keith Richards woke up one day in Connecticut unable to move his arm, and thought he was having a heart attack; it proved to be cramp. Mick went to an outdoor party at a friend's property in Kent, where he chose to seclude himself with a companion in the garden shed. The long-awaited Beijing concerts were cancelled because of the SARS panic. June saw the first of the European shows: Vienna (where the government issued a stamp in the Stones' honour), Paris, London. Later in the month, the band's head of security and Keith's long-time friend Jim Callaghan fell foul of the German police for allegedly selling VIP passes for large sums of cash. 'The Stones didn't give a shit about that, but they also didn't need the grief about unreported income, which is why [Allen Klein] went to jail,' I was authoritatively told. After thirty-one years' service, Callaghan was abruptly terminated, or 'placed on indefinite leave of absence, pending further enquiries', as the band's press release put it. Mick turned sixty that July. Someone should have checked to see if he had a grotesquely ageing picture of himself stashed in his attic, as he still sprinted tirelessly up and down the stage, singing in key as he did so, and pausing only to leer at an animated, scantily clad character who appeared on the video screen during 'Honky Tonk Women'. The figure in question rode a huge cartoon of the band's tongue logo as if it was a bucking bull and then, at the end of the song, the lips swallowed her whole, spitting out her black high-heeled shoes.

On 20 September, the band finally played at Twickenham stadium, after cancelling the night before when Mick lost his voice, just forty years after a sparsely attended gig down the road at Eel Pie Island. In the interim, their fee had risen from £15 to a reported £6million. They'd also seen off seven British prime ministers and eight US presidents. Charlie gave a backstage interview to the British radio presenter Charlie Gillett, and afterwards sent him a handwritten thank-you note signed with his name and the words 'Drummer for the Rolling Stones', as if his job title might not be immediately familiar. The applause went on so long at the end of the show that Keith Richards eventually came back in his bathrobe as the fans yelled for another encore. There was as much chance that they would get one as that Mick and Keith would go home together on the District Line. The *Licks* tour formally ended on 2 October, in Zurich, although the Stones eventually regrouped a month later to close out a harbour-front festival in Hong Kong, marking their debut on Chinese soil. The first song they played was 'Brown Sugar'.

At the end, they came out for a final bow to the 13,000-strong crowd. The four of them held their fists aloft and shouted something back in to the din.

But no one heard. Their words were drowned by cheers.

Early in June 2004, Mick and Keith were sitting down in Mick's château in France to write some songs for a new album – their first in eight years – when Charlie Watts' wife Shirley called them from the family farm in Devon. Charlie had throat cancer. 'There was a pregnant pause, like what do we do?' Keith says. Michael Cohl was soon on the line, and there was some talk of cancelling both the planned recording sessions and ensuing tour. But the band who were still comfortably out-selling their competition at the box-office didn't attain that position simply through a combination of rampant nostalgia and aggressive marketing. They were, even in their well-heeled sixties, fiercely dedicated professionals. Jagger and Richards had often worked through their crises in the past, whether by turning a night in jail in to a prolific songwriting session or by going on stage just hours after learning of the death of a son. They did so again now. 'I thought for a minute and said, no, let's start,' Keith adds. 'Charlie would be very pissed if we stopped just because he was incapacitated for the moment. It wouldn't be good for Charlie and, shit, we've got some songs to write. That's the way we did it.'

Meanwhile, Mick Jagger's vocal disdain for the 'constant shit' of rehashing the past and snide remarks about those who 'milked the 60s only for the money' did not keep him from accepting a commission to write music for the remake of the seminal 1966 film *Alfie*. Mick relaxed his self-imposed ban on revisiting the scene of his youth by contributing a total of eleven songs, one of which – 'Old Habits Die Hard' – won him a slew of awards including a Golden Globe. The film itself was a box-office bomb on its release in October 2004. During this period, Charlie underwent radiotherapy treatment in London and Ron Wood was on and off the wagon. A friend watched Woody celebrate at a Christmas party in Ireland by filling a pint mug of vodka, adding a few drops of fruit juice ('for the vitamins') and then downing it at impressive speed. He was back in detox early in 2005. Mick and Keith were left to work on together in Mick's home studio, recreating some of the French-basement vibe of *Exile*, if on a significantly higher budget. Keith announced he was getting on better than ever with 'Brenda', although, he noted, the latter still preferred a 'glass wall and a control room with all these fucking computers' to record in.

Early in 2005, Jagger and Richards took the tapes for the new record – now going under the title *A Bigger Bang* – for sweetening at Ocean Way studios in Hollywood. Don Was worked with Mick in one room and with Keith in another one. Michael Cohl brought representatives of the mortgage company Ameriquest to a meeting with the Stones at the Bel Air hotel to discuss their underwriting the new tour. Seats for this were priced at $75 to $450 (more, in some markets), and sold out almost instantly. Ticket buyers would soon be reading of the sponsor's current activities. In June 2005, Ameriquest put aside $325million to settle a predatory-lending lawsuit, in which thirty federal and State prosecutors had accused it of gouging customers by charging 'hidden fees and radically higher than promised interest rates'. It would be fair to say that the ensuing press coverage, depicting the company as 'ethically bankrupt', 'voraciously aggressive' and 'complete vultures' did not make an immediately obvious fit with the spirit of the Woodstock generation. That same day, President Bush named Ameriquest's chairman and CEO, Roland Arnall, a man with no previous diplomatic experience, as US Ambassador to the Netherlands. Arnall and his wife Dawn had previously contributed some $5.5million to Bush's successful re-election campaign. In television ads that ran throughout the tour, a middle-aged Ameriquest executive in a suit and tie appeared on screen to explain how 'really, really proud' he and his colleagues were to be involved with the Stones, as the band itself mimed away in the background. A reporter from *Maxim* later asked Mick Jagger why he had decided to do business with so controversial a sponsor. 'They offered us the most money,' Mick said. In an even more curious association, the Stones went on to premiere the video for 'Streets of Love', the first single off their new album, on the long-running daytime-TV soap opera *Days of Our Lives*, a show popular with American housewives. 'It's the perfect vehicle for promoting the band,' the press release noted proudly.

In April 2005, Mick Jagger was in London setting up the tour and working with his movie-production company on a remake of the 1939 film *The Women*. Keith Richards was in Parrot Cay, an exclusive resort in the Turks and Caicos Islands with one hotel and eight private residents: Keith, Paul McCartney, Bruce Willis, the ex-model Christie Brinkley, a Russian mobile-phone tycoon, and three Wall Street bankers. Charlie Watts successfully completed his cancer therapy in London, often walking the 5 miles from his hotel to the clinic and back again and pausing to chat with anyone who greeted him. Few people outside the band knew how serious Charlie's health problems had been until he had solved them. Ron Wood emerged from rehab in Ireland and put together a two-CD compilation of his life's work he called *The Essential Crossexion*; of the thirty-seven tracks, only two featured his time with the Stones. On 3 May, all the band members passed their mandatory pre-tour physicals. A week later, they walked out on stage at New York's Juilliard School of Music and played three songs, which served as the official announcement. Following the Stones' set, a marketing manager from Ameriquest came out to tell the invited audience that merely by being there they were somehow 'making the American dream come true', and assuring them that his company's 'core sales strategy' (no-nonsense pragmatism with a populist veneer) was the 'perfect fit' for the Stones. The band themselves were unable to confirm or deny this, having already left the scene in four separate limos.

There's a seam of music critics for whom the release of a new Rolling Stones album represents not just an artistic event but a sort of saint's vision. Hence, perhaps, some of the more effusive reviews which greeted the appearance of *A Bigger Bang* in September 2005. *Rolling Stone* called it 'not a good album considering the band's age, [but] a straight-up classic, with no qualifiers or apologies necessary for the first time in a few decades'. There was some excited talk in the *New York Times* and elsewhere about a song called 'Sweet Neo Con', which supposedly 'personally offended' President Bush with its unflattering allusions to the Iraq war. The ensuing debate was only the latest attempt by an interested group to claim for itself a band with a nearly perfect 43-year track record of political apathy. Much like 1991's 'Highwire' before it, 'Sweet Neo Con' offered lyrics of almost masterly vacuity, relying instead on crashing blues-guitar chords, wailing harmonica and a large degree of critical goodwill. (It was, perhaps, distinguished by its use of the word 'Halliburton' in a rock song.) Its principal composer again demonstrated his keen eye for the avenues down which his public might be inclined to roam, without showing any interest in exploring them himself. In the 147 concerts that followed over the next two years, 'Sweet Neo Con' failed to make a single appearance. President Bush later remarked genially that he had 'never heard of' the song.

If the Stones had ever been in revolt against the sort of effete, toffee-nosed twits they satirised in 'Play with Fire', it was not from the standpoint of social democracy, nor as advocates of the down-trodden. Even in the 1960s, saving the world, ending the Vietnam War and stopping the arms race always had to be fitted in by the band to any spare time left over from the demands of their high-powered business managers and the endearments of groupies. 'Everybody's talking, showing off their wit/The moon is yellow, I'm like jello/Staring down your tits', Mick Jagger crooned in a more representative moment on *A Bigger Bang*, among other such refer-ences to his storied social life – the women in these songs have 'burglarised my soul', 'wipe the floor with me' and are a 'danger-ous beauty/painfully beating up booty'. ('I was awful bad,' Mick himself admits at one point, leaving us to guess at the details.) There are one or two fair, faux-*Exile* rockers, 'Back of My Hand' reani-mated the oldest blues chords on earth to good effect, and Keith's endearingly slurred vocals closed the whole (at sixty-four minutes, perhaps overlong) production on 'Infamy'. *A Bigger Bang* hit number 2 on the British chart, number 3 in the US, and eventually sold around 3 million copies worldwide.

The Stones opened their tour on 21 August 2005, with two shows at Boston's venerable Fenway Park. A baseball game sched-uled at the venue three days later had to be delayed due to the extensive damage caused to the outfield by the band's 200-ton stage structure, a virtual town at the rear of which loomed two steel and glass towers looking like silver ribbons curled in to cylindrical stacks, flanking an 80-foot-high video screen. The whole backdrop was sufficiently vast that 400 fans could be accommodated on balconies discreetly built in to the twin turrets, adding another $250,000 to the band's nightly receipts. Two sets of special-effects panels showed a variety of computer-generated graphics alongside live footage of the musicians, predominantly Mick. There were pyrotechnic blasts, huge speaker clusters, hundreds of lights. The first number per-formed was 'Start Me Up'. The Stones got the name of their latest tour right: on 5 December 2005, when everyone went home for a month's break, Michael Cohl announced that the forty-two concerts to date had grossed over $162million, shattering the record set by *Bridges to Babylon*. Although the band had rarely been troubled by any post-hippyish qualms about commercialising themselves, only now, perhaps, did they come to nakedly cash in. Among several other novel marketing initiatives over the next year, Ameriquest and Michael Cohl sold Arnold Schwarzenegger a luxury box for several concerts, so that he could in turn offer seats to his friends and supporters in exchange for a $100,000 contribution to his re-election campaign. Although Mick Jagger signed off on the arrangement, that didn't stop him from periodically poking fun at the 'governator', shouting out at one show that he'd been caught 'selling bootleg T-shirts and scalping tickets' outside the hall. Throughout the tour, Mick seemed to want to maximise revenues on the one hand, and to insist it was all really about 'four guys having fun' and 'not giv[ing] a shit about the business side' on the other. Nobody has said the man was without contradictions.

On 5 February 2006, the Stones provided the mood music at Super Bowl XL in Detroit, performing ecstatically received oldies (and one off the new album) to an American viewing audience of 142 million. Rather justifiably, the organisers had been keen to erase the memory of Janet Jackson's infamous 'wardrobe malfunction' of two years earlier by engaging artists felt unlikely to expose themselves on national television. Their confidence was well placed. At the pre-game press conference, Mick Jagger assured the 600 media representatives present that the band would be on its best behaviour during the show. Being Mick, he also noted that there were those who were concerned at the possibility of him saying 'fuck' on stage. No way would he refer to 'fuck' or 'fucking' in public, Mick stressed, several times. He was as good as his word. The Stones later used the occasion to perform a somewhat raspy 'Start Me Up' and two other numbers. The only disrobing came when Mick took off his black tail-coat to sing 'Satisfaction'. There was a moment when his skimpy silver vest separated from his strides, allowing a glimpse of his girlishly flat 28-inch waist. Other than that, nothing malfunctioned. If, like Jackson, he wore any nipple jewellery, he mercifully kept it to himself. The lone controversy was when the TV network turned down Jagger's mike as he sang the words 'cocks' and 'cum' (not sequentially, it should be noted), lest they shock the viewing audience. Coincidentally, on the night of the first-ever Super Bowl, in January 1967, the Stones had been censored while performing 'Let's Spend the Night Together' on the *Ed Sullivan Show*. Despite increasing age and wealth, Mick and the boys were still gleefully offending what was left of the Establishment. Thirteen days later, the Stones performed to an estimated audience of 1.6 million fans huddled on a wet beach in Rio de Janeiro. Many young women in the crowd sported T-shirts or other items daubed with slogans stressing how warmly they would respond if, like Luciana Morad, Mick chose to impregnate them. Others dispensed with modesty altogether and customised their messages across their bare chests. On 8 April, the Stones finally got to perform in mainland China, with a concert at the relatively intimate 8,000-seat Shanghai Grand Stage. Censorship was again in play: the Chinese Government was apparently fine with the schoolboy sexual puns, but concerned about Mick's rousing contribution to the miscegenation debate in 'Brown Sugar'. After a heated discussion, the band dropped the number and performed a bluesy and insolent 'Bitch' instead.

On 18 April, the Stones performed a comparatively rare concert in Wellington, New Zealand, the country Mick had stigmatised as 'a dump' forty-one years earlier. Pending their European shows, the band members and their entourage then took over all ten bungalows of the exclusive Wakaya Club in Fiji, which each cost around $5,000 to $7,000 a night, inclusive of unlimited fresh fruit and alcohol. Around dusk on 26 April, Keith Richards was relaxing with a tropical cooler on a branch some 6 feet up the side of a banyan tree while his wife and the Wood family prepared lunch a few yards away on the beach. Keith dismounted from his perch successfully, but then hit the sand harder than expected, fell backwards, and grazed the trunk of the tree with his head. Three days later, he developed a migraine. Keith suffered a seizure in bed that night, and on the morning of the 30th an air ambulance flew him to Ascot Hospital in Auckland, a four-hour journey. A source familiar with the facts says that the patient arrived in the emergency room 'strapped on a gurney, heavily bandaged, with a wild look in his eyes'. Asked if he knew what was the matter with him, Richards replied, 'My head hurts like a motherfucker.'

Three days later, Keith was considered stabilised. The doctors then performed a two-and-a-half-hour operation to drain blood from his brain. Following the life-saving procedure, they reattached Keith's scalp with six titanium bolts and put him on a heavy morphine regimen, a not wholly disagreeable experience for him. The surgeons then advised Keith to abandon his forty-year cocaine habit and to take a minimum of six months' rest. He agreed to the former condition, but was back on the road with the Stones on 11 July, just over nine weeks later. Comedians did a brisk trade in Keith jokes over the spring, suggesting that he had fallen out of a 'fifty-foot-high coconut tree' and 'suffered permanent brain damage – although how can you tell?' The band's insurance company made good some $14million in lost receipts as a result of changes to the tour itinerary. When they picked up again in Milan, Keith looked happy but frail, and took a stool for several of the slower numbers. The Auckland neurosurgeon and his team flew in and watched the show proudly, and perhaps anxiously, from the wings. In a possible reference to his misadventure, Keith added 'Slipping Away' to the repertoire. Mick sang 'As Tears Go By' in cod-Italian. Later he brought out the local soccer star Marco Materazzi, who had been knocked cold in a recent World Cup game and said: 'Materazzi and Richards have something in common tonight – they both had head-related problems.' All sorts of sensational stagecraft ideas, including a great many projections and flashing lights, were strategically placed to elicit a few gasps of admiration from the crowd, but the overriding emotion was surely one of relief at simply seeing the band back where they belonged.

Keith followed his return from cranial surgery by taking a cameo – as Johnny Depp's father – in *Pirates of the Caribbean: At World's End*. It was a role for which he seemed to have been on permanent audition for the last twenty years. Meanwhile, Mick played himself in the American TV comedy series *The Knights of Prosperity*.

After that, the Stones played another forty shows in Europe and North America during 2006. Their tour contract specified that all four band members have their own customised dressing room, and that a 'clearly designated name-sign be affixed' to each: 'The Work-Out Area' (Mick), 'Camp X-Ray' (Keith), 'The Cotton Club' (Charlie) and 'The Recovery Room' (Ron). Jagger was further to be 'physically absent from the playing area and its surrounds' during Richards' nightly two-song mini-set. Mick often took the opportunity to pop backstage and strap on an oxygen mask before coming back for the second half of the show.

Keith's near-death experience also apparently made him and his bandmates think about their heirs. In August 2006, Jagger, Richards and Watts sat down with Prince Rupert and their reclusive Dutch accountant Johannes Favie to create a pair of private Amsterdam-based foundations that would allow them to pass on their assets tax-free when they died. The fact that the Stones were concerned about their money would possibly not have come as a surprise to anyone who had bought a $400 concert ticket or browsed the band's officially licensed products ranging from Mick Jagger 'quality resin' bobblehead dolls and 'It's Only Rock 'n Roll' lava lamps down to a line of 'personally approved' ladies underwear, among other exotica. Not that any intimations of mortality meant that Keith Richards, for one, was quite finished enjoying himself, as the singer-entrepreneur Jimmy Buffett found one day that summer when he looked up in to the blue Caribbean sky and saw Keith gleefully swooping overhead in the passenger seat of a restored World War Two Heinkel bomber.

The Stones played a block of five sold-out British concerts in August 2006. In general, they were a brilliantly effective exercise in decline management. At sixty-three, Mick seemed to have enhanced his natural hair tone from silver to rich chestnut, but he retained that extraordinary musculature, a tangle of bungee cords and suspension-bridge cables rippling out of a washboard-flat torso, as he prowled in that unmistakable gait. Keith, for his part, still struck at his guitar in curt, shocked gestures, often snapping his left hand away altogether and jabbing the air with it. An enormous pro-portion of the band's live power continued to be due to Charlie's undemonstrative but precise drumming, filled, like Keith's riffing, with little strategic bursts of silence. After thirty years opinion still varied as to how good, technically, Ron Wood was, but his caper-ing stage presence added to the visual thrills.

Perhaps the worst you could say about the Stones in concert was that they tended to dumb down some of their classic tunes instead of giving them their original, layered treatment. The studio 'Brown Sugar' was a dynamic mix of acoustic and electric, enjoying what Mick aptly called a 'slinky' rhythm, and leaving most of the heavy lifting to Charlie's bass drum. Now the audience got the overexcited riff and a few shouted variants of the chorus, but not much else. Similarly, 'Honky Tonk Women' needed sleek, propulsive guitar, and didn't really get it in the formidable but lumbering version the Stones wheeled out on stage. The song had been a Maserati; now it was a runaway Mack truck. The playful bounce of 'Start Me Up' all too often became a steamroller. Listen to the kinetically thrilling first fifteen seconds of the recorded 'Jumpin' Jack Flash', stripped to the essentials and steadily building momentum, and then listen to the in-your-face live intro of the same song. In all, an odd series of arrangements, which many people were very taken by.

On 29 October, the Stones comfortably filled the 2,800-seat Beacon Theatre in New York. Bill Clinton again served as MC, and Martin Scorsese filmed the concert for a rock-documentary he called *Shine a Light*. Minutes before the show, 83-year-old Ahmet Ertegun, the man who had effectively rescued the Stones' career when they were down and out both in 1971 and 1977, tripped over in the backstage hospitality suite – nicknamed the Rattlesnake Inn – and hit his head on the floor. While the band ran on, Ertegun was rushed to Manhattan's Presbyterian Hospital; although initially listed in stable condition, he fell in to a coma and died there six weeks later. After a second performance at the Beacon, Mick Jagger flew to London for twenty-four hours in order to be at his father Joe's bedside. He, too, had recently fallen, and then developed pneumonia. Mick rejoined the band in Las Vegas on 11 November, only to hear that Joe had just died. He was ninety-three. The Stones played their full two-hour set as scheduled that night. It was later revealed that Mr Jagger left the bulk of his £380,000 estate to his younger son Chris, whose career as a musician stalled in the 1970s, and not a penny to Mick – who was, however, made executor of his father's will. (In May 2007, the two brothers startled the forty or so customers in the Bull's Head pub in Barnes, south London, by getting up on the makeshift stage one night to duet on *Sticky Fingers'* 'Dead Flowers'.) Joe Jagger's funeral arrangements were held back in order to allow the Stones to complete a final five *Bigger Bang* North American concerts. On 25 November, there was an end-of-tour party in Vancouver where Mick spoke of there having been 'no serious mishaps' during the previous year. Keith corrected him, to some mirth, by pointing at his head. Three days later, a black-suited Mick presided over his father's funeral at St Mary's church in Teddington, Surrey, where he was joined by L'Wren Scott, Jerry Hall, Bianca and Marsha Hunt. Six of Mick's children and two of his four grandchildren also attended. Charlie Watts represented the band. James Brown, the 'godfather of soul', died on Christmas Day of that year. In 2006, Mick had lost three out of what may have been his four biggest male influences, and nearly lost the fourth.

On 21 April 2007, Doris Richards died of cancer at the age of ninety-one. 'We knew me mum was going,' Keith recalled, 'and so my daughter Angela says, "Dad, take the guitar out. Play to her. Go in to her room." So I went up there and sat on the hospital bed and played my best. And I played the old songs, the old dance-hall songs. The next morning, she came out of her sleep for a moment, and my daughter was there and asked her, "Did you hear Dad play for you last night?" And me mum says, "Yeah, he was out of tune."'

That same month, ruminating on his family losses, Keith told a British music magazine that he had previously inhaled his late father's remains mixed with cocaine. 'I couldn't resist grinding him up with a little bit of blow. My dad wouldn't have cared,' he said, adding, 'It went down pretty well.' In the subsequent furore, Keith indignantly protested that he'd been 'having a joke' or been 'taken out of context', before eventually revealing that perhaps he actually had snorted some of Bert's ashes after all, after they blew on to a garden table just as he was about to scatter them around an oak tree.

Meanwhile, the Stones began the eighth and final leg of their tour, having already played in thirty-two countries over a period of twenty-one months. On 10 June, they headlined at the Isle of Wight festival, but declined to do the same at Glastonbury after organisers failed to meet the band's 'reduced' £1million appearance fee. Several Spanish, French and Italian stadium shows followed. In the same week as *Forbes* magazine placed the Stones at the top of its music moneymaking list, Mick Taylor was pictured by a British tabloid trudging home to his 'run-down cottage' after doing his shopping at Asda. P.J. Crittenden, owner of the Dirty Water club in Tufnell Park, where Taylor's band sometimes played, said: 'Mick is a lovely guy. People interested in him fall in the 30 to 45-year-old category. Although enthusiastic, they are not exactly a legion.'

The band Taylor had left thirty-three years earlier was now so expert in serving up heritage rock that it managed to give the impression, simultaneously, of belonging to a bygone era and thus having all the charm of the 1960s at their most appealing, while consistently showing its mastery of state-of-the-art technology, if not always of contemporary music styles. It was also quite versatile. On 21 June, the Stones packed the 62,000-seat Estadi Olímpic Lluís Companys in Barcelona; Mick zigzagged around the stage, continually waving hello with his thin, elegant arms, while Keith stood stock still, creating mountainous walls of sound with tiny swipes at his guitar. Later in the week the band played to a more select audience of 480 at a private party for Deutsche Bank employees held at the nearby Catalan Art Museum. They were reportedly paid $5.6million for their services. Mick told the small but appreciative crowd: 'Thank you for having us. The best part is it's coming out of your bonuses.' Over the next month, the Stones would perform in such previously aloof and forbidding rock and roll markets as Montenegro, Serbia and Romania, causing celebratory riots wherever they went. The only note of censure came in Gothenburg, Sweden, where Markus Larsson, music writer of the *Aftonbladet* newspaper, gave the concert a poor review. Among other things, Mr Larsson suggested that Keith Richards appeared 'a bit confused' on stage. Keith fired back in an open letter, saying that the critic should withdraw his remarks and 'admit it was a good show'. Larsson in turn wrote, 'It is Richards who should apologise', since fans had each paid around $150 'to see a rock star who can hardly handle the riff to "Brown Sugar" any more.'

After two years, 147 shows and a gross of $560million, the *Bigger Bang* tour finally wound up with three sellout concerts at London's O2 Arena, a few miles from where the band had plugged in for the first time forty-five years earlier. In general, the British critics were more forgiving than some of their foreign counterparts. 'The music is still risky, edgy, very much a living organism,' Andrew Perry wrote of the final show in the *Daily Telegraph*. 'During "Tumbling Dice", Keith Richards – the fans' favourite, who received a standing ovation for lighting up a cigarette – delivered a solo possibly from another song, or maybe another galaxy. It sounded amazing. He's still way out there.' Between them, Keith and Woody blasted out some particularly rude cones of noise that night. It was 26 August 2007. The press again deployed their 'This Could Be the Last Time' headlines in the days ahead.

Each of the Stones was said to have earned some $45million, or £30million, for his services since August 2005 – although court documents would later put Ron Wood's net worth at £36million, down from a high of £75million earlier in the decade, due largely to bad investments, personal habits, and a subsequent costly divorce settlement. Woody was also thought to have spent some £1.5million on his revolving-door detox therapy during the period. Apart from the money, one possible reason the band had stayed together so long was that away from the stage they saw very little of each other. Mick immediately went back to his film production company, his parties and his cricket. Keith was content to spend much of his time sprawled in a hammock on one or other of his Caribbean estates, occasionally emerging to paste a few inimitable

guitar licks on to a friend's album, and eventually to begin his memoirs. Charlie retreated behind the ivy-clad walls of his farm in
Devon, where he preferred to relax with his horses and sheepdogs
rather than carousing with what he had once called 'those awful
rock and roll people'. Only Woody, the band's perennial new boy,
seemed to still spend his days and nights in the dogged pursuit of a
rock lifestyle characterised by his heroic consumption of alcohol,
cigarettes and inappropriate young women. And even he
announced, incredibly enough, that he was now in to 'organic
nosh'.

In October 2007 Wood published his autobiography *Ronnie*, a
consistently cheery if occasionally also impressionistic account of his
time with Jeff Beck, the Faces and the Stones. It was an engagingly
slurry romp through the past forty years. To get some of the flavour,
you might imagine a skinny, 60-year-old man hanging around, say,
a south London pub, telling people about his life. He relates slightly
improbable stories of having toured the world with various musician friends, drinking impressive amounts of alcohol and sometimes
passing the time by playing doctor with the local women. Once up
on stage with his mates there is more drink, often served by a uniformed bartender, and a whole series of consequent misadventures
in exotic locales. The booze and the women always have a beneficial effect. Eventually he is recognised as a creative artist, with
private jets and a large entourage at his disposal. The former president of the United States commissions him to paint his portrait.
Fame and fortune, but also a series of highly complicated international business disasters, follow. He squanders most of his money.
The only difference between this man and Woody is that while one
might be a bore, the other remains an impish and lovable survivor
of a time when pop stars tottered around on high heels and women
were 'chicks' or 'the old lady'. His book was tremendous fun to
read.

Meanwhile, Keith Richards grew a moustache and helped his
wife Patti, now fifty-two, successfully battle bladder cancer. Keith
later told a British trade magazine, 'I ain't got any favourite crappy
new bands.' There was a generous minimum excrement-quota to

Keith's daily language, but, even so, he seemed to be aiming for a new world record here. His uncompromising verdict on the current music scene: 'Everyone's a load of crap. They're all trying to be somebody else and they ain't being themselves. The Libertines, Arctic Monkeys, Bloc Party? Load of crap, load of crap. Posers, rubbish. There ain't nothing out there that's worth shit. I listen to the real shit, I don't listen to bullshit. I listen to my shit, baby, Motorhead, reggae, Moroccan music. All kinds of shit.' Keith was to comment of the Stones, 'They're the only ones I care about. I can't wait to get back on the road with those bastards, who happen to miraculously be one of the best bands in the world. I dunno how the hell it happened.'

In February 2008, the Stones met for a rare off-tour event to celebrate the premiere of Martin Scorsese's concert documentary *Shine a Light* at the Berlin Film Festival. Mick Jagger took the opportunity to expound on drugs in general and the troubled singer Amy Winehouse in particular. 'When we were experimenting with dope, little was known about the effects. In our time, there were no rehab centres. Anyway, I didn't hear about them.' Mick said he couldn't fathom how the younger generation, knowing the dangers of drugs, could still be users. Keith Richards similarly advised Winehouse to 'get her act together'. He expressed concern about the singer's descent in to addiction, warning her she could end up looking as 'wrinkly and wasted' as he did. However, Keith drew the line at total abstinence. 'I smoke my head off,' he confided. 'But that's my benign weed. That's all I take, that's all I do. But I do smoke, and I've got some really good shit.'

The Stones' worldwide goodwill tour to promote Scorsese's film was stately, dignified, proud and slow. In a marked reversal of his stage technique, Mick sat still for extended periods, often wore a suit and glasses, made no particular effort to entertain anyone, and spoke at length of his family and his spiritual life. According to published reports, Mick now 'practise[d] Buddhism and meditation every day. He says it's the first thing he does when he gets up in the morning.' Keith Richards credited his own rude health to 'not eating much, drinking a lot [and] good weed'. His fifty-year Marlboro habit had effectively rendered his tastebuds redundant, so regular doses of pub food, with plenty of HP Sauce, remained his preferred diet. Around this time, Richards appeared in a series of glossy advertisements for the French luxury fashion house Louis Vuitton. It was hard to say which was the more shocking, the original commission or Keith's decision to donate his fee to the Climate Project, an environmental action group founded by Al Gore. In Devon, Charlie Watts denied reports that he had left the band, which he characterised as 'codswallop'. 'Why should I quit?' Charlie asked. 'It seems that whenever we stop I get ill. The last time we had a break I got throat cancer. I do all my exercises, I don't smoke and I don't drink . . . I think we should carry on.'

Mick, too, was clearly in for the long haul: he might reflect to film-festival audiences that the Stones had hit their creative peak in the late 1960s, but he had no intention of becoming what he called 'an old fart boring people down the pub'. It was not in his nature or that of the band's financial managers to wallow in nostalgia too long; both depended on a continuing dynamism for their survival. Although Mick turned sixty-five in July 2008, he was able to supplement his state pension by signing a new contract that week with Vivendi's Universal Music Group, which paid the Stones $15million upfront and guaranteed them a reported $120million over four years. Mick himself was now believed to be worth £225million, or $340million, and was thought unlikely to sire any more heirs – 'I have inherited many fantastic children and that's enough,' L'Wren Scott said.

Not one to rest on his laurels, Mick went on to pursue several more personal artistic projects, including his movie-production company's long-delayed adaptation of Clare Boothe Luce's *The Women*. Broadly in the vein of *Sex and the City* (although, unlike that romp, with not a single man in sight), it was released in September 2008. The critics were unimpressed. A.O. Scott of the *New York Times* spoke for many when he called the film 'a witless, straining mess', while to *Rolling Stone* it was a 'misbegotten redo' and 'a major dud'. Despite or because of the mostly sour reviews,

The Women grossed a respectable $48million worldwide, twice its production budget. Mick also tirelessly promoted the first overview of his solo music career. Perhaps immodestly, if unambiguously, called *The Very Best of Mick Jagger* – a contradiction in terms, Keith felt – it peaked at number 79 on the *Billboard* chart, some 76 places lower than had been the case for the Stones' *A Bigger Bang*.

While Mick still generally shunned introspection, Keith was now busy piecing together various lost parts of his life – such as the 1970s – for his autobiography. More or less drug-free, he fortified himself for the task with large doses of vodka and the odd energy-enhancement pill in the morning. As a further aid to the creative process, a ghostwriter named James Fox was signed on. Temperamentally unsuited to the gerbil existence of a professional author, Keith also allowed himself certain relaxations in this period, including a raucous night on stage at the Musicians Hall of Fame concert in Nashville, where he joined the re-formed Crickets for spirited performances of 'Peggy Sue', 'Not Fade Away' and 'That'll Be the Day'. Charlie Watts and Bill Wyman were subsequently reunited at a London gala dinner for the former England cricketer Ian Botham. Bill was now a bespectacled old gentleman of seventy-two who divided his time between managing his burger restaurants, touring with a small-scale blues band he called The Rhythm Kings, and selling a range of 'top of the line' metal detectors priced at £120. He continued to express his relief at having left the Stones when he did, although he noted that, unlike them, he 'had to work for a living'.

While the surviving charter members of the Stones were all in the money, Ron Wood seemed to lurch from one financial or personal crisis to another in 2008–09. Woody had been hit by a number of family losses over recent years, culminating in the November 2006 death from cancer of his 69-year-old brother Art, one of the regular guest vocalists at the old Ealing Jazz Club and a seminal influence on Ron's music career. Since 2003, Wood had also lost both parents, his brother Ted and his ex-wife Krissy (who died of an accidental overdose in 2005), while there were apparently issues with his grown daughter Leah, a model, who reportedly moved to

Australia without first mentioning the fact to her parents. It's possible Wood suffered a late middle-aged crisis of sorts after coming off the road in 2008. In June, he walked out on Jo, his wife of twenty-three years, to live with Ekaterina Ivanova, a blonde, 19-year-old Russian cocktail waitress he met in a Soho lap-dancing bar. In July, he was back in rehab. In August, Woody packed up his remaining guitars at his £10million mansion in Kingston-upon-Thames, put his Irish estate on the market, and set up home with Ivanova in what CNN called a 'luxury $8million love-nest in central London', but which was actually a small flat in Belsize Park, followed in turn by a mock-Gothic castle Woody rented from the Lacoste sportswear family in suburban Cobham, Surrey.

The Stones' troublesome second-guitar spot had already accounted for Brian Jones and Mick Taylor, and now Wood, too, seemed to be in a fast-falling lift that paused only for him to periodically alight at various detox centres. The British press soon learned that it could feed on this long-running rock folly by yielding to it in certain ways. Between July 2008 and December 2009, there were frequent stories about Wood's 'tempestuous' sex life, and specifically about his penchant for sketching his 'uninhibited' young lover. Various newspapers helpfully provided archive photographs of Ivanova in the nude. One well-known Sunday tabloid later bribed a hotel chambermaid for a pair of her knickers. Exactly what it meant to do with them remained unclear, but cash changed hands. Ivanova told the *News of the World* she was 'really in love' with both Ron and his music, although she couldn't immediately say which Stones song might be her favourite. Both parties were binge drinkers, and in time there were reportedly late-night rows that shattered the peace both of Belsize Park and Cobham. Jo Wood, who went on to become a fixture on *Strictly Come Dancing*, appears to have viewed the whole saga with a mixture of stoical good humour and mild relief. 'That girl did me a favour,' Jo commented in 2009. 'She's become me, having to look after Ronnie full-time.' Wood did manage a little music in this period, guesting with Pearl Jam in August 2009 and then staging a Faces reunion at the Royal Albert Hall, with Mick Hucknall replacing Rod Stewart on vocals, and Bill Wyman on bass.

Mick Jagger had occasionally disparaged *Exile on Main Street* over the years, but early in 2009 he decided the time had come to reissue the album with ten previously unreleased tracks and an accompanying documentary. Don Was agreed to produce the project, and in due course looked out of his window to see 'two Mack trucks full of tapes backing up to the door.' Mick Taylor came out of semi-retirement to help tidy up archival material such as the swaggering 'Plundered My Soul', which became the best 'new' single the Stones had released in decades. Both Keith and Bill were on board, while Charlie announced only that his two favourite destinations outside his farm were his tailor and his shoemaker, and that he owned neither a phone or a 'machine thing', as he called a computer. Shopping was Charlie's only known vice, and he remained on track to become the first major rock star to celebrate a golden wedding anniversary.

Having made determined efforts over the years to portray Brian Jones' drowning as a murder, the Stones' legendary fixer Tom Keylock died that 2 July, which happened to be the fortieth anniversary of Brian's death. By a mild coincidence, Keylock's old boss and occasional foe Allen Klein followed just two days later. He was seventy-seven, and had dementia. Mick's good friend Michael Jackson also died that summer. As usual, none of these various losses seemed to bother the Stones. Most of the band's original entourage had long since moved on, although Andrew Oldham still had a daily satellite-radio show which he broadcast from his home in Colombia, and often collaborated with the Argentinian singer-songwriter Charly Garcia, popularly known as El Bigote Bicolor or 'the Bi-coloured Moustache'. Oldham also wrote a book about Abba.

A distressing episode in the Ron Wood household saga followed in September 2009, when Ekaterina Ivanova was said to have threatened suicide following a late-night disagreement at the couple's Gothic folly in Cobham. According to a report published in the *Daily Mirror*, Ekaterina was heard shouting: 'I'm going to kill myself. You're going to find me dead.' Ron replied: 'Fuck off home, you slag.' A spokesman for Surrey Police said, 'Officers attended the address and no offences were alleged and there were no arrests.' In a subsequent incident, 62-year-old, grandfather-of-six Woody was said to have appeared on the street one night 'his face swollen, screaming at the top of his lungs, spitting out abuse, waving his arms wildly, and drumming on his head with his fists'. While Mick and Keith had mellowed, Ron still obliged the press by apparently living like a 1970s rock and roll cliché. On 11 November Jo Wood filed for divorce, noting that her marriage of twenty-four years had broken down and that she found it intolerable to live with her husband. The subsequent settlement reportedly cost Ron £6.5million.

In the early hours of 2 December 2009, the police arrested Wood following an alleged assault on Ivanova outside the normally staid surroundings of the Bengal Lancer restaurant in Claygate High Street, close to the couple's rented home. It was claimed he had threatened to stub out his cigarette in his girlfriend's face, called her an unflattering name, and subsequently dragged her 'gurgling' and 'choking' towards a parked car. Wood spent the remainder of that night in a cell at Staines police station. He was eventually given a caution for common assault. Ivanova went on to confirm that she had 'reluctantly split' from the man she now characterised as an 'evil goblin [with] bad boozy breath'. 'It started off really exciting,' she announced of her sixteen-month relationship. 'His body is very good for his age and he was very youthful in bed. But towards the end it got in to a routine, especially as he was always drunk. He'd try it on with me and he stank of rum, which I hate. Sometimes I'd go through the motions but sometimes I'd just push him off. I'd stopped fancying him.' It seems reasonable to suggest that in general terms Ron and Ekaterina's affair had not been a sustainable model to follow for a mutually fulfilling, long-term partnership.

In the winter of 2009–10, the Stones either collectively or individually picked up a number of lifetime-achievement awards, everything from a Chinese Government cultural citation to a British radio 'roll of honour' gong and, the capstone of this phase of their career, a new Dartford housing estate having the roads named after their classic songs – Ruby Tuesday Drive, Little Red Walk and Sympathy Street, among others. Mick was in the studio polishing the *Exile* tapes, while Keith talked about going back on the road. 'Maybe we'll search for a different way,' he said. 'Maybe not the stadiums any more. You can't go around in lemon-yellow tights forever.' When a British newspaper later reported that Keith had given up alcohol, the guitarist immediately rang back to set the record straight. 'The rumours of my sobriety are greatly exaggerated,' he said, indignantly. Meanwhile, Charlie played a low-key series of concerts in Europe with blues-jazz ensemble The ABC&D of Boogie-Woogie, named after the initials of the four musicians in the band. 'This is what I really want to do,' Charlie now insisted. 'Honestly, I couldn't care less if it were over with the Stones.' Ron Wood lost no time in dating another Russian-born woman, 26-year-old Hannah Kamelmacher, before stepping out with a Brazilian polo coach and aspiring actress named Ana Araujo, who was thirty. 'We're both Geminis, so we're good together,' Woody observed. In Rio, his girlfriend's father Manuel Pinto told reporters that he was a big Stones fan and he hoped the couple would get married someday. At fifty-seven, Mr Pinto was six years younger than his prospective son-in-law. In June 2010, Woody, having left Ana Araujo for a 24-year-old hair stylist named Nicola Sargent, began hosting his own well-received Saturday-night show on London's independent Absolute Radio. Ron's double life as an elder statesman of rock music and a perpetual teenager got another public airing that September, when British newspapers published photos of him, drink and cigarette in hand, frolicking with his bikini-clad partner while on holiday in Spain. A seventh studio solo album, *I Feel Like Playing*, followed later that month, with guests like Bobby Womack, Billy Gibbons and Slash all dropping by to have fun on an amiable party collection of rock, reggae and blues. Warmly reviewed, it did not trouble the charts.

Exile did rather better on its reissue in May 2010, entering the UK chart at number one exactly thirty-eight years after it first occupied that position. Some of the newly released outtakes, such as 'Plundered My Soul', were treated in the music press and elsewhere like the discovery of an Eleventh Commandment, possibly because up until then the Stones, unlike other bands, had generally left their discarded recordings and intriguing rejects in the vaults. Jagger and Richards talked the album up to the media, and were on hand for the premiere of the *Stones in Exile* documentary at New York's Museum of Modern Art. In all, the project was so successful that the Stones soon went on to follow the same protocol with their 1978 masterpiece, *Some Girls*. Keith also revealed that he was waiting for the nod from Mick to start working on new material. 'I usually get a call from Himself saying, "Let's make something, let's do something" because without his actual "want to do it", there's not much point,' he said.

Jagger then did the rounds at the Cannes Film Festival, where he charmed audiences by speaking to them at length in very passable French. (He could also say 'Having a good time?' in seventeen languages.) Mick liked to make news, and by now he was effortlessly good at it. When one of the PR handlers urged him during a 'bull session' for a Cannes press conference to 'be dull, Sir Mick', he replied honestly, 'Being dull is very hard for me.' As well as reflecting both on the album and the state of the contemporary music scene, Mick urged the British Government to legalise cannabis on the Isle of Man, calling for a social experiment to see if it prevented drug-related crime. 'In England they always try out new mobile phones in the Isle of Man,' Mick said. 'They've got a captive audience. So I say you should try the legalisation of drugs there and see what happens.' Somehow, the authorities have yet to take up this imaginative proposal. Later in the summer, Ron Wood was present to collect a Classic Rock 'Reissue of the Year' award for *Exile*, an album he didn't play on. By then Keith was busy reading his autobiography and Mick was escorting his 11-year-old son Lucas around the soccer World Cup in South Africa, where they were joined by Bill Clinton for several matches. Hedging his bets, Mick variously appeared sporting English, US and Brazilian national colours, earning him the playful title 'The Angel of Death' when all three sides crashed out of the tournament. Some of the media also complained that Clinton was a 'Stones-slut' and that he'd 'sold out' by seeming to follow the band members around the world, 'fawning on them as if he were a groupie'.

In May 1979, in the course of what became a protracted divorce hearing, Los Angeles superior court judge Harry Shafer had called Mick someone who enjoyed a 'quintessentially peripatetic' lifestyle. It was a verdict that still held thirty-one years later. Essentially, Mick divided his time between his homes in London, the Loire Valley and Mustique, although there were frequent excursions further afield. Along with his travels in the likes of Mongolia and Tibet, he also enjoyed the perhaps more louche attractions of his daughter Jade's estate on Ibiza, the Mediterranean retreat where the mantra was '*No pasa nada*' (No problem), and the all-purpose adjective was 'amazing'. The island's pervasive spirit of freedom, laziness and decadence made it the getaway of choice for 1960s hippies, although by 2010 it was also home to the deposed king of Spain, sundry Arab oil sheikhs and the model Kate Moss, among others. Swimming costumes were not mandatory on the resort's beaches. Mick sometimes joined Jade for the summer party she threw each year for 500 guests at her luxury villa, although she later moved both her family and her jewellery-design business to New York, where she could be seen in advertisements for a block of 'laid-back condominiums' named 'Jade', priced at between $600,000 and $1,900,000 each. Mick made his own occasional New York home in the Royal Suite of the Carlyle hotel. He had first become acquainted with it when dating Jerry Hall in the late 1970s. After safely returning his son Lucas to his mother following the World Cup, Mick was successively in Los Angeles, Paris, Dublin – and Luang Prabang in Laos, where he reportedly spent three weeks on 'a spiritual trip . . . He dined in the hotel library away from guests and went out only to visit temples and meditate with monks.'

A year of introspection for the Stones, which saw the re-release both of *Exile* and of the classic 1974 film of the band on stage in America, ended with the publication of Keith's autobiography *Life*. It proved an engaging and wildly successful project, and confirmed that its author cared more about the big picture than he did about the fine detail of his life and career. Among other factual slips, Keith got both the date he met Mick at Dartford station and of Bert Richards' death wrong, confused the timing and circumstances of the 1967 police raid on Redlands, gave an only partially convincing description of his childhood home, and listed himself as having been born in London. At one point Keith relates a long and rather intricate story about having once met Tommy James of the Shondells on Sunset Strip in Los Angeles, where James was 'trying to hand out things about the draft . . . Obviously he thought he was about to be fucking drafted. This was Vietnam War time.' Keith goes on to credit this encounter, and others like it, for significantly raising his political consciousness during the period. I asked Tommy James about the incident. 'It never happened,' he said. Although Keith's book gave a certain amount of ammunition to those who felt he might have fried his memory in the early 1970s, it was also a lively and nicely mock-innocent account of his life and times which fully deserved to sell over a million copies in hardback. One of the few dissenting reviewers was Markus Larsson, the music critic who had publicly exchanged views with Keith after a Stones concert in Sweden three years earlier. On 9 November, Larsson went to interview the author at Le Meurice hotel in Paris. The details of what followed are unclear, due to conflicting testimony, but it seems fairly certain that Larsson identified himself to Keith and that Keith then terminated their session by 'jokingly tapping' the journalist on the head. The audio recording of the incident captures only the sound of a dull thud, followed by that of a door rather loudly closing. The year ended with an animated debate both about this alleged assault, and whether Mick Jagger really was under-endowed, as Keith claimed.

On 13 February 2011, Mick made a triumphant debut on the Grammy Awards stage at the Staples Center in Los Angeles, paying tribute to the late Solomon Burke with a full-service rendition of 'Everybody Needs Somebody to Love'. The Stones had recorded the number on their second album, forty-six years earlier. A gaudily clad showband lined up from one side of the stage to the other, and a chorus of beehive-haired backing singers could be seen bopping up and down in the wings. Before he launched in to the song, Mick stood still on stage with his back to the crowd while wearing a fur-trimmed, black floor-length cape. He then whirled around, flung off the cape and hollered, 'I'm so glad to be here tonight! I'm so glad to be in your wonderful city!' It was vintage Jagger. At a time when most modern rock stars dress like they work in the stockroom at their local Tesco, Mick could be relied on to keep the spirit of James Brown alive with a whole series of dramatic leaps, splits and slides that would have spelled a trip to the chiropractor for the average 67-year-old. The audience loved it.

Later that year, Mick announced the formation of a side-group called SuperHeavy, in which he was one of four featured vocalists. The band, which also included Dave Stewart, Joss Stone and A.R. Rahman, the film composer best known for his score to *Slumdog Millionaire*, played its first preview show on 30 June 2011 at the old Muppet studios in Hollywood. Stewart informed the press that he had been inspired by the 'mystic sounds washing in to the bay' near his home in Jamaica, and that everyone had been enthused by the idea of fusing these with Indian orchestration. Mick subsequently appeared for the recording session for the band's single 'Satyameva Jayate' (Truth alone triumphs) with a garland of flowers around his neck. He sang the song's lyrics in Sanskrit.

There was thought to be little fear of Keith Richards following suit when in March 2011 he, in turn, reactivated his band the X-Pensive Winos. 'Dirty-ass rock and roll' remained his forte, he noted. Keith also completed another cameo alongside Johnny Depp in the latest instalment of the *Pirates of the Caribbean* franchise, *On Stranger Tides*. His character was arguably the most swashbuckling thing about the film, which opened in May to largely negative reviews. Keith's trailer on set at Pinewood studios was that same brocaded lair strewn with Tibetan prayer-shawls, crates of vodka, scuffed biker boots, books, cassettes and thick cigarette smoke that had been his preferred habitat for some forty years. Between takes he occasionally stole an hour of sleep, often with his acoustic guitar cradled on his lap. Keith was in a good mood at the *Pirates* premiere in Los Angeles. 'Not everybody that likes pirate movies necessarily likes rock 'n' roll, right, so this all gives me another chance to communicate with the people,' he said. 'Now everywhere there's all these kids who know me as Captain Teague, not as Keith Richards. "That's Jack Sparrow's dad!" And that's cool, man.'

During this period Mick, Keith and their colleagues did collaborate on a version of Bob Dylan's song 'Watching the River Flow' as part of a new charity album in tribute to Ian Stewart. However, the session fell some way short of a full-scale Stones reunion. According to a source familiar with the project, 'First Keith recorded his guitar part in New York. Then the tape was emailed to Mick in France, and he sent it back with a vocal and harmonica track. Charlie and Bill later added their contributions at separate studios in London, and everything was mixed courtesy of FedEx. At no time did any of the band actually meet.'

As Stu himself had noted, 'Most overnight sensations in the rock business manage to fuck up royally within a year.' One week they're playing to thousands, quoted breathily in *People* and on TV, surrounded by aides and toadies, courted and cosseted like a head of state, and the next they're auditioning for panto. Although the Stones had fairly clearly avoided this fate, it seems safe to say that by 2011–12 even the band's most forgiving fans were forced to conclude that their best creative days were behind them. It wasn't just that Mick and the rest were getting on a bit; even some of their children were middle-aged. Marlon Richards was now forty-two, happily married, with his father's angular face and flinty stare, as well as a farmhouse near Keith's in West Wittering. Although Marlon had arguably not fulfilled the promise as a professional photographer some had seen in him and he'd glimpsed in himself in the early 1990s, he'd come out of it all remarkably well given the chaos of his upbringing. 'What did Keith and Anita do wrong?' a family friend remarked in the *Daily Mail*. 'Marlon was supposed to wind up a really nasty piece of work, and he's a fabulous guy, polite, gentlemanly and witty.'

In August 2004, Keith's sparsely clad 19-year-old daughter Theodora appeared on the cover of *Nylon* magazine with her arm draped around Mick's 20-year-old daughter Elizabeth. The pose recreated one adopted by their fathers thirty years earlier in the likes of *Rolling Stone* and other outlets. Lizzy Jagger later went on to grace the June 2011 issue of *Playboy*, an act of 'artistic self-fulfilment', apparently, for which she wore only a pair of thigh-high boots and bunny ears. Lizzy's younger sister Georgia had since posed topless to advertise the American jeans company Hudson. Ron Wood in turn announced in 2011 that his 35-year-old son Jesse, the bass player in a rock band called The Black Swan Effect, had entered rehab. In an unusual example of family bonding, they reportedly went through at least one detox programme together. 'We're helping each other out,' said Woody, who had sought treatment for drink or drug addiction seven times. Somehow fittingly, 44-year-old Serafina Watts was an irreproachable mother of one, while Bill Wyman's son Stephen, now fifty, was back on friendly terms with his father following a period of coolness at around the time of the Patsy and Mandy Smith saga. Mick Taylor, for his part, was thought to have a 'distant' relationship with his two adult daughters. Brian Jones was known to have a minimum of six children, all now in their late forties or early fifties, three of them named Julian, at least one of whom was still determined to prove that his father had died at the hands of a homicidal builder rather than merely succumbing to a combination of alcohol, sleeping pills and warm water on that fateful summer night in 1969.

Other Stones insiders and camp followers enjoyed mixed fortunes over the years. Bianca Jagger emerged from a lengthy exploration of New York café society to become an outspoken human-rights advocate whose current causes, according to published sources, include 'genocide, the war in Iraq, the war in Afghanistan, the war on terror, war crimes against humanity, crimes against future generations, the former Yugoslavia, Sri Lanka, Central America, Iran, Iraq, India, children and women's rights, the rights of indigenous peoples, climate change, the rainforest, renewable energy, corporate social responsibility, the erosion of civil liberties and human rights, global debt and the death penalty.' Significantly different to her days propping up the dance floor at Studio 54. Anita Pallenberg survived the 1970s and went on to parody herself as the devil in the British sitcom *Absolutely Fabulous*, in which Marianne Faithfull appeared as God. Mick's friend Donald Cammell, who wrote and co-directed *Performance*, committed suicide in April 1996, allegedly shooting himself in the head and then asking for a mirror so that he could watch himself bleed to death. There is a roughly similar incident in his film. He was sixty-two. The Stones' long-time collaborator Billy Preston died in 2006, aged fifty-nine, after struggling for years both with his health and his repressed homosexuality. A friend of Keith's, guitar-maker Ted Newman Jones, is currently serving a twenty-year sentence in a Texas jail on a range of drug and parole-violation charges. Various members of the Hell's Angels still occasionally appear on television or in print to threaten the 'limey bastards' with dire retribution for Altamont.

All the Stones' parents are deceased. Bill Wyman turned seventy-five in October 2011, and reflected with satisfaction that at least he'd walked before they made him run. Mick Taylor, now sixty-three, could sometimes be seen playing in small clubs, and joined Bill and Charlie for a one-off London gig dedicated to Ian Stewart in March 2011. Mick Jagger and Keith Richards didn't show up. The Glimmer Twins still regularly exchanged tapes and song ideas, even on the days they had nothing else in common. Tom Keylock remembered Keith once saying to Mick in the 1960s, 'We must talk to each other as much as we can. When one of us dies, there'll be some things the other one will never be able to talk about with anyone else.' The press increasingly compared them to an elderly married couple. Brian Jones was in Cheltenham, on a green hill overlooking the church where he'd sung as a choirboy. The old flat at Edith Grove had been turned in to a battered-women's refuge.

When Mick Jagger had sat down with Prince Rupert Loewenstein in July 1981 to budget the Stones' finances, they'd made the assumption that the amount the band would make from touring would gradually decline. After all, 'they'll lose interest eventually', Mick had noted of his core audience. But the long-expected down-turn never came. As if by magical suspension, Mick's own fame and fortune remained as high as ever, with an annual royalty flow and a healthy property-and-investment portfolio estimated in 2012 at £240million. This impressed or amused some observers, and outraged others. But even critics generally agreed that Mick was much more than just a singing accountant who had somehow gotten lucky over the years. Kicking seventy, he remained staggeringly creative – whether developing and producing films, reading widely, writing the script of a project he called *Tabloid* dealing with a Rupert Murdoch-like news tycoon, speaking on everything from state terrorism to esoteric geological issues concerning wave formations, or appearing on video in a flamingo-pink suit to strut out his latest single. The renaissance sweep of his activities was arguably what made him the driven, restless individual he was. As one American magazine profile wrote, 'When [Jagger] begins to feel pleasantly relaxed or satisfied, some danger sign goes up, some inner voice says no, and he feels called back in to the quest for new worlds to conquer.' Or, as Charlie Watts put it more crisply: 'You'd imagine Mick would be the happiest guy in the world, and yet a lot of the time he isn't. Being with him I know.'

That Mick was sometimes less besotted than Keith with the rock and roll lifestyle the preceding pages have, perhaps, shown; and in the 1980s and beyond a reaction set in which portrayed the 'Human Riff' as a permanently sozzled and lovable old rogue and his longtime partner as an uptight poseur. This, too, was an inadequate picture. Although he looked so wizened as to resemble a Red Indian chief, Keith stubbornly refused to conform to rock and roll stereotypes. 'I'm a much broader character than people think,' he said in his 'elegantly wasted' heyday. 'It's not all *ah-har!* and slitting throats in dark alleyways. I make a very nice cup of tea.' In 2012, Keith's own nest-egg was estimated at £190million, or $290million, some $12million of which came from his North American book sales, making him one of the most commercially successful authors alive. He sometimes tells interviewers that if he had it all to do again he would forgo the guitar and become a librarian.

In December 2011, the Rolling Stones released *Live in Texas*, a concert film taken from the *Some Girls* tour thirty-three years earlier.

As that rose in the charts, hard-core fans around the world became increasingly like old-time Kremlinologists, using the internet to analyse such titbits as the arrangement of the photographs in Keith Richards' book, Mick Jagger's online postings and what Charlie Watts may or may not have told an Austrian newspaper interviewer, among other cryptic details, in an attempt to understand the inner workings of an opaque organisation like the Stones – and more specifically, if and when the band would ever play again. One more substantial clue came in a 2011 lawsuit filed by Michael Cohl against Live Nation, the production company he'd left amid some acrimony three years earlier. In court documents, Cohl claimed his former employers had tried to 'interfere' in his relationship with his friends Mick, Keith, Charlie and Ron and steal away 'the crown jewel' of an agreement he had made to promote a fiftieth-anniversary Stones tour. This suggested rather clearly that there was a tour to promote, although, seeming to immediately deflate the fans' expectations, Cohl also claimed that his feud with Live Nation (who paid him a $9.8million severance fee) had since 'destroyed' certain negotiations between the Stones and himself. Hopes had been raised apparently only to be dashed again. But not for long. On 7 September 2011, all four band members appeared for a long-awaited summit at the London offices of their company Marathon Music. A crowd of excited reporters and paparazzi jostling at the front door disturbed the peace of the building's normally hushed reception area, with its ornate coffee tables covered in carefully fanned copies of *The Wisden Cricketer* and *Country Life*. Copious product was soon in place to cash in on the band's milestone, including more archival live recordings from the *Tattoo You* tour, and an exclusive deal with Google to promote and distribute various 'official' bootlegs. The inevitable followed. And so the Stones roll on, with some of its members enjoying their status and others paying the price for being in the greatest rock and roll band in the world.

BIBLIOGRAPHY

Berry, Chuck, *Chuck Berry: The Autobiography*, New York: Harmony, 1987

Bockris, Victor, *Keith Richards*, New York: Poseidon, 1992

Bonanno, Massimo, *The Rolling Stones Chronicle*, London: Plexus, 1990

Booth, Stanley, *Keith*, New York: St Martin's Press, 1995

—, *The True Adventures of the Rolling Stones*, New York: Random House, 1984

Carr, Roy, *The Rolling Stones, An Illustrated Record*, London: New English Library, 1976

Charone, Barbara, *Keith Richards*, London: Futura Publications, 1979

Clayson, Alan, *Charlie Watts*, London: Sanctuary Publishing, 2004

Cooper, Michael, with Terry Southern and Keith Richards, *The Early Stones*, New York: Hyperion, 1992

Dalton, David, *The Rolling Stones*, New York: Knopf, 1981

Davis, Stephen, *Old Gods Almost Dead*, New York: Broadway Books, 2001

Elliott, Martin, *The Rolling Stones: Complete Recording Sessions 1963–1989*, London: Blandford, 1990

Faithfull, Marianne, and David Dalton, *Faithfull*, Boston: Little, Brown, 1994

Flippo, Chet, *On the Road with the Rolling Stones*, New York: Doubleday, 1985

German, Bill, *Under Their Thumb*, New York: Villard Books, 2009

Greenfield, Robert, *A Journey Through America with the Rolling Stones*, New York: Dutton, 1974

—, *Exile on Main Street: A Season in Hell with the Rolling Stones*, Philadelphia: Da Capo, 2006

Hall, Jerry with Christopher Hemphill, *Tall Tales*, London: Elm Tree Books, 1981

Hector, James, *The Complete Guide to the Music of the Rolling Stones*, London: Omnibus Press, 1995

Hotchner, A.E., *Blown Away: The Rolling Stones and the Death of the Sixties*, New York: Simon & Schuster, 1990

Jackson, Laura, *Brian Jones: Golden Stone*, London: Smith Gryphon, 1992

Jasper, Tony, *The Rolling Stones*, London: Octopus Books, 1976

McLagan, Ian, *All the Rage*, London: Sidgwick & Jackson, 1998

Mankowitz, Gered, *Satisfaction: The Rolling Stones Photographs*, London: Sidgwick & Jackson, 1984

Norman, Philip, *The Stones*, London: Elm Tree Books, 1984

Rawlings, Terry, Keith Badman and Andrew Neill, *Good Times Bad Times*, London: Complete Music Publications, 1997

Richards, Keith, *Life*, New York: Little, Brown, 2010

Rolling Stones, The, *A Life on the Road,* New York: The Penguin Group, 1998

Sanchez, Tony, *Up and Down with the Rolling Stones*, New York: William Morrow, 1979

Sandford, Christopher, *Mick Jagger: Primitive Cool*, London: Gollancz, 1993

—, *Keith Richards: Satisfaction*, London: Headline, 2003

Scaduto, Anthony, *Mick Jagger*, London: W.H. Allen, 1974

Trudeau, Margaret, *Beyond Reason*, New York: Paddington Press, 1979

Warhol, Andy, *The Andy Warhol Diaries*, New York: Warner Books, 1989

Wood, Ron, with Bill German, *The Works*, London: Fontana, 1988

Wyman, Bill, with Ray Coleman, *Stone Alone*, London: Viking, 1990

SOURCES AND CHAPTER NOTES

Source one for the life and times of the Rolling Stones is the roughly 400 songs written and performed over the course of fifty years. If nothing else, the book aims to pay due credit to the music as well as the men. Although it lacks the band members' direct involvement, it is just possible it's no worse off factually as a result. When one reads Mick Jagger reminiscing in 2011 of the Stones' professional debut, 'It was just me and Keith, Brian [Jones] and a backing band. I remember it exactly. I was nineteen years old. Ricky Fenson on bass. Carlo Little on drums and Nicky Hopkins on piano . . . The gig was amazing. The drummer was going mad and Nicky was rocking his electric piano and I remember the crowd going absolutely wild,' one realises he may be just as much in thrall to the Stones' myths as anybody else.

The following notes show at least the formal interviews, conversations and/or other material mined during the two years of concentrated research for the book. I should particularly thank the now late Tom Keylock and the late Frank Thorogood, both of whom shed light on the day-to-day life of the Stones in the 1960s. As well as those listed, I also spoke to a number of people who prefer not to be named. Where sources asked for anonymity – usually citing a healthy respect for the Rolling Stones' lawyers – every effort was made to get them to go on the record. Where this wasn't possible, I've used the words 'a friend' or 'a colleague', as usual. Once or twice, I've resorted to the formula of an alias. (The reader should be assured that every fact stated in the book has been sourced, and for obvious reasons corroborated to the very fullest extent possible, before publication.) No acknowledgement thus appears of the help, encouragement and kindness I got from a number of quarters, some of them, as they say, household names.

CHAPTER 1

Among periodicals consulted were *Billboard*, the *Daily Mail*, *Details*, the *Guardian*, *Jazz News*, *Melody Maker*, *Q*, the *Seattle Times*, *The Times*, *The Weekly*, the *Wall Street Journal*. Some of the specific sources for the childhoods of Mick Jagger and Keith Richards – their mutual friend Dick Taylor, for one – spoke to me at the time of my biographies of Jagger and Richards which first appeared in 1993 and 2003 respectively. I interviewed the late Joe and Eva Jagger in October 1991. I should thank Pytor Sachin for his insights in to the Rolling Stones' visit to Moscow in 1998, and Ron Simms for his recollections of 1950s Dartford. I visited the scenes of each of the original Stones' upbringing. Tony Smith, formerly headmaster at Dartford Grammar School, very kindly put his records of the young Mike Jagger's attendance there at my disposal. I remember a long conversation with the late John Peel in which he spoke about Brian Jones, and what Brian had told him about his childhood and musical education. Both Companies House and the UK Family Records Centre supplied archive material. Keith Richards' memoir *Life*, cited in the bibliography, albeit occasionally straying from the strict chronological record, is as good an account of the period 1943–62 as any, and obviously informed by Keith's diaries of the era. The late Carlo Little did not play drums for the Stones on their Marquee Club debut. He did, however, supply several amusing and generally affectionate stories about the band at that time. Charlie Watts did not speak to me; he did once describe me as 'really macabre', a compliment I turned over in my mind for many years afterwards.

CHAPTER 2

For events from 1943 until fame struck, exactly twenty years later, I'm grateful to the late Joe and Eva Jagger, and to Mick Jagger's former assistant Janice Crotch; to a Dupree family relative; an old source at Livingstone Hospital, Dartford; former members of the staff of Cheltenham Grammar School; and the dozens of those who spoke to me either in 2010–11 or at the time of my Jagger and Richards biographies, notably Bob Beckwith, Alan Deane, Alan Etherington, Alex Gibb, Eileen Giles, the late Charlie Gillett, the late Dick Heckstall-Smith, Peter Holland, Paul Jones, Matthew Kite, the late Carlo Little,

Robin Medley, the late Yehudi Menuhin, Cecilia Nixon, David Pracy, Chris Rea, Mike Richards, Clive Robson, Walter Stern, Dick Taylor. I spoke to Mick Jagger's former girlfriend Chrissie Shrimpton at the time of my Jagger biography. The *Dartford Chronicle* was a mine of information; a visit to the UK Family Records Centre finally settled such essential points of record as Bill Wyman's correct date of birth. Number 102 Edith Grove is greatly modified from its 1962 squalor, but still just about recognisable as the low-rent crucible of the Rolling Stones. The band did their first organised rehearsals at 34 Alexander Road, Bexleyheath, surely a deserving site for a blue plaque fifty-odd years later. The old Crawdaddy Club has been absorbed in to a wine bar. Secondary sources included Keith Richards' *Life*, Stephen Davis' *Old Gods Almost Dead*, Philip Norman's *The Stones*, Alan Clayson's *Charlie Watts*, Bill Wyman's *Stone Alone* and my own *Mick Jagger: Primitive Cool*, all as cited in the bibliography. The late Tony Sanchez's *Up and Down with the Rolling Stones*, if labouring under its author's note of simulated moral outrage, is as good an account of the band's early days as any other. A number of the Mick Jagger quotes, both here and elsewhere in the book, came from his *Rolling Stone* interview of 14 December 1995. While Robert Fraser may have felt closer to Paul McCartney towards the end of his life than he did to Mick Jagger or Keith Richards, both the Stones were warmly supportive to him over the years.

Other secondary sources included the *Chicago Tribune*, the *Daily Mail*, the *Daily Mirror*, *Haagsche Courant*, *Portsmouth Evening News*, *Rolling Stone*, *The Times*, *Wall Street Journal*, the *West London Advertiser*. Companies House provided records of the Stones' long-standing financial edifice, Nanker Phelge Limited. Mary Wilson very kindly put her personal memories of the Stones' pivotal performance at the TAMI show of October 1964 at my disposal. I should also par-ticularly thank both Robert Stigwood and Decca Records for their help.

Andrew Loog Oldham returned my email.

CHAPTER 3

Interviews and/or taped conversations, some conducted at the time of my Jagger and Richards biographies, took place with Allan Clarke, Lol Creme, the late Adam Faith, Chris Farlowe, Alex Gibb, Nick Gough,

Ryan Grice, Jeff Griffin, Debbie Guest, Alan Hazen, the late Al Hendrix, David Jacobs, Edith Keep, the late Tom Keylock, Cecilia Lewis, the late Carlo Little, Gered Mankowitz, Ted Neely, Mike Oldfield, Andy Peebles, Anthony Phillips, the late Wilson Pickett, Terry Reid, Mike Richards, Ronnie Schneider, Don Short, Chrissie Shrimpton, Eric Stewart, Robert Stigwood, Carol Ward, Walton Wilkinson. The UK National Archives established some of the immediate background and consequences both of the famous raid on Keith Richards' home Redlands of February 1967, and of Mick Jagger's arrest at 48 Cheyne Walk in May 1969. I should again thank the staff both of Companies House and the UK Family Records Centre.

Keith Richards has often spoken or, more recently, written engagingly of a number of episodes from the Stones' early years. It's perhaps pedantic to point out that some of these stories differ in tone if not in broad fact from the memories of other people who were there. To give just one example, Keith speaks effusively of his first, paint-soaked meeting with Muddy Waters, which took place at Chess Studios in Chicago in June 1964. It's only fair to say that a number of those who knew Waters best, including Marshall Chess, aren't so sure of the specifics of the story. Chess remembers Keith, perhaps significantly, downing a large amount of sour mash whiskey on the historic day in question.

Printed sources included *Billboard*, the *Daily Express*, *Havering Post*, the *News of the World*, *Neus Deutschland*, *Nova*, *Queen*, the *Sydney Morning Herald*, *Time*, *The Times*, *Variety*, *Vogue*. I should acknowledge the help of the Gulf Beach Hotel of Clearwater, Florida, where Keith Richards dreamt up 'Satisfaction', the Royal Navy Officers Club of Portsmouth, UK, and the archives of the *Ed Sullivan Show* in New York. I visited Redlands.

Keith Altham's quote 'The Loog was in the throes of moving . . .', very slightly amended for sense, first appeared in the *New Musical Express* of 5 August 1966; Steve Leber's 'I did the tours . . .' quote appears in Fred Goodwin's magisterial book *The Mansion on the Hill* (Times Books, 1997); the peerless line 'A Rimbauesque declension of the shadow world of illicit sexuality' appears in Stephen Davis' as elsewhere book *Old Gods Almost Dead*; Marianne Faithfull's 'Jagger was the last person in the world . . .' is from A.E. Hotchner's book *Blown Away*; the quote beginning 'There were about twenty people there . . .' appears in Bill Wyman's book *Stone Alone*.

There is no suggestion, whatsoever, that Keith Richards' interest in World War Two militaria was ever anything more than a visual style appreciation – one shared by many people around the world.

'Stupid Girl' (Jagger–Richards)
© ABKCO Music, Inc

'Let's Spend the Night Together' (Jagger–Richards)
© ABKCO Music, Inc

CHAPTER 4

The Stones' purple patch was recalled by, among others, Dick Allen, Paul Bibire, John Birt, the late William Burroughs, the late Albert Clinton, Terry Clymes, the late James Coburn, Alan Deane, Judy Flanders, Nick Gough, Jeff Griffin, Tommy James, Joan Keylock, the late Tom Keylock, the late Alexis Korner, Dave Mason, Terry Reid, Don Short, Don Taylor, the late Frank Thorogood, Johnny Winter, Tony Yeo. On an institutional note, I'm grateful to the UK National Archives, HM Prison Service and the FBI – Freedom of Information Division. I should also thank Noel Chelberg for his always canny deconstruction of the Rolling Stones' songs, and David Waldman, formerly HM Coroner for East Sussex. I visited Cotchford Farm.

Secondary sources included the *Daily Express*, the *Daily Mirror*, *Life*, *Melody Maker*, *Metro*, the *News of the World*, *Rolling Stone*, *Sounds*, the *Sunday Telegraph*, *The Times*, *Vogue* and, particularly, both Stanley Booth's *The True Adventures of the Rolling Stones* and Albert & David Maysles' *Gimme Shelter* (Home Vision Cinema). I'm grateful to Stanley Booth for taking the time to speak to me about the Stones.

The Peter Swales quote beginning 'Brian Jones was just a wreck ...', the George Chkiantz quote 'He beat up Suki right off ...' and the Christopher Gibbs quote 'She jolly nearly died ...' all appear in Stephen Davis' book *Old Gods Almost Dead*. The Christopher Gibbs quote about 'stopping at various hostelries along the way ...' appears in the book *According to the Rolling Stones* (San Francisco: Chronicle Books, 2003); Keith Richards' quote beginning 'I would take a barbiturate to wake up ...' is from his book *Life*. The Mick Taylor quote beginning 'I couldn't believe it ...' is taken from his interview with *Mojo* of November 1997.

As stated in the text, there's no suggestion that the late Allen Klein or any representative working on his behalf acted in any way illegally or improperly in their management of the Stones. By far the band's greatest objection was that funds weren't always wired from New York as quickly as they might have liked.

Nor is there any suggestion in the book that Mick Jagger or Keith Richards ever expropriated any other musician's work, even if from time to time, and in keeping with standard songwriting practice, they accepted the help freely given them. Their guests' session fees were always paid in full.

'Parachute Woman' (Jagger–Richards)
© ABKCO Music, Inc

CHAPTER 5

Comment on the Stones' exile, and *Exile*, came from, among others: Dick Allen, Ross Benson, Paul Bibire, Stanley Booth, Angie Bowie, Vanetta Fields, Judy Flanders, Alex Gibb, Eileen Giles, Jeff Griffin, the late Al Hendrix, the late Joe and Eva Jagger, Phil Kaufman, the late Tom Keylock, the late Steve Mariott, Dave Mason, Bill Plummer, Terry Reid, Ronnie Schneider, Don Short, Winston Stagers, the late Frank Thorogood, Peter Tork, Bill Truscott, Lisbeth Vogl, Alan Weyer. I also spoke to a source, who prefers not to be named, intimately familiar with the domestic arrangements at Keith Richards' Riviera lair, Nellcôte. On an institutional note, I should acknowledge the help both of the Hotel Byblos and of the FBI – Freedom of Information Division, which clarified certain points of record about the Stones' problematical US immigration status around 1970–74. I'm also grateful to the Edgewater Inn, Seattle, and to the source familiar with the late Bill Graham.

The quote saying that Bill Wyman would 'simply ask the most attractive woman at the dinner table . . .' is from Robert Greenfield's book *Exile on Main Street*; The Keith Richards quotes beginning 'At first I thought Bianca . . .' and 'I was a bit unpredictable in those days . . .' both appear in his book *Life*; Tony Sanchez's quote beginning 'Keith and I would take the children . . .' is from Sanchez's book *Up and Down with the Rolling Stones*, all as cited in the bibliography.

Secondary sources included *Billboard*, the *Daily Mail*, the *Daily*

Mirror, *Life*, *Rolling Stone*, the *Seattle Times*, *The Times* and the *Toronto Star*. Some of the brief quotes attributed here to Keith Richards first appeared in Victor Bockris' biography of him; Keith's own views on Mick Taylor are summarised in the Rolling Stones' book *A Life on the Road* (New York: The Penguin Group, 1998). I should also credit *The Early Stones* by the late Michael Cooper, with text by Terry Southern and comments by Keith Richards (New York: Hyperion, 1992).

'Midnight Rambler' (Jagger–Richards)
© ABKCO Music, Inc

'Casino Boogie' (Jagger–Richards)
© EMI Music Publishing Ltd.

'Sweet Black Angel' (Jagger–Richards)
© EMI Publishing Ltd.

CHAPTER 6

The Stones' personal and creative highs – and the nadir of *Black and Blue* – were crisply brought home by Ross Benson, Stanley Booth, Geoff Bradford, Bebe Buell, the late Peter Cook, Alan Deane, the late John Diefenbaker, Alex Gibb, Nick Gough, Jeff Griffin, Bob Harris, the late Furry Lewis, Chris Page, Graham Parker, Don Peltz, Wayne Perkins. I'm particularly grateful to the last. A source uniquely familiar with the late Steve McQueen's thoughts put McQueen's views on the Rolling Stones, and the 'Star Star' furore, at my disposal.

Secondary sources included *Billboard*, *Life*, *Melody Maker*, the *New York Times*, *Q*, *Rolling Stone*, *Variety*, *Vogue*, and virtually every UK and Canadian tabloid in the period immediately leading up to, and following, 27 February 1977. I happened to meet Keith Richards myself the week before his ill-fated trip to Toronto.

Other published sources included Bebe Buell with Victor Bockris, *Rebel Heart* (New York: St Martin's Press, 2001), Stephen Davis' *Old Gods Almost Dead* and Chet Flippo's *On the Road with the Rolling Stones*.

Keith Richards' quotes beginning 'Mick Taylor left us in the lurch . . .' and 'I wasn't about to ask questions . . .' are both from *Life*; Tony Sanchez's quote beginning 'As soon as the cure had been effected . . .' is from his book *Up and Down with the Rolling Stones*; Del Taylor's quote beginning 'The idea was that Alexis . . .' is from Harry

Shapiro's *Alexis Korner: The Biography* (London: Bloomsbury, 1996); Anita Pallenberg's 'Keith was very calm . . .' quote appears in Victor Bockris' book *Keith Richards*. Mick Taylor's quote beginning 'When I told the office I was going . . .' is from his interview in the *Daily Mail* of 13 September 2009; the Mackenzie Phillips' ('There was no telephone . . .') quote first appeared in *Night and Day* of 7 October 2001.

I'm again grateful to the UK National Archives for material concerning Keith Richards' arrest and trial on assorted drugs charges in the period February 1977 to October 1978; previously, to the Public Affairs office of the Canadian Government; to the FBI – Freedom of Information Division; and to the US Department of Justice.

CHAPTER 7

The Rolling Stones' trials and tribulations, and their first great comeback, were vividly recalled by, among others: Dick Allen, Tom Andrews, the late Hal Ashby, Paul Bibire, Pete Brown, the late Peter Cook, Alex Gibb, Jeff Griffin, Bob Harris, Roger Hayes, Alan Hazen, Tommy James, Baird Jones, Lenny Kaye, Chris Page, Andy Peebles, Terry Reid, Tim Rice, Don Short, the late Andy Warhol. I'm grateful to the source at the old Harbour Castle hotel, Toronto, and to the Lewisboro, New York, Police Department. Keith Richards' lawyer Austin Cooper very kindly responded to the few fact-checking questions I asked him.

Published sources included *Billboard*, *Esquire*, *The Facts*, *Life*, the *Los Angeles Times*, the *New York Post World*, *Q*, *Seattle Times*, the *Toronto Star*, *The Times*, *Variety*, *Wall Street Journal*. I should once again mention Chet Flippo's book *On the Road with the Rolling Stones*.

The quote beginning 'Mick looked after me . . .' and the quote beginning 'I fell asleep under the booth . . .' are both from Keith Richards' book *Life*; the quote beginning 'He was lying there wearing these things . . .' appears in *Tall Tales*, by Jerry Hall with Christopher Hemphill (London: Elm Tree Books, 1981).

I watched *Green Ice*.

'Before They Make Me Run' (Jagger–Richards)
© EMI Music Publishing Ltd.

'All About You' (Jagger–Richards)
© EMI Music Publishing Ltd.

CHAPTER 8

Primary sources included Dick Allen, the late Hal Ashby, Don Bates, Alex Bennett, the late Jeffrey Bernard, Tony Bill, Pete Brown, Jack Bruce, the late William Burroughs (16 February 1995), Neil Conti, Alan Deane, Anton Fig, Ryan Grice, Jeff Griffin, Johnny Johnson, Edith Keep, David Kelly, Gered Mankowitz, Nick Miles, Andy Peebles, Terry Reid, Tim Rice, David Sinclair, the late Peter Smith, Tony Smith, Don Taylor, Carol Ward, Adele Warlow. Ernie Watts was one of those who described his experience of playing and touring with the Stones in 1981–82. The Jagger–Richards feud of c. 1984–89 was well detailed in *Rolling Stone* and *USA Today*, among others. I also read the *Daily Mirror*, the *New York Times*, the *Seattle Times*, the *Sun*, *The Times*, the *Toronto Star* and the *Washington Post*. I'm grateful both to a source at the US Drugs Enforcement Agency and to the UK Family Records Centre, the latter of which supplied details of Mick Jagger's quite prolific role as a father.

Published sources particularly included Ian McLagan's book *All the Rage*, Bill German's book *Under Their Thumb* and the Rolling Stones' own *According to the Rolling Stones*, all as cited in the bibliography.

Bill Wyman's quote beginning 'I found her descent . . .' is from his book *Stone Alone*; Gered Mankowitz's reported speech involving his discussions with the Rolling Stones office ("Mick's just got up, and he's in the bath . . .") is from his book *Satisfaction*; I also spoke to Gered Mankowitz at some length at the time of my 1993 Jagger biography.

I should particularly acknowledge the late Cat Sinclair.

CHAPTER 9

Help in recalling the Rolling Stones' comeback years came from Don Bates, Byron Berline, Alex Bennett, the late William Burroughs, Allan Clarke, the late Peter Cook, Jan Even, Alex Gibb, Nick Gough, Jeff Griffin, Roger Hayes, the late Joe and Eva Jagger, Lenny Kaye, Edith Keep, Chuck Leavell, the late Carlo Little, Chris Page, the late Harold Pinter, Bill Plummer, Terry Reid, Tim Rice, David Sinclair, Dick Taylor, Don Taylor, Charles Vann, Carol Ward, Alan Weyer. I enjoyed a 'VIP' pass to the Stones shows in Seattle and Vancouver in December 1994. I'm grateful to Mick Jagger's then secretary Janice Crotch, and to A&M Studios, Companies House and the Hollywood Roosevelt hotel.

Secondary sources included *Billboard, Fortune, Guitar Player, Musician, People, Q, Rolling Stone, Seattle Times*, the *Seattle Weekly*, the *Sunday Times, Vanity Fair, Variety*, the *Wall Street Journal*.

The comments by Ron Wood's former manager first appeared in largely the form given here in the *Daily Mail* of 25 October 2008. Keith Richards' quote beginning 'We were getting to the dress rehearsals ...' and the Don Was quotes beginning 'It was a total stand-off ...' and 'The only time any of them ...' (the latter very slightly amended for sense) are taken from Keith Richards' book *Life*. Ron Wood's quote beginning 'Bill said, "Fuck you lot ..."' is from *According to the Rolling Stones*. Bill Wyman's quote beginning 'The big money wasn't there yet ...' is from his interview with the *Daily Telegraph* of 10 January 2008.

'Back to Zero' (Jagger–Richards–Leavell)
© Promopub B.V. (PRS)

'Had It with You' (Jagger–Richards–Wood)
© Promopub B.V. (PRS)

'Kow Tow' (Jagger–D. Stewart)
© Promopub B.V. (PRS) & BMG Music Ltd/Arista Music, Inc

'Let's Work' (Jagger–D. Stewart)
© Promopub B.V. (PRS) & BMG Music Ltd/Arista Music, Inc

'You Don't Move Me' (Richards–S. Jordan)
© Promopub B.V. (PRS)

'Wired All Night' (Jagger)
© Promotone B.V.

'Sweet Thing' (Jagger)
© Promotone B.V.

CHAPTER 10

Parting comment from Byron Berline, Neil Conti, the late John Entwistle, Alan Hazen, Tommy James, Edith Keep, the late Tom Keylock, Imran Khan, Chris Page, Wayne Perkins, Bill Plummer, Terry Reid, David Sinclair, Carol Ward. I'm grateful, too, to Terry Lambert, Vince Lorimer and the Villars. I should also particularly acknowledge the kind help of Keith Richards' former employee Bethany Staelens. The late and irreplaceable Charlie Gillett recalled the story of his interview with Charlie Watts. Sam Cutler kindly returned my email.

Published sources included Bill German's *Under their Thumb*, Robert Greenfield's *Exile on Main Street* and the Rolling Stones' *According to the Rolling Stones*; the last named is a gripping first-hand account of the band's career, if not one burdened by excessive self-doubt on the authors' part. Secondary published sources included *Billboard*, *Chicago Tribune*, the *Daily Mail*, the *Independent*, the *Los Angeles Times*, *Sunday Express*, *The Times*, *Wall Street Journal*, *The Weekly*.

The quote beginning 'There was a pregnant pause . . .' is taken from Keith Richards' *Life*. The quote beginning '[Keith Richards] scratched his head . . .', very slightly amended for sense, is from Nigel Williamson's article 'Alive and Kicking' in the *Guardian* of 5 December 2003; the quote beginning 'Mick is a lovely guy . . .' is from the *Daily Mail* of 28 January 2007; the quote about Keith Richards 'starting a song in the wrong key . . .' is from *Rolling Stone* of 17 October 2002; the Keith Richards quote beginning 'I ain't got any favourite crappy new bands . . .' is from *New Musical Express*, April 2007; the Charlie Watts quote insisting he doesn't own a 'machine thing' is from *Details* of March 2010.

'Salt of the Earth' (Jagger–Richards)
© ABKCO Music, Inc

'You Don't Have to Mean It' (Jagger–Richards)
© Promotone B.V.

LIST OF ILLUSTRATIONS

All illustrations courtesy of Getty Images, except for:

INDEX

Christopher Sandford has reviewed and written about music, film and art for thirty years. A regular contributor to titles on both sides of the Atlantic, who has also been profiled in *Rolling Stone* magazine, he's published acclaimed biographies of Mick Jagger and Keith Richards, as well as of Eric Clapton, David Bowie, Bruce Springsteen, Steve McQueen, Roman Polanski and Imran Khan, among others. His bestselling life of Kurt Cobain is currently in production as a feature film. A dual national, Christopher divides his time between Seattle, Surrey and Lord's cricket ground. He's married with one son.